TEACHING CLASSICS WORL

Also available from Bloomsbury

COMMUNICATIVE APPROACHES FOR ANCIENT LANGUAGES
by Mair E. Lloyd and Steven Hunt

FORWARD WITH CLASSICS: CLASSICAL LANGUAGES IN SCHOOLS AND
COMMUNITIES
edited by Arlene Holmes-Henderson, Steven Hunt and Mai Musié

STARTING TO TEACH LATIN
by Steven Hunt

TEACHING CLASSICS WITH TECHNOLOGY
edited by Bartolo Natoli and Steven Hunt

TEACHING LATIN: CONTEXTS, THEORIES, PRACTICES
by Steven Hunt

TEACHING CLASSICS WORLDWIDE

SUCCESSES, CHALLENGES AND DEVELOPMENTS

Edited by Steven Hunt and John Bulwer

BLOOMSBURY ACADEMIC

LONDON • NEW YORK • OXFORD • NEW DELHI • SYDNEY

BLOOMSBURY ACADEMIC
Bloomsbury Publishing Plc
50 Bedford Square, London, WC1B 3DP, UK
1385 Broadway, New York, NY 10018, USA
29 Earlsfort Terrace, Dublin 2, Ireland

BLOOMSBURY, BLOOMSBURY ACADEMIC and the Diana logo are trademarks of
Bloomsbury Publishing Plc

First published in Great Britain 2025

Cover image: *The Dialogue of Titokowaru and Socrates* by Marian Maguire, 2010.
Lithograph 570 x 760 mm
Reproduced courtesy of the artist

A catalogue record for this book is available from the British Library.

Library of Congress Cataloging-in-Publication Data
Names: Hunt, Steven (Classicist), editor. | Bulwer, John, editor.
Title: Teaching classics worldwide : successes, challenges and developments /
edited by Steven Hunt and John Bulwer.
Description: London ; New York, NY : Bloomsbury Academic, 2024. |
Includes bibliographical references and index.
Identifiers: LCCN 2024019557 (print) | LCCN 2024019558 (ebook) |
ISBN 9781350427617 (paperback) | ISBN 9781350427624 (hardback) |
ISBN 9781350427631 (pdf) | ISBN 9781350427648 (ebook)
Subjects: LCSH: Classical philology—Study and teaching. | Classical
literature—Study and teaching. | Civilization, Classical—Study and teaching. | LCGFT: Essays.
Classification: LCC PA74 .T43 2024 (print) | LCC PA74 (ebook) |
DDC 938.0071—dc23/eng/20240624
LC record available at https://lccn.loc.gov/2024019557
LC ebook record available at https://lccn.loc.gov/2024019558

ISBN: HB: 978-1-3504-2762-4
         PB: 978-1-3504-2761-7
         ePDF: 978-1-3504-2763-1
         eBook: 978-1-3504-2764-8

Typeset by RefineCatch Limited, Bungay, Suffolk
Printed and bound in Great Britain

To find out more about our authors and books visit www.bloomsbury.com
and sign up for our newsletters.

CONTENTS

Contents

ACKNOWLEDGEMENTS

The editors would like to extend their sincere thanks and gratitude to all the contributing authors and to all those who helped in any way put this book together. Word-of-mouth recommendations, suggestions and advice were received from numerous people, including: Jane Ainsworth, Ronnie Ancona, Yoseph Ariya, Ignacio Armella, Francisco Javier Hernandez Astete, Elvira Mendez Chang, Armand D'Angour, Sally Davies, Hannah Dech, Surya Pratap Deka, Šime Demo, Melinda Dszeleky, Ahmed Fahmy, Harriet Fertik, Maria-Eleftheria Giatrakou, Anatoly Grablevsky, Steven Green, Dexter Hoyos, Jo Jones, Georgy Kantor, Dániel Kiss, Dániel Kozák, Christian Laes, Peter Liddel, Helen Lovatt, Helen McVeigh, Botan Maghdid, Katrin Michaelsdottir, Andrew Moorhouse, Llewellyn Morgan, Mai Musié, Edward Nolan, Michael Kwadwo Okyereasante, Barbara Pokorná, Lucy Pollock, Steph Rasmussen, Susana Reisz, Ilse van Rooyen, Eleni Sanida, Carmel Serracino, Eva Schough Tarandi, Nidhi Singal, Csaba Szabó, Melinda Székely, Laila Tims, Thang Tu, Karl Watson, and Justine Wolfenden.

The editors would also like to thank Alice Wright and Lily Mac Mahon and the rest of the staff at Bloomsbury, without whose support this project would not have come to fruition.

CONTRIBUTORS

Suzanne Adema is Assistant Professor in Latin at Leiden University, and research Fellow in the NWO Gravitation Project 'Anchoring Innovation'.

Margaret Baird is Head of Classics at North London Collegiate School, Jeju, South Korea.

Evelien Bracke lectures in ancient Greek literature at Ghent University, and particularly works on inclusive Classics education.

Raimonda Brunevičiūtė was Professor at the University of Lithuania. She has taught Latin at university and secondary school. Her research includes the history of teaching Latin and humanitarian education in Lithuania, during the Soviet period.

Nada Bulić is Associate Professor in Classical Philology at the University of Zadar, Croatia.

John Bulwer taught in the European Schools in Bergen (NL) and Brussels and is a former president of Euroclassica.

Daniela Canfarotta holds a PhD in pedagogical and didactic teachers' training, and is a Latin/Greek teacher at classical high school 'Scaduto' in Bagheria, Italy.

Franck Colotte is former Associate Teaching Professor in Classics Education at the University of Luxembourg.

Paula da Cunha Corrêa is Associate Professor of Greek Language and Literature at the University of São Paolo.

Irine Darchia is Associate Professor in Classics at the Institute of Classical, Byzantine and Modern Greek Studies of Ivane Javakhishvili Tbilisi State University, Georgia.

Vesna Dimovska is Full Professor in Classics at Ss.Cyril and Methodius University in Skopje, North Macedonia.

Paulo Donoso is Assistant Professor in the History Institute at the Pontificia Universidad Católica de Valparaíso, Chile.

Dimitar Dragnev is a PhD student (Sofia University), teaching Latin at New Bulgarian University and in three schools in Sofia, Bulgaria.

Elena Ermolaeva is Associate Professor in Classics at Saint Petersburg State University, Russia, and Vice-president of Euroclassica (2012–15).

Attila Ferenczi is Associate Professor at the Department of Latin, Eötvös Loránd University, Budapest, Hungary.

Bärbel Flaig teaches at the Gymnasium Fridericianum Rudolstadt, where she is responsible for the planning of the teaching. She graduated from the Eberhard-Karls-University of Tübingen and the Sorbonne at Paris.

Theodor Georgescu is Associate Teaching Professor in Classical Philology at the University of Bucharest, Romania.

Margaret-Anne Gillis has taught Latin for thirty-two years at Barrie Central Collegiate and Innisdale Secondary School in Barrie, Ontario, Canada.

Peter Glatz is teacher of Classics at the monastery of Wilhering, teacher trainer at Linz, founder of Amici Linguae Latinae, President of the Austrian Classics Association, and member of the executive committee of Euroclassica.

Zoltán Gloviczki is Chancellor of the Apor Vilmos Catholic College, Hungary. He has taught theory and methodology of Latin teaching for twenty years.

Rasmus Gottschalck is former Chairman of Klassikerforeningen, the Danish association for Classics teachers.

John Hayden is a former head of high school Classics. He was awarded a Woolf Fisher Fellowship in 2015 for making Classics relevant for twenty-first-century learners.

Katja De Herdt works at Ghent University as a senior lecturer in the fields of didactics of Classics and Modern Greek. Her research interests include active Latin, vocabulary acquisition and text comprehension.

Axel Hörstedt, PhD in Latin, is High School Lecturer in languages in Uppsala, Sweden, and President of the Swedish Classics Association.

Arlene Holmes-Henderson MBE is Professor of Classics Education and Public Policy at Durham University, UK.

Steven Hunt is Associate Teaching Professor of Classics Education at the University of Cambridge, UK.

Pantelis Iacovou is the Subject Lead and PGCE consultant of Classics at Harris Federation. He is Head of Classics in three secondary and two primary schools in Essex, UK.

Simon Idema is the head of Latin at St Mary's School, Waverley, in Johannesburg, South Africa. He completed his MA in Ancient Languages with Latin at the North West University in 2023 and is currently working on promoting Latin as a school subject and establishing better relations with schools and universities that still offer Classics in South Africa.

Alex Imrie is Tutor in Classics at the University of Edinburgh, and the Scottish regional organizer for Classics for All.

Leslie F. Ivings is a former History Master at Carlton College and a member of the Classical Association of South Africa.

Anders Klarskov Jensen is the current chairman of Klassikerforeningen, the Danish association for Classics teachers.

Nijolė Juchnevičienė is Associate Professor in Classical Philology at Vilnius University, Lithuania.

Contributors

Gifty Etornam Katahena is an Assistant Lecturer in Classics and its Reception at the University of Ghana.

Shiro Kawashima is Associate Professor in Classics at Kyoto University, Japan.

Aisha Khan-Evans is Senior Lecturer in Classics Education at King's College London, UK.

Svetlana Kočovska-Stevoviḱ is Associate Professor in Classics at Ss. Cyril and Methodius University in Skopje, North Macedonia.

Antje-Marianne Kolde is Professor in Greek and Latin Didactics at the Haute Ecole Pédagogique du canton de Vaud, Switzerland.

Ilkka Kuivalainen teaches Latin and History in Ressun lukio, Helsinki, Finland.

Leslie Lagos is Assistant Professor in the History Department at the Universidad de Concepción, Chile.

Li Hui, PhD, is an Associate Professor and the Director of the Department of Latin at Beijing Foreign Studies University. Her research focuses on Sinology and Latin language and literature.

Li Qiang is Associate Professor in IHAC (Institute for the History of Ancient Civilizations) at Northeast Normal University, China.

Liu Jianchang is an undergraduate in the School of History and Culture at Northeast Normal University, China.

Sanja Ljubišić is Associate Professor of Classical Philology at the Faculty of Philosophy, University of Banja Luka, Republic of Srpska.

Robert Luther is a retired schoolteacher (Latin and French), Helsinki, Finland.

Álvaro Matías Moreno Leoni is Associate Professor of Ancient History at the National University of Río Cuarto and a researcher at Consejo Nacional de Investigaciones Científicas y Técnicas, Argentina.

Botan Maghdid is a Lecturer at Soran University, Iraq, specializing in history, with a focus on historiography and ancient Middle East history.

Louise Maguire is a Latin teacher and current Chair of the Classical Association of Ireland – Teachers.

Katarzyna Marciniak is Full Professor at the University of Warsaw, Poland, and the head of the Our Mythical Childhood programme.

Zdravka Martinić-Jerčić is Principal of the Classical Gymnasium in Zagreb and co-author of several textbooks of Latin and Ancient Greek.

Lisa Maurice is Associate Professor and Head of the Department of Classical Studies, Bar-Ilan University, Israel.

Obert Bernard Mlambo is Associate Professor of Classical Studies at Rhodes University.

Nicolas Meunier is Assistant Professor at the Université catholique de Louvain. His main interests lie in archaic Latin and Roman historiography.

Mariano Nava is retired Professor in Classics at the University of Los Andes, Merida, Venezuela.

José Luis Navarro has been Professor of Classics at the Universidad Autónoma of Madrid and at High School CARLOS III (1979–2019) and is a former President of Euroclassica.

Diego Alexander Olivera is Assistant Professor of Ancient History at the Autonomous University of Entre Ríos, Argentina.

Boris Pendelj is a Serbian scholar and translator who is involved in the journal *Lucida intervalla*, which publishes original research in all areas of classical studies.

Susana Marta Pereira is a secondary education teacher, in the areas of Classical Studies, Latin and Greek. She is a researcher in the area of Classical Language Didactics at the University of Lisbon, in the Centre of Classical Studies and is the president of the Clenardus Association.

Louella Perrett is Head of Languages at Saint Ignatius' College, Riverview, Australia, and President of the Classical Languages Teachers' Association (NSW).

Paul Pietquin is Lecturer in Ancient Greek and Latin Didactics at the University of Liège, Belgium.

Danny Pucknell is Lecturer in Classics, Ancient History and History at a Further Education college in Wales.

Teresa Ramsby is Professor of Classics at the University of Massachusetts Amherst in the USA.

Arto Rantamaa teaches English and Latin in schools in Vantaa, Finland.

Natalia María Ruiz de los Llanos is Associate Professor of Greek and Latin Language and Literature at the National University of Salta, Argentina.

Vibeke Roggen is Associate Professor at the University of Oslo, specializing in philology, Latin translation and the work of the priest Niels Thomessøn.

Janusz Ryba is Assistant Professor at the Jagiellonian University, Poland, and Latin teacher at Bartłomiej Nowodworski I High School in Cracow.

Miran Sajovic was Full Professor of the Chair of Ancient Latin Christian Literature at the Salesian Pontifical University.

Seda Şen is Assistant Professor in American Culture and Literature at Başkent University in Ankara, Turkey.

Mali Skotheim is Assistant Professor of English at Ashoka University, near Delhi, India; her PhD (Princeton, 2016) is in Classics.

Dimitrios Stamatis is Post-Doctoral Researcher in Classics Education at the National & Kapodistrian University of Athens, Greece.

Contributors

Barbara Strycharczyk is a teacher of Latin and Ancient Civilizations at 'Strumienie' High School in Józefów, Poland.

Amber Taylor is a Primary Teacher at Hollybank Primary, NI, and Outreach Officer of the Classical Association in Northern Ireland.

Tatiana Alvarado Teodorika is a María Zambrano fellow at the Complutense University of Madrid. She is deputy editor and scientific secretary of the journal *Classica Boliviana*.

Geir Þ. Þórarinsson is Adjunct Lecturer in Classics at the University of Iceland.

Florence Turpin, member of the CNARELA (*Coordination nationale des associations régionales de langues anciennes*) board and the Euroclassica committee, teaches Classics in a high school in Montpellier, France.

Néstor Urrutia is part-time Professor at the Universidad Diego Portales and Universidad Alberto Hurtado, Chile.

Charlotte Vanhalme is Associate Professor of Didactics of Classical Languages (Université libre de Bruxelles) and Applied Didactics Teacher (Pedagogical Departement, Haute Ecole Ferrer). She builds bridges between classical languages and contemporary society.

Martina Vaníková is Assistant Professor in Latin Linguistics and Didactics at the Charles University in Prague, Czech Republic.

Horatio Caesar Roger Vella is Full Professor of Latin and Greek at the University of Malta.

Goran Vidović is Associate Professor of Classics at the Department of Classics, Faculty of Philosophy, University of Belgrade, Serbia.

Eirik Welo is Senior Lecturer in Ancient Greek at the University of Oslo, Norway.

Chandima Wickramasinghe is Professor in Western Classical Culture at the University of Peradeniya, Sri Lanka.

Anna Wojciechowska is a teacher of Latin and Ancient Culture at Mikołaj Rej XI High School in Warsaw, Poland.

Drago Župarić is Associate Teaching Professor in Classics Education at the University of Sarajevo, Bosnia and Herzegovina.

INTRODUCTION

John Bulwer and Steven Hunt

We should like to thank all our contributors who have given their accounts of Classics teaching from all over the world. As the momentum of the project grew, we began to come across many more places where some form of Classics is taught than we first envisaged. On reading the chapters for the first time our reactions were often of surprise and a sense of learning something new. There turns out to be more worldwide activity in Classics than we thought, and it seems that Classics is truly a world subject. There are of course many different approaches and reasons for the continuing study of the subject, and no single rationale covers everything, but the languages and cultures of ancient Greece and Rome continue to resonate *in toto orbe terrarum*.

The book covers all five continents and includes as many individual countries as we could manage. We tried to contact a suitable person to write about their national tradition in every likely country we could think of and if there are some missing it is not for want of trying. Many are well known for their commitment to teaching Latin, Greek and classical culture in some form, but others began to emerge, and their detailed and extensive chapters opened up new vistas that were often new to us. Where we started looking at curriculum provision and practices at the secondary school level, we found in many cases an even richer discussion about the status of classical education, its wider purposes and the ways in which it makes a contribution to a lively debate about what education means in each country. Further reading at the end of each section provides a round-up of books, articles and websites which give a flavour of what we have found for those places where Classics, while not mainstream, still impacts in some way on contemporary society. The Graeco-Roman world – and neighbouring ancient societies – maintains its grip on the human imagination through art, literature and other forms of reception: this is a form of education in itself.

We hope that our readers will include practising teachers, researchers in education history and practice, education policy-makers in government, politicians, academics in Classics, history, and other disciplines. The temptation will be to go straight to individual chapters on specific countries, but we hope that readers will go beyond this to read about other countries and continents to see how their specific interest fits into a global context.

In western European countries, close to the Mediterranean sources, we see approaches ranging from conservation to innovation which provide a contrasting view to the United States of America, the United Kingdom and other anglophone countries. We have been agreeably surprised by the fascinating chapters (often giving illuminating sketches of the previous history of Classical Studies in their country) from South America, China, Japan and some African countries, and we have found the chapters from eastern Europe to show extraordinary strength and resolve in often difficult circumstances. We were not expecting the study of Latin to be quite as widespread as we found it: in that sense, Latin remains a 'world language' and it is certainly not quite as dead a language as so many media commentators like to make out. Ancient Greek fares less well: numbers in schools where it is provided have been historically small and the impression one gets is that unless an enlightened head teacher or principal is willing to bear the cost of keeping it, the language may only be found in universities in the future. By contrast, in China, the strongest interest seems to be in Ancient Greek rather than Latin, although interest in the ancient world as well as its languages seems to be growing.

There are recurrent themes that many if not all chapters deal with. There exists for many a difficulty in the recruitment and retention of pupils for courses in ancient languages and cultures and there is universal pressure to justify the subject in the face of competing subjects, particularly 'useful' ones that are thought to lead to well-paid jobs. There is often an expectation on young people to take STEM subjects (Science, Technology, Engineering, Mathematics) to the detriment of the humanities including Classics. In some countries there is a question of elitism or class difference: in some countries learning Latin or Greek is seen as a marker of class and that the subject is limited to a certain social group. This may extend to the subject being seen as a marker of traditional values and in some cases of racial distinction or colonial oppression. For many there may also be an historical connection to the Catholic church. There is even an association with right-wing politics. On the other hand, some may see it as a marker of democratic values or even as the sign of philosophical and unworldly romantics. This question of class may then lead the subject to be seen as difficult and therefore reserved for only the brightest pupils. This particularly affects systems which practise academic selection, but many chapters do not indicate this as a divisive factor any longer. The extension of Classics into primary education shows how material from the ancient world can be suitably adapted to any appropriate level and need not be made to be intellectually challenging to all. Many countries keep Classics for the secondary sector, or even beyond that into higher education where instruction in the languages may begin.

Teachers will find that the problems that they face in their own system may be duplicated elsewhere and they may be able to see how the problem has been dealt with. Alternatively, they may see that what seems to be to them a major problem, is not at all a problem elsewhere.

We use the term 'Classics' to refer to the study of the languages (Greek and Latin), literatures and cultures of the ancient Mediterranean world. Terminology differs in different languages and countries. Some refer to 'Latin' as the subject on the timetable (which may well include more than language and literature), others to languages and cultures, others to ancient languages, others to Classical Civilization as a non-linguistic study with texts read in translation. It may well be time to retire the word 'Classics' in favour of a more precise formulation but for the present it will have to do. The individual chapters will use a wide variety of terms for the subject, and these may well reveal changing attitudes to the way it is regarded and taught: whether the traditional link to the mother tongue or first language of education is retained and whether the course content is extended to include more than grammar, syntax and vocabulary. 'Greek' throughout refers to Ancient or Classical Greek, unless otherwise stated.

This volume is about beginning to learn about Classics: the languages and cultures of the ancient world. It is clear from the chapters that this beginning may occur at different stages of education. Some countries are beginning to have a provision for Latin and Greek in primary school; at an appropriate level, schools are introducing ancient languages including Greek to young children in a context of mythology and literacy enhancement. Others firmly remain in the tradition of beginning Latin in secondary school, followed by the possibility of Greek at a later stage. Non-linguistic courses can begin at different stages but often towards the final level of secondary school (teenagers love Greek tragedy which can speak directly to their concerns). Elsewhere there may be little or no provision in schools, so the first exposure to the ancient world may begin at university level where intensive courses in the languages may be provided.

This shows that levels of achievement in Classics described here may vary widely, between the introductory courses at primary level and the cutting edge of highly academic research at the most prestigious universities at the other. We are concerned here with these beginners' courses, and continuing up to intermediate and advanced level at whatever stage they may appear.

Relations between universities and schools are another thread that runs through the accounts. The chapters show that where there is cooperation, collaboration and understanding between the two sectors there seems to be more success in promoting Classical Studies and in recruiting and retaining students. If universities regard Classics teaching at school primarily as a preparation for university studies, such collaboration is likely to be difficult to achieve. If the universities recognize that not all the young people following a Classics course at school will go on to become specialists, then collaboration to ensure that all those young people take away a positive memory of their studies is more likely to occur, and then perhaps a good number of them will pursue their studies further.

The existence of a national curriculum imposed by the ministry of education is a feature of the educational system of some countries, but not all. Where there is an officially sanctioned programme of study in which Latin and other Classical subjects are included, the involvement of politicians and other policy-makers is more important. In other places without such a centralized system there is perhaps more opportunity for individual initiative and decision-making, but the official backing for the subject is lacking. There is a useful debate to be had here over which situation is more favourable to the promotion of Classical studies and individual chapters provide plenty of case studies.

Professional teachers of ancient languages will find that questions of methodology and practice occur in different ways in many places. Questions of how Latin and Greek should be pronounced; whether and how much Latin or Greek should be spoken in the classroom; whether the use of a dictionary should be allowed in examinations; whether translation into the target language of Latin or Greek should be required; which type of learning should be followed: grammar/translation or reading/comprehension; should the languages be decoded like a puzzle or should a more natural reading method be encouraged; how much emphasis should be placed on civilization/cultural aspects as opposed to pure language learning; whether it is possible or desirable to teach Classics without a language requirement at all. It takes time to make changes in teaching practices: each new generation of teachers represents some thirty or forty years of experience gained in their own schools and those in which they work. Assessment methods – especially national examinations – are often a drag on innovatory practices. Social media has already served to rupture long-held views with its constant babble of voices, views and enterprise. The impact of Artificial Intelligence (AI) on teaching and learning is only just beginning to be understood. Perhaps more prosaically, the most important question of all for many teachers of which textbook should be used finds its echo in nearly all countries, though of course the answer is rarely if ever the same. The lists of references at the end of the chapters show the textbooks in use in each country and it is notable that some are in international use, while the majority come from the country itself using its first language of education. The most often used internationally seems to be Ørberg's *Lingua Latina per se illustrata* (Ørberg 2011).

The language of publication is English, perhaps the academic equivalent to Latin today. We should like to thank all the authors for their patience and skills in writing in their second or third language, and for their tolerance and understanding of our demands as editors to create consistency in their texts. The chapters from France and Switzerland were originally written in French and have been translated by John Bulwer.

Some chapters mention the organizations for international cooperation between countries. First, FIEC (*Fédération Internationale des associations d'Études Classiques*) is a post war initiative supported by UNESCO to restore relations between international academic communities (fiecnet.org). It holds triennial meetings, most recently in London 2019, Mexico City 2022 (online) and Wrocław 2025. Euroclassica (founded in the 1990s) attempts to do the same for teachers in schools across Europe (euroclassica.eu). Euroclassica meets annually and among other activities sets a yearly Latin and Greek test at beginners and intermediate level. This is open to pupils at all schools in Europe to take at an appropriate stage in their learning and is certificated by Euroclassica. Examples of past test papers are available on the website and are provided in a multilingual format.

A recent chapter in *The Cambridge Critical Guide to Latin Literature* (Fuhrer 2024) on national traditions gives an overview from a predominantly Swiss/German viewpoint and shows the depth of tradition of Latin studies in countries all over the world, as our chapters do too with the authors setting out their national traditions in their own words. With this firmly embedded, such an historical foundation of educational and cultural capital further shows that the Latin and Greek heritage cannot be so easily dispensed with.

What begins to emerge is that Classics is not a monolith and has many different aspects. Yet all over the world there is a connection to the ancient world and the influence of ancient Mediterranean culture can be felt in many diverse places. It has even been suggested (half-humorously) that Latin should become the official language of the European Union (Ramanadane 2021). Children and young people will all read foundational texts for their own countries as part of their first language learning, but these will be different for each tradition. However, some reading of Greek myths and some texts from the ancient world may be read in many diverse regions and thus form a common reading pattern all over the world, showing a continuing influence of the ancient Mediterranean. Many contributors write of the difficulties facing them in their country in the light of curriculum reform and the demands of a modernizing educational programme, and the often fierce opposition of policy-makers and politicians. Nevertheless, they then go on to describe the tenacious and enterprising initiatives their Classics teachers, universities and associations are undertaking: reforms of teaching materials, use of new technology, innovative teaching strategies, flexibility in timetabling, exploitation of new areas available in the curriculum, extra-curricular activities and many others. Classics clearly refuses to go away completely, but in changing circumstances undergoes a kind of Ovidian metamorphosis and by adapting and improving comes back in a different guise.

References

Fuhrer, T. (2024), 'National Traditions', in R. Gibson and C. Whitton (eds), *The Cambridge Critical Guide to Latin Literature*, Cambridge: Cambridge University Press, 447–515.

Ørberg, H. (2011), *Lingua Latina per se illustrata*, Indianapolis, IN: Hackett Publishing Company.

Ramanadane (2021), 'Et si la langue officielle de l'Union européenne devenait. . . le latin?' Available online: https://www.lefigaro.fr/vox/culture/et-si-la-langue-officielle-de-l-union-europeenne-devenait-le-latin-20210208 (accessed 22 February 2024).

PART 1
EUROPE AND RUSSIA

AUSTRIA

Peter Glatz

The situation of classical languages in Austria: facts, figures, framework

There are no documents or resources for the primary level. There is not yet an Austrian equivalent to *Minimus* (Bell & Forte 1999) for primary schools. In Austria, Latin is offered as a language subject at all types of general secondary schools (*Allgemeinbildende Höhere Schulen* – AHS), currently at a total of 353 schools: *Gymnasium* (high school), *Realgymnasium* (secondary school), *wirtschaftskundliches Realgymnasium* (economic secondary school) and *Oberstufenrealgymnasium* (upper secondary school). Latin is occasionally taught at other types of schools (e.g. at commercial academies as an optional subject for a minimum of ten hours per week). Students have to take the subject to a final examination only in *Gymnasium*, either from the 7th grade (six-year long Latin, L6) or from the 9th grade (four-year short Latin, L4).

Whether Latin is not just offered as L4 at other types of high school but is actually taught, depends on parameters specific to each school: if the school only offers Latin as a second foreign language, every student must complete the Latin course. If modern foreign languages (French, Spanish, Italian, Russian) are offered as optional alternatives, the existence of the subject depends on the numbers necessary to open a class (set independently by the school), and the choice of the students in a year group. Here, just as with the choice of language in the 7th grade of high school, there is a competition with modern foreign languages. The Austrian school system does not allow you to deselect a foreign language, once you have chosen it, before taking the final school-leaving examination.

The total number of hours per week in L6 (7th to 12th grades) is usually nineteen, of which seven are in secondary level I (four in 7th grade, three in 8th grade) and twelve in secondary level II (three each from the 9th to 12th grades). The number of schools with L6 varies greatly depending on the federal state: Salzburg, Lower Austria and Vienna still have a relatively high number of schools with L6. In L4 (9th to 12th grades) the total is twelve hours per week, three per school level. However, many schools use their autonomy to open timetable spaces and increase the time to thirteen hours. However, the twelve hours per week can also be reduced by a maximum of two hours per week independently of the school, so the minimum number is ten. Schools can use their autonomy to depart from the guidelines, but the schools are very careful to adhere to the minimum number of ten hours per week, as this is the only way to avoid the university admission test. Since the standards in the final state examination for classical languages are based on the level of performance after twelve hours per week in the entire upper level, the majority of schools have twelve hours per week of Latin in the upper level (cf. Lošek 2011: 43). These requirements apply equally to all federal states. Unfortunately, L6 has been under serious pressure in recent years.

Greek is offered at a few humanistic high schools with L6. There are currently no Greek lessons in the federal states of Vorarlberg and Burgenland; in the remaining seven federal states there is at least one school with Greek.

The University Eligibility Ordinance (*Universitätsberechtigungsverordnung*) regulates how many hours in the AHS you can take to avoid taking the additional examination in Latin

(*Latinum*) or in Greek (UBVO § 2 Paragraphs 2 and 3): 'The additional examination in Latin ... is not applicable if the student of Latin has successfully completed at least ten hours per week at a secondary school [...] The additional exam in Greek ... is not required if the student has successfully attended Greek for at least ten hours per week at a secondary school after the 8th grade' (Lošek 2017).

After a historic low of 52,514 Latin students in secondary schools in the 2001/2 school year, the number rose sharply until the 2007/8 school year, reaching a maximum of 72,375, and then continued to decline again. In the 2020/1 school year (these are the most recent figures available), the number of Latin students (L6+L4) was still 55,757 out of a total student population of 212,264. Latin is still the language most taught at general secondary schools after English (French: 41,806, Spanish: 27,211) (see extensive figures in Lošek & Seitz 2020). The number of learners of Greek is at a very low level, which is exacerbated by the decline in L6. In 2020/21, when 14.65 per cent of students attended L6 in the 7th and 8th grades, the number of Greek students was 734, which is at least a slight increase compared to the previous year. Since the baby boomer generation of teachers is increasingly retiring, there is already a noticeable shortage of Latin teachers. This is very unfortunate because Latin teaching has been completely modernized over the last twenty years and has therefore been exposed to fewer criticisms, but now there is a risk of reductions due to the lack of personnel.

Curriculum development

Since 2000 there have been significant curriculum developments. In 2000 the curriculum for the lower grades (5th to 8th grades) was recreated, and in 2004 the curriculum for the upper grades (9th to 12th grades). A decisive change in the 2004 curriculum was the switch from author-based reading to topic-centred modular reading. While one classical author used to be read per semester, the curriculum modules now include texts from classical antiquity to the present, and the reading of Medieval and Neo-Latin texts is also specifically included. However, there is no longer any requirement for an author. Finally, in 2016, the curriculum for the upper grades (9th to 12th grades) was redesigned to be competency-oriented, followed in 2023 by the competency-oriented curriculum for the lower grades (L6 in 7th and 8th grades).

The upper school curriculum modules of L6 and L4 are listed below. According to the curriculum, in the 12th grade there is only one competency module.

Latin long form (L6)

9th grade | 1st and 2nd semester
Figures and personalities from mythology and history
Austria Latina
Encountering and dealing with strangers

10th grade | 3rd semester – competence module 3
Myth and its impact
Eros and Love

10th grade | 4th semester – competence module 4
Rhetoric, propaganda, manipulation
Comedy, jokes, mockery, irony

11th grade | 5th semester – competence module 5
Politics and society
The origin, idea and meaning of Europe

11th grade | 6th semester – competence module 6
People in their everyday lives
Technical languages and specialist texts

12th grade | 7th semester – competence module 7
The search for meaning and happiness
Religio

12th grade | 8th semester – competence module 7 (!)
Reception in language and literature

Latin short form (L4)

5th grade | 1st and 2nd semester
Focus: basic language education

6th grade | 3rd semester – competence module 3
Focus: basic language education

6th grade | 4th semester – competence module 4
Basic language training and beginning to read original texts based on the first reading module
Key texts from European intellectual and cultural history

7th grade | 5th semester – competence module 5
The cheerful and the profound
Politics and rhetoric

7th grade | 6th semester – competence module 6
People in their everyday lives
Love, lust and passion

8th grade | 7th semester – competence module 7
Forms of coping with life
Myth and reception

8th grade | 8th semester – competence module 7 (!)
Technical languages and specialist texts

For the module 'The cheerful and the profound' in L4, for example, texts by the following authors are presented in the textbook *Medias in Res* (Kautzky and Hissek 2021): Erasmus of Rotterdam, Johann Freinsheim, Justinus, Macrobius, Valerius Maximus, Lhomond, Suetonius, Catullus, Martial, Petronius, Phaedrus, Odo of Cherington, Carmina Burana, Hugh of Orleans, Petrus Alfonsi, Ricardus Bartholinus. The series concludes with Nuntii Latini from recent years and Latin comics (Wilhelm Busch, Hägar the Horrible, Donald Duck, Asterix).

For the module 'Politics and Rhetoric' in the textbook *Words and Actions* (Glatz & Keplinger 2007) Latin texts on politics and rhetoric for L4 are offered, including, among others, the following: Cicero, *De re publica* 1, 39; Erasmus of Rotterdam, *Querela pacis*; Thomas More, *Utopia*, 2.7; Gerardus Alesius, *Ad Americanos post ruinam turrium geminarum*; Benedict XVI *Deus caritas est*, 28 etc.

Assessment

After redesigning the curricula, a pan-Austrian working group from SODALITAS (*Bundesarbeitsgemeinschaft Klassischer Philologen und Altertumswissenschafter Österreichs / Federal Working Group of Classicists in Austria*), created a new competency model for L6, L4 and Greek. Based on the two competence areas 'translation' and 'interpretation', the following sub-competencies were defined:

1. Translating: Recognizing, assigning, structuring, recording and understanding, transferring, formulating. The first four steps of the complex translation process cannot be directly observed in written work; only the last two sub-skills of recoding come into play in the assessment.

2. Interpreting: collecting and listing, analysing and structuring, summarizing and paraphrasing, contrasting and comparing, supporting and proving, discussing and taking a stand, creative editing and design.

Consequently, the assessment scheme for written work also had to be redesigned in detail and adapted to the competency model. According to an idea by Walter Freinbichler and Peter Glatz, with a total of 60 points, 36 points were assigned to the translation text and 24 points to the interpretation text. For the translation text, 12 points are allocated to understanding the meaning, 18 points to lexis, morphology and syntax and 6 points to the quality of the target language. The translation text tests the students' linguistic competence, but the interpretation text does not have to be translated. It serves to demonstrate interpretative skills based on the text. The purpose of submitting two different texts is to require proof of the two skills translation and interpretation as independently as possible from one another. According to test theory, the demonstration of one competency must not influence the demonstration of another competency. When interpreting a text, tasks can also be set relating to the cultural context of the text (cf. the detailed presentation in Freinbichler et al. 2012, in Lošek et al. 2018 and in Consensus 2023).

After the renewal of curricula, the creation of competency models and new performance assessment formats for class work, the central school leaving examination was consequently redesigned. The written standardized competency-oriented maturity examination (SKRP) in Latin and Greek has been running since 2014 to the great satisfaction of everyone involved, not least the Federal Ministry of Education, Science and Research. Students take the SKRP in classical languages voluntarily by choosing Latin or Greek as their fourth written subject (in addition to the obligatory exams in German, modern foreign languages and mathematics). The number of entries in Latin is very encouraging and is constantly at just over 2,000. The tasks for L6 and L4 differ in terms of the linguistic and content-related complexity of the tasks. Unfortunately, only very few candidates are taking Greek (under twenty across Austria). However, this also has to do with the fact that good Greek students often compete in Latin and then it is no longer possible to compete in Greek.

The oral maturity examination (*Mündliche Reifeprüfung*, MRP) has also been completely renewed since 2015. Proof of translation competence is not provided here. The oral summary of the essential content of the examination text is considered a reproduction effort, as only texts previously discussed in class may be submitted for the MRP. The cultural studies tasks are based on previously agreed themes to which the Latin or Greek text passages presented are assigned. The current number of subject areas is eighteen for L6 and fourteen for L4. Instead of skills, we talk about three requirement areas (*Anforderungsbereiche*) that every task must contain:

(I) reproductive performance (represent subject-specific facts, determine the type of material, extract information from material, use technical terms, apply working techniques, etc.). In short: reproduction of learning material.

(II) transference (explain connections, link and classify facts, analyse materials, distinguish factual from value judgments). In short: apply skills to an unknown problem that has not been addressed in class.

(III) achievement in the area of reflection and problem solving (discuss facts and problems, develop hypotheses, reflect on one's own judgement). In short: development of independent thoughts on a problem area.

(Federal Ministry for Education and Women 2014)

Tertiary sector

In Austria you can study the classical languages Latin and Greek at four university locations:

University of Graz, Institute for Antiquity, Department of Classical Philology,
University of Innsbruck, Institute for Classical Philology (Latin and Greek Studies) and Neo-Latin Studies,
University of Salzburg, Institute for Classical Philology,
University of Vienna, Institute for Classical Philology, Medieval and Neo-Latin.

The position of classical languages in the public sphere

Whether Latin is compulsory or can be chosen depends on the type of school. There is always at least one alternative option to Greek. Since practically the entire scene has been completely renewed in the last twenty years, the public perception is good, even if the previous highly elitist approach to the subject has had a continuing negative impact for many years to this day (it is seen as a 'selective subject'). The decision-makers in recent years and the parents of our schoolchildren have often had bad experiences in their own lessons.

Latin still has a somewhat elitist reputation but is no longer perceived in the class-struggle sense of an elite that is isolating itself. The arguments for classical languages are still as follows: Latin is a prerequisite for various university studies (law, pharmacy, medicine, history, religion, German, many languages); Latin offers a deeper insight into the German language; modern Latin lessons are cultural and European lessons. The main argument put forward against classical languages is that the content is useless for further professional life and that STEM subjects should be promoted.

In response to the counter-arguments, the advertising line *#sprichlatein* for L6 was developed at the Vienna University of Economics and Business: advertising flyers, posters, banners (see www.latein.edugroup.at). Image videos are being planned. A promotional flyer for Greek provides basic information and testimonials from prominent personalities for learning Greek.

The magazine *Cursor* from the *Amici Linguae Latinae* association is aimed at an education-oriented audience and seeks to influence decision-makers positively for classical languages. The association SODALITAS serves to network and pool forces throughout Austria. A homepage will be created soon. The publication *Circulare* is published three to four times a year and the didactic publication *IANUS* is published once a year. The best counter-argument is good teaching in classical languages. The majority of teachers work very hard to ensure that the subjects are taught sustainably in the predominantly free education market.

Current trends

The almost complete focus on linguistic work was relaxed in favour of the cultural-historical parts of the lesson. In order to enable more students to successfully participate in lessons, texts are not continuously recoded. Work with differentiated materials in the sense of internal differentiation, work with bilingual texts and interdisciplinary projects are encouraged. Reading (simplified) original texts is increasingly required in the basic course. The digitalization of teaching in classical languages is progressing successfully. A relatively new and promising trend is the moderate reintroduction of *Latine loqui* or active Latin, in the interests of efficient language learning. The increased circulation promotes retention rates when learning basic vocabulary. This also causes the internalization and consolidation of grammar and, in general, the perception of Latin as a natural language.

Numerous new Latin textbooks have been published in recent years. The current clear market leader (approximately 80 per cent) *Medias in Res* (Kautzky & Hissek 2021) has initiated a complete turnaround in the textbook market. Modern preparation and a complete reorganization of the content have contributed significantly to the success in recent years. Visualization, clear structuring of the lessons, concentration on the essentials, detailed commentary on the learning vocabulary including foreign vocabulary, clear presentation of the (reduced) grammar, sufficient exercises in language and interpretation and, last but not least, a good pinch of humour have achieved success. The criticism is that the lesson texts in the basic course are consistently non-original. The *Medias in Res* textbook offers a complete programme for L6 and L4 including a wide range of additional digital materials. As a result, numerous publishers have resumed the publication of Latin textbooks based on or continuing *Medias in Res: Expressis Verbis* (Grobauer et al. 2014), *Ex Libris* (Kronberger-Schmid & Knabl 2018), *Lege et Intellege* (Klug et al. 2018), *Artes* (Bauer-Zetzmann et al. 2014) and *Contactus* (Glas & Oswald 2022). The publishers rely on (simplified) original texts in the lessons, *Contactus* also offers vocabulary with some visual support.

In addition to the products from textbook publishers, two books for interdisciplinary project teaching have also been published in recent years. *European Symbols – United in Diversity. A*

Schoolbook for European Students (Glatz & Thiel 2015) is written in English and offers examples of the reception of antiquity from twenty European countries. The common roots in the culture of antiquity are intended to make the connection between European countries visible. The book is used in several European countries, including Austria and also within the framework of Erasmus+ projects. Also, *Adventure Latin: Fascination Archaeology* (Glatz et al. 2023) looks at the Roman heritage in Upper Austria. As a counterpoint to the previous book, this publication offers a look at the region's Roman past. Museum education and school lessons are essentially interlinked here, and various museum visits are prepared at high school level.

In the area of Greek lessons, there is little commitment from textbook publishers due to the low number of students. The most commonly used book for the basic course is *Kantharos* (Fink et al. 2016). In addition, *Mythologia* is increasingly being used (published in Germany by the Lower Saxony Association of Classical Philologists in collaboration with the KWR Foundation). In the area of reading there are four books from the öbv publishing house: *Philosophy, Greek Historiography, The Greek Drama* and *From the World of Christianity, Greek texts from the New Testament*. However, all books do not correspond to the current status of the competency model.

Translation competitions in L6, L4 and Greek are held in each of the nine federal states. The top two winners in each category are eligible to take part in the nationwide competition, which runs over four days including preparation units and a supporting programme and is organized by SODALITAS. There is also the Benedictus Latin Competition every third year in Melk Abbey, in which all students in Lower Austria, all denominational high schools in Austria and all Benedictine high schools in the German-speaking area, are eligible to take part. There are no specific scholarships, from either the state or from private sources.

What lessons have been learned from the Covid pandemic? Digital media has made it possible to keep schools running. The quality of conventional face-to-face teaching could not be achieved, not least due to the fact that, on the one hand, the technology does not always work perfectly, and on the other hand the screen cannot adequately replace personal encounters. The conclusion was that the students were really looking forward to going to school again. In addition, significant numbers of less independent students who generally need more guidance in the learning process were disadvantaged. Nevertheless, the pandemic has encouraged the digitalization of school teaching. In the new lower school curriculum for 2023, there was a clear commitment to the topics of 'computer science education' and 'media education'.

Further training

Until a few years ago, new teachers only had to teach two classes independently in their first year of service. The rest of the time they sat in with their supervising teachers and had plenty of time to reflect. Since 2019, teachers in their first year of service have had to take on full and even increased teaching obligations. There is little time for adequate supervision. As a result, many young colleagues opt for reduced teaching obligations, which further increases the already noticeable shortage of teachers. Further training for in-service teachers is not offered at universities, but at teacher training colleges, of which there is at least one in every federal state. These training courses are planned by experienced teachers who lead the working group in the respective federal state and determine the specific training needs. The school directors are responsible for approving the number of training days.

Networking

Teaching projects involving several schools happen rarely. A very important one is the 'Long Night of Antiquity' promotional initiative, which takes place every two years and is based on the annual 'Long Night of the Museums', which to date has mainly taken place in Vienna. The teachers at the schools are very well networked via the establishment of working groups in the federal states and throughout Austria. Over 1,050 teachers can currently be reached via Moodle. Collaboration with local museums is maintained at various schools, e.g. in Upper Austria with various projects (see above). More intensive collaboration between school and university was institutionalized at the University of Graz with the 'Graz Latin Days'. The 'Graz resource of antique fables' (GRaF) is a remarkable product of the Graz collaboration. A good example of collaboration between school and university is the already completed Innsbruck project 'In Dialogue with Antiquity – Inscriptiones Antiquae. Scientific and didactic processing of the largest collection of urban Roman inscriptions in Austria', in which three Innsbruck high schools were significantly involved.

Conclusion

Due to enormous efforts in the last twenty years, Classics in the Austrian school system have almost been completely reorganized and so have consolidated their situation. The decline in long-form Latin is a disappointment, as is the low number of students in Greek, but publishers have taken up the upward trend in Latin by publishing numerous new textbooks.

The Latin and Greek lessons at the AHS in Austria are taught by committed colleagues who are increasingly confident and well-connected in the new media, but the general problem of a shortage of teachers is particularly noticeable in the classical subjects. SODALITAS tries to promote classical subjects at school and university through various advertising initiatives. The modern textbooks and media for Latin are up to date and the new Austrian curricula are modern, attractive, competency-oriented and balanced in terms of the relationship between language and culture. They thus offer the ideal basis for productive and, above all, meaningful language, literature, culture and European lessons using the classical languages Latin and Greek.

References

Bauer-Zetzmann, M. M., K. Diwiak, K. Goda, S. Graf, U. Trojer, M. Einfalt and R. Oswald (2014), *Artes*, Wien: Verlag Hölder-Pichler-Tempsky GmbH.

Bell, B. and H. Forte (1999), *Minimus: Starting out in Latin*, Cambridge: Cambridge University Press.

Consensus (2023), Legal basis and guidelines for competency-based performance assessment and performance assessment in the classical languages Latin and Greek. Available online: https://www.matura.gv.at/downloads/download/consensus (accessed 29 February 2024).

Federal Ministry for Education and Women (2014), The competency-oriented oral maturity examination in the subjects of Latin and Greek. Recommended guidelines and examples for topic pools and examination tasks, Wien: Österreichischer Bundesverlag Schulbuch GmbH & Co. KG.

Fink, G., G. Heil, K. Pirker, W. Elliger and T. Meyer (2016), *Kantharos*, Wien: Österreichischer Bundesverlag Schulbuch GmbH & Co. KG.

Freinbichler, W., P. Glatz and F. Schaffenrath (2012), Grundsätze des Korrektursystems zur schriftlichen Reifeprüfung in Griechisch und Latein [Principles of the correction system for the written school leaving examination in Greek and Latin]. Available online: https://latein.schule.at/portale/latein/unterricht/leistungsbeurteilung/detail/-b9474ebce2.html (accessed 14 May 2024).

Glas, R. and R. Oswald (2022), *Contactus*, Wien: Verlag Hölder-Pichler-Tempsky GmbH.

Glatz, P. and K. Keplinger (2007), *Worte und Taten: Lateinische Texte zu Politik und Rhetorik* [Words and actions: Latin texts on politics and rhetoric], Wien: Österreichischer Bundesverlag Schulbuch GmbH & Co. KG.

Glatz, P. and A. Thiel (2015), *European Symbols – United in Diversity. A Schoolbook for European Students*, Linz: Euroclassica.

Glatz, Peter (2018), Das Korrektursystem in den klassischen Sprachen Griechisch und Latein. In: Lošek, Fritz/Glatz, Peter/Niedermayr, Hermann/Weyrich-Zak, Irmtraud, Entwicklung von Testsystemen in den klassischen Sprachen. In: Günther Sigott (Hg.), Language Testing in Austria: Taking Stock. Sprachtesten in Österreich: Eine Bestandsaufnahme, Verlag Peter Lang, Berlin 2018 (Reihe: Rüdiger Grotjahn, Claudia Harsch, Günther Sigott, Language Testing and Evaluation, Vol. 40), S. 266–72.

Glatz, P., A. Thiel and S. Traxler (2023), *Abenteuer Latein Faszination Archäologie. Römisches Erbe in Oberösterreich* [Adventure Latin: Fascination Archaeology. Roman heritage in Upper Austria], Linz: unknown publisher.

Grobauer, F.-J., H. Gschwandtner and W. Widhalm (2014), *Medias in Res: Expressis Verbis*, Graz: Leykam Buchverlag.

Kautzky, W. and O. Hissek (2021), *Medias in Res! L4. 7. Texts*, Graz: Leykam Buchverlag.

Klug, J., R. Kurtz and I. Zins (2018), *Lege et Intellege*, Wien: Verlag Hölder-Pichler-Tempsky GmbH.

Kronberger-Schmid, B. and A. Knabl (2018), *Ex Libris*, Wien: Österreichischer Bundesverlag Schulbuch GmbH & Co. KG.

Lošek, F. (2011), Latein im 21. Jahrhundert. Ein Grenzgang zwischen 'toter Sprache' und lebendigem Trendfach [Latin in the 21st century. A borderline walk between a 'dead language' and a lively trendy subject]. Review of developments in Austria (with a focus on interdisciplinary teaching), in E. Rauscher (ed.), *Teaching as dialogue: From the connection between subjects to the connection between people*, Baden: Pädagogik fur Niederösterreich, 213–38. Available online: https://www.matura.gv.at/index.php (accessed 29 February 2024).

Losek, F. (2017), 'Austria Latina. Von einer "sterbenden Sprache" zum Trendfach und zum Vorzeigemodell: Altsprachlicher Unterricht in Österreich' [Austria Latina. From a 'dying language' to a trend subject and a model: Classical language teaching in Austria], *Cursor*, 13: 42–7.

Lošek, F. and M. Seitz (2020), 'Latein – Zahlen bitte!' [Latin – numbers please!], *IANUS*, 41: 62–81.

Sigott, G., ed. (2018), *Language Testing in Austria: Taking Stock*, Berlin: Peter Lang.

Sörös, M., M. Seitz, R. Glas, W. Kuchling, R. Oswald and A. Lošek (2018), 'Aspekte der Implementierung der neuen Testsysteme in den klassischen Sprachen' [Aspects of the implementation of the new test systems in classical languages], in G. Sigott (ed.), *Language Testing in Austria: Taking Stock*, Berlin: Peter Lang, 287–322.

Weblinks and further reading

Grazer Repetitorium antiker Fabeln (collaboration between school and university): https://gams.uni-graz.at/context:graf.

Latin edugroup: Austrian specialist portal for teachers, students, parents and interested parties: https://latein.edugroup.at.

'Long Night of Antiquity' promotional initiative: https://langenachtderantike.at.

Niedermayr, H. (2014), 'Generalprobe rundum gelungen! Hintergründe zur schriftlichen Reifeprüfung Latein im Haupttermin 2014' [Dress rehearsal was a complete success! Background to the written Latin school leaving examination in 2014], *Latin Forum Innsbruck*, 83/4: 1–13.

Niedermayr, H. and A. Pinter (2012), 'Herausforderungen der neuen schriftlichen Reifeprüfung –Tipps für eine zielführende Vorbereitung' [Challenges of the new written school leaving examination – tips for effective preparation], *Latin Forum Innsbruck*, 76: 1–13.

Principles of the correction system for the written school leaving examination in Greek and Latin: https://www.matura.gv.at/downloads/download/grundsaetze-des-correctionsystems-zur-schriftlichen-reifepruefung-in-griechisch-und-latein-aktualiert.

Promotional publication of the magazine 'Cursor. Magazine for Friends of the Latin Language and European Culture' of the Amici Linguae Latinae: https://latein.schule.at/portale/latein/aktuelles/detail/amici-linguae-latinae-magazin-cursor.html?no_cache=1&cHash=01ea7eaeb57e1b1200d4b09e05039fe7.

Sparkling Science Project, 'In Dialogue with Antiquity – Inscriptiones Antiquae. Scientific and didactic processing of the largest collection of urban Roman inscriptions in Austria' (collaboration between school and university): https://www.sparklingscience.at/de/show.html?--typo3_neos_nodetypes-page[id]=331&--typo3_neos_nodetypes-page[subpage]=links-downloads.

Standardized competence-oriented school-leaving examination (SRP): https://www.matura.gv.at/?id=105.

BELGIUM

Evelien Bracke, Katja De Herdt, Charlotte Vanhalme, Nicolas Meunier and Paul Pietquin

A Tale of Two Communities

Introduction

In Belgium today, a classical education inherently refers to a classical *language* education, while any teaching of antiquity without the languages (the British *Classical Civilization* and similar programmes) tends to be confined to history lessons. In spite of numerous external pressures on the subject area over the past decades, Latin and Greek language studies at secondary school continue to hold sway in both the Flemish- and French-speaking Communities – though enrolment numbers for Greek have been dwindling in the past decades. Since education in Belgium is devolved entirely and is therefore regulated and financed not by the federal government but by its separate Flemish and French Communities, this chapter will discuss them separately, as Classics teachers in both Communities are responding to different educational policies and challenges. (As the German Community is very small, we have excluded it from our discussion.) Let us first, however, acknowledge the parallel contexts in which education takes place in both parts of the country.

Indeed, in both Communities, schools are clustered in four non-private educational networks. The largest of these is the Catholic educational network. A smaller network consists of non-denominational schools funded by the Communities themselves; and two final (even smaller) networks are the local provincial/municipal schools, and independent schools (Cibois 2018; Laes 2019). Primary and secondary school each last for six years (Year 1 to Year 6). Classical language teaching is predominantly present in the first two educational networks, less so in the two smaller ones. In all educational networks, the secondary education level is divided into four school types: the General Secondary Education type, with a broad education in preparation for Higher Education; Technical Secondary Education and Vocational Secondary Education which offer more practice-based education; and Art Secondary Education. It is only students in the General Secondary Education type who get the opportunity to study Latin in the first year of secondary school, and afterwards possibly also Greek (see separate discussions), provided they choose a Latin/and or Greek pathway. All General Secondary schools in Belgium indeed offer different educational pathways from the second year onwards, such as

15

Mathematics-Sciences, Economics-Languages, or indeed combinations with Latin and Greek, such as Latin-Greek, Latin-Mathematics, Latin-Modern Languages, etc. The first year is a broad year in which students may try out different options, though in reality, it is difficult for most students to move to Latin, for example, in the second year if they have not tried it in the first. All pathways have a similar core programme (French and Dutch, English, a number of compulsory hours of Mathematics and Sciences, and Physical Education), yet beyond that their programmes vary widely. Any pathways with Latin or Greek will offer on average three to four hours of either language a week. Not all schools offer all pathways (Greek particularly is being removed in many schools because of low student numbers), which can create issues for teachers trying to cater to student needs. Indeed, while Latin student numbers are relatively positive in both communities, teaching hours are under pressure because of an increasing focus on STEM (Science, Technology, Engineering and Mathematics) subjects and – in some schools – decreasing student numbers. Teachers in both parts of the country nonetheless work hard to bring the latest didactic innovations into the classroom, primarily in order to offer a programme competitive to STEM, but also to offer Latin and Greek to increasingly multidiverse and multilingual pupil groups (see the following discussions).

In short, it is clear that Latin and Greek teaching in both communities takes place in similar educational structures, with similar outside pressures. Let us now discuss both communities separately.

The Flemish-speaking Community

Student numbers

Pathways with Latin remain popular in most secondary schools in the Flemish Community: around 9 per cent of all secondary school students have studied Latin in any given year in the past decade, though after Year 2 and again after Year 4 there is a significant drop in numbers as students, having received an introductory training in Latin, opt for more scientific studies (Classica Vlaanderen 2023). Greek is a different matter: even twenty years ago, fewer than 2 per cent of all secondary school students studied it, and in the past decade that percentage has hovered around 1.2 per cent. The main reason for this low uptake is that Greek is only accessible to those students who have already opted for Latin. It is possible for Latin-Greek students to drop Latin in favour for a Greek pathway (e.g. Greek-Mathematics) in the fifth year of secondary school, but it is not possible to study Greek without first having studied Latin. Students tend to opt for a pathway combining a classical language with a scientific focus, which tends to be detrimental for Greek studies in many schools. Research consistently reveals that students who have taken a secondary-school pathway with Latin or Greek are more likely to succeed at university studies (Declercq & Verboven 2010; Hauspie 2021), which bolsters the societal consensus of classical languages as a rigorous option at secondary school. At the same time, research also demonstrates that students with a lower socio-economic status are less likely to study Latin than their peers, so there is some class-related bias in who gets to study Latin (and hence Greek) at secondary school (Boone 2011). Initiatives such as the Ghent University Ancient Greek – Young Heroes project attempt to provide at least an introduction to Greek among non-traditional target groups (primary school pupils with a lower socio-economic status, or secondary school students that do not attend the General Secondary Education school type) (Bracke 2023).

Didactic approaches: policy and practice

The Flemish Community government imposes learning content and outcomes to determine what students should learn in any core subject; these outcomes are then interpreted by the respective educational networks who formulate guidelines for their teachers. No clear consensus exists about the ultimate outcome of classical language studies – for students to understand and reflect on original texts – and the interpretation of this policy by the different educational networks has led to quite different approaches in the first three years of secondary school. Catholic school teachers (where 85 per cent of classical language students study) have long held on to the grammar-translation method, while Communities-funded educational network teachers – from the 1960s onwards – have taken a wholly reading-based approach, in which grammar is only introduced functionally, in and through the text. To this end, they teach by means of (slightly adapted) authentic text from the beginning, while the Catholic educational network favours a more gradual transition from textbook stories to unadapted texts. This different vision of beginners' language teaching remains the key point of difference, since didactic differences have faded incrementally in the past fifteen years. Indeed, the Catholic network too now posits that grammar should always be taught in the function of reading. This revolutionary development has ensured that beginners' Latin or Greek in most schools now focuses on reading / translation, with less emphasis on grammar and rote learning. The latter is regretted by some teachers, as recent research into self-reported didactic practice of Classics teachers by De Herdt and Vereeck (forthcoming) reveals. As for reading strategies, most teachers favour a 'linear' reading method, in which the word order of Latin or Greek sentences is maintained when analysing, interpreting and translating sentences (see, for example, the reading method developed by Kristien Hulstaert (2019)). Finally, learning outcomes posit that translating is not the only way for students to demonstrate text comprehension: while oral translation remains common classroom practice, most teachers have stopped focusing wholly on translation in assessments.

The textbooks largely follow a reading-comprehension approach. Catholic schools mostly favour *Pegasus Novus* series (Ackermann et al. 2019) for Latin and the Universa-published books (*Mythoi, Logoi* and *Historia* (Halsberghe et al. 2020)) for Greek, though some teachers still teach grammar deductively and with a strong focus on forms, thereby straying from the intended didactic approach of the book. Teachers in Communities-funded schools, by contrast, largely work with their own learning materials. The Flemish school system provides individual teachers with a lot of freedom to shape their subjects, so even within one school, different didactic approaches may be observed. A very small but growing number of teachers (particularly in the Catholic educational network) are also starting to use the Active or Living Latin method, by means of Ørberg's *Lingua Latina per se illustrata* (2011), which tallies with the international trend towards spoken Latin. Living Greek is as yet not taught in Flanders.

With regard to textual emphasis, the Latin and Greek learning outcomes of Catholic and Communities-funded educational networks (Years 3–6) impose on teachers only a limited number of canonical authors or genres to be read, again leaving a lot of freedom for teachers to develop their own curriculum on the basis of their individual interests. For Greek, for example, in the Catholic educational network, only Herodotus is compulsory reading in Years 3–4, and Homer, Plato and Sophocles or Euripides in Years 5–6. In the Communities-funded educational network, only epic and tragedy are compulsory in Years 5–6 (see learning outcomes below). The reading of *some* post-classical texts (even just a few fragments) has also become compulsory in both the Catholic and Communities-funded educational networks in the past few years. In reality, it appears again that much depends on the individual teacher: there is a lively Facebook community of Classics teachers on which teaching materials (also for post-Classical texts) is regularly shared, and some teachers have also worked on developing further materials together with academics with an expertise on certain texts (see e.g. www.dcg.ugent.be/lesmateriaal/ and www.kleiotijdschrift.net). Particularly for Latin, broadening antiquity chronologically has become more common. A similar redirection is also slowly starting to take place for Greek studies, but is slower to spread, because texts tend to be less well known and for students the linguistic gap is more difficult to cross.

A final development is the increasing number of non-native Dutch speakers starting to study Latin. Traditionally a 'white' subject, Latin classes have started to become more diverse, particularly in large cities. This has led to teachers broadening the horizons of their subject area not merely chronologically but also geographically as well as content-wise (Bierten 2022). The international drive towards more inclusive Classical language education can thus also – slowly – be discerned in Flemish education, also since emphasis on this issue is increasingly being addressed in teacher training.

Teacher training

Both Flemish universities offering Classical Studies – Ghent University and the Catholic University of Leuven – also offer Latin and Greek teacher-training programmes. Via the 'educational pathway', third-year Bachelor students can start taking pedagogy modules, which lead – via a two-year or shortened one-year Educational Master's (EduMa, 60 ECTS) – to a degree allowing teachers to teach in all six years of secondary school. EduMa students are required to write a wholly or partially educational thesis, in which they make a contribution to the Flemish educational field. The alternative Educational Bachelor in Latin leading to a degree allowing teachers to teach in only the first four years of secondary school, which was long offered by a number of Further Education Colleges, has suffered cuts in the past decades. The final college (*Arteveldehogeschool*) to drop Latin teacher-training only did so in 2022, leading to fewer options for students wanting to become Latin teachers. As only small groups of students choose to study Latin or Greek at university, and even fewer of those choose to become teachers, many schools are struggling to fill vacancies, which is slowly starting to lead to a lack of teachers for Classics.

The French-speaking Community

Student numbers

Similar to Flanders, a relatively large proportion of secondary school students still study Latin in the French-speaking Community. Up-to-date figures are unfortunately not publicly available. The latest known figures put the proportion of Latinists at between 10 per cent among 14–16-year-old students and 5 per cent among 16–18-year-old students (see https://enseignement-latin.hypotheses.org/10573). The number of students doing Greek is lower, and decreasing. Generally speaking, in schools that offer a Latin pathway, the teaching of Greek does not begin until Year 3 or 4, again creating the issue of Greek being taught solely *after* Latin. An unusual but striking exception in the educational landscape is Schola Nova, a private school that organizes its secondary education around a mastery of Latin as a modern language (URL below).

Didactic approaches: current and core

In all educational networks, the content taught corresponds to the philological learning of translation and interpretation skills through lexical and grammatical work. The aim is for students to be able to translate (with the help of a dictionary) and comment on a text from antiquity presented in its original language. The cultural, historical, artistic and linguistic content is developed on the basis of authentic translated texts. Although the great flexibility of the programmes allows for a wide range of authors to be read, from Plautus to the humanist Renaissance, Classical authors remain the preferred choice, especially for assessment purposes. Each educational network has its own programmes, often containing pedagogical, didactic and methodological guidelines, and offering examples of lesson sequences. The *Fédération Wallonie-Bruxelles*, for example, encourages the use of certain approved textbooks through subsidies and lists recommended tools on a dedicated website (URL below). In addition, recently published handbooks are also geared more towards a particular educational network, without being exclusive. These include *Sur les traces d'Ulysse* for Greek lessons (Bibliothèque nationale de France 2023), and *Prosper & Felix* (Pellegrini 2018) for Latin lessons in the early years of learning.

Digital technologies (such as Wooclap, use of tablets, videos, etc.), game-based teaching (escape games), Active Latin methods, and tools adapted to specific learner profiles (dyslexia, dyspraxia, ADHD) are increasingly becoming part of teaching habits, to a greater or lesser extent depending on the school's project and the profile of each teacher. Moreover, teacher-training courses are designed to raise awareness among future teachers and stress the need to master these elements. The *Fédération Wallonie-Bruxelles* also devotes substantial resources to enabling existing teachers to acquire these areas of expertise.

Of note is the education reform currently under implementation, the *Pacte pour un Enseignement d'Excellence* [Pact for Excellence in Education]. This introduces a Common Core up to Year 3 in secondary school. From 2026 onwards, two hours of Latin will be compulsory in Year 2 (for students aged 13–14) in all educational networks. Greek is not directly part of the Common Core and will therefore no longer be taught before Year 4 in the best of cases (the organization of options in the post-Common Core period – Years 4, 5 and 6 – is not yet known at the time of writing). One of the major challenges teachers of ancient languages are facing is the great disparity in levels of knowledge of the language of instruction, in this case French, by students from a wide range of cultural backgrounds. The fight against the lowering of standards and against inequalities has indeed become one of the objectives of the Pact for Excellence in Education reform. As a result, the Common Core innovatively combines four hours of French and two hours of Latin per week within the same reference framework, but with parallel objectives. High hopes are placed on the mutual reinforcement of these two language courses, Latin and French, through increased collaboration between them. More information on the connection between French and Latin in the Common Core may be found in *Caractères*, 67 (2023). This explicit objective will extend current practices which are already producing tangible results, such as the tandem project teaching Latin through the medium of English to French- and Dutch-speaking students under the aegis of ULB E.COL.E (URL below).

The perceived elitism associated with ancient languages is a legacy that does not reflect the current position. The reform imposing the Common Core will provide Latin for all, by means of new reference frameworks that reasonably integrate societal issues without making them the exclusive concerns. A happy thematic medium has been found, sensitive to changes in our society and its concern for inclusiveness, without distorting the spirit and tradition of classical studies. The reference frameworks address themes such as the place of women in antiquity, interculturality, and environmental issues.

Teacher training

Current teacher training corresponds to a number of didactic courses of 30 ECTS, integrated as a specialization into the Master's degree in Classics or added as a supplement for graduates of the Master's degree in Classics with other specializations (such as Modern Greek, Italian, Publishing, etc.). It includes general courses in pedagogy and didactics, as well as courses in didactics specific to ancient languages and their practical applications. Courses include observation practicum [teaching practice] followed by collective critical feedback, then active supervised and assessed practicum in different schools, with different class levels, including Greek and Latin. Once they have obtained their degree, teachers benefit from in-service training, focusing on the didactics of classical languages or on cross-disciplinary methods. Some educational networks provide teachers of ancient languages with a pedagogical adviser. It should be noted that some teachers in the field are directly involved in drafting curricula, teaching tools and reference frameworks for the benefit of their colleagues.

The Pact for Excellence in Education also includes a reform of teacher initial training. This involves a joint degree programme between universities and the teaching departments of the Further Education Colleges, with each system contributing its specific expertise to the other. In concrete terms, practicum courses will be increased with more active hours, while a Master's thesis will have to include a mandatory didactic dimension, as is already the case in Flanders. At the same time, research partnerships between colleges and universities will be expanded. We should also mention a positive feature that distinguishes teachers of ancient languages. For teachers who took up their post in 2005 (taking all education levels and fields of study together), the average number of teachers still in post after five years was only 31 per cent, while in contrast, 93 per cent of Greek and Latin teachers who started their careers in 2013 were still in post five years later (88 per cent held a teaching qualification and 5 per cent only a degree in ancient languages).

Conclusion

In spite of external pressures, Classical education in Belgium remains a vibrant field, with innovative practices in both Communities driven by engaged teachers. With pressures from STEM pathways as well as an increasingly diverse student population, a growing emphasis on broadening antiquity has led to different policies and practices in both Communities. Teachers' commitment and passion (see a list of teachers' associations below) are, however, underpinned by a flexible curriculum framework in both Communities, which allows for many intellectually stimulating and emotionally motivating initiatives. This dynamism is reflected in many extra-curricular activities, such as the use of museum resources, appropriately adapted to the needs of teachers and the public concerned (for example, the *Cinquantenaire* Museum of Art and History in Brussels and the Gallo-Roman museums in Tongeren, Velzeke and Ath), school trips to Rome, Greece, Trier, or the South of France, and taking part in various competitions offered by Classical pedagogy organizations, which focus on translating authentic texts or on cultural aspects. This personal drive by teachers often keeps students engaged and committed to the subject area.

References

Ackerman, J., L. De Paep and M. Hillewaere (2019), *Pegasus Novus 1*, Kapellen: Pelckmans.

Bibliothèque nationale de France (2023), 'BNF Essentials. Homère, sur les traces d'Ulysse'. Available online: https://essentiels.bnf.fr/fr/litterature/antiquite/523f3805-7ddb-43de-90c6-d1e964e8b833-homere-sur-traces-ulysse (accessed 5 November 2023).

Bierten, R. (2022), 'Latijn in tijden van superdiversiteit. *Hic & Nunc*'. Available online: https://hic-nunc.be/nl/artikels/latijn-in-tijden-van-superdiversiteit (accessed 5 November 2023).

Boone, S. (2011), 'Sociale ongelijkheid bij de overgang van basis- naar secundair onderwijs: Een onderzoek naar de oriënteringspraktijk', Vlaams ministerie van Onderwijs en Vorming.

Bracke, E. (2023), *Classics at primary school: A tool for social justice*, London: Routledge.

Cibois, P. (2018), 'L'enseignement du latin en Belgique'. Available online: https://enseignement-latin.hypotheses.org/10573 (accessed 5 November 2023).

Classica Vlaanderen (2023), 'Classica Vlaanderen'. Available online: http://www.classicavlaanderen.be/informatie/cijfermateriaal/index.html (accessed 20 October 2023).

Declercq, K. and F. Verboven (2010), 'Slaagkansen aan Vlaamse universiteiten: tijd om het beleid bij te sturen?' Vives KU Leuven. Available online: http://www.classicavlaanderen.be/informatie/cijfermateriaal/slaagkansen.pdf (accessed 5 November 2023).

De Herdt, K. and A Vereeck (2024), 'Van grammaticaal naar genietend lezen? Recente tendensen in de Vlaamse lespraktijk Latijn'. *Lampas*, 57 (2): 124–50.

De Kesel, M., J.-L. Dufays and A. Meurant, eds (2011), *Le curriculum en questions. La progression et les ruptures des apprentissages disciplinaires de la maternelle à l'université*, Louvain-la-Neuve: PUL.

Halsberghe, J., H. Leroux and W. Vervoort (2020), *Mythoi*, Wetteren: Universa.

Hauspie, C. (2021), *The transfer effects of Latin on study achievement in Flemish Higher Education*, MA Diss., University of Ghent.

Hulstaert, K. (2019), 'Reading, seeing and understanding Latin', *Journal of Latin Linguistics*, 18 (1–2): 61–83.

Laes, C. (2019), '*Quo vadimus*? Latin and Greek in Flemish secondary schools', *Cursor*, 15: 58–60.

Ørberg, H. (2011), *Lingua Latina per se illustrata*, Bemidji, MN: Focus Publishing.

Pellegrini, J. (2018), *Prosper & Felix*, Mont-Saint-Guibert: Uitgeverij Van In.

Vanhalme, C. (2020), 'Comment conjuguer le présent actif des compétences en langues anciennes au mode des cours de philosophie et citoyenneté ?', in B. Sans and C. Vanhalme (eds), *À l'école de l'Antiquité, Hommages à Ghislaine Viré*, Bruxelles: Latomus, 241–54.

Websites

Learning outcomes set by the Community governments

Flemish-speaking Community:

- The Catholic educational network: https://pro.katholiekonderwijs.vlaanderen/didactiek-en-leerplannen/so/vakken

- The Communities-funded educational network: https://pro.g-o.be/themas/leerplannen/

French-speaking Community:

- Segec: https://enseignement.catholique.be/secteur/langues-anciennes/
- Wallonie-Bruxelles Enseignement: https://www.wbe.be/ressources/ressources-pedagogiques/programmes-et-referentiels
- CEPEONS: https://www.cpeons.be/node/189

Teachers' organizations

- ACFLA (*Association de la Communauté Française [aka Fédération Wallonie-Bruxelles] pour les Langues Anciennes*): https://www.facebook.com/groups/43648340615/?locale=fr_FR
- FRPGL (*Fédération Royale des Professeurs de Grec et de Latin*): http://fpgl.be
- VLOT (*Vereniging van Leerkrachten Oude Talen*): https://www.vlot-vzw.be/

Resources

Fédération Wallonie-Bruxelles:

- Resource platform dedicated to the FW-B educational community: https://www.e-classe.be/.
- Subsidies webpage: www.enseignement.be/index.php?page=28586.
- Kleio. *Tijdschrift voor oude talen en antieke cultuur* [Journal of Ancient Languages and Ancient Culture]: www.kleiotijdschrift.net.
- Schola Nova https://www.scholanova.be/fr/presentation.
- ULB E.COL.E: www.ulb.be/fr/plateforme-collaborative-ulb-e-col-e/tandem-de-classiques.
- University of Ghent. Materials for Latin and Ancient Greek: www.dcg.ugent.be/lesmateriaal/.

BOSNIA AND HERZEGOVINA

Drago Župarić and Sanja Ljubišić

Introduction

Federation of Bosnia and Herzegovina

The education system in Bosnia and Herzegovina is quite decentralized, since the country consists of two entities: the Federation of Bosnia and Herzegovina (consisting of 10 cantons) with the Republic of Srpska (which is administratively divided into regions) and the Brčko District (as a separate district). In the Federation of Bosnia and Herzegovina, the competence for education is decentralized and under the control of individual counties. Education is organized through four basic levels:

1. Preschool upbringing and education.
2. Basic education.

3. Secondary education.

4. Higher education.

In recent years, there has been a noticeable decline in the birth rate and population, which has reduced the number of pupils and students. For example, the total number of students enrolled in regular elementary schools and schools for children with special needs in the school year 2022/23 amounted to 169,775 students, which represents a decrease of two per cent compared to the previous school year (Institute for Statistics 2022).

Latinity in Bosnia and Herzegovina is an under-researched area, but one that forms an inseparable part of our cultural heritage. Learning the Latin language is included in the school curriculum of secondary education, primarily in *gymnasiums*, medical schools and some vocational schools. During the two-year programme, there are usually two hours per week of Latin in both classes, or distributed as two hours in one year and one hour in the second year. In the Catholic School Centres, the possibility of learning Greek is also offered, with a mandatory one hour per week during the two-year course. Since the student population is decreasing, so is the number of students attending these subjects. In Bosnia and Herzegovina, the Franciscan Classical High School in Visoko preserves classical education, with a focus on Latin and Greek (three hours per week).

In higher education, Latin is usually taught during two semesters at philosophy faculties. For example, at the Faculty of Philosophy in Sarajevo, students studying history and archaeology must also choose Latin or Greek, and Italian language students are required to attend Latin lectures.

Greek is taught during two semesters at the Faculty of Philosophy in Sarajevo. It is a compulsory subject for students studying the Latin language and Roman literature, and for philosophy students. Students of archaeology and history can choose Greek as an elective subject, with one hour of lectures and two hours of exercises per week.

At a high academic level, the University of Sarajevo and the University of Mostar offer a study programme in Latin language and Roman literature. However, this programme has seen a significant drop in the number of enrolled students in recent years, which is a consequence of the pressure on the humanities and the growing challenges in finding jobs on the labour market. For example, during the winter semester of the academic year 2022/23, a total of 52,874 students were enrolled in higher education institutions, which represents a decrease of 4.9 per cent compared to the previous academic year. This decline threatens the viability and future of this study programme (Institute for Statistics 2023).

Republic of Srpska

In the Republic of Srpska, the majority are state schools, with a few private and religious schools whose diplomas are recognized by the state. The Ministry of Education and Culture of the Republic of Srpska and the Republic Pedagogical Institute of the Republic of Srpska regulate curricula, programmes and textbooks in state schools. These institutions supervise primary and secondary education, while higher education is supervised through the Agency for Science and Higher Education. In the Republic, classical languages are studied in secondary schools and colleges.

Primary school education lasts eight years and is mandatory for children aged seven to fifteen. Classical languages are not studied at this level of education. Secondary education lasts from two to four years and includes different types and forms of education. It is attended by students aged fifteen to eighteen, and is not compulsory. In secondary schools where classical languages are taught, especially Latin, there are different courses. *Gymnasium* is divided into general, social-linguistic, scientific-mathematical and computer-informatics courses. The Latin language is taught in the general and social-linguistic route pathway during the first two grades, while in the natural-mathematics and computer-informatics pathway, the Latin language is taught only in the first grade.

Greek and Latin were studied only in the Catholic School Centre (KŠC) in Banja Luka from 2007 to 2012, after which, due to a lack of staff, Greek was abolished, and only the Latin language remained in all four grades. In professional schools, such as those specializing in economics and medicine, Latin is taught only in the first grade.

At the higher educational level, classical languages, including Latin, are studied at the Faculty of Philosophy and Philology of the University of Banja Luka and the University of East Sarajevo. At the Faculty of Philosophy in Banja Luka, Latin is studied as part of the Study Programme for History, during the first four semesters of the undergraduate course, and during the two semesters of the Master's course, depending on the academic field or department. At the Faculty of Philology in Banja Luka, Latin is taught within the Department of Romance Studies, during four semesters. Following the 2022 education reforms, the curriculum for French language students was shortened to two semesters in the third year. Latin is also studied independently at the Department of French language and literature and Latin, including Latin morphology and syntax and Roman literature.

According to the Republic Institute of Statistics of the Republic of Srpska, a drop in the birth rate was observed, which resulted in a decrease in the number of pupils and students at the beginning of the school year in 1997/98. In 2010, significantly more students were enrolled in primary schools, secondary schools and higher education institutions, but over time that number has decreased. Data from 2020/21 show a significantly reduced number of enrolled pupils and students. That reduction is the result of economic and socio-political factors that led to frequent population migrations.

Classics in the high school

Federation of Bosnia and Herzegovina

Classical subjects have their important place in *gymnasium* [high school] education, and they are also present in some vocational high schools, if this is determined by the curriculum (e.g. School of Agriculture, Nutrition, Veterinary and Service Activities Sarajevo).

Teachers often respond to the arguments for and against learning classical languages. Arguments for include: provide cultural and historical value, develop language skills, encourage philosophical thinking and facilitate the learning of other languages. Arguments against include: may be considered less relevant in the modern world, may be challenging for students, do not necessarily lead to employment in certain industries and may be unavailable due to lack of resources. The decision to study classical subjects depends on personal interests and resources.

Classical language teachers respond to criticism of the relevance of the Latin language in the modern world by emphasizing that classical languages contribute to general education and the development of critical thinking, and that the challenge of learning classical languages develops important life skills such as patience and perseverance. They also point out that studying classical languages can provide the foundations for a variety of careers, including education, linguistics, archaeology and philosophy, despite the lack of direct jobs.

Republic of Srpska

In the Republic of Srpska, classical languages, such as Latin, face a limited presence in the education system. Curricula were reduced, and Greek was dropped from the curriculum. Latin remains compulsory only in certain secondary schools, including *gymnasia* with different majors. Compulsory Latin is taught in high school as follows: general major two hours per week in first and second grade (total 144 hours); science and mathematics course two hours per week only in first grade (72 hours); computer science major two hours per week only in first grade (72 hours). According to the 2018 Curriculum, compulsory Latin language is taught in the following majors: socio-linguistic major two hours per week in first and second grade (total 144 hours), general major two hours per week in first grade (72 hours), science and mathematical major two hours per week in first grade (72 hours), computer science major two hours per week in first grade (72 hours). Also, compulsory Latin language is taught in vocational, economic and medical schools. In an economic school with the profession of business-legal technician, the Latin language is taught in the first grade two hours a week (68 hours). In a medical school that educates different profiles (medical technician, pharmaceutical technician, dental technician, cosmetic technician and physiotherapist), Latin is taught in the first grade for two hours a week (68 hours). Elective courses in classical languages are not widely available, except in the Catholic School Centre (KŠC), where Latin is taught as a compulsory subject: 2+2 classes in the first and second, and 1+1 in the third and fourth grades.

The perception of classical languages in Bosnian grammar schools is worrying, given the trends in the education system. Modern times are more inclined towards the natural sciences and computer science, which has resulted in the reduction or even the abolition of classes devoted to classical languages. The classical *gymnasia* that once taught Greek and Latin no longer exist, while in the remaining *gymnasia* Latin classes were held only with many restrictions.

Humanities were suppressed, and classical languages, the foundations of humanistic education, were also affected. Critics of the education system favour a pragmatic approach, aimed at educating the profiles needed in the labour market, which is dictated by employers. Even the students themselves often consider the Latin language 'dead' and unnecessary, mainly due to the perception of difficulties in learning it.

A minority advocates the study of classical languages as the foundation of general education, emphasizing the contribution of the Greeks and Romans to the science and culture of the modern world. Teachers of classical languages try to popularize the learning of these languages and bring them closer to students through the context of ancient civilization, including history, literature, art and culture. Also, there are opportunities for occupations and jobs that require knowledge of classical languages in the fields of education, science, culture (archives, museums, libraries) and tourism, which is often associated with archaeological sites from the ancient era in the area.

Trends in Classics education

Federation of Bosnia and Herzegovina

Trends in education in Bosnia and Herzegovina are directed towards technology integration, active teaching, personalized learning and inclusive education in order to provide better educational opportunities for all students. Classical language teachers use a variety of methods to facilitate learning, including authentic texts by classical authors for a better understanding of the language and culture, and grammar textbooks with examples and exercises for practical application. This modernizes education according to global guidelines, preparing students for future challenges.

Here are some grammar books with examples and exercises for practical application:

- Samouković-Jusufbegović, B. and S. Dević (n.d.), *Latinski jezik za 1. i 2. razred medicinske i zdravstvene struke* [Latin language for 1st and 2nd grade medical and health profession], Sarajevo: "OKO".
- Salopek, D., Z. Šešelj and D. Škiljan (1997), *Orbis Romanus,* Zagreb: Profil.
- Basic, I. and F. Međeral (2013), *Elementa linguae Latinae medicae,* Zagreb: ŠK.
- Bagarić, J. (2004), *Latinski 1–2: udžbenik za gimnaziju* [Latin 1–2: textbook for high school], Sarajevo: Sarajevo Publishing.
- Bagarić, J. (2019), *Linguae Latinae elementa,* Zagreb: ŠK.
- Arnautović, O. (2012), *Latinski jezik 1–2* [Latin language 1-2], Sarajevo: Svjetlost.
- Gortan, V., O. Gorski and P. Pauš (2011), *Elementa Latina*, Zagreb: ŠK.
- Martinić-Jerčić, Z. and D. Matković (2013), *PROMETEJ* [Prometheus], Zagreb: ŠK.

Pedagogical approaches in the teaching of classical languages include encouraging understanding of word meaning and sentence construction, connecting language elements with classical stories and myths, encouraging creative writing in classical language, group learning for interaction and cooperation among students, and emphasis on regular practice of reading, writing and speaking. Teachers adapt their approaches and materials to facilitate the learning of classical languages.

During the pandemic lockdown, digital technology had a significant impact on the teaching of classical languages. Some positive aspects include access to online resources, online learning and creative tools. Lessons from the lockdown include the importance of flexibility in teaching, the key role of teachers, the need to study online teaching, sharing experiences and emergency preparedness. Balancing digital tools with traditional approaches remains key to fully understanding classical languages.

Classical language teachers have stood out for their adaptability and commitment during the pandemic. They used innovative methods and digital resources to enrich the learning experience, providing students with useful tools for successful language learning. To maintain engagement, lecturers encouraged collaborative learning through online platforms. They maintained regular communication with students and their parents through e-mail, online conferences and social networks. These valuable practices and digital resources not only helped preserve the quality of classical language teaching during the pandemic, but also became an integral part of the teaching process after returning to classrooms.

Republic of Srpska

The teaching of classical languages in the Republic of Srpska used to be conducted face-to-face, using the grammar-translation method. Teachers presented grammar rules that students had to learn and apply to sentences and texts related to a specific grammar lesson.

The oldest curriculum for *gymnasia* dates back to 1993 and contained a gradual progression in language concepts from simple to complex grammatical structures. Apart from textbooks, other teaching aids such as audio-video recordings, radio and television shows and films were also recommended.

However, these teaching programmes were considered outdated, so in 2011 and 2012, the Ministry of Education and Culture of the Republic of Srpska implemented a project to modernize the teaching contents for the first and second grades of grammar schools, including the Latin language subject. This project resulted in new curricula that emphasized grammatical topics, operational goals, programme content, and their connection to other subjects. Also, emphasis is placed on creating a favourable working atmosphere, encouraging student independence in concluding rules, understanding language concepts in the context of civilization, and group work.

The teaching of Latin in schools is often based on the traditional grammar-translation method, which is considered outdated. This approach focuses on theoretical knowledge and analysis of grammatical rules, with an emphasis on text translation. However, nowadays this method is considered dry and limiting. It is recommended to introduce other methods, such as direct and combined.

The direct method, which is used in learning modern languages, is difficult to apply with Latin because it is no longer in wide use as a spoken language. Also, the vocabulary of the Latin language does not follow today's civilizational and cultural-technological changes.

The combined method, which is based on logical thinking, connecting previously acquired knowledge with new ones and analogy with the mother tongue (Ljubišić 2016), seems to be a more acceptable option for teaching Latin. Teachers usually choose this method, which allows flexibility and adaptation of teaching to the needs of students. Latin textbooks approved by the Ministry of Education and Culture of the Republic of Srpska are most often used as teaching aids in the classroom.

The approved textbooks for high school are:

- Simeunović, A. (2006), *Latinski jezik za prvi razred gimnazije* [Latin language for the first grade of high school], Istočno Sarajevo: Zavod za udžbenike i nastavna sredstva.

- Šijački-Manević, B. (1998), *Gramatika latinskog jezika* [Grammar of the Latin language], Belgrade: Zavod za udžbenike i nastavna sredstva.

- Pakiž, M., T. Kiselički-Vaš and M. Kisić (2005–12), *Latinski jezik za drugi razred gimnazije* [Latin language for the second grade of high school], Belgrade: Zavod za udžbenike i nastavna sredstva.

The above-mentioned textbooks were designed according to the indirect method (grammatical-translation).

In the textbook for the second grade of high school, which deals with syntax, an innovative approach can be observed. The text is conceived in the form of a comic with the main characters Tranion, a cunning slave from Plautus' comedies, and the imaginary character History, as a teacher of life. They have a conversation in the 'speech-bubbles' on the pictures. These dialogues are for learning Latin grammar. The textbook also includes elements of Roman literature, the story of the founding of Rome, Greek myths that were covered by Roman writers, and the names of people from the tombstones of ancient Singidunum. This approach makes the textbook more attractive to students, stimulates their curiosity about the main characters and dialogues, and encourages them to use grammar explanations and vocabulary to better understand the content.

Books which are approved studies for secondary vocational schools are based on professional terminology:

- Gemaljević, O. (2023), *Latinski jezik za medicinske, veterinarske i poljoprivredne škole* [Latin language for medical, veterinary and agricultural schools], Belgrade: ZUNS.

- Jagić, V. and V. Marković (n.d.), *Latinski jezik za prvi razred medicinske škole, zanimanja laboratorijsko-sanitarni, zubno-stomatološki, farmaceutski, fizioterapeutski, akušersko-ginekološki i medicinski tehničar* [Latin language for the first year of medical school: laboratory-sanitary, dental, pharmaceutical, physiotherapeutic, obstetric-gynecological and medical technician], Belgrade: Data Didakta.

During the time of the pandemic in the 2019/20 and 2020/21 school years, digital technology has become essential for teaching in the Republic of Srpska. The Ministry of Education and Culture of the Republic of Srpska and the Republic Pedagogical Institute cooperated with the Radio/Television of the Republic in order to organize distance learning through television broadcasts. Short video lessons were also created and distributed to students. Teaching was conducted through the Microsoft Teams platform and Google classroom through which pupils and students were directly involved in teaching, but was also a place where they could find materials used by teachers and professors. The experience of teachers and students shows that this type of teaching is demanding and difficult, and that nothing can replace live interaction in the classroom.

Teacher training

Federation of Bosnia and Herzegovina

Students of the Latin language and Roman literature on Master's studies must participate in pedagogical and didactic activities during their studies. These include high school internships, high school Latin teaching and college teaching. In addition, during their studies, students must make written preparations for classes.

Teachers of classical languages go through university programmes that systematically prepare them for teaching Latin and other classical languages. These programmes provide thorough theoretical and practical knowledge to ensure high quality teaching. During their studies, teachers have the opportunity to conduct their own research in order to advance their professional development and deepen their understanding of the subject. Also, cooperation with colleagues from different schools and countries encourages the exchange of experiences, materials and ideas and contributes to the development of creative teaching methods. This enables classical language teachers to be informed of best practices and to improve their skills in order to provide high quality teaching to their students.

Republic of Srpska

In the Republic of Srpska, there is no special methodical training for future teachers of the Latin language. Up until now, it has not been the practice of their education after schooling, so they are left to themselves, to their acquired knowledge, talent and imagination. It is planned that in the future, with the support of the Faculty of Philosophy in Banja Luka, an educational round table for teachers of the Latin language will be held. Through various workshops and lectures, the professional training and development of Latin language teachers would be enabled, who, based on the good experiences of others, would apply some innovations in the teaching process.

Wider participation

Federation of Bosnia and Herzegovina

Students of the Faculty of Philosophy in Sarajevo have at their disposal a rich library with relevant literature and critical editions of Latin texts. In Bosnia and Herzegovina, we do not have competitions in classical languages at the county or state level. However, I know that the students at the Franciscan Classical High School from Visoko participated in the Euroclassica international competition. In that *gymnasium* there is also a 'Greek corner' stocked with educational material and books in the Greek language.

Republic of Srpska

Secondary schools and faculties in the Republic of Srpska achieve successful cooperation with the University Library, Archive and Museum there. History students undertake field-work where they deal with sources in the Latin language and archaeological sites in the Republic.

The Faculty of Philology of the University of Banja Luka, which founded the Centre for Hellenic Research (CHI) in 2021 with the support of the Embassy of Greece in Bosnia and Herzegovina, is particularly noteworthy. After the Faculty of Philosophy in Pale, University of East Sarajevo, it is among the first centres of its type in the Republic. CHI focuses on the multidisciplinary study of Hellenic culture from antiquity to the present and has a wide range of activities, including scientific research, teaching and cultural projects (University of Banja Luka 2021). CHI aims to promote the study of Hellenism and its role in the creation of European identity, as well as to promote the Greek language and culture. In addition to numerous lectures and exhibitions, CHI organized the first School of Ancient Languages and Cultures in 2022, intended for high school students from all over Bosnia and Herzegovina. The school included Greek and Latin language courses, workshops inspired by ancient heritage, and a visit to the Roman baths in Laktaši and the Republic of Srpska Museum.

In addition to CHI, the promotion of the Greek language and culture is also dealt with by 'Greek Corners', which were established at primary and secondary schools in the Republic of Srpska and Bosnia and Herzegovina (Prijedor, Doboj, Derventa, Zvornik, Visoko, Višegrad and Šamac).

Conclusion

Federation of Bosnia and Herzegovina

The experience of teaching classical languages in Bosnia and Herzegovina indicates the need to adapt to modern methods and technology in order to attract new generations of students. The flexibility of the curriculum and administrative framework and the preservation of social contact between teachers and students are also important. Continuous education of teachers and exchange of experiences are crucial and teaching classical languages is challenging because it is increasingly difficult for students to acquire language content. The experience of teaching during the pandemic accelerated changes in programmes and organization, showing that quality can be maintained or even improved under difficult conditions.

In our country, there is a lack of additional literature on classical pedagogy. Before the pandemic, the practice was to organize an annual lecture on a specific topic at the Faculty of Philosophy in Sarajevo, as an illustration of the best methods, in which professors of classical languages would participate, but now there is no such thing. This lecture and the accompanying discussion were organized by members of the professorial team from the Department of Latin Language and Roman Literature.

Republic of Srpska

We can conclude that there is concern about the decline of interest in learning classical languages and humanities. A group of enthusiasts, especially professors of classical languages, is working to promote these subjects and change the negative perception that they are useless and unnecessary. Their teaching approach focuses on encouraging the spirit of inquiry and students' interest in the ancient past, culture, civilization, mythology, literature and other aspects that include classical languages.

The key point is to focus on the students and adapt the teaching to their cognitive abilities in order to adopt the grammar rules and apply them to the texts. Also, the importance of not only the language side of learning is emphasized, but also the approach of ancient civilization and its heritage in order to convey to students the importance of these subjects for the modern world. Classical language teachers should go through additional education and acquire new competencies in order to improve the teaching process. The need to strengthen the creativity of teachers and students and their involvement in the learning process, connecting acquired knowledge with other subjects and teaching in an interesting and creative way is also emphasized. This approach is aimed at adapting the teaching of classical languages to the twenty-first century and the interests of today's students.

References

Boban, L., J. Grubeša and J. Jurčić (2022), *Specifičnost latiniteta u Hercegovini* [Specificity of Latinity in Herzegovina], Mostar: University of Mostar.

Institute for Statistics (2022), First Results, Institute for Statistics of the Federation of Bosnia and Herzegovina, year XIV, number 12.1, Sarajevo.

Institute for Statistics (2023), First results, Institute for Statistics of the Federation of Bosnia and Herzegovina, year XVI, number 12.3, Sarajevo.

Knezović, P. (2013), 'Polivalentnost latinskog jezika u Bosni i Hercegovini' [Polyvalence of the Latin language in Bosnia and Herzegovina], *Kroatologija*, 4 (1–2): 24–55.

Ljubišić, S. (2016), 'Specifičnosti Metoda u Nastavi latinskog Jezika' [Specifics of the Method in Continuing the Latin Language], *Naša škola*, 1–2: 115–25.

University of Banja Luka (2021), 'Elaborat o potrebi i opravdanosti osnivanja Centra za helenska istraživanja kao podorganizacione jedinice Filološkog fakulteta Univerziteta u Banjoj Luci' ['Elaboration on the necessity and justification of establishing the Centre for Hellenic Research as a sub-organizational unit of the Faculty of Philology of the University of Banja Luka']. Available online: https://unibl.org/sr-lat/vesti/2021/12/otvoren-centar-za-helenska-istrazivanja (accessed 5 November 2023).

BULGARIA

Dimitar Dragnev

Introduction

Bulgaria is situated on the south-east corner of the Balkan peninsula, a place where Greek and Latin has been in use for many centuries by Greeks, Romans, local inhabitants – Thracians – and other populations even before the foundation of the First Bulgarian State around 680 CE. Latin, and most significantly Greek, continued to be a major cultural factor throughout the next centuries. This rich classical tradition is only partially reflected in the contemporary Bulgarian educational system today.

Today Bulgaria is a unitary state and the education system is centralized and guided by the Bulgarian Ministry of Education and Science. There are around 700,000 students in all forms of school education (the overall population is just below seven million people in the country, census of 2021). The general structure of the education system consists of seven years of primary education, five years of secondary education (in *gymnasium*, in high school, in vocational school or in another institution of secondary education) and tertiary education (universities and colleges). Education in Bulgaria (compulsory until age sixteen) is secular and free in state-owned and municipal schools. However, some additional expenses are incurred (e.g. for purchase of textbooks in secondary education, which costs will be almost fully covered after 2024). The private schools and universities charge fees, although they offer students scholarships. The vast majority of the pupils and the students attend the state schools and universities (for further description see Eurydice 2023).

The state education standards determine the levels of necessary general and vocational preparation. They relate to various elements of the educational environment including educational contents, textbooks and school aids, teachers' licensing and qualification, the assessment system and inspecting (Eurydice 2023). However, neither the current law on pre-school and school education which came into force in 2016, nor the subsequent ordinances of the Ministry of Education and Science, explicitly mention any of the classical subjects – Latin, Greek or Ancient Culture – which have been part of the curriculum of the Bulgarian schools since the foundation of the current Bulgarian state in 1878. The former law on people's education (in force between 1991 and 2016) was also mute on the presence of Classics in Bulgarian schools. Therefore, in fact, nowadays it is up to each educational institution to put Latin and Greek into their respective curriculum either as a 'foreign language' or in another form.

Status of classical subjects

According to the estimate of the author, currently around 1,000 students are studying Latin and/or Greek in Bulgaria. The official numbers for 2023 in Sofia (the ancient Roman city of Serdica, today the most populous city and the capital of Bulgaria), where the vast majority of the students are concentrated, is 735 (around 320 of them in the upper level of primary education) for Latin and 307 for Ancient Greek (Prohazkova 2023). However, these numbers do not seem to reflect all the forms in which the ancient languages are provided. The number of Greek students has been relatively steady and the number of Latin students has been slightly rising over the last years, but since 2019 there has been a great development and an amplification of the ways of incorporating Latin and Greek into the school curricula, of which further details will be provided below. There are also between fifteen and twenty students admitted to the Bachelor and Master programmes of Classics (Classical Philology) at Sofia University 'Saint Clement of Ochrid' ('Sveti Kliment Ohridski' in Bulgarian), which is the sole place providing coherent instruction in this field.

Teaching

The majority of secondary level students of Latin and Ancient Greek in Bulgaria are those of the National Gymnasium for Ancient Languages and Civilizations 'St. Constantine Cyrill the Philosopher' which is a unique educational institution in many ways. A state-owned school, defined as a 'school of culture' and as a 'cultural institute' by the country's legislation, it is governed both by the Ministry of Education and Science and the Ministry of Culture with close ties to Sofia University, which provided it with the additional honorary name of 'National Classical Lyceum'. It was founded in 1977 by some leading scholars of Sofia University and the Bulgarian Academy of Sciences who persuaded the communist governors that the future of scholarship in Bulgaria would be doomed without proper knowledge of Classics. Its curriculum (drafted by the scholars and improved over the years by the teachers and university professors with the support of the long-time director Gergina Toncheva) has remained generally unscathed for over forty years since its foundation, despite the political turbulences and many attempts to annihilate the school. The five-year curriculum obliged every student to have four lessons per week of Latin for five years and four lessons of Greek for four years (after the first year). The classes of Ancient Civilization (three times a week) in the third year were also one of the highlights of the curriculum. This enabled the teachers to read authors such as Caesar, Sallust, Cicero, Seneca, Ovid, Xenophon and others in the higher classes. For the last two years in the curriculum there were six lessons a week (the so-called 'profiles'), which the students were obliged to select according to their preference and once selected, they became obligatory. Students interested in classical languages could choose the profile of Latin with Italian or the profile of Greek with Modern Greek, in which they had three lessons a week more than the other students both for Latin/Greek and for Italian/Modern Greek. So, a student could graduate from the high school with up to 899 hours of Latin or 755 hours of Ancient Greek, gaining some experience of reading Livy, Tacitus, Horace, Catullus, Pliny or, respectively, Homer, Hesiod, the tragic and the comic poets, Plato, Aristotle, Herodotus and Thucydides. Old Bulgarian (Old Church Slavonic), a language of utmost importance to Bulgaria, closely connected with Latin and Greek, was and still is a part of the curriculum. Also, the students are given the opportunity to participate in the annual school competition (Olympiad) in both classical languages.

However, the introduction of the current Law on pre-school and school education in 2016 saw the obligatory reduction of the curriculum of Latin and Greek in the high school, because of the general reorganizing of the educational system. This saw the merger of the classes of Ancient Civilization with the classes of Latin and Greek and their reorganization and/or reduction. The students also lost the possibility of choosing Latin and Greek as their 'profile' in the last two years. Whereas the opportunities in the secondary education for this high school were reduced, the new law gave it the possibility to admit students in the upper level of primary education, where Latin and Ancient Civilization are studied with a timetable of one or two hours per week. Not all the students from the primary level, though, will continue in the secondary level of the school.

The application of the current law has also had a positive side, since it provided a simpler way of introducing new subjects in the schools. This is applicable also to classical languages and prompted some schools to introduce Latin in various forms. In the beginning of September 2021, the Minister of Education of Bulgaria approved new school curricula (composed by the author of this article in closer collaboration with professors of Sofia University and with the advice of other high school teachers), which allow all the secondary schools in Bulgaria (if they wish) to offer obligatory classes of Latin. This is the first positive initiative of this kind in the country since the Second World War.

The approval of the curricula is prompted by 17th School 'Damian Gruev' in Sofia, which introduced Latin for its students in early 2017 and then admitted its first class of students.

The material is distributed into three levels – A.1, A.2 and B.1.1 according to the CEFR (Common European Framework of Reference for Languages). The schools can use these curricula from the ninth until the twelfth (and last) grade. These documents allow not only the teaching of grammar, but also introduce some spoken and written elements into class. Level B.1.1 has a generous timetable and therefore is divided into four obligatory modules, which bear the names 'Oral communication', 'Written communication', 'Language and culture', 'Linguistic practice'. Furthermore, teachers are free to organize the programme of a further fifth module. The schools which want to choose Latin as an obligatory subject must provide the students with at least 288 hours throughout the four years, which could grow up to 671 with some other options (see the links to the curricula at the end of this chapter).

The students can also sit a State Maturity Exam in Latin, which includes written exercises – reading and translation, listening and composition of two small texts in Latin with guidance. This exam occurred in 2022 for the first time after more than seventy-five years.

Moreover, it has become a lot easier to introduce, with funding from the state, Latin lessons as optional subjects for the students who want to study the language for a year or more. Significant successes have been recorded in Sofia: in 9th French Language School 'Alphonse de Lamartine', in First English Language School, in the National Gymnasium of Sciences and Mathematics 'Acad. Lyubomir Chakalov', in 164th Spanish Language School 'Miguel de Cervantes', but also in Plovdiv (ancient Philippopolis) in Humanities Gymnasium 'Saint Cyrill and Saint Methodius'. Greek has also been offered in Sofia in 9th French Language School 'Alphonse de Lamartine' and in a language high school in Haskovo. In some cases, the students who voluntarily attended these lessons showed remarkable achievements which prompted the school management to introduce Latin as an obligatory subject into the curriculum.

Other students are studying in the Humanities High School 'Konstantin Preslavski' in Varna (ancient Odessos), in the theological seminaries of Sofia and Plovdiv and in some other *gymnasia* which provide vocational instruction in the field of human or veterinary medicine, where Latin is studied for professional purposes only. There have been some private schools who have offered Latin over the years, most significantly the French Lycée 'Victor Hugo' in Sofia, which follows the curriculum of the French state.

The aforementioned 17th School 'Damian Gruev' has been teaching Latin (one or two hours a week) to some younger students (the upper level of primary education) with success.

Nowadays, in Bulgaria there is no public debate over the role of Classics and its contribution to the education of young people, nor, as already hinted, are they perceived by the state as strategically or particularly important. This gives more freedom for teachers and students to implement their initiatives, if they meet the support of the school community (and if the community does not deem the languages 'difficult' and therefore less attractive). Actually, the teachers and the professors are challenged to respond to a growing interest by some students who want to study Latin and/or Greek, because they want to pursue a study in a relevant field, where these languages are needed, or simply because they are just interested in these languages, frequently incited by a plethora of materials available to them via books, podcasts, YouTube, Instagram and even TikTok videos, the products of an international community in which they want to participate.

Resources

The most popular textbooks in recent times are *Latin for Beginners* (Atanasova & Yordanova 1996), *Ancient Greek for Beginners* (Bogdanov & Stefanov 1988), and *Ancient Greek for Beginners* (Slavova 2013). They include elements of grammar-translation and reading methods (which remain the most popular methods among the teachers) and are used both at the secondary level and in the universities. Since 2014 the immensely popular textbook *Familia Romana* (Ørberg 2011) came as innovation in the *gymnasia*, in the high schools, and in the universities. This textbook now has a wider use because of the requirements of the above-mentioned curricula to include writing and speaking elements in the classroom. For the advanced students, who are occupied with reading of authors, there are separate textbooks.

For the younger students (the upper level of primary education), teachers frequently compose their own materials. Textbooks such as *Via Latina* (Aguilar & Tárrega 2022) and the website *Legonium* by Anthony Gibbins (www.legonium.com) are in use. The focus at this level remains more on interactive learning with even the use of music in the classroom – the grammar is rather postponed.

The Covid-19 lockdowns in recent years did not affect the teaching of classical subjects much. They encouraged the teachers to convert some of their didactic materials for online use, but also incited the students to search and to take advantage of the great number of materials and courses available to them on the world wide web.

Teacher training

In Bulgaria, the position of 'teacher' requires a completed higher education and an education qualification degree of 'Master', 'Bachelor' or 'Specialist' in a major from a professional direction in accordance with the classifier of higher education and professional direction and in the 'teacher' or 'pedagogue' professional qualification area (Eurydice 2023). As already mentioned, the only institution which currently provides Bachelor or Master degrees in Classics (Classical Philology) is Sofia University. Therefore, almost all the schoolteachers of Latin and Greek have this degree in Classics from Sofia University, usually together with the professional qualification; they are meant both to become skilled professionals in classics and to have the ability to teach at secondary level, which combination is one of the significant traits of the Bulgarian teachers. The teacher training is a part of the Bachelor degree in Classics and is designed as a module with the name 'Didactics of classical languages' and consists of some twenty-four disciplines, of which eight become compulsory once the module is selected by the students (which usually happens to be the case). The compulsory disciplines are the following: History of Classical Education in Bulgaria, Didactics of Latin, Didactics of Greek, Online Databases and Resources for Classics, Psychology, Pedagogy, IT in Classics Teaching and Bulgarian Textbooks, and Programmes in Classics and Classical Civilization. Additionally, the student must undergo a didactical practicum, consisting of 120 hours, preparing lessons and teaching in a high school.

Some teachers in the *gymnasia* which provide vocational instruction (e.g. Latin in the field of the veterinary medicine) are not trained classical philologists and they are teaching Latin only as an additional subject to their main discipline – usually another foreign language, in which they possess a graduate degree.

Because of the relatively scarce number of teachers of Latin and Greek in Bulgaria, there is no further specific teacher training or professional development which aims particularly at these subjects. The teachers could either organize internal training courses in which they (or some university professors) – in an informal manner – share experiences with their colleagues (this happens only occasionally), otherwise they could visit 'general' teacher training courses, e.g. for language teachers, provided by public or private institutions. However, these courses have nothing to do with the specifics of the classical subjects.

Support and collaboration for teaching

The pillar of Classics in Bulgaria has been the Chair of Classics, part of the Faculty for Classical and Modern Philologies at Sofia University, which in 2021 celebrated its hundredth anniversary. As already mentioned, it provides the necessary instruction for all future teachers and also shares its expert capacity in matters regarding teaching of Classics whenever it is needed. Many high school students are regularly attracted to the initiatives of the Chair. Over the last twenty years, the Chair has also launched some initiatives for more narrow partnerships in Classics teaching in the region.

Bulgaria has re-installed its membership in the European Classics teachers' association Euroclassica, through the Association for the Development of the University Classical Education (ADUCE/ARUKO). ADUCE has members both from the teachers' community and from different academic fields. It organized two significant events (in 2017 and 2023) in order to attract more public attention to the problems of Classics teaching and to provide an opportunity for sharing of experiences.

The main activity outside formal education, which has brought together students, teachers, and professors from different high schools (and universities), has been the Summer School of Classical Languages (www.schola.bg). It has taken place ten times since 2014, attracting as many as seventy students in 2019 from Bulgaria and abroad every year. Typically, it lasts eight to nine days, in which the main objective is to read as much Latin and Greek as possible. Leading scholars (also mainly from Bulgaria) in the field of Classics and its adjacent disciplines are invited to deliver one or two lectures every day. The poetry lessons, combined with music and introductory courses to other ancient languages, are among the programme's highlights.

The Summer School has played a role as a platform for introducing active methods in Classics teaching since its inception. The experience gained at the Summer School later made some teachers more confident to use these methods in the classroom. It evolved also into other initiatives, such as Summer School of Classics and History for younger (5–7 grade) students at 17th School 'Damian Gruev' in Sofia, held by the same team of organizers, and it provided some of the inspiration for an analogous event in neighbouring Serbia.

Being part of the international Classics community is of utmost importance for the development of the Bulgarian educational institutions. Over the last ten years the Bulgarian schools and universities have maintained partnerships with institutions such as the Accademia Vivarium Novum in Italy, where some high school and university students spent a year or more, bringing home colourful and valuable experience afterwards. There have been common activities also with Het Baarnsch Lyceum (Netherlands), Schola Nova (Belgium), Greko-latinskiy kabinet (Russia) and Oxford Latinitas (United Kingdom).

Traditionally, Bulgarian students from the National Gymnasium for Ancient Languages and Cultures have participated and gained prizes at international high school students' competitions such as the Certamen Ciceronianum (Arpino), Certamen Horatianum (Venosa), Certamen Ovidianum (Sulmona) in Italy, and at the former Annual European Student Competition in Ancient Greek Language and Culture (Greece). In the last ten years a handful of high school and university students have participated successfully also in Latin composition competitions, some of them initiated in Bulgaria.

The theatrical troupe 'Alter Ego', founded in 1982 at the National Gymnasium for Ancient Languages and Cultures by Ognian Radev, a teacher of Ancient Greek and Ancient Culture, had obtained wide popularity among the Classics community in Europe for its nearly thirty years of existence. The director with the help of some teachers and with the high school students as actors staged some of the Plautus comedies entirely in Latin at European festivals in Italy and Spain, and in Bulgarian at occasional domestic events. Since the death of Radev in 2015 there have been different attempts to continue this tradition, albeit with other kinds of productions.

Finally, Bulgarian high school students participate in the relevant initiatives of the Bulgarian Academy of Sciences, such as collaborating with the scholars of the Academy on their projects in the field of Classics. They also participate in archaeological excavations of ancient sites in different regions of the country, the result of various partnerships with the National Archaeological Institute and with the regional museums of history.

Conclusion

As already mentioned, Bulgaria has a rich tradition of Classics teaching, which is influenced by its historical milieu, by the fate of the country throughout the late nineteenth century and the whole of the twentieth, and by the contemporary tendencies of education in the region and in Europe as whole. Classics in Bulgaria survived severe setbacks in the past, which narrowed the paths towards a broader distribution of Classics in the schools, especially after 1945. However, because of the relatively small number of institutions involved in Classics, in recent times the most distinctive characteristic of Classics teaching in Bulgaria has been the close interaction between universities and schools. This interaction has been realized on many levels, even on a personal level, where university professors teach at secondary level and vice versa – high school teachers teach some courses at the university. This gives a unique versatility to the people engaged in the dissemination of the knowledge of Classics, which, in turn, promises further development of this field in the schools: a development adequate to the rich classical heritage of the country and to the demands of contemporary students.

For further reading, see Panova (2016), which sheds light on the history of the Classics teaching in Bulgaria, giving an explanation about the processes which are a basis of the current tendencies in the country. For another shorter review of the current situation, see Dragnev (2022).

References

Aguilar, M. and J. Tárrega (2022), *Via Latina*, Madrid: Cultura Clasica.

Atanasova, I. and L. Yordanova (1996), *Латински език за начинаещи* [Latin for Beginners], Sofia: Open Society Foundation.

Bogdanov, B. and R. Stefanov (1988), *Старогръцки език* [Ancient Greek for Beginners], Sofia: Public Education.

Dragnev, D. (2022), 'Crescunt in Bulgaria studia Latina', *Cursor: Zeitschrift für Freunde der lateinischen Sprache und europäischen Kultur*, 1 (18): 22–3. Available online: https://latein.schule.at/fileadmin/DAM/Gegenstandsportale/Latein/Dateien/Cursor_18_online_LQ.pdf (accessed 30 November 2023).

Eurydice (2023), *National Education Systems: Bulgaria*. Available online: https://eurydice.eacea.ec.europa.eu/national-education-systems/bulgaria/overview (accessed 30 November 2023).

Ørberg, H. (2011), *Familia Romana,* Indianapolis, IN: Hackett.

Panova, N. (2016), 'The Foundation of the National Gymnasium for Ancient Languages and Civilisations in Sofia: between Tradition and Ideology', in E. Olechowska and D. Movrin (eds), *Classics and Class: Greek and Latin Classics and Communism at School*, Ljubljana: DiG Publishing House, 167–91.

Prohazkova, Y. (2023), 'К-поп културата засили интереса към корейския, английският още е №1 за следване в чужбина [K-pop culture has intensified the interest in Korean language, English is still number 1 for studying abroad]', *24 chasa*, 7 March. Available online: https://www.24chasa.bg/bulgaria/article/13929148 (accessed 30 November 2023).

Slavova M. (2013), ΕΛΛΗΝΙΖΕΙΝ [Ancient Greek], privately published.

Organizations

The current curricula for Latin in the high schools can be seen through these links:

Latin A1: https://mon.bg/upload/21882/UP-Latinski-A1.pdf

Latin A2: https://mon.bg/upload/27647/UP_Latinski_A2_11-12kl_03092021.pdf

Latin B11: https://mon.bg/upload/27646/zap1885_LatE_B11_11-12kl_03092021.pdf

The special curricula for the National Gymnasium for Ancient Languages and Civilizations: https://mc.government.bg/page.php?p=58&s=81&sp=21&t=555&z=616

CROATIA

Nada Bulić and Zdravka Martinić-Jerčić

Introduction: *Qui sumus*

The teaching of classical languages and culture in Croatia has been associated, since the beginning of Croatian literacy, with the conversion of the population to Christianity. It has held a prominent place in all educational systems throughout Croatian history due to its geographical position on the border between the Greek and Roman worlds and Croatia's complex historical circumstances. Latin, in particular, is embedded in the foundations of Croatian identity, as it was the official language of the Croatian Parliament until 1847, as well as of the Catholic Church, the predominant religious institution in the Republic of Croatia. In addition, the Croatian Latin tradition, and with it the rich creative literary and scientific activity during the Renaissance and the Enlightenment, are a strong traditional pillar of educational programmes. As a result, content concerning the Latin language and grammar is more prevalent than that of Greek in modern educational programmes.

Most educational institutions in the Republic of Croatia are state funded, while a smaller number are private or religious. All educational programmes, whether public or private, are defined and their implementation is supervised by three umbrella state institutions – the Ministry of Science and Education, the Education and Teacher Training Agency, and the Agency for Science and Higher Education. The education system in the Republic of Croatia is organized into three levels:

1. Primary school: a general education programme, eight years in duration, attended by children aged seven to fourteen.

2. Secondary school: programmes may last three, four or five years. Schools are classified according to their programme as vocational (industrial, craft, technical), art, or grammar schools (general, language, classical, mathematics, physics, computer science, biology and chemistry). They are attended by students aged fifteen to eighteen.

3. Tertiary, or higher education: higher education programmes (university or professional studies) are conducted at polytechnical schools and universities. They are divided into three levels: Bachelor's (three or four years), Master's (one or two years, or may be integrated into Bachelor's programme with a five-year duration) and Doctoral studies (three years).

The significant decline in population in recent decades, which now amounts to 3,871,833, is also reflected in the school population, with 305,929 students attending primary school, 145,053 secondary and 173,243 tertiary level students (49,797 in vocational studies and 123,446 university students) (Croatian Bureau of Statistics 2021). Content of classical civilization and literature in translation, traditionally considered an essential part of general culture, is incorporated into the teaching curricula of subjects related to history and literature and is present at all levels, adapted to the students' age group. Croatia also has special classical programmes at all educational levels in which classical languages and literature are taught.

At the primary school levels, classical programmes are carried out in special classes, in which Latin is taught from the fifth to the eighth grade (children aged eleven to fourteen), and Greek in the seventh and eighth grades (children aged thirteen and fourteen). Classical programmes are conducted in thirteen primary schools, twelve of which are in Zagreb and one in Požega, attended by about eighty to 100 children in each generation (according to observations made by the authors of this text in 2021). At the secondary level, the classical programme is carried out in sixteen classical grammar schools for a duration of four years (ages fifteen to eighteen), with a total of about 2,500 students enrolled in classical programmes. The eight-year programme for Latin and six-year programme for Greek is carried out only by the Gymnasium classicum Zagrabiense, the oldest school in the region (founded in 1607).

Statistical indicators warn of a continuous trend of decline in the number of children interested in this programme due to a steep demographic decline in the appropriate age group, and because of political and economic developments. The decline in weekly classes in not only classical languages and literature, but also other subjects in the humanities, is the result of the promotion of STEM (Science, Technology, Engineering and Mathematics) subjects on a global level at the expense of the humanities.

At the higher education level, study programmes in classical philology or, separately, Latin or Greek language and literature, are conducted at the University of Zagreb and the University of Zadar. In recent years, all study programmes have recorded a significant drop in the number of students enrolled, which calls into question the existence and sustainability of study programmes as a result of pressure on the humanities and the narrowing of employment opportunities in the job market.

Quantum, quot, quia

In classical programmes, a mandatory class schedule of Latin and Greek is prescribed with the accompanying literary and historical and civilizational context. In primary school this consists of three hours a week of Latin for four years, and three hours a week of Greek for two years. In the classical grammar secondary school both Latin and Greek are studied for three hours a week for four years. Furthermore, Latin is compulsory for two years at two hours a week in all grammar schools, attended, in Croatia, by 44,012 students. Grammar school programmes represent the largest base of classical education. The mainstay of these programmes is language and civilizational content. Latin is also compulsory in medical vocational schools (which have programmes for nurses and midwives as well as medical laboratory, veterinary, pharmaceutical, dental, and health technicians) where it is taught for two years, at two hours per week. The emphasis of the programme is on the technical terms of the profession and the history of medicine in ancient times. Classical subjects are offered as elective subjects or extra-curricular activities in schools in which teachers have the initiative and willingness to get involved.

Traditional/classical programmes are perceived in two ways by the public. In part of the media, on social networks, and in public debates, they are perceived as distant from modern life, burdened with redundant and useless data. It has been noted that the negative perception in part of the public, but also among students, comes from the notion that knowledge of classical languages and culture is not practical knowledge that can be used to ensure an independent existence as quickly as possible. There is a widespread notion that with the knowledge of classical languages, one can only find work in education. The income from such work is relatively modest because salaries in the public sector are directly linked to the GDP (State Bureau of Statistics 2023). For this reason, the efforts of teachers of classical languages are focused on changing this attitude. By affirming ancient heritage in different contexts, they attempt to contribute to creating a broader picture, developing critical thinking, a culture of tolerance, and communication in public space. Also, in cooperation with other institutions, they try to present to students and the public the spectrum of occupations and specific jobs for which knowledge of classical languages is necessary and desirable, along with the usual and most widespread idea of working in education. Attention is drawn to jobs in heritage institutions, archives, libraries, museums and in translation. Teachers also draw attention to the attractiveness of the tourism sector, given the archaeological wealth and tourist orientation of Croatia, where knowledge of classical languages and culture in the jobs of tourist guides and organizers of cultural events will provide a significantly higher salary. At the same time, the public has a sense of their own national identity being rooted in ancient tradition, especially the Roman and Croatian Latin tradition, thus preserving the identity of a small nation in an increasingly globalized world. The consequences of globalization highlighted in public and scholarly literature (Katunarić 2014) requests that teacher's direct content in the curriculum towards the national heritage. In this sense, the activities of teachers are aimed at spreading awareness of the ancient heritage as a root of cultural identity and a building element of national identity. In the student population, this is done by including the national Latin tradition in teaching content, and in the general public through activities aimed at popularization.

Quo modo

The perception of educational programmes as outdated and not adapted to the demands of modern life was the impetus for the last curricular reform of primary and secondary education, implemented in 2019. The reform guidelines enabled a more flexible approach and greater freedom for teachers in terms of creating and teaching content, resulting in new educational models (Jokić & Dedić 2018). Although most of the members were the same, expert teams for classical languages (separately for Latin and Greek) focused on placing students and classical text at the centre of the teaching process.

The new curricula of classical languages emphasize the comprehension of text and consider grammar, vocabulary and civilization content to be tools for easier understanding of the text. In addition, manuals and teaching tips give priority to greater student activity in the teaching process and put the teacher in the role of moderator. It is recommended that lessons be divided into several smaller activities, to give priority to pair and group work, and, to a lesser extent, lecture-style classes. The curriculum approach encourages that material be aimed at enforcing connections both with other classes and with real life. Therefore, both classical language curricula and teaching recommendations have the same aim.

Based on these principles, new textbooks were created between 2019 and 2021, and some existing ones were adapted to the new curriculum requirements. Latin textbooks published for classical grammar schools are as follows: *Minerva Origines* (Bagarić & Gjurašin 2020), *Minerva Forum* (Bagarić & Matković 2020), *Minerva Opes* (Martinić-Jerčić et al. 2021a), *Minerva Fines* (Martinić-Jerčić et al. 2021b). Greek textbooks published for classical grammar schools are as follows: *Prometheus Mythos, Epos, Logos* (Martinić-Jerčić et al. 2019), and *Prometheus Kosmos* (Martinić-Jerčić et al. 2021c). The textbooks *Lingua Latina per se illustrata pars I et II* (Ørberg 2011) were also approved for this Latin programme, although the topics do not follow the recommendations outlined in the curriculum.

Textbooks approved for use in other grammar schools are as follows: *Linguae Latinae elementa 1 and 2* (Bagarić 2020), *Hereditas linguae Latinae* (Milanović 2019), and *Lingua Latina per se illustrata pars I* (Ørberg 2011). New textbooks for primary schools have not been written, with the only approved textbook being Ørberg's *Lingua Latina per se illustrata pars I*, which does not follow the recommended topics for that curriculum, so teachers have to create class materials themselves. At this level the most used textbook for Latin is *Orbis Romanus* (Salopek et al. 2008), and for Greek, *Prometheus* (Martinić-Jerčić et al. 2019). The textbook

Elementa linguae Latinae medicae (Bekavac Basić & Međeral 2012) has been used in medical vocational schools for several decades.

In practice, teachers are mostly familiar with three basic approaches to teaching classical languages, the grammar-translation approach, the reading (text comprehension) approach, and the communicative approach (Hunt 2016), and in their work they usually try to combine two approaches and adapt their teaching to the new curriculum (Martinić-Jerčić 2019). Methodological literature on the topic suggests strategies and examples of activities for the analysis and understanding of text in specific teaching units, pointing out ways to interpret the text with an emphasis on the continuity of western European heritage from antiquity to the present day and the connection between the ancient and modern worlds (Martinić-Jerčić & Tvrtković 2016).

Textbooks that are currently used in classes were generally created with the reading approach in mind (i.e., text comprehension), but can be adapted for use with other methods as well. Ørberg's textbook was famously created as an alternative to the grammar-translation approach but is versatile and can be used with both the communicative and reading approaches.

The Covid-19 pandemic accelerated the digitalization process and the introduction of digital teaching tools. At that time, with the support of the Ministry of Science and Education and the Education and Teacher Training Agency, over 500 video lessons for Latin and Greek were created, and during the strict lockdown in 2020, part of that material was also broadcast on public television as part of remote learning. About fifteen teachers participated in the recording of these fifteen- to twenty-minute video lessons. After the pandemic, some digital tools are still used in classes in formative or summative evaluation, and video lessons are used as a supplement to classes or in the flipped classroom method. In addition, remote platforms such as Teams, Google Classroom, etc. are used as shared repositories to store individual materials and additional teaching content. As much as these methods of teaching are necessary and the only ones that could be used during the lockdown, the experiences of remote schooling have undoubtedly shown that classroom teaching is irreplaceable, but also that some distance learning methods can be very successfully applied in normal times (Jokić 2023).

Ab inuicem

During their studies of Latin and/or Greek, prospective teachers must attend courses in which they are introduced to the approaches, forms, methods and strategies of teaching classical languages and the foundations of educational science. They are then obliged to teach several lessons under the tutelage of a mentor. In their first year of work teachers have the status of trainees and, following this, they must pass a professional exam in an authorized school held by the Education and Teacher Training Agency. Teachers in secondary schools write this exam at the Gymnasium Classicum in Zagreb, and those in primary schools at J.J. Strossmayer Elementary School in Zagreb. Their further professional progress depends on their interests and personal commitment. The Education and Teacher Training Agency organizes two national assemblies every year, and at least two to three more are organized at the county and inter-county level, where teachers can participate in lectures and workshops held by university instructors or colleagues from other schools and hear examples of good practice and new ideas. The most innovative teachers always independently research and come up with new knowledge that allows them to create new teaching materials and devise new approaches to teaching.

Quid facimus

Primary and secondary schools, especially classical grammar schools, work hard to popularize classical languages through school, inter-school and national projects. Thus, schools often launch projects and organize events that promote Roman and Greek culture or Croatian heritage based on ancient culture. At the national level, several Classical Language Festivals have been organized since 2007 in which students of all ages and from all types of schools celebrate ancient culture and classical languages with creative performances in Split, Hvar and Skradin. Certain schools regularly organize events or competitions dedicated to ancient culture. For example, the Gymnasium Classicum in Zagreb offers three elective courses: Ancient Drama, Ancient Costume Design, and Ancient Heritage, in which students deepen their knowledge of ancient culture. Every year, students of Ancient Drama prepare a play based on the works of ancient authors and perform it on stage. Other classical grammar schools throughout Croatia celebrate Days of Antiquity, or Greek or Roman Evenings to showcase the great creativity of all students and teachers.

Trips to sites in Croatia, Rome and Greece are part of the curriculum of all classical grammar schools. Some schools also cooperate with museums, scholarly institutes, and/or institutes of higher education. All this contributes to the greater visibility of schools with classical programmes to the public and in the media.

Faced with the challenges of creating a positive atmosphere to the public and with the problems of how to attract and retain students, higher education attempts to respond to these challenges by refreshing programmes with special content, enhancing civilizational content, working more on sources using digital processing tools and digital databases, and organizing workshops to read documents and inscriptions, thus practically applying linguistic knowledge. Extra-curricular activities are frequently carried out in archives, museums and archaeological sites, by organizing guest lectures from related professions, and by strengthening cooperation with the departments of history, archaeology, art history and philosophy. Student surveys regularly conducted by the Department of Classical Philology at the universities of Zagreb and Zadar have positively changed the impression of the static and hermetic nature of the programme previously held among students. An effort is also made to strengthen individual approaches to teaching to obtain a positive result from each student. To create a positive atmosphere with the public, universities have intensified activities aimed at popularization by organizing various events. The general public and tourists are presented with the achievements of antiquity in everyday life in an appealing way, for example the processing of glass, clothing, cosmetics and the culinary arts, by presenting the living aspect of the language through the translation of contemporary poetry into classical languages, organizing poetry reviews, through public readings of classical literature in the original and translation, organizing playrooms for children of kindergarten age with games inspired by antiquity, organizing workshops for school-aged children on a topic from antiquity or the reception of antiquity in modern times. These activities have resulted in media coverage and the presence of the Department of Classical Philology and the university in general in public life, and contributed to the contemporary appearance of both the programme and the institution. These measures have had a certain effect because the enrolment results this year, despite the economic and demographic situation, indicate that the downward trend has stopped.

Conclusion: *Quo vadimus*

In conclusion, the experience of teaching classical languages in Croatia, passing through long phases and recording ups and downs, shows that in a time of rapid changes due to accelerated technological development, it is necessary to keep up with the times, and to follow and maximally apply modern teaching methods and technological tools to attract and maintain the interest of children and young people. This implies curriculum flexibility, the ability to quickly adapt to such changes, as well as an administrative framework that can support this course. At the same time, it should be firmly kept in mind that social contact is irreplaceable, both between teachers and students, as well as between students themselves, which is why it is necessary to encourage groupwork and not lose the feeling for the student as an individual.

Such a system requires that teachers undergo continuous education (Odak et al. 2023) and an exchange of experiences. Regardless of the approach taken to teaching classical languages, the main challenge in teaching is to balance grammar, civilization and text, because students find it increasingly difficult to acquire vocabulary, grammar and language content. The experience of teaching during the Covid pandemic in Croatia pushed and accelerated qualitative changes in both the curriculum and in the organization of classes and taught us that it is possible to make significant progress even under difficult circumstances. It remains to be seen in the future what the overall effect of all the measures taken will be on the teaching of classical languages, the number of students, and society as a whole.

References

Bagarić, J. (2020), *Linguae Latinae elementa*, Zagreb: Skolska Knjiga.

Bagarić, J. and M. Gjurašin (2020), *Minerva Origines*, Zagreb: Skolska Knjiga.

Bagarić, J. and D. Matković (2020), *Minerva Forum*, Zagreb: Skolska Knjiga.

Bekavac Basić, I. and F. Međeral (2012), *Elementa linguae Latinae medicae*, Zagreb: Skolska Knjiga.

Bišćan, I. and Ž. Plužarić (2021), 'University teachers and the pandemic: academic and psychological challenges', Agency for Science and Higher Education, University Computer Centre of the University of Zagreb and University of Rijeka, Zagreb. Available online: https://www.azvo.hr/images/stories/publikacije/Visoko%C5%A1kolski_nastavnici_i_pandemija_akademski_i_psiholo%C5%A1ki_izazovi_AZVO_Srce_UNIRI.pdf (accessed 18 October 2023).

Croatian Bureau of Statistics (2021), 'Population by school attendance and sex, by towns/municipalities, Census 2021'. Croatian Bureau of Statistics, Available online: https://www.google.com/url?sa=t&rct=j&q=&esrc=s&source=web&cd=&ved=2ahUKEwj2u5Cs57mBAxUng_0HHUqhDxYQFnoECBAQAQ&url=https%3A%2F%2Fpodaci.dzs.hr%2Fmedia%2Ftd3jvrbu%2Fpopis_2021-stanovnistvo_po_gradovima_opcinama.xlsx&usg=AOvVaw3TCg5X9BnjtZ19--DvfvbS&opi=89978449 (accessed 18 October 2023).

Hunt, S. (2016), *Starting to Teach Latin*, London: Bloomsbury Academic.

Jokić, B. (2023), *Project Changes in the Organization of the Education Process Caused by the Covid-19 Pandemic: Effects on the Educational Experiences, Welfare and Aspirations of Students in the Republic of Croatia* (EWAchange). Final results of the EWAchange project, *Growing up in (post)pandemic times: experiences from Croatia* 2023. Available online: https://wwwadmin.idi.hr/uploads/Odrastanje_u_ppv_iskustva_iz_Hrvatske_IDIZ_f6b0d1f2e8.pdf (accessed 18 October 2023).

Jokić, B. and Z. Ristić Dedić (2018), *Comprehensive Curriculum Reform: Original Ideas and Processes*, Zagreb: Friedrich Ebert Stiftung.

Katunarić, V. (2014), 'Dancing and Calculating: Culturally sustainable development and globalization in light of two paradigms of socio-cultural evolution', *Croatian International Relations Review*, 20 (70): 5–29.

Martinić-Jerčić, Z. (2019), *Approaches to the teaching of classical languages, Utile cum dulci*, Collection in honour of Pavlo Knezović, Croatian Studies, Zagreb: University of Zagreb.

Martinić-Jerčić, Z. and T. Tvrtković (2016), 'Prodesse et delectare in the teaching of Latin language and literature – a new approach based on old foundations', *Croatologija*, 7: 75–90.

Martinić-Jerčić, Z., D. Matković and M. Gjurašin (2019), *Prometheus Mythos, Epos, Logos*, Zagreb: Skolska Knjiga.

Martinić-Jerčić, Z., D. Matković and M. Gjurašin (2021a), *Minerva Opes*, Zagreb: Skolska Knjiga.

Martinić-Jerčić, Z., D. Matković, M. Gjurašin and T. Maleš (2021b), *Minerva Fines*, Zagreb: Skolska Knjiga.

Martinić-Jerčić, Z., D. Matković, M. Gjurašin and T. Maleš (2021c), *Prometheus Kosmos*, Zagreb: Skolska Knjiga.

Milanović, Z. (2019), *Hereditas linguae Latinae*, Zagreb: V.B.Z.

Odak, I, I. Marušić, J. Matić Bojić, S. Puzić, H. Bakić, N. Eliasson, B. Gasteiger Klicpera, K. Gøtzsche, A. Kozina, I. Perković, N. Roczen, G. Tomé and M. Veldin (2023), 'Teachers' Social and Emotional Competencies: A Lever for Social and Emotional Learning in Schools', *Sociologija i prostor*, 61, 226 (1): 105–22.

Ørberg, H. (2011), *Lingua Latina per se illustrata*, Cambridge, MA: Focus Publishing.

Salopek, D., Z. Šešelj and D. Škiljan (2008), *Orbis Romanus*, Zagreb: Profil-Klett.

State Bureau of Statistics (2023), *Average net and gross salaries by level of professional education and by activity in 2020*, State Bureau of Statistics. Available online: https://podaci.dzs.hr/2021/hr/10045 (accessed 18 October 2023).

CYPRUS

Pantelis Iacovou

The educational framework in Cyprus generally adheres, with marginal variations, to the pedagogical directives and curricular structures of Greece. The enduring educational interdependence between the two countries persisted even when Cyprus gained independence in 1960 (Zekas 2017). Nevertheless, after the island's independence, there has been an endeavour towards emancipation from Greek educational influences. Despite this trend, it has not significantly impacted the teaching of Ancient Greek and Latin. It is essential to highlight that until 1976, both Greece and Cyprus used 'katharevusa', characterized as a purist variety of Modern Greek. This form aimed to purify the language by eliminating foreign elements and systematizing its morphology through the use of the ancient Greek polytonic system and classical inflection. Consequently, classical subjects, particularly Ancient Greek, held significant influence in schools and society. However, the adoption of demotic Greek in 1976 marked a shift, as it constituted a more simplified and monotonic version of the language which subsequently had an impact on classical teaching.

This chapter will specifically address the teaching of classical subjects within state-maintained schools, which constitute 86 per cent of the country's educational institutions as reported by the Ministry of Education (MOEC n.d.). The primary education is mandated for children aged five years and ten months before 1 September of the upcoming school year, while secondary education is offered to students aged twelve to eighteen. The latter is organized into two three-year cycles: *Gymnasium* and *Lyceum*. The *Gymnasium* cycle is mandatory for all students aged twelve to fifteen. Within the *Lyceum* phase, students have the option to choose between two distinct pathways: academic and vocational. Both cycles incorporate cross-curricular programmes and various extra-curricular opportunities to foster a more comprehensive and global development of students' personalities. Classical education is most prominent on the academic pathway and possesses a fundamental role in Greek Cypriot education irrespective of potential political changes. According to Sinno (n.d.), of the approximate 46,000 students at *Lyceum*, the number of students has decreased from 663 in 2019 to 281 in 2023 for Latin, and from 544 to 250 over the same period for Ancient Greek (Table 1).

Sinno (n.d.) also reports that the numbers of those entering for Classics at the University of Cyprus has also suffered, with 270 candidates for thirty-five places in Classics in 2019 decreasing to 181 for thirty-one places in 2023. Byzantine Studies, History and Archaeology, and Philosophy have also seen reduced numbers of applicants (Table 2).

All state-maintained schools in both primary and secondary sectors follow the national curriculum which is designed around specific learning pillars and taught through utilizing government-endorsed books. More specifically, the Ministry of Education and Culture (MOEC n.d.) advocates that the basic responsibility of Primary and Secondary Education is to help pupils become acquainted with their civilization, religion and tradition. This instrumentalization of Classics teaching across the phases also has the intent to develop respect and love for the

Table 1. Number of students at *Lyceum*, studying Ancient Greek, Latin and History

Year	Ancient Greek	Latin	History
2023	250	281	621
2022	298	323	682
2021	454	504	1,163
2020	438	540	1,293
2019	544	663	1,408

Source: Sinno (n.d.).

Table 2. Number of students (candidates / places) entering for 'classical studies' at the University of Cyprus

	Faculty of the University of Cyprus			
Year	Classics	Byzantine / Modern Greek studies	History and Archaeology	Philosophy
2023	181/31	178/22	193/49	170/7
2022	195/33	182/26	211/57	186/11
2021	243/35	229/36	254/63	231/18
2020	225/35	200/27	225/70	203/12
2019	270/35	251/39	274/70	252/14

Source: Sinno (n.d.).

national heritage, inculcation of tolerance and awareness relating to cultural otherness. Ultimately, a standardized approach to achieving academic homogeneity and consistency across the country is entrenched.

The teaching of classical subjects in Cyprus has historically held a significant place in the educational system. In primary and *Gymnasium* schools, all students are to follow the same curriculum across the country and are required to attend all mandatory subjects in order to complete successfully the compulsory phase of education in Cyprus. The ministry has designed a Classics curriculum that is deeply rooted in history and culture. Therefore, the teaching of Classics regardless of its form, functions as the vehicle for developing students' historical literacy, but also historical epistemological understanding to achieve the cultivation of historical thinking and historical consciousness.

In the first phase of education, Classics is taught through the subject of Ancient/Modern History. Students in Years 3 and 4 begin to engage with history from early on with the study of Prehistoric periods (2,500,000 BCE to fourth century CE) twice a week for 80 minutes (2 × 40 minutes). By the conclusion of Year 4, pupils are able to identify the developments of humankind and society from the Neolithic period until the end of the Roman Empire with a clear focus on the major events from each era relevant to Cyprus and the classical world more broadly (MOEC 2019). Beyond the teaching of history, students in primary education are taught classical mythology alongside their history lessons and they become familiar with the creation myths, the Olympian gods, Odysseus and the Trojan War and how this led to the creation of the first kingdoms in Cyprus. The objective is not only for students to excel in recalling mythological elements related to the periods they study, but also to discern the key differences between myth and reality. The emphasis lies in understanding why myths were created in the first place and how these narratives echo in historical contexts.

The same principles and methodologies are also followed in Years 5 and 6. Precisely, the development of coherent knowledge of important characteristics, phenomena and events of the various historical periods at the local and global level from the Byzantine Era to the present is sought. While all the aforementioned historical periods are also taught in *Gymnasium* and *Lyceum*, what makes them different is the heightened emphasis on nurturing students' critical skills and their ability to analyse sources.

The subject of History during the first cycle of middle education (Years 7–9) reinforces the content students were taught during their primary years. Pupils are taught two periods a week except for Year 9 who are timetabled for three periods on a weekly basis (3×40mins). The content of history follows a chronological sequence beginning from:

- First Grade (Year 7): The Stone Age–The end of the Roman Empire.
- Second Grade (Year 8): Romans in Cyprus/Byzantine era–Ottoman Empire.
- Third Grade (Year 9): Renaissance in Europe–The induction of Cyprus into the European Union in 2004.

It is noteworthy to mention that Year 8 and 9 students are required to sit an examination in History in order to move to the next stage of their education. These exams are designed by the ministry and therefore, state schools are obliged to follow faithfully the analytical curriculum without any deviation. These exams are marked with the highest degree of confidentiality by being sent to different schools for marking to avoid any conflict of interest.

At the *Gymnasium* and *Lyceum*, the presence of Classics becomes more multifaceted and obtains a much more prominent role within the curriculum. The purpose of teaching Ancient Greek in the two cycles of secondary education is the path towards linguistic self-awareness of the student and subsequently to complement students' understanding of the subtleties of Modern Greek (MOEC 2023a). This comparative analysis of the two forms of Greek language becomes the cornerstone in developing linguists who are able to discern the influences of those languages to the modern European languages. The Ministry of Education (MOEC 2023a) postulates that the key cultural vocabulary that Greece bequeathed to the West was not mere words, but ideas and conceptions – in which students could recognize the stamp of 'Greekness'.

During the three years of *Gymnasium*, students are not only required to delve into the study of history but are also immersed in the realm of Ancient Greek Language and Literature, with a dedicated allocation of two periods for each component, totalling four periods of forty minutes each. This time allocation remains consistent throughout their middle school education, albeit with some variations in the allotted time for language acquisition. However, what is subjected to change across each year is the set texts and progressive elevation of linguistic complexity. Firstly, the teaching of Ancient Greek literature is delivered from translation which is accompanied by comprehension and interpretation questions. The curriculum unfolds with a sequential exploration of all twenty-four books of Homer's *Odyssey* in Year 7, followed by Homer's *Iliad* in Year 8, and culminating in the study of the Euripides' 'Helen of Troy,' in Year 9. What adds an intriguing dimension to this curriculum is the careful choice of this tragedy. The Ministry of Education (MOEC 2017) argues that this particular play interweaves elements from both tragedy and comedy, providing students with a 'lighter' version of the tragic genre compared to, for example, *Oedipus*.

The deliberate focus on the Homeric epics and this specific tragedy serves the overarching purpose of developing students' intertextual comparison skills and through exposing students to the depictions of Helen in Homer and Euripides (MOEC 2023a). It serves also as a means of illustrating the influence the Cypriot literature was susceptible to in antiquity (i.e., colonized by the Achaeans). This is further reinforced through the study of the Cypriot epic texts in which students actively engage in first-hand experiences that unveil the inextricable links between Cypriot literature and its Greek counterparts in epic and drama. However, the assessment landscape for the subject diverges from the standardized approach in History. Unlike the nationally assessed field of history, Ancient Greek assessment is at the discretion of individual teachers throughout the two semesters in the year. This nuanced approach allows for a more personalized and varied evaluation of a student's understanding and proficiency in the subject.

For the second cycle of secondary education (*Lyceum*), classical subjects are presented at both foundation and higher levels, determined by the student's chosen orientation. This updated system, introduced in 2015 (MOEC n.d.), draws inspiration from the twentieth century model but is far from a mere replication of the options available fifteen years ago. Instead, it incorporates modernizations and introduces new subjects, aligning with contemporary trends in scientific fields. The first year of *Lyceum* involves thirty-five teaching periods, with thirty-one dedicated to core courses, mirroring those in *Gymnasium*. The remaining four periods require students to select two subjects from two teaching periods each, falling under four Orientation Course Groups (OCGs). This flexible system allows students to delve deeper into two subjects of their interest, with an additional two teaching periods each. Classics is part of the first OCG, encompassing the teaching of Ancient Greek and History. However, students who opt out of the first OCG must still study Ancient Greek at a foundation level for two forty-minute periods each week.

In the second and final year of *Lyceum*, students choose one of six OCGs. Each OCG consists of four courses, with each spanning four periods (a total of sixteen periods). Students have the right to change OCGs from the 1st to the 2nd grade, provided they take an entrance exam for the chosen subjects. A notable trend is the tendency of students to maintain the same OCG throughout the three years of *Lyceum* education. Consequently, in the second and third years of *Lyceum*, Classics OCG introduces Latin as a compulsory subject and one additional option, which could be either additional Literature, Philosophy or a foreign language. It is worthwhile to note that efforts are being made to encourage more students to take up Latin. This initiative is particularly directed at students in the Arts stream and the rationale behind this is the close connection of Latin to the Renaissance and the revival of classical influences in art.

The course of Ancient Greek Literature from translation is clearly upgraded in *Lyceum*, in the sense that it ceases to be merely an opportunity for acquaintance with the literary nature of texts in general. Instead, it specifically highlights two aspects of these works (MOEC 2023a): firstly, the cultural value that each of the studied texts holds within the context of antiquity and the present; and secondly, the technical-narrative structure of the work as a representative of the particular literary genre of antiquity to which it belongs. During the first and second year of *Lyceum*, students engage with Thucydides' 'The Melian Dialogue' and Sophocles' *Oedipus Rex* through translation, both at foundation and higher levels. However, in the third year Classics students are taught *Protagoras* by Plato and *Pericles Funeral Oration* by Thucydides from both translation and the original.

At the foundation level, Ancient Greek language lessons also constitute the final year for those not opting for it as an OCG. Students are required to approach the process of translating the Ancient Greek text not by memorizing a ready-made translation, but by understanding segments of it which subsequently will enhance students' work in Modern Greek (MOEC n.d.). The evaluation of those linguistic mechanisms extends beyond grammatical and syntactic phenomena to include etymology and vocabulary, as well as knowledge of the specific historical and factual elements. Efforts also extend to gaining a linguistic understanding of fundamental terms from other subjects taught. This includes Mathematics, Physics, Chemistry, Biology, Economics, English and French. In this context, teachers emphasize vocabulary related to the chosen Orientation courses. Conversely, at the higher tier (OCG), a comprehensive review and deepening of already familiar grammatical and syntactical phenomena are essential for enabling students to recognize structures in specific textual genres and understand their cross-linguistic function.

In the assessment process for the second cycle of middle education, students undergo a minimum of two written assessments per semester. The second semester includes both teacher assessments and the comprehensive national exam based on students' OCG. At the end of the first year, all students are required to take exams in Modern Greek and Mathematics (either at the foundation or high level), irrespective of their chosen Optional Course Group (OCG).

For students enrolled in the OCG that encompasses all classical subjects during the second and third years of *Lyceum*, the exams include Modern and Ancient Greek, History, Latin, and one of the aforementioned optional subjects. According to MOEC (2023b), the assessment criteria for Ancient Greek and Latin involve evaluating students' translation skills on both prescribed and unseen text. Beyond translation proficiency, students are required to provide linguistic observations, addressing grammatical, syntactic and lexical aspects of the unseen text, along with questions on linguistics and interpretation derived from the set texts. Additionally, students are also required to transfer an unseen extract from Modern Greek to Ancient Greek and Latin and vice versa. A notable difference in the assessment criteria is that, for Ancient Greek, students are assessed in a spelling proficiency test of an unseen author, whereas in Latin, students are not required to translate any unseen text (MOEC 2023c).

Beyond the formal assessment system outlined earlier, students specializing in classics have the unique opportunity to enhance their proficiency and appreciation for the subject through active participation in the annual Pan-Cyprian competition in Ancient Greek Language. This competition is open to *Gymnasium* students and those at the *Lyceum* level who have chosen classics as their field of study. Participants are encouraged to either craft their own original texts, drawing inspiration from Greek literature and engaging in meaningful dialogue, or undertake an assessment focused on a specific author (e.g. *Pericles* by Plutarch) for contextual and linguistic analysis. This competition not only allows students to explore captivating themes and values relevant to modern life but also cultivates a profound and enduring appreciation for classical subjects.

Teaching methodology, teachers training and new initiatives in Ancient Greek and Latin

The overarching teaching methodology and approach of teaching Greek and Latin in the Cypriot educational system is the grammar-translation approach. This involves a guided process by the teacher and active, conscious and creative involvement by the student. Moreover, an inductive approach is followed when teaching complex grammatical concepts where students are gradually led from simple to complex, from specific to general, from recognition and observation to rules. The original Greek text is provided both in regular typography and in a transcription known as 'κατὰ κῶλα' or by meaningful-syntactic units (MOEC 2023a). This approach which was introduced in 2020 is particularly useful for the precise understanding of the long and symmetric ancient discourse. The division of the continuous text into sections or 'κῶλα' (main clauses, subordinate clauses and adverbial participial phrases) reveals each structural component of even the most complex sentence and their hierarchical relationships. Before 2020, this used to be done during the guided reading of the teacher, but now ancient texts are presented in a way that highlights form, content and logical articulation of discourse, all bound in a unity that cultivates exploratory learning and actively engages the student in knowledge acquisition. It thus makes the thematic units of the language visible with clarity while simultaneously illuminating their syntactic composition.

In examining the current state of teaching methodology in Cyprus, what is particularly notable is the incorporation of recent pedagogical approaches with technology into the instruction of classical subjects. Despite the substantial growth observed in the technological landscape, with the creation of numerous educational programmes that are designed to enhance the teaching process, the educational system in Cyprus lags in embracing technology (Stylianou 2023). An interesting outcome of the pandemic was the widespread adoption of professional emails by all teachers, a practice previously uncommon. In the post-Covid-19 era, there is no additional complementary action plan to further integrate technology into education. Recognizing the importance of technology in education, especially in subjects such as Greek and Latin, where enrolment numbers as stated above have declined, the ministry must invest in providing schools with the necessary equipment. This investment aims to actively engage students in these subjects, fostering a dynamic and interactive learning environment.

The designated teaching methodology for Classics is introduced to every teacher right at the outset of their recruitment process. Similar to curriculum design, teacher recruitment is overseen by the government. A recent development in the recruitment process, aimed at addressing the growing waiting list for teacher appointments, now mandates that every teacher, regardless of their specialization, must undertake a series of subject-specific exams and an examination focusing on pedagogy. The primary goal is to ensure the selection of teachers with the most robust subject knowledge. Those with the highest results are prioritized on the appointment list and are the first to be contacted when there is a demand for teachers. Prior to their school placement, future teachers are required to undertake a year-long training programme facilitated by the University of Cyprus. Specifically, the training for Classics teachers includes mandatory pedagogical seminars and two school placements involving the observation of experienced teachers. Upon completion of the training, secondary education teachers are required to attend four pedagogical seminars annually, consisting of two led by government inspectors and two on 'school inset days'. This training is reinforced by the Cyprus Pedagogical Institute (2015) which organizes numerous optional seminars. However, concerning teachers' development into senior leadership positions, Cyprus follows a somewhat anachronistic approach. This progression is only initiated after sixteen years of service in their current position, requiring a combination of years of service, inspector ratings, and a mandatory interview.

The cooperation between academia and school education is highly beneficial, effectively narrowing the gap between these two phases, a distinction often observed in other countries. Nonetheless, the success of this collaboration between universities and school education is not always guaranteed, as it heavily relies on the orientation and goals of the government at the time. For instance, when a reform for Ancient Greek occurred in 2008 within the context of a broader educational restructuring implemented under the administration of Minister Andreas Demetriou, the academic circles were the first to initiate this well-received initiative. The endeavour to create and implement a new curriculum for Ancient Greek was led by Professors Antonis Tsakmakis and Vaios Liapis. The new reform which was adopted by the MOEC in 2010, was the only time a reading approach was to be followed. Precisely, it introduces students to Ancient Greek through texts constructed from the beginning and written in a dialogical and visual form (Petrides 2015). In addition, there was notably the absence of theory concerning morphology and syntax. Instead, the focus is on linguistic learning and the enhancement of ancient cultural knowledge, primarily through the text of each unit. In this sense, a text-centred approach is implemented. According to Zekas (2017) to achieve this goal, both intrinsic and extrinsic factors were facilitated such as (a) the type of texts, their themes and content, the vocabulary they encompass, and the syntax on which they are structured; (b) the illustrations accompanying the text, as well as the targeted questions that form the basis of the teaching. Despite, its successful completion for the three years of *Gymnasium*, as evidenced by positive reactions from students, parents and educators, the developments from that point onward were not equally auspicious as the newly elected government in 2013 proceeded in the withdrawal of the course by 2015 returning to the traditional grammar-translation approach.

In conclusion, Cyprus has exhibited unwavering dedication to the preservation of classical education, proving resilient in the face of political shifts, broader curriculum changes, and a certain reluctance to embrace the most recent pedagogic approaches. The enduring vitality of classical teaching in Cyprus can be attributed to historical ties between Cyprus and Greece, the impact of language shifts, and the enduring significance of classical education. Recognizing the integral role of classical subjects in fostering cultural heritage, historical literacy, and linguistic self-awareness has been a key factor. The collaboration between academia and school education, coupled with an alignment of teaching practices with academic developments, presents a model that could yield positive results not only for Cyprus but also serve as an inspiration for sustaining Classics worldwide.

References

Cyprus Pedagogical Institute (2015), Development of a Unified Policy for the Training of Educators. Available online: https://www.pi.ac.cy/pi/files/epimorfosi/seminaria/sxoliki_vasi/EPAGGELM_MATHISH/2015_03_23_protasi_epangelmatiki_mathisi_ekpaideftikon.pdf (accessed 14 November 2023).

MOEC (2017), Teachers' and Students' Ancient Greek Textbooks. Available online: https://latim.schools.ac.cy/index.php/el/yliko/didaktiko-yliko2 (accessed 15 October 2023).

MOEC (2018), Teachers' and Students' Latin Textbooks. Available online: https://latim.schools.ac.cy/index.php/el/yliko/didaktiko-yliko2 (accessed 10 November 2023).

MOEC (2019), History in Primary Education. Available online: https://istod.schools.ac.cy/index.php/el/istoria/programmatismoi (accessed 29 October 2023).

MOEC (2023a), Ancient Greek curriculum in Middle education. Available online: https://archm.schools.ac.cy/index.php/el/archaia/programmatismoi (accessed 15 October 2023).

MOEC (2023b), Structure of Pancyprian Classical exam. Available online: https://archeia.moec.gov.cy/mc/938/odigos_exetaseon_tomos_b_2023.pdf (accessed 10 November 2023).

MOEC (2023c), Latin curriculum in Middle education. Available online: https://latim.schools.ac.cy/index.php/el/latinika/programmatismoi (accessed 15 October 2023).

MOEC (n.d.), Structure of the secondary education. Available online: https://nop.moec.gov.cy/index.php (accessed 10 November 2023).

Petrides, A. (2015), Reform and Counter-Reform in the Teaching of Ancient Greek (Cyprus). Available online: https://antonispetrides.wordpress.com/2015/02/27/ancient-greek-reform-and-counter-reform/ (accessed 12 November 2023).

Sinno, M. (n.d.), Statistics in Cypriot education. Available online: http://www.statscy.com/pagstats/index.html (accessed 1 November 2023).

Stylianou, M. (2023), Digital education in Cyprus post Covid. Available online: https://www.academia.edu/106332334/Ψηφιακη_εκπαιδευση_στην_Κυπρο_στην_meta_covid_19_περιοδο_1 (accessed 12 November 2023).

University of Cyprus (n.d.), Programme of Teaching Training. Available online: https://www.ucy.ac.cy/paidagogiki/programme/ (accessed 18 November).

Zekas, C. (2017), 'The teaching of Ancient Greek in Cyprus', in K. Tsalakanidou (ed.), *Studies in Greek Linguistics*, 38, Thessaloniki: Aristotle University of Thessaloniki, 79–92.

CZECH REPUBLIC

Martina Vaníková

Brief historical outline

The uninterrupted tradition of teaching Classics in the Czech Lands was disrupted by the socialist school reform in 1953. After a partial liberalization in the 1960s, there was further decline in the 1970s and 1980s when the number of schools offering Latin in their curriculum dropped close to zero. Following the revolution in 1989, there was a sudden interest in Classics. The reform of education in the democracy was inspired both by the Western education system and the pre-war tradition, including the restoration of teaching Latin. However, the enthusiasm did not last long. Nowadays, there is a wide offer of subjects such as informatics, spoken languages and economic subjects in high schools, and in the overall atmosphere of economic pragmatism Latin (not even speaking about Greek) hardly defends its position in schools. On top of that, the parents and grandparents of the current students mostly did not have any Classics teaching themselves and do not demand it.

Czech educational system

Czech education typically consists of the mandatory elementary school (age 6–15) and secondary school (age 16–19). The elementary schools are divided into two stages: the first stage (age 6–10) and the second stage (age 11–14).

As for secondary schools, there are vocational schools (2–4 years), professional schools and *lycea* (four years), grammar schools (*gymnázium*) and practical schools. Grammar schools are universal secondary schools, graduates of which typically study at universities. Most grammar schools are four-year secondary schools (for students who completed elementary schools), but there are also eight-year grammar schools for pupils after the first stage of elementary school, i.e. age 11–19, and a few six-year grammar schools for pupils aged 13–19.

Except for some vocational schools and practical schools, the students graduate with the so-called *maturita* examination, which is a pre-requisite to further post-secondary or tertiary education. The *maturita* examination has been a matter of heated discussion in all levels of society for the past ten years. At the time of writing, the *maturita* examination consists of the 'common part' (standardized tests from Czech language and literature, Mathematics or foreign language examination) and the 'school part' (any two subjects from the particular school's offer). Most of the universities do not take the results from the *maturita* examination into consideration and have their own criteria and entrance examinations.

Greek

According to the statistics of the Ministry of Education, Youth and Sports (2020), the numbers of students who learn Greek in their secondary schools varies from zero to five in the past fifteen years. If there is any Greek at a grammar school, it is usually an extra-curricular activity taught by an enthusiastic Latin teacher and learned by enthusiastic students, both in their free time.

Latin at elementary schools (age 6–15)

Latin is not being taught in primary schools – with a very few exceptions of extra-curricular Latin lessons offered by keen teachers of history or French.

After the first stage the pupils either stay four more years in the elementary school to complete their compulsory education, or they continue to an eight-year *gymnázium* [grammar school], or they stay two more years at the second stage of their elementary school and then switch to a six-years' *gymnázium*. At these six- or eight-years' *gymnázia*, the Latin teaching is as common as in the secondary (four-year) *gymnázia*.

Latin in secondary education (age 16–19)

The statistics of the Ministry of Education, Youth and Sports (2020) show the gradual decline in the number of students learning Latin in all types of high schools from 3 per cent of all students that learn at least one foreign language (15,266 students) in 2003 to 1.8 per cent (7,100 students) in 2018. The overall number of secondary school students who learn at least one foreign language is approximately 97 per cent. Unfortunately, these statistics include all types of secondary schools. Out of these, it is mostly just the *gymnázia* that offer Latin (with the exception of medical schools that offer medical Latin).

A major decline in Latin teaching coincided with the application of the new 'Framework Educational Programmes' to high schools in 2009 (Research Institute of Education in Prague 2007). Based on these documents, the schools limited the number of 'unnecessary lessons' to be able to fulfil the obligatory requirements. It resulted in reducing Latin even more. This new framework does not even include Latin. According to Žytek (2014):

> Latin was pushed to the margin of interest first in the general educational documents. After four years of school programmes that have been developed based on the Framework Educational Programmes, we can say that Latin was pushed to the margin even in the school praxis.

The length and frequency of the Latin instructions in the schools therefore mainly depends on how much the Latin teachers themselves are able to introduce in their school, but also on the school director's stand towards humanities and Classics and also on the school's tradition.

Applicants to the Classics programmes at the Czech universities

According to the four Czech universities that offer a BA in Classics and/or Latin, the number of applicants to the Latin programmes has decreased from the total of around 300 applicants in 2006 to the current total of around 80 applicants (there has been no further decrease between 2014 and 2018).

Latin is no longer a part of the entrance examinations to either humanities or medical studies. The *maturita* examination in Latin does not give the students any extra advantage in the admission process. Nor do the individual departments of Classics require any previous knowledge of Latin. The only exception is the Institute of Greek and Latin Studies at the Charles University, which has a Latin examination as a part of their admission process to the

Latin Studies programme, and students with the *maturita* examination from Latin are admitted without any further testing.

Latin teachers

With the exception of a few church schools, Latin teachers typically either teach Latin in addition to another (major) subject such as History or Czech Language and Literature, or they teach Latin only part-time. The teachers in the Czech Republic are generally required to gain a Master's from a pedagogical faculty where they specialize in one or two subjects, or a Master's from a specific field and to get a teaching certificate after a one- or two-year course. As for Latin, the pedagogical faculties are not an option, for they do not offer Latin as a specialization. Therefore, the possible ways to fulfil the requirements to become a Latin teacher are either to graduate from special pedagogical Master's programmes at the departments of Classics (at Charles University in Prague or the Masaryk University in Brno) or to graduate in Classics (Latin) at Master's level and gain an additional teaching certificate. There is no imminent lack of Latin teachers in Czech schools, but there are several Latin teachers at secondary schools who have not graduated yet and teach during their Master's studies.

Latin at *gymnázia*

Latin is taught at one-third of grammar schools, with only a minority of them (mostly church schools) having Latin in their school curricula as an obligatory subject for all students. At some schools, the student takes Latin as an optional subject. In other cases, students have to choose between Latin and other subject(s), but most of these schools offer Latin only as one of many optional subjects or an extra-curricular one. The organization of the Latin classes at *gymnázia* varies from one class a week for one year to two classes a week for four years, with the average of two classes a week for two years. Very often at those schools, where students take one or two years of Latin, the Latin teachers open an extra-curricular Latin in the second or third year for those students who want to take the *maturita* in Latin or plan to study Latin at university.

Framework Educational Programmes, the school curricula and Latin

In 2009 the Czech educational system was profoundly changed by introducing the Framework Educational Programmes (FEP) to both elementary and secondary schools. These documents serve the school directors as a base for creation of their school's curricula. There is not a single mention of Latin in the FEP documents, which means it is absolutely up to each school director if and how they include Latin in the school curriculum. This also means that Latin teachers are free to choose their subject matter. In schools where Latin is a part of the school curriculum, the Latin teachers have to set up a plan for Latin lessons which is a part of the school curriculum. At the schools where Latin is just an extra-curricular subject, there is usually just one Latin teacher who is free in the matter.

Due to the limited time allowance, the content of the courses is often limited to the basics of grammar (it is not an exception that the teachers do not manage to get to the perfect tense with the students), the main emphasis being on the reading of made-up texts and on work with vocabulary. However, teachers try to incorporate ancient mythology and the daily life of the

Romans. The medieval pronunciation is used almost exclusively (in the universities, the students of Latin use either the *pronuntiatio restituta* or the medieval one, depending on their field of study).

Teaching materials

In the Czech Republic, there is a serious lack of quality textbooks for Latin, which is a frequent complaint of both the teachers and the students. Most teachers use more than one textbook; some prepare their own materials. There are three most used textbooks, of which two are in Czech. Ørberg's *Lingua Latina per se illustrata* (2010) is sometimes used. The most used of the two Czech books, *Latina pro střední školy* (Seinerová 1997), is brief, cut down to basic grammar and basic vocabulary, visually and content-wise unattractive, but thin and manageable in the limited time-allowance. The second one, *Latina pro gymnázia* (Pech 1994), is the exact opposite – very detailed, overwhelming, full of information, dense. Thanks to its density, there is a good chance that even more motivated students find something that attracts them. However, it needs a very good teacher so that the students do not get scared away. Both these textbooks are based on the grammar-translation method. As for Ørberg's Latin-only textbook, it is very hard to use it in the limited time, but teachers often choose it for its attractive story that works as a motivation. However, as far as I know, not many teachers who work with this textbook use the Direct Method to learn Latin, for which this book was designed, but they use the grammar-translation method mixed in with the elements of the Direct Method.

School/university partnerships

The departments of Classics at the Czech universities take actions to support Latin at the grammar schools (and even elementary schools). The future Latin teachers from the pedagogical Master's programmes fulfil an extensive praxis with the best Latin teachers at grammar schools as a mandatory part of their study programme. These teachers get back to the university students to discuss their teaching methods and challenges. The Classics departments organize courses of further education for Latin high school teachers. There are 'open days' at the departments of Classics, with lectures and workshops for those interested in Latin and Ancient Greek.

Students from grammar schools have the possibility to attend a semestrial programme at the university called '24 hours with the Faculty of Arts, Charles University', which means they spend 24 teaching hours at the faculty, according to their choice. Their grammar schools free them from their school programme and let them attend the classes at the university. The Classics department hosts around five students every year.

The biggest yearly event in Classics in the Czech Republic is 'The Latin Day' organized by the Classics department of Charles University. This traditional and popular event is attended every year by hundreds of high school students from all over the country along with their teachers. They spend a day listening to lectures on various topics regarding Latin and ancient Rome given by specialists from the universities and the Academy of Sciences.

There are a few theatre groups connected to the departments of Classics that present theatre pieces at the schools or to a wider audience (original theatre plays in Latin, plays by Plautus in Czech, Jesuit theatre plays). There are already a few Latin movies produced by one of these groups, and these are often used in Latin classes at the schools. There is also a national contest *Certamen Latinum* in Latin for high school students organized by the Czech state in cooperation with the Classics departments and the Czech Association of Latin Teachers (ALFA).

Conclusion

Studying Classics has a long tradition in the Czech Republic. However, in the present atmosphere of 'education pragmatism', there is a low demand for Latin at high schools from parents and students and only a little support from school directors. Latin is also ignored in the state Framework documents and except for those schools, which have Latin among the obligatory subjects, Latin teachers struggle to keep Latin alive at their schools. Still, approximately one-third of *gymnázia* offer Latin at least as one of the extra-curricular subjects although there is a strong need of a new Latin textbook that would meet the expectations of the present generation of students. There are four departments of Classics at the Czech universities which have a constant (low) number of students which manage to produce enough graduates to fulfil the need of Latin teachers. The Latin departments support the high school Latin by organizing events for students and offering further education to the Latin teachers. As for Greek, there are only very occasional extra-curricular seminars offered by the Latin teachers.

References

Ministry of Education, Youth and Sports (2020), *Statistická ročenka školství – výkonové ukazatele* [Statistical yearbook of education – performance indicators].
Ørberg, H. (2010), *Lingua Latina per se illustrata,* Rome: Accademia Vivarium Novum.
Pech, J. (1994), *Latina pro gymnázia* [Latin for High School], Praha: Leda.
Research Institute of Education in Prague (2007), 'Framework Education Programme for Secondary General Education (Grammar Schools)'. Research Institute of Education in Prague – VÚP. Available online: http://www.nuv.cz/file/161_1_1/ (accessed 5 November 2023).
Seinerová, V. (1997), *Latina pro střední školy* [Latin for Secondary Schools], Praha: Fortuna.
Žytek, J. (2014), 'Konec latiny na českých gymníziích?' [The end of Latin in Czech grammar schools?], *Lidové noviny,* 18 January.

DENMARK

Rasmus Gottschalck and Anders Klarskov Jensen

The Danish school system

The Danish school system is divided into two parts: a primary school from 1st to 9th (or 10th) grade followed by a secondary education separated in a practical branch meant for vocational training and a theoretical branch aiming at further studies at a higher education. The theoretical branch usually has the form of an upper secondary school of three years, called *gymnasium*. The term *gymnasium* covers different kinds of schools depending on the study focus, the four most common types being the higher Commercial Examination, the higher Technical Examination, the higher Preparatory Examination (a two-year alternative to the usual three-year programme) and the general *gymnasium*. The classical subjects Latin, Greek and Classical Studies (see below) are all placed in the general *gymnasium*.

In Denmark, the pupils begin school at the age of six and after an introductory year start in first grade at the age of seven. Many primary schools also offer a 10th grade, originally meant as an alternative to the *gymnasium* but today mostly used by pupils that prefer an extra year in primary school, though often spent in a boarding school (*efterskole*), before possibly continuing to a secondary education. Annually, approximately 100,000 pupils finish 9th grade. Of these, around 60 per cent continue directly to one of the secondary educations while a third prefer to spend a year in 10th grade. Annually, around 64,000 pupils attend secondary education. Around 72 per cent choose one of the four kinds of *gymnasium* and of these around 60 per cent, approximately 28,000 pupils, choose the general *gymnasium*, by far the most popular among all secondary educations.

The present *gymnasium* follows the reform of 2005 (modified 2017) that introduced so-called study programmes (*studieretninger*), the idea being that two, three or four main subjects are gathered as a focus in each study programme. The schools are free to combine subjects within natural science, political science, languages and art although the Ministry of Children and Education has limited the number of official study programmes to eighteen different combinations. Typical combinations are: biology-chemistry, English-political science, mathematics-political science, English-German, English-French, English-Spanish-Latin. One study programme also has Latin and Greek as its main subjects.

A study programme should not be confused with a school class. A school class of thirty pupils might easily contain two, even three, study programmes, some of the pupils having for example a study programme of mathematics-physics, the other half English-music or one half having English-German the other half Latin-Greek. The pupils will thus be together when taught compulsory subjects as history, Danish literature, geography, etc. but divided when taught the specific disciplines of their study programme.

When the pupils start in the general *gymnasium*, a part of their school programme during the first three months is an introductory course that includes an introduction to general linguistics, formally called a basic course in general knowledge of languages (*Almen sprogforståelse*), an introduction to natural science as well as a presentation of the study programmes offered by the school. When the introductory course ends, typically around 1 November, the pupils choose the study programme they wish to follow for the rest of their time in the *gymnasium*. Whether a study programme is opened or not depends on the number of pupils interested and the willingness of the school direction. Popular study programmes with political science, mathematics or biotechnics are almost always opened but study programmes with less requested subjects are always at risk of not opening. The number and kind of study programmes are decided by the school direction. In Denmark, the *gymnasia* have a high degree of independence, and a school direction is solely responsible, not only for the study programmes, but also for the number of teachers and the general economy of the school.

Classics in the Danish school

In primary school, Latin remained a compulsory subject until 1979, at that time a one-year subject in 9th grade. Although Latin formally remained in primary school as an optional subject, today it has almost disappeared. It is still possible to have Latin in a few primary schools and regularly Latin courses are offered in the so-called youth schools (*ungdomsskoler*), an institution shared between neighbouring schools offering different optional after-school activities, but in reality, few pupils today begin their secondary education with any knowledge of Latin.

The situation is remarkably different in the *gymnasium*. No less than three classical subjects are represented in the general *gymnasium*: Latin, Greek and Classical Studies. It makes no difference whether the schools are public or private, and the difference should not be overemphasized. Around 10 per cent of the approximately 150 general *gymnasia* of the country are private, but the study programme and the national exams are identical. All *gymnasia* are economically supported by the state according to the number of pupils they educate, the main difference between public and private *gymnasia* being that private schools receive less money from the state than public schools due to the school fees paid by parents with children in private schools.

During the three-month introductory programme, twenty hours of Latin are compulsory for *all* pupils in the general *gymnasium* as part of the introductory course in general linguistics. The Latin lessons make up half of the course while the other half mainly focuses on the Danish language and usually is taught by one or more of the other language teachers in the school, though it happens that the Latin teacher handles the full course. The teachers responsible for the course are supposed to cooperate to make sure that it is presented as a unit to the pupils. The general aim of the course in general linguistics is to improve the pupils' theoretical comprehension of languages, giving them a basic introduction to central topics such as morphology and syntax, word formation, loan words and foreign words, a basic knowledge of language families and the interrelation between the European languages. The formal role of Latin in this context is to exemplify and concretize these fields. This is done by reading easy, adapted Latin texts, usually revolving around important themes, events or personalities from the ancient world, the formal aim being to demonstrate the relation between language and culture.

It is possible to choose Latin as an elective on different levels in the general *gymnasium*. Quite a few pupils choose Latin for one year, so-called C-level, as an additional subject to their main study programme. In 2020, 3,717 pupils graduated with Latin as a one-year elective; in 2023 the number had grown to 4,261 pupils. This number, considered quite high for Danish standards, is partly due to the fact that pupils with at least three foreign languages, among them Latin, are allowed to replace a science subject or to have less mathematics than usually required, which may be attractive for some pupils. Latin for two years, so-called B-level, and Latin for three years, so-called A-level, both without Greek, do exist in some schools, but the present school structure defined by study programmes often makes it difficult to open long lasting study programmes with single subjects.

Denmark has no real tradition for choosing Greek without Latin. During the former school programme (before 2005) it was a theoretical possibility to have Greek at A-level without Latin, used by a few pupils, but for the moment no schools offer this possibility. Nevertheless, recently some schools have started to open Greek classes as a one-year elective. Greek at C-level is new in the Danish school system and the future will show how this initiative develops.

The pupils most interested in antiquity choose Classics as their study programme after having finished the introductory programme, thus having Latin and Greek as their main subjects for the rest of their time in the *gymnasium*. Around twenty schools offer a study programme of Classics and annually around fifteen schools open a new study programme of

Classics, each typically consisting of eight to fifteen pupils. Thus, between 100 and 150 pupils annually finish *gymnasium* with Latin and Greek at A-level. This might sound like a small number but is considered acceptable given the existing school structure and that the pupils have both Latin and Greek at A-level.

Without doubt, most characteristic for Classics in Denmark is the third classical subject: Classical Studies (*Oldtidskundskab*), a one-year compulsory subject for *all* pupils in the general *gymnasium*. The teaching of Classical Studies is based on classical Greek texts in Danish translations, as well as Greek art, but it also includes a few Roman texts and Roman art. Moreover, in order to demonstrate the classical tradition, the pupils are presented to post-ancient texts inspired by ancient ones. In its present form, the teaching is arranged around five themes chosen individually by the teachers (though Homer and at least one Roman text must be represented). One theme might include either one or more ancient Greek texts, possibly supplemented by Roman texts. Typical themes are: democracy, forms of government, rhetoric, Platonic ideas, heroic ideals, fate, love, the good life and the good state. An Epic theme might include selected songs of Homer, possibly a book of Vergil's *Aeneid* and passages or poems of modern literature inspired by Homer, e.g. passages from Margaret Atwood's *The Penelopiad* and a poem by a modern Danish author. A tragedy theme could include Sophocles' *Oedipus* and sections of Max Frisch's *Homo Faber* or *Antigone* and Jean Anouilh's play of the same title. All texts are in Danish translation. The teachers are free to choose post-ancient texts from any period and any country they wish, the only constraint being that the ancient text read in this context should be clearly visible in the post-ancient texts. Films are also often included to demonstrate the ancient influence, e.g. Woody Allen's *Match Point* or Joel and Ethan Coen's *O Brother, Where Art Thou*. One of the five themes is an art theme. Typically, the teacher presents either Greek architecture or sculpture to the pupils supplemented by post-ancient architecture or art influenced by ancient artistic or architectural ideals.

The formal aims of Greek, Latin and Classical Studies in the Danish Upper Secondary School are described in the school programme published by the Ministry of Children and Education. According to this, Latin, Greek and Classical Studies are perceived as a central contribution to the pupils' general knowledge of antiquity as a foundation for the ideas and concepts of literature, art, values, and ways of thinking that have played a defining role for the subsequent periods of Western civilization until today. This insight enables the pupils to better understand their own culture and to see themselves as part of a bigger, international community and in this way to better understand other cultures with another history and other cultural ideas and values, thus developing the democratic education of the pupils. Moreover, Classics provide the pupils with a fundamental understanding of the discussions about the organization of a society, different forms of government and democracy, in antiquity as well as today.

Specifically for Latin and Greek (but not for Classical Studies), the direct access to the ancient sources describing these values is emphasized. Working with Latin and Greek gives a grammatical insight, knowledge about the Greek and Latin vocabulary for the languages in the Western world, including the unique role of Latin in European history, and a linguistic structure that is very useful when learning other languages. A basic impression of these aspects of Latin and Greek is already introduced during the basic course in general linguistics.

One of the central discussions revolving around Classics in Denmark particularly touches upon the three months introductory programme, including twenty compulsory Latin lessons. The formal reason for keeping the introductory programme is to give the pupils a fair chance to choose the right study programme that will qualify them for their preferred further education, e.g. at the university or at the business school, enabling them to begin their further education directly after having finished the *gymnasium* without having to supplement their school education with new subjects (that they could have had in school if they had chosen the right study programme). But critical voices question if the introductory programme is really necessary. According to these, the pupils already have a sufficient impression of the subjects of the *gymnasium*, being relatively similar to the subjects of primary school. Such voices would like to see the introductory programme removed from the school programme so that the pupils could choose and start in their study programmes from the beginning of the *gymnasium*. This discussion involves Classics very much because Latin teachers generally fear that Latin, Greek and the whole classical study programme would disappear from upper secondary school if the pupils are not introduced to Latin (and Classics) at the beginning of the *gymnasium*.

Another discussion concerns the existence of Classical Studies as a compulsory subject in the Danish general *gymnasium*. Classical Studies was introduced in the *gymnasium* with the school reform of 1903 and was meant as a compensation for pupils not having Latin and Greek as their primary subjects but modern languages or natural science instead. During the last decades, every time a new school reform has been passed, a discussion has taken place regarding whether Classical Studies should be preserved or replaced by another subject – e.g. a kind of general culture subject – or simply just removed to create more room for the other school subjects. The discussion always results in several newspaper articles, radio interviews and sometimes even books published in favour of Classical Studies. So far, Classical Studies has been preserved thanks to politicians who have been responsive to arguments about the importance of the classical ideals, not least the Athenian democracy and democratic debate, and the influence of these ideals on Danish culture and history. Nevertheless, the existence of Classical Studies should especially be ascribed to the direction of the Association of Classical Teachers (*Klassikerforeningen*) that at every moment of reform in schools has played an active role for the continuous existence of Classics in the Danish *gymnasium*.

Current trends in Classics teaching today

Traditionally, textbooks in both Greek and Latin intend to bring the pupils as quickly as possible to the ancient texts without spending too much time on adapted texts. The pupils thus learn a lot of the necessary Greek and Latin grammar while reading original texts. This approach is not only due to the limited number of lessons available but also to the idea of *autopsy* founded by Denmark's greatest philologist, Johan Nicolai Madvig (1804–86), according to whom true understanding of antiquity and true education must be through the sources themselves. An example of this is the still much used textbook for Greek, *Prologos* (Tortzen 2007), containing around thirty short chapters with passages of original Greek texts starting with poems by Anacreon and extracts of two of Lucian's dialogues and ending with Hesiod, Xenophanes and Sappho. The book is supposed to supplement the Greek grammar, *Basis* (Tortzen 2020), reprinted several times, and today being the standard grammar for beginners in Greek used in all school classes and at many Greek beginner's courses at university. The beginner's book for Latin, *Ludus* (Christensen & Tortzen 1999), uses the same principle as *Prologos* bringing the reader to original ancient Latin texts after a few introductory lessons. The *autopsy* approach is perhaps the reason why the only internationally well-known Danish beginner's book in Latin *Lingua Latina per se illustrata* (Ørberg 2019), focusing on learning Latin by an immediate understanding by adapted texts, never has been much used in Denmark. But considering the generally increasing interest for oral Latin, this might change.

Due to the growing number of pupils choosing Latin as a one-year elective, mentioned above, several new Latin textbooks have been published to supplement the existing materials. What characterizes these new publications is their close alignment with the details of the school programme set by the Ministry of Children and Education, making them readily applicable. Often, these textbooks are extensively didacticized to alleviate the workload of teachers, which has been increased in later years. *Latinbogen* [The Latin Book] (Pedersen & Svenningsen 2022) includes preparatory exercises for pupils to solve before translating a Latin text into Danish, e.g. finding out which tenses or cases are present in the Latin text. This makes it clearer for pupils how they are supposed to approach the original text and what is expected of them. *Latin – her og nu* [Latin – Right Now] (Jørgensen & Jensen 2021) strives to make Latin literature relevant for the pupils by incorporating memes and other well-known features of popular culture. In *Græsk – her og nu* [Greek – Right Now] (Jensen 2023), exercises involve translating Danish into Greek. While a practical use of Greek is not a learning goal, it is believed that adopting this teaching tool from modern foreign languages will make the ancient language appear less alien and intimidating and allow the pupils to feel, by creating their own sentences in Greek, that they master Greek in a new way.

Classical Studies also sees its fair share of publications. Originally, no real introductory book existed and was – to a certain degree – undesirable due to the ideal of *autopsy*. It sufficed to read translations furnished with small introductory chapters giving the necessary historical and cultural background, thus keeping the ancient text as a focus. Nevertheless, though *autopsy* is still the ideal approach in Classical Studies, today several introductory books on ancient culture, literature and art exist, e.g. *Paideia* (Andreasen & Poulsen 2012), *Antik Mytologi* [Ancient Mythology] (Tortzen 2009) and *Græsk kunst* [Greek Art] (Fich 2008) to mention a few examples. Some recent publications include didactic suggestions for creative ways of working with the texts. Some have a methodical awareness suggesting to pupils and teachers what methods to use on different kinds of texts, e.g. *Metode i Oldtidskundskab* [Methods in Classical Studies] (Sørensen 2021).

It is a common pedagogical practice to vary the teaching in some way or another, especially in schools with long lessons of 100 minutes or more. This variation may take very different forms depending on the teacher's preferences and ideas. The pupils are used to working in groups or in pairs. In that case, the Latin and Greek pupils help each other translating the text, assisted by the teacher. The pupils of Classical Studies may be asked to rewrite a dramatic passage of Homer into their own style – if you were Achilles in the first song of the *Iliad* how would you express yourself to Agamemnon, using as much as Homer's text as possible? – or to see a passage, e.g. of the *Odyssey* or a Catullus poem, from another angle than the one presented in the text, or to prepare and perform an episode of a tragedy. Quizzes making groups compete against each other are usually popular and often a useful way to make the pupils do their best to remember what they have been taught recently. Cooperative Learning exercises that engage the whole class at the same time are quite widespread as well. Nevertheless, the teachers are aware of the advantages of a more traditional kind of teaching and that some pupils prefer this. Tests are rare in Classics in general, but the Latin and Greek classes regularly have quite long written exercises to do at home.

Digital learning plays a central role in today's *gymnasium*, with pupils using computers for most of their schoolwork. As useful as computers are, they can easily distract and therefore pose a didactic problem in the classroom. Many teachers, particularly those teaching Latin and Greek, prefer an analogue approach, requiring the pupils to use pen and paper when working with the ancient texts. According to these teachers, this enhances the pupils' immersion. There is an on-going debate in Denmark about the use of computers in the classrooms, with some politicians aiming to reduce their prevalence. During the lockdowns of 2020 and 2021, teachers as well as pupils who went through whole courses with video communication realized the importance of a face-to-face conversation in a learning environment.

Teacher training

Teaching Latin, Greek and/or Classical Studies requires a Master's degree from a university including one or more of these subjects. In Denmark, most Master's degrees meant for teaching include two subjects. A permanent position in a school requires one year of teacher training including theoretical courses on pedagogics alternating with teaching in practice in a classroom. For the practical part, the candidate is assisted by (usually) two experienced teachers that regularly follow and supervise the teaching of the candidate while the candidate likewise regularly observes the teaching of the two supervisors. Moreover, the teaching of the candidate is observed three times by an external teacher that together with a member of the school direction compiles a final report on the teaching competences of the candidate. The year ends with a written one-week exercise on a pedagogical subject hosted by the Ministry of Children and Education.

However, for the moment there is a high demand for Latin teachers, especially since all pupils in the *gymnasium* must follow the aforementioned introductory programme including twenty lessons of Latin, and some schools therefore face challenges in meeting the teacher capacity for all classes. Consequently, it is not unheard of for university students of Latin to teach some of these classes. To address this issue, Danish universities have established a supplementary education programme enabling teachers (of modern foreign languages, for example) to obtain a degree in Latin in less time than usually required.

Cooperation

Denmark is a small country – around six million inhabitants – and many teachers of Latin and most teachers of Greek are familiar with each other. The Association of Classical Teachers plays an important role in bringing teachers together from across the country. The Association organizes several seminars every year, providing a platform for teachers to engage in professional discussions, and covering topics such as the national written examination and various approaches to teaching certain authors or genres. The Association also publishes a periodical, entitled *Logos*, issued three times a year, containing academic and didactic articles, book reviews, messages from the national adviser and more. The direction of the Association also includes a university representative to maintain a connection between the *gymnasium* and the university. Furthermore, the Association annually hosts a range of competitions in Latin, Greek and ancient culture that all schools may participate in. There is generally a sense of unity among the Danish teachers of Classics; the classical subjects are considered precious and vulnerable, and this sentiment certainly motivates the teachers to put in an extra effort to inspire the pupils and make the classes a positive learning experience.

Conclusion

In Denmark, the classical subjects are currently considered to be in a good place. Many pupils choose Latin as a one-year elective, Greek as a one-year elective has recently been introduced, and an acceptable number of schools have the study programme that includes both Latin and Greek at A-level. Moreover, Classical Studies remains compulsory for all pupils in the general, *gymnasium* and is generally a subject appreciated by the pupils. Several new textbooks contribute to the pedagogical evolution of the classical subjects and discussions and exchange of teaching experiences and material are on-going between teachers across the country, at meetings organized by the Association for Classical Teachers and via social media. This cooperation between teachers plays a very important part in helping these subjects not only survive but thrive.

Related reading on Classics in Danish schools may be found in Gottschalck (2019), Hansen (2022) and Tortzen (2001). All statistics mentioned in this article come from The Danish Ministry of Children and Education, currently available online. We would like to thank the current national adviser of Classics in Denmark, Allan Uhre Hansen, for following the work on this article and sharing his opinion with us, and former president of the Association of Classical Teachers, Erik Kristensen, for his linguistic assistance.

References

Andreasen, B. and J. R. Poulsen (2012), *Paideia*, Aarhus: Systime.

Christensen, B. and C. G. Tortzen (1999), *Ludus, Introduktion til Latin* [Ludus, Introduction to Latin], Copenhagen: Gyldendal.

Fich, H. (2008), *Græsk kunst* [Greek Art], Aarhus: Systime.

Gottschalck, R. (2019), 'Greek in Denmark', in F. Oliveira and R. Martinez (eds), *Europatrida*, Imprensa da Universidade de Coimbra / Coimbra University Press, 59–70.

Hansen, A. U. (2022), 'The Status of Latin in Denmark', *Latinitas, Series Nova*, X, Volumen Prius, 167–70. Pontificia Academia Latinitatis in Civitate Vaticana.

Jensen, A. K. (2023), *Græsk – her og nu* [Greek – Right Now], Copenhagen: Praxis.

Jørgensen, K. B. and L. T.-P. Jensen (2021), *Latin – her og nu* [Latin – Right Now], Copenhagen: Praxis.

Ørberg, H. (2019), *Lingua Latina per se illustrata, pars I: Familia Romana,* Montella: Edizioni Accademia Vivarium Novum (1st edition 1981, Grenaa: Domus Latina).

Pedersen, L. A. and S. A. Svenningsen (2022), *Latinbogen, Grundbogen til Latin C* [The Latin Book, Introduction to Latin C], Aarhus: Systime.

Sørensen, M. (2021), *Metode i Oldtidskundskab* [Methods in Classical Studies], Frederiksberg: Frydenlund.

Tortzen, C. G. (2001), 'Translations and Classical Civilization in the Danish Gymnasium', in H. Holmboe and S. Isager (eds), *Translators and Translations,* Aarhus: Aarhus University Press / The Danish Institute at Athens, 45–51.

Tortzen, C. G. (2007), *Prologos, Introduktion til græsk* [Prologos, Introduction to Greek], Copenhagen: Museum Tusculanums Forlag.

Tortzen, C. G. (2009), *Antik mytologi* [Ancient Mythology], Copenhagen: Gyldendal.

Tortzen, C. G. (2020), *Basis, Græsk grammatik for begyndere* [Basis, Greek for Beginners], Copenhagen: Museum Tusculanums Forlag.

FINLAND

Ilkka Kuivalainen, Robert Luther and Arto Rantamaa

Introduction This article was written in 2019 and only very minor changes have been made since then.

Greek has not been taught in Finnish schools for several years. In the state schools there are two possible levels to study Latin but it is always an optional subject. The number of pupils who study foreign languages other than English in Finnish schools has decreased considerably lately. There are two official languages in Finland, Finnish and Swedish, and all pupils have to study both in school. In addition, all students have to choose a modern language, which is mostly English. There are many pupils who find it demanding to choose yet another language.

Schools

In some schools there is a long tradition of Latin teaching. There are also families where members of several generations have studied Latin. At the same time a considerable portion of the Latinists has for a long time been pupils who are the first in their family to study Latin. The reasons why the pupils choose Latin are very varied. Many are interested in the classical history and culture, some in languages and there are pupils with a very special interest in, for example, birds or flowers and who wish to understand the Latin terms. The opinion that Latin is required for future students of law and medicine is receding and Latin is rather seen as a subject that gives the pupils a possibility to understand many things than as a necessary practical tool. Some of the pupils who succeed well in their Latin studies show a clear talent for languages, others have a mathematical mind. The balance between girls and boys who choose Latin in the same school may vary much from year to year, but the relative number of boys who choose Latin may be greater than that of boys who choose other optional languages.

In accordance with the general curriculum the pupils can study Latin for two lessons a week during the three last years of the elementary school. For a few years now it has not been possible to choose both Latin and a modern language (for example German or French). It is too early to say how this will reflect on the choices of the pupils, but it is possible that it will have a negative effect on the status of Latin. After the elementary school the pupils can choose to continue their Latin studies in the upper secondary school. Many pupils however do not choose to continue with Latin after the elementary school.

The other option is to study Latin during the three years of the upper secondary school where the studies are based on courses. In general, the greatest possible number of Latin courses is eight, but there are great differences between schools. The pupils decide after each course whether they wish to continue their Latin studies or not. At the end of the upper secondary school the pupils can choose to include Latin as one of the subjects in their matriculation examinations, but the number of pupils who take this option each year is counted in tens.

At all levels there is a minimum number of pupils required to start or to continue to study the subject and this number can vary from school to school. Even if there are pupils who wish to study Latin, they are often too few to make it possible. In some cities there is a well-functioning system which makes it possible for pupils from different upper secondary schools to come together to study Latin in one of the schools. In general, the teachers think however that it is easier to keep up the interest in Latin if the teacher and the pupils work in one and the same school.

The first Latin texts that are studied are written to be used in teaching. Later the pupils study modified or authentic classical, medieval or later texts. At all levels language and culture are studied together, with an emphasis on aspects of the classical (or later) culture that are relevant today. The linguistic studies involve among other things a knowledge of grammatical terms and of a vocabulary that is found in different languages, and an ability to analyse complex sentences. Since the frequency of words derived from Latin is relatively small in Finnish (although it is larger in Swedish) the Latin vocabulary is more useful to the pupils in learning foreign languages than in learning Finnish. Especially in the later courses, the pupils get acquainted with different literary genres and rhetorical and poetic stylistic devices. When needed they are also encouraged to compare the message of the first reading of the text with what is known about the actual situation to which the text alludes.

In the elementary school and the first courses in the upper secondary school the pupils acquire a basic knowledge of Latin and of life in classical Rome. They study both the private and the public life of the Romans, for example work, leisure and school life. When it comes to culture, they study among other things Greek and Roman mythology. During the later courses in the upper secondary school the pupils develop their knowledge of, for example, Roman history, famous Romans and classical culture and literature. The history, development and importance of Latin from antiquity through the Middle Ages and the Renaissance to modern times and the position of Latin in, for example, Christianity, the law and sciences are also studied. Naturally the pupils also get acquainted with the history of Latin in Finland.

Resources and teaching materials

The use of information technology and of social media in the teaching of Latin varies according to the interests of the teacher. There is a long tradition in Finland of translating well-known both national and international songs and poems into Latin. There is, for example, a Latin version of the Finnish national anthem and the late professor Teivas Oksala has rendered *Love Me Tender* and other songs remembered in connection with Elvis Presley in Latin. The brilliant Latin translation of *Kalevala* by Professor Tuomo Pekkanen may be regarded as the finest example of this tradition. All these texts may be used to enhance the interest of the pupils in Latin and to show them that Latin may still be used actively in many ways. The *Nuntii Latini Radiophoniae Finniae Generalis* (Finnish Radio News in Latin) bulletins were well known in the world and have been used in classrooms by many teachers.

Assessment

The main aims of the subjects are enumerated in the general curriculum, but the Finnish teachers of all subjects, and especially of the optional subjects, enjoy a relatively great freedom when it comes to, for example, teaching methods and materials. The same freedom applies to the assessment of how the pupils progress in the subjects. The assessment uses the grades 4 to 10, where 4 is not sufficient and 10 is excellent. The assessment takes into account everything the pupil does: activity during classes, homework, written and oral presentations, written tests and examinations. The general curriculum attaches great importance to the self-assessment of the pupils. It is customary for the teachers to discuss individually with the pupils their strengths and where they need to improve their work in the subject. This takes time but is generally accepted to be very good for the motivation of the pupils.

The matriculation examination is the only case where the assessment is based solely on a written examination. The number of participants in the matriculation examinations has diminished as in the other optional languages as well. During the past twenty years the highest number of students to take part in the examinations was in 2004: the shorter Latin course had 118 participants in the spring and 55 in the autumn, altogether 173 participants. The longer course had 28 participants that year; the highest number for that examination was in 1999 with 45 participants. The latest numbers are much lower. In the spring of 2018 and 2019 only 24 and 28 for the shorter Latin course, and in the autumn of 2018 and 2019 only eight. The number of participants in the longer course examinations has varied more but has been under ten for several years. It will not be possible to pass the the longer course examination after the spring of 2025.

The matriculation examination in Latin has been in digital form since the spring examinations 2019, but the structure is nearly the same as before. There is a translation of a Latin text into the mother tongue (Finnish or Swedish). The translation stands for around 77–96 marks where the highest possible total mark is 209. The second task is a reading comprehension with answers in the mother tongue. There are also questions on syntax and morphology. The last questions are multiple-choice questions. The students do the examinations on their own laptops and they are allowed to use printed dictionaries. The new digital form of the exams has made it possible to link pictures to the texts. The most recent topics have been, for example, the school years of Augustine of Hippo, Romulus, Antony and Cleopatra, excerpts from *Satyricon* and *Germania* in the shorter course, and in the examination of the longer course Nero and Agrippina, Alexander the Great, Charlemagne and the death of Cicero.

In some schools there are also Latin clubs. Their main aim is to foster the interest of the pupils in the classical culture and classical languages and to give them the rudiments of Latin grammar and vocabulary. In Finland there is also a well-functioning system of learning institutions for adults and Latin is taught in several of these. Some of the pupils have university degrees, some have studied other languages, and some have studied Latin before and wish to brush up their knowledge of Latin while others may have very little experience of academic studies. Normally there are no tests and examinations in these institutions. The pupils and teachers may decide relatively freely the aims and methods of the courses, and in many cases small but determined classes pursue their studies for several years.

Teachers

The training of teachers contains a university degree in the subjects the teacher is going to teach, pedagogical studies and practising in a school. There are teachers who teach only or mostly Latin, but most Latin teachers teach at least one other subject. Many teach other languages or history, but there is no norm deciding which subjects can be combined. There are more qualified Latin teachers than there are positions for them.

Most of the Latin teachers are the only teachers of the subject in their school and many are the only teacher in the town. Therefore, many of them feel keenly the need of collaboration with other Latin teachers. This is partly provided for by the Association of Latin teachers in Finland (*Latinankielen opettajien yhdistys – Latinlärarnas förening r.y*). The Association organizes training courses every other summer and during these courses the teachers get a chance to meet and discuss with both colleagues and university teachers. More seldom arranged but also very important are the courses arranged in Rome and Athens as a collaboration between the Association and the local Finnish institutes.

Extra-curricular

There is an interest in Finnish society concerning Latin and the classical heritage. At the same time authorities, parents and pupils are especially interested in subjects that are expected to be of measurable practical use to the pupils. Because of the complicated grammar Latin is considered a difficult subject that requires hard work. Many young people feel insecure about the future and they feel the importance of a good education leading to a degree. It seems that the success of the pupils in school and especially in the matriculation examination will be of even greater importance than before when the students apply for the right to study subjects at university level. It is quite possible that this will lead to a situation where many pupils with an interest in and ability to learn Latin feel that they should rather apply themselves to subjects, like advanced mathematics, that will be of greater help to them when they apply for entrance at a university.

Conclusion

The obligatory education was prolonged a few years ago. It seems that this change has not affected the study of Latin in any remarkable way. Latin is a small subject in the Finnish school system, but it is important to many pupils.

FRANCE

Florence Turpin

Introduction

The French education system is centralized. In all teaching establishments, both primary and secondary, and at all levels, everyone must follow ministerial decisions and government instructions and guidance. These decide the teaching levels, the curriculum, the recruitment of teachers, the subjects to be taught, the number of hours per week for each subject, and the setting of examinations to receive official certificates. In principle, all pupils have access to the same teaching as schools are free of charge and attendance is obligatory from three to sixteen years. A small minority choose private fee-paying education, but most of these schools have a contract with the state administration, which means they must conform to the public education system. Their teachers are paid by the state.

After spending three years at nursery, pupils enter primary school for five years. There are no examinations. They are then admitted to a lower secondary school (*collège*) at eleven years, and after four years they take an intermediate examination, the DNB (*Diplôme national du brevet*). At the end of this stage, they are directed towards different educational branches: either to a professional or vocational one, or to a general or technological one. These courses lead to the Baccalaureate examination at eighteen, which acts as a certificate for final school leaving and university entrance. It is possible to pass from one branch to another. The Baccalaureate requires three years at upper secondary school (*lycée*). After the final year, pupils can continue their studies which are dependent on their examination results, their applications and the number of places available. They then obtain places on courses in higher education institutions (for the majority) in post-bac vocational courses, or in preparatory courses (*classes préparatoires*) which lead to entry into the most prestigious institutions (*les grandes écoles*). These are mostly independent of the universities. Higher education is less uniform than secondary education at school and universities have a degree of autonomy. The programmes and the character of the teaching and learning can vary considerably from one university to another, but the structure of the courses must conform to a certain pattern: an undergraduate degree in three years, a Master's degree in two, followed by a thesis. Entry into the teaching profession is by a national competitive examination and students who apply to be candidates must be prepared methodically, particularly as they are set according to a fixed programme.

Although there are some instances here and there in primary school, or even in nursery school (see, for example, Duchemin et al. 2023), the teaching of Classics (*Langues et Cultures de l'Antiquité* – LCA) only really begins in the lower secondary school (*collège*). In the first year, an optional course of two hours a week has recently been established, called *Français Culture Antique*. Its emphasis is on helping pupils improve their French as their first language of education through close attention to the origin of words. The course content is ambitious and deserves to be taught to all pupils in the sixth class (the first year of *collège*), but the lessons are offered only in a small number of schools with different timetable arrangements. Latin is offered in the second year (one optional hour a week). In the following two years it becomes an option of three hours a week. Greek can be chosen in the fourth year of *collège* in addition to or instead of Latin, with the same weekly timetable provision. Joint teaching of the two languages has been established in a number of schools with a special timetable. However, in many *collèges* the timetable requirements of LCA are not respected. Furthermore, it is not always possible to take Latin, and especially Greek, because of a lack of teachers. It is not surprising, therefore, that the number of pupils who choose these options is decreasing, especially as there is only one option available for certification in the *Diplôme national du brevet* in Classics (LCA): Latin *or* Greek.

Classics is not taught in the vocational branches, but only in the general and technological branches of the upper secondary school (*lycées*). In the first year, pupils can choose an option of LCA/Latin and/or LCA/Greek, along with other options with an allocation of three hours a week. In the second and third year of *lycée* these options can be continued with the same timetables. In addition, in the second year, pupils following the general paths have to choose three special subjects: Art, Mathematics, Physics/Chemistry, Life and Earth Sciences, Humanities, Literature, Philosophy, etc. At this point they can opt for Literature and Languages and Culture of Antiquity (*Littérature et Langues et Cultures de l'Antiquité* – LLCA) in either Latin or Greek, with a timetable allocation of four hours a week. This special subject can be taken in the last year of *lycée* with a timetable of six hours a week, along with another special subject with the same timetable allocation. Special subjects form part of the Baccalaureate and candidates must take a national written examination with a high coefficient or weighting for the final overall Baccalaureate mark; other optional subjects are accredited through continuous assessment and have less importance in the final mark. In 2022 there were 225 candidates for Greek and 507 for Latin. However, only a few *lycées* offer the LLCA special subject, and even when it is offered, the timetable is not always respected. The LCA options are often in the same situation and, as in the *collège,* the numbers are decreasing, particularly in Latin, according to the figures published in 2022 in the *Enquête du Syndicat National de l'Enseignement secondaire sur les LCA* (SNES 2022). This confirms the already disappointing figures in the *Rapport Charvet* (Charvet & Bauduin 2018). Charvet and Bauduin (2018) note in particular that the decrease in numbers takes place mainly in the move from *collège* to *lycée*: 15 per cent of pupils in the last year of *collège* take Latin but only 5 per cent in the following first year of *lycée*. Many higher-level literary courses at *lycée* and most universities offer students courses in the teaching of French (first language), Latin and Greek.

Classical languages and literature

Classics teaching in France (LCA) is always optional. This has been the case for decades and there is no question of making it obligatory. It is open to all pupils in secondary education, which is rare in Europe, and in 2018 12 per cent followed a Classics (LCA) course. The state of LCA teaching has been made worse in recent years by successive reforms. However, even if the type of education does not have the same prestige that it had before, its critics (who do not hesitate to declare that the discipline is elitist, that the learning of the ancient languages is dull and too difficult, and that there is no need to learn ancient languages and cultures) are obliged to recognize that the intellectual contribution of this type of learning is considerable. Furthermore, the criticisms of the teaching of Classics are not much echoed in the country itself, and Classics teachers are not ashamed to teach their subjects – even if they are concerned with societies where there were many enslaved persons and where women played a minor role. Pupils are convinced that it is a way to get to know the civilizations and languages which have fashioned the history of Europe, and to reach a better understanding of the contemporary world. It is a path which offers the study of ancient worlds which are both distant and yet almost nearby. They also know, especially those from a disadvantaged background, that this study will lead them to a stronger mastery of their first language, French, and so to greater success in their education. This has been demonstrated by statistics published in the report by Charvet and Bauduin (2018). In response to the arguments of the 'Modernists', supporters of Classics reply that it is not just about training more Classics teachers – even if they are needed – but to give to the pupils who choose it the possibility of a moment of reflection to reach a firmer understanding of their place in the world in which they live. It is not a question of presenting to them models of languages and cultures to admire or imitate, but to give them the means to compare different systems and to contribute to the formation of their critical instincts. However, all these arguments which ought to favour the access to Classical Studies are not sufficient and there are many obstacles to overcome. Successive reforms have rarely improved the situation, even when improvements were expected: once the timetable has been reduced, it is difficult to return to the full allocation later. In theory, all pupils should have access to all options in the *collège* and then in the *lycée* of their choice, but in practice there are large disparities across the country. In addition to the joint teaching of Latin and Greek which already exists in both *lycée* and *collège*, the *Mare Nostrum* project has been set up to promote the teaching of Classical Greek more widely. We will give more details below.

Teaching methods and resources

At the *collège* and then in the *lycée*, the programmes and the teaching methods for all academic subjects are drawn up after a long and complex procedure within the *Conseil Supérieur des Programmes* and validated by the Minister of Education. They are published in the Official Bulletin and must be applied in all establishments. The inspectors have a particular duty to check that teachers are following the programmes. In the *collège* the programmes for Classics (EDUSCOL 2023) aim for pupils in Latin to acquire elements of literary, historical and artistic culture, to read, comprehend, translate and respond to original texts, and to understand the function of the language. Pupils are expected to be able to not only translate an authentic Latin text into French, but also to situate literary texts in their historical and cultural context and to interpret them. In Greek, after one year's teaching, they should be able to recognize key elements of language in a given passage of a short and accessible text, as well as to translate simple sentences into French. They should also know how 'to deal with texts and language systems' (EDUSCOL 2023a). The authors of textbooks, who are often teachers themselves, conform to the instructions and take account of 'accompanying resources for the programmes' (EDUSCOL 2023a) published by the ministry and available online. All these resources are available to teachers and pupils in print or digital format.

There is also a teaching programme for the option French and Ancient Culture (*Français Culture Antique*) published in the Official Bulletin (Ministère de l'Éducation Nationale et de la Jeunesse 2021). The teaching resources follow the three parts of the programme: lexical (Greek and Latin roots for all curriculum subjects, Greek and Latin roots for the learning of French); grammatical (comparison of French to Latin to understand the structure and the function of a sentence, comparison of French to Latin to understand the principle of grammatical agreement, comparison of French to Latin to achieve mastery of correct spelling); and literary, cultural and artistic (birth and rebirth of the world; representation of the origins of the universe and of mankind; war and peace between gods and mortals; understanding of what unites and divides, representations of eternity; imaginings of the cycle of life).

For the joint teaching of Latin and Greek, colleagues have been inspired by the method established by Marie-France Kalantzis and the working group set up by the Academy of Besançon. The course structure is linked to the introduction of the programmes at the *collège* and the *lycée* and the resources are available online from the Academy of Besançon (ECLA 2023). They contain schemes of work, exercises of graded difficulty for the different levels of *collège* or the beginning of *lycée*, and offer ideas to colleagues. The pedagogical content is progressively updated. An example is of a project based on the theme to be studied in the fourth cycle of *collège*, entitled 'From Myth to History'. The scheme of work allows comparisons to be made between the two languages and contains extracts from Ovid's *Metamorphoses* (2. 15–34) and Lucian's *Dialogues of the Dead* (10, Hermes and Helios). In the Ovid extract, Phaethon discovers the palace of Phoebus; after entering the marvellously constructed doors of the palace, he notices, in astonishment, Phoebus surrounded by his court formed of the Days, Months and Years. In the Lucian extract, on the order of Zeus, Hermes asks Helios not to take his usual course and to remain at rest for three days; Zeus needs a longer night with Alcmena. Beginning with a review of the lexical field of time in the two languages, pupils are asked to work on the etymology of a certain number of first-language French words and on the third declension in Latin and Greek. This is the moment to introduce or revise the conjugation of verbs in the imperfect, to work on some figures of style and to bring together lexis, morphology and commentary. This joint teaching, practised mainly in the *collège*, has been well received; it has been encouraged above all in the south-east of France. It can also be taught in the *lycée*, but it does not qualify for inclusion in assessment for the Baccalaureate.

At the *lycée* the programmes are based on the confrontation between the ancient and modern worlds, with a reading-comprehension approach which blends language and culture together. In this optional subject, pupils are mainly required to reflect, in the first year of the *lycée*, on humankind in general, in the second year on the political and religious environment of the individual, and in the final year on the place of humankind in the universe. The progressive acquisition of knowledge and understanding of the language is strictly graded as appropriate for each level.

For the teaching of the 'special subject' (*Littérature et Langues et Cultures de l'Antiquité –* LLCA) the levels of achievement are of course more demanding than for the optional subject. In the final year of the LLCA, the programme consists of the study and comparison of two works (renewed every two years) which relate to antiquity and to any epoch and country as long as they are linked thematically. For example, in LLCA Latin for 2023/24, Virgil's *Aeneid* Book 6 and J. M. Coetzee's *The Age of Iron* are studied for the theme of the descent to the underworld and the promise of a new era; while in LLCA Greek, Homer's *Odyssey* Books 19 and 20 are linked to the *Naissance de l'Odyssée* by Jean Giono. Furthermore, three set themes are studied throughout the year: humankind, the world, fate; belief, knowledge, doubt; and the Mediterranean (presence of the ancient world), along a number of lines of study – for example, for the third set theme is the knowledge of the major geographical and cultural reference markers through a comparison of the ancient and contemporary worlds.

The joint teaching of Latin and Greek (ECLA) is not the only feature common to *collège* and *lycée*. A project called *Mare Nostrum* was developed in 2022 in order to permit the European alliance of the ancient languages announced by the Education Minister (Ministère de l'Éducation Nationale et de la Jeunesse 2023). This project brings together four different countries (Italy, Greece, Cyprus and France) and is designed to contribute to the humanistic education of pupils who will develop their awareness of the classical heritage at the heart of our society (EDUSCOL 2023b). Pupils will have one extra hour on their weekly timetable in the course of which they will learn with different language teachers and put together a personal project which can be accredited for the DNB and the Baccalaureate. It is too soon to evaluate the experience, but teachers have enabled pupils to discover, reinforce and link the learning of Latin, Provençal, and Italian through linguistic, cultural and artistic workshops. The resources have been put on line on the platform *Odysseum* 'the digital home of the humanities' (Odysseum 2023). *Odysseum* can be consulted by anyone, whether they are a teacher, pupil or just a fan of the ancient world.

Odysseum echoes many other projects, in particular 'the Humanities in the text', an academic and pedagogical programme which aims to construct a digital anthology of Greek and Latin texts, with translation and commentary suitable for teaching in *collège, lycée* or in higher education (Worms et al. 2023). The anthology may also contain two or three interpretations and copyright-free images, short videos or a podcast. Research teams are exploring active methods for teaching Latin and even Greek (see the website antiqdialog (2023) for examples of these innovative practices in French schools today).

Higher education has also developed its use of digital technology. During the Covid pandemic, most courses were available only online. In more normal times, the majority of universities offer courses in person, although some use distance learning. Some trial partnerships between the preparatory classes for literature and the universities are being carried out.

Teacher training

Although there is an elite path (two years of preparatory classes and admittance to the *École Normale Supérieure* by competitive examination), the training of teachers of Classics takes place in the universities which offer courses consisting of both French literature and Classical languages and literature. The arrangement of the teaching and learning (the literary programmes, the cultural history and the ancient history courses) vary from university to university. Many student teachers are late beginners in Latin and/or Greek. At the Sorbonne, for example, for the first degree, after three years (*licence*) students must achieve a certain number of credits each semester (ECTS: European Credit Transfer and Accumulation System) in French, Greek and Latin language and literature, to which they add a modern language, and various optional subjects such as a certificate in computer and internet use. For the two following years (Master's 1 and Master's 2) the base disciplines are studied in more depth and are complemented by the addition of information technology and pedagogy. Students must also present a dissertation. They also prepare to take the professional entry examination for teaching, principally the CAPES (*Certificat d'aptitude professionnelle à l'enseignement secondaire*) for the majority, and also the *Agrégation* in Classics or in grammar. After a year's training they are qualified to teach in the *collège* or *lycée*. Teachers in higher education at university are recruited after submission of a thesis. However, these careers in education do not attract many students because the life of a teacher is becoming more and more difficult and is becoming less well remunerated. The shortage affects all disciplines but the number of candidates for the examination in Classics is particularly low, because the examinations for the CAPES seem unattainable for the rare students who present themselves as candidates.

Developments in Classics teaching

Innovative teaching is inspired and led by several associations and notably by the regional associations coordinated by CNARELA (*Coordination nationale des associations régionales de langues anciennes*). The associations produce analytical documents, projects, new methods, videos, and lessons on all aspects of Classical antiquity (mythology, history, literature and language learning) which can be found on the CNARELA website (CNARELA 2023). The associations spread the word about the European Certificates for Classics from Euroclassica: ELEX and EGEX (Euroclassica 2023). They organize competitions, festivals, Classics Days, visits to archaeological sites, talks and conferences, literary cafés, school or university trips, and study days in partnership with museums and archaeological sites. They take an active part in the continuing professional development of teachers, which is organized annually in each academy and delivered in general by experienced secondary or university teachers.

Conclusion

In conclusion it cannot be denied that Classics teaching in France has considerable advantages at its disposal. A willing and well-advised pupil can benefit from a highly formative course thanks to dynamic teachers who, in spite of often very difficult working conditions, continue to fight for their pupils and allow them to blossom and become well-informed and intelligent citizens. If the institution, which is expected to support this subject, showed the necessary authority and willingness to put into practice the ambitions that it asserts, it could offer a real foundation of education. Unfortunately, the planned reforms for 2024 and the following years seem to renew the risk of depriving pupils and students of this essential learning.

References

Antiqdialog (2023), 'Antiqdialog'. Avalable online: https://antiqdialog.hypotheses.org/ (accessed 14 October 2023).

Charvet P. and D. Bauduin (2018), 'Rapport sur la valorisation des langues et cultures de l'Antiquité: les humanités au coeur de l'école'. Available online: https://www.vie-publique.fr/rapport/37138-les-humanites-au-coeur-de-lecole-rapport-sur-la-valorisation-des-lang (accessed 14 October 2023).

CNARELA (2023), 'Coordination nationale des associations régionales de langues anciennes'. Available online: https://cnarela.wixsite.com/cnarela (accessed 14 October 2023).

Duchemin, L., A. Durand and B. Franceschetti (2023), 'The Nausicaa experience: Teaching Ancient Greek in French preschools and primary schools', *Journal of Classics Teaching*, 49: 1–4.

ECLA (2023), 'ECLA: Enseignement conjoint Latin/Grec. Académie de Besançon'. Available online: http://lettres.ac-besancon.fr/?cat=82 (accessed 14 October 2023).

EDUSCOL (2023a), 'Langues et cultures de l'Antiquité'. Available online: https://eduscol.education.fr/2365/langues-et-cultures-de-l-antiquite (accessed 14 October 2023).

EDUSCOL (2023b), 'Mare Nostrum – croiser les langues de l'Antiquité et les langues vivantes régionales et étrangères'. Available online: https://eduscol.education.fr/3245/mare-nostrum-croiser-les-langues-de-l-antiquite-et-les-langues-vivantes-regionales-et-etrangeres (accessed 14 October 2023).

Euroclassica (2023), EUROCLASSICA. Available online: https://www.euroclassica.eu/ (accessed 14 October 2023).

Ministère de l'Éducation Nationale et de la Jeunesse (2021), Bulletin Officiel 27: 8 juillet 2021. Available online: https://www.education.gouv.fr/bo/21/Hebdo27/MENE2118785A.htm (accessed 14 October 2023).

Ministère de l'Éducation Nationale et de la Jeunesse (2023), 'Apporter une culture humaniste à chaque élève' Available online: https://www.education.gouv.fr/apporter-une-culture-humaniste-chaque-eleve-324653 (accessed 14 October 2023).

Odysseum (2023), 'ODYSSEUM. Le site des ressources des langues, cultures et civilisations de l'Antiquité'. Available online: https://odysseum.eduscol.education.fr (accessed 14 October 2023).

SNES (2022), 'Bilan chiffré de l'enquête du SNES-FSU sur les LCA en 2022'. Available online: https://www.snes.edu/article/bilan-chiffre-de-l'enquete-du-snes-fsu-sur-les-lca (accessed 14 October 2023).

Worms, F., A. Dan and C. Mauduit (2023), 'Les Humanités dans le texte'. Available online: https://www.translitterae.psl.eu/humanites-dans-le-texte/ (accessed 14 October 2023).

GEORGIA

Irine Darchia

It is generally recognized that classical languages and culture are the bases of European and Western civilization, and had a great impact on different historical and cultural traditions in many other countries around the globe. From the earliest times, Georgia (ancient Colchis and Iberia) had close relations with other areas of the ancient world and there is much mythological, geographical and historical information about ancient Georgia in Greek mythology and literature. Georgia has long been a partner of ancient Greece, Rome and Byzantium, privileged to belong to European civilization through these historical and cultural contacts. Therefore, studies of classical civilization are closely related to studies of the history, literature and culture of Georgia.

It is believed that Ancient Greek was taught and spoken in Georgia as early as the fourth century, when a well-known Rhetoric School in Phasis existed (Kaukhchishvili 1940; Nutsubidze 1956). As Themistius mentioned in his *Orationes*, he himself 'reaped the fruits of rhetorical study in a place far more obscure than this one, not a refined Greek place, but one on the outskirts of Pontus near [the River] Phasis. There, as the poets have told us in amazement, the Argo arrived safely from Thessaly, and there she was taken up into heaven' (Them. Or., XXVII 332d–333a; Penella 2000: 165).

In 2001, after archaeological excavations in the ancient capital of Georgia, Mtskheta, a 'writing set' was found in the yard of the Svetitskhovli Cathedral (Stonetomb N 14) dated as third to fourth century and decorated with representations in relief of the nine silver-gilt Muses, miniature silver figures of Homer, Demosthenes and Menander and an openwork gold plaque with Greek inscriptions. This writing set and its iconography illustrate the role Greek language and culture historically played in Georgia in terms of sharing and promoting writing and knowledge.

Students of the well-known Georgian medieval educational centres – the Ikalto and Gelati Academies – studied Greek language and culture in the eleventh to twelfth centuries, while Georgian writers, historians and philosophers in the Middle Ages (first of all Ioane Petritsi) were well acquainted with ancient Greek myths and literature, which is obvious in their works. We may assume that a knowledge of Ancient Greek served as the basis for their education.

Teaching classical languages was common in the nineteenth century when Georgia was under the rule of the Russian Empire. According to materials in the Georgian press, following the educational policy of the Russian Empire, thirty-nine hours a week were given to the study of ancient Greek and Latin languages in the theological seminary, and only eight hours to native Georgian. This caused great public dissatisfaction (Andronikashvili 1881: 2). Classical languages continued to be taught in Georgian *gymnasiums* after the country gained independence in 1918, but the situation changed radically in the 1920s, after Georgia was occupied by the Red Army and lost its independence in 1921.

Georgia then became part of the Soviet Russian Empire and under pressure from Soviet ideology, teaching classical languages was seen as an attribute of Western culture and was discontinued. Attempts were made to restore the teaching of Ancient Greek and Latin at the secondary level of education or to create specialized schools where classical languages would be taught under the supervision of university professors in the 1950s and the 1980s, but these attempts failed (See Darchia & Shukhoshvili 2018: 105–11, for a short history of teaching classical languages in Georgia).

Despite the centuries-old tradition of teaching classical languages and culture, during the Soviet period these disciplines were preserved and developed only at university level and teaching in general education schools only became possible after the collapse of the Soviet Union. This process turned out to be quite long considering the serious political and economic crises of the late twentieth and early twenty-first centuries with their inconsistent general education reforms.

After the transition from the Soviet system to a democratic free-market economy and after transformations in the education system, Georgia established a centralized model of general education governed by the Ministry of Education and Science (MoES) through its departments, agencies and regional educational resource centres that represent today the MoES in sixty-nine regions. Since 2005, Georgia has provided a twelve-year general education system where grades 1 to 9 are obligatory basic education.

There are around 2,100 public and 250 private schools in Georgia with almost 550,000 students in grades 1–12. Georgia has a unified National Curriculum, a system developed and introduced in 2005. Today, the Third Generation National Curriculum operates in schools across the country. The National Curriculum is an obligatory document for all public and private schools and defines level-based educational results to be achieved by students (at the end of grades 4,6,9 and 12). It gives full flexibility for schools to develop school curricula and strategies for achieving standards. The general education programme has three levels: elementary (grades 1–6) with sub-level (grades 1–4); lower-secondary/basic (grades 7–9); and upper-secondary/high school (grades 10–12).

The National Curriculum is a modern document with a student-centred approach and formulates educational results through knowledge, skills and attitudes to be developed. Subjects taught in schools are: the mother tongue (including minority languages), a first foreign language (English), a second foreign language (selected by schools from a list), the Georgian state language (for ethnic minority schools), maths, STEM subjects, civic education and social science subjects, as well as arts, music and sports. Information and communication technologies (ICT) is a standalone subject as well as integrated into other subjects as an important competence. The National Curriculum introduces compulsory and elective subjects, including World History, Cultural Studies, a third foreign language and many others, which schools can also select from a list prepared by the National Curriculum.

This general overview of the National Curriculum illustrates its flexible and favourable structure for introducing Ancient Greek and Latin as a third language and for offering Classics like Greek and Roman Mythology, Ancient Literature and History, Ancient Culture/ Civilization, etc., as elective subjects.

Despite the openness and flexibility of the National Curriculum, classical languages and subjects are only gradually being established within the general education system of Georgia, a process influenced by several objective and subjective factors. Among these, the traditions of a seventy-year Soviet regime has not been easy to change, and an insufficient awareness by the school community about the importance of classical subjects are factors that have meant a lack of interest in antiquities is due to the attitude that this is a non-pragmatic field.[1]

The Ancient Greek language, one of the optional subjects, was taught for only a few years, in 2004 to 2009, in two schools, one private and one public. One was in Tbilisi and the other in Khashuri, in central Georgia's Shida Kartli region (the St Ilia True Gymnasium and Khashuri Primary School N 9). Ancient Greek was taught as part of a 'learning circle' that included volunteer students in grades 6–11 (approximately 15–20 per school each year). *The Ancient Greek Language*, which was developed by the Georgian classicist Ketevan Abesadze, based on a German teaching methodology and textbook, was used during learning and teaching.

This short period of teaching ancient Greek would not be possible if it were not for the Organization for the Promotion of Greek Language (https://www.odeg.gr/), which organized a European, and later an international, competition in Ancient Greek from 2002 to 2010. The winning students and teachers from all participating countries were invited to an award ceremony in Athens with all travel and accommodation expenses covered by the organizers. The competition was held at different times through support and involvement by the President and the Chair of the Parliament of the Hellenic Republic, the Ministries of Education of Greece and Cyprus, Euroclassica and various Greek organizations (see details of the competition at https://www.odeg.gr/diethnis-diagonismos-arxaion-ellinikon.html). It was the desire to participate in this competition that prompted the two schools to begin teaching Ancient Greek in 2004, with the support of the Institute of Classical, Byzantine and Modern Greek Studies of Ivane Javakhishvili Tbilisi State University (TSU), and this process continued until the competition and award ceremony were held in Athens, which made it inspiring and motivating to teach Ancient Greek (Darchia 2018: 13–22).

The most popular subject related to Greek and Roman antiquity is Mythology, which has been taught in a large number of public and private schools and for the longest time since 1997, and is still taught as an elective subject in various grades (from the 3rd to the 10th grade in the following schools: Public School No. 53, St Ilia True Gymnasium, School *Mermisi*, Batumi School *Nike*, Tbilisi Classical Gymnasium, Guram Dochanashvili International School, Tetritskaro No. 2 Public School, etc.). In classes of Mythology, groups range from ten to thirty-five, for courses one to two hours per week on average. Teachers usually rely on the ten-volume series, *The World of Ancient Greek Myths,* written by Georgian classicists and published by the publishing programme *Logos*, and on a textbook on mythology specially developed for the 8th grade (authors: Zurab Kiknadze and Nana Tonia). At the same time, *Ancient Greek Mythology* by Nikolai Kuhn, popular since Soviet times, is also used. Teachers also use materials prepared themselves (such as simplified mythological stories), or show cartoons, movies, etc.

In addition to teaching Ancient Greek Language and Mythology, Greek Civilization was taught one year at the 44th public school named after the Kakabadze brothers. Ancient Literature was also taught at the Tbilisi American Academy as part of an interdisciplinary block of disciplines. The Antiquity Club functioned at this Academy for almost ten years, where interested students were introduced to the history, literature and culture of ancient Greece and Rome, as well as Latin *sententia*.

A new and important stage in teaching the Classics began around 2010, when several private schools in Tbilisi made Latin and other related disciplines an integral part of their curriculum, taking into account the best German and Swiss, British and American experience. The motivation of private schools was determined not only by the understanding of the general importance of classical education, but also by the advantage the Classics give to applicants when enrolling in leading universities abroad.

Since 2011–13, teaching ancient philosophy in the 12th grade has been integrated into the compulsory subjects 'Great Ideas' (ten hours per week) and 'History of Western Philosophy' (five hours per week), in the American Academy of Tbilisi. The courses are taught using a Reader prepared by the lecturer himself and by Norman Menchert's universally recognized book *The Great Conversation* (Menchert 2010).

Latin is taught as an optional subject in three private schools in Tbilisi. Since 2012, in the 6th Authorised German School's 8th grade, for three hours a week; since 2017 in the American School of Advanced Studies (former American High School) of the European School, from 8th to 12th grades, for two hours a week; and since 2020, Latin is taught in the University of Georgia (UG) School from the 7th to 10th grades, two to four hours a week, according to the level of education (55, 73 and 14 pupils respectively have been studying Latin in the Academic Year 2023/24). In the American School of Advanced Studies there is a specialized group for intensive learning. The number of pupils studying Latin here increased by 2.5 times, from 29 in 2017 to 73 in 2023. The Latin study programme of the 6th Authorised German School is based on German and Swiss curricula and follows a special programme developed by the teacher. It starts with simple phrases and finishes with extracts from Roman authors.

The handbook *Lingua Latina* (2008) developed by the Georgian classicists, Manana Pkhakadze and Levan Berdzenishvili, is used in learning and teaching. The following handbooks are also used: *VERBA LATINA* (Gardapkhadze & Cheishvili 2018) and *Schola Latina* (Cheishvili & Pkhakadze 2016–17).

The handbook *Familia Romana per se illustrata* (Ørberg 2011) is used in the American School of Advanced Studies and the UG School. According to observations by the teachers, the interaction with the original texts arouses student interest and motivation, which makes Ørberg's method particularly attractive. The UG School also offers a wider variety of textbooks, combining traditional and relatively new, 'natural method' of language instruction. The *Cambridge Latin Course* (CSCP 1998), *Exercitia Latina* (Ørberg 2005), *Fabulae Syrae* (Miraglia 2011), *Wheelock's Latin* (LaFleur 2011), *Latin Stories Designed to Accompany Frederic M. Wheelock's Latin* (Groton & May 1998), *Introducing Cicero* (Scottish Classics Group 2002), *A Latin Reader for the Lower Forms in Schools* (Hardy 1889) and the Latin edition of A. A. Milne's *Winnie the Pooh* / Winnie Ille Pu (Lenard & Milne 2015) are all used and adjusted to the needs of the learners of each group.

Since 2013 the American School of Advanced Studies of the European School offers an obligatory Classics course. From 2022 some studies of the Reception of Classics have been added to the Syllabus. Currently, 188 students are studying this subject, for 2–3 hours a week (according to their level of education). In addition to the handbooks, some international online sources are used. The Classics course is taught using the books on *Greek and Roman Civilizations* and *Greek Myths* by Heidi Dierckx (2012), *D'Aulaires' Book of Greek Myths* (d'Aulaire & d'Aulaire 1962), *D'Aulaires' Greek Myths Student's Book* (Lowe & Lowe 2006), and Stephen Fry's *Mythos* (2018) and others, as well as various online resources.

The following methods are used: presentations, working on the text, text analysis, discussion, debate, 'natural method' of language instruction, comprehensive input, grammar-translation methods, and the Ranieri-Dowling Method, etc. In the lower classes, natural methods, including conversation are used, while in the higher grades more attention is paid to grammatical material.

To make learning Latin more fun, teachers use other methods as well. For example, after explaining a few verses of Catullus, students are asked to complete tasks in Latin in the style of Catullus (disconnect the noun and the epithet from each other, use litotes, synchysis, etc.), which makes the learning process enjoyable. Teachers also use game methods (Vinco; Quizlet match); students are given Latin names; and they play the so-called 'hangman' game using Latin words.

In addition, the teachers try to teach Latin in the context of European languages having the following slogan: 'We already know Latin. We need to remember and seek it out.' Some students note that while being abroad, i.e. in Italy or Spain, they already partially understood words that locals used although they had never learned these languages. They also say that after their Latin studies they intend to continue learning a Romance language. One teacher proposed to integrate the Classics with painting classes, by asking students to paint their favourite mythological stories and characters as they imagined them, thus increasing their interest, motivation and creativity.

Students at the American School of Advanced Studies actively participate in school competitions (namely the Iliad and Odyssey Competition), within the Golden Fleece Festival jointly organized by the Greek Embassy and Tbilisi State University. They participated in the International Classics Competition (Lytham St Anne's Classical Association – UK) three times and won all three. In 2023, the School became a member of Lytham St Anne's Classical Association – UK and several students attend the lectures offered by this association. In addition, an International General Certificate of Education (IGCSE) Classics course is now offered in line with the British analogue.

Students at the American School of Advanced Studies have the opportunity to visit museums and archaeological sites of Greece and Italy, offered and organized by the school administration. At other schools, students carry out study visits to the museums and places of Georgia where they become acquainted with examples of ancient culture through artefacts and sites reflecting the historical and cultural ties of Georgia with Greece and Rome in antiquity, such as Dzalisa, Vani and the National Museum of Georgia, etc.

As there are only a few secondary schools today where Latin and other Classical subjects are taught, and the number of teachers in these subjects is limited, there are not enough resources to establish a specialized professional organization. Therefore, teaching Classical Languages and Culture at the secondary school level in Georgia is promoted by the Institute of Classical, Byzantine and Modern Greek Studies of the Ivane Javakhishvili Tbilisi State University (TSU), which became a member of Euroclassica in 2023. Along with teaching activities, the Institute deals with research and science communication and collaborates with the public and private secondary schools of Georgia where all Classical subjects are delivered by current MA and PhD students, graduates, lecturers and professors of the Institute.

On 24–6 February 2021 the TSU Institute of Classical, Byzantine and Modern Greek Studies organized an online International Conference 'Teaching Classical Languages in the 21st Century – Vitae Discimus', which was the first time an open and public dialogue on Classics learning and teaching was launched in Georgia. Various pedagogical and methodological approaches were discussed and analysed by more than thirty participants from ten countries, including Georgia, Germany, the UK, Italy, Belgium, Netherlands, Ukraine, the USA, Columbia and Japan. Relevant recommendations and suggestions were offered to Georgian university and school teachers of classical languages.

The TSU Institute of Classical, Byzantine and Modern Greek Studies annually organizes an open competition in Classical Languages, called 'Victoria', in which students of different Georgian higher educational institutions and secondary schools participate. The winners receive a certificate, publications of the Institute and other gifts. From 2024, the Institute will organize Euroclassica exams (https://www.euroclassica.eu/portale/euroclassica/eccl.html).

Besides language competitions, the Institute regularly offers other events and activities for Georgia's secondary schools, for example the cultural and educational festival called 'Golden Fleece', organized by the Institute since 2013. Students take part in the festival which aims to introduce Greek culture among Georgian youth. Many conferences, public lectures, contests, competitions, movie projections and theatrical performances are held during this festival.

The TSU Institute of Classical, Byzantine and Modern Greek Studies plans to strengthen collaboration with secondary schools, to supervise teaching and learning of Classics subjects in order to support the design and development of relevant curricula; teaching and learning methodology; update handbooks and other teaching materials; and offer free training courses for school teachers. The first pilot training course in Ancient Literature for school teachers was conducted in 2022 by the Institute staff, and more are planned for the future. Of course, there are some other possibilities for teachers' professional development. One of the teachers of the American School of Advanced Studies underwent a college board specialized training course for Latin teachers (https://apcentral.collegeboard.org/professional-learning/workshops).

For some Georgian secondary schools, the Ørberg method of instruction appears most effective, especially for beginners. Thus in 2023 the TSU Institute of Classical, Byzantine and Modern Greek Studies began cooperating with the Accademia Vivarium Novum (https://www.vivariumnovum.net/en), and signed an agreement to begin implementation of exchange programmes, with face-to-face and online training courses for students, lecturers and school teachers.

After analysing the history and current situation of teaching Classics in the general education schools of Georgia, the following conclusions can be made.

Teaching Classical Languages/Classics – the scope, content, methodology – in the general education schools of Georgia has been directly related to the socio-political situation in the country. It was well developed under the influence of the relevant policy of the Russian Empire, and maintained during a short-term independence, then was hindered and prohibited due to pressure from Soviet ideology.

Teaching classical disciplines in independent Georgia (since 1992) can be conventionally divided into two stages. The first stage covers the period from the end of the 1990s until 2010, when teaching was carried out relatively unsystematically and inconsistently, based on the initiative of individual principals and teachers. The second stage began after 2010 when Classics disciplines were firmly, systematically and consistently established within the curriculum of several private, and mostly international, schools.

Teaching Classical Languages and Culture is still geographically limited and mostly concentrated in the capital, Tbilisi. Teaching these subjects in the regions outside of Tbilisi, for example in Batumi, Khashuri and Tetritskaro, remains quite rare and exceptional.

There are far more opportunities for pupils in Georgian private schools to study Classics than for the pupils in public schools, which means these disciplines are considered part of an 'elite' education. However, internationalization in its various forms – participation in international competitions or in excursions abroad, a desire to continue studies abroad, harmonization of Georgian curricula with international standards, etc. – should be regarded as a trigger for the systematic introduction and development of Classics in the schools of Georgia.

There are different types of Georgian-language textbooks compiled by the Georgian classicists that are currently used by Georgian-language public and private schools, although international schools, in line with their English-language instruction, use the more widely recognized English-language textbooks.

Various local and international conferences, competitions, quizzes and similar educational and competitive events, as well as excursions to antiquity-related areas of Georgia and abroad, also contribute to popularizing the Classics by increasing student interest and motivation. The openness and flexibility of the National Curriculum could be effectively explored to promote and disseminate the Classics in the future.

New plans to introduce subjects such as 'Ancient Greek Language', 'Masterpieces of Ancient Literature and Mythology', etc. are underway in some schools. In order to improve the positions of Classics in the general education schools of Georgia, it is important to strengthen communication with the school community and to raise awareness within the Georgian public on the importance of Classics. This could be done through joint efforts of the classicists, the university community and alumni of Classics programmes, while international cooperation and shared experiences also play an important role in this long and challenging endeavour.

Note

1 Since no research has been conducted on teaching the Classics in Georgia and there are no statistical data, the author of the article had to identify and contact the school teachers who taught the Classics in different schools since the end of the twentieth century. They answered a specially developed questionnaire and some were interviewed. The author is especially grateful to those colleagues, school teachers and university lecturers who participated in the survey and provided valuable information, namely (in alphabetical order): Tea Dularidze, Levan Gigineishvili, Anina Gogokhia, Giorgi Kakhishvili and Nino Kikvadze, Ekaterine Kobakhidze, Tatia Mtvarelidze, Dachi Pachulia, Manana Pkhakadze, Nana Tonia, Tamar Tskhvediani, Irine Tsiklauri and Giorgi Ugulava. Also, special thanks to the education specialist, Natia Jokhadze, who consulted the author regarding the National Curriculum, and to Tamara Cheishvili, who shared the materials of the project SCISCITATOR that she is involved in.

References

Abesadze, K. (2007), *The Ancient Greek Language*, Tbilisi: Logos.

Andronikashvili, L. (1881), 'The Case of our Schools', *Droeba*, 145: 1–2, Tbilisi: Melikishvili Publishing House.

Cheishvili, T. and M. Pkhakadze (2016–17), *Schola Latina*, Vols I–IV, Tbilisi: Logos.

CSCP (1998), *Cambridge Latin Course*, Cambridge, Cambridge University Press.

Darchia, I. (2018), 'Teaching Ancient Greek Language in Georgia', in I. Darchia, *Issues of Teaching Classics (Collection of Papers)*, Tbilisi: Publishing Programme Logos, 13–22.

Darchia, I. and M. Shukhoshvili (2018), 'Classical Studies in Soviet Georgia', in I. Darchia (ed.), *Issues of Teaching Classics (Collection of Papers)*, Tbilisi: Publishing Programme Logos, 105–11.

D'Aulaire, I. and E. d'Aulaire (1962), *D'Aularies' Book of Greek Myths*, London: Random House.

Dierckx, H. (2012), *Greek and Roman Civilizations*, Greensboro: Mark Twain Media.

Dierckx, H. (2012), *Greek Myths*, Greensboro: Mark Twain Media.

Fry, S. (2018), *Mythos*, London: Penguin.

Gardapkhadze, K. and T. Cheishvili (2018), *VERBA LATINA*, Tbilisi: Logos.

Grotoan, A. and J. May (1998), *Latin Stories Designed to Accompany Frederic M. Wheelock's Latin*, Mundelein, IL: Bolchazy-Carducci.

Hardy, H. (1889), *A Latin Reader for the Lower Forms in Schools*, London: Macmillan.

Kaukhchishvili, S. (1940), 'Center of Rhetorical Education in Ancient Georgia', *Bulletin of Georgia State Museum*, 10B, Tbilisi: Tbilisi University Press.

Kiknadze, Z. and N. Tonia (2006), *The World of Ancient Greek Myths*, Tbilisi: Logos.

Kun, N. (1914), *Ancient Greek Mythology* [*Что разсказывали греки и римляне о своих богах и героях*], Moscow: I.N. Kushnerev.

LaFleur, R. (2011), *Wheelock's Latin*, New York: Collins.

Lenard, A. and A. A. Milne (1958), *Winnie Ille Pu*, Malton: Methuen.

Lowe, C. and L. Lowe (2006), *D'Aulaires' Greek Myths Student's Book*, Louisville, KY: Memorial Press.

Menchert, N. (2010), *The Great Conversation: A Historical Introduction to Philosophy*, 6th edition, Oxford: Oxford University Press.

Miraglia, L. (2011), *Fabulae Syrae*, Indianapolis, IN: Hackett Publishing Company.

Nutsubidze, S. (1956), *History of Georgian Philosophy, Volume 1*, Tbilisi: Tbilisi University Press.

Ørberg, H. (2005), *Exercitia Latina*, Indianapolis, IN: Hackett Publishing Company.

Ørberg, H. (2011), *Lingua Latina per se illustrata*, Indianapolis, IN: Hackett Publishing Company.

Penella, R. (2000), 'The Private Orations of Themistius', *Transformation of the Classical Heritage*,
    Berkeley, CA: University of California Press.
Pkhakadze, M. and L. Berdzenishvili (2008), *Lingua Latina*, Tbilisi: Logos.
Scottish Classics Group (2002), *Introducing Cicero*, Bristol: Bristol Classical Press.

GERMANY

Bärbel Flaig

Germany consists of sixteen federal states with sixteen different ministries of education and culture and sixteen different education systems.

Types of schools in Germany

This is noticeable not only for the length of time in primary school (four or six years), but also in the diversification of secondary schools. There are different variants in the individual federal states, from a strict separation into different types of schools with different vocational goals (*Regelschule*/regular school: *Hauptschule* and *Realschule* with more practical training, and *Gymnasium* to prepare for higher education and the *Abitur* or final leaving certificate) to the different types of comprehensive/community school. Students are allocated to the classes according to their performance and final goal after a common start.

The range of classical languages in the individual types of schools

The types of schools in which Latin and Greek are taught are the *Gymnasium* and, for some time now, also the comprehensive/community school, as the continuation up to the *Abitur* has been strongly promoted in these schools in recent years. The *Gymnasia* offer Latin from grade 5 (classical and modern language grammar schools), and in many federal states it is also offered as an early second foreign language from grade 5 or 6. The older variant from grade 7 onwards also exists again, after the attempt to have the *Abitur* taken nationwide after eight years of school in grade 12 failed in many federal states. The so-called G8 (*Abitur* after eight years) still exists in Thuringia and Saxony (where G9 never existed), but in all other federal states the G8 was retained only for gifted students or completely abolished. The main reason the initiative failed was that most attempts were made to spread the same amount of learning as in G9 (*Abitur* after nine years) over a shorter period, which was extremely problematic from the outset.

Latin is still offered as a third foreign language from grade 8 or 9 and as a new language from grade 10, 11 or 12, although not in all federal states. Greek is only available as a third foreign language from grade 8 or 9, except in special grammar schools, and as a new language from grade 10, 11 or 12. In addition, many schools also have voluntary study groups (AGs) in both ancient languages.

In comprehensive/community schools, Latin is increasingly being offered as a second foreign language in the high-achieving learning groups working towards the *Abitur*. Occasionally, there are even courses at vocational high schools, which is because students with Latin as a second foreign language want to take a vocational *Abitur* in these schools.

Importance of classical languages in schools

Latin is still extremely popular with parents and students and is in third place in the ranking behind English and French. In recent years, Spanish has moved forwards and is also becoming increasingly popular as a second foreign language – in addition to the variant of the third or fourth foreign language, which has been practised for some time.

English is taught from the third grade at the latest in primary school and in addition to the international schools, there are also individual primary schools that offer English from grade 1 onwards. It is therefore continued in secondary school as a first foreign language. In the border area with France, French is still compulsory in primary schools instead of English. If Latin or French/Spanish is chosen as the first foreign language, English is taught in parallel with fewer hours so that the students do not forget English until the second foreign language begins officially.

Greek has been increasingly threatened in recent years. It is now only offered at individual *Gymnasia*, mostly traditional classical grammar schools, or study groups (AGs) alongside Latin. There is also the approach of giving a choice between Latin and Greek. However, this only takes place at grammar schools for the highly gifted on the grounds that an ancient language is chosen because of its cultural function. However, this approach has globally no significance.

Anyone who takes Latin or Greek in the *Abitur* must prove their knowledge by translating an original Latin/Greek text into German as well as interpreting a text, which is usually given bilingually.

Reasons for learning Latin

The fact that Latin is still in an advantageous position is because it is still required for many fields of study at many universities (https://www.bildungsserver.de). Although the universities in individual federal states have also often reduced their requirements for Latin language skills (usually a *Latinum*, which has compulsory written and oral examinations according to uniform federal requirements), the traditional entrance qualifications at the old universities have still not changed and even the new universities at least rely on 'Latin knowledge' for all courses of study related to language, history and other cultural content.

At school, students learn more about the cultural advantages in a Europe that is growing together as well as the educational value of ancient languages. These are also aspects that are important to the parents of the students, who often have no idea of their future career aspirations, when choosing a language.

A second, widespread argument, especially in favour of Latin, is an improved mastery of the mother tongue. Since it is a learning objective, especially in Latin, to create a linguistically good translation of an original Latin text into the mother tongue, the students are forced to deal with their own language, to juggle with words and to find good correspondences and formulations. This expands the vocabulary in the mother tongue, improves the knowledge of synonyms and antonyms and helps to develop a better writing style. Teachers also point out at promotional events for the subject that grammar skills are improved by learning Latin, as one must deal with grammatical functions and constructions that often do not exist in the first language, and therefore appropriate means of expression must be found. However, through the search for a suitable and coherent translation, the students must first become clear about the use of their first language, which they learned as a child in everyday contact with their respective environment. This results in cognitive penetration and systematization of one's own language and an improved mastery of one's first language of education. This is also helpful for other subjects – not only in the field of languages.

A third argument, which is often put forward, is that mastery of Latin vocabulary is helpful in learning other languages, especially Romance languages. Since German and English are Germanic languages, both of which have been significantly influenced by Latin, but especially English, this is an argument that seems plausible to many German native speakers. Latin also has the 'advantage' that you usually do not have to speak it and can still read other languages well with the vocabulary you have learned.

Textbooks and their conception

In Germany, there are many textbooks that are currently approved for Latin. Among the most recent are *Salto* (Haselmann et al. 2021), *Campus* (Utz & Kammerer 2021), *Cursus* new edition (Hotz & Maier 2020), *Prima* (Utz & Kammerer 2020a), *Prima nova* (Utz & Kammerer 2020b), *Adeamus!* (Berchtold et al. 2018), *Via mea* (Pinkernell-Kreidt et al. 2016) and *Pontes* (Behrens et al. 2016, 2020) for the first and second foreign languages. In addition, there are abbreviated textbooks for Latin as a third foreign language or Latin that begins late or at university, e.g. *breVIA* (Jitschin et al. 2018) or *Prima brevis* (Utz & Kammerer 2017).

The new generation of textbooks relies on shorter, image-supported texts that are easier to grasp. The individual sentences for the introduction of grammar have been abandoned, they are introduced in the text, followed by practice with slightly modified example sentences from the text. Tasks for the preparation of an interpretation are now standard and follow a gradient, from simple elaboration from the text (especially for beginners) to stylistic investigations with indication of the function in the extract, to partial interpretation tasks with the inclusion of information texts in German as background knowledge. In this way, the translation of the text for study is supplemented by various content-related tasks and a deeper understanding of the text is achieved, which is the basis for an interpretation.

Following the textbook work, almost all publishers offer reading books with adapted original texts. However, there are also modern editions of the popular school authors with small text excerpts, pictures and exercises including the practice of prosody from all relevant publishers.

New, modern textbooks for Greek are now available: in addition to *Kairos kompakt* (Weileder & Heber 2022), *Dialogos* (Kussl et al. 2020) and *Kantharos* (Hollerman & Utzinger 2018), which is still the most popular textbook. Developed especially for the teaching of Greek in schools, these textbooks are also used in the courses of the universities. However, many Greek teachers/lecturers also work with their own material according to the hours assigned to them or according to the aims of the course (language or culture course).

Language course or culture course?

While Latin in Germany is still primarily a language course that is characterized by historical and cultural elements that are laid down in the curriculum programmes, in Greek there is often a tendency towards it becoming a cultural subject even at school level. The language as such is still learned, but it is often compromised. Not all the subtleties of the language are taught anymore, so that students are able to read the original, but are no longer able to write or translate Greek themselves, as is still required in Greek studies. In some federal states, Modern Greek is included in the curriculum, while other states are content to include the later periods.

Didactics and methodology

In the classroom, there are still some differences to the didactics and methodology of modern foreign languages, which is mainly because Latin is usually not spoken, and communication is not a goal formulated in the curricula. However, there are now also audio recordings and videos in Latin, as well as software for practising vocabulary and grammar. In the meantime, digital development is very gratifying. There are programmes that learners can use independently for repetition and/or consolidation. These are often used in schools in the classroom, too.

Methodologically, teaching has evolved in recent years under the influence of modern foreign languages. For example, group work, lectures with PowerPoint and Smartboard, and discussing translations are now standard practice in many classrooms. Input from the teacher is no longer the only resource, but a wide range of teaching options can be used. This also applies to the material.

Materials in the classroom

In addition to the textbooks, musical means (e.g. creating a rap song), playful forms of repetition of vocabulary or grammar (e.g. making or creating puzzles), but also theatrical elements, are used. In addition, the new digital media offer many forms and variants that can be used in the classroom to motivate students. It is not for nothing that the Federal Competition for Foreign Languages of Education and Talent includes the ancient languages. In the *Team* section, a play or radio play can be created, also in Latin or Greek. In the *Solo* competition, as in modern foreign languages, there is a task where candidates fill in the blanks on a text/topic and there is an audio text with multiple choice questions.

The students enjoy these forms and like to come to Latin lessons. Since the students who take Greek are older, the main goal is more to teach cultural skills – which is why most of them take the subject.

Studies and degrees

Studying Latin in school has become popular again in recent years. The classical language is often combined with German, English or French, but also with history. Greek, on the other hand, is almost exclusively chosen for school use in a triple combination, mostly with Latin. Since the number taking Greek in schools has declined considerably, this is understandable.

There are currently two recognized qualifications for the teaching profession. At some universities, a first state examination is still offered with about ten semesters of standard periods of study (including examinations). In recent years, however, this has been replaced at many universities by a Bachelor's/Master's degree programme based on the European model, which already includes practical parts. This is followed by a so-called traineeship at one or more schools, which prepares graduates for practical work at the school and is completed by a second state examination or a teacher-training examination.

Further education and training

In Germany, there are continuing education courses for teachers in every federal state, which are either run by a teacher-training institute or by the regional association that operates under the umbrella organization of German Classical Philologists (DAV, https://altphilologenverband. de). In addition to the further development of the curricula and their implementation, the usual content is lesson development and the further development of the examinations (https:// www.iqb.hu-berlin.de). At the moment, there are increasing efforts to develop a comparable *Abitur* for the whole of Germany through establishing common educational standards and the harmonization of *Abitur* examinations. However, since only mathematics, German, English and French have so far been developed, this does not yet affect the ancient languages. On the one hand, this is an advantage, as teachers are freer in the arrangement and selection of topics, but on the other hand, there is no comparability within the state. Even the contents differ from one federal state to another.

The willingness of individual teachers to undergo further training is also reflected in the standard assessments. It is also possible for a principal to instruct a teacher to attend a particular training course if he or she feels that this is necessary.

Otherwise, there are in-school training courses that are organized within the school either by the school management or by the staff council. While the focus of the training on the part of the school management is usually on aspects of school development, the aim of the training on the part of the staff council is primarily the personal development of the teachers, either in the direct personal area (e.g. resilience training) or in the area of more recent developments (e.g. AI use).

Cooperation between schools

There are two main reasons why schools work together. The first important reason is to make the transition from primary to secondary school as smooth as possible. This is achieved through reciprocal visits, but also taster lessons in class groups or to introduce the new subjects. This is also the purpose of the 'Open Days'. There is a great deal of interest on both sides with an increase in cooperation, as when speakers are invited who are interesting for both schools (e.g. local grammar school and regular school) but who are only affordable in cooperation (e.g. top-class scientists such as Manfred Spitzer or lecturers from abroad).

There are many links with museums, theatres, cinemas, universities and companies, but also cooperation agreements that stipulate the contributions of both sides. In some cases, students are also supported by companies, who arrange internships or award high school graduates in the hope of attracting them to the company as future employees or by steering their career aspirations.

Competitions and offers

In addition, there are also competitions for all subjects. In Latin and Greek they are organized by the regional associations and the DAV in addition to the Federal Foreign Language Competition. Other courses, including interdisciplinary ones, are common in Germany. They are often not limited to one subject but bring together students with different interests in a topic (https://www.nationalstiftung.de/projekte/schulbruecken/). These interdisciplinary offers are often international and are run through ERASMUS. The topics that are treated on in such groups are often free, so that different school subjects can be included. Especially in the linguistic field, often not only modern foreign languages are included in the presentations, but also ancient languages, mainly Latin. This is interesting for the students because they notice that a school subject can be taught quite differently in another country and has a different focus – especially for an ancient language in Italy or Greece, for example.

Conclusion

To sum up, it can be said that the ancient languages still have a high status in Germany, although more for Latin than Greek. Newer didactics with their new methods still manage to interest the younger generations in the ancient world. What is missing is a systematic approach to ancient languages in primary school, which is now widespread in the UK. It remains to be seen which languages the students will choose in the next few years, but this is also influenced by the various school reforms, and politics. So it remains exciting!

References

Behrens, J., M.-L. Bothe, I. Gottwald, B. Guthier, A. Hellwig, W. Schubert, D. Schücker-Elkheir, W. Siewert, C. Strucken-Paland and K.-W. Weeber (2020), *Pontes*, Stuttgart: Klett.
Berchtold, V., M. Schauer and M. Janka (2018), *Adeamus!*, Berlin: Cornelsen.
Haselmann, H., P. Jitschin, F. Hennerici, G. Laser and S. Losch (2021), *Salto*, Göttingen: Vandenhoeck and Ruprecht.
Hollerman, M. and C. Utzinger (2018), *Kantharos*, Stuttgart: Klett.
Hotz, M. and F. Maier (2020), *Cursus*, Bamberg: Buchner.
Jitschin, P., G. Laser, S. Lösch and B. Scholz (2018), *breVIA*, Göttingen: Vandenhoeck and Ruprecht.
Kussl, R., W. Scheibmayr and B. van Vugt (2020), *Dialogos*, Braunschweig: Westermann.
Pinkernell-Kreidt, S., J. Kühne and P. Kuhlmann (2016), *Via mea*, Berlin: Cornelsen.
Utz, C. and A. Kammerer (2017*)*, *Prima brevis*, Bamberg: Buchner.
Utz, C. and A. Kammerer (2020a*)*, *Prima*, Bamberg: Buchner.
Utz, C. and A. Kammerer (2020b*)*, *Prima nova*, Bamberg: Buchner.
Utz, C. and A. Kammerer (2021), *Campus*, Bamberg: Buchner.
Weileder, A. and M. Heber (2022), *Kairos kompakt*, Bamberg: Buchner.

GREECE

Dimitrios Stamatis

Between tradition and political expediency

Classics are obviously no longer considered to be the main pillar of Western civilization, at least in the way they were since the Renaissance Humanistic reform until quite recently. As early as the nineteenth century the influence of the classical world and the value of the relevant studies was declining, particularly in the US where it was often criticized for elitism (Becker 2001; Nash 2007). However, although the discipline was evolving even in that period, and kept on broadening its scope including further academic subjects under its purview – mainly thanks to the effect of the 'New Philology' movement, which turned the inherently theoretical object into becoming more systematic in its methods and more scientific in its scholarship (Rommel 2001; Stray 1996) – nowadays the criticism against the classical studies seems to be reviving, and indeed with a more severe tone, which adds to their already disadvantageous position with regard to the 'positive' sciences.

In particular, they are criticized for structural racism as they appear to promote the ideas of white supremacy and Western civilization – since the number of people from other races or of women who deal with Classics is considered relatively small – while silencing or deliberately downplaying slavery, the treatment of women as inferior beings, post-colonialism, etc. Moreover, Classics are often judged as outdated from a methodological point of view and unattractive taking into account modern needs of society (Chaniotis, cited in Papadopoulos 2021).

Interpreting the most recent 'resounding' blow to the prestige of Classics worldwide, namely the abolition of the compulsory study of Greek and Latin for the newly entering students of classical studies at the renowned University of Princeton, professor of Classics Dan-el Padilla Peralta emphasized that in our era these studies must become more inclusive, and thus to include other forms of classicism, such as 'black studies', gender studies, and deeper study of cultures beyond the Mediterranean (Padilla Peralta 2019; Poser 2021; Kokkinidis 2021; Ioannides 2021; Dreher 2021).

Nevertheless, having transformed its original – mainly linguistic – dimensions into a broader cultural science that connects or enables the most active cultures globally to be united under the scope of research, classical education nowadays seems to aim mostly at providing future generations not only with the most precious and tested values of humanity, but also with a fresh method of treating modern problems. In other words, it comprises the background of a futuristic philosophy. Beyond the recognized linguistic value of the study of Greek and Latin texts, which constitutes the core of the specialized vocabulary of other sciences, such as legal studies and medicine, the immersion in the original principles of political philosophy and mostly ethical philosophy should not be considered as simple and outdated knowledge. Especially nowadays that humanity struggles to establish regulatory principles by which great technological achievements such as Artificial Intelligence, the Internet or Biotechnology should be regulated, it seems necessary to look back to the 'melting pot' of antiquity in order to elaborate ethical rules and refined philosophical concepts and reconsider our beliefs.

Never before was the promotion of classical studies of such importance as today. Particularly in Greece, where classical civilization thrived, classical studies were constantly and continuously highly appreciated over time, even in difficult circumstances – or, to put it more accurately, especially in those ones. However, after the foundation of the modern Greek state in 1830, the engagement of students with the ancient cultural legacy was considered as 'the umbilical cord' that joined new generations with their national glorious past. After all, the value of Classics as a reinforcement of the national ideology during the Independence War (Koliopoulos et al. 2023) has been proven many times afterwards, while its 'sanctification' since then as a legacy and a 'national ark of the covenant', was exploited in almost every national danger, such as in the unfortunate war of 1897 or the years before the outbreak of the Second World War.

In any case, this tight bond of Greek education with the Classics, which were deeply respected as the most preferable field by the most apt pupils, belongs to the past. In a series of educational reforms, classical studies were gradually dispersed in favour of technocratic training, which is easily measurable and valued in economic terms. Recurring changes throughout the previous century affected secondary education, where Greek courses were replaced by modern translations. Moreover, the teaching hours of Greek and Latin were gradually decreased. Progressive governments, historically, choose to reduce the teaching hours of Greek and especially Latin, while conservatives tend to make these subjects compulsory and increase their teaching hours.

Even during the Greek Independence War, the revolutionary councils were forming the Educational Curricula for the new state so that they would include national tradition and at the same time emphasize that they belonged to the European context. In this light, the teaching of Latin in Greek schools, alongside that of Ancient Greek, was decided in 1829, as the outcome of a report 'on Greek Education' prepared by a committee of five eminent scholars under the chairmanship of Anthimos Gazis. The plan stipulated a three-level educational system. It is noteworthy that this committee began to meet in 1824 – the third year of the Greek Revolution – with the scope of the new state orientating the interests of society towards the ideas of the Enlightenment, at the urging of the eighteenth-century scholars Korais and Moisiodax, so that Hellenism aligns its education with that of the rest of Europe (Bouzakis 2007; Karakasis & Sarra 2017; Stamatis 2021).

Although the Latin language and literature are absent from the Kapodistrias government's Educational Programme (1828–31), things changed when the new state was governed by the first king of Greece, Otto, and during the years of the Bavarian rule. Classicism prevailed, and thus, most programme hours of the Greek School (three years) and *Gymnasium* (three years) were dedicated to Greek and Latin. The curriculum, launched by the German educationist and supporter of Greek independence, Friedrich Thiersch, emphasized Ancient as well as Modern Greek, while Latin was also introduced, making up approximately 80 per cent of the programme, and leaving only the remaining 20 per cent to mathematics and natural sciences (Mavrogordatos 1983). However, at the turn of the century, an urban perspective of school prevails, which provides a shift in more practical directions and the adaptation of secondary education to the requirements of economic development.

Already in 1884, the reform made by the Trikoupis progressive governance limited the teaching of Latin only to the last grade of the Greek School, in the pursuit of economic development based on industrialization. Nevertheless, it is notable that thanks to the rise of patriotism after the defeat of the Greeks in the war of 1897, the teaching hours of Latin were substantially increased (from twelve to sixteen) (Karakasis & Sarra 2017). The bold attempt of the Theotokis government in 1900 to turn education in a more practical direction met with strong opposition, to the extent that the law-drafts were not approved. The abolition of Ancient Greek in primary school was in essence the bone of conflict (Tsoukalas 1977; Bouzakis 2007).

Later, during the first administration of the Venizelos government, the educational reform by the Minister Tsirimokos was not voted for, due to the many negative reactions caused by the abolition of the classicistic orientation of the curriculum. It was the first time that Latin courses became optional in high schools. The Prime Minister himself stated in the Parliament that 'Latin is necessary for someone who intends to become a professor; to study Roman Law. For everyone else Latin is 100 per cent useless' (Karakasis & Sarra 2017). These draft laws sought to adapt education to economic needs by reducing the number of general education graduates and channelling students to urban schools. In the introductory report, the reforming educator

Glinos, for the first time, points out the danger of unemployment of the educated and the degradation of university degrees. The Philosophy School of Athens, the Associations of parents, students and merchants protested. Yet, the reform is thwarted by an external factor: enrolment in lower schools remains stagnant. The obsession of society with traditional educational orientations is proved to be stronger than the will of the government. Venizelos, realizing that the reform does not acquire consensus, exclaims: 'I will abolish 80 *Gymnasiums* even if I am overthrown' (Pesmazoglou 1987: 240).

The change in the political scene in 1932 with the conservative government of Tsaldaris and the subsequent military governments formed by the dictator Metaxas cancelled Venizelos' reform and made Latin compulsory again.

After some indecision that occurred in the two post-war decades, prime minister Papandreou's educational reform, introduced by reforming educator Papanoutsos in 1964 institutionalizes the establishment of the vernacular in the educational process. Greek is now taught through translations and Latin becomes optional. Furthermore, the Latin course was abolished in junior high schools and is only taught in the last two grades of the senior (*Lyceum*). However, it remains mandatory for the candidates to the Schools of Philosophy, Law and Religion. The changes were met with strong reactions from the opposition as well as by many organizations that supported classicism (Anderson 1965).

The junta from 1967 to 1974 strongly promoted Classics, but at the same time these subjects were stigmatized as carriers of extreme nationalist views. Nevertheless, the thorough documentation of the reform's introductory report is impressive, especially in relation to the value of learning Latin. It is objectively the most comprehensive of the educational programmes to date. Specifically, the rational and practical aspect of Latin along with the disciplined structure of the language are highlighted in an attempt to identify in them the principles of the regime. Yet, the usefulness of Latin while learning Romance languages, and furthermore its importance as carrier of the Greek spirit in the West are explicitly noted for the first time, and also in scientific terminology. Astonishingly, the syllabus requires overview of the whole works from which the taught passages are extracted, as well as the teaching of Roman culture and literature (Karakasis & Sarra 2017).

The educational reform of 1976 attempted to direct the large volume of students towards technical-vocational education. Examinations to enter senior high school were introduced. Latin is offered as an optional subject in the last two classes of the general senior high school, while it is compulsory in all three classes of the Classical senior high schools (an institution that was later abolished).

All educational reforms after 1964 focus mostly on the examinations taken to enter tertiary education. Since 2006, the passing mark for admission to University Schools has been introduced, which increases the number of candidates that fail, dramatically. Variations of this system are still active today. As far as Greek is concerned, in the course of time various anthologies of texts were taught in the *Lyceum*: besides Lysias' oration *On the refusal of a pension to the invalid*, Sophocles' *Antigone* and *Oedipus Rex*, as well as Pericles' funeral oration by Thucydides, in recent years Lysias' speech *For Mantitheus* is taught, as well as a selection of philosophical texts mainly by Plato and Aristotle. The introduction of Euripides' *Alcestis* or *Trojan Women* instead of *Helen* in junior high school and Lysias' *Against Eratosthenes* and Demosthenes' *On the Freedom of Rhodians* in the *Lyceum* is planned for 2025. In 1984, when the system of thematic collections of subjects was established, the anthology of texts by Paschalis and Savvantidis was introduced for the Latin course of preparation. It consists of fifty units to be taught in the last grade – nowadays, they are shared in the last two grades. Since 1999, the collection has been enriched with a brief introduction to Roman literature by Nikitas.

Recent reforms implemented by the progressive government in 2018 led to the abolition of Latin in senior high school, a fact that provoked strong reactions mainly from the academic teaching staff, the conservative opposition and the press close to it, but also from broader parts of Greek society, who assessed the measure as a blow afflicting national identity. Nevertheless, although the subsequent change of government in 2019 completely restored Latin to the curriculum and reinstated the course as a nationally examined subject for the admission of students to higher education schools in the humanistic field, the choices of the candidates in the following years have not confirmed the government's intentions. Specifically, according to the most recent statistics concerning the National Examinations, in the year 2022 Humanities were chosen by 19.1 per cent fewer candidates than those in 2021. Moreover, according to the 2021 Report of the Hellenic Authority for Higher Education (*EΘAAE*), only 13.04 per cent of students chose to study Arts and Humanities (the third choice in order of preference of Greek students), while in 2019 the corresponding percentage amounted to 13.45 (the same position). Still, the corresponding statistics for EU students show a similar decline in their choice of the Arts and Humanities sector: only 11.5 per cent of the enrolled students in the EU chose to study Arts and Humanities (fourth in order of preference), while in 2019 the corresponding percentage amounted to 12.15 (same position). Moreover, the announcement of the most recent examination results for admission to the Classics departments in Greece certified in an indisputable way the crisis that plagues them. Specifically, candidates are admitted to the Classics departments in the University of Athens having scored around 13,000 points, while a decade ago they needed above 17,000. For the respective departments in provincial universities, they need around 8,000 points, a fact clearly revealing that more and more Greek students show preference for other fields, at the expense of classical studies, which are claimed by more average, or even weak students. The aforementioned data suggest that the great exodus from classical studies in Greece is a facet of a wider – at least European – phenomenon. Absolutely similar trends are observed in countries with a long tradition in classical studies, such as France and Italy.

However, the problem seems to have various dimensions, as the relationship of Greek students with linguistics in general seems to be going through a serious crisis. In particular, mainly in secondary education, pupils show a general reluctance to compose long texts as well as to deeply study essential chapters of grammar and syntax, as a result of which their speech turns out to be unreadable and uninspired (Markantonatos 2019). Surprisingly, fifty-six Greek university professors, in a public letter on 24 May 2016, requested that the teaching of Greek from the original at least in junior high school be abolished and replaced by more teaching hours spent on Modern Greek courses or Ancient Greek from a translation. The proposal, made during a period of progressive governance, aimed rather at upgrading the course of Modern Greek. However, it identified the teaching of Classics as the cause for the linguistic weakness of the pupils. In the letter, predominantly negative arguments and criticism against the usefulness of classical courses as unsuitable for foreign language pupils as well as for those from underprivileged social classes are used. This particular argumentation was exploited by both political factions, distorted according to their beliefs, ultimately leading to a barren tug-of-war. However, research showing that the teaching of Ancient Greek in high school does not improve the performance of students in the *Lyceum* deserves attention (Bardani 1999; Koxarakis 2000).

The solution to the riddle lies precisely in the identification of a continuing weakness of the Greek state: the lack of a consistent national and long-term strategy for education which is bold enough to go beyond its international commitments to its financial state. Greek governments, aware of the special position that classical antiquity has in the mindset of Greek people, tend to project it as a defining element of modern Hellenism, and accordingly a main pillar of Greek education, while essentially seeking to exploit it as a slogan exclusively for political expediency.

These governments have been obviously trying to prevent the tendency of Greeks to follow the curriculum of a general education and to orientate them towards technical education, driven by business needs. For this purpose, 'classical' subjects are systematically undermined through reforms such as the abolition of the polytonic system in 1982; they are also devalued through outdated and inappropriate textbooks (Bardani 1999), while the schools that teach them are downgraded and their numerous graduates become *de facto* candidates for long-term unemployment. In addition to the infrastructure deficiencies, the cuts led to the decline in status of the teaching staff. Particularly during the years of the Covid-19 pandemic, the language level of the students collapsed due to the lack of interactivity and the obsolescence and ineffectiveness of online distance education. At the same time indifference was shown for any change of the outdated and inherently problematic textbooks. (The current Greek textbooks were distributed in 2007–8, while the Latin textbook was distributed in 1984.) It is absolutely illuminating that from 2001 to 2009 the Greek state instituted an 'Annual European Student Competition in Ancient Greek Language and Literature' for the Upper (*sic*) High schools in Europe. In 2012 it seems to have waned, having failed to win the recognition and acceptance of teachers, according to the UNESCO report *Annex to 2012 Greek statistics* (Michaelides & Zekos 2016: 548). Quite interestingly though, a similar competition –restricted to one of the prefectures of Athens – has been held by the private American College of Greece since 2017.

Obviously, the policies undermining classical studies in Greece stem mainly from the state's constant and steady pursuit of producing mainly technical labour and economic technocrats, rather than intellectuals and scholars, who are understood as effective in exercising criticism to the status quo. Furthermore, these policies are drawn up in the context of the political confrontation between the left-wing rhetoric that considers classical studies the prerogative of a plutocratic elite, which through them reproduces inequality and racist perceptions, and the right-wing slogan of an education of *Excellence* (Ἀριστεία).

Finally, international developments in the field of classical studies cannot be ignored. The retreat of classical studies before sciences worldwide, due to the technocratic turn of education dictated by the prevalence of global market rules, no doubt prompts these government decisions. In addition, the current discussion about the establishment of private universities in Greece can be judged as highly controversial, since it will result in the minimization of the state costs; yet, it will force universities to operate in a competitive environment, seeking self-financing. Thus, knowledge will become a marketable product. On the contrary, the work of political and social culture, the cultivation of morals and the course of social justice and integration are activated by humanistic education.

To sum up, the status of classical studies in Greece is a part of and reflects global developments on education. Nevertheless, it differs somewhat because of an inherent characteristic of the temperament of the Greeks, to which we shall refer in the next paragraph. Classical studies worldwide are threatened with abolition or with optionalization. Such demands appear to emanate from equally afflicted subjects which appear to be marginalized, and by newly-created scientific fields which seek to be established. Classical studies are criticized under the following pretexts: as elitist, racist, outdated, or uninteresting. In fact, classical studies develops critical and unbiased questioning of many of the issues which are relevant to global society. Furthermore, the in-depth understanding of sources and terminology that they promote leads to compelling argumentation. The defence of human rights and the contribution of humanities to the self-determination of nations is contrary to the aims of the global market.

However, despite the limitations of the international economic situation, the deep relationship of modern Greeks with tradition, and the general conception regarding the contribution of classical literature to the national struggles, has thwarted several attempts aimed at abolishing Classics from the programme or even converting them to optional subjects.

Therefore, can such policies ignore the choice of multinational companies such as Apple and IBM to train their IT executives by teaching them Greek? It was only recently that Facebook added the Ancient Greek language option to the ones that can be used by the users of this specific social medium. Now, young people all around the world can use it, if they have already been familiar with the language. All the above show a new trend and a need that has to be satisfied. It is definitely not too late for a brave decision that will affect the national strategy for education over time. Classical education has the potential to support the needs of future generations, of the Greek youth that needs the solid sustenance of the global wisdom that was the heritage of classical Greece to humanity. It depends on the Greek state to give back to the classical studies the status they had in the place that classical civilization was born. It will definitely set the foundations for a new, exquisite era.

References

Anderson, C. A. (1965), 'Access to Higher Education and Economic Development', in A. H. Halsey, J. Floud and C. A. Anderson (eds), *Education, Economy, Society: A Reader in the Sociology of Education*, New York: The Free Press/London: Collier Macmillan Limited, 252–68.

Bardani, S. (1999), Η διδασκαλία της Ελληνικής γλώσσας μέσα από αρχαία, βυζαντινά και λόγια κείμενα [The teaching of the Greek language through ancient, Byzantine and scholarly texts] in Σεμινάριο 20: Η γλωσσική κατάρτιση και αγωγή των μαθητών στη δευτεροβάθμια Εκπαίδευση [Seminar 20: The language training and teaching of students in secondary education], Athens: Grigoris, 57–69.

Becker, T. (2001), 'Broadening Access to a Classical Education: State Universities in Virginia in the Nineteenth Century', *The Classical Journal*, 96 (3): 309–22.

Bouzakis, S. (2007), *Εκπαιδευτικές Μεταρρυθμίσεις στην Ελλάδα* [Educational Reforms in Greece]. 'Τεκμήρια – Μελέτες της Νεοελληνικής Εκπαίδευσης» ['Evidence – Studies on Modern Greek Education'] 1 (1), Athens: Gutenberg.

Chaniotis, A. (2021), [Radio-broadcast] 18 April, cited in P. Papadopoulos *Με το πρώτο στην Ευρώπη και τον Κόσμο* [With the first in Europe and the World].

Dreher, R. (2021), 'Suicide of The Humanities', *The American Conservative*, 3 May. Available online: https://www.theamericanconservative.com/suicide-of-the-humanities-dan-el-padilla-peralta-classics/ (accessed 25 September 2023).

Ioannides, S. (2021), 'Interview with Dan-el Padilla Peralta: Classical studies needs structural changes', *Ekathimerini*, 12 September. Available online: https://www.ekathimerini.com/opinion/interviews/1167721/classical-studies-needs-structural-changes/ (accessed 21 September 2023).

Karakasis, E. and A. Sarra (2017), 'Τα Λατινικά γράμματα στο Ελληνικό σχολείο: Πορεία μέσα στο χρόνο' ['Latin grammar in the Greek school: Progress through time'], *Δωδώνη: Φιλολογία*, 42–4: 289–304.

Koliopoulos, I., K. Svolopoulos, E. Chatzivasiliou, T. Nimas and C. Scholinaki-Helioti (2023), *Ιστορία του νεότερου και του σύγχρονου κόσμου (από το 1815 έως σήμερα)* [History of the modern and contemporary world (from 1815 to the present)], Athens: ΙΤΥΕ Διόφαντος.

Kokkinidis, T. (2021), 'Removal of Greek, Latin at Princeton Sparks Debate on Classics in the US', *The Greek Reporter*, 6 September. https://greekreporter.com/2021/09/06/greek-latin-princeton-sparks-debate-classics/ (accessed 21 September 2023).

Koxarakis, M. (2000), *Η αποτελεσματικότητα της διδασκαλίας της Ελληνικής Γλώσσας μέσα από αρχαία, βυζαντινά και λόγια κείμενα: Εμπειρική έρευνα αξιολόγησης* [The effectiveness of teaching the Greek language through ancient, Byzantine and scholarly texts: Empirical evaluation research], Athens: Grigoris.

Markantonatos, A. (2019), 'Κλασικά Γράμματα: Ωρα Μηδέν' ['Classic Letters: Zero Hour'], *ΤΟ ΒΗΜΑ*, 14 July.

Mavrogordatos, G. Th. (1983), 'Ο Διχασμός ως κρίση Εθνικής Ολοκλήρωσης' [Disunity as a crisis of National Integration], in D. Tsaousis (ed.), *Ελληνισμός, Ελληνικότητα: Ιδεολογικοί και Βιωματικοί Άξονες της Νεοελληνικής Κοινωνίας*, [Hellenism, Hellenicity: Ideological and Experiential Axes of Modern Greek Society], Athens: Estia, 69–80.

Michaelides, T. and N. Zekos (2016), 'Ο βαθμός εδραίωσης των Πανελλήνιων Μαθητικών Διαγωνισμών στην Ελληνική Εκπαίδευση και διερεύνηση της στάσης της μαθητικής κοινότητας' ['The degree of consolidation of Panhellenic Student Competitions in Greek Education and investigation of the attitude of the student community'], in D. Kolokotronis (ed.), *2nd Pan-Hellenic Congress for the Promotion of Innovation in Education*, Larissa 21–3, II: 546–54.

Nash, M. (2007), *Women's Education in the United States, 1780–1840*, New York: Palgrave Macmillan.

Padilla Peralta, D. (2019), 'Racial Equity and the Production of Knowledge. SCS Annual Meeting: *The Future of Classics*'. Available online: https://static1.squarespace.com/static/5f04d36c7eb60c2415efa0f1/t/5f70d7ff8bc6782718859284/1601230847948/Padilla+Peralta+SCS+2019+Future+of+Classics+Equity+and+the+Production+of+Knowledge+ed+w+tables.pdf (accessed 9 November 2023).

Papadopoulos, P. (2021), 'Υπάρχει μέλλον για τις κλασσικές σπουδές;' ['Is there a future for classical studies?'], *EPT News*, 2 October. https://www.ertnews.gr/eidiseis/ellada/yparxei-mellon-gia-tis-klassikes-spoudes/ (accessed 25 September 2023).

Pesmazoglou, St. (1987), *Εκπαίδευση και Ανάπτυξη στην Ελλάδα 1948–1985: Το ασύμπτωτο μιας σχέσης* [Education and Development in Greece, 1948–1985: The asymptote of a relationship], Athens: Themelio.

Poser, R. (2021), 'He Wants to Save Classics from Whiteness. Can the Field Survive?' *The New York Times Magazine*, 2 February. Available online: https://www.nytimes.com/2021/02/02/magazine/classics-greece-rome-whiteness.html (accessed 23 September 2023).

Rommel, G. (2001), 'The Cradle of Titans: Classical Philology in Greifswald and its History from 1820', *Illinois Classical Studies*, 26: 169–78.

Stamatis, D. (2021), '*Graecia capta* . . . Latin Studies in modern Greece: An international passport to the Western world', *Cursor*, 17: 29–30.

Stray, C. (1996), 'Culture and Discipline: Classics and Society in Victorian England', *International Journal of the Classical Tradition*, 3 (1): 77–85.

Tsoukalas, K. (1977), *Εξάρτηση και Αναπαραγωγή: Ο κοινωνικός ρόλος των Εκπαιδευτικών Μηχανισμών στην Ελλάδα (1830–1922)* [Dependence and Reproduction: The Social Role of Educational Mechanisms in Greece (1830–1922)], Athens: Themelio.

UNESCO (2012), *World Data on Education 2010/11: Greece*, Geneva: UNESCO.

HUNGARY

Attila Ferenczi and Zoltán Gloviczki

Introduction: historical background

Although it was as part of the Habsburg Empire that Hungary arrived in the early Modern Age, the leading stratum of Hungarian society, who spoke Hungarian and claimed a Hungarian national identity, had no desire to be absorbed into the Austrian imperial elite. Up to the nineteenth century age of national romanticism and revolution, this conflict with a power that was foreign from both a linguistic, and (partly) cultural point of view, ensured an unusual place and role for the Latin language: instead of communicating in German, which was met with protest, or Hungarian, which the ruling power would not accept, Latin was used in an official capacity as a sort of compromise solution and with this became both a part of everyday life and a means and symbol of national resistance. At the same time, the critical attitudes of the Enlightenment, the growing role of national languages, and the rise and spread of the natural sciences vis-à-vis what was formerly a humanities-focused education, all made their influence felt in Hungary, as elsewhere. Nevertheless, the first document to regulate public education, the 1777 *Ratio Educationis* of Empress of Austria and Queen of Hungary Maria Theresa, upheld Latin as one of the subjects that, being practical, should be retained. In the words of Mór Jókai, one of Hungary's most popular nineteenth century writers, if Hungarian was the nation's 'mother tongue', then Latin had become 'that of its fathers', which explains the exceptional fact that in Hungary it remained the official legal language of the nation until as late as 1844. Thus, instruction in Latin served first and foremost expressly practical objectives as a vehicle for ordinary official verbal and written communications, though the simultaneously coalescing new humanism, which emphasized the aesthetic and moral qualities of both Latin and Greek, was not without some influence in the matter. It was this latter movement that laid the solid foundation for classical language education to preserve its role as a dominant subject throughout the development of the modern schools of the nineteenth and twentieth centuries.

The switch to teaching in Hungarian in secondary schools occurred only in the early nineteenth century; until then, all textbooks were written in Latin, which remained the primary language of verbal communication in lessons, as well. This historical background would also place Latin into an unusual situation later: for a very long time it remained the subject occupying the greatest number of hours per week, a statistic that would decrease only with reference to the scientific secondary schools created in 1883. In humanities schools, Greek remained an elective subject until the end of the Second World War, though, beginning with the Education Act of 1924 and in parallel with the continued polarization of the school system, both subjects faded gradually and generally into the background in comparison to modern languages. Still, both the tradition for the classical languages and acceptance of them remained strong: the Education Acts of 1924 and 1934, the second of which placed a strong emphasis on national traditions, both evaluate the classical languages – and Latin in particular – as strong, indispensable pillars of Hungarian education. Ultimately, the decline in the influence of these languages must be viewed in light of the number of hours of each taught in eight-form secondary schools: the central curriculum of 1938 prescribed twenty-nine hours per week (in total, distributed over eight years) of Hungarian language and literature; seventeen hours of history (over six years), thirty-four hours of Latin in boys' schools, and twenty-six in girls' schools (over eight years for both).

In the post-Second World War Soviet 'sphere of interest' and post-1948 dictatorship, mandatory instruction in Latin was removed entirely and elective Latin eliminated from forms five through eight, in part due to the introduction and democratization of the eight-form elementary school. Although Latin was now in part associated with the disparaged Catholic church and former social elite, which the regime regarded as hostile, even between 1950 and 1957, the darkest period in Hungarian political life, one could still study Latin as an elective, in parallel with the required Russian. Under the latter language's strategic domination, the number of hours in which Latin was studied and methodological reforms applied to it corresponded roughly to those experienced by other (living) foreign languages, most of them likewise associated with 'hostile' Western Europe. It was the 1960s' de-escalation of tensions, therefore, that explains the reform of 1966–7, which introduced a curriculum, textbooks and educational materials reflecting contemporary findings in modern language instruction. At the same time, the global modernization efforts of the age resulted in a decline in the role of Latin overall, including both decreased opportunities, and total teaching hours dedicated.

Such trends notwithstanding, during the 1970s, the study of Latin experienced a sort of social renaissance, including a gradual expansion of course hours. Until the early 1980s, the general rule was five hours every two weeks, with secondary schools teaching the 9th to 12th forms offering Latin as a second foreign language in addition to Russian in the first two forms and as a general elective in the second two. Another, novel strategic paradigm for Latin instruction had as its primary objective the application of an aesthetic approach: curricula introduced for the 1978/79 academic year targeted the reading and literary interpretation of mainly original classical texts, following less than a year of reading edited practice texts. Here, the end in view was that students should be able to understand, at an aesthetic level, the – amply annotated – writings of Horace and Tacitus following just four years of study at a pace of two or three hours per week. Though with the changes in study habits and academic requirements that have arisen in the interim, this expectation would seem ever less realistic, still, the notion resulted in a coherent, carefully thought-out conception that was fully developed in its own right, as well as a series of corresponding textbooks that were developed in the space of just a few years.

Development of the present situation

Nevertheless, there is still today a measure of ongoing cultural guerrilla warfare over the question of Latin education, though what was formerly a battle with bureaucrats is today one of societal demands. As ever, the movement is headed by the Hungarian Society for Ancient Studies, which formerly organized a national academic competition with the aim of popularization until in 1984, it managed to get the subject listed among those of the national competition schedule. Since 1990, it has supported Hungarian students participating in the Cicero Competition in Arpino and has even won the battle to have a matriculation in Latin and/or official language certification represent an advantage in the university admissions process. In the meantime, the percentage of students studying Latin in Hungary in 1984 – i.e. during the final years of communist rule – was 4.1 per cent of the total secondary school population.

The fall of the communist system in 1990 led, as one might expect, to a transformation of the Hungarian school system. The Education Act of 1990 both terminated the compulsory study of Russian, leaving Latin in a significantly stronger position among elective languages, and enabled the opening of both privately funded schools in addition to existing state-funded ones, and new church schools in addition to those already available. One of several side-effects of this process was that certain parts of society, after more than forty years of communist rule, sought to resurrect cultural traditions that had been swept away by force following the Second World War, one of the most important pillars of which was Latin. Thus, for the length of a decade, Latin enjoyed something of an unnatural boost in popularity to the point of being made compulsory in a number of secondary schools. There were even years where it was the third most-studied foreign language after English and German and, not infrequently, the first – and therefore foundational – language a student would encounter. The 1990s witnessed the publication of a number of Latin textbook series, materials that were frequently – and, given the lack of precedents, understandably – as unscientifically constructed as they were innovative. During this period, the state provided free re-training for former Russian teachers in order to ensure them an opportunity at a marketable job. Latin emerged from this programme a success story, as many practising teachers of Russian were able to earn credentials in its instruction.

After its exclusion in 1945, the ancient Greek language never made its way back into any curriculum, though some secondary schools still offer it in the form of a leisure time, extra-curricular activity led by enthusiastic teachers of Latin.

The years following the turn of the millennium brought with them a measure of market-based sobriety, in which cultural nostalgia was increasingly replaced by practical concerns on the part of the social environment. Speakers of Hungarian, an isolated Finno-Ugric language, can communicate with neither the populations of surrounding countries, which all speak Indo-European languages, nor the speakers of other Finno-Ugric languages living much further away, as none of the languages of this group are mutually intelligible in even the most limited sense. One of the greatest educational problems for Hungarian society is related to its knowledge and use of foreign languages. Surveys consistently show that a much smaller percentage of Hungarians can communicate (or claim to be able to communicate) in a foreign language than is the case in other European countries of similar levels of development. This circumstance negatively influences social productivity and, from the point of view of the individual, represents his or her greatest obstacle to success in the labour market. While prior to the fall of communism, the near-complete social consensus was to blame compulsory Russian instruction for this situation, the very disappointing statistics of the past few decades have demonstrated that the deficiency stems rather from deeper social, cultural and didactic causes. For this reason, it may truly seem to a family looking to select a language for their children that, in fact, any living foreign language will serve them better than Latin. Paired with this is the observation that, at the societal or even overall educational level, no one has yet managed to interpret and position the potential objectives and possibilities for twenty-first century Latin education more broadly and in more modern fashion. Together, these factors explain the dramatic decline represented by Tables 3–5.

Table 3 gives the number of students of Latin among all participants in Hungarian public education. (Until 2008, the National Core Curriculum permitted students to study Latin as their first foreign language undertaken; from 2009 onwards, Latin is elective only as second or third foreign language.) In Hungary, in all school types where Latin is offered, public school studies conclude at the end of the twelfth grade with an examination of matriculation. Table 4 presents the number of examinations taken in Latin, indicating also the examination level. The examination can be passed at two different intermediate levels, which together correspond to the Common European Framework of Reference for Languages (or CEFR) level B1, and at one advanced level, which corresponds to CEFR level B2. Table 5 concerns language examinations possessing state accreditation. In Hungary, specifically to address the above-mentioned societal problem related to foreign language knowledge, fluency in foreign languages can be measured via state-accredited examinations, the certifications associated with which have conferred advantage in the college admissions process, resulted in higher wages in certain jobs, and until recently, were required for receiving a diploma from an institute of higher education.

In 2022, the total number of students taking Latin was 2,931, representing 0.57 per cent of all students of the affected age group (14–18-year-olds), and only 1.5 per cent of students attending college preparatory secondary schools, i.e. schools that offered a matriculation examination. For comparison: the same statistic for 1984 was 4.1 per cent!

Table 3. Students learning Latin in public education

Year	Students learning Latin	% of all students (14–18 years)
2005	11,441	1.72
2006	11,795	1.77
2007	11,207	1.69
2008	11,086	1.7
2009	10,459	1.59
2010	10,855	1.64
2011	9,946	1.53
2012	8,951	1.43
2013	8,064	1.38
2014	6,430	1.17
2015	5,113	0.98
2016	4,965	0.93
2017	4,564	0.88
2018	4,218	0.84
2019	4,621	0.93
2020	3,495	0.73
2021	3,091	0.6
2022	2,931	0.57

Source: © Attila Ferenczi and Zoltán Gloviczki 2023.

Table 4. Matriculation examinations in Latin

Year	Number of exams (Latin, B1)	Number of exams (Latin, 21)	Exams (Latin overall)	% of all exams (B1)	% of all exams (B2)	% of all exams (overall)
2010	490	121	611	0.11	0.44	0.13
2011	401	81	482	0.09	0.28	0.1
2012	382	83	465	0.09	0.23	0.1
2013	443	72	515	0.11	0.19	0.11
2014	380	50	430	0.1	0.13	0.1
2015	250	44	294	0.07	0.05	0.06
2016	284	42	326	0.08	0.1	0.08
2017	200	46	246	0.06	0.11	0.06
2018	322	36	358	0.09	0.09	0.09
2019	244	28	272	0.07	0.06	0.07
2019	244	28	272	0.07	0.06	0.06
2020	184	36	220	0.06	0.06	0.05
2021	176	43	219	0.05	0.06	0.05
2022	180	42	222	0.05	0.06	0.06

Source: © Attila Ferenczi and Zoltán Gloviczki 2023.

Table 5. Examinations with state accreditation in Latin

Year	Exams (Latin)	% of all exams taken
2014	113	0.09
2015	118	0.09
2016	86	0.06
2017	91	0.08
2018	77	0.06
2019	83	0.07
2020	70	0.08
2021	69	0.08
2022	49	0.06

Source: © Attila Ferenczi and Zoltán Gloviczki 2023.

Present conditions

Today, all education regulations that apply to the development of skill competency in Latin were developed prior to the turn of the millennia and in the years immediately subsequent. As early as 1995, the fst version of today's National Core Curriculum offered a sense of the waning significance to be accorded to Latin with respect to what it termed 'more modern subjects'. In its first wording, the curriculum not only does not mention Latin as an existing subject, but also embeds the concept of foreign language study in general within the phrase 'living foreign languages'. Later, under pressure from the aforementioned Society for Ancient Studies and the Hungarian Academy of Sciences, the consolidated curriculum – in the interim subjected to triennial review and multiple far-reaching reforms – would include Latin first at a level of a mention, and then, in the more detailed supplementary regulation, in its entirety. Although its final role in the central content-related regulations was the result of a serious ongoing education policy battle, at the same time, the opportunity of placing Latin instruction within a modern regulatory framework enabled the re-expression of the role, objectives and methods of Latin instruction in terms of a modern approach. With this, Latin instruction was fitted into an educative conceptual framework centred on competency acquisition as part of a system of means for general language development. Of particular significance from this standpoint is the set of generally innovative, competency-based, centrally administered matriculation examination regulations introduced in 2002, which are not only considerably more creative than their predecessors, but also lay down what stands as a modern system of requirements for language use and instruction to this day.

Today, Latin features in Hungarian curricula as an elective second foreign language, a separate Framework Curriculum having been drafted for each of the three types of secondary school – the four-year secondary school (forms 9 through 12), six-year secondary school (forms 7 through 12), and eight-year secondary school (forms 5 through 12) – and a course entitled Our Latin Heritage introduced for students in the first two years (forms 5 and 6) of eight-year secondary schools. Although recent curricula have offered little leeway for secondary schools to implement individual, non-standard plans, it is nevertheless an important affirmative gesture that in those schools where directors decide to offer Latin teaching and where students can elect to take Latin in place of one of the 'living languages', the subject may be taught as a second language at a time investment of at least three hours per week. It bears mention that, although education legislators have provided the opportunity for Latin instruction, it has not been made compulsory for anyone. The decision is instead left up to the schools, whose primary concern is generally the wishes and demands of the parents.

With regard to content, the internal structure of Latin instruction in Hungary has remained consistent for decades, consisting largely of one-third grammar, one-third translation from Latin into Hungarian, and one-third cultural history. The slow, but pervasive modernization of pedagogical habits experienced across the field of education has had its effect on Latin teachers as well. One clear sign of this is the Upper Secondary School Leaving Examination system, in continuous operation since 2005, which has taken unambiguous steps towards the introduction of a competency assessment exam. Despite this slow methodological rejuvenation, the current (one and only) Latin textbook is the *Latin language book for high schools* (Horváth & Nagy 2021). It is the only book to have, for administrative reasons, state accreditation. Although it is professionally reliable, the book represents a serious burden, as despite recent changes in theory and approach, it is – apart from a reduced number of texts – practically identical to the series developed in the 1970s. This textbook series defines the content of the various framework curricula. Though certainly it would fall to the Hungarian Society for Ancient Studies and the field of Latin instruction in general to develop a modern textbook, the funding for such a project is currently unavailable. Also absent is any consensus on the part of the Latin teaching community as to the direction in which instruction might move beyond its traditionally conceptualized canonical-aesthetic educational objectives.

At the same time, the new two-year course of study entitled Our Latin Heritage may represent within the framework curriculum just such an opportunity for didactic and conceptual progress. The curriculum prescribes that eight-year secondary school students begin their studies in history in the seventh form, and it is for this that the Our Latin Heritage course is to prepare them. The notion represented in the curriculum is to introduce a fifth and sixth-form subject that sets the stage for both history and Latin language studies, but that is short and can be interpreted and concluded internally. The secondary title of the course is The Latin Foundations of European Culture, suggesting that it will contribute indirectly to the attainment of such developmental objectives as are considered primary to the studies of history and the Latin language: in particular an understanding of the vestiges of Roman culture (*Pannonia provincia*) in Hungary and exploration of the relationship of Latin to Hungarian history. Ultimately, the goal of the course is to provide age-appropriate information that piques students' curiosity and to develop the competencies that will enable students to continue their studies in history and Latin.

Teaching Latin in higher education and teacher training

The situation with higher education is characterized by phenomena somewhat similar to those outlined above. During the interwar period, entrance into humanities departments was contingent upon a matriculation examination in Latin. Thus, students who had attended schools specializing in the sciences and therefore did not have this certification were forced to make up for this gap in knowledge privately in order to procure certification prior to the university application process. Latin was required for admission to departments offering degrees in both law and medicine. After the Second World War, a desire for equality of opportunity led to the option that these competencies be acquired specifically as part of one's university studies. Accordingly, students were universally referred to a four-semester Latin Matriculation Examination Equivalency course as part of their regular studies. Later, the number of disciplines requiring a knowledge of Latin began to decrease. Those for which it was a continued requirement included: history, ethnography, art history, archaeology, philosophy and, of course, the neo-Latin languages.

The situation today reflects continued changes in approach. In the medical field, Latin teaching has shifted from general language studies to instruction in pragmatic medical onomastics, taken two hours per week for a total of two semesters. In legal studies, Latin instruction has been reduced to a course of just half a year. In the humanities, too, two-semester courses without qualifying examinations have become the norm. In Hungary, not one MA programme except for Classical Philology requires a knowledge of Latin. Still, the 2005 introduction of a bi-level course corresponding to the Bologna Process created the opportunity of gaining admission to the university faculty of classical philology without any prior knowledge of Greek or Latin at all. As a result, in the years that have passed since then, the percentage of students who commence learning both languages in higher education has risen continuously.

At the introduction of the Bologna Process in Hungary, teacher training was also converted to the bi-level system; however, after a few years, the monolithic five-year system was re-introduced. Today, university students training to be Latin teachers take many of their core courses together with students on the disciplinary philological track, supplemented with courses in pedagogy and methodology. After their qualification exam, Latin teachers have the opportunity of taking part in pedagogical workshops organized by the Hungarian Society for Ancient Studies and other organizations.

Reference

Horváth, M. and F. Nagy (2021), *Latin nyelvkönyv a gimnáziumok I-IV. osztálya számára* [Latin language book for high schools I-IV], Budapest: Oktatási Hivatal.

ICELAND

Geir Þ. Þórarinsson

Introduction

The education system in Iceland resembles those of neighbouring countries in Scandinavia, with compulsory education for children six to sixteen years old, followed by a voluntary upper-level secondary school and higher education at the college and university level. Classics is virtually non-existent at the compulsory level and only offered regularly at a single upper secondary level school. An undergraduate programme in Classics is offered at one university.

Classics in the curriculum

The Icelandic National Curriculum Guide for Compulsory Schools (Ministry of Education, Science and Culture 2014) does not mention any classical subjects, e.g. Ancient Greek or Latin language or literature. It is assumed that children will study history as part of social sciences, but the curriculum guide stipulates nothing with regard to the content and very little teaching material is available for classical topics suitable for children at this level. In 2021, however, the Directorate of Education published a brief introduction (32 pages) to ancient Greek civilization which is intended for the upper-level compulsory forms (Sigurjónsson 2021).

Until recently, the upper secondary level was four years of study, but since 2016 all upper-level secondary schools in Iceland have been shortened to three years. There are thirty-eight schools that offer education at the upper secondary level. A few are traditional *gymnasia*, which aim to prepare students for higher learning, but there are also vocational schools, music and art schools, and comprehensive schools at the upper secondary level. Matriculation from any upper secondary level school, however, will grant access to tertiary education.

The general section of the Icelandic National Curriculum Guide for Upper Secondary Schools (Ministry of Education, Science and Culture 2012) does not mention classical subjects either, but history and foreign languages are discussed in separate sections of the curriculum guide.

History is not considered a core discipline at the upper secondary level and schools are not obliged to offer history as an elective, although academic study programmes in *gymnasia* and comprehensive schools must offer a minimum of two semester long courses or six credits (108–144 hours) in history. Of the four courses envisioned in the curriculum guide as potential course offerings, classical civilization may form a part of SAG103, which will cover the period from the dawn of history to 1800, and SAG303, which will cover select topics in social and cultural history. However, it is not clear to what extent ancient history or classical civilization more specifically is represented in the curriculum across the upper secondary level, as individual schools are given leeway to choose historical topics to cover in the courses offered. Nor is it clear to what extent ancient history may have been sacrificed when the upper-level secondary schools transitioned from four-year to three-year schools.

The National Curriculum Guide for Upper Secondary Schools section on foreign languages (Menntamálaráðuneytið 1999) is almost exclusively dedicated to discussion of English, Danish, Norwegian and Swedish, German, French and Spanish within the school system. It only briefly mentions that language tracks within *gymnasia* may offer Latin as well as 'other languages'. Concerns have been raised about cuts to foreign languages at the upper secondary level as a result of the transition from four to three years of study. Latin courses have in the past occasionally been offered as electives in a few schools, but such electives are currently nowhere on offer.

One upper secondary school, however, Menntaskólinn í Reykjavík, does offer a language track, which has a common first year and then divides during the second year of study into a modern language track and an ancient language track. During the first year, all students must take Latin. The modern language track will continue Latin for another year, whereas the ancient language track will continue to take two more years of Latin. Additionally, students in the ancient language track may elect to have two years of Greek, and all students of the ancient language track will have two years of classical studies where they study a selection of classical literature and a selection of ancient philosophy in translation.

Menntaskólinn í Reykjavík is generally considered to be among Iceland's finest *gymnasia* and has a reputation for preparing students well for higher learning. Its ancient language track is a long-standing tradition. The school was founded in its current location in 1846 as 'The learned school in Reykjavík' (but was more commonly known as the Latin school). Its pre-history may be traced back much further, all the way to the bishopric in Skálholt in 1056. Yet the ancient languages themselves are often regarded as relics of the past and much like the humanities generally their usefulness will often be questioned compared to other disciplines, especially the natural sciences, which are considered to be more practical and to 'open more doors' in higher education. This is reflected in enrolment numbers. Typically, a cohort in the ancient language track will include anywhere from half a dozen to a dozen students. At the university level, there are typically between eight and twelve active Classics majors.

Current trends

A grammar-translation approach remains common but is used in combination with a reading-based approach. At the secondary level, students will usually first encounter Latin through the only textbook available in Icelandic, *Latnesk lestrarbók*, a reader, coupled with *Latnesk málfræði* (Ármannson 1994a and 1994b) originally published in 1940 and 1941, respectively. During their second year of Latin, students on the ancient language track at Menntaskólinn í Reykjavík progress to the *Oxford Latin Course III* (Balme & Morwood 2006), and in their third year they will read book I of Caesar's *Gallic War*, Cicero's first oration *Against Catiline*, as well as a selection of poems by Catullus and Ovid.

There is no available textbook for Ancient Greek in Icelandic. At the secondary level, *Athenaze* (Balme et al. 2016) has been used in the past, but currently students start with *Greek to GCSE 1* (Taylor 2016) in their first year, and read selections from Herodotus, Homer and the New Testament in their second year.

Not only are textbooks in Icelandic for the most part unavailable, so are dictionaries in Icelandic. There has never been an Ancient Greek–Icelandic dictionary and the only Latin–Icelandic dictionary available, *Nucleus Latinitatis* (Gram & Árnason 1994), came out in 1738 and is not really suitable for use in schools, although it is available in reprint. As a result, students must rely on foreign dictionaries, most often in English. The preferred dictionary for Latin is *Cassell's Latin Dictionary* (Simpson 1968) whereas for Greek, students at the secondary level might use *The Pocket Oxford Classical Greek Dictionary* (Morwood & Taylor 2002), and at the university students might use Liddell and Scott's *Intermediate Greek–English Lexicon* (2001) or even *The Cambridge Greek Lexicon* (Diggle 2021). However, internet resources have proven quite useful here, especially *Logeion*.

Students on the ancient language track at Menntaskólinn í Reykjavík will also have two years of classical studies, where they are exposed to classical literature in translation. Typically, they will read in Icelandic translation from Homer's *Iliad* and *Odyssey*, Vergil's *Aeneid*, Ovid's *Metamorphoses,* Euripides' *Medea,* and some of Plato's dialogues.

At the university level, both Latin and Greek are taught *ab initio*. Language instruction methods have been similar to the secondary level, combining grammar-translation approaches and reading-based approaches. Mastronarde's *Introduction to Attic Greek* (2013), has been used since the 1990s. In Latin, the Icelandic reader by Kristinn Ármannsson is no longer used, for several reasons, including the fact that it excludes foreign exchange students and others not proficient in Icelandic from participating. Using an English language textbook, on the other hand, allows international students to enroll, which is important when enrolment numbers are low. Students may choose to submit any assignment and take the exams in English and the classroom can be bilingual when needed, using both Icelandic and English as languages of instruction. In recent years, Shelmerdine's *Introduction to Latin* (2013) has been used in the beginners' course (KLM101G Latin I), replacing *Wiley's Real Latin* (Maltby & Belcher 2013), which was used for a few years. The textbook is covered from beginning to end in the beginners' course in the autumn semester and is followed by a selection of Latin prose in KLM201G Latin II in the spring semester. The spring semester course is intended to achieve four main objectives: to reinforce the students' understanding of Latin and their grasp of Latin grammar, to introduce them to authentic Latin texts, to give them an appreciation of variation in style and sentence structure, and to enhance reading techniques and strategies.

Instructors have often found it useful to point out, exaggerate even, the similarities between the grammar and syntax of Greek and Latin on the one hand and Icelandic grammar and syntax on the other. This is thought to benefit students because it gives them something to which to relate, not unlike when the etymology of cognates or of borrowed words is used to help students learn vocabulary. After all, there are indeed a number of similar grammatical and syntactical features in Icelandic, the native language of the vast majority of students, and the conceptual scheme originally used to describe Icelandic grammar is derived from classical grammar. Linguists, however, have for decades increasingly deviated from applying classical grammatical theory to Icelandic, because it is considered in many ways deficient, turning instead to modern linguistic theories in order to describe more accurately the complexities of Icelandic grammar and syntax. The majority of graduates in comparative linguistics, however, will have little or no knowledge of the classical languages. Furthermore, there is less and less emphasis on teaching Icelandic grammar and syntax to children at the compulsory and secondary level. As a result, students of the classical languages today may well be less likely to benefit from speaking Icelandic, a language that shares many features with Greek and Latin, than they were thirty to fifty years ago. This, however, is speculation and has not been studied. On the contrary, it might be argued that students benefit from the study of classical languages precisely because it is apt to furnish them with increased awareness and depth of understanding of their own language.

During the last decade, at the university level, there has been a trend to reduce emphasis on summative assessment with greater emphasis placed instead on formative assessment; and in recent years pre-recorded lectures have been used increasingly, freeing up time in the classroom for other activities. During Covid-19 lockdowns in 2020–2022, teaching migrated online. This deprived instructors of the use of whiteboards during class meetings. In KLM201G Latin II this fact was countered with the use of PowerPoint, which could easily be shared on screen in Microsoft Teams. Reading techniques and strategies could be discussed by highlighting different elements of the texts so that they visually 'pop out' so to speak, e.g. conjunctions, grammatical subjects and main verbs, main verbs and several direct objects, several accusative and infinitive constructions depending on a single main verb, main verbs and verbs in dependent clauses following the sequence of tenses, etc. Since slides can easily be shared with students, which may be useful for review purposes, they remain in use and continue to be shared after teaching returned from cyberspace to the physical classroom.

Teacher training

In Iceland, certified teachers at the primary or secondary level must have either a Master's degree in education or they may earn a Teacher Certificate in addition to a Master's degree in their field of study. By and large, instructors in Classics, at the secondary level as well as at the university, have graduate degrees in Classics and have all studied abroad. The University of Iceland does not have a graduate programme in Classics, nor is Classics taught at any other university in Iceland. Moreover, the University does not offer Master of Teaching degrees (MT) or a Master of Education degree (MEd) in Classics, although such degrees are offered for several other languages in the Faculty of Languages and Cultures within the School of Humanities as well as within the School of Education. An MT degree is offered in History in the Faculty of Philosophy, History and Archaeology, which may very well prepare teachers to teach non-language-related classical subjects at the upper secondary level, e.g. ancient history or classical civilization. The University, on the other hand, does offer to its faculty a postgraduate diploma (30 ECTS) in Teaching Studies for Higher Education as a form of professional development. Although much therein is applicable to the teaching of Classics, there is no available training specifically in the teaching of Classics.

Cooperation

No classical organization exists in Iceland yet. The University of Iceland has an informal classical colloquium which is intended to bolster dialogue among scholars interested in classical topics who are spread out in different faculties within the University. Teachers from the upper secondary level (i.e. Menntaskólinn í Reykjavík) have been invited and have actively participated, but contact and communication between the upper secondary level and the University, albeit genial, have remained informal.

Conclusion

The Classics community in Iceland remains small but stable. Translations of classical literature continue to be published very gradually and thus become available to the public. But much important work remains to be done, such as making available dictionaries and grammars in Icelandic. Lack of resources in Icelandic and lack of funding indeed pose a challenge. Graduate students must still study abroad, and currently there are two Icelandic students working to complete their PhDs in the UK. This is invaluable to the Classics community. However, equally important for the survival of Classics in Iceland is a different kind of success story, *viz.* the graduates who upon completion of their degrees in Classics go on to work various kinds of jobs; because ultimately the survival of Classics depends on a convincing answer to the question, 'What can I do with a degree in Classics?' Over and above the lack of resources and the lack of funding, this is the most difficult challenge we face.

References

Ármannson, K. (1994a), *Latnesk lestrarbók*, Reykjavík: Mál & menning.

Ármannson, K. (1994b), *Latnesk málfræði*, Reykjavík: Mál & menning.

Balme, M. and J. Morwood (2006), *Oxford Latin Course, Part III*, Oxford: Oxford University Press.

Balme, M., G. Lawall and J. Morwood (2016), *Athenaze*, Oxford: Oxford University Press.

Diggle, J. (2021), *The Cambridge Greek Lexicon*, Cambridge: Cambridge University Press.

Gram, H. and J. Árnason (1994), *Nucleus Latinitatis, qvo pleræqve Romani sermonis voces, ex classicis auctoribus aureæ argenteæqve ætatis, ordine etymologico adductæ, & interpretatione vernacula expositæ comprehenduntur, in usum scholæ Schalholtinæ*, edited by G. Kvaran and F. Magnússon, Reykjavík: Orðabók Háskólans.

Liddell, H. and R. Scott (2001), *An Intermediate Greek–English Lexicon*, Oxford: Clarendon Press.

Maltby, R. and K. Belcher (2013), *Wiley's Real Latin: Learning Latin from the Source*, Oxford: Wiley-Blackwell.

Mastronarde, D. (2013), *Introduction to Attic Greek*, Berkeley, CA: University of California Press.

Menntamálaráðuneytið (1999), Aðalnámskrá framhaldsskóla: Erlend tungumál. Menntamálaráðuneyti. Available online: https://www.stjornarradid.is/media/menntamalaraduneyti-media/media/ritogskyrslur/aferlendtungumal.pdf (accessed 19 November 2023).

Ministry of Education, Science and Culture (2012), 'The Icelandic National Curriculum Guide for Upper Secondary Schools – General Section', Mennta- og menningarmálaráðuneyti. Available online: https://www.stjornarradid.is/media/menntamalaraduneyti-media/media/ritogskyrslur/adskr_frsk_ens_2012.pdf (accessed 19 November 2023).

Ministry of Education, Science and Culture (2014), 'The Icelandic National Curriculum Guide for Compulsory Schools – with Subject Areas. Mennta- og menningarmálaráðuneyti. Available online: https://www.stjornarradid.is/media/menntamalaraduneyti-media/media/ritogskyrslur/adalnrsk_greinask_ens_2014.pdf (accessed 19 November 2023).

Morwood, J. and J. Taylor (2002), *The Pocket Oxford Classical Greek Dictionary*, Oxford: Oxford University Press.

Shelmerdine, S. (2013), *Introduction to Latin*, London: Focus Publishing.

Sigurjónsson, H. Þ. (2021), 'Grikkland hið forna', Menntamálastofnun. Available online: https://mms.is/ (accessed 19 November 2023).

Simpson, D. (1968), *Cassell's Latin Dictionary: Latin–English, English–Latin*, London: Cassell.

Taylor, J. (2016), *Greek to GCSE 1*, London: Bloomsbury Academic.

IRELAND

Louise Maguire

Introduction

It is tempting to begin a discussion of the classical subjects in Ireland with allusions to a romanticized past. A past where Greek and Latin were taught in informal and illegal schools to Catholic children excluded by law from education, or to focus on the formalization of education under the Irish Free State in 1922 and the subsequent church-controlled dominance and focus on Latin, and even the first four decades of a nascent nation where the elite had far greater access to classical subjects, and Greek and Latin held the key to university education. However, we will restrict our view to the highly formalized and democratized system in place since Donogh O'Malley, the then Minister for Education (1965–8), in an unauthorized speech, promised free second-level education for all children in Ireland. This was followed quickly by the realization of this goal in 1967, and the widespread centralization of curriculum and policy across the education sector (Fleming & Harford 2014). The widening of access to education saw a sharp decline in classical subjects, but we will see in this chapter how the trend has been reversed, and how new life is being breathed into the subjects.

Education in Ireland is currently divided into four categories, Early Years, Primary, Secondary, and Third-Level. School is compulsory from age six to sixteen, or until three years of secondary have been completed. In practice most children attend school for thirteen or fourteen years, from age four or five, to eighteen, and the state funds one year of Early Years and all of primary and secondary education. Although there are private offerings at all levels, every child has a constitutional right to a free education.

Status and trends of classical subjects

There is no formal provision for classical subjects within Early Years, or at primary level, but Greek myths commonly feature in 'readers' and textbooks as part of the study of English Language. In addition, anecdotal evidence from teachers around the country, and across educational contexts, indicates that children are reading ancient-world inspired texts such as *Percy Jackson* (Riordan 2005) and *The Eagle of the Ninth* (Sutcliff 1954) before age thirteen. In some cases, we have had children present at second-level having read *The Song of Achilles* (Miller 2017) and books by historians Tom Holland and Mary Beard.

At second-level there are two formal stages. The Junior Cycle, which leads to a Profile of Achievement, and Senior Cycle, which can be structured as the Leaving Certificate Vocational

Programme, the Leaving Certificate Applied, or the Established Leaving Certificate, which is the route taken by the vast majority of students. Classical subjects are available within both of these cycles, though only within the Established Leaving Certificate at Senior Cycle. The tri-partite structure at Senior Cycle is currently under review, with moves to allow more interconnections across the three models.

O'Malley's reforms of 1967 had unintended consequences for the classical subjects at second-level as the dominance of the church in curricular decision-making was (somewhat) reduced. At the same time the Second Vatican Council (1962–5) facilitated Mass being said in the vernacular, greatly reducing the presence of Latin in the everyday life of a majority of the population. A final blow was struck when Greek or Latin were dropped as a requirement for entry into university in 1973. The numbers are stark: in 1972, 9,106 students presented for Leaving Certificate Latin; this has reduced to eighty students in 2023.

The decline in numbers studying classical languages fuelled an idea that the subjects were academically challenging and socially elite. Classical Studies, a non-language course, was introduced in the 1980s at both junior and senior levels, with the hope of reversing this trend and perception. It was first examined in 1983 at Intermediate Certificate, which became Junior Certificate, and then Junior Cycle. Despite a review raising concerns in 2004 and citing 'lack of awareness about the subject' and 'perceived difficulty' as possible reasons for the decline in numbers, the course remained largely unchanged until 2020 when it was re-imagined as Classics. Thankfully, as a result of years of lobbying by the Classical Association of Ireland Teachers subject association, and strong support from many of our colleagues at third-level, the subjects have undergone significant change in recent years, with two fully new courses now being taught, and two in the final stages of approval.

This new Common Level subject combines the old subjects Classical Studies, Latin and Greek. The course structure is unique across Junior Cycle. All learners take Strand 1, which covers myth and daily life in ancient Rome and Greece, and then can choose Strand 2, the Classical Studies route, where they learn about the city of Rome and the Homeric world, or Strand 3, where they can study Latin or Greek. The approach to the languages has been completely overhauled. While they still allow for a challenge for strong learners, the common level approach has allowed much greater differentiation and accessibility. We have moved completely away from rote learning and into a space where students can learn to parse, decode and translate at a level in line with other Junior Cycle languages. Anecdotally this seems to be greatly improving retention into Senior Cycle, as well as broadening the appeal of Latin and Greek to a wider range of abilities.

In addition to a terminal examination, students undertake two Classroom Based Assessments (CBAs), one in each of the second and third year. Students and teachers alike are particularly in favour of CBA1, which allows students to retell or recreate a myth in any format they wish. We have had everything from traditional written accounts to graphic novels, jigsaws, digital creations, myths relocated to Irish secondary schools, sculptures and a 1980s Synth rock ballad about Athena and Arachne. The second CBA is a study of an ancient monument for Strand 2, or a portfolio of learning for Strand 3. The introduction of CBA2 has been postponed on a rolling basis to allow for schools recovering from the upheaval of the pandemic. The final exam is a well laid out, multi-faceted exam which allows for differentiation across the whole spectrum of candidates. The new Junior Cycle is now fully embedded and we have had two full exam sittings. The exam has an excellent layout which builds from lower to higher order tasks, and is also visually inviting and reassuring.

At Junior Cycle there are only four compulsory subjects with a terminal exam: English, Gaelige (Irish), Mathematics and History. Various subjects falling under the umbrella of wellbeing, for instance PE, are also compulsory, but not examined. With stiff competition amongst subjects, Classics had just 1.2 per cent of candidates, and is relatively stable when compared to combined numbers for the Classical Studies, Latin and Greek in previous years. Typically, it takes 'new' subjects some time to embed and anecdotally we are seeing increased numbers choosing the subject this year. The three-year span of Junior Cycle also means a delay in seeing a real difference in student numbers, as exam candidature is the most reliable figure.

Leaving Certificate Classical Studies was first examined in 1985, and far from being the hoped-for renaissance, saw numbers plummet from 1,585 in 1995 to 657 in 2016. The Leaving Certificate Classical Studies curriculum review noted that the subject had been 'declining steadily over the last twenty years'. Upon completion of the new Junior Cycle Specification attention was turned to Leaving Certificate Classical Studies, with an understanding that the classical languages would be reformed immediately thereafter. Progress on the languages has been markedly slow – of which more later.

The new Classical Studies course has been well received. Students study four inter-related, interdependent strands: the world of heroes; drama and spectacle; power and identity; gods and humans. The new specification allows for research and higher order thinking, while also giving access to popular topics such as Roman gladiatorial games and Julius Caesar. While there is always a delay in seeing how a new course will be received, and the numbers who ultimately chose to take it, anecdotally subject teachers are reporting a significant increase in the number of incoming fifth years who have chosen to study the subject for their Leaving Certificate. In a welcome turn of events, it seems that Classical Studies is drawing students from history, as there is less focus on essays produced in an exam setting. With a two-and-a-half-hour exam it is much more student friendly. There are two essays and source questions at higher level and one essay and source questions at ordinary level. In addition, a newly introduced research essay carries 20 per cent, and is submitted months before the terminal exam. It gives students a real insight into the research element of studying the ancient world. It also allows Classical Studies to compete in a real way with History and Religion, both of which had the advantage of introducing a pre-submitted component years before Classical Studies did. The 2023 sitting saw a marginal increase in numbers, but, as above, typically it takes 'new' subjects some time to embed, and after years of decline even static numbers are to be welcomed.

The new Classics and Classical Studies specifications are both structured around learning outcomes, with no set material at Junior Cycle, and minimal prescribed material at Senior Cycle. This move was mandated by the Department of Education and Skills (DES) and proved a daunting ask for students and teachers alike. However, with both subjects now live and examined at least once we see a little less trepidation. Junior Cycle proved an easier win with students as they are younger and it is a low-stakes exam. At Senior Cycle however, with a terminal examination that directly ties to entry to third level, there has been slower acceptance amongst both students and teachers. There are no guaranteed questions, nor is there any clarity around how many marks each section holds. An admirable attempt by the DES to prevent 'teaching to the exam' is oddly coupled with an exam that is a high-stakes gamble to earn a place at third-level. It seems in some instances that students have only accepted the situation out of trust in experienced, established teachers. The fact that all students sit the same exam also gave rise to some camaraderie as teachers and students realized that whether it was a rising tide or a sinking ship, we were all swimming together. The (forced) 'early adoption' of new trends may prove to be a blessing, though, as Latin and Greek, along with Arabic, will be the first specifications to allow for 40 per cent pre-submitted work, a huge advantage in appealing to students.

Official numbers from 2022 indicate a significant spread (unpublished numbers from the Central Statistics Office, provided in private correspondence). There are thirty-one fee charging schools, six schools within the Delivering Equality of Education in Schools programme (designed to target communities with the greatest risk of educational disadvantage, hereafter DEIS schools), and an additional forty-eight non-fee-charging schools. In addition, we have noticed a trend whereby Classics/Classical Studies is being offered in new Educate Together schools. Educate Together is a patron body which is relatively new to second-level provision, characterized by, amongst other things, no religious instruction. The embracing of Classical subjects in these schools is a welcome, but unsurprising, development. The subject specifications and content of Classics/Classical Studies offer an excellent base from which to explore ideas of ethics, philosophy, society and the context of the ancient world, and offer an excellent curricular alternative where religion is not offered.

Collaborative activities

The coalface of widening access to classical subjects has been championed in recent years by Dr Bridget Martin (www.accesscassics.ie). Martin is Director of the Access Classics outreach programme run by Dr Martin based in University College Dublin (UCD). Created by Tasneem Filaih, Martin and Dr Christoper Farrel, the enthusiastic team started this project with the intention of bringing Classical Studies and the classical languages to more, and a wider range, of students. Access Classics' three core aims are designed to address the low levels of uptake of classical subjects and the knock-on effect this, combined with Brexit and a subsequent loss of international students, has had at third-level. These aims are:

- to encourage and facilitate the uptake of Classics, Latin and Greek at second- and third-level;

- to work with schools that currently do not or cannot offer Classics as part of their official curriculum to provide their students opportunities to explore the ancient world; and

- to provide support for second-level teachers of Classics through teaching resources and individualized support.

The award-winning Access Classics was piloted on this premise in 2019, but has grown to be much more than a university outreach programme's usual remit. It won the University College Dublin Values in Action award in 2020 and was a finalist in the Best Education Outreach award at the 2021 Education Awards. The success of the pilot programme across three diverse schools allowed Martin and her team to expand to other schools, and to date they have connected with over forty schools. It allows students to visit the UCD Classical Museum, take part in hands-on sessions, dip their toes into the classical languages and much more. Sessions can take place remotely, and the team are sometimes able to visit schools. The ongoing project focuses particularly on introducing students in DEIS schools to Classics, and Martin's personal commitment to ensuring equality of access is proving a great success and her inextinguishable enthusiasm, has reignited belief amongst teachers in the value and possibility of bringing our subjects to a wider cohort of children.

Teacher training and professional development

Several universities in Ireland offer undergraduate and postgraduate degrees across a range of classical disciplines. But only two offer a Professional Master's in Education (PME) in Classics, and no university offers a PME in, or even a module on the pedagogy of, classical languages. The registration of teachers is a tightly controlled process in Ireland. A combination of a crisis in teacher recruitment, very few options for taking the PME in Classics within the country, scant recognition of foreign teaching qualifications, prohibitive costs, and a two-year time commitment on top of a basic degree has led to a sharp decline in new teachers coming on board. Nonetheless, the Classics Association of Ireland (CAI) continues to promote the profession, to support new teachers, and to encourage those with classical subjects in their degree to teach it along with their other subjects (which is permitted under the complex and myriad rules governing the profession).

The Classical Association of Ireland Teachers (CAIT) is the subject association for teachers of classical subjects in Ireland. The association is run entirely on a voluntary basis, by an annually elected committee. Originally conceived of as a branch of the CAI, the teacher's association now operates independently as a sister organization. The CAI remains as a group for Classics devotees organizing events and trips, while the purpose of the CAIT is to provide tangible support to those teaching the classical subjects at second-level. Initially the CAIT focused heavily on advocating for, and contributing to curricular reform, while providing ongoing support in the form of teaching resources, ongoing informal professional development opportunities, and an annual conference.

The annual conference is a low-cost two-day event of workshops, talks and resource sharing. The most recent years have focused on the introduction of the new specifications. As the vast majority of teachers of the subjects are operating solo in their schools it provided a much-needed opportunity to share best practice, discuss new developments, and as an informal check-in. As the committee is run by active teachers the events are always tailored to the most immediate needs of a given year. Some funding is available through the Teachers Professional Network, but the association also relies on legacy funding to keep the event as low-cost as possible. The event is always free for teachers undertaking the PME.

In addition to recognizing that teachers need support, the CAIT understands that students are often in small classes, or in a minority in their schools. With this in mind, in an attempt to foster reassurance and peer support the association runs a Senior Cycle revision day for both Classical Studies and Latin every year, with support from University College Dublin and the University of Dublin. While these are important academically the real benefits are in bringing the students together and giving them an insight into third-level. The association also runs an annual competition, the Young Classicists Award, open to all ages as groups or individuals, and an Ides of March table quiz open to all schools. The quiz, held as close as possible to the Ides of March, has proven to be popular with over 200 students attending the most recent one.

The advocacy for and implementation of reform of the specifications merits an article in itself but suffice to say the CAIT, having successfully ushered in the much-needed new specifications, are on the cusp of welcoming new courses in Latin and Greek at Senior Cycle. With this in place the association has continued to provide and expand its resources and supports for teachers: PDF textbooks, podcasts, resource-sharing evenings, online classes for teachers to upskill in Latin and Greek, an online forum, and a central repository for sample questions in the works. All of these resources are provided free of charge.

The landscape for classical subjects in Ireland has shifted dramatically in the last five years. Teachers have faced an uphill struggle to get new curricula in place, and were faced with the additional challenges of widespread changes in both the formatting of courses and the expectations in assessments, all while weathering a pandemic. We have adapted though, and would encourage teachers in other jurisdictions to advocate for change where it is needed and to be open to the challenges of reform. Our discipline is endlessly adaptable and can continue to enrich the lives of our students no matter how many times we need to adjust and adapt. *Ad astra per aspera.*

References

Fleming, B. and J. Harford (2014), 'Irish educational policy in the 1960s: a decade of transformation', *History of Education*, 43 (5): 635–56.

Miller, M. (2017), *The Song of Achilles*, London: Bloomsbury.

Riordan, R. (2005), *Percy Jackson and the Olympians* [Book series 2005–23], London: Puffin.

Sutcliff, R. (1954), *The Eagle of the Ninth*, Oxford: Oxford University Press.

ITALY

Daniela Canfarotta

Introduction

Today, teaching ancient languages involves taking on a complex role, which requires knowledge of multiple factors. The famous Austrian philosopher Ludwig Wittgenstein said: 'The borders of my language are the borders of my world.' The more languages a person knows, the wider the boundaries of the world will be for them. Knowledge of classical languages gives a diachronic, profound gaze on reality. It helps a person to grasp its meaning and depth, because it forces them to deal with the new all the time, even though this 'newness' happened centuries ago. Tradition and innovation are constantly present in the study of Latin and Greek. How true this is will be seen by my analysis of the history of teaching classical languages in Italy.

Education system in Italy

Education in Italy is regulated by the Ministry of Education, University and Research (MIUR). Schools may be public or private. According to MIUR (2022), in total there are 8.5 million students enrolled in Italy, 10 per cent of whom are foreigners.

The Italian system has different levels of study: *Scuola primaria* (Primary school, ages 6–11) and *Scuola secondaria* (First Grade Secondary school, for students aged 11–14 years, and

Second Grade, for ages 14–19). From the 2010/11 school year, the reform of the Second Grade came into force. The Second Grade is now divided into five-year courses: High Schools (*licei*), Technical and Professional Institutes, and Vocational Education and Training Courses (IFP) under regional jurisdiction. The Technical and Professional Institute is a type of school which provides technical preparation and a professional qualification for access to various sectors of work.

Second Grade secondary schools include six types of *liceo* (High School): classical, scientific, linguistic, human sciences, artistic and musical. They are the most popular choice amongst both male and female students: a year ago, 57.8 per cent of students preferred a *liceo* compared to technical and professional institutes.

Latin and Greek in the school curriculum

In 2021/22 enrolments in the *licei* decreased from 6.5 per cent to 6.2 per cent, 26 per cent of enrolments were in scientific *licei* (a decrease from 26.9 per cent the previous year) and 7.4 per cent opted for the linguistics *licei*. The human sciences *licei* has grown from 9.7 per cent to 10.3 per cent. On the other hand, technical institutes have risen to 30.7 per cent of enrolments, from 30.3 per cent a year ago. Interest in professional institutes also grew, by almost one percentage point, from 11.9 per cent to 12.7 per cent.

As for gender differences, most of the girls choose a *liceo*, with a preference for the scientific (26 per cent). Technical institutes follow (21 per cent) and other high schools (20 per cent). Professional institutes are at 17 per cent. The proportion for the classical *licei* has fallen to 15 per cent. Boys, on the other hand, prefer technical institutes, with 43 per cent enrolled. This is followed by the scientific *licei* (24 per cent), professional institutes (21 per cent) and other high schools (6.5 per cent). Classical *licei*, on the other hand, stands at 6 per cent, nine percentage points fewer than for girls.

Optionally, in lower secondary school, it is possible to introduce the study of Latin to enhance the legacy of the Greek and Latin tradition, understood not only as a heritage of the past, but as a key to interpreting and reading the contemporary world.

The *liceo* provides a generic education of five years, in preparation for access to university. It is currently one of the last types of school in Europe where it is compulsory to teach Latin and Greek languages and literature. The teaching of Latin and Greek differs in the number of hours per week in classical, scientific, and human sciences high schools. Latin is taught:

- five hours a week in the first two years and four hours a week in the last three years of the classical *liceo*;
- three hours a week in the five-year period of the scientific *liceo*;
- three hours a week in the first two years and two hours a week in the last three years of the human sciences *liceo*; and
- two hours a week in the first two years of the linguistic *liceo*.

Greek is only offered in the classical *liceo*, with four hours a week in the first two years, and three hours a week in the last three years. Table 6 shows that the number of hours per week dedicated to the study of Classics is higher than that of all other subjects.

Table 6. Organization of subjects of the classical *liceo*

Subject per week	First biennium (hours)		Second biennium (hours)		Last year (hours)
	1st year	2nd year	3rd year	4th year	5th year
Language and Italian literature	4	4	4	4	4
Language and Latin culture	5	5	4	4	4
Language and Greek culture	4	4	3	3	3
Language and foreign culture	3	3	3	3	3
History	2	2	3	3	3
Geography	1	1	–	–	–
Mathematics	3	3	2	2	2
Philosophy	–	–	3	3	3
Physics	–	–	2	2	2
Natural Sciences	2	2	2	2	2
Physical education	2	2	2	2	2
Religion or another alternative subject	1	1	1	1	1
Total hours	**27**	**27**	**31**	**31**	**31**

Source: © Daniela Canfarotta 2024 starting from MIUR 2010, Annex C.

Classical subjects as a contribution to the education of young people in Italy

In Italy classical subjects have been perceived as a contribution to the education of young people in different ways, depending on the historical period. Education reforms have mirrored these perceptions. Originally, the classical *liceo* derived from the single secondary school established by the Casati Law in 1859, later reorganized in the Gentile Reform of 1923 and the Bottai Reform of 1940. Although it was the Casati Law that ensured that literary and humanistic themes prevailed in the *liceo*, it was Gentile's approach that made classical culture the essential element of a prestigious school. Gentile followed the neorealist philosophy, of which Benedetto Croce was the greatest exponent. The neorealist philosophers considered that literary and historical disciplines were the only ones capable of providing true knowledge. That is why only graduates at the classical *liceo* had free enrolment in *any* faculty of the university, while those who came from the scientific secondary school could not enrol in any of the letters or jurisprudence.

Bottai's reform (1940) established the three-year lower grade upper school and the classical high school was structured as a five-year school. In 1969, access to the university was liberalized and enrolment in each faculty was granted to all high school graduates (Briguglio 2011).

In the reforms of the last twenty years, the Ministers of Education have tried to update the curriculum of the classical high school to bring it closer to changed sentiments and different cultural context.

(a) The Berlinguer Reform (MIUR 2000) oriented the curriculum offer towards a more multicultural society. The Minister supported the need for a radical renewal of the classical high school.

(b) The Moratti Reform (MIUR 2003) had a strong personalized orientation and gave new importance to teachers' professional training.

(c) The Gelmini Reform (MIUR 2010) instituted the competence level model, began experimentation with work-experience placements, and valued professional training even more (Briguglio 2011).

(d) The Renzi Reform (MIUR 2015) included several measures aimed at improving student competences, school management practices, the role of teachers, and the transition of students from school to work (OECD 2019).

Therefore, key citizenship competences (European Council 2018) are expected to be certified in the second year of the classical *liceo*. These help students to become aware of their growth in transversal, metacognitive and relational competences, and they are also useful for employment.

According to the profile of classical *liceo*, at the end of the course of study, in addition to achieving common learning outcomes, students must:

(a) recognize the value of tradition as a possibility of critical understanding of the present;

(b) acquire knowledge of classical languages for the understanding of Greek and Latin texts, through the comprehensive study of their linguistic structures (morphosyntactic, lexical, semantic);

(c) know how to argue, interpret complex texts and solve different types of problems, even distant from the disciplines specifically studied; and

(d) be able to reflect critically on the forms of knowledge and mutual relationships, and to locate scientific thinking even within a humanist dimension.

The challenge in classrooms is to maintain a balance between the dimension of knowledge and of competences and not to separate them. In fact, if the former prevails the teacher acquires the role of 'dispenser' of knowledge and this does not end up giving personal meaning to what the student learns, because he/she will do so by memorizing it and then forgetting it. But, if only the competences are highlighted, the risk is of promoting a utilitarian approach, which neglects the student's freedom and responsibility (Castoldi 2009). The approach, therefore, is very important, because it influences the type of didactics that the teacher will choose in class.

Approaches for the study of Latin and Greek

The debate on teaching classical languages has often focused on finding the best method. The main linguistic-grammatical approaches and their applications in the teaching of Latin and Greek will be analysed below.

1. The grammatical-translation approach (Alcalde Mato 2011) is based on the deductive-normative learning of the grammatical rules of the language. It consists of the study of morphology and syntax, and the translation of sentences and passages suitably chosen,

because it considers translation as the necessary and indispensable moment for the understanding of a text. It is the most widespread method in Italian classical *liceo* classrooms because it starts from the text and focuses on it at a morphosyntactic and lexical level. Starting from an exact understanding of the Latin language, the student arrives at the best translation into Italian. The quality of this final rendering is one of the dimensions of the evaluation of the translation from the Latin/Greek to the Italian language. The most popular manuals of this model are *Corso di lingua latina. Dalla grammatica alla traduzione* (Pepe & Golin 2005) and *Il mio latino* (Tantucci & Roncoroni 2018). However, Mangiavini and Bettoni (2009) state that linear thinking and a transmissive logic are no longer useful for the challenges of the twenty-first century.

2. The natural model (Balbo 2007) proposes that language is alive, spoken and aimed at the communication of meanings. The approach is mainly inductive: grammar must be 'discovered' – that is a point of arrival. The teacher 'tells' the culture and reads some texts which offer ideas for themed conversations.

3. The 'nature method' or inductive-contextual approach of *Latino Vivo* [Living Latin] by Ørberg (2010) consists of explaining the norm through its use and not vice versa. In this way, it emphasizes the path of discovery that the student must follow in order to master the learning of the rule. It is an inductive method. Generally, the person who applies it does not consider it appropriate to use the dictionary and it is preferable that the student memorize the terms he finds in the use of the different texts. The grammar rules, illustrated in the manual *Lingua Latina per se illustrata* (Ørberg 2010) are established in Latin. An interesting innovation is the use of *Pensa* [Reflection-exercises], which are exercises of reflection and linguistic manipulation in each chapter, in which Latin questions are asked about the text read and the answer is always requested in Latin. This proposal is practicable even if a different grammatical model is used in the classroom. This practice allows you to apply the concept of case, pay attention to verbal morphology and, sometimes, to reformulate sentences, consolidating the lexicon, the true *punctum dolens* of teaching classical languages. The nature model is distinguished from the 'natural' method because it provides for the deepening of morphosyntactic knowledge without going through the mediation of the mother tongue (Balbo 2007). Among the objections posed to the nature method, the following stand out: we work on artificial and non-authored texts; using Latin as a communicative language is anti-historical; the subdivision of grammatical knowledge does not follow the traditional ministerial programmes (according to which grammar should be known within the first two years of high school); and translation is placed in the background (contrary to what traditional programmes envisage). Others argue that the effectiveness of this method can only be verified if this approach is followed for the entire five years. By contrast, it often happens that a teacher adopts the model for the first two years and then in the last three a new teacher takes over who adopts the grammar-translation method.

4. The valential grammar approach (Tesnière 1959/2001) follows a more descriptive-functional method, based on the heuristic definition of functional syntactic relationships. It is based on two principles: the sentence is considered as a unit of

observation, and it identifies the verb as the central constituent element of the sentence. The method offers weak and strong points: the fact that the notional definitions of the grammatical categories are excluded to replace them with definitions of a syntactic type is certainly positive as it focuses on identifying the relationships between the various elements of the sentence. However, the description of the morphological part is weak. An interesting manual with this approach is *Ratio* (Azzoni et al. 2012).

5. The neo-comparative approach (Ricucci 2015) makes it possible to improve metalinguistic reflection with a contrastive approach to the descriptive systems of languages, to find elements of convergence between them.

6. The Martinet (1972) functionalist model considers language to have a 'double linguistic articulation', because it divides the linguistic choices that a sender makes into two categories. On the one hand, we have the units carrying meaning (moneme: lexical, if we consider the root which contains the information of meaning common to a series of elements and is defined as lexeme; and grammatical, if we consider the functions of the cases and the verbal endings, for which we speak of morpheme), while on the other hand we have the sound dimension (and we consider units that have no meaning, the phonemes). The advantage of this method lies in the fact that languages are considered as a tool for communication, i.e. for the transmission of experience from one person to another. However, this model is more suited to the teaching of modern languages because it focuses on the synchronic perspective of language study, whereas it is less suitable for teaching an ancient language, which starts from the diachronic perspective. The most important supporter of this model is Ghiselli, who wrote the new edition of *Il libro di latino* (1995).

7. Models based on the generative-transformational grammar of Chomsky (1965) have helped to explain, for example, why terms applied to the same case can perform different functions; other advantages concern the clearer explanation of aspects of the analysis of the sentence and of some grammatical constructs. Among the most problematic aspects of this approach, we must underline an excessive abstractness in the structural descriptions. Furthermore, it seems that the productive linguistic competence is favoured more than the receptive one towards which the teaching of Latin in Italy tends today (Giordano Rampioni 2010).

8. The models of 'brief eclectic teaching' combine characteristics of valential grammar and contrastive methodology. Therefore, analogies and differences between Latin and Italian are highlighted and a lot of importance is given to the lexicon, both in a synchronic and diachronic perspective. Latin language and civilization are often integrated, and the lexicon is presented in a functional perspective for the study of culture (Cova 1995). The most popular examples of this model are: *Lingua e cultura latina* (Flocchini et al. 2020), Diotti's *Lingua magistra* (2008) and Diotti and Diotti's *Plane discere* (2014), *Il latino* (Dionigi et al. 2011) and *Il nuovo latino a colori* (Conte & Ferri 2014). Among the advantages is its cost-effectiveness: the grammar course can be condensed into two years, perhaps dealing with and clarifying the syntax of the cases at the beginning of the third year. Among the weak points, we highlight the presence of what have become very well-known texts as, over the years, students have

had the opportunity to share the translations and solutions of the exercises on online platforms. This now makes it necessary to shift the weight of assessment not so much to a good translation, but to a correct morphological and syntactic analysis of the sentence.

As can be seen from the synthetic analysis, each didactic model has its advantages and disadvantages. Probably the best solution for the good teacher of classical languages is to exploit the potential of each one.

During the Covid-19 pandemic, teachers were forced to use technology in ordinary teaching. New experiments have been born that focus more and more on students as protagonists of learning (Canfarotta & Lojacono 2022; Monella 2020). The need to renew teacher training has emerged overwhelmingly.

Teacher training

To become a Latin and Greek professor in Italy, the following steps must be followed: (a) obtain a five-year degree in Classical Literature; (b) participate in a public competition to obtain the qualification to teach Latin and Greek; (c) complete a teaching trial year in a public school. After all this, the teacher is hired in the school for an indefinite period.

The most serious problem of the Italian teacher is that career advancement is rather poor and the salary low. A comparison of data from European countries shows that in Italy the salary differences between the beginning and the end of the career are small (European Commission 2022). In fact, salary increase is based on years of service or based on the number of assignments carried out in school, in addition to the traditional eighteen hours of classroom instruction per week.

In recent times, the idea of the teacher-researcher is making headway. With serious scientific preparation, a teacher-researcher can document their own didactic and educational innovation (Canfarotta & Lojacono 2022). However, educational policies do not provide for additional compensation for those teachers who carry out research, which means them dedicating extra time beyond their ordinary teaching commitments.

School collaborations

Collaboration between schools is an aspect that in Italy has progressively intensified over the last ten years, in the belief that this is a benefit for both individuals and communities (Valli et al. 2018). The specific nature of these relationships, called 'purpose networks', can vary a lot, both in relation to the subjects involved (school and school, school and local associations, school and political institutions) and in relation to the reasons which lead to the creation of a network in the first place. An important change in this line will take place in the coming months with the adoption of the Guidance Guidelines, relating to the 'Reform of the guidance system', in the context of Mission 4.1 of the National Recovery and Resilience Plan, funded by the European Union – Next Generation EU (Ministerial Decree 22 December 2022, No. 328). It is an ambitious project to bridge the mismatch between what is learned at school and the world of work. It establishes that teachers of every subject use orientation teaching, which develops students' orientation competences, as well as disciplinary ones. The orientation competences are those that enable you to know how to govern your own training experience (analyse, predict, plan, decide, evaluate) (UNESCO 1970).

From an orientation perspective, the didactic activity starts from the experiences of the students, rather than with the transmission of knowledge, and is enhanced by the teaching laboratory, flexible times and spaces. A vertical curriculum will be organized which will link the orientation objectives of the different school levels (preschool, primary, secondary, university and tertiary education). This change could have interesting repercussions on the teaching of Latin and Greek: students will be able to experience more directly that the skills they develop while studying classical languages are also useful for work.

For the diffusion of classical culture, the Italian Association of Classical Culture (AICC) was founded in 1897 in Florence. It is made up of university and school teachers, students and citizens who believe in the values of classical culture and is under the aegis of UNESCO. In recent years the activity of the Association has focused on the ever-wider involvement of schools. The hope is that classical culture can also be made known to students who do not usually study Greek and Latin.

Conclusion

Italy is the homeland of Latin culture and the main heir of the Greek one. At school, this is evidenced by the weekly number of hours dedicated to these subjects: as many as four types of high school out of the six existing in Italian secondary schools provide for the study of Latin and Greek, in different quantities and forms.

However, in recent years students have struggled to choose these subjects, because they are considered 'useless' compared to the real needs of contemporary society. The progressive reduction of the Latin and Greek classes is a real problem. Educational research, educational policies and teachers in the field have often highlighted this concern. The solution perhaps lies in a set of factors to be taken care of in the classical high school classrooms: didactic innovation (laboratory teaching and use of technologies), updating of contents (translating texts closer to the students' interests), more frequent visits to Italian archaeological sites, and relationship care between teachers and students (orientation teaching).

The hope is that recent education reforms and new teacher training will give new impetus to the teaching and learning of classical languages in Italy.

References

Alcalde Mato, N. (2011), 'Principales métodos de enseñanza de lenguas extranjeras en Alemania', *Revista de Lingüística y Lenguas Aplicadas*, 6 (1): 9–24.

Azzoni, L., B. Nanni and L. Montanari (2012), *Ratio. Un metodo per il latino*, Bari: Laterza Edizioni Scolastiche.

Balbo, A. (2007), *Insegnare Latino. Sentieri di ricerca per una didattica ragionevole*, Novara: UTET Università.

Briguglio, A. (2011), 'Dal ministero Berlinguer alla riforma Gelmini: note cursorie per riflettere sugli itinerari della formazione e dell'istruzione in Italia', *Quaderni di Intercultura*, 3: 1–25.

Canfarotta, D. and C. Lojacono (2022), 'Formative assessment and key competences for a conscious recovery after Covid-19: An Action-Research at a school in Italy to enhance reflection starting from mistakes', *Journal of Classics Teaching*, 24 (47): 72–80.

Castoldi, M. (2009), *Valutare le competenze. Percorsi e strumenti,* Roma: Carocci.

Chomsky, N. (1965), *Aspects of the Theory of Syntax,* Cambridge: The MIT Press.

Conte, G. and R. Ferri (2014), *Il nuovo latino a colori,* Milan: Mondadori Education.

Cova, P. (1995), 'Didattica breve e grammatica latina 1', *Nuova Secondaria*, 9: 69–71.

Dionigi, I., L. Morisi and E. Riganti (2011), *Il latino,* Bari: Edizioni Laterza.

Diotti, A. (2008), *Lingua magistra,* Milan: Edizioni Scolastiche Bruno Mondadori.

Diotti, A. and E. Diotti (2014), *Plane discere,* Milan: Edizioni Scolastiche Bruno Mondadori.

European Commission (2022), 'Teachers' and school heads' salaries and allowances in Europe – 2020/2021. Eurydice Facts and Figures', *European Commission/EACEA/Eurydice*, Luxembourg: Publications Office of the European Union.

European Council (2018), 'Recommendation on Key Competences for Lifelong Learning', *Official Journal of the European Union*, Brussels: European Council.

Flocchini, N., P. Bacci and M. Moscio (2020), *Lingua e cultura latina,* Milan: Rizzoli Education.

Ghiselli, A. and G. Concialini (1995), *Il libo di Latino,* Rome: Laterza.

Giordano Rampioni, A. (2010), *Manuale per l'insegnamento del Latino,* Bologna: Patron.

Mangiavini, M. and M. Bettoni (2009), 'Lingue classiche, complessità e competenze', *Interaction Design and Architecture(s) Journal – IxD&A*, 7–8: 48–50.

Martinet, A. (1972), *Elementi di linguistica generale,* Bari: Edizioni Laterza.

Ministerial Decree 22 December 2022, n. 328 (2022), 'Adoption of the Guidelines for guidance, relating to the reform 1.4 Reform of the guidance system'. Available online: https://www.miur.gov.it/-/decreto-ministeriale-n-328-del-22-dicembre-2022 (accessed 5 November 2023).

MIUR (2022), 'Iscrizioni all'anno scolastico 2022/2023'. Available online: https://www.miur.gov.it/-/iscrizioni-all-anno-scolastico-2022-2023-i-primi-dati-crescono-i-tecnici-e-i-professionali-il-56-6-degli-studenti-sceglie-i-licei (accessed 5 November 2023).

MIUR (2015), 'Legge 13 luglio 2015, n. 107. Riforma del sistema nazionale di istruzione e formazione e delega per il riordino delle disposizioni legislative vigenti.' Available online: https://www.gazzettaufficiale.it/eli/id/2015/07/15/15G00122/sg (accessed 5 November 2023).

MIUR (2010), 'Regolamento recante revisione dell'assetto ordinamentale, organizzativo e didattico dei licei.' Available online: https://www.gazzettaufficiale.it/gunewsletter/dettaglio.jsp?service=1&datagu=2010-06-15&task=dettaglio&numgu=137&redaz=010G0111&tmstp=1276687571279 (accessed 5 November 2023).

MIUR (2003), 'Legge 28 marzo 2003, n. 53 Delega al Governo per la definizione delle norme generali sull'istruzione e dei livelli essenziali delle prestazioni in materia di istruzione e formazione professionale.' Available online: https://www.gazzettaufficiale.it/eli/id/2003/04/02/003G0065/sg (accessed 5 November 2023).

MIUR (2000), 'Legge 10 febbraio 2000, n. 30. Legge-quadro in materia di riordino dei cicli dell'istruzione.' Available online: https://www.gazzettaufficiale.it/eli/id/2000/02/23/000G0063/sg (accessed 5 November 2023).

Monella, P. (2020), *Metodi digitali per l'insegnamento classico e umanistico,* Milan: EDUCatt.

OECD (2019), *OECD Skills Strategy 2019: Skills to Shape a Better Future,* Paris: OECD Publishing.

Ørberg, H. (2010*), Lingua Latina per se illustrata – Familia Romana,* Montella: Edizioni Accademia Vivarium Novum.

Pepe, L. and D. Golin (2005), *Corso di Lingua latino. Dalla grammatica alla traduzione*, Milan: Mondadori Education.

Ricucci, M. (2015), 'Ritorno al futuro: la riflessione metalinguistica tra latino e lingue moderne nel metodo neocomparativo', *Scuola e Lingue Moderne (SeLM)*, 7: 15–22.

Tantucci, V. and A. Roncoroni (2018), *Il mio Latino,* Milan: Mondadori Education.

Tesnière, L. (1959/2001), *Èlements de Syntaxe structurale,* trans. G. Proverbio and A. Trocini Cerrina, Paris: Klincksieck.

UNESCO (1970), *Concluding recommendation of the Unesco Congress, Bratislava.* UNESCO.

Valli, L., A. Stefanski and R. Jacobson (2018), 'School-community partnership models: implications for leadership', *International Journal of Leadership in Education*, 21 (1): 31–49.

LITHUANIA

Nijolė Juchnevičienė and Raimonda Brunevičiūtė

School system

According to the Law on Education of the Republic of Lithuania (2023) the education system of Lithuania includes:

- Pre-school education – at the request of the parents/guardians – provided in accordance with a pre-school education programme.

- Pre-primary education, provided to a child when he/she reaches the age of five years by 30 April in the calendar year in question.

- Primary education, provided within the framework of a four-year primary education programme implemented in accordance with the Primary Curriculum Framework, the General Curriculum for Primary Education, and the General Education Plans. Primary education may be combined with art, music, sports or other education. A child will start primary education when he or she reaches the age of seven in the calendar year in question. Primary education is the first part of the basic education core curriculum and covers the four-year period of basic education; the second part covers the two-year period of basic education. It may include modules of vocational training programmes.

- Secondary education, based on a two-year secondary curriculum, consists of compulsory and optional general education subjects and possible vocational training modules. Secondary education may be combined with art, music, sports or other education. Secondary education will be obtained by completing a secondary education programme and passing the matriculation examinations.

Formal (pre-primary, primary and secondary) and/or non-formal (pre-primary, pre-school and other non-formal) education programmes may include non-traditional education, which is based on a distinctive pedagogical system or elements thereof, and usually includes primary and secondary education. Non-traditional education includes ecology and environmental technology education, humanistic culture education through artistic activities, education based on Jesuit pedagogy in Lithuania, Catholic education, classical education (from 2015), Waldorf pedagogy in Lithuania, Montessori pedagogy in Lithuania, Suzuki talent education in Lithuania, education for innovative entrepreneurship, sports and health education, and land cadets in Lithuania.

Vocational training can be both initial and continuing. Initial vocational training is formal, generalized and designed to provide the first qualification. It is provided to apprentices who have completed primary or secondary education. For pupils who have completed primary education, it may be combined with secondary education. Initial vocational training may also be provided for pupils aged fourteen or over who have not completed primary education.

Higher education studies are carried out on the basis of accredited study programmes. A student may study in instalments at different higher education institutions.

Formal education schools in the Republic of Lithuania are divided into groups: general education schools, vocational education institutions, and higher education institutions. Types of general education schools: primary school, elementary school, post-primary school, *gymnasium*. Primary schools are schools that provide a basic education programme or a programme of both basic education and primary education. The pre-*gymnasium*-type schools are schools that offer the first part of the basic education curriculum or the first part of the basic education curriculum and the primary education curriculum. The *gymnasium* includes schools providing the secondary education programme accredited in accordance with the procedure laid down by the Minister of Education, Science and Sport and the second part of the primary education programme.

Classical studies in schools and universities

At present (2023), there are 232 primary schools, 176 grammar schools and 395 *gymnasia*. Latin is generally taught as an elective subject in *gymnasium* III–IV, and in some schools also in *gymnasium* I–II. Greek generally is not taught at secondary schools and *gymnasia*, except for a few voluntary schoolchildren groups in some schools (not included in the general programme), and as an elective subject in the Classical *gymnasium*. Classical culture is not a separate subject in schools (except Classical *gymnasia*), but various aspects of it are included in the general educational courses (history and literature). Greek is studied in higher education studies (Classical Philology and Philosophy).

The trend over the last fifteen years has been that the number of schools teaching Latin as an optional language has halved, but the number of pupils choosing to study Latin has increased by around 30 per cent (Table 7). The first Classical *gymnasium* was opened in 2015 after the Concept of Classical Humanities Education, initiated by the Lithuanian Classical Association, was approved by the Ministry of Education, Science and Sport of the Republic of Lithuania.

With the establishment of the Abraomas Kulvietis Classical Gymnasium in 2015 in Vilnius, the capital of Lithuania, and the Vytautas Magnus University School of Classical Education in 2021 in Kaunas, the second largest city in Lithuania, the number of students who study Latin and classical subjects at school has substantially changed. According to the Ministry of Education, Science and Sport, in school year 2022/23 the Classical Education School in Kaunas had a total of 114 pupils enrolled in the classical education programme: 48 pupils in grade V, 23 pupils in grade VI, 22 pupils in grade IX, and 2 pupils in grade X. The Classical Gymnasium in Vilnius had 753 pupils enrolled in the classical education programme: 102 in grade V, 126 in grade VI, 105 in grade VII, 117 in grade VIII, 91 in grade I *gymnasium*, 82 in grade II, 76 in grade III, and 54 in grade IV.

At present (2023), there are eleven state and seven non-state university higher education institutions, and twelve state and seven non-state non-university higher education institutions (colleges) in Lithuania. Higher education institutions have autonomy; there are no unified curricula for higher education in Lithuania. Each higher education institution allocates as many credits for the teaching of Latin as necessary for the profession concerned (study programmes in medicine, law, philology, philosophy, history). The only higher education institution running a Classical Philology study programme (Bachelor studies, four years), a Classical Studies study programme (Master studies, two years), and PhD study programme in Classics (four years) is Vilnius University (VU).

The tradition of teaching classical languages and culture in Lithuania coincides with the establishment of Vilnius University by the Jesuits in 1579 (Academia et Universitas Vilnensis

Table 7. A comparison of the Latin language teaching statistics

School year	2006–2007		2007–2008		2022–2023	
Region (R) or City (C)	Number of schools	Number of students	Number of schools	Number of students	Number of schools	Number of students
Vilnius (R)	3	29	3	32	–	–
Vilnius (C)	1	31	2	109	3	817
Kaunas (C)	3	61	3	41	2	137
Klaipėda (C)	4	138	4	88	1	22
Panevėžys (R)	2	18	–	–	–	–
Panevėžys (C)	1	3	2	26	1	20
Šiauliai (C)	1	19	2	46	–	–
Šiauliai (R)					1	21
Alytus (C)	2	19	3	33	1	19
Lazdijai (R)	1	13	–	–	–	–
Varėna (R)	1	9	–	–	–	–
Kėdainiai (R)	1	10	–	–	–	–
Raseiniai (R)	2	53	–	–	–	–
Kretinga (R)	1	13	1	7	1	13
Skuodas (R)	1	13	–	–	–	–
Šilutė (R)	2	106	2	152	1	93
Pasvalys (R)	1	27	1	33	1	11
Joniškis (R)	2	17	2	16	1	8
Tauragė (R)	1	5	1	40	–	–
Mažeikiai (R)	1	5	1	8	1	6
Plungė (R)	1	12	1	24	–	–
Telšiai (R)	2	43	1	24	1	12
Molėtai (R)	1	3	–	–	–	–
Utena (R)	2	26	2	36	–	–
Zarasai (R)	1	32	1	30	–	–
Švenčionys (R)	2	52	1	31	–	––
Trakai (R)	1	40	1	59	–	–
Ukmergė (R)	1	5	1	5	–	–
Jurbarkas (R)	–	–	1	7	1	22
Šilalė (R)	–	–	1	15	–	–

School year	2006–2007		2007–2008		2022–2023	
Region (R) or City (C)	Number of schools	Number of students	Number of schools	Number of students	Number of schools	Number of students
Anykščiai (R)	–	–	1	20	1	24
Elektrėnai (R)	–	–	1	8	–	–
Jonava (R)	–	–	–	–	1	26
Kaišiadorys (R)	–	–	–	–	1	5
Total	**42**	**822**	**39**	**899**	**19**	**1256**

Source: © Nijolė Juchnevičienė 2023.

Societatis Jesu). The Jesuit model of humanities education, which had existed in the European educational system since the sixteenth century, was transferred to Lithuania. The VU Printing House is considered the centre of the Latin press in the Grand Duchy of Lithuania (GDL). In the sixteenth century, the Vilnius University Printing House published 87 Latin prints, in the seventeenth century 554 and in the eighteenth century 412. Neo-Latin literature in Lithuania was strongly influenced by Roman literature, had links with the neo-Latin literature of central and western Europe, and was concerned with the realities of Lithuanian political and cultural life. *Latinitas* became an integrating principle of the identity of the intellectual and political classes in GDL. It provides an account of the Roman descent of Lithuanians, sustains the claim for political sovereignty, and indicates the European civilizing process, thus becoming part of social identity as well (Knieža 2020).

After the liberation from tsarist Russia, in the period of the first independent state of Lithuania (1918–40), the orientation towards teaching Classics and the European classical tradition was a factor incident to the European identity of Lithuania. This tradition was cut off in 1940 when Lithuania was annexed by the Soviet Union under the conditions of the Molotov–Ribbentrop pact and re-occupied by the Soviet Army after the Second World War. Immediately after the re-occupation, the system of secondary education changed; the changes were predominated by ideological and political factors (Brunevičiūtė 2009). The non-state owned educational institutions (primary schools, craft schools, kindergartens, secondary schools) were nationalized; the curricula of primary and secondary schools were changed and 'unnecessary and socially insecure' subjects, such as Latin and Greek, were excluded. Vilnius University, which was the oldest university in the territories controlled by the USSR, was reshaped according to the model of Soviet universities and fell under strict Communist Party control (Juchnevičienė 2013).

Nevertheless, the Department of Classical Philology, officially established in 1805, has never been closed down and was the main factor in maintaining and promoting classical languages and culture, not only as university study subjects but also as a component of general education. Due to its activity, since the 1970s, schools with intensified teaching of certain subjects were introduced, and among them the so-called humanitarian schools with compulsory classes in Latin. Latin was supposed to be taught sixty-eight hours per year in grades IX and X, and sixty-six hours per year in grade XI, in total 202 hours (Brunevičiūtė 2009). There were up to ten humanitarian schools in Lithuania until the announcement of the independence of Lithuania from the USSR in 1990, after which the system of education in Lithuania changed. The establishment of an independent education policy in the Republic of Lithuania aimed to preserve Lithuania's European identity and ethnic core of culture, integrate it into the European cultural context, and ensure a high standard of education. Required conceptions were framed: the Concept of Types of Schools (1990), the Law on Education of the Republic of Lithuania (1991), and the Guidelines for Education Reform (1993). Fundamental guidelines of these documents had to ensure that education should be based on humanistic values, democratic principles and universally recognized human rights, and should be oriented towards openness to European cultural traditions. Humanities were regarded as a key instrument to ensure the achievement of these objectives. However, in practice, the content of education did not include programmes of intercultural education and greater integration into the European cultural context, and so the attitude towards the teaching of classical disciplines was not essential or determinative (Brunevičiūtė 1999). Thus, during the period of restoration of the national education system (1990–6), there was a tendency to exclude the teaching of classical subjects from the secondary compulsory curriculum, but the institutions were free to teach Latin as an elective subject.

Since 1997, the second phase of the reform of the Lithuanian education system has begun. The number of grammar schools, which were divided into real, arts and humanities profiles, increased; and the offer of humanities subjects increased as well, but Latin and other classical subjects were not included in the curriculum of the humanities. In secondary schools and *gymnasia*, that sought to maintain the tradition of teaching it, Latin has been taught as a second foreign language. Throughout the period, Latin was taught according to a curriculum drawn up as early as 1962.

Trends in Classics education

In 2010 a public discussion with the state institutions on the teaching of classical subjects at schools was started by the Lithuanian Classical Association. Thus, the conference at the Parliament of the Republic of Lithuania (Seimas), titled 'Challenges and Prospects for Classical Education', was organized for the first time, together with the members of the Lithuanian Parliament, Ministry of Education, and Vilnius City Municipality. On 5 March 2010, the concept of Non-Traditional Education was approved by the Minister of Education, Science and Sport and a curriculum of Ancient Culture and Latin for secondary education in grades IX–XII was prepared by the Department of Classical Philology and the Classical Association. Unfortunately, this programme has not been approved. Nevertheless, the Classical Association and the Department of Classical Philology made every effort to revive the tradition of classical humanitarian education, and in June 2015, by the Order of the Minister of Education and Science of the Republic of Lithuania No.V-638 the concept of Classical Humanitarian Education, that was prepared by the Association together with teachers of Latin, was approved. This empowered the establishment of Lithuania's first classical grammar school (Vilnius Abraomas Kulvietis' Classical Gymnasium), which encompasses elementary, primary and secondary education. Classical education includes the following elements: Art Expression (35 lessons per year) in primary education; Ancient Culture (35 lessons per year), Latin (35/70 lessons per year) in Primary I; History of Culture (35 lessons per year), Latin (35/70 lessons per year) in Primary II; and History of Culture (35 lessons per year), Latin (35/70 lessons per year) in Secondary Education. After six years (in 2021) another classical *gymnasium*, the School of Classical Education of Vytautas Magnus University, was established in Kaunas. The school's classical education content consists of compulsory subjects complementary to the general education content: Art Expression (grades I–IV); Ancient Culture (grades IV–VIII), History of Culture (grades I–IV *gymnasium*), Latin (grades V–VIII), Latin or Greek (compulsory elective, grades I–IV *gymnasium*); Hebrew (a separate class of Emmanuel Levinas: grades I–IV, grades V–VIII, *gymnasium* I–IV), and other compulsory elective subjects, such as Rhetoric or Philosophy, in *gymnasium* I–IV.

As part of the renewal of the content of the Lithuanian general education curriculum from 2023/24, for the first time in the secondary education framework of Lithuania, the General Curriculum of Latin Language and Ancient Culture (Order of the Ministry of Education, Science and Sport of the Republic of Lithuania, August 2023) has been introduced as part of the list of nationally developed general programmes of subjects for the free choice of the *gymnasium* (grades III–IV), which can be carried out in any Lithuanian grammar school and thus creates the pre-conditions for the broader availability of Classics. The main innovation of the present programme is its orientation towards both the Latin language and the basics of classical culture. This will help to meet the needs of students seeking to acquire general philological knowledge, which gives a deeper understanding of how languages work, an appreciation of linguistic relations (including the mother tongue) to better understand European cultural identity, and to be able to recognize its founding cultural code, as well as to develop intercultural competence.

Educational innovations that promote the modernization and individualization of education in the implementation of the curriculum content or the development of teacher qualification are carried out in cooperation with academic institutions, namely the Department of Classical Philology of Vilnius University, along with the Ministry of Education, Sport and Science, its educational assistance institution, the National Agency for Education, and by exchanging good practices with partner schools, such as the Francois Couperin Lycée in Fontainebleau, France, and the Mario Cutelli Classical Gymnasium in Sicily.

Resources

At present, there is a discussion with Hands Up Education, a non-profit organization working with and for Classics teachers, about the possibility of translating their online textbook *Suburani* (Hands up Education 2021) into Lithuanian. Some schools use *European Symbols* (Glatz & Thiel 2015), a joint schoolbook for European students, containing contributions from twenty European countries (including Lithuania) with a stress on the classical cultural legacy in every country. Recently there has been an increasing interest in Ørberg's *Lingua Latina per se illustrata* (2011), in which the inductive teaching method is used. Instead of translating single sentences, students read a coherent Latin text that grows in complexity over time, adding new words and illustrating each new grammatical form and syntactic structure with various contextual examples.

Still, the main textbook for schools remains *Vox Latina* (Kuzavinis & Valkūnas 1973), using the traditional grammatical approach, which for many Lithuanian teachers seems more fitting, because of the phonetical, grammatical and lexical affinity of Latin to Lithuanian, which is the oldest living Indo-European language. The communicative approach to learning Latin, used in many schools around the world, is not used in Lithuanian schools, but at VU it is one of the methods used to some extent to develop Latin and Greek language skills, such as the oral production of text. Students have access to the Latin–Lithuanian dictionary (KALBA n.d.), the United Latin–Lithuanian Dictionary from the seventeenth to the twenty-first centuries (Thesaurus Latino-Lituanicus n.d.), a Greek Hexameter Analysis tool (Strockis & Tverijonas 2012) and other resources.

Teacher preparation

During the period of the first independent state of Lithuania (1918–40), the orientation towards Classics and the European classical tradition was an essential factor. The education system was modelled on that of Finland, Switzerland and other countries. In 1939, the last year before the occupation, five types of *gymnasium* were introduced: the Humanitarian Gymnasium (reinforced Latin), the Realgymnasium (reinforced science and mathematics), the Classical Gymnasium (reinforced ancient languages), the Enhanced Foreign Language Gymnasium and the Commercial Gymnasium. In the Classical Gymnasium, Latin was taught for seven years, and Greek for five years. Courses and seminars were set up to train the teachers of Classical subjects. According to The Law on Secondary Schools, Latin was required for admission to Vilnius University (Brunevičiūtė 1999). This tradition has influenced the content of education in the modern Lithuanian education system.

After the Soviet occupation of Lithuania, the links with European cultural legacy were treated as ideologically harmful, and a new Soviet identity of the 'Soviet Lithuania, Republic of workers and peasants' was created. Still, the Department of Classical Philology of Vilnius University prepared up to five specialists every year, with a major in Lithuanian Philology and a minor in Classical Philology. So, when at the end of the 1970s the ten so-called humanitarian schools were established, these graduates started to teach Latin at schools, and the Department was engaged in their professional development. Until now there is no study programme qualifying for teaching classical subjects, and all the teachers are graduates of the Department of Classical Philology. The Lithuanian Classical Association, established in 2007, brings together teachers of Latin and helps to keep a dialogue with public institutions and society. It aims to uphold and promote the tradition of classical studies and research in Lithuania in cooperation with public and educational institutions of Lithuania, as well as other national and international organizations. Every year, since 2011, the Association has organized refresher courses for teachers of Latin. The classes are taught by the Vilnius University staff and by teachers from other institutions, including the University of Edinburgh, Berlin Freie University, University of Saint Petersburg, Schola humanistica in Padova and the Hands Up Education Group. As a result, modern approaches and new textbooks found their way into Lithuanian schools. At the very end of 2023, a new refresher course programme, prepared by the Association together with the National Agency for Education, started; it has been approved to run for three years.

Community engagement

Another trend of the Association's activity is directed towards schoolchildren and towards society in general, to enhance the appreciation of classical languages and culture. Since 2009, the Association has organized a yearly competition for schoolchildren in the Latin language and classical culture. It brings together students and teachers from all over Lithuania. In 2011, following an appeal by the Association, the Classical Competition was given national status and is organized by the Association in partnership with the Ministry of Education, Science and Sport. Since 2014, the Classical Association has organized the ELEX (Euroclassica ECCL) competition in Lithuania; only fifty students from four schools participated in the first competition, while in the most recent one there were nine schools and up to 350 students. Since 2022, in cooperation with the national broadcaster LRT (Lithuanian Radio and Television), the Association has organized a national quiz on ancient culture, and since 2012 a yearly summer school for *gymnasium* students – the Classical Academy. Up to thirty-five students from various regions come to Vilnius University to listen to lectures on a topic chosen for the year and to take part in the seminars. Additionally, since 2012, 'The Classical Club' has run a monthly event for the general public (during every school year, with a break during the pandemic), where anyone can listen to lectures by writers, professors, politicians, teachers and other cultural representatives, and take part in discussions afterwards on topics chosen by the Classical Association. All these activities became very popular in Lithuania, and interest in classical languages and culture is increasing. This is evident in the doubling number of students entering Classical Philology and Classical Studies study programmes.

References

Brunevičiūtė, R. (1999), *Klasikiniai humanitarinio ugdymo pagrindai: lotynų kalba:* monografija, Kaunas: KTU.

Brunevičiūtė, R. (2009), 'The Effect of Teaching Latin on the Education System in Lithuania during the Soviet Period', *Literatūra*, 51 (3): 109–23.

Glatz, P. and A. Thiel (2015), *European Symbols*, Horn: Euroclassica/Amici Linguae Latinae.

Hands Up Education (2021), *Suburani*, Haverhill: Hands Up Education.

Juchnevičienė, N. (2013), 'Classical Philology in Early Soviet Lithuania: Between the European Tradition and Reality', in G. Karsai, G. Klaniczay, D. Movrin and E. Olechowska (eds), *Classics and Communism. Greek and Latin behind the Iron Curtain,* Ljubljana-Budapest-Warsaw, 169–86.

KALBA (n.d.), Latin–Lithuanian Dictionary: https://ekalba.lt/lotynu-lietuviu-kalbu-zodynas/.

Knieža, S. (2020), 'The Intrinsic and Extrinsic. Latinitas in the Research of the Grand Duchy of Lithuania', *Literatūra,* 62 (3): 93–110.

Kuzavinis, K. and L. Valkūnas (1993), *Vox Latina,* Vilnius: Šviesa.

Lietuvos Respublikos švietimo įstatymas (1991), m. birželio 25 d. Nr. I-1489 Vilnius. Aktuali redakcija nuo 2023-07-06 iki 2023-08-31 [Law on Education of the Republic of Lithuania. 25 June 1991. No. I-1489 Vilnius] Available online: https://eseimas.lrs.lt/portal/legalAct/lt/TAD/TAIS.1480/asr (accessed 15 December 2023).

Ørberg, H. (2011), *Lingua Latina per se illustrata*, Indianapolis, IN: Hackett Publishing.

Strockis, M. and M. Tverijonas (2012), Greek Hexameter Analysis tool: http://www.thesaurus.flf.vu.lt/eiledara/index.php.

Thesaurus Latino-Lituanicus (n.d.), Latin–Lithuanian Thesaurus: http://www.thesaurus.flf.vu.lt/

Organizations

Vilniaus Abraomo Kulviečio klasikinė gimnazija [Vilnius Abraomas Kulvietis Classical Gymnasium]: https://kulviecio.vilnius.lm.lt/.

VDU klasikinio ugdymo mokykla [VMU School of Classical Education]: https://vduklasikinis.kaunas.lm.lt/.

Lotynų kalba ir Antikos kultūra. Bendroji programa [Latin and Ancient Culture. General Programme]: www.emokykla.lt/bendrosios-programos/visos-bendrosios-programos/56.
Societas Classica: https://www.klasikai.lt/apie-mus/.
National Agency for Education, refresher course programme: https://www.nsa.smm.lt/wp-content/uploads/2023/11/Lotynu-kalbos-ir-antikos-kulturos-PKT_FIN.pdf.

LUXEMBOURG

Franck Colotte

The Luxembourgish education system and Classics

Heir to the Jesuit tradition, the teaching of Latin in the Grand Duchy of Luxembourg is, in its current configuration, the one in Europe with the highest number of teaching hours (which would have seemed like a pittance to practising teachers in the nineteenth century, when they had a weekly timetable of up to ten hours!). Continuing the traditional teaching method based essentially on the reasoned study of how the language works and its morphosyntactic structures, it therefore trains first and foremost 'student-translators' capable of deciphering – ideally without translation tools such as a dictionary and/or normative grammar – both prose and poetry texts of increasing difficulty, right up to the authors studied for the *baccalauréat* (Cicero and Seneca for prose; Virgil and Lucretius for poetry). The translational (i.e. lexico-philological) method of teaching in Luxembourg, which has disappeared or is in the process of disappearing in a number of European countries, requires pupils to make a considerable effort. For, since they are immersed in a multilingual environment (which characterizes the country in general), they are required to translate an ancient language into a language other than their mother tongue, in this case French (which is the language of teaching and translation, but rarely the mother tongue of the learner). In such an alloglossic context, the mode of operation of translation – and its level of demand – is therefore high, in view of the defining characteristics mentioned above.

However, the humanist idea underlying such a teaching system is also, and above all, that of sight-reading, as one would do with a text written in a modern language. This survival lays the philological foundations for the second objective of teaching Latin in Luxembourg, namely the training of a 'pupil-reader' capable of applying to an extract of prose or poetry a battery of strategies for reading, analysing and interpreting texts, whether in terms of their rhetorical framework, stylistic ornamentation, narrative or argumentative strategies. The text is no longer simply an object to be read, but also an object to be read and interpreted. The text is no longer just a philological end in itself, but a multi-dimensional springboard on which the most diverse interpretative, reflexive, communicative and other strategies are based. These two dimensions combine and complement each other so as not only to maintain the high level of translation practised in Luxembourg, but also to adopt the reading techniques and strategies applied in the other language and literature courses taken by pupils (whatever their cycle). This two-pronged approach, adopted by a large proportion of the teaching staff, is helping to revitalize a teaching discipline that is aware of the challenges it faces. This includes the learning of French, which has been in decline for many years, and the new technology, which is changing the traditional way of doing things, particularly from the point of view of the essential 'sorting' of information and documentary sources. Thus, situated 'at the confluence of two rivers' – that of tradition and modernity, to paraphrase Chateaubriand's famous phrase – the teaching of Latin in Luxembourg draws its richness and diversity from both the roots of an in-depth knowledge of the language (which structures the mind and enables its subtleties to be understood) and the necessary interpretative contextualization that constitutes a wide cultural context. Without claiming to be absolute, it is nonetheless a question of transforming the way pupils look, through direct and personalized access to the text, at what is supposed to become a category of thought. This should lead, through the broadening and structuring of a cultural heritage, to enrichment and interpretative depth.

Table 8 shows the number of Latinists for the 2022/23 school year (abbreviations refer to individual schools). The totals for the previous years were as follows: 689 (2021/22), 713 (2020/21) and 718 (2019/20).

Table 8. Number of high school students for Latin 2022/23

High Schools	6th	5th	4th	3rd	2nd	1st	Total
LCD	2	8	1	3	2	1 (1 LMRL)	17
AL	33	28	36	23	–	8 (1 LMRL)	128
LJBM	8	8	7	3	(2 LGE)	2	30
LHCE	8	5	11	3	(1 LGE)	–	27
LNBD	10	7	3	7	(1 LHCE)	–	27
LGE	16	15	13	16	7 (1 LHCE)	5	72
LCE	13	9	9	6	3	5	45
ALR	11	8	9	7	–	– (AL)	35
LMRL	30	11	10	15	–	(1 AL)	66
LAML	32	10	12	11	4	–	69
EPF	3	3	8	–	(3 LGL)	–	17
LRSL	7	8	3	3	(1 LGL)	–	21
LN	4	4	4	3	–	–	15
LMA	–	2	–	–	– (1 LRSL)	–	2
LGL	27	18	13	17	10 (1 LRSL)	2	87
LEM	4	8	2	3	–	–	17
LGK	2	2	2	1	–	–	7
MLG	3	4	1	–	–	–	8
Total	**218**	**165**	**154**	**123**	**31**	**23**	**714**

Source: © Franck Colotte 2023.

Perception of Classics

Since 2002, secondary education in Luxembourg has provided for a minimum of four years of study of Latin for those who are in the option branch or section containing Latin: this corresponds to a total of 16.5 hours a week. Since 2002, the timetable has been distributed as follows: 1st year: 6 hours a week; 2nd 4.5 hours; 3rd 3 hours; 4th 3 hours; 5th 3 hours; 6th 3 hours, with a maximum of six years, corresponding to a total of 22½ hours per week, culminating in the written and oral examinations for the Luxembourg baccalaureate. The vast majority of pupils in the Latin or Classical section follow a four-year course. Latin studies are divided into two distinct phases: firstly, in the lower cycle, pupils are essentially introduced to the grammatical system of the Latin language (vocabulary, morphology, syntax) – an introduction which is based on the translation of texts into easy Latin (in the same way as there are adapted texts for beginners in French as a foreign language). Then, in the upper cycle, pupils begin the study of Latin literature by reading extracts from some of the great authors: Caesar, *Bellum gallicum*, Cicero, speeches against Verres and Catiline, Ovid, *Metamorphoses*, etc. The fourth year of secondary school occupies a pivotal position in this structure: here, pupils complete their study of the language by studying some complex aspects of Latin syntax, while at the same time being introduced to the reading of authors by translating simplified extracts from Latin authors such as Caesar, Cicero and Pliny the Younger. By the end of their third year in the upper cycle, pupils in the classical section have completed their compulsory Latin course and receive a certificate attesting that they have studied Latin for four years; this certificate is generally accepted as equivalent to the *Kleines Latinum* in Germany. Pupils interested in Latin and wishing to have a good classical training for university studies can continue to study Latin in the last two years of secondary school. They will read texts by Latin philosophers (Cicero and Seneca) and poets (Virgil and Horace). At the end of the final year of secondary school, they will sit a Latin test in the secondary school leaving examination, which will include a written translation into French of a seen text and an unseen text, and an oral translation and commentary on a seen text. The last two years are a complex phase, in the sense that the reading of a particular extract from a text serves firstly as an exercise in morphosyntactic deciphering, and secondly and above all as a way of putting it into conceptual, diachronic, cultural, mythological and other perspectives. Once the translation has been completed – and therefore once students have become familiar with the text to which they have already devoted a certain amount of time – they are placed at the centre of a complex learning process that enables them to establish certain key concepts, some aspects of Roman *realia*, and make the link with modernity in the broadest sense of the term (from the Renaissance to the twenty-first century). It is this essential contextualization that is the major challenge facing Latin teachers today (while preserving the purely philological dimension), as well as being the most fruitful way of building a broad general culture that can be transferred to other educational and/or cultural contexts.

Current trends

The teaching of Latin places a great deal of emphasis on traditional philological learning based on the study of a large number of morphosyntactic structures necessary for the correct understanding and translation, initially of simplified extracts, then of original texts by poets (e.g. Virgil, Lucretius, Ovid) and prose writers (e.g. Cicero, Seneca, Tacitus). For the first three years, teaching is based essentially on the series *Invitation au latin* (Gason et al. 1997). This will one day pose a problem in terms of books, as these French textbooks will not be published *ad vitam aeternam*, for editorial and/or budgetary reasons. In addition, there is a vocabulary booklet in line with the texts in these textbooks, written by Luxembourg teachers and published by the Ministry of Education, Children and Youth. This is the responsibility not only of the teachers themselves, but also of the National Latin and Greek Curriculum Committee (CNPLG), which, with its consultative and partly decision-making powers, acts as an intermediary between the teachers and the ministerial authorities. The CNPLG is made up of a president, a secretary and a representative from each secondary school where Latin is taught, i.e. around fifteen traditional and general *lycées*, representing a total (all levels combined) of around 700 Latin pupils (a minority within the educational establishment). These figures are on a par with a country the size of a medium-sized French *departement*, with around 660,000 people (at the start of 2023) living in the Grand Duchy (to whom are added around 212,000 cross-border workers every day). These figures, which have remained constant for a number of years, are obviously in no way comparable to the much higher statistical figures for neighbouring countries.

What models does the Luxembourg school system follow when it comes to ancient languages? Referring to the article by Violaine Houdart-Merot (2003), we could say that the Luxembourg system follows a hybrid model combining the 'humanities' of nineteenth-century France, evolving from Latin translation to French explanation, and the 'methodical reading' that emerged in the 1980s, insofar as the Luxembourg system requires the reading methods used in French classes (and modern languages in general) to be applied to ancient texts. Latin teaching thus borrowed from the so-called modern / Romance languages their analytical tools and their metalanguage, while persevering in the affirmation of a 'true' and unique meaning of the text to be translated. Translation is also seen as a kind of 'literary act', demonstrating both 'rigour' and 'finesse', while respecting the structures of the original text as much as possible, and thus distancing itself from translations that are a little (too) far removed from the original text. This is sometimes the case with the *Collection des Universités de France* (CUF) of *Les Belles Lettres*, or the *belles infidèles* as they have been known since the seventeenth century, which 'to please and conform to the taste and decorum of the time, are versions "revised and corrected" by translators who are conscious (too conscious, no doubt) of the superiority of their language and their judgement' (Horguelin 1981).

What about the teaching of Greek? The aims of teaching Greek are threefold. At a linguistic level, the teaching of Greek aims to translate authentic Greek texts, by mastering how the language works through the study of literary, philosophical and historical texts. At a cross-curricular level, learning Greek develops students' analytical and synthesizing skills, and encourages their capacity for abstraction, especially as it promotes systematic reflection on the richness and complexity of this ancient language in relation to the target language, and facilitates understanding of the countless technical terms (e.g. scientific, philosophical, IT) present in modern languages. From a cultural point of view, learning Greek enables students to deepen their literary, historical and philosophical knowledge of classical antiquity and leads them to reflect on it from both a synchronic and a diachronic perspective, all the more so as the values thus transmitted – along with those of Latin antiquity – constitute a cultural heritage and an observation grid that are essential for a better understanding of the foundations of other cultures and for warning against one-track thinking. As part of a classical humanist education, Greek helps to enrich students' general culture and prepares them for university studies.

From a didactic point of view, the new series of three *NOVA ITINERA* textbooks, launched in 2020, proposes new pedagogical paths between the tradition of books and digital innovation. Underpinned by this hybrid dimension, the aim of these textbooks is not only to teach the basic morphosyntactic structures in a rigorous manner, but also to put them into perspective by discovering and assimilating contexts (historical, archaeological, cultural, civilizational, etc.) and uses that to provide an enhanced and extended vision of the study of Latin. The *realia* on show are Italian, Roman, etc., but also from Luxembourg and the Greater Region. In this way, the paths of small- and large-scale history cross within a large whole, which is thus given stimulating cultural depth. The *NOVA ITINERA* series is made up of both printed textbooks and the *PEARLTREES* platform (http://www.pearltrees .com/), which is an editable digital complement (bringing together various resources that can be used in lessons, *ad libitum*, as documentary extensions). Without losing sight of the teacher's essential freedom to teach, the series proposes a progression and sets a framework whose components, available on the *PEARLTREES* platform, are both linguistic and edutainment.

Training and professional development

Teacher training for secondary school teachers (particularly in Latin) is based on the following model: future teachers first complete four or more years of higher education in the subject of their choice. To enter the teaching profession, they must then pass a competitive examination organized by the Ministry of Education.

Candidates who have passed this competitive examination complete a two-year teaching placement, during which they teach at a *lycée* while following the teacher training course for secondary school teachers at the *Institut de formation de l'Éducation nationale* (IFEN). This training is organized in modules and leads to a certificate awarded on the basis of a portfolio assessed by a committee. At the end of the training period, appointed teachers are given a one-year period of further training to consolidate their professional skills.

Teacher training for secondary school teachers prepares them for three fundamental tasks: the construction of knowledge and the development of pupils' skills; regulation and assessment as well as the socialization of young people; and classroom management. It is organized according to the following principles:

- academic training in the form of modules;
- alternating training (theory-practice; school-training institute); and
- gradual integration of the trainee into the teaching profession through a system of supervision.

It covers four different areas:

- academic areas relating to the knowledge of the teaching profession;
- general didactics with a view to providing personalized care for learners;
- didactics relating to the subjects taught; and
- institutional issues relating to the school's legislative framework and society's expectations.

Collaborative practices

Founded in 2014, the, *Association luxembourgeoise des professeurs de latin et de grec* (ALPLG), is constituted in 2023 of an executive committee including a President (Franck Colotte), a Vice-President (Daniel Reding), a Treasurer (Fabienne Fatello) as well as a Secretary (Lydia Keilen). Its aims are to represent Latin and Greek teachers in the Grand Duchy of Luxembourg, and to defend and promote ancient languages and culture. This mission is based firstly on the prospect of Latin and Greek becoming deeply rooted in Luxembourg's school culture:

- Linguistic mastery: Latin and Greek help students to master not only the French language, but also the many modern languages that these foundational languages feed into. Latin and Greek give access to a precise and detailed understanding of vocabulary, to the etymology of international scholarly language, and to an original system of thought and expression.

- A cultural foundation: the French arts and humanities syllabuses emphasize the links between modern and contemporary culture and the fundamental works of antiquity. As for the pupils themselves, they will find that Latin and Greek open them up to scientific, political and philosophical reflection.

- A humanist spirit: even more broadly, Latin and Greek are languages of culture that help us to understand European identity. These sources of a shared past thus contribute to the formation of a sense of history and judgement, by learning both distance and proximity.

With this in mind, the ALPLG's ambition is to defend ancient languages, not only in schools, but also in public opinion, by holding or promoting school and university events designed to highlight the interest and the (recreational) cultural dimension of these disciplines, as demonstrated by the *Prix Henri Kugener*. Presented in memory of the eminent Luxembourg Latin scholar Henri Kugener, the 'Henri Kugener Prize' competition, established for the first time in 2008/09, is aimed at third-year secondary school classes in Luxembourg. It aims to stimulate pupils' interest in the Graeco-Latin world, promote Latin in contemporary culture and create interaction around the Latin language.

Conclusion

Backed by a long philological tradition, Classics in the Grand Duchy of Luxembourg find their strength in a teaching system that strives, thanks in particular to the large amount of time available, to provide pupils with morphosyntactic and cultural *impedimenta* designed to enable them to play a dual role: to be both pupil-translators and pupil-readers of texts that promote not only knowledge of the ancient world, but also its permanence within our modern world.

In this way, Luxembourg is privileged in the gently declining climate that currently characterizes the teaching of ancient languages in Europe, even though, like every country, it is experiencing problems and has had to face up to new challenges for a number of years. The situation of ancient languages in Luxembourg bears witness to the composite interest in what Jürgen Leonhardt (2010) calls 'retro-cultures' – a translation of the German *Retrokulturen* – that people in the twenty-first century have in the buried continent of classical culture.

In such a context, the role of the teacher is to show how Latin is a living subject, capable of being integrated into the modern world, with its place in today's linguistic and cultural mix. You can rap in Latin, you can perform a play from the classical Greek repertoire, you can write text messages in Latin, you can create games based on antiquity, you can talk and exchange ideas with young Europeans of your own age, you can discover the Roman *realia* of Luxembourg and the Greater Region in a constructive and convivial way, and, in the end, you can say with Jacques Gaillard (1993): 'Antiquity is among us. You met it not only on holiday in Rhodes, Naples or Vaison, but in the ordinary consumption of a familiar world. It is in our language, in our values, in our desires, in our leisure activities. It's in the objects, it's in the images, it's in our symbols, often discreet, sometimes triumphant, an obligatory reference or a subtle afterthought.'

References

Gaillard, J. and J. Cousteix (1993), *Grammaire du latin, Lycée*, Paris: Éditions Nathan.
Gason, J., A. Lambert and H. Trézigny (1997), *Invitation au latin*, Paris: Magnard Collèges.
Horguelin, P. (1981), *Anthologie de la manière de traduire. Domaine français*, Montréal: Linguatech.
Houdart-Merot, V. (2003), 'Textes traduits et traduction dans le secondaire: des destins liés', *Le français aujourd'hui*, 142: 19–28.
Gaillard, J. (1993), *Beau comme l'antique*, Paris: Actes Sud.
Leonhardt, J. (2010), *La Grande histoire du latin. Des origines à nos jours* (trans. B. Vacher), Paris: CNRS Editions.

MALTA

Horatio Caesar Roger Vella

Introduction

Classics in Malta is taken to mean Latin and Greek, that is, languages. Traditionally, only languages were taught in Malta, as these languages were considered to be useful for the formation of Catholic priests. But these subjects disappeared from the schools' curriculum and the University of Malta, when the government in the late seventies and eighties was then led by architect Dom Mintoff, who introduced 'educational reforms' and imposed such questions as 'Why should the state employ people to teach a few students? What is the use of Latin, or even Ancient Greek, for a totalitarian state? What better than call such subjects as 'mental sport'?' When his government suspended the studies of all Arts, Sciences and Theology subjects from the university, immediately afterwards government, private and church schools suspended their curricula in Latin studies. In the case of the Church schools, this measure was then considered as consonant with their own misguided interpretation of Vatican II reforms. The Vatican never suspended the study of Latin from church schools, nor the Latin Mass, but simply allowed and recommended the celebration of Mass in the vernacular language. For these actions taken in the seventies and eighties, Classics came to a standstill in Malta and in its sister island, Gozo.

Even the Maltese lawyers went through a similar transition. When in the past lawyers showed their pride in quoting Latin *dicta*, now the opposite situation still exists where today's lawyers are expert in nothing except Law, and when at Court I cited a Latin *dictum*, I was asked to render it in Maltese! The same experience was met by historians who, today, are stuck when they face notarial records in Latin, or even the records which the Knights of St John left behind them in Malta in 1798. This situation was beneficial to me, as private individuals, Law Courts themselves and the Church Curia commissioned me on many occasions until the present day, after returning to Malta from the University of Zimbabwe in 1989, to transcribe and translate Latin documents into Maltese or English. The demand to transcribe and translate Latin documents, particularly wills and contracts, has recently increased due to the increase in property sale. Documents in Latin remain sole proofs of ownership and location of otherwise lost sites. It is unfortunate that my service has been used to reduce green spaces from these islands.

Returning Classics to Malta

I happen to have been the last student studying Classics at the University of Malta in 1979, when I graduated PhD. My BA course did not consist just of Latin and Greek languages, but also the History of Mediterranean Civilization (especially that of Greece and Rome), Philosophy, Archaeology and Literature. With no hope of teaching Classics in Malta anymore, I emigrated to war-torn Rhodesia, which then became Zimbabwe, and there I taught four different subjects related to Classics: Latin, Greek, Classical Studies and Africa in Antiquity. The last two subjects were taught in English, the first of which, Classical Studies, was identical to what was taught to other students at the University of Malta and what is still taught at St Martin's College (a secondary school) in Malta, namely, Classical Culture and Civilization. To justify further the teaching of Classics in Africa, we taught yet another subject, namely, Africa in Antiquity, which meant the Civilization of Egypt, Libya and Carthage from Prehistoric times to the coming of the Vandals. In this capacity I claim that I taught Egyptology as well, which included Egyptian Pictorial Art.

Equipped with all this training and vast experience in all aspects of the Classics and other related subjects, after ten and a half years I returned to Malta when a change of Government brought about a change of ideas about Classics and other subjects previously thought to be non-economical. Indeed, this experience helped me 'to defend the bridge' alone, because for many years I taught Classics here at the University of Malta alone, and that for twenty hours per week.

Here in Malta, I, alone as a full-time classicist, re-introduced the subject of Classics, being Latin and Greek, with other ingredients such as Archaeology, History, Philosophy, Literature, Art and Sociology. Topics here included Sources for Archaeology, Literary Criticism, Pictorial Art, Mythology, and Women in Antiquity. Addressed to Classics students, these last components were taught in English, but gobbets from Latin and Greek sources were presented to them for examination. In addition to Classics, I was also teaching Classical Culture and Civilization, a course in Classics taught in English and without the study of the languages, as well as History of Mediterranean Civilization, which included Greek and Roman civilization.

The University of Malta offers Classics to students with or without a background acquired in the schools. Its Classics programme brings students' level from zero knowledge to degree level in just three years, with possibility of postgraduate studies. In October 2014, it celebrated its twenty-fifth anniversary since it launched this programme by means of an international conference held on the 11th and 12th of December, at the Valletta Campus of the University of Malta under the auspices of the Rectorate and the Malta Classics Association.

Teaching Classics Worldwide

When Malta was about to join the European Union in 2004, I was asked by the Rector of the University to represent Malta at an international conference held in Athens and Delphi, when Greece had the presidency of the Union, to discuss the study of Classics within the European Union. In May 2010, the Malta Classics Association was formed, and I was elected as its first Executive President for the first two years. Two years later I served the Association in the same capacity for another two years. In August 2014, the Malta Classics Association joined Euroclassica, a Confederation of Classical Associations. Since then, I served the Association again as its President for a further two-year period, from 2020 to 2021.

Teaching and learning Classics

Classics, therefore, is the study of the languages, history, culture, philosophy, archaeology, literature and art of the Greeks and Romans. It, therefore, does not mean just Latin and Greek; but it gives these two languages great and due importance for being both mother-languages and for providing scientific terminology to several modern disciplines. Above all, the process of studying the languages provides the student with several other hidden tools. These are abilities to comprehend the etymology of words, the structure of simple and complex sentences, the requirements of grammar and syntax in these sentences, the position of emphasis, the structure of paragraphs, essays and speeches, philosophical arguments and rhetorical devises. Consequently, a Classics student meliorates in his or her other languages, in spelling, expression and delivery of speeches, and is evidently equipped with a vast repertoire of fundamental mythological, historical, literary and philosophical references and Greek and Latin maxims to relate to any subject he or she may happen to tackle.

Since the launching of the present Classics programme thirty-five years ago, the University of Malta has helped students to graduate in Classics in undergraduate and postgraduate levels. These are not necessarily employed directly in the classical field: but they are still giving a useful contribution to society in the civil service, to which Classics has always been considered as the best training, especially in Britain, and in the teaching of other subjects; also in politics, administration, journalism, the creative industries and the sciences, including Librarianship and Archival Studies.

The Malta Classics Association believes including Classics within our education curriculum will finally bring up our Maltese students to the level of our neighbours, students from the European Union who, at present, far and wide surpass ours in their knowledge and appreciation of their classical roots.

In the old days, one could not enter the University of Malta to study Classics without an A-Level in Latin, and an O-Level in Greek (Advanced Level and Ordinary Level are equivalent to British public examinations taken at 18+ and 16+ years). With a scholarly background from Great Britain, I was privileged to enter with A-Levels in both languages. But in 1989, no student was expected to possess an O-Level in either Latin or Greek, as for more than ten years these languages were no longer studied at school. So, the new system which I introduced not only helped students to learn at university Latin or Greek, but both Latin and Greek in just three years, reaching the level of a Bachelor degree just as in the old times. This system could not work without a great effort made by myself alone, teaching the two languages from O-Level to a high quality praised throughout the years by our external examiners. Many of our students became my colleagues, others continued their studies in Europe, where the level of their languages was much more admired by the host universities in comparison with the level of their own students in that country. Recently, we had four students furthering their studies in Classics in Great Britain, now we have one studying at Leiden.

New frontiers

After twenty years of producing students and lecturers in Classics, the time was ripe to introduce a new subject which would be taught in the sixth form (the last two years of secondary education, 16–18 years), where for two years students may opt to study Classical Studies at Intermediate Level before entering the university. But this Classical Studies was different from that of the same name which I taught in Zimbabwe, for with us here it meant elementary Latin and Greek, and a wide spectrum of what made the Greeks and the Romans the people we know about. In this way, students were introduced to Latin and Greek and, at the same time, were not frightened by too much language.

The idea was successful, for not only the Junior College of the University of Malta taught it, but also the Government introduced it in its sixth forms both in Malta and on the island of Gozo. The teachers, of course, are my ex-students and presently my colleagues. Our next step is to introduce Classics in the secondary schools, perhaps in the line of Classical Studies taught at the sixth form. This would lead to an O-Level in Classical Studies. We also hope to introduce Classics to schools at the primary level under 'mild' titles such as 'Ancient civilisation', 'Greek Mythology', 'Ancient Literature', 'Ancient Architecture' and 'Classical Archaeology' and the like. Especially regarding the latter subjects, Malta and Gozo would be ideal for the introduction of this new subject since these islands were precisely inhabited by the Greeks and the Romans for many centuries, and many archaeological remains and museums of Greek and Roman antiquities are still with us as a vivid illustration of our past.

One must remember that for many years now a different subject, Classical Culture and Civilization, has been taught at St Martin's College (a private school) to Maltese and international students with great success. The Director and owner of one of these schools was in fact a member of the Malta Classics Association and its Honorary President and benefactor.

At the same time, a group of ex-students and colleagues met for the first time in 2010 to form the Malta Classics Association. This was very important, for it ensured that Classics could reach the whole society through the distribution of its academic journal, the *Melita Classica*, its newsletter and now Facebook. Lots of courses are given to the public throughout the year to people of all ages, and we continually offer public lectures in various parts of the island as well as dramatic performances from Classical sources through the great efforts of my ex-student and now full-time colleague, Dr Carmel Serracino. This colleague has also been instrumental in introducing into our university curriculum conversational Latin and Greek, Drama and Modern Greek. The Malta Classics Association constantly organizes public lectures. Indeed, a recent public lecture, delivered by myself at the University of Malta, was about 'Those Sacred Numbers', about the moon and our activities which depend upon the changing phases of the moon, with many references to Greek, Roman and Hebrew sources. The attraction to this lecture was that the lecture coincided with other various occurrences, namely, that of a full moon, a lunar eclipse and the fiftieth anniversary of the first landing on the moon by Man. In addition, I sang the Homeric Hymn to Selene in Greek, and Catullus' poem to Diana in Latin. The attendance was a record of more than 300 people.

So, the interest in Classics in Malta has been increasing all the time. This year I teach Latin to eleven students in the first year, a high figure when compared to previous years. Their only motivation is the fact that in three years they will be knowledgeable of two languages, apart from their interest in the history and society of the Greeks and the Romans, penetrating into the classical spirit which arose from the Greek sense of excellence, and from Roman law and value of *gravitas*. Jobs will be very few for them, but they know that Classics would help them in their other subjects which they would teach in schools.

Apart from teaching Classics at sixth form and university, Classics is considered here a good certificate to have because the effort to get a Degree in Classics is well known to be more demanding than that required for other subjects. All know that Greek and Latin are not easy subjects, and word is passed round from student to student that the subject is a very serious one, but very rewarding too. All students are proud to have passed Latin and Greek with us for the simple reason that they cannot but work hard to graduate in this subject. Needless to add, the lecturers have been giving their utmost to attract students through their expertise and dedication.

The Malta Classics Association, affiliated with Euroclassica, has in its statutes the obligation to foster an interest in Sanskrit. In fact, it has been teaching Sanskrit as one of its own courses, even if this subject has never reached the schools. Sanskrit Philosophy is also taught at the Philosophy Department of our university by the husband of one of our founder members.

Classics at the university

I turn now to explain how I succeeded to re-introduce Latin and Greek studies at the University of Malta when I was teaching on my own and when I was asked to teach the level of a BA degree in just three years. I also decided to work things in a way to cut down expenses for the Government by introducing the alternating scheme of Latin and Greek years in the first two years, in such a way that second-year students (who will, at a given year, have covered Greek) would join first-year students studying Latin. Then, students for both the General and the Honours degrees would further their knowledge in both Latin and Greek languages together in the third year, together with several other units which are partly based on surveys delivered in English, and partly on Greek and Latin sources. Such units include the following: Classical Epic, Classical Art and Archaeology, Sources for Ancient Art and Archaeology, Greek Mythology, Classical Mythology in Pictorial Art, Greek and Roman Civilization, History of Greek and Roman Literature, Prosody and Rhetoric, Greek and Roman Philosophy, Classical Literary Criticism, Classical Sciences and Women in the Classical World. These units, already involving both Latin and Greek, serve to complement the other direct training in translating advanced Greek and Latin passages into English, and in translating English passages into Greek and Latin through Prose Composition. In addition, a set of Greek and Roman authors, offering a wide spectrum of genres, are analysed, explained and commented upon by various part-time lecturers, my ex-students, and myself. These genres include the following: Satire (Petronius and Aristophanes), Philosophy (Plato and Cicero), Historiography (Herodotus and Livy), Drama (Euripides and Plautus), Epic (Homer and Vergil), Narrative (Xenophon and Caesar), Elegy/Lyric (Catullus and Horace), and Oratory (Demosthenes and Cicero).

It has to be added here that from a few years ago, a dissertation has been introduced. This addition could only work provided the grammar and syntax hours were reduced. In addition, a new course was introduced for the first-year students, called 'Introduction to Classics'. I participate in it by teaching Classical Malta, namely, the archaeology and inscriptions found in Malta and Gozo, and all the literary references to the islands made in Latin or Greek.

Perhaps one should ask how we are able to teach all this stuff in three years to students who start from zero level in Latin and Greek. The answer is found in methodology. Old fashioned teachers were dumbfounded to hear that I teach the four conjugations at one go in one lesson. But through this method, I show students how economical it is to learn Greek and Latin in just two years of the three-year programme faster and easier and more intelligently and deeply than the five years it took me at school, when shortly afterwards my fellow schoolmates forgot all.

The Department of Classics and Archaeology at the University of Malta has at present the following work force: Professor Horatio Vella, Full Professor, full-time; Dr Carmel Serracino, Senior Lecturer, full-time; Dr Jurgen Gatt, Lecturer, part-time; Mrs Maria Fenech, Lecturer, part-time. Mrs Fenech is also the Lecturer of Classical Studies taught at Intermediate level at the Junior College of the University of Malta. One should note that lecturers teach their course every other year. This method also enables us to train a variety of part-time lecturers in their own preferred fields.

Conclusion

Since 1989, over thirty years ago, first alone, and gradually through the help of my ex-students, I have succeeded in setting up a programme in Classics (Latin and Greek) taught over three years from zero level to a BA degree. Postgraduate degree programmes also exist for both MA and PhD degrees. The student numbers have been increasing ever since. The teaching of Classics has now spread to the sixth form level as well as to private secondary schools. It is hoped that Latin Studies (with some Greek) will be introduced sometime in government schools, Mythology and Ancient History in the primary schools. Malta has its own association, the Malta Classics Association, since 2010, which has been affiliated to Euroclassica since 2014, and Malta was the host country for Euroclassica's annual conference held in August 2015 in Valletta.

Organizations

Euroclassica: https://www.euroclassica.eu/
Malta Classics Association: https://classicsmalta.org/

NETHERLANDS

Suzanne Adema

A Selfie with Sappho

Introduction

The formal Dutch curriculum for Greek and Latin is a combination of language and culture, as is reflected in the official titles: *Griekse Taal en Cultuur* (GTC) [Greek Language and Culture] and *Latijnse Taal en Cultuur* (LTC) [Latin Language and Culture]. Their outcomes are not (only) aimed at knowledge and skills; the main goals are intercultural awareness and personal development. A key phrase in curricular publications of the last four or five decades is 'reflection on your own world through the unknown'. That is, use antiquity as a grindstone to help develop your own ideas.

The emphasis on these intercultural and personal goals is why a recent curriculum committee chose to name their report 'Selfie with Sappho' (VCN 2019). The explanation of this title reads:

> Delving into Sappho's poems and her world encourages you to think about yourself and your own world. Together with Sappho you look in the mirror of your screen and who do you see? The school subjects GTC and LTC enable students to enrich the image they have of themselves and their environment with people and texts from antiquity.

At the moment, a curriculum reform is taking place in the Netherlands, for all subjects. The committee for Greek and Latin takes 'Selfie with Sappho' as their basis. In this contribution, I describe the current curriculum and practices, ongoing debates and, where possible, sketch the directions in which the new curriculum seems to develop.

The Dutch educational system, numbers of Greek and Latin students

The Dutch educational system roughly has three secondary school types of four, five and six years respectively. The six-year type, *vwo*, prepares for university programmes, and it is only in this six-year type that Greek and Latin are offered, in the subtype of *vwo* called *gymnasium*. The open data on Dutch secondary education show that in 2021 about 57,000 students were following a *gymnasium* education, out of a total of 930,000 secondary school students.

In the Netherlands, forty-two schools exclusively offer the *gymnasium* subtype, so-called independent gymnasia. In sum, approximately 30,000 pupils attend these schools. Note that these are not private schools, they are funded in the same way as any other school. If a student at an independent *gymnasium* would like to drop Greek and Latin, they need to leave their school and continue their *vwo* education at another school. Another 27,000 pupils follow a *gymnasium* education at schools that also offer the other subtype of *vwo*, as well as the five-year *havo* and four-year *vmbo*. When students at these schools drop both Greek and Latin, they can stay at the same school and finish their *vwo* education.

In 2021, about 39,000 students took the national final examinations for *vwo*. Of these 9,500 finished the subtype of *gymnasium*: about 7,000 took the final Latin examination (on Cicero's *Pro Sexto Roscio*) and 3,000 took the Greek examination (on Euripides' *Bacchae*). There was an overlap of at least 700 students who took both. These numbers are pretty representative for the numbers of the last five to ten years. But whereas the *gymnasium* used to be the only *vwo* subtype for students craving cognitive challenges, the educational landscape has changed in recent years: variants such as the bilingual *vwo*, the *technasium* and *coder class* are becoming increasingly popular and are serious competitors for the *gymnasium*.

Debate: accessibility and social equality

Although all Dutch primary and secondary school students meet the Greeks and Romans as part of the formal history curriculum, not all of them have the opportunity to learn their languages. Not everyone is given the opportunity to 'take a selfie with Sappho'.

Teachers and tests in the final years of primary school are decisive at which school types eleven- and twelve-year-old children will continue their education. Thus, the opportunity to study Greek and Latin depends on how you perform cognitively at a relatively young age. Moreover, it seems to depend on chance as well, as Lidewij van Gils shows (Van Gils 2023). Her results are based on a survey completed by more than 1,700 secondary school students. Van Gils concludes that first generation students do find their way to a classics education, but that this is, in a large number of cases, the result of a series of coincidences. Many primary school students, their parents and, possibly, teachers do not seem to be aware of the existence of the *gymnasium*, and the subjects Greek and Latin.

The accessibility of the *gymnasium* is part of a larger societal debate on social equality in education in the Netherlands (see also e.g., Burgersdijk 2022; Remie 2022; Van Gils 2023, for further references). The larger debate, held by educational experts, sociologists and politicians, mostly concerns the relatively early moment of separating students according to their cognitive skills. As part of the standpoint that selection at a later age (e.g., 14 or 15) would be better, some contributors argue for the abolition of independent *gymnasia*, often also denying any value to Greek and Latin at the same time. Another argument to abolish *gymnasia* is the idea that they foster social inequality, as they allegedly maintain a socio-cultural elite of generations of people sending their children to these relatively small and mostly well-performing schools.

School leaders and classicists respond to the standpoint on early selection by proposing that the *gymnasium* could be seen as a type of education specifically catered for early cognitive bloomers, who need challenges to learn and stay happy – just as there are school types for students who thrive in a more practical education. In addition, they point out standing practice and experiments with later enrolment at the *gymnasium*.

The accessibility of the *gymnasium* could and should be improved. Schools and classicists acknowledge this and have already developed initiatives to indeed draw and keep a more heterogeneous population. The Stichting Het Zelfstandig Gymnasium (SHZG), in which the independent *gymnasia* are united, has, for instance, initiated action research in collaboration with the Free University (Amsterdam). They explore a range of interventions to increase the diversity of their population and the feelings of belonging of all students (Waldring et al. 2022). Among these interventions are the following:

- Strengthen contact with a wide range of primary schools, e.g., by means of workshops or student ambassadors.
- Initiate pre-secondary school classes for eleven-year-olds.
- Help students with planning and homework.
- Create an inclusive programme of curricular and extra-curricular activities to increase social cohesion.

On their website, the SHZG summarizes the findings of an intermediate conference (June 2023) with the 'honest conclusion' that there is still a lot of work to be done, adding the positive note that schools are joining forces to address these issues.

The subjects of Greek and Latin are closely connected to the *vwo* subtype of *gymnasium*. So, whenever the *gymnasium* is discussed, the value of Greek and Latin needs to be put to the fore as well. The 'Curriculum Mirror' of 2017 lists often named merits of the Greek and Latin curriculum (Van der Plaat 2017, with further references). Apart from insight in language systems and close readings skills, these are a flexibility of mind when approaching something new or different and the ability to put one's own time and world view in perspective. The imagery of influential west-European culture is better understood with knowledge of Greek and Roman antiquity. Other merits mentioned are the ability to read and appreciate complex literature, understand human motives and actions, and, of a slightly different nature, acquire complex study and organizational skills.

An internal debate: assessment and the unseen translation

Whereas the debate on accessibility concerns society at large, another Dutch discussion is much more confined to classicists. It concerns the unseen translation as part of the national assessment. An unseen translation makes up 50 per cent of this test and the grading method is a rather strict model prescribing how to assign 1, 2 or 3 points for a short clause or word group. Results of the unseen translation have drastically deteriorated over the past decades (Kroon & Sluiter 2010).

There is a group of classicists that wants to keep the unseen and a group that does not. People who are against the unseen do not just adhere to this opinion because of bad examination results. They argue that an unseen translation does not assess text comprehension, but, rather, the (almost mechanical) skill to convert chunks of Greek or Latin into chunks of Dutch. People who want to keep the unseen focus on the value of linguistic skills and precision fostered by translating and express the concern that the subjects and language skills will be hollowed out when it is cancelled.

The discussion flared up in 2009, after the publication of reports on possible curricular reforms (Kroon & Sluiter 2009, 2010). They proposed to discontinue the unseen translation, because training for this part of the examination compromises the time that can be spent on fostering intercultural awareness and personal development. After heated debate, the unseen remained part of the assessment.

Since then, Suzanne Luger has investigated the complexities of translating as part of the Latin curriculum. Building on the idea that translating is an iterative process, Luger has developed and empirically tested possible interventions to teach students to produce translations that are not a series of converted chunks, but coherent texts. Luger separates the *classroom activity of translating* from the *assessment method of the unseen*, arguing that the classroom activity should be part of the curriculum, but that translating an unseen text is not a fitting assessment method of text comprehension (Luger 2020).

At the moment (Autumn 2023), the debate about the unseen is in full swing again. In the current reform proposal, there is less space for the unseen as an assessment method. The committee does, however, stress the value of translating as a classroom activity, an activity in which students and teachers collaboratively come to a deeper understanding of the original text. The coming year will show how the field currently feels about the unseen translation as an assessment form.

The situation in and outside the classroom: teaching materials and activities

The six years of *vwo* are rather strictly divided into two parts of three years in the Netherlands, and so are the schoolbooks for Latin and Greek. For the first years (the *onderbouw*), there are about five school methods on offer for Latin, a little less for Greek. For about ten years, the Ørberg method for Latin has also been used in several schools.

Dutch school methods look attractive, and full colour pictures of artefacts and paintings illustrate and help to clarify the texts. Grammar and vocabulary are offered with a focus on reading and translating, in the Greek/Latin-Dutch direction. A chapter typically introduces relevant cultural information and new grammar and vocabulary, after which students practise in specific exercises. Students spend most time, generally, applying this knowledge while translating texts. These texts are adapted from original Greek or Latin texts or written specifically for the method. Comprehension questions about these texts range from explaining grammatical and text linguistic features to cultural questions.

Although some lower year school methods include exercises on comparing an original text with a given translation, most school methods and schools do not start offering unadapted texts until the last three years (the *bovenbouw*). In their sixth year, all students prepare for the national assessment by reading the same set of texts. The set consists of about twenty pages (from the Oxford Classical Text edition) in the original language and twenty-five pages in translation. The author changes every year (e.g., Homer, Herodotus, Euripides for Greek, Vergil, Livy, Cicero for Latin). The national assessment consists of questions about the set texts (50 per cent) and an unseen translation (50 per cent), as discussed above.

In the fourth and fifth year, students read thirty pages in the original language and forty-five pages in translation. Teachers are free to choose the texts – from Homer to Neo-Latin. Fourth year texts in Greek could be stories from the New Testament, fables or Lucianus' *Dialogues of the Dead*. For Latin, these may be fables, Ovid, Caesar but also hagiography (e.g., St Martin of Tours) or Erasmus' colloquies. In the fifth year, texts will usually be from a classical author. Teachers can use schoolbooks or make their own material. Teaching materials contain, apart from the texts, introductions and cultural information, quite extensive annotations and text comprehension questions. Added to these are PowerPoint presentations and, more and more, YouTube videos in which a teacher talks students through the syntax of a text. The popularity of these videos understandably increased during the pandemic.

An important tool for students in higher years is a dictionary: they are allowed to use a dictionary in class and during tests. For tests, paper dictionaries are obligatory, but for class and homework both the online Latin–Dutch Dictionary and the Greek–Dutch Dictionary are available (see below for URLs). Students rely heavily on their dictionary, and problems and possible solutions of their dictionary use were investigated by Daniël Bartelds (2024). He proposes a pedagogy based on a cognitive apprenticeship between teachers and students. Amongst his advice are the following points: demonstrate dictionary use by thinking aloud on a regular basis, observe students while they use the dictionary and let them reflect on their dictionary use. Moreover, he argues that insights from situated problem-solving, and the form of cognitive apprenticeship are useful for other parts of the Classics curriculum as well.

Dutch schoolbooks tend to focus on translation and text comprehension, and do not generally contain ready-made assignments that foster intercultural awareness and personal development. To fill this gap, Kokkie van Oeveren developed a tested approach to help teachers design their own materials (Van Oeveren 2019a). In this approach, teachers choose texts and other sources from antiquity around a theme that is relevant and appealing to students. After reading and studying the materials from antiquity, students engage in activities that help them formulate the ideas in the text and to form their own ideas on the theme under investigation. An example of a theme is "(alleged) threats to society", connected to Livy's Bacchanalia episode (Van Oeveren 2019b).

Teachers generally do not solely stick to cognitive activities, nor do they confine their teaching to the classroom. Especially in lower years, students learn and process information about antiquity in active and creative ways. They craft Roman houses, paint pottery or re-enact a visit to the baths (*thermae*) in the Dutch open-air museum Archeon. Classrooms tend to be filled with the results of their projects, such as infographics, mosaics and sugar cube temples. Apart from (international) excursions, teachers organize visits to Greek tragedies or other plays inspired by antiquity. Several theatre groups in the Netherlands have specialized in performances and workshops specifically aimed at students, with great success.

Becoming a Classics teacher in the Netherlands

In the Netherlands, there are four undergraduate and Masters programmes in Classics, and about 100 first-year students start their BA in one of these programmes each year. It is compulsory to have taken the final school exam in Greek or Latin to enter these programmes. Most students have taken both, others train extra during their first year. If you want to study the ancient world at the university level but did not take a final exam in Greek or Latin, there are several other possibilities, such as Ancient Studies in Amsterdam or Ancient Near East Studies in Leiden (see also Schulz et al. 2023).

In 2014, the publication *Een gouden standaard voor de gymnasiumopleiding* [The gold standard for high school teaching] saw the light. This 'gold standard' presents curricular suggestions and practical recommendations, as well as standards for teacher training and professional development. Even though the publication is over ten years old by now, its 'golden road' to becoming a teacher of Greek and Latin is still valid: it leads from taking Greek and Latin in secondary school, via a three-year Bachelor in Greek and Latin Languages and Cultures (GLTC) and a one-year Master in Classics and Ancient Cultures to a one-year Teaching Training Master. After this trajectory, the student has become a fully qualified teacher of Greek and Latin. Another possibility is to qualify as a Latin teacher, after an undergraduate and MA in Ancient Studies with Latin.

Far from all 100 first-year students follow the trajectory to teacher qualification, and a relatively large number of new teachers make a career switch, out of education, in their first five years. In fact, the shortage of qualified Classics teachers is an existing and increasing problem in the Netherlands. There is a general shortage of teachers in the Netherlands, and Classics has the questionable honour of being in the top ten. There was a shortage of 53 full-time Classics teachers in 2022, with an estimated shortage of 166 teachers in 2031.

The shortage is why universities took the initiative, in cooperation with the ministry, to develop a programme for teachers of other subjects to obtain added qualifications in Greek and Latin. This three-year programme, *Scholae*, has since its start in 2007 resulted in a fresh group of qualified teachers, but their numbers are, unfortunately, not enough to solve the problem. At the moment, schools need to resort to unwanted solutions like unqualified teachers, students (even in their first or second year) or combining classes.

Professional development

Ties between classicists are strong in the Netherlands. Teaching materials and ideas are exchanged among teachers on social media and can also be found in the Dutch journal for classicists *Lampas* and the website Quamlibet. Classics departments regularly contribute to post-graduate teacher training. Together with the Vereniging Classici Nederland, they organize a yearly two-day conference for teachers. Museums, publishers and distributors of school methods offer training, for instance on excursions, on using active Latin or on more general topics. Excursions to Italy and Greece specifically aimed at teachers are organized as well.

Teachers who like an academic challenge may apply for a grant enabling them to do academic research for part of their week, resulting in a dissertation after about five or six years. This research, funded by the Dutch Government, may concern a classics topic, but can also be an educational research project. Apart from the above-mentioned projects (Van Oeveren 2019a; Luger 2020; Bartelds 2024), a fourth project, by Chelsea O'Brien (2023) focused on the ability to bounce back after a setback in reading and translating Latin. Sandra Karten currently investigates the role and possibilities of classics in cross-curricular and interdisciplinary education (see Schulz et al. 2023).

The future of Greek and Latin in the Netherlands

As we have seen, all school subjects are being reformed in the Netherlands, and so are Greek and Latin, but translating will remain part of the curriculum as a classroom activity. The unseen translation as part of the national assessment is, yet again, subject of a hot debate among Dutch classicists. In this respect, the final outcome is not yet clear, but the focus of the curricula will remain on intercultural awareness and personal development. Greek and Latin will still be characterized by a combination of language, text, culture, history and myth.

Despite worries on the accessibility of Classics and the ever-growing teacher shortage, I hope to have shown that there is reason for optimism: Greek and Latin are and will be part of our curriculum, and Dutch classicists at schools and universities form a close-knit network of committed and enthusiastic professionals. There are means to focus energy into making these subjects and their related school type known to children from all layers of society. Thus, many future children can be given the opportunity to think about Greeks, Romans, humanity and themselves.

References

Adema, S., R. Bekker, X. Van Eckeren, M. De Ferrante, H. Van Gelder, H. De Gier, C. Van Oeveren, M. Simons, J. Splinter, P. Van Uum and B. Van der Wijk (2019), *Selfie met Sappho*, Vereniging Classici

Nederland. Available online: https://klassieken.nu/wp-content/uploads/2019/10/Rapport-VCN-Volgteam-Selfie-met-Sappho.pdf (accessed 7 November 2023).

Bartelds, D. (2024), *Zinnig Zoeken. Een cognitieve benadering van woordenboekdidactiek Grieks* [Sensible Searching. A Cognitive Approach to a Dictionary Use Curriculum for Ancient Greek], Dissertation, Leiden University. (Including three chapters and a summary in English.)

Burgersdijk, D. (2022), *Gymnasium. Geschiedenis van een eliteschool* [Gymnasium. History of an elite school], Amsterdam: Athenaeum.

Crump, L. (2008), 'A contemporary subject for contemporary Europe: the much-disputed role and relevance of Latin at Dutch gymnasia', in B. Lister (ed.), *Meeting the Challenge*, Cambridge: Cambridge University Press, 31–43.

Kits, K., S. Luger, M. Simons, H. Neven and P. Zijlstra (2014), *Een gouden standaard voor de gymnasiumopleiding* [A gold standard for grammar school education], Werkgroep Gouden Standaard.

Kroon, C. and I. Sluiter (2009), *Tussenrapport van de verkenningscommissie klassieke talen* [Interim report of the exploratory committee on classical languages], Leiden: Enschede. Available online: https://www.stilus.nl/examen/x-0101.pdf (accessed 7 November 2023).

Kroon, C. and I. Sluiter (2010), *Het geheim van de blauwe broer: Eindrapport van de verkenningscommissie klassieke talen* [The secret of the blue brother: Final report of the exploratory committee on classical languages], Leiden: Enschede. Available online: https://bgv.aob.nl/wp-content/uploads/2013/03/het_geheim_van_de_blauwe_broer_def.pdf (accessed 7 November 2023).

Luger, S. (2020), *Lost in Latin translation. Teaching students to produce coherent target texts*, Dissertation, University of Amsterdam.

O'Brien, C. (2023), *Dealing with setbacks. Exploring academic buoyancy in Latin students who are cognitively gifted*, Dissertation, University of Amsterdam.

Remie, M. (2022), *Het gymnasium. Het verhaal van een eigengereid schooltype* [The gymnasium. The story of a headstrong school type], Amsterdam: Prometheus.

Schulz, V., S. Adema, L. van Gils, S. Karten and H. Baumann (2023), 'Latein in interdisziplinären Lehrplänen' [Latin in interdisciplinary curricula], *Forum Classicum*, 2: 134–40.

Van der Plaat, A. (2017), Klassieke Talen, in E. Folmer, A. Koopmans-van Noorel and W. Kuiper (eds), *Curriculumspiegel 2017*, Enschede: SLO, 203–26.

Van Gils, L. (2023), 'At the gymnasium through your football buddy's aunt. Accessibility of classical education in the Netherlands', *Journal of Classics Teaching*, 49: 52–5.

Van Oeveren, C. (2019a), *Ithaka gaf je de reis . . . Op weg naar reflectie op het eigene en het vreemde in het literatuuronderwijs klassieke talen* [Ithaka gave you the journey . . . Towards reflection on the familiar and the foreign in classical language literature education], Dissertation, Vrije Universiteit Amsterdam. (Including a summary in English.)

Van Oeveren, C. (2019b), *Ithaka gaf je de reis . . . Docentenmateriaal Deel III, Livius' Bacchanalia*, Enschede: SLO.

Van Oeveren, C. and M. Ferrante (2022), *Startnotitie klassieke talen* [Initial note on classical languages], Amersfoort: SLO.

VCN Volgteam (2019), *Selfie met Sappho*, Open Access.

Waldring, I., P. Scheltema and J. van Zwieten (2022), *Startnotitie 2.0. Richting kansengelijkheid op het Gymnasium* [Starting note 2.0. Towards equality of opportunity at the Gymnasium], SHZG and VU University. Available online: https://www.gymnasia.nl/app/uploads/2023/02/Notitie-1-aangevulde-versie-Startnotitie-Kansengelijkheid-2.0.pdf (accessed 1 November 2023).

Websites

Archeon: https://www.archeon.nl/index.html.
Greek–Dutch Dictionary: https://woordenboekgrieks.nl/.
Lampas: https://www.aup-online.com/content/journals/01658204.

Latin–Dutch Dictionary: https://www.latijnnederlands.nl/.
Quamlibet: https://www.quamlibet.nl/.
Vereniging Classici Nederland: https://vcnonline.nl/.

NORTH MACEDONIA

Vesna Dimovska and Svetlana Kočovska-Stevovik̇

Introduction

The teaching of Classics in the territory of present-day Republic of North Macedonia does not have a very long tradition. In the period between 1945 and 1982, when the country was part of former Yugoslavia, Latin was taught as a compulsory subject in *gymnasia*, in two academic years with two classes per week. Greek, on the other hand, was part of the curriculum on a few occasions only: in the Classics classes in a *gymnasium* in the capital Skopje, which existed in the period between 1948 and 1956 and in the period between 1976 and 1982, and in the classes of so-called Cultural Studies that functioned in the 1980s. In the Classics class, known as 'Classical *gymnasium*', Latin and Greek were taught for four years, with a weekly quota that was no less than three lessons per week for each of the two classical languages in all of its stages of existence. In the curricula of the Cultural Studies class, Latin and Greek were taught for two academic years, with a weekly quota of two lessons. From 1982 up to today each consecutive educational reform has been to the detriment of classical education: in secondary education Latin has progressively had a smaller number of lessons, while, with the demise of the Cultural Sciences qualification in the early 1990s, the teaching of Greek as a compulsory subject has been almost completely excluded from curricula in secondary education.

In higher education, Classics have been taught continuously since 1946, when the Institute of Classical Studies was established within the Faculty of Philosophy in Skopje. The trend of gradual reduction of the importance of classical education in Macedonian society had an impact on higher education too. Thus, while in the past Latin was a compulsory subject not only for the students who decided to study Classics, but for students enrolled at the Departments of History, Art History and Archaeology, Romance Philology, and General and Comparative Literature, today it has the status of a compulsory subject only for the students studying Classical Philology or Latin.

Classics in schools and universities today

For now, Classics can be studied at all three levels of education, but to a degree that cannot be considered satisfactory. As part of the nine-year primary education (6–14 years of age) classical languages are not taught, but students acquire some basic knowledge about ancient history and culture as part of the syllabus for History in sixth grade (11–12 years). Sixth-grade students have the opportunity to deepen their knowledge about Classics through the syllabus for the subject of Classical Culture in European Civilization. Unfortunately, this is an elective subject and to our knowledge, it is chosen less frequently than the other two subjects available to students: Ethics of Religions and Introduction to Religion. In four-year secondary comprehensive education (14–18 years), some classical topics are covered as part of the subjects Mother Tongue and Literature, History, and Art, which in *gymnasia* are compulsory for all students. In the second year in *gymnasium*, there is an elective subject Classical Language, when students have the option to choose whether to learn Greek or Latin. Which of these two languages will be studied, should they choose the subject, depends on the student's interest. This subject is on the list of electives together with four others (Information Technology, Elementary Algebra and Geometry, Speaking and Writing, and Ethics), and as experience so far shows, it is chosen less often than the other subjects on offer. Not infrequently, due to the insufficient number of students (the minimum for a group to be formed is fifteen), even those who choose this subject are forced to take another subject from the list of electives. On the rare occasion when a group is formed, students prefer to study Latin in the classes for classical languages.

Whether *gymnasium* students will study classical languages in their continued studies depends on which of the six areas they choose in the third year: Natural Sciences and Mathematics, combination A or B; Social Sciences and Humanities, combination A or B, and Languages and Arts, combination A or B. One of these six packages (Languages and Arts, combination A) envisages the studying of one of the two classical languages in two academic years, with a weekly quota of two lessons. As part of this subject, entitled Classical Language (Latin or Greek), students always study Latin, mostly at the suggestion of the subject teacher. One-year's study of Latin, with a weekly quota of two lessons, is also envisaged in two other elective packages (Natural Sciences and Mathematics, combination B, and Social Sciences and Humanities, combination A). The subjects Classical Language (Latin or Greek) and Latin in the above-mentioned three packages are on the list of so-called electives, but in fact they do not have the status of electives, because their studying is obligatory for all students who elected the package that includes them. In addition to *gymnasia*, Latin is taught in vocational secondary medical and veterinary schools, where it has the status of a compulsory subject. In these schools, it is taught for one year, with two lessons per week.

In higher education, Classics are taught at only one university in the country – the State University of Ss Cyril and Methodius in Skopje (UKIM). At the Institute of Classical Studies within the Faculty of Philosophy at this university, Classics can be studied in three education cycles: undergraduate, postgraduate and doctoral studies. In the first cycle of studies, the learning of classical languages at UKIM is compulsory only for the Classical Studies students, while Greek is taught as a compulsory at the Orthodox Theological Faculty. Latin and Greek, together with a series of other subjects in the field of Classics (Daily Life in Ancient Times, Reception of Classical Culture, Ancient Drama, Ancient Rhetoric, Ancient Mythology, Introduction to Latin Epigraphy) are on the so-called list of free elective subjects and can be chosen by all UKIM students. Classical languages do not have the status of compulsory classes even in the second and third cycle courses. In addition to UKIM, Latin can be studied at the Goce Delchev State University in Shtip, where, as part of undergraduate studies in Archaeology, Italian Language and Literature and French Language and Literature, it has the status of an elective subject, which can be attended for only one semester. Also, at the State University in Tetovo, there are Latin courses present as a compulsory or elective subject (taught in Albanian) in two or four semesters in the Faculty of Philology.

Teachers – supply and pedagogy

As can be seen in this overview, in the Republic of North Macedonian education system, Classics are represented at a level that cannot be considered satisfactory. Classics under-representation in education is not due to the lack of staff. A total of 260 students have graduated from the Institute of Classical Studies (fzf.ukim.edu.mk/институт-за-класични-студии) since its inception in 1946 until today, most of whom acquired a university diploma in the last twenty years. Due to the trend of progressively reducing the lessons in classical languages after independence in 1991 until the present, fewer than 10 per cent of active classical philologists are employed in the education sector.

The analysis of the staff's engagement shows that, in the last decade, they have been facing an insufficient number of lessons and, as a result, they cannot have full-time jobs. This is not so much a result of educational reforms, but a result of demographic processes: due to the declining birth rate and the rising trend of people moving out of the country, fewer children enrol in primary and secondary schools in the country than a decade ago, which results in a decreasing number of classes in school. In the academic year 2019/20 only five classical language teachers in the entire country have the full quota of lessons (twenty to twenty-three lessons per week) in their original schools. A small number of them have also a full quota of lessons but in addition to their original school, they were employed in other, primary or secondary schools, as teachers for the elective subjects of Classical Culture in European Civilization or Classical Language. Most of the teachers, particularly in smaller towns, do not have a full quota of lessons, despite the fact that some of them work in several different towns in the country. Often the inability to have full-time employment and the low salaries force teachers to look for other sources of income, which in many cases affects the quality of teaching.

Because teachers are not sufficiently motivated to improve the quality of teaching, lessons in Latin today are very rarely different from the Latin lessons in the past. Even though teachers are advised to abandon the traditional approach, which is not adequate to the times and the context in which young generations are educated, teachers very rarely show willingness to abandon it and to move from a grammar-based course to a reading course for studying Latin. The dominance of the traditional approach is due, to a certain extent, to the teachers' fear that, if they change the approach, they would not be able to cover the entire syllabus, which in the case of Latin envisages that in the first year of studying almost the entire Latin morphology is taught in only seventy-two lessons per year. Although the Latin syllabus envisages for the students to gain knowledge about Roman culture and civilization, teachers of Latin pay much less attention to this content. The application of the traditional approach to teaching and the sacrificing of the content about culture and civilization in favour of the language leaves the impression on students that the goal of the Latin course is to learn Latin grammar, and not that learning grammar is necessary for them to be able to read and understand texts in Latin.

In addition to teaching methods, this impression is also based on assessment. During the school year, teachers assess students' knowledge through oral exams and written tests. The final mark is mostly based on the result that the students get at the written test at the end of each half term, which consists of various questions on grammar and a translation of several sentences from Latin into the teaching language (Macedonian or Albanian). It often happens that the teacher, in order to make it easier for the students to acquire the content, gives them the option to use a dictionary for the written tests, thus relieving them of the duty to learn vocabulary. In many cases this means that students are able to decline, for example the noun *res, rei, f.* in cases or are able to give a definition how to make an indicative imperfect of the verb *video, vidi, visum 2*, but when they encounter the forms *rebus* or *videbatis* in a text, they are not able to translate them properly. The assessment method additionally reinforces the students' impression that the goal of Latin classes is to learn Latin grammar. Thus, the stereotype already prevailing among students that the studying of Latin is unnecessary is further reinforced.

Education policy

Some of the challenges that the teaching of Classics faces are the same challenges that the entire education system in the Republic of North Macedonia faces. These challenges have been recognized and defined in the latest national Strategy on Education 2018–2025 (Стратегија за образованието за 2018–2025 и Акциски план 2018) and some of them are as follows: the curricula are overburdened and there are still syllabi that are antiquated, do not permit an integrated approach to studying ideas, do not develop sufficiently generic and key competences, and do not support modern approaches to teaching; the dispersion of secondary schools is inadequate, which results in an excessive number of students (up to 40 per class) in some schools or a very small number in others; teachers do not get adequate practical preparation during their initial training or internship; the assessment of the curriculum and syllabus quality and student assessment are not consistent in terms of all relevant factors; reforms in comprehensive secondary education (*gymnasia*) are not always coherent/consistent with reforms in primary education, etc. Of the specific challenges, the greatest one is how to break the stereotype that Classics today are an anachronistic discipline, unnecessary in the modern world of globalization, modern technologies and progress based on a strong economy. Unfortunately, this stereotype is equally present in the public, among parents, as well as in the institutions in charge of educational policies. Another major challenge is also related to the stereotype / prejudice that the studying of classical languages is too difficult and requires a lot of time, and that the didactical and methodical approach is contrary to the general tendency among young people for achieving quick and easily visible results and progress in some other fields or subjects. The demotivation of Classics teachers is also a major problem, which is due to the low salaries in education (particularly secondary education), the feeling that there are no prospects and the lack of options for career advancement, as well as too many administrative duties. Thus, many teachers are not stimulated to invest greater efforts for innovations in teaching, for inventive methods and after-school activities. Although some of them really invest great efforts and creativity in teaching, the majority practise a rather traditional teaching method.

In the last twenty-seven years, since the country became independent and the political system changed from one-party to multi-party, it is evident that the changes in the authorities results in relatively frequent changes in educational policies and the politicization of education, which negatively affects the situation in Classics education. These changes in educational policies, strongly dependent and linked to political changes, often impose reforms and changes with a short lifespan, and do not allow for implementation of long-term coherent and consistent strategies and monitoring of the effect of these changes. Sometimes interventions are made in the content, the curricula or textbooks with adaptations and along models taken from education systems in other European countries, without creating autochthonous education policies for the long-term. The creation of education policies rarely involves people competent in classical education or who have had a classical education themselves. They have the opportunity to participate in public debates on certain laws or other documents; however, their remarks or opinions are usually lost in the multitude and are not implemented in the end. Recently, there are various non-governmental organizations trying to influence education policies, but they are mostly focused on creating conditions for international cooperation, mobility and the implementation of projects. One gets the impression that the changes in education policies (whether initiated by institutions or under the influence of the civil society sector) are mostly within the frame of general tendencies and the current market conditions, avoid deep cuts and reorientations, and do not respect the scientific aspect sufficiently. The above-mentioned Education Strategy and Action Plan 2018–2025 (Стратегија за образованието за 2018–2025 и Акциски план 2018) should be given a chance, but it seems quite general and cannot have a strong impact by itself on classical education specifically.

There is no specific analysis about how much classical education impacts social mobility so we can only make general conclusions. Generally speaking, in the Republic of North Macedonia, higher education permits respected jobs, however people with faculty degrees and higher education levels do not necessarily gain economic or social improvement. People with higher education in humanities are oriented towards professions in the field of culture, education, media and sciences – sectors where income is not enviable. The same applies to teachers of classical languages and culture employed in all levels of education, while the absorption of these profiles on adequate positions in the labour market is limited.

In the last fifteen years young people have been increasingly oriented to technical disciplines, conditioned by the situation on the labour market, where there are incomparably more job openings that are much better paid in the sector of information technology, business, banking and trade. So young people based on their judgement and under the influence of parents and peers, even in secondary education, prefer subjects or courses that enable them to study at one of the popular study programmes later on. Generally speaking, the interest for studying humanities is decreasing every year, and, consequently, so is the interest for studying classical languages and culture in secondary education, most probably due to the fact that this type of education does not provide a career where one can make fast and significant progress, gain good social status and material wellbeing. Another important fact needs to be mentioned: emigration, mainly of young and educated people, which has grown to a worrisome extent, and which also affects the number of students studying classical languages, as well as the perception that a classical education does not offer prospects for finding work abroad.

The efforts to apply new pedagogical or methodical approaches in the teaching of classical languages and culture are not completely missing. The Ministry of Education and Science and the Bureau for Development of Education, for all teachers in primary and secondary education, organize training events, courses, seminars and counselling. However, they are generally focused on specific aspects of pedagogical work, the introduction of some novelties, or changes of an administrative character, such as the introduction of the electronic school register, changes in the model of periodical planning of classes, general pedagogical techniques or methods, and the inclusion of students with disabilities. For teachers of specific subjects there are seminars when more than 30 per cent of the curriculum content is changed, when new subjects and new textbooks in their field are introduced. For instance, in 2010/11 there was a series of training events for teachers of Classical Culture in European Civilization, when it was included for the first time on the list of elective subjects.

Support for Classics in schools

In addition to state institutions, there has been assistance about new approaches and methods of teaching classical languages offered by the non-governmental organization Association of Classical Philologists (Antika), as part of their regular activities, or through special projects such as the *Docendo discimus I and II* summer schools, which were held in 2006 and 2007, along with the didactic handbook that resulted from these summer schools in 2008 (Systasis 2008). The electronic scholarly periodical *Systasis* (www.systasis.org) regularly publishes articles on topics related to pedagogical approaches or didactic examples in the field of classical languages. In 2019, another project was implemented: *Hermes*, about the presentation of content treating ancient cultural heritage (epigraphic, literary and artistic) in various subjects in secondary education, through field visits to archaeological sites, museums and the theatre (https://hermes.org.mk/).

The use of information technology and social media for teaching purposes was also promoted by the Hermes project, and work should certainly continue in this area. There are really good and beneficial individual examples of teachers who personally create and maintain websites, blogs or similar electronic tools with content that help students to acquire and expand their knowledge of classical language and culture, but these efforts were incidental and motivated by individual teachers' enthusiasm, and are not general practice or part of a broader targeted activity. Several such projects, available for other teachers to use, deserve to be mentioned: a project by a teacher in the Resen *gymnasium*, who made several creative videos on studying Latin on his YouTube channel (Nopixel 2023); the blog Mithos (Nachkovski 2023), written by a teacher in Kumanovo, who teaches the subject Classical Culture in European Civilization; or the TV documentary-feature series *Ancient Medicine in Heraclea*, written by a group of classical philologists and teachers of Latin and Greek from Bitola. The show was made by a local TV station, and was later broadcast on another channel with national concession. In the last couple of years, there have been Facebook groups which promote events, content, ideas and information that are useful for classical language teachers as well. It should also be mentioned that curricula and newer textbooks give teachers greater freedom to combine content, be more creative and even use social media and information technology when teaching.

In addition to the partnership with Antika, mentioned above, the schools teaching classical languages cooperate with the Ss. Cyril and Methodius University, more specifically the Faculty of Philosophy, where the Institute of Classical Studies is located. The Faculty provides logistical support for the activities of Antika, such as the organization of national competitions in classical languages for students in *gymnasia* and medical vocational secondary schools. Competitions for the European Certificate for Classics have been held for the last fifty years, while professors and students from the Institute occasionally visit secondary schools to give lectures, workshops or presentations. In 2019 the Faculty of Philosophy launched a one-year project 'Identifying the needs and potentials for reviving the classical gymnasium in Macedonia', that would result in a study and a concrete initiative for re-opening the classical *gymnasium*, where the two classical languages and classical culture will be taught for four years with an adequate number of classes. This cooperation between Antika, the university and individual education institutions aims to address the challenges in teaching classical languages and raise awareness in society about the importance of a classical education.

References

Стратегија за образованието за 2018–2025 и Акциски план 2018 [Education Strategy for 2018–2025 and Action Plan 2018], Министерство за образование и наука, Скопје (Strategija za obrzovanieto za 2018–2025 i Akciski plan (2018), Ministerstvo za obrazovanie i nauka, Skopje) [Ministry of Education and Science, Skopje (Education Strategy for 2018–2025 and Action Plan (2018)]. Available online: http://mrk.mk/wp-content/uploads/2018/10/Strategija-za-obrazovanie-MAK-WEB.pdf (accessed 26 October 2023).

Nachkovski, N. (2023), *Mithos*. Available online: https://mythosmk.blogspot.com/ (accessed 12 October 2023).

Nopixel (2023), Часови по латински јазик [Latin Language Classes]. YouTube video. Available online: латински во лозјето на татко ми (accessed 12 October 2023).

Systasis (2008), 'Docendo Discimus – Development and Implementation of Master Studies in Didactics of Classical Languages'. Available online: https://www.systasis.org/pdfs/posebni/docendo2008cel.pdf (accessed 12 October 2023).

NORWAY

Vibeke Roggen and Eirik Welo

Introduction

This chapter describes and evaluates the organization and present state of Classics teaching in Norwegian schools. We provide some historical background to make it easier to understand the status of the classical languages in the Norwegian educational system and in Norwegian society in general.

Our country has a weak intellectual tradition in general and was the last country in Europe to get a printing house, as late as 1643. Moreover, Norway's first university was established only in 1811, during the last phase of what Ibsen (1867) calls 'the 400 years' night', when Norway was ruled by Danish kings (*c.* 1400–1814). In the subsequent union with Sweden (1814–1905), Norway was allowed its own government, which was, however, situated in Stockholm, and without ministers of defence and foreign policy. Independence was obtained in 1905, after more than 500 years of foreign rule.

The dominant nationalistic ideology of the late nineteenth and early twentieth centuries did not favour the classical tradition. A famous novel, with the self-ironic title *Poison* [*Gift*], attacks the school system of its day as old-fashioned: Classics are presented as a foreign tradition, opposed to the sagas of Snorre Sturlason (*c.* 1179–1241) and Norway's own history as an independent country in the Middle Ages (Kielland 1907). In a famous classroom scene, the pupil little Marius is not able to conjugate *monere* in the passive. A well-known quotation, so destructive to Latin in Norway, includes his last words: '*Mensa rotunda*, said little Marius and died.' (Kielland 1907: 228; Sejersted 1986).

In the law of education of 1896, Latin could easily have been excluded from the school system. However, the church minister sneaked it back in, so to speak, and in 1919, a classical side (Latin, with or without Greek) was included in the *gymnasium* (three years, for youth aged 15–19), on an equal footing with the modern language and science sides (Ekrem 1997: 70). This system continued for sixty years.

The position of Classics was weakened significantly through a revision in 1978 (Rian 1986). The *gymnasium*, with its specialization, was replaced by more of an 'à la carte menu'. The upper secondary school has no specialized branches for intellectual subjects as Natural Science or Classics anymore, and it is no longer called *gymnasium*. And unfortunately, there is something of an anti-intellectual trend in Norway, particularly on the left wing in politics. One idea is that good school results are hereditary, and therefore, good grades should not decide access to the best schools. The so-called uniform school (*enhetsskolen*) should last for all the thirteen years at school: each class should contain pupils with all kinds of school results, not only during the mandatory years, but even the last three. Needless to say, this ideology is believed to have weakened the intellectual level considerably, not least in the case of electives, as for example Latin.

Another reason for the negative trend in the classical languages, particularly from the 1970s onwards, was the lack of innovation. The classical languages were not seen as relevant or useful by politicians and the general public, especially considering the effort needed to make pupils master them, and the classical community was not able to counter these views effectively. Ancient Culture and 'international words' (German: *Wortkunde*) from Greek and Latin were included in the curriculum, but this was carried out too late (Weidemann 1987: 49). Dissemination of classics to the general public might have improved the situation but was weak or lacking at the time.

Classics in schools today

Today Norway has ten years of compulsory schooling. Pupils start in the year they turn six. They attend primary or elementary school ('children's school') for seven years, followed by three years of lower secondary school ('youth's school'). From the eighth grade, pupils can choose one foreign language, in addition to English. Classical languages are not among the options at this stage. Upper secondary school (three years) has curricula for Latin and Greek (two years) and for Ancient Culture (*Antikkens kultur*) (one year).

In addition to the mandatory subjects, the pupil can choose among elective subjects that their school offers. Subjects that are not mandatory have to compete for pupils. In such a system, it soon became impossible to offer *both* Latin and Greek at the same school: the group size in both subjects became too small, and because of the funding system ('the money follows the pupil') the few schools with such competence could not afford to give both of them and began to offer Latin only. Greek has not been taught in Norwegian schools since around 1980. Today, Ancient culture is offered at one school and Latin at six schools in the country as a whole – in most cases in the so-called 'cathedral' schools, founded in the Middle Ages. There are examples of economic support from local authorities for schools offering Latin, but this is not the norm. The curriculum covers two years as a maximum in upper secondary school, and two of the schools offer only one year. To sum up, the situation for classical subjects is vulnerable and depends on individuals. When a teacher retires at a given school, the subject may disappear there. For various reasons, Norway is often characterized as 'the upside-down country' (*Annerledeslandet*) – a description which fits the situation for the classical languages as well. No one argues for mandatory Latin, but the opposite scenario is equally absurd: that no teenager in Norway should be given the opportunity to learn Latin at school (Sejersted 1986).

Classical subjects from school are not required for any kind of higher education. For many years now, it has been necessary to teach not only Greek, but also Latin from beginner's level at the universities which offer classical languages (in Oslo, Bergen and Trondheim). The reason is, as is shown above, the extremely weak position of Classics in the school system.

To our knowledge, none of the international schools in Norway offer classical subjects. At the French school in Oslo, Greek was taught at a time when no Norwegian schools offered it anymore. Now, however, neither Greek nor Latin is taught.

Recruitment for courses in Latin and Ancient Culture has been relatively stable. In the last ten years, on average around seventy pupils have taken Latin 1 per year nationally. The corresponding number for Latin 2 is twenty-five, one reason being that two of the six schools offer only one year of Latin, but also that the drop-out rate from the first to the second year of Latin is high. Another problem is that there are clashes between elective subjects on individual pupils' timetables. Latin tends to lose, since it is not mandatory for any kind of higher studies. On average, twenty-three pupils have taken courses in Ancient Culture annually over the last ten years. Only one school in Norway, Bergen Cathedral School, offers this subject regularly.

Since the same pupils are often interested in both Latin and Ancient Culture, a school offering both courses runs the risk of small group sizes. Some schools have solved this problem by offering only Latin, over two years, while one school offers one year of Latin in combination with one year of Ancient Culture. A third way of meeting the challenge of small group sizes has been tried out in Oslo and Bergen. Extra Latin classes were scheduled for the afternoon and opened up to pupils from other schools in the region. This scheme attracted pupils from a variety of schools, and even though each school would only contribute a few pupils, the group would be big enough to run the course. This option has, however, not been offered regularly in recent years.

There is hardly any public debate about the importance of Classics. On attempts to improve the situation, see below.

Trends and resources in teaching Classics

The mission statement of the Norwegian Education Act (*Opplæringsloven*) contains the following passage: 'Education and training shall help increase the knowledge and understanding of the national cultural heritage and our common international cultural traditions' (Opplæringsloven 2010: 5). The phrase 'our common international cultural traditions' must refer primarily to the cultural tradition from Greece and Rome.

The Norwegian commercial book market for Latin textbooks is small. The incentive for publishers to develop teaching materials in Latin is therefore dependent on government initiatives. This is even more so since the pupils in Norway do not buy textbooks but borrow them from their school. Responsible for this area are the Ministry of Education and its executive agency, the Norwegian Directorate for Education and Training (*Utdanningsdirektoratet*). The latter has for many years now favoured purely digital teaching material in its funding, which is not in accordance with the wishes of teachers and pupils when it comes to a subject such as

Latin. Salen (2013) shows how Norwegian publishers at an early stage underestimated the difficulty involved in developing digital teaching materials of high quality for classical subjects. According to teachers' responses to a questionnaire in 2023, *Pegasus Latin 1–2* (Weidemann & Petersen 2021–2), the teaching materials supported by the Directorate, is actually not in use. Instead, teachers use various textbooks. The Latin course *OMNIBVS* (Roggen et al. 1996), in Norwegian, is still used by the schools, even though it is no longer in print.

In writing this chapter, we interviewed teachers who are currently teaching Latin in upper secondary school (*videregående skole*) in Norway. These teachers kindly shared their thoughts on the opportunities and challenges of teaching Latin today and commented on what they see as important trends, internationally and nationally, within their professional field. The teachers use different textbooks as the basis of their courses. While the above-mentioned *OMNIBVS* has been widely used in earlier years, *Familia Romana*, the first part of Ørberg's *Lingua Latina per se illustrata* (Ørberg 1955) has gained in popularity during recent times. One of the reasons for this change may be that *OMNIBVS* is in need of revision. Moreover, the new curriculum for Latin (effective from 2021) puts more emphasis on spoken Latin and the teachers see Ørberg's book as more suitable for this purpose. Some of the teachers speak to their pupils mainly in Latin from day one, while others mix Latin and Norwegian.

All the teachers report that they teach Latin grammar by means of presentations which they make themselves to supplement the available textbooks. One of the teachers is involved in creating an international network around spoken Latin, connecting teachers and classes across borders. The teachers report that while they have some contact with other Latin teachers, especially in the area in which they are based, there is less contact between schools on an institutional level. Pupils in Bergen, Oslo and Trondheim may follow courses in Latin and take exams at the respective universities. All the teachers we have spoken to mention the increased importance of the active use of spoken Latin in the classroom as an international trend which is of direct relevance to their teaching style. They also mention that the new official curricula for Latin and Greek and for Ancient Culture make a sharper differentiation between ancient culture and the classical languages as school subjects. (A new textbook for ancient culture is being developed to conform better with the new curriculum.) Latin is more clearly defined as a language while there are fewer competence goals related to language in Ancient Culture. The teachers see both good and bad sides to this development.

In 2022 appeared a new and comprehensive Latin grammar written in Norwegian, Vibeke Roggen's *Latinsk grammatikk* of 900 pages (Roggen 2022). Her ambition is to present Latin grammar alongside the history and culture of the language. The main tool to achieve this is the use of quotations, translated and commented, almost 4,000 in number. The grammar includes paradigms and explains Latin grammar from beginner's level up. It is written for learners, professionals and everyone interested in Latin, even those who do not intend to learn the language. Teachers can find material for their teaching of grammar, and the book may also be used by pupils.

Teacher training and development

In Norway, teacher training is a requirement for obtaining a permanent position in public schools. The training includes both general pedagogy and didactics related to the specialization of the student. However, for decades, Latin didactics (not to mention Greek) was not offered anywhere in Norway. It took years of struggle to change that fact. Didactics in Latin was offered as a pilot in 1999 at the Department of Teacher Education and School Research (*Institutt for lærerutdanning og skoleforskning*) and permanently from the Autumn term 2016. But alas, most years there are no candidates.

As to professional development opportunities, there are no systematic courses or similar arranged by the authorities. A seventy-hours course for teachers was offered in 1999, after oral Latin had been introduced in the school curriculum, alongside other changes. The course took place partly in Rome and partly at a hotel in Norway. The University of Oslo offers a day of lectures and seminars for teachers each year, to which staff members in the Classics department contribute. The Foreign Language Centre (*Fremmedspråksenteret*) and the Directorate for Education and Training have arranged a few events related to Classics as well. See also next section.

Schools working together and with classical organizations

The most important classical organization is the Classical Association of Norway (*Norsk Klassisk Forbund*), which is a nationwide organization whose aim it is to promote the understanding of antiquity and the classical tradition in the context of European and national culture. The Association will strive to support the classical subjects and thematic fields in schools, at universities and university colleges and in society as a whole. Membership is open to everyone who supports the aim of the Association and pays the membership fee.

One main goal for the Classical Association of Norway, since its founding in 1986, has been to build bridges between schools and universities, including competence building and promotion of Classics. Every other year, the Classical Association arranges an excursion to 'a country of antiquity', that is, an area which was part of the Roman Empire and where remaining monuments and buildings can make the past more vivid. Norwegian archaeologists and local guides have made the excursions a valuable arena for learning more about the classical world. The participants in the trips also contribute to the programme, according to their special competences. Teachers have always been given priority for taking part in these excursions and some schools have supported the participation of teachers financially. Among the sites visited are Rome, Sicily, the Naples area, Athens and surroundings, western Turkey, Roman Britain, Provence, Syria, Jordan and Tunisia.

The Classical Association of Norway publishes a periodical, *Klassisk forum*, which comes out twice a year and contains both research and popular contributions. The columns are open to articles and surveys about the situation for classics in Norwegian schools. The Association also arranges yearly seminars on themes relevant to Classics teachers.

To a certain degree, there is cooperation between schools and universities. In Bergen and Trondheim, pupils have the option to follow introductory courses in Latin and take an exam at the local university. The Department of Classics at the University of Oslo has signed a cooperation agreement with the Oslo Cathedral School – the only school in the capital where Latin is offered. The agreement gives gifted pupils the opportunity to follow intermediate Latin courses at the university and take exams during their senior year at school (after having successfully completed two years of Latin there). Each year, a scholar from the university gives a lecture on a relevant subject to the pupils at the Cathedral School. These lectures may be attended by all, not only by the pupils who study Latin.

In 1993, a conference with the title 'The future for classical studies in Norway' (*Fremtiden for de klassiske studier i Norge*) was held at the Norwegian Institute in Athens. The background was a vacant position as Professor of Medieval Latin at the University of Bergen: among the applicants there was not one Norwegian. One concrete result of the conference, however, was the Programme for Ancient Studies (*Antikkprogrammet*), funded and administered by the Research Council of Norway, with the aim of supporting studies related to antiquity at the universities, and not least the classical languages. Among the activities were scholarships offered to students for taking a beginner's course in Greek or Latin, if relevant for their studies in general.

In 1994, the so-called Resource Office for Greek, Latin and Ancient Studies was opened at the University of Oslo. Important aims were to promote Latin, and even Greek, as school subjects, and to secure a better position for ancient culture in schools (Roggen 1995: 35). Among the means were initiatives towards 'neighbouring' subjects, regarding the relevance of one or both classical languages, in addition to dissemination to the general public. The office, funded by the humanities faculties at the universities in Norway and the Ministry of Education, was active for some years and played a part in making Classics more visible.

There have traditionally been close ties between the classical organizations in the Scandinavian countries. Meetings and conferences arranged by these organizations or by classical scholars in the universities are arenas for discussion and exchange of information. For example, Eirik Welo presented a paper on 'The classical languages in Norway: status and opportunities' at the tenth Swedish Philology Congress in 2018, an event which also featured reports about the status of classics teaching in other Nordic countries. As always, comparison showed that Norway stood out with its extremely low number of pupils who study Latin.

Conclusion

The teaching of Latin and Ancient Culture occupies a small place in Norwegian schools today. The situation is not, however, too dark. The number of pupils has remained stable for at least the last ten years, and Latin courses are regularly offered at a small group of schools across the country (except for the northern part of Norway). These schools have knowledgeable and enthusiastic Latin teachers who provide their pupils with valuable experiences. The challenges for Latin and Ancient Culture as school subjects are to some extent structural: although there exist curricula for both Latin, Greek and Ancient Culture, it is difficult for the same school to offer all three. Consequently, Greek is not offered at any school in Norway, while the second year of Latin competes with Ancient Culture. Another challenge concerns the teacher profession. The small number of teachers of classical subjects and the geographical spread make it difficult to keep up relationships. The Classical Association of Norway, even though it is not primarily a teachers' organization, aims to be an ally in the fight for expanding classical subjects in Norwegian schools.

There is also an historical challenge: the situation for the classical languages in Norway has been described here as very special, due to the political and cultural history of our country. Latin and Greek have been described and defined as something foreign, which has nothing to do with Norway – the land of the Vikings. The position for the classical languages in school curricula was weakened around the turn of the century, 1800–1900, in connection with the fight for national independence from Sweden, and the nation-building processes both before and after 1905. Nevertheless, the classical languages had a secure position in the *gymnasium*, until this kind of school was abolished in 1978.

The way ahead lies, we are convinced, in strengthening the ties between classical teachers across the country and internationally. The ties which exist between schools and universities should also be strengthened, and everyone with a passion for the classical languages and the cultural impact of the ancient world should speak up in public about the rewards of getting to know them. *Fluctuat, nec mergitur!*

References

Ekrem, I. (1997), 'Latinens rolle i norsk skole 1537–1896' [The role of Latin in Norwegian schools 1537–1896], *Klassisk forum*, 1: 60–79.

Ibsen, H. (1867), *Peer Gynt*.

Kielland, A. (1907), *Gift* [Poison], Mindeudgave (Collected Works), vol. 2, 163–295 (1st edn 1883).

Opplæringsloven (2010), Education Act. Available in English online: https://www.regjeringen.no/contentassets/b3b9e92cce6742c39581b661a019e504/education-act-norway-with-amendments-entered-2014-2.pdf (accessed 15 October 2023).

Rian, B. (1986), 'Latin som C-språk' [Latin as C language], *Klassisk forum*, 2: 55.

Roggen, V. (1995), 'Nomen atque omen eller Ressurskontoret GLA' [Nomen atque omen or The Resource Office GLA], *Schola*, 2: 31–5.

Salen, E. (2013), 'Antikken i skolen' [Antiquity in School], *Klassisk forum*, 2: 87–96.

Sejersted, H. (1986), 'Lille Marius i dag' [Little Marius Today], *Klassisk forum*, 2: 54.

Weidemann, E. (1987), 'Latinen lever fortsatt i norsk skole' [Latin is still alive in Norwegian schools], *Klassisk forum*, 2: 49–53.

Online resources

Classics Forum (Klassisk Forum): https://www.klassiskforbund.no/klassisk-forum.

Curriculum for Latin or Greek (Læreplan i latin eller gresk): https://www.udir.no/lk20/ask03-01.

Curriculum for Ancient Culture (Læreplan i antikkens kultur): https://www.udir.no/lk20/ask02-01.

The Classical Association of Norway (Norsk Klassisk Forbund): https://www.klassiskforbund.no.

The Foreign Language Centre (Fremmedspråksenteret): https://www.hiof.no/fss/english/.

The Norwegian Directorate for Education and Training (Utdanningsdirektoratet). https://www.udir.no/in-english/.

Official statistics for student enrolment in classical languages: https://www.udir.no/tall-og-forskning/statistikk/statistikk-videregaende-skole/fagvalg-i-videregaende-skole/fagvalg-vgs-fylker-skoler/.

Teaching materials

Eitrem, S. (1926), *Latinsk grammatikk* [Latin Grammar], Oslo: Aschehoug; revised edition by E. Kraggerud and B. Tosterud, Oslo: Aschehoug, 1997.

Frihagen, A., B. Rian, V. Roggen and B. Tosterud (1997), *OMNIBVS 2*, Oslo: Aschehoug.

Ørberg, H. (1955), *Lingua Latina per se illustrata*, Indianapolis, IN: Hackett.

Roggen, V. (2022), *Latinsk grammatikk* [Latin Grammar], Oslo: Cappelen Damm.

Roggen, V., E. Kraggerud and B. Tosterud (2015), *Latinsk ordbok* [Latin Dictionary], Oslo: Cappelen Damm.

Roggen, V., R. Hesse and G. Haastrup (1996), *OMNIBVS 1*, Oslo: Aschehoug.

Roggen, V., P. Ravnå, S. Sande and T. S. Thorsen (2010), *Antikkens kultur* [Ancient Culture], Oslo: Aschehoug.

Weidemann, E. and T. Petersen (2021–2), *Pegasus Latin 1–2*, Oslo: Tell.

POLAND

*Katarzyna Marciniak, Janusz Ryba, Barbara Strycharczyk
and Anna Wojciechowska*

The Polish case, or the Classics as a common wealth

With her utmost respect for liberty and freedom, Poland deemed herself a natural heir to the Roman Republic. Although her system was monarchical for most of her history, with the passing of time she made her kings rule, but not govern: *Rex regnat, sed non gubernat*, as allegedly expressed by Jan Zamoyski, the founder of the famous Academy of Zamość, where the Classics were taught also to less well-off students. As early as in the seventeenth century, the connection with ancient republican ideas was reflected in an element of the country's very name: *Rzeczpospolita* – 'Commonwealth'. This element, preserved in the official nomenclature of the Polish state to our day (*Rzeczpospolita Polska*), is an exact cognate of the term *res publica* – 'republic'. Therefore, the Classics were much more than a trifling component of education in Poland. They were the foundation for all activities. They determined the way of life.

A special role in this context was played by the Latin that had become part of a code in which 'the political people of the First Republic [*I Rzeczpospolita* – the Polish-Lithuanian Commonwealth] interpreted the world and, in particular, made self-interpretations of the political system they had created and of the system of values they adhered to' (Axer 2004: 155–6). No wonder that Daniel Defoe, in *The Compleat English Gentleman*, made this heart-warming observation: 'they all [the Poles] speak Latin, and a man that can talk Latin may travel from one end of Poland to another as familiarly as if he was born in the country' (Defoe, ed. Bülbring 1890: 114).

At the time of the publication of *The Compleat English Gentleman*, Poland was fighting for freedom by trying to throw off the yoke of the three partitioners (Austria, Prussia and Russia) that had removed her 100 years earlier from the world map. The short period of independence following the First World War ended with the tragedy of the Second World War, after which Poland, though theoretically free, was forced under the yoke of the USSR. In all those dark times, the Classics were a source of light. People cared to learn about them as tools enabling 'the captive minds' (a term by the Nobel *poeta laureatus* Czesław Miłosz) to strive for freedom in its spiritual dimension, to nourish the sense of community, and to maintain links with the truly democratic West.

And what is the situation of Latin, Greek and Ancient Culture in Polish education today, when the country can fully exercise her freedoms and is a member of the European Union? The next sections will provide us some answers. However, we make no claim to exhaust the topic. And yet, in one aspect we are confident. While Defoe's observation on the usefulness of knowledge of Latin while travelling through Poland needs to be revised (both for the hosts and the travellers), the community based on the ancient heritage has survived, as attested also by the present chapter. It was written by three teachers from differing Polish cities (Kraków, Józefów and Warsaw) and types of schools (both public / co-educational and not-public / single-sex ones) along with a classical scholar who is a former student of one of these teachers and a lasting collaborator of all of them within the 'Our Mythical Childhood' programme established at the Faculty of 'Artes Liberales', University of Warsaw (OMC 2023). Thus, our reflections are practice-based. With them we wish to pay respect to the community of passionate educators in Poland and the world over, as by joint effort we increase our opportunities to make our ancient masters and modern students meet – as well as to care for each other and show the next generations how to use the force of Graeco-Roman heritage. For as much in the past as today, the Classics are our common wealth. Except that today they need us – and we need them – like never before.

Introduction

The education system of Poland comprises an eight-year primary school, compulsory from the age of seven, and three types of secondary school, of which the key one for the Classics is the four-year high school (the attempt of 1999 to modify this system by shortening both primary school and high school and introducing a three-year lower secondary school called *gimnazjum* was withdrawn in 2017). Students can choose between public and non-public schools and home schooling. The universities operate within the Bologna Process. The content and outcome of the education stages are defined by the Polish Qualifications Framework.

The primary school is divided into two phases (grades 1–3 and 4–8) and it ends with a compulsory 8th-grade exam in Polish, Maths, and a foreign language. The next educational stage takes place in secondary schools, whose programmes depend on their type. The secondary schools preparing for the national exit examinations bearing the Latin name *matura* (that is, high schools and technical schools) are subject to curricular branching, which means that students read the compulsory subjects at a basic level and two or three subjects at an extended level. High school graduates are entitled to take the *matura* exams (which are not compulsory as such), while technical school graduates have the right to sit, in addition to the *matura*, vocational qualification examinations. The *matura* exams are taken at the basic level in written form (Polish, Mathematics and a foreign language – and from 2027 Latin will also be included in the foreign language group) and in oral form (Polish and a foreign language). Moreover, each student can choose a maximum of six subjects, the exams in which are taken at an extended level. The choice of the subjects and the result of *matura* decide on enrolment at university.

After the Second World War the classical languages were increasingly marginalized in Poland. The return to the democratic freedoms in 1989 did not halt this process. The number of hours of Latin was gradually reduced, and Greek was almost completely removed from Polish schools and can no longer be taken as part of the *matura* exams. For comparison, in the 2014/15 school year 9,943 students learnt Latin as a compulsory and 8,650 as an elective subject. In 2017/18 these numbers fell to 8,256 students for the compulsory and 5,493 for the elective subject. In 2009/10 the situation was much better: 23,505 students opted for the compulsory and 22,655 for the elective subject, which shows the dynamics of the marginalization of Latin in Polish schools (ICEIN 2023). As for Greek, it can now be taught solely as an elective subject. According to the data made available by the Polish Ministry of Education and Science, in 2022/23 Latin was taught in 201 schools in Poland, while Greek only in two (Gov.Pl 2023). The number of schools offering Latin is monitored by the Polish Philological Society (PTF), one of whose statutory aims is to foster the Classics in education (PTF n.d.). Some changes in the choice of subjects offer cautious hope. Besides, even in such difficult circumstances, the ancient heritage is strong in Polish education due to its general content and to the quality of teaching.

Between obligation and optionality

Despite the marginalization of Latin and Greek, the classical tradition is still an important part of education in Poland because of the aforementioned role of the ancient heritage in her history and culture. It is therefore present in the core curricula in as many as four aspects.

1. The first one concerns the elements of ancient culture which are present in the curricula of humanistic subjects (mainly Polish and History), implemented in both primary and secondary school. This content is compulsorily taught in every school (also in non-public schools), which means that the entire population of primary and secondary school students is familiar with it. For instance, in elementary school students learn (ORE 2017):

   - Polish class: chosen Greek myths, including the creation of the world, Prometheus, Sisyphus, Demeter and Kora, Daedalus and Icarus, Herakles, Theseus and Ariadne, Orpheus and Eurydice. As optional reading Olaf Fritsche's time-travel novel *Jagd auf den Schatz von Troja* [The Treasure of Troy] (Polish trans. 2017).

   - History class: Greece and Rome (next to Mesopotamia, Egypt, Israel, India and China) as examples of ancient civilizations with various religious systems of beliefs, governance types, achievements in material and spiritual culture (philosophy, science, law, architecture, art and literature).

   The high schoolers at the basic level learn (ORE 2018):

   - Polish class: Greek myths, according to the famous elaboration by Jan Parandowski (Marciniak 2015), selections from Homer's *Iliad* and *Odyssey*, chosen poems by Horace, and Sophocles' *Antigone*.

   - History class: geography of ancient Greece, societal organization of Athens and Sparta, various forms of expansion in the Greek world (Greek and Phoenician colonization, Greek–Persian wars, Alexander the Great's conquests), Greek beliefs, the societal organization of ancient Rome (including the issue of slavery, colonial expansion, the rise and fall of the Roman Empire), Christianity, Byzantium and the cultural achievements of Greeks and Romans.

2. The second aspect is related to the implementation of the elective education at the extended level. In addition to Polish and History pursued at the extended level, the Ministry allows the addition of one subject out of four: Philosophy, Latin and Ancient Culture, Fine Arts and Music. This additional subject is taught at the basic level in the first year of secondary school. The choice of subject is made by the headteacher, taking into account the tradition and offer of the school, the successes of students in subject Olympiads and other competitions, as well as the availability of a teacher with appropriate qualifications (in some secondary schools, Latin happens to be removed from the offer when the Latin teacher retires). A very serious 'competitor' to Latin and Ancient Culture is Philosophy. In this configuration, the students learn about antiquity in the following scheme (ORE 2018):

   - Polish class: fragments of Aristotle (*Poetics, Rhetorics*), Plato (*Republic*), Virgil (*Aeneid*), St Augustine (*Confessions*), and – in full – *The Clouds* by Aristophanes.

Parandowski makes a come-back at this stage (including the myths and legends of Rome).

- History class: the geographical conditions of the birth of the civilizations of the ancient East and Greece, Cretan and Mycenaean cultures, Pericles' Athens, Alexander the Great, Hellenistic culture, the origins of Rome (including the Etruscans, Roman army and Roman expansion), the reception of classical antiquity in the contemporary world, the concept of citizen, Byzantium, and the influence of Islamic civilization on Latin and Byzantine civilizations.

- Philosophy class: the etymology of this term, major disciplines (metaphysics/ontology, epistemology, ethics, philosophy of nature, philosophical anthropology, philosophical theology, aesthetics, political philosophy), the notion of *arché*, the Ionian philosophers of nature (Thales, Anaximander and Anaximenes), the Eleatics, the first philosophical disputes (monism versus pluralism; variabilism versus statism), the reception of the ancient philosophers in modern and contemporary philosophy, atomism, Socrates, Plato's philosophy as a paradigm of anti-naturalistic metaphysics and a basis for later philosophers, Aristotle's philosophy as an attempt to reconcile previous philosophical oppositions, Epicureanism and Stoicism as two paradigms of ethics, sceptical tropes as a timeless challenge to epistemology, the beginnings of philosophical theology (including Plotinus and St Augustine), the birth of aesthetics (proportion, *mimesis*, *katharsis*); fragments of Plato (*Apology of Socrates* or *Crito, Phaedo, Timaeus, Symposium, Republic* and *Phaedrus*), Aristotle's *Nicomachean Ethics* and *Poetics*, Diogenes Laertius and, as optional reading, selections from Epicurus, Epictetus, Seneca, Marcus Aurelius or St Augustine.

3. The third aspect is the elective subject Latin and Ancient Culture. In practice, it can be chosen by the headteacher and the pedagogical council (and sometimes by students), and assigned to a specific class profile (e.g., Classics, humanistic, biological). According to the regulations, once chosen, it becomes compulsory for the given class/students and is implemented in accordance with the core curriculum. The basic level can only be taken in the first class at a rate of thirty hours per cycle (one hour per week for two semesters). The extended level comprises 240 hours per cycle (two hours per week for eight semesters). It should be noted that these are *de facto* two separate subjects and the extended level is not an extension of the basic one, as is the case with other subjects. The extended level prepares students for the *matura* exam. Statistically, this subject is most often implemented in high school and this can be seen precisely in the *matura* statistics. In 2022 the exit exam in Latin and Ancient Culture was taken by 153 students, 133 of whom were high school graduates and twenty were technical school graduates.

The main contribution of the subject of Latin and Ancient Culture in both approaches is to provide students with a more in-depth humanistic education, encompassing, on the one hand, knowledge of the Latin language and the culture of ancient Greece and Rome, and, on the other, the ability to grasp and understand the role of the ancient heritage for the development of modern and contemporary culture, as well as of the Polish language. In order to secure these aims, three main areas of learning objectives have been defined: linguistic, cultural, and societal competences. Within the linguistic skills, the main learning objective is to achieve a knowledge of grammar and the ability to receive, understand and translate Latin texts. The core curriculum includes a catalogue of grammatical issues that students should master within each level, and, in addition, a canon of Latin texts has been created for the extended level. Topics concerning ancient culture are divided into thematic blocks regarding mythology, ancient history, Greek and Roman literature, philosophy, material culture and everyday life, as well as the reception of classical antiquity.

4. The fourth aspect is the elective subject of Latin implemented instead of a second modern language. There are currently no data available that would permit us to analyse this aspect. It is a ministerial innovation in the Polish educational system and has been in place since 1 September 2023. This subject can be implemented in grades 7 and 8 of primary school and in secondary schools. It is also planned to introduce a written *matura* exam in this subject from 2027. The learning content in the core curriculum is also divided into three areas: linguistic, cultural, and societal competences. The main emphasis is placed on Latin reading comprehension and knowledge of vocabulary, although this subject does take into account the importance of understanding the reception of antiquity and the ability to discern and identify elements linking modern languages and contemporary culture with the civilization of the Greeks and Romans, as well.

A fact of paramount importance is that in many schools (both public and non-public ones) the subject of Latin and Ancient Culture (i.e., the course that is crucial for Polish classical education) is implemented via the teachers' original programmes that go far beyond the core curriculum and take into account the needs of the given school, the interests and abilities of the students, and the cooperation of teachers in teaching teams and with external institutions. For instance, the non-public female High School 'Strumienie' in Józefów and the public co-educational XI Mikołaj Rej High School in Warsaw work according to the programme *Ad fontes*, being the fruit of the cooperation between these two schools' teachers of Latin and Ancient Culture. This programme includes content that helps students to achieve full idiomatic proficiency in the Polish language and emphasizes the interdisciplinary nature of learning about antiquity in line with the *artes liberales* model. This is also an excellent demonstration of teamwork within diversity, as the students from these schools get to know each other in the process and learn to respect various worldviews. Of course, their learning milieux are different. The 'Strumienie' Association also operates a primary school. In 2021/22, taking into consideration the benefits of studying Latin and Ancient Culture as perceived by the high schoolers and their parents and teachers, the management included Latin in the curriculum of the 5th grades (one hour per week) with a possibility of continuation in the 6th and 7th grades. In the 'Strumienie' High School, Latin and Ancient Culture belongs to the compulsory subjects and is implemented at the basic level for the 1st grades with sixty hours. It is continued in the 2nd and 3rd class as an elective subject at the basic level (120 hours, chosen by 50 per cent of the students) or at the extended level (240 hours, chosen by 10 per cent of the students who prepare for the *matura* exam in this subject and for the Latin Language Olympiad).

As for Mikołaj Rej XI High School, it belongs to a small group of schools – together with Bartłomiej Nowodworski I High School in Kraków – that in the 1980s started boldly experimenting against the flow: like Bartłomiej Nowodworski High School, for more than thirty years, Mikołaj Rej High School has been developing a Classics profile class (Marciniak & Strycharczyk 2021), with Latin at the rate of 270 hours in the four-year cycle and an in-depth presence of the ancient culture in the curricula of other subjects (especially Polish and History). In this school, around ninety students (from *c.* 550) choose this profile. Every year, one third of its graduates decide for the *matura* exam in Latin and Ancient Culture and usually the same students take part in the Latin Language Olympiad beforehand (often with great results which translate into the highest score at the *matura* without sitting this examination if they are the Olympiad laureates). Some of these students also continue classical education by choosing a university curriculum with Greek and Roman components. In the 2023/24 school year, Mikołaj Rej High School opened its first Classics class, in which Latin has the status of a second foreign language.

Nonetheless, classical education, and the humanities in general, is a subject of heated debates, the results of which are sometimes difficult for Classics. At some schools, for example, the future of humanities classes is uncertain, despite the successes of their students and graduates – not only because of local education policy, but also due to the great popularity of science subjects among young people. Opponents of the teaching of Latin at school claim that it is an anachronistic subject and a relic of the past, and that logical thinking, usually associated with Latin, is now better fostered by maths and philosophy. Learning Latin is also perceived as extremely difficult, requiring the sacrifice of time or even forgoing other, more 'attractive' activities. Last but not least, parents and students sometimes make the argument about the uselessness of teaching a 'dead' language, instead hinting at the need to include another modern language into the curriculum.

If Latin is given a chance, however, it quickly becomes apparent that this subject is an excellent investment in a young person's development on many levels. Not only does its propaedeutic function manifest itself, enabling pupils to learn modern languages (including their mother tongue) faster and to have a greater vocabulary and idiom, but also Latin fosters interdisciplinary education, from maths through history to arts. Above all, it is the key to perceiving, reading and understanding a particular code of cultural communication that, along with the Graeco-Roman tradition, has reached almost all regions of the world. Removing Latin from school therefore deprives young people of the opportunity to acquire some crucial competences that not only facilitate, but are in fact indispensable for understanding both ancient, modern, and contemporary culture, including pop culture, which is so attractive for young people and which, *nota bene*, draws them into antiquity through a 'back door': movies, games and TV series with ancient threads – all of which are good reference points in class. Last but not least, Latin supports the youth in societal and civic education. All this may be difficult, but school is a place where students can have a unique chance to learn – in a controlled environment, with support from teachers and colleagues – how to face difficulties, ask questions, practise patience, gather experiences and discover the value of cooperation and diversity. In short, Latin develops important competences in terms of both mind and character that will help students form their identity and find their way into the future with an understanding of the past.

Arriving at such reflection and awareness sometimes requires from the teacher a new approach to work with both students and their parents, but the challenge is well worth this effort. And it bears fruit also for the teacher, who has to learn how to draw students into antiquity and who often discovers in the process his/her own new competences and the beauty of cooperation both at school and with external partners.

Between tradition and innovation

Regarding the teaching of Latin in Poland, whether at the primary, secondary or tertiary level, we should speak of the use of the so-called eclecticism and methodological differentiation. This consists in combining elements of various teaching methods and adapting them to the individual needs of the given teachers and their students who learn to comprehend the text meaning, translate into Polish, and write simple phrases in Latin. A very important and distinctive aspect of classical education in Poland is an intercultural approach, which makes the linguistic, cultural and communicative competences as equal in the teaching process. The *Latinitas viva* [Living Latin] trend is also present. Its proponents, under the auspices of the PTF, organize courses and workshops, mainly in the form of summer schools. Such activities popularize the Classics, but do not constitute a systemic or institutional training – rather, they are its attractive complement.

The above methods have provided the framework for the textbooks that are widely used in Polish schools. Among the most popular ones, mention should be made of the *Homo Romanus* series (Ryba et al. 2017) and the *Cognoscite* series (Ryba & Klęczar 2020). These aim at integrating linguistic and cultural contents, thus referring to the textbooks used in the teaching of modern languages. The Latin texts in these books are authentic: they are based on the ancient sources, with the grammatical, syntactic and lexical structures adapted to the level of the students' proficiency. *Porta Latina* (Wilczyński et al. 2007), on the other hand, pays homage to more traditional teaching methods in the Classics (see Domagała et al. 2021; Ryba 2010). This textbook consists of two parts. The first contains readings, exercises and a handy glossary; the second contains preparations of sources with a grammatical commentary. Some innovations have entered this textbook, as well. For instance, in the section *Ars poetica aut quod libet*, students are offered short poetic fragments, inscriptions and riddles. In addition, *Porta Latina* includes a few spoken language texts and song lyrics (Ryba 2010). Teachers in Poland also make use of foreign textbooks, such as *De Romanis* (Radice et al. 2020), and, in order to make the learning process more attractive, *Lingua Latina per se illustrata* (Ørberg 2003). Those teaching Latin in Biology and Chemistry profile classes also use academic textbooks designed to deal with a specialized language, mainly medical. Mention should also be made of 286 pieces of supporting materials for Latin and Ancient Culture that are available on the Ministry's Integrated Educational Platform (ZPE n.d.).

Finally, our conversations with teachers have shown that yet another approach is more typical than atypical: instead of using a specific textbook for the full course, they prefer to prepare their own materials based on different textbooks and ancient sources. This creativity and freedom (of course within the framework ensuring the implementation of the core curriculum) attest to the teachers' educational passion – and this is one of the keys to the survival, against all odds, of Latin in schools (for further discussions on Classics, see Ryba (2019, 2020, 2021 and 2022).

One more aspect needs to be mentioned – one that is marginal in the quantitative sense, but important for the idea of a community based on the code of antiquity: the individual scheme of learning, to which both highly talented students and those with special educational needs are entitled. But even outside this scheme, Latin teachers spend time in working with students individually, often *pro bono*. The sense of mission is very strong. Hence, teaching innovations are almost always the result of the teachers' initiative. They must be approved by the school pedagogical council and are usually implemented without external funding, while the teachers, *nolens volens*, become their leaders and thus also role models for the students in following their passion. Some innovations are linked to cooperation outside school and will be discussed in the section 'The power of the community'. A special kind of innovation is that of scholarly trips, both in Poland (e.g., students discover the Renaissance ideal city of Zamość, they learn the roots of Polish culture in Kraków, or follow the ancient threads in the Royal Castle in Warsaw) and abroad (also with the support from the Erasmus+ School Mobilities Programme). Mikołaj Rej and 'Strumienie', for instance, revive the tradition of the nineteenth-century 'Grand Tour', crowning education: the classes go for a study trip to Rome (for Rej's Classics class this twenty-year long tradition was interrupted only by the pandemic). Their trips become big educational projects. The students prepare for the trip in advance, and it can be stated that each year, for the whole week, Rome is their classroom. Moreover, in 2022/3, a Polish-Classics class from Rej also took part in a study trip to Athens. Educational travel as part of the Latin and Ancient Culture curriculum is also organized by the Bartłomiej Nowodworski High School. Since 2016, the Classics-profile students have been participating in trips to Italy, where they visit the most important monuments of Rome and of Campania. A trip to Greece is also planned for the future.

A very important element of the contemporary didactics of classical languages and ancient culture is the application of new technologies and ICT tools in the teaching process. They had already been in use in Polish schools for many years, but during the Covid-19 pandemic that forced remote teaching for a while, they were developed and new tools were spread or added. Most still accompany teachers who are open also to the students' ideas on how to make the best use of the ICT tools in the classroom: a collaborative account on Instagram, a blog or a website, an online interview with a scholar or an artist (who are sometimes even the school's graduates) are attractive and enrich regular lessons. The pandemic, however, has made it perfectly clear that school is first and foremost a place where the students and the teachers meet. We have a great desire to be together, build a community, and explore our ancient heritage face to face.

Teacher training and professional advancement

The standard of teacher training in Poland is governed by the Regulation of the Minister of Science and Higher Education (in 2021–3 the Minister of Education and Science), updated in August 2022 in order to take into account the current situation: the post-pandemic spread of distance learning opportunities and the challenges faced by teachers in the face of the war in Ukraine. Approximately 200,000 immigrant children started attending Polish schools after their traumatic run for their lives following Russia's attack on 24 February 2022 – their quick adaptation to the school milieu was of paramount importance for their psychological wellbeing.

The teacher's educational track includes content-related, psychological-pedagogical, and didactic preparations. The content-related preparation is a study curriculum in the given field (BA and MA cycles or a unified five-year MA cycle). For a secondary school teacher an MA degree is required. The psychological-pedagogical preparation includes specialist courses in pedagogy and psychology of childhood and adolescence in the amount of 210 hours (90 hours psychology, 90 hours pedagogy, 30 hours professional training). The didactic preparation comprises the basics of didactics and voice emission (60 hours) and specialist didactic preparation for teaching a specific subject, including 150 hours subject didactics and 120 hours professional training if the subject is taught at all educational stages, or 90 hours subject didactics and 60 hours professional training if the subject is taught only in primary or secondary school. Until the school year 2022/23, the educational track for the profession of a teacher of Latin and Ancient Culture was carried out exclusively on the MA cycle of studies, and the qualifications obtained conferred the right to teach only in secondary schools. The introduction of the possibility of teaching Latin as a second foreign language in primary school (grades 7–8) makes it necessary now to introduce changes at Polish universities in order to address this stage.

Teachers pursue professional advancement, which as of 2022 has three grades: beginning teacher, appointed teacher, and certified teacher. In addition, there is an honorary title of Professor of Education, which can be awarded to certified teachers who distinguish themself by the quality of their work and professional achievements. Teachers are obliged to continuously improve their qualifications and are subject to evaluation. As part of their in-service training, they can obtain the qualifications of a member of the district examination board and participate in expert teams that evaluate exams, including the *matura*. In addition, teachers participate in various courses, training and workshops that are organized by governmental institutions, public and non-public training centres, universities and schools (e.g., in 'Strumienie' High School, a group of teachers, mainly of foreign languages and Maths, participate in a course in Latin and Ancient Culture, conducted online by a Latin teacher). Good practices include teachers working together in a subject team. As there are few schools in Poland that employ more than one Latin teacher, they usually work in an interdisciplinary team. This type of cooperation is a challenge for all the members, but it also brings great benefits to them, in terms of broadening their horizons and increasing empathy, which is further beneficial to their students.

The power of the community

A powerful source of support for the Classics at school arises from various forms of collaboration. They allow exceptional results to be achieved even in difficult circumstances. Teachers' workshops and conferences create space for the exchange of experiences, which are also discussed via social media.

A shared sense of mission and an ethos of responsibility for educating new generations is always vivid among the staff of cultural institutions, such as museums or libraries, and they are open to cooperation, even though – just like schools – they struggle with numerous challenges. Owing to this, and to the teachers' creativity, students can broaden their horizons outside classroom, as much as the location of the given school permits. They visit local cultural institutions, branches of the National Museum and theatres. The hospitality of the managers of these institutions enables unforgettable experiences – for example, the Museum of King Jan III's Palace at Wilanów hosts the final of a rhetoric competition, in which Mikołaj Rej and 'Strumienie' students take part. The schools situated in the province have to make a greater effort (including financially) in order to reach certain cultural attractions; however, now ever more attractive local initiatives flourish. Moreover, the distance is shortened at least to some extent thanks to the Internet resources. For instance, the teachers of Mikołaj Rej and

'Strumienie' contribute to Wilanów's online offer and co-create educational materials for the Palace's website, from where the teachers in the whole country can draw freely.

An aspect of collaboration of paramount importance for the development of classical education in Poland regards the contacts between the school and the university. This works in two ways. On the one hand, the students of the MA cycle at Classics departments who wish to specialize in teaching Latin and Ancient Culture accomplish their internships in the school setting under the supervision of experienced teachers. On the other hand, schools may take part in ventures organized by the university departments or the local PTF branches, in various regions of the country and sometimes also with an international contribution. Examples of such ventures include the National Latin Language Olympiad and (for its laureates) the international *Certamen Ciceronianum Arpinas*; reading the Classics sessions within the European Festival of Latin and Greek (https://festival-latingrec.eu/); the Ancient League (*Liga Starożytnicza*) – a programme for secondary school students who discover certain aspects of classical antiquity by participating in a competition organized by the Institute of Classical Philology in Toruń, the Toruń PTF Branch, and the 'Traditio Europae' Foundation; the Institute of Classical Philology Laboratory at the University of Warsaw – a cycle of open online lectures of popularizing character; and the patronage of the University of Warsaw's Faculty of 'Artes Liberales' over the Classics classes at Mikołaj Rej High School with the involvement of the classes from this and other schools in the Faculty's international research projects, especially within the 'Our Mythical Childhood' programme. And precisely via the example of this programme we wish to show the potential of research-driven education.

'Our Mythical Childhood' is dedicated to researching the role of classical antiquity in children's and young adults' culture. Established in 2011, it has been carried out within the Loeb Classical Library Foundation Grant (2012–13), the Alexander von Humboldt Foundation Alumni Award for Innovative Networking Initiatives (2014–17), and the European Research Council Consolidator (2016–22) and Proof of Concept (2023–5) grants. A cooperation between the school and university has always been among our priorities. Thus, each year we design a different educational project that we can embed in the programme's current stage (OMC 2023). Throughout the school year, high schoolers carry out their first research under the guidance of their teachers, with the kind permission of the school management. Along with Mikołaj Rej, we cooperate with 'Strumienie' and Bartłomiej Nowodworski high schools; at one stage the Nicolaus Copernicus University Academic Junior and Senior High School in Toruń joined us. Owing to these kinds of experiences we all – the students, teachers and scholars – could broaden our horizons and develop soft skills and empathy, especially regarding teamwork in different work milieux (public and non-public schools, the academic environment) and the most pressing needs in education. Moreover, the students gained a deeper knowledge about the Classics by following traces of the reception of myths in Warsaw urban space; they developed creativity by designing advertising campaigns with the heroes and gods from classical mythology; they discovered their artistic talents by staging the story of Pyramus and Thisbe from Shakespeare's *A Midsummer Night's Dream* in Latin; they practised communication skills by taking part in reportages.

It is worth emphasising that three projects gave fruit in the form of the first research publications of the students. In 2018/19 they studied the bibliographical materials and the school notes of a Polish boy who died in Auschwitz, where he had been sent for his participation in clandestine education during the Second World War. In 2019/20 they followed in the footsteps of Publius Cornelius Nepos and presented four figures from Polish history outside the core curricula – the people who had studied the Classics and who still might be attractive for youth – among them Krystyna Skarbek, the audacious secret agent appreciated by Winston Churchill and Ian Fleming, the author of James Bond novels (hence the title of the book prepared by the students *De viris mulieribusque illustribus* (Marciniak 2019)). In 2020/21–2021/22 (an extension due to the pandemic), the students worked on the Classics and environmental issues – a theme that turned out particularly important in the context of the Covid-19 lockdowns and of the young people's voice on the climate crisis (see the book, *Naturae cognoscere causas* (Marciniak et al. 2021)). Along with the publications, the presentation of the high schoolers' works took place during the programme's workshops and conferences at the Faculty of 'Artes Liberales' in Warsaw, with the participation of the scholars who build the 'Our Mythical Childhood' team from America, across Europe, Africa, Asia, and on to Australia and New Zealand. Such joint meetings and discussions show students the beauty of intercultural relationships, teach them respect for diversity, and inspire teachers and researchers to further actions aimed at broadening and strengthening our Classical community.

The potential here is great, as attested also by our most recent endeavour – the project 'The Modern Argonauts: A Multicultural Educational Programme Preparing Young People for Contemporary Challenges through an Innovative Use of Classical Mythology'. It will result in an international handbook of mythology understood as a treasury of cultural code that enables dialogue on current pressing and often difficult themes (Modern Argonauts 2024). For instance, Poseidon will invite us to talk about water pollution and Midas will touch on the topic of responsibility for ways our civilization generates profits. At the present phase, the lessons prepared by the experts from the 'Our Mythical Childhood' team are tested at schools worldwide, from an Italian *liceo classico* through a technical mechanics school in Poland to an evening school in Cameroon. The Classics component is enriched by some references to the mythical traditions of other cultures and encourages integration beyond the borders of time, countries and generations. A truly mythical journey and all are welcome on board.

Conclusion, or new beginnings

For every student who is given a chance to learn about the ancient heritage, a new adventure begins. This adventure brings some concrete profits, such as specific knowledge and skills. Yet far more important is how it helps young people face timeless questions about the meaning of the world and the nature of human beings, including their own identities.

The students' meeting with the past is also, each time, a new beginning for antiquity, which is thus given a chance to live on, both in and for subsequent generations. And this is a new beginning for scholars, teachers, parents, and tutors, too, as they get a chance to look at the past from the perspective of young people and connect with them through the ancient code. Win-win only.

In this chapter we tried to offer the keys to such an approach. In sum: Latin and Ancient Culture blossom when they are treated as an interdisciplinary subject; an individual approach to the implementation of the core curriculum content is crucial (schools are not the same and each of them has slightly different educational needs, and the special needs of the students must also be taken into account); it does good to leave the classroom from time to time in order to learn about the Classics 'in practice', and by this also the outside world is 'drawn into' school; cooperation between school and university is of paramount importance for the full development of the Classics' potential in education; we learn from each other also in the international perspective.

It turns out that, although we no longer commonly speak Latin, the community built on the Classics understood as our common wealth still exists, and the present times allow us to experience it even more easily, as we travel to various parts of the world or learn about classical reception in various cultures through the available media. What is more, by working together (*quod est demonstrandum* by this volume, too), we are stronger and can achieve more. In this context, Defoe's observation is still valid (maybe only with minor updates in italics): 'A *person*, who *knows the ancient tradition,* may travel from one end of Poland to another as familiarly as if *s/he* was born in the country.' And vice versa – the Poles knowing the ancient tradition find themselves as if in a family among the inhabitants of all the regions from which this volume's authors and you – its reader – come.

References

Axer, J. (2004), 'Łacina jako drugi język narodu szlacheckiego Rzeczypospolitej' [Latin as the second language of the noble nation of the Polish-Lithuanian Commonwealth], in J. Axer (ed.), *Łacina jako język elit* [Latin as the language of the elites], Warsaw, OBTA–DiG, 151–6.

Defoe, D. (1890), *The Compleat English Gentleman*, ed. K. Bülbring, London: Nutt.

Domagała, S., M. Loch and K. Ochman (2021), 'Latin Teaching in Poland – a New Renaissance with Communicative Approaches', in M. Lloyd and S. Hunt (eds), *Communicative Approaches for Ancient Languages*, London: Bloomsbury, 161–78.

Fritsche, O. (2017), *Skarb Troi* [The treasure of Troy], trans. A. Wziątek, Wrocław: Wydawnictwo Dolnośląskie (first edn in German 2007).

Gov.Pl (2023), Poland's Data Portal. Available online: https://dane.gov.pl/pl (accessed 12 December 2023).

ICEIN (2023), IT Centre for Education and Science, Języki obce i języki mniejszości narodowych. Available online: https://icein.gov.pl/archiwalne-dane-statystyczne/ads-jezyki-obce-i-jezyki-mniejszosci-narodowych/ (accessed 12 December 2023).

Marciniak, K. (2015), '(De)constructing Arcadia: Polish Struggles with History and Differing Colours of Childhood in the Mirror of Classical Mythology', in L. Maurice (ed.), *The Reception of Ancient Greece and Rome in Children's Literature: Heroes and Eagles,* 'Metaforms: Studies in the Reception of Classical Antiquity', Leiden and Boston: Brill, 56–82.

Marciniak, K., ed. (2019), *De viris mulieribusque illustribus: Schools Endeavour Educational Materials,* trans. J. Dutkiewicz, 'OBTA Studies in Classical Reception', Warsaw: Faculty of 'Artes Liberales', University of Warsaw.

Marciniak, K. and B. Strycharczyk (2021), '*Macte animo!* – or, The Polish Experiment with "Classics Profiles" in Secondary School Education: The Warsaw Example', in L. Maurice (ed.), *Our Mythical Education: The Reception of Classical Myth Worldwide in Formal Education, 1900–2020,* 'Our Mythical Childhood', Warsaw: Warsaw University Press, 237–91.

Marciniak, K., J. Ryba, B. Strycharczyk, O. Strycharczyk and A. Wojciechowska, eds (2021), *Naturae cognoscere causas: Schools Endeavour Educational Materials,* trans. J. Dutkiewicz, 'OBTA Studies in Classical Reception', Warsaw: Faculty of 'Artes Liberales', University of Warsaw.

Modern Argonauts (2024), The Modern Argonauts: A Multicultural Educational Programme Preparing Young People for Contemporary Challenges through an Innovative Use of Classical Mythology. Available online: https://modernargonauts.al.uw.edu.pl/ (accessed 4 February 2024).

OMC (2023), Our Mythical Childhood. Available online: http://omc.obta.al.uw.edu.pl/ (accessed 12 December 2023).

Ørberg, H. (2003), *Lingua Latina per se illustrata*, Indianapolis, IN: Hackett Publishing Inc.

ORE (2017), Ośrodek Rozwoju Edukacji [Centre for Education Development], Podstawa programowa kształcenia ogólnego dla przedszkoli i szkół podstawowych [General education curriculum for kindergartens and primary schools]. Available online: https://www.ore.edu.pl/2017/12/ppko/ (accessed 12 December 2023).

ORE (2018), Ośrodek Rozwoju Edukacji [Centre for Education Development], Podstawa programowa kształcenia ogólnego dla liceum, technikum i branżowej szkoły II stopnia [General education curriculum for upper secondary, technical and upper secondary vocational schools]. Available online: https://www.ore.edu.pl/2018/03/podstawa-programowa-ksztalcenia-ogolnego-dla-liceum-technikum-i-branzowej-szkoly-ii-stopnia/ (accessed 12 December 2023).

PTF (n.d.), Polskie Towarzystwo Filologiczne [Polish Philological Society]. Available online: http://ptf.edu.pl/nauczanie-laciny-stan-prawny/ (accessed 12 December 2023).

Radice, K., G. Lord, A. Cheetham and S. Kirk (2020), *De Romanis*, London: Bloomsbury.

Ryba, J. (2021), 'Greek and Roman Mythology in Classical Education in Poland after 1945', in L. Maurice (ed.), *Our Mythical Education: The Reception of Classical Myth Worldwide in Formal Education, 1900–2020*, 'Our Mythical Childhood', Warsaw: Warsaw University Press, 209–36.

Ryba, J. (2022), 'Drogi i bezdroża nauczania języka łacińskiego w latach 1945–2021' [Roads and wildernesses of teaching Latin in the years 1945–2021], *Języki obce w szkole*, 2: 5–13.

Ryba, J. (2010), '*Libri amici, libri magistri. . .* Analiza porównawcza wybranych podręczników do nauczania języka łacińskiego stosowanych w szkołach polskich i włoskich' [*Libri amici, libri magistri. . .* Comparative analysis of selected textbooks for teaching Latin used in Polish and Italian schools], *Języki obce w szkole*, 3: 79–87.

Ryba, J. (2019), 'Języki klasyczne i kultura antyczna w zreformowanym liceum ogólnokształcącym' [Classical languages and ancient culture in the reformed high school], *Eos*, 106 (2): 315–23.

Ryba, J. (2020), *Język łaciński w średniej szkole ogólnokształcącej w latach 1945–2004* [Latin language in secondary general education in the years 1945–2004], Kraków: Wydawnictwo Uniwersytetu Jagiellońskiego.

Ryba, J. and A. Klęczar (2020), *Cognoscite*, Kraków: Draco.

Ryba, J., E. Wolanin and A. Klęczar (2017), *Homo Romanus*, Kraków: Draco.

Stuligrosz, M. (2022), 'Łacina (jeszcze nie) umarła' [Latin is (not yet) dead], *Forum Akademickie*, 1: 33–5.

Toczko, R. (2022), 'Niewidzialna sieć tradycji antycznej' [The invisible network of ancient tradition], *Forum Akademickie*, 1: 30–2.

Wilczyński, S., E. Pobiedzińska, and A. Jaworska (2007), *Porta Latina*, Warszawa: Wydawnictwo Szkolne PWN.

ZPE (n.d.), Integrated Educational Platform of the Ministry of Education and Science. Available online: https://zpe.gov.pl/ (accessed 12 December 2023)

The research results presented in this paper have been obtained within the project 'The Modern Argonauts: A Multicultural Educational Programme Preparing Young People for Contemporary Challenges through an Innovative Use of Classical Mythology' led by Katarzyna Marciniak at the Faculty of 'Artes Liberales', University of Warsaw, with funding from the European Research Council (ERC) under the European Union's Horizon Europe Research and Innovation Programme – ERC Proof of Concept Grant (Grant Agreement No. 101122976).

PORTUGAL

Susana Marta Pereira

nil novi sub sole

In our present times Languages and Humanities seem to be neglected for Science and Technology courses, and both teachers and parents redirect students towards courses that are said to make them more employable. This utilitarian view of education does not always provide the expected results and, in the short to medium term, ends up having nefarious consequences in the way humanity sees itself and how it supports humanist values. Whenever we ignore our past and look at it as if it were something useless and without relevance, we end up being, in a sense, overwhelmed with an admirable but ephemeral new world, where everything is illusory and without support. It is in this respect that the teaching of Latin in Portugal, as has been the case in other European countries, has been relegated to the old and the outdated, supposedly without any practical usefulness. Contemporary society and the decision-making powers, rooted in educational policies, consider the teaching of classical languages as something that should be restricted to an elite and unnecessary for students that need tools to enter the job market.

The lack of teachers in recent years in the country, has made the situation even worse. If it was already difficult to open Latin and Greek classes in schools, with the worsening shortage of teachers, it has become almost impossible. Latin and Greek teachers, in Portugal, are also Portuguese teachers, because their pedagogical training belongs to the so-called recruitment Group 310 (Latin, Greek and Portuguese). Considering the scarcity of mother tongue teachers, these teachers are much more aimed at teaching Portuguese. If there is a lack of Portuguese teachers in a school, the Ministry of Education does not authorize the opening of Latin classes, as it considers that it cannot provide the human resources for the other subjects. Therefore, at this moment, in Portugal, it is even more complicated to open Latin classes.

For Greek, the situation is in a slightly better position, despite being moribund, because it is only possible to learn this subject as an option in the last year of secondary education, with just three classes per week of forty-five or fifty minutes. Some schools are able to offer it if they have more than twenty students. Latin has three classes of ninety minutes each, over two years, starting from the tenth year (which is the first year of secondary education). These classes can occupy many hours in a teacher's schedule that otherwise could be directed to teaching Portuguese.

Furthermore, the last government changed access to higher education and students now only need to take three exams to complete secondary education and apply for university. Portuguese is one of the three, which has become mandatory for all students to complete secondary education. Since the Latin exam is not a mandatory entry requirement for any higher education course, not even for Classical Studies, students prefer and are channelled towards subjects considered more accessible, to help them obtain higher grade averages. Unfortunately, in recent years, political decisions have been channelled to address the lack of teachers in schools and the situation of teaching Latin and Greek has been neglected, as it is considered not essential. If the situation was already bad before these problems, it will now tend to get worse or to simply eradicate the teaching of these subjects from the national curriculum completely.

These curricular choices which are followed in schools on behalf of the Ministry of Education reveal a deep lack of knowledge of these languages' journey and their importance. Learning Latin and Greek allows one to read, in their original form, founding texts, treaties that changed the world, revolutionary scientific works, and an entire patrimony that reveals to us the human thought from ancient times to the present. Knowing the etymology of words is knowing the archaeology of the human thought, questioning values that rule over us and understanding the journey that humanity has gone through.

At a time when, every day, we witness situations of war, unthinkable a few years ago, where we see history repeating itself and where the political banner of recent years from the Ministry of Education is the discipline of citizenship, one cannot understand that they do not have the ability to recognize the importance of teaching these subjects in the curriculum: two languages that allow us to access ancient texts that put the history of the world and the history of ideas into perspective, which confront us with other cultures that were foundational and fundamental to the history of the world. How can we understand that someone considers the subject of citizenship important and then completely disregards the teaching of classical languages, leading them almost to extinction?

The situation of classical languages in Portugal is catastrophic and, if nothing is done by the entities that have the power to change the educational policies, there is a risk they will disappear from the Portuguese education system. In 1996 around 13,000 students took the national Latin exam, and the subject was already weakening by then. However, twenty years later, in 2016, only thirty-four students took the national Latin exam throughout the entire country and in 2023 only six Latin exams were held *nationwide*. The decrease in the number of Latin students in secondary education in almost three decades has almost led to the extinction of the teaching of this language in the Portuguese education system.

However, the problem around teaching Latin is not restricted solely to the reduced number of students, but is part of a more profound and structural issue. Various factors contributed to this situation. First of all, the subject of Latin appears as an option in a group of subjects such as Geography, English, Spanish, History and Culture of the Arts, among others. Secondly, the national Latin exam is not a mandatory requirement to access any university course. In the field of Classical Studies, it is reduced to being an option, and any student can enrol without having had Latin or Greek in their subject pathway. The third factor is the teacher supply. Despite the latest decisions which allow a university student to teach the subject, without finishing their degree and with only 40 ECT (40 credits in the European Credit Transfer and accumulation System) in Latin, someone is not considered a teacher unless they enter into a teaching career.

Ever since the entry into force of the Bologna process, in order to have a job as a professional teacher, a university student must possess a degree in their specialist subject and hold a professionalizing Master's degree. In the first year of this Master's, they are required to take a set of subjects related to the intended scientific field, to specific didactics and the field of Educational Sciences. In the second year, the future teacher must undertake a pedagogical internship during one school year, without receiving any payment, where two advisers supervise them – one to supervise the practical component in a classroom context, and another at the university, who follows the scientific and theoretical component. At the end of those two years, the future teacher must write a report on Supervised Teaching Practice and proceed to defend it at the university in front of a jury composed of several university teachers in the area and supervising teachers from primary and secondary education. A university student can only become a qualified teacher after going through this path to teach in public and private Portuguese schools. Teachers can specialize in three teaching levels: 1st Cycle, 2nd Cycle, and 3rd Cycle of primary education; and secondary education. The 1st Cycle of primary education lasts for four years and is for children aged six to nine. The 2nd Cycle of primary education lasts for two years, for children aged ten and eleven, while the 3rd Cycle of primary education lasts for three years for children aged twelve to fourteen. Secondary education lasts for three years for teenagers aged fifteen to seventeen. At the end of secondary education, the student is subjected to a specific examination that contributes to their final grade point average. These examinations are a mandatory prerequisite for entrance to university. Until 2013, all university students who intended to start a teaching career and wanted to teach Latin and Greek had to enrol into a professional Master's course titled 'Masters in Teaching Portuguese and Classical Languages in the 3rd Cycle of Elementary Education and in Secondary Education'. This way, universities combined the professionalization in Teaching Classical Languages (Greek and Latin) with Teaching Portuguese. Therefore, their professionalization in the area of classical languages continued and teachers had a greater likelihood of getting a job in teaching Portuguese, as the teaching of Latin and Greek was residual. Consequently, the conjunction of these two subjects gave the teacher a deepened knowledge of their mother tongue, as Portuguese is a Romance language, and allowed the renewal of teacher training in the field of classical languages.

In 2014, with Decree Law 79/2014, the structure of this training was altered, changing its name to 'Masters in Teaching Portuguese in the 3rd Cycle of Primary Education and in Secondary Education and Latin in Secondary Education'. Thus, the ability to gain a professional qualification in Greek was removed, the amount of teaching of Latin was reduced, and a new area solely in teaching Portuguese was created. This change makes it possible for professionalizing teachers in Latin only for secondary education, removing the 3rd Cycle professional qualifications and roundly excluding the possibility of having professionalized teachers in Portugal teaching Greek. Furthermore, the division of the professional qualifications of subjects into separate Portuguese and Latin areas led to teachers choosing only Portuguese teaching as an option, taking into consideration the statistics of Latin teacher vacancies in the country (as well as their own personal and academic investment).

Today it can be seen that the 2014 changes have had a direct repercussion in the initial training of Latin teachers. The numbers prove the calamitous state of the initial teacher training and a complete abandonment of an investment on behalf of the universities that provide them. During the last decade the country went from having four universities that trained Portuguese and Latin teachers to just one: in 2023, only the University of Coimbra offers this possibility. Since 2020, the number of students there has not exceeded ten. Over time, it will become unsustainable to maintain a Master's degree in teaching Portuguese and Latin to just one or two students per year. The costs of human resources will be enormous and there is no higher institution that can support this expense.

In recent years, with the evaluation of Master's degrees by external entities, universities, in order to keep teaching Master's degrees open, have found themselves forced to invest in the area of didactics and pedagogy. Thus, despite this area not being valued in higher education, some university professors invest in activities connected to initial and continuous teacher training and writing scientific articles on didactics.

This situation reveals some inconsistencies, since it is not only by holding colloquia, congresses, lectures and annual courses that we may renew pedagogies and seriously invest in teacher training. Even so, after a few years of delay in relation to the rest of some European countries, some university teachers in Portugal are already beginning to embrace active methodologies for teaching classical languages, but still in a very timid way. It was only after some professors from renowned foreign universities adopted these methodologies that Portuguese university professors began to look at active methodologies.

However, the Clenardus Association has engaged in the promotion and teaching of classical languages. Clenardus is an association of teachers of classical languages, in which secondary and university teachers, historians and archaeologists linked to the ancient world collaborate, on a voluntary basis, and have developed training in the area of teaching classical languages, using active methodologies. Since 2016, they have provided Latin and Greek training to over 500 teachers. This association managed to establish a protocol with the General Directorate of Education, so that the training provided can be recognized for teachers' career progression. In this way, the Clenardus Association has helped many teachers return to studying Latin, this time through active methodologies, after many years of absence.

However, it remains very difficult to convince university professors, who occupy decisive positions in universities, that these more active methodologies facilitate learning and encourage motivation, both for students and professors. In an era where significant learning activities are theorized over and teaching methodologies are being rethought, teacher training is still being carried out in expositive courses where teachers have a passive role. Teachers would be better served if they were able to take an active role in sharing experiences and reflecting on their own practices, and there should be a place for specialists in teaching and pedagogy, with field experience, to promote a more reflective practice and encourage new methodologies so as to acquire and improve their knowledge and skills. Well-meant but isolated activities, such as congresses and *colloquia,* are less effective at feeding into teacher training and in the long term making it efficient and benefiting the teaching of classical languages in the Portuguese education system. It seems to me that it is urgent to make a plan for the continuous training of classical languages teachers that can update their knowledge and provide them with tools that can be adapted to their context and can motivate students to learn those languages. Until this happens, nothing will change, and students' lack of motivation and teachers' lack of interest will keep being perpetuated. The number of students that are enrolled in Latin in secondary school is not promising either.

However, in an attempt to revive the teaching of classical languages, in 2015, the former Minister of Education Nuno Crato, in collaboration with various partnering entities, decided to allow schools, if they wanted, to integrate into their curriculum from the 1st Cycle the new subject 'Introduction to Classical Languages and Culture' (ICLC). This subject is optional and each school can choose to integrate it or not in their curriculum. The following guidance can be read on the Directorate-General of Education website:

> Recognising the relevance of classical languages and culture in training children and youth, the School Groups/Non-grouped Schools can take into consideration said component, integrating it in Educational Projects as a 'School offer'. To achieve the component – hereby designated as Introduction to Classical Languages and Cultures – each School Group/Non-grouped School will structure and develop its own programme, in accordance with its Educational Project.

> (Directorate General of Education 2015)

This political measure opened a bigger possibility for the learning of classical languages in the Portuguese Public Educational System, especially in primary education in Portuguese public schools. In the last few years, the number of national and international private schools has grown exponentially in the country. These schools have replicated the curriculum of their countries of origin and integrated Latin as a subject since primary education, some in the 1st Cycle. As a result, it has only been in private schools that there was the possibility to integrate

Latin as a subject in curricula starting from primary education. With the ICLC this possibility has now extended to public schools. Several years before, however, in 2011, there had been some isolated cases in public schools. These included the project *Pari Passu*, developed by the 2nd Cycle in Escola Secundária Rodrigues de Freitas in the city of Porto, and the 'Latin Free Course', using the methodology from the *Cambridge Latin Course*, in Escola Secundária de Pedro Nunes in Lisbon, for 3rd Cycle and secondary education students. Various integration formats of studying Classical Languages and Cultures in Portuguese public schools have been surging in the almost ten years after the possibility of integrating the subject was allowed through the ICLC. Some public school teachers, by resilience and resistance noticed that their schools were not adhering to this experiment, becaue they were refused permission to open secondary school Latin classes. Instead, they have to channel their teachers to teach Portuguese. In response, they managed to open clubs or extra-curriculars. For example, the Escola Secundária du Bocage offers a Latin Club, which has more than eighty students, who participate in this activity in their free time. Classes are given *pro bono* and due to the stubbornness of the teacher who insists on not giving up.

However, the difference that still exists between the number of students that learn Latin in private schools and in public schools is noteworthy. While in a private school, the school management has complete liberty to implement Latin or Greek in its curriculum; in public schools there are limitations, and it can be complicated to integrate the subjects, despite the Ministry of Education offering the possibility.

Beyond the possibility to teach Latin and Greek to primary education students, there is also the gap between the educational policies from the Ministry of Education and initial teacher training. The same Ministry that placed the possibility of learning Latin and Greek in primary education removed the possibility of entering the job market for teachers professionalized in primary education by eliminating the teaching professionalization in this study cycle. As has been mentioned above, teachers are professionalized solely in Latin in secondary education and do their internship only in this cycle. There they develop didactic issues and their pedagogical practices, rooted in studies and methodologies developed for that study cycle. To add to that, they now see the possibility of entering the job market, in public or private schools, to lecture in a subject that they never had any kind of training or experience in. It is unclear how a teacher who does not have full command of the materials will be able to teach using them. Additionaly, there is the problem of pedagogical practice. Without having had a classroom context experience, it is difficult to ensure that a future teacher will be able to adjust, select and define strategies for a subject that requires specific pedagogical and didactic knowledge for certain age ranges. Nor can the validating authorities assume that teachers are didactically competent to teach this subject. These are questions of some complexity and they cannot be answered with generalities. They demand responsibility and a serious investigation.

The problem with teachers' initial training is just the tip of the iceberg. The training of teachers who are at the moment teaching Latin or Greek is unknown, as teaching the subjects is not confined to classical language teachers. Any teacher in any area, without having had Latin or Greek in their training, can teach them. When it comes to continuous training, the problem is even more complex, as most teachers have not taught Latin for over a decade or have simply never taught it. It should be noted that, despite the changes to the Master's degree in teaching classical languages which started in 2015, there are no records of internships developed by active teachers in primary education previous to the change, with rare exceptions of internships implemented in free courses or observing and teaching supervised classes in primary education. It was carried out in this way because it was not considered relevant as the number of Latin students in primary education was minimal. Now, it becomes a pertinent and pressing question, as it takes into consideration that public schools have the possibility of integrating the subject of ICLC in this study cycle. In effect, the following questions arise: what training do teachers have to teach classical languages and cultures in primary school? And, if there is not a specific programme, which programmatic content is taught? How are contents planned and what are the reasons behind choosing the teachers who teach them? How are these contents applied in a classroom context?

It should be noted that the instructions given by the Ministry of Education are vague and open up the possibility of countless different practices. In the official page that the Ministry of Education dedicates to ICLC, the content is organized in two general topics, a term used by the Ministry itself, the first being 'Civilization and culture' and the second 'The inheritance of classical languages: We all speak Latin and Greek'. The former is limited to mythology, gods, heroes, and the presence of Graeco-Roman culture in our everyday life. In the latter, we find Latin expressions with current usage, etymologies, day-to-day words, reference to syntactic structure and building short sentences. This is no mandatory programme, but merely programmatic instructions. Thus, there is no methodology in classical language teaching, but only very sparse indications that seem to be deemed as necessary to access the knowledge of Latin. While there is no specific programme and the programmatic instructions are very vague, the following instruction for linguistic knowledge has been published: 'Engage in expression (written, oral, corporeal, musical . . .) of knowledge related to classical languages and culture] (Directorate-General of Education 2017).

It is unclear how a student can engage in written and oral production in a language if they only know words and build small sentences. Is it through Latin expressions of current usage that you have access to classical languages? In short, in each school each teacher can interpret and teach the subject as they wish. In itself, this option is not completely prejudicial, because it allows teachers to integrate the subject in the context where it is inserted. However, there is a risk that the subject becomes merely a gathering of vague terms, rooted in frugal expressions, mythology and curiosities at a curricular level. Yet the Ministry of Education advises that the subject is structured in a logic of progression in the learning of culture and of language. The question remains: which methodology is to be applied in learning the Latin language? If one analyses the programmes and the programmatic content of the different training actions, congresses or lectures that have been announced ever since the possibility of integrating this subject in schools came up, it can be determined that the beneficiaries are mainly teachers who belong to various subjects: ICLC does not require a specific group of teachers. In this way there is a presumed path on behalf of the university institutions that develop these initiatives, by legitimizing that teachers from diverse areas can teach the subject. In the first instance, it is immediately understood that the organizing institutions, in general, stated that there are not enough Recruitment Group 310 (Latin and Greek) teachers to feed these initiatives, and that therefore the universities and schools should help themselves with teachers who are interested in teaching ICLC whether they had Latin and Greek in their academic training or not. If this is the case, then if any teacher in any disciplinary area can teach Latin or Greek regardless of having had them in their academic training or not, then there seems little motivation for future young teachers to professionalize themselves at all. Should not we rethink the goals in introducing this subject in the Portuguese educational system? Should not we act in conformity with those goals? Do we only want students in primary education to have access to classical culture and some notion of classical languages? Do we want students to choose Latin in the field of Languages and Humanities in secondary education? Do we want more students graduating in Classical Studies in universities? Do we want more teachers professionalized in the area of Classical Languages and, consequently, more teachers specialized in teaching that subject?

All these questions are interconnected and, to be able to alter the national panorama, a strategic plan should be developed. Strategies can be continuously rethought, but there will only be more classical studies students at universities and candidates to teacher training in classical languages if there are job opportunities at schools and there have to be more students studying Latin and Greek so that there can be jobs for these teachers.

One of the ways to contribute to this increase in the number of job vacancies for classical languages teachers would be by creating a subject programme – even if open to diverse methodologies – with teaching content that demanded the specific training of specialized teachers in the area. Only in this way would the search for staff in the area of initial and continuous teacher training increase. This training would always have to be connected to the renewal and development of pedagogical practices taking into consideration students' motivation, appealing to new technologies and using orality as a teaching tool. There is, however, an undisputed truth. Despite the catastrophic situation and the disparate situation of Latin teaching in public and private education in Portugal, classical language teachers themselves have been the driving force, often at financial and personal cost, that has kept Latin teaching connected to its oxygen. These teachers are the ones who can keep Latin teaching in some schools, despite knowing that, if other serious measures are not taken, death is nearby and that the end is inevitable. They are the ones who look their students in the eye and understand what is being denied to them, the ones who try to tackle the difference, ever more accentuated, between public and private students, taking the knowledge of the classical language, culture and mythologies to students of all socio-economical classes, by believing only school and knowledge allow for full social mobility and that the cradle cannot determine the intellectual and social class one belongs to. These teachers are spread throughout the entire Portuguese territory, including Madeira and the Azores archipelago islands. They are teachers who saw their core training being a missed opportunity and were conditioned, for decades, to teach solely Portuguese. It is on their resilience and resistance that it can be affirmed that there is still Latin teaching in Portugal. However, these teachers are, for the most part, aged around fifty to sixty years old. If nothing is done, in the next two decades, the teaching of Latin and Greek will disappear from Portuguese schools.

References

Directorate-General of Education (2015), available online: https://www.dge.mec.pt/introducao-cultura-e-linguas-classicas (accessed 5 March 2024).

Directorate-General of Education (2017), available online: https://www.dge.mec.pt/introducao-cultura-e-linguas-classicas (accessed 5 March 2024).

Theodor Georgescu

Introduction: classical languages in schools

Romania has a uniform education system for primary and secondary education throughout the country. Classical languages are currently studied in the lower secondary cycle (*gymnasium*) and in the upper secondary cycle (high school). High school graduates can also take Latin and Greek in higher education (universities).

In lower secondary school there is only one Latin language class (in the 7th grade, 12–13-year-olds) entitled 'Elements of Latin Language and Romance Culture'. The syllabus for this subject, which is compulsory for all pupils in Romania, combines linguistic aspects with those of Roman civilization. It also offers a diachronic linguistic perspective from Latin to Romance languages, with an emphasis on the Romanian language.

The upper secondary cycle (high school) in Romania is divided into the following coursework directions: the theoretical coursework (humanities or science), the technological coursework (technical / services / natural resources / environmental protection field) and vocational coursework (military, theological, sports, artistic or pedagogical area). Latin and Greek are studied as given in Table 9 and 10, respectively.

Table 9. Latin at the high school level – allocation of lessons

Coursework	Area	Specialization	Number of classes per week (Roman numerals represent the school year: IXth–XIIth)
Theoretical	Humanities	Philology	1 (IX, X, XII), 2 (XI)
Theoretical	Humanities	Social Sciences	1 (IX, X)
Vocational	Theological	Orthodox Theology	1 (IX–XII)
Vocational	Theological	Church Music	1 (IX–XII)
Vocational	Theological	Roman Catholic Theology of Romanian Language	2 (IX, X, XI)
Vocational	Theological	Roman Catholic Theology of Hungarian Language	2 (IX, X), 1 (XI, XII)
Vocational	Theological	Greek Catholic Theology	1 (IX, X, XI)
Vocational	Theological	Reformed Theology	1 (IX, X)
Vocational	Theological	Pentecostal Theology	1 (IX, X)
Vocational	Theological	Baptist Theology	1 (IX, X)

Source: © Theodor Georgescu 2023.

Table 10. Greek at the high school level – allocation of lessons

Coursework	Area	Specialization	Number of classes per week (Roman numerals represent the school year)
Vocational	Theological	Orthodox Theology	1 (IX–XII)
Vocational	Theological	Church Music	1 (IX–XII)

Source: © Theodor Georgescu 2023.

Since 2010, students in Romania no longer have the option of choosing Latin among the subjects in which they take the baccalaureate examination, despite numerous efforts in society to reintroduce this possibility.

The Latin language class in lower secondary school is part of the common curriculum for all pupils in Romania. Latin and Greek language classes in upper secondary school are only taken by students who have opted for the respective coursework or specialization. However, the number of philology classes is low in high schools and decreasing. It is estimated that less than 10 per cent of students in Romania currently study Latin in high school and only students in theological high schools study Greek. With the reduction of humanities classes in high schools in favour of science or technological classes, the number of those studying a classical language is decreasing year by year.

In addition to the public education system, by far the largest in Romania, a private system is also developing. Some of these private schools are beginning to introduce classical languages into their educational offer, a tendency that is also a result of the continued restriction of classical language study in the public system.

Trends in Classics teaching

The presence of classical subjects in the curriculum has varied over time, as has the perception of the need for these classes. Following the example of France and Germany before the Second World War, Romania offered students the opportunity to study classical languages with a significant number of classes per week. After 1946, when Romania came under the influence of the Soviet model, classical languages dramatically lost their importance in education. Only a few humanities high schools continued to offer Latin language classes, and only for a limited period of time. In the 1970s, a Latin class was reintroduced in the lower secondary school cycle (*gymnasium*) in order to emphasize that Romanian language belongs to the Romance family. After the 1989 Revolution, as a reaction to the previous situation during the communist period, the perspective changed radically in favour of the classical languages. Many high schools were reintroduced with a humanities coursework and the number of Latin classes increased to three per week for the philological curriculum. Moreover, students in the science coursework also studied Latin, although with a smaller number of classes per week and only in the first two high school grades. Humanities students also had the option of choosing Latin as a subject for the Baccalaureate exam, and this option was very popular with students.

Since the 2000s the authorities have introduced several reforms that have had the effect of reducing the three hours of Latin to one hour, and since 2010 the possibility of taking the Latin examination at the Baccalaureate has been eliminated. As a result of this situation, the number of teachers has also decreased significantly, leading to a situation where Latin is taught by teachers with a background in other subject areas: Romanian, modern languages, history.

Perception of Classics

The perception in society about the role of classical studies in education can be summarized in the form of two main trends. Many people still believe that classical languages provide students with the cultural foundation necessary for a good quality humanities education. Latin is considered a fundamental subject for the humanities, especially for philology classes. Another part of society, without denying the formative role of the classical languages, believes that they should be studied exclusively at university by people who are interested in an ultra-specialization. For them, there are other important subjects to be studied in secondary education.

Those in the first category generally make the following arguments in favour of classics in school:

a. Cultural arguments: classical languages are the foundation of European culture. Through classical languages Romanian culture is connected to the great culture of the West. Young people thus have access to the cultural foundations of civilized Europe.

b. Educational and pedagogical arguments: Latin, with its highly ordered and coherent grammatical system, orders the mind and thus helps the whole educational process. Latin is a 'gymnastics of the mind', it teaches you to learn.

c. The national argument: Latin must be taught in school in order to understand the origins of Romance languages. Romanians have a duty to learn Latin, because the Romanian language comes from Latin.

Those who propose the removal of classical languages from the curriculum argue mainly that the education system needs to keep pace with the evolution of society. One of the preferred expressions is 'correlation with the labour market'. They believe that classical languages do not help students to meet the needs of today's society. In addition, students take two important examinations on which their future depends (at the end of secondary school, the 'national evaluation', and at the end of high school, the 'Baccalaureate') in subjects such as mathematics, Romanian and so on. Many believe that pupils should have in school only the subjects that are required in these exams, and classical languages are not evaluated in either of these exams. Others believe that some notions of Latin language should be studied within the subject of Romanian language, not as a stand-alone subject. In conclusion, their opinion is that classical languages should be maintained only at university level, and that new subjects now demanded by part of society should be introduced in high school.

Classical languages teachers in Romania continue to argue for the usefulness of the classical subjects in the national curriculum. They assert that the legitimate need to modernize education does not deny the benefits of studying Latin and Greek. On the contrary, more than ever, students in this age of rapid change need fundamental benchmarks that provide a solid foundation in an education that often fails to find its intended purpose and outcomes. In their view, classical languages help students to structure their minds and then perform in whatever field they want to work in. In addition, they convey a set of values. It is also completely wrong to maintain as part of the curriculum only those subjects which are apparently related to the 'needs of today's society' or to the 'labour market', because a civilized society cannot dispense with the cultural foundations which have formed it. In addition, the classical subjects must be studied as independent subjects and not as content within other subjects (Romanian, history, etc.), as this is the only way they can be studied coherently and show their value. It would also be a great mistake to study these subjects only at university level, as their formative role is most effective in the period of pupils' education (11–18 years), i.e. in secondary school and high school.

Classroom practice

In their approach to lesson design, teachers are guided mainly by the national mandatory syllabus – approved by the Ministry of Education – which contains not only the targeted scientific content and skills/competences, but also the methods, learning activities and assessment tools. Additionally, students in Romania have as their main tool for learning classical languages the school textbook validated by the Ministry of Education. In Latin, for middle and high school, there are at least two student books in force for each grade (each teacher can choose which textbook to use). The situation for Greek is similar, but the offer is on the whole more limited. The textbooks are compiled in accordance with the curriculum set by Ministry of Education experts.

As far as Latin is concerned, in secondary school pupils learn elements of Latin (morphology and vocabulary) in connection with Romanian and other European languages. Linguistic notions are taught in relation to aspects of Roman civilization and values passed on by ancient authors. In the 9th grade, the systematic study of Latin grammar begins with elements of morphology (noun, adjective, pronoun, verb [active voice], prepositions, conjunctions) and themes of culture and civilization (mentalities, political concepts, myths, legends, symbols). In the 10th grade the study of morphology focuses on the passive voice and moves on to the study of sentence and phrase syntax. Institutions and mentalities specific to the period of the Republic's crisis are also studied. In both 9th and 10th grades most of the texts used for language practice are adapted from Caesar's *De bello Gallico*. In the 11th grade, students continue to focus on the study of syntax and on reading and interpreting excerpts from Cicero (40 per cent), Titus Livius and Petronius, while translated/bilingual texts from Seneca, Tacitus and Apuleius are used for literature class projects. Finally, in the 12th grade students focus on Latin poetry with excerpts from, Catullus, Vergilius, Horatius and Ovidius (the exile poetry), while Lucretius and Ovid's *Metamorphoses* are used for literature class projects.

As for Greek, taught only in Orthodox high schools, morphology and syntax are taught gradually over four years, and students consolidate their grammar knowledge with texts mainly from Xenophon, the New Testament, Plato and St Basil the Great.

In addition to the textbook, classics teachers can also use Open Digital Resources (ODR) which they can adapt for the classics. After the Covid-19 lockdown experience, it has become possible for remote students to participate in lessons through different platforms, and students who either do not have a qualified Latin/Greek teacher at school or do not have these subjects in their curriculum can participate in lessons offered by other teachers.

Each teacher adapts their teaching method according to the school and students where they teach. Often personal worksheets are used, which have proven their effectiveness over time and the charismatic personality of the teacher often ensures the success of the Latin lesson. A dynamic teaching style and a constant reference to the present age provide the prerequisites for success. Also, many students learn classical languages by entering national school competitions or preparing for some international competitions (such as *Certamen Ciceronianum Arpinas, Certamen Ovidianum Sulmonense* or *Certamen Horatianum*).

Teacher training and professional development

In Romania there are very few opportunities to improve your skills as a Classics teacher. The Ministry of Education does not offer such programmes, and training is more of a personal adventure. Several years ago, there were teacher training courses for Latin teachers (along with training courses for several other disciplines), but these were discontinued as they were not considered cost-effective.

The most fruitful meetings of classical language teachers take place during national competitions dedicated to these subjects. Every year teachers prepare students for the Classical Languages Olympiad, with separate sections for Latin and Greek, and for a competition dedicated to the poet Ovidius (*Certamen Ovidianum Ponticum*). Also, traditionally teachers from the University of Bucharest and teachers from pre-university education prepare students to participate in international Latin language competitions.

Classical languages are studied in universities in major cities: Bucharest, Iasi, Cluj, Napoca, Craiova and Timisoara. In these universities there are classical philology departments where students study Latin and Greek equally. The number of students in these sections varies between ten and twenty.

Classical philology departments are striving to keep this domain as a unitary specialization, by allowing the study of the two languages together, at the same level, although there is pressure to separate Latin and Greek so that they can be studied in other combinations: e.g. major English-minor Greek // major Latin-minor German, etc. There is, in addition, the possibility for students from other majors (modern languages, Romanian language) to opt for Latin as a minor. In addition, students in some majors such as Romance languages or theology have a minimum number of Latin and/or Greek courses in their study programmes.

There are also private or public initiatives that support the study of classical languages in the form of training camps or courses offered by universities. Among these, we would like to point out that from 2023 the University of Bucharest is offering free courses in Latin and Greek, primarily for pupils, but the participants are very diverse: students, PhD students and enthusiasts of all ages. These Latin and Greek language courses offer the possibility to participate both in person and online, so participants come from all over Romania, including Romanian students studying abroad. This initiative has been a real success, proving that there is a real desire on the part of students to study classical languages in the absence of a centralized educational offer.

In Romania there is also an organization representing teachers of classical languages, the Classical Studies Society (*Societatea de Studii Clasice*), which carries out activities for the promotion of classical languages.

Conclusion

In Romania, the study of classical languages flourished after 1989, compared to the period of the previous socialist type of education. After the 2000s, however, as a result of an extensive process of educational reform, classical languages entered a steep decline, both in the pre-university and university systems. The current situation is that of trying to keep the field afloat with a decreasing number of people, under constant pressure from the authorities who want to reduce the field even more markedly. The community of classicists in Romania fights to keep Romania connected to the European tradition of classical culture. As public education tends to reduce the weight of the classics in favour of new disciplines 'imposed by the labour market', private initiatives or university departments promote the study of classical languages, thus responding to a demand that the public system does not satisfy.

Organizations

Certamen Ciceronianum Arpinas: https://certamenciceronianum.it/en/.
Certamen Horatianum: https://www.liceovenosa.edu.it/scheda-progetto/certamen/.
Certamen Ovidianum Sulmonense: https://www.iisovidio.edu.it/pagine/xxii-certamen-ovidianum-sulmonese.

RUSSIA

Elena Ermolaeva

The modern system of teaching classical languages and ancient culture in Russian schools has developed as a result of different tendencies, on the one hand, reviving the best of the classical Gymnasium tradition, which was destroyed after the revolution of 1917, and on the other, following modern European – mainly German, English, and Italian – pedagogical strategies. The rebirth of classical education began in the late 1980s, during the Perestroika. In 1989, the Classical Gymnasium of St Petersburg (*Gymnasium Classicum Petropolitanum* http://610.ru) was founded by the historians Leonid Zhmud and Lev Lurie and other enthusiastic teachers under the auspices of the city authorities. Professors Iakob M. Borovsky (1896–1994) and Alexander I. Zaicev (1926–2000) were behind this initiative. In 1990, the first private Orthodox Classical Gymnasium Yasenevo was opened in Moscow by the Orthodox Educational Society Radonezh; in 1993, a private classical Gymnasium was founded in Moscow by the classicist Yury Shichalin. Besides, there are several other public and private schools that teach both Latin and Greek, and several dozen schools and classes that teach only Latin. The latter can be divided into those with a deep level of studying Latin, with a more general course, and those offering Latin as a small part of a cultural programme familiarizing pupils with the ancient civilization.

As for Greek, the situation is different. Orthodox church schools, supported by the Russian Orthodox Church and the Patriarchate, offer such courses more often than state schools. The main purpose of their programmes is to study the language of the New Testament and the Church Fathers, Orthodox worship and Byzantine Greek. Mostly, these schools are private and very small.

Most of the schools with Classics are in Moscow – the best known are Yury Shichalin's Classical Gymnasium and school No. 1507 – and in St Petersburg. Several exist in the reginal centres – Kaluga, Saratov, Nizhny Novgorod, Dzerzhinsk, Petrozavodsk, Vologda, etc. – where the teaching of classics is often mainly dependent on enthusiastic teachers.

There is no unified system of teaching Greek, Latin and ancient culture in our country, each school follows its own way. As for Latin, many schools are guided by the methodological recommendations of Alexander Podosinov, the author, together with Natalia Shchaveleva, of a Latin textbook, popular in Russia, *Lingua Latina* (1993, 2021) and one of the initiators of the All-Russian Latin Language Olympiad. In schools, where classical languages are studied as electives, the teachers are often free to choose their methods.

Now, I will go into more detail about several schools to show the different levels of teaching as well as their different goals, methods, textbooks and forms of student motivation.

The most profound study of classical languages is in the Classical Gymnasium of St Petersburg (CGSP), where Ancient Greek and Latin languages are compulsory subjects and are taught according to the unified programmes developed at the school itself. It is a state school, pupils are selected through entrance examinations that determine their general development and aptitude for logical thinking (mathematics at the school is very serious). They start studying in Grade 5 (10–11 years old) and continue for seven years up to Grade 11 (17–18 years old). From Grade 5, pupils are given lessons in ancient civilization, mythology, and Greek and Roman history. Likewise, Latin begins in Grade 5 and continues until the final year, with four to five academic hours per week in Grades 5–7 (covering Latin grammar and syntax), three hours in Grades 8–11 (reading ancient authors: Caesar, Cicero, Ovid, Horace, Livy, Virgil, Tacitus, and Petronius). Greek starts in Grade 7 (12–13 years old) and continues throughout with three hours per week to Grade 11. The curriculum aims to teach Greek grammar and syntax for three years, after which students begin reading texts in the original: Attic prose excerpts from Xenophon's *Anabasis*, *Memorabilia* or *Institutio Cyri* and the works of Plato, Lysias, and Lucian, followed by Homer in Grade 10, and, in the final year, Herodotus and a tragedy of Euripides or Sophocles, or a comedy of Aristophanes. Verification of knowledge is carried out by means of grammar tests, translations from Russian into Latin and Greek, and a final oral examination after almost every level. Such examination involves translation of an unseen text (with a dictionary), a grammar test, and translation of a text that has been read during the year (without a dictionary). After Grade 10, there is a written test on Homer, including translation, grammar tasks, and converting the Homeric dialect into Attic. There is also an obligatory year-long course on the history of Greek and Latin literature. (Budaragina & Ermolaeva 2021; Ermolaeva & Pushel 2021).

I have taught classical languages and literature in this school since 1991. At the beginning, we used xeroxed copies of pre-revolutionary textbooks for Russian Gymnasia; later several modern German textbooks have been translated into Russian by our teachers Vanda Kazanskene and Aleksandr Chernoglazov, such as Person (1967), Stehle (1950) and Holtermann and Baumgarten (1986). In recent years, we moved on to creating our own textbooks and selections of texts. The school has published a witty collection of grammar, linguistic, lexical, and translation assignments (Zelchenko 2011). The Greek grammar for Grades 7–8 (St Petersburg, 2023) was written by Nina Almazova, who teaches both at the University of St Petersburg and in the CGSP. I am finishing a textbook on Homer's and Herodotus' language and style.

Another school with both classical languages is St Philip's School in Moscow. In 2000, this private school was founded by Mikhail Povaliaev, now vice-director and, since 2005, president of the Russian Foundation for Education and Science. Key teachers of classical languages in this school for many years were classical scholars Alexey Belousov, Grigory Belikov, and recently Maria Abramovich. Latin is taught here as a compulsory subject from Grades 5 to 11, three hours per week in Grades 5–7, two hours per week in Grades 8–11. Greek is studied as an optional subject only from Grade 8, two hours per week. The Latin textbooks are Ørberg's *Lingua Latina per se illustrate, Familia Romana* and *Roma Aeterna* (Ørberg 2011); the Greek textbook is *Athenaze* (Balme et al. 2016).

Alexey Belousov describes his personal experience of teaching classical languages at the school, which led him to the decision to replace the conventional method of teaching with a 'direct' and 'natural' method, and reflects on the modern teenager's motivation to learn Latin:

> I believed that the methods my teachers had learned were beautiful, unshakeable and the crowning achievement of European classical pedagogy for five hundred years. Therefore, if a child doesn't learn the material, you have to 'force' him with bad marks, up to expulsion if necessary. In 2008, I started teaching Latin at the St Philip's School, a private school in Moscow, where the very external environment was quite different from my previous schools. And though the former method worked with some of the pupils, it failed with those children who needed any other motivation than the lofty words about 'the classics as the basis of true European and Russian culture'.
>
> Imagine the average urban child in an environment for which it is commonplace that Latin and Greek are 'dead' languages, which are absolutely unnecessary for social life and material success. Add to this the fact that our child's parents were themselves brought up by some works of Russian literature and Soviet propaganda that Latin and Greek were instruments of torturing children in the classical gymnasia of tsarist Russia. This environment, in which the modern teenager lives, is a powerful demotivating force, which is almost impossible for a teacher, whose main motivator remain only bad and good marks, to overcome. It took me, a person who is quite stubborn in their beliefs, almost two years to realize all this. That's when I first got my hands on Hans Ørberg's *Lingua Latina per se illustrata*, after some reflection, I decided to replace the previous textbooks at the St Philip's school.
>
> (Belousov 2020: 307)

The practice of living Latin by the pupils and teachers of Belousov's Gymnasium at the Vivarium Novum (Luigi Miraglia, Italy) twice a year strengthened his own confidence in the correctness of the method. Socializing and then often friendship with high school students in European countries has in some ways increased the motivation to learn classics. Besides, Alexei Belousov, referring to Eleanor Dickey's work (2016, 2018) writes on the need to use more back-and-forth translation in teaching (Belousov 2020).

Here is a story about another school. Dr Pavel Evdokimov, a teacher of Latin at the Moscow 'Intellectual' state school from its foundation in 2003, reports on his school:

> Latin has been taught since 2003, ancient Greek during 2010–2012 and then since 2016. The teaching of ancient languages is optional and is carried out within the framework of the system of additional education. There is no upper limit, if pupils who have started studying an ancient language want to continue, they will be engaged with it at any grade and age. Usually, it is relatively massive in Grades 5–7 and literally piecework in Grades

8–11. The classes are usually two times per week for forty minutes. The difficulty in scheduling the second half of the day is very high, it is not always possible to find a convenient time for everyone, so it happens that a pupil manages to come to only one lesson a week.

In this school the main focus is on the Latin textbook (Podosinov & Shchaveleva 1993, 2021), and A. Kozarzewski's (1981) Latin textbook for the Soviet universities and materials from Ørberg's *Familia Romana*. For Greek, the teacher Maria Fedortsova selectively uses *Athenaze* (Balme et al. 2016) and F. Wolf et al.'s (2004) and Kozarzewski's (2002) textbooks. Each teacher works in his/her own way creatively, relying rather on his/her own programmes, supplementing them with interesting materials from different textbooks and manuals. There are no exams and credits as mandatory elements of certification, the role of independent certification for beginners is usually played by the ELEX and EGEX of Euroclassica.

Pavel Evdokimov says that the administration has changed twice in the twenty years of the school's history, and currently no one has expressed doubts about the necessity of teaching ancient languages. Nevertheless, there is a problem of adequate payment for teachers' efforts. The administration is ready to pay a certain amount of money to the teachers, realizing that in fact they are overworking, working in small groups, sometimes additionally with those who, due to the schedule, cannot get to classes. In their turn, teachers of ancient languages create periodic 'informational occasions' to report to higher authorities and the parental community how many pupils took part in the Olympiad or received the Euroclassica ELEX and EGEX certificates, or completed research works based on their knowledge of ancient languages.

From 2011 to 2020, the school had a practical experience on history and culture of the Mediterranean in Cyprus. As part of the trip, pupils and teachers spent ten days travelling to ancient and medieval monuments, holding classes in museums, and a seminar called 'Homeric Readings' (https://librarius-narod.ru/m/150214.php). Together with students from the Russian-speaking school 'Pythagoras' Disciples' they performed an excerpt from Aristophanes' *The Frogs* in the ancient theatre of Kourion in Cyprus. The school has an educational archaeological museum where a fair share of the exhibits and units are replicas or original objects from the ancient period. Periodically, in late spring, costume competitions for fifth graders, 'The Olympic Games' is held, where sports events are combined with historical and cultural ones.

In recent years, circumstances have not favoured classical education, and the teaching of classical languages has been reduced in several schools and universities. However, there is a reverse trend as well. For example, the administration of the Vologda Multidisciplinary Lyceum supports the teaching of Latin in every possible way. Its curriculum for the study of Latin in Grades 5 and 6 of the humanities section is two academic hours per week by subgroups; and in the 6th grade, one more hour per week is added for the whole class to prepare pupils for the exam in Latin language. The structure of the exam is as follows:

1. Reading and translation of an unfamiliar coherent text.
2. Grammatical analysis of underlined forms.
3. Reading by heart a passage from Latin authors (Catullus, Phaedrus, Horace).
4. Idiomatic expressions (150 in total). Translation of ten expressions from Russian into Latin and their historical commentary.

Moving to Grade 7, pupils no longer have Latin as a compulsory subject in the schedule but can choose it as an additional programme: 'Advanced Latin language study. Olympiad preparation'. This programme is developed by Natalia Komleva for students of Grades 6–8, who have a special interest in the study of Latin and ancient culture.

A few words about a recent bold initiative. In 2023, a private Orthodox school 'Sophia' was opened in St Petersburg by Priest Daniil Vasilevsky, a graduate of the Department of Classical Philology of the University of St Petersburg. He introduced Latin from the first grade (7–8 years old). Teachers Anna Chernovskaya and Polina Sirota (a graduate from the Classical Gymnasium of St Petersburg) start with a playful introduction to children of the first grade, which proceeds as if Latin is not just an academic subject, like mathematics or reading, but rather a secret cipher that almost no one understands, and is all the more interesting to master it together knowing strict rules of Latin. The children draw their own illustrations to the Latin alphabet, colour special books with mythological stories, and play with pictured cards for Latin words. The teachers create their own programme, inspired by the *Cambridge Latin Course*.

Extra-curricular activities are also an important source of classical education in Russian schools. The Annual All-Russian Olympiad on Latin Language and Ancient Culture for pupils of Grades 5–11 is held in Moscow and every fourth year in St Petersburg. The Olympiad is held in two stages: the first one is a qualifying round in schools, the winners of which come to compete in the main round in Moscow or St Petersburg. The organizers of the Olympiad are the Moscow City Department of Education, Moscow State Linguistic University, Moscow State University, Russian State University for the Humanities, St Petersburg Classical Gymnasium and the Orthodox Svyato-Tikhonovsky University. Winners of the Olympiad receive diplomas and valuable prizes. The twenty-sixth Latin Olympiad, which was held on 13 April 2024 in the Classical Gymnasium of St Petersburg, was attended by 86 students from ten schools of Moscow, St Petersburg, Vologda, Semenovsk and Serpukhov.

The association of school teachers of classical languages, *Societas Russica Magistrorum Linguarum Classicarum* (https://librarius-narod.ru/pro/srmlc.php), as a member of Euroclassica, aims to promote classical education. The association takes part in the annual Euroclassica Greek and Latin examinations, while the Euroclassica congress that took place in St Petersburg in September 2007 contributed to the popularity of classical education and brought new members into the Russian association. One of the projects of the *Societas Russica* was the Summer School in Classics (*Academia Classica Aestiva*) for pupils all over Russia with the aim to popularize ancient languages and civilization. It has been held from 2009 to 2020 annually. The Summer School was a successful and lively experience of socializing and sharing ideas and knowledge of classicist colleagues, especially the young, mostly from St Petersburg and Moscow. Several students participating in it became teachers of Classics and / or classical scholars, like Daria Kondakova (PhD Oxford, 2022) and Arseny Vetushko-Kalevich (PhD Lund, 2019).

The last Summer School was held via Zoom on the reason of the Covid-19 lockdown. This reduced all the activities of the Summer School, seminars, theatre performances, games and competitions, but gave the advantage of inviting lecturers from different countries. Now, we are making efforts to resume. To summarize the experience of teaching Classics during the lockdown period: the years of distance teaching were exhausting for teachers and children, but at the same time, after it, we started to use digital opportunities more actively, especially in the schools that have computers and screens in every classroom.

Finally, some words about teacher training and professional development opportunities. In Russia there are four universities which have Departments of Classics: the Moscow State University, Russian State University for the Humanities (Moscow, since 1993), the HSE Institute for Oriental and Classical Studies (Moscow, since 2017), and St Petersburg State University. Since 1995 the Classical department of Moscow State University holds annual conferences and seminars on reading ancient authors for the professional development of teachers of Classics from all regions of Russia; in 2021 and 2022 the meetings were held online. The Volga Region Centre of Greek-Latin Linguacultural Studies exists at Nizhny Novgorod State University. Its main task is assigned to the methodological support of training, retraining and professional development of teaching staff of the classical cycle in various educational institutions of the Volga region.

One of the most renowned centres for the study of antiquity in Russia is the *Bibliotheca classica Petropolitana* (BiCl) (http://www.bibliotheca-classica.org/en/node/107), founded in 1993 by the classical philologist Alexander Gavrilov (St Petersburg State University; Institute of History of the Russian Academy of Sciences) to revive the traditional study of the ancient heritage in Russia and to strengthen the classical philology in St Petersburg University and the Academy of Sciences. The BiCl houses a publicly accessible reference library of about 30,000 volumes and more than 30,000 digital books and articles. It publishes the scholarly journal *Hyperboreus* and the humanistic almanac *Ancient World and Us*. Among the many projects of the BiCl were *Corpus inscriptionum regni Bosporani: Album imaginum*, published in 2004, and the *Dictionary of St Petersburg Classical Scholars (1819–1920)*, published in 2021. There is a unique situation in St Petersburg, as the BiCl and the Classical Gymnasium share the same building and are in close contact; some the BiCl staff teach Classics at the school. Thus, the teachers at the school have the opportunity to develop professionally and the students to get acquainted with classics with the assistance of professional scholars (Budaragina and Ermolaeva, 2021).

In sum, it seems to me that a teacher of classics is like a λαμπαδηφόρος [torch-bearer] who tries to keep the fire alive and pass it on to their students.

References

Balme, M., G. Lawall and J. Morwood (2016), *Athenaze: An Introduction to Ancient Greek*, Oxford: Oxford University Press.

Belousov, A. (2020), 'From personal teaching experience classical languages by "natural" method', *Aristeas*, XXI: 297–327.

Budaragina, O. and E. Ermolaeva (2021), 'Classics in St Petersburg', in A. Fricke, M. Reith and G. Vogt-Spira (eds), *Latein und Griechisch im 21. Jahrhundert*, Darmstadt: Wissenschaftliche Buchgesellschaft (WBG), 269–79.

Dickey, E. (2016), *An Introduction to the Composition and Analysis of Greek Prose*, Cambridge: Cambridge University Press.

Dickey, E. (2018), *Learn Latin from the Romans. A Complete Introductory Course Using Textbooks from the Roman Empire*, Cambridge: Cambridge University Press.

Ermolaeva, E. and L. Pushel, (2021), 'Classical Languages, Culture, and Mythology at the Classical Gymnasium of Saint Petersburg', in L. Maurice (ed.), *Our Mythical Education: The Reception of Classical Myth Worldwide in Formal Education, 1900–2020*, Warsaw: Wydawnictwa Uniwersytetu Warszawskiego, 189–208.

Holtermann, H. and H. Baumgarten (1986/93, 2016), *Ianua nova*, Göttingen and St Petersburg: Vandenhoeck & Ruprecht.

Kozarzewski, A. (1981), Учебник латинского языка [Textbook of the Latin language], Moscow: Moscow University Publishing House.

Kozarzewski, A. (2002), Учебник древнегреческого языка [Textbook of Ancient Greek], Moscow: Greco-Latin Cabinet.

Ørberg, H. (2011), *Lingua Latina per se illustrata. Familia Romana* and *Roma Aeterna*, London: Hackett.

Person, K. (1967/93, 2013), *Propulaia: Griechisches Unterrichtswerk,* Stuttgart and St Petersburg: Klett.

Podosinov, A. (2006), 'Latin in the Secondary School Humanitarian Cycle,' *Educational Studies Moscow. National Research University Higher School of Economics*, 4: 192–9.

Podosinov, A. and N. Shchaveleva (1993/2021), *Lingua Latina. Introduction to Latin Language and Ancient Culture*, Vols I–V, Moscow: Progress.

Stehle, M. (1950/93), *Griechische Sprachlehre,* Stuttgart and St Petersburg: Klett.

Wolf, F., N. Malinauskene, A. Lyubzhin and Y. Shichalin (2004), Древнегреческий язык: начальный курс [Ancient Greek: initial course], Moscow: Greco-Latin Cabinet.

Zelchenko, V. (2013), 'Gymnasium Classicum Petropolitanum,' *Hyperboreus*, 19 (1–2): 289–96.

Zelchenko, V. (2011), Древнегреческий язык: Задания и тесты [Ancient Greek: Tasks and Tests], St Petersburg: Progress.

SERBIA

Goran Vidović and Boris Pendelj

In Serbian secondary education, classical languages are part of the traditional and uniform school curricula, within which the vast majority of the same subjects have been mandatory since at least the late 1980s. Despite individual revisions or attempts at educational reforms since the early 2000s, high school teaching practice of classical languages has not sufficiently progressed in terms of focus and methodology. The presentation below will be accompanied by some of the findings from responses by fifty-seven high school Latin teachers to a survey conducted in September 2023. Since Greek is mostly a separate case, it is best addressed individually. On the university level, classical languages are studied as the mandatory component of classical philology and as more or less elective at various other programmes (Romance Languages, History, Archaeology, etc.)

Institutions and courses

Various Latin courses are mandatory in several secondary school programmes. 'General' Latin is included in the most comprehensive and intensive national secondary education programme, taught in the four-year general education high schools, a version of the German *Realgymnasium* (henceforth, RG). It is by far the single most populous on the national level: currently, 145 public schools offer RG programmes, accounting for close to 30 per cent of the student body (see figures below). Currently, RG subjects include Serbian (sometimes also an ethnic minority) language and literature, Mathematics, English, another foreign language, Latin, History, Geography, Biology, Psychology, Philosophy, Sociology, Physics, Chemistry, Information Technologies, Visual arts, Musical education, and Physical education. Slight, predefined differences in weekly number of classes and years studied of different subjects result in three

RG 'concentrations': Natural Sciences (NS), Social Sciences and Humanities (SH), and a combination of these two ('mixed'). About one half of all RG students enrol in NS, where Latin is studied only in the first year (RG1), while the other half is comprised of those who choose SH or mixed, where Latin is continued in the second year (RG2). RG Latin is thus conceived of as more pertinent to humanities than the sciences. Although not explicit in the subject title, the RG Latin also includes regular lessons in Roman civilization.

Next, 'Latin for Specific Purposes' is taught for one year (typically the first) in two different vocational secondary school programmes. Various paramedic, healthcare, pharmaceutical, laboratory, veterinary and agricultural technicians in eighty-six public schools study customized 'biomedical' Latin (BM), with reduced grammar, overwhelmingly technical vocabulary, special attention to prefixes/suffixes and compound derivations, and examples and readings geared towards the field of study (anatomy, pathology, botany, etc.). Since the Serbian legal system is Continental, based on Roman law, Latin with jurisprudential focus (J) is taught in programmes for paralegal associates; these programmes enrol about a third of students in twenty-eight public high schools that offer various combinations of law, business and administration subjects. The J Latin is oriented towards Roman legal texts, with emphasis on analysing and memorizing Latin legal vocabulary, formulae and maxims. This is also a preparation for Law School, where Roman law features prominently.

Some schools in the country offer a modified RG philological programme, with strong focus on – a 'major' in – one modern language and literature (henceforth, PhG). The PhG programme includes all four years of 'philological' Latin (officially titled 'Latin Language with Elements of Classical Civilization'), which in the first three years covers more thoroughly the grammar that the RG programme covers in two, while the fourth year is devoted solely to readings from classical authors. Currently, there are seven such schools in the country, each of which enrols about one combined PhG class per year (students from the same class with different language majors), while another two schools, specialized in philology exclusively, enrol about one class for every language major (in total, 6–7 such classes each year), including one class of Classical Philology major (more below). On average, around 600 students enrol in PhG programmes every year (for total figures, see below). Additionally, one Catholic high school in the country (Subotica) has mandatory, four-year PhG Latin (though currently not Greek).

Greek instruction is always paired with Latin, in two types of programmes. One is the Classical Philology option of the PhG (henceforth, PhGCl), currently offered by two specialized philological secondary schools, heirs to the tradition of classical *gymnasium* (abolished in the late 1970s): The Philological Gymnasium in Belgrade and the Gymnasium of Sremski Karlovci (Karlovačka gimnazija), each of which enrols one PhGCl class every year. PhGCl students study Latin and Greek in all four years, three times a week. PhGCl Latin is similar to PhG Latin (i.e., RG1-2 programme extended to three years), but is more thorough not only since it is studied three times a week but because lessons in civilization are separated into its own subject, 'Introduction to Classics', which also includes mythology and literature. Likewise, in the third year, PhGCl language instruction is complemented twice a week by a separate subject, Translation Exercises, a joint course for both Greek and Latin, where teachers can alternate between the two or approach them comparatively in the same session. Finally, like Modern Language PhG students, the PhGCl students in their fourth year study Rhetoric and Oratory, where they also learn history of rhetoric, the bulk of which is devoted to Graeco-Roman tradition.

The only other place where Greek and Latin are integrated is outside the state education system, in four ecclesiastical secondary schools for junior clergy of the Serbian Orthodox Church. The five-year programme includes two years of 'theological' Latin and Greek geared towards ministerial and theological training. The Greek is the New Testament and patristic *koiné*, while Latin is primarily Biblical and Medieval. Teachers are mostly members of the clergy, graduates from the Church's Faculty of Orthodox Theology, though some are Classics Department graduates.

Secondary school and university programmes: enrolments

The total number of public secondary schools in Serbia is 454, of which Latin is taught in 269: 145 RG Latin, 86 BM Latin, 28 J Latin, 9 PhG Latin, of which two teach PhGCl Latin and Greek (the exact number of private schools is not presented since they constitute a minority and typically offer more than one programme). According to official 2022/23 data of the Public Statistics Agency (www.stat.gov.rs), 28.1 per cent of all high school students in Serbia (including both public and private schools of all profiles, without ecclesiastical schools) are studying RG programmes; 14.2 per cent attend biomedical vocational schools, and 16.7 per cent law, business and administration schools, of which an estimated one-third study Latin. With these numbers combined, we arrive at over 50 per cent of all high school students nationwide who study Latin at least in their first year. To offer some illustrative estimates, since there are around 60,000 students entering Serbian high schools every (recent) year, that means that over 30,000 study RG1/BM/J Latin every given year for the first and the last time. To this we add those who are at that point in their second year of study (RG2), that is, the second-year RG students in SH and mixed programmes (who make up about a half of all second-year RG students), so approximately 9,000. This, therefore, amounts to close to 40,000 students studying Latin any given year, for 2 × 45 minutes weekly. Another approximately 600 study PhG Latin; lastly, two classes study PhGCl Latin and Greek, for 3 × 45 minutes weekly.

At the tertiary level, Classical Philology as a distinct university programme is studied only at the Faculty of Philosophy's Classics Department (University of Belgrade), operational under different names and institutions since 1875 (henceforth, CD). The CD's comprehensive programme in Classical Philology is rare in the region, and unique in the country. Besides covering instruction in classical languages and literature, courses range from Indo-European linguistics to Modern Greek, and include, among many others, Biblical philology, Byzantine studies, and reception studies.

Following national demographic trends since the 1990s, enrolment in the Faculty of Philosophy has been steadily declining, and more rapidly since the mid-2000s. At times enrolling over thirty students, the CD now enrols fewer than fifteen.

Outside CD, classical languages are taught by CD graduates at several philological and other humanities departments in the country. Classical Greek is taught at the Department of Modern Greek Studies at the University of Belgrade, while the University of Belgrade and other universities in the country (Novi Sad, Niš, and Kragujevac) offer Latin in Romance Languages departments, and both languages at the departments of History, Archaeology, Philosophy and Art history. In these programmes, classical languages are either elective or sometimes mandatory for two semesters and elective for another two. According to some calculations, Latin is studied every year by somewhere between two and three hundred

Romance Language students nationwide, by about a hundred from other humanities departments (Archaeology, etc.), and Greek by about fifty. Graduates from these departments with all four semesters qualify for teaching high school Latin (PhGCl Latin and Greek are reserved for classicists).

CD graduates also sometimes teach Greek and Latin in the Orthodox Church's high schools, as well as on the tertiary level at the Faculty of Orthodox Theology, where classical languages are studied up to four semesters (its annual enrolment is about 200 students). Lastly, in some Law Schools and Medical Schools CD graduates also teach remedial Latin courses to entering students who had no high school Latin.

Textbooks and approaches

In Serbia, every subject in schools with state curricula is regulated by the Department of Education and specialized governmental agencies, in cooperation with high school teachers and university professors. Yet even though relevant regulatory documents prescribe only the guidelines and frameworks, with considerable leeway for content and methodology interventions, let alone classroom practice, actual high school teaching often depends on the available textbooks. This is particularly visible in the case of Latin.

The single most important factor of the current state of RG Latin instruction is the legacy of the only two textbooks in circulation for over twenty years and a household name for nearly forty, Vulićević and Maskareli (1978) and Vulićević and Maskareli (1979) for RG1, RG2 respectively. As products of their time (indeed, earlier times), these old-school, black-and-white textbooks with occasional images presented grammar with superb competence and accuracy, but in the order and the level of detail of grammar manuals—including the exceptions, irregular and less frequent forms. Even though the readings are stratified (longer texts, shorter anecdotes, exercise sentences, proverbs), the mere layout gave the impression of prioritizing grammar instructions, with readings in the service of memorizing the forms. Whether or not that was the intention, for decades RG Latin teachers have been reducing them to this, perhaps understandably: simpler to teach and easier to grade, morphology is a tempting shortcut for managing classes sometimes counting up to thirty students, and at some earlier times even more. This tedious and unstimulating practice was able to survive since the subject is mandatory (see students' impressions below).

Two new textbooks that emerged since the 2000s brought visible, though partial improvements. Pakiž and Dimitrijević (2003/19) for RG1 (henceforth Pakiž 1) and Pakiž et al. (2006/20) for RG2 (henceforth Pakiž 2) made one perhaps small step for Latin instruction but considerable for Latin in Serbia by visually updating the traditional text-only approach to an illustrated 'graphic novel' design. Besides being visually more attractive and, thus, memorable – text is often arranged in speech balloons, 'bubbles' – such an approach contributed to wrapping Latin instruction in a narrative structure, a sequence of stories with a sense of progress and purpose. A typical Pakiž 1 unit consists of a situation presented in bubbles and a short prose passage, followed by the unit's vocabulary, grammar explanation with short examples, translation exercises (Latin to Serbian and vice versa), and a thematically related lesson in classical civilization. In Pakiž 2, the prose passages are longer and based on original sources, with some adaptations. Both textbooks include a comprehensive vocabulary in both directions.

Yet, despite the refreshing take of these two textbooks, the fact that they retained the old order and selection of grammar units of the long-lasting, iconic Vulićević and Maskareli textbooks, and for some time coexisted with them – the latter were officially discontinued in 2017 – contributed to slowing down the change in attitude to learning Latin. The implicit reasoning remains that texts serve as a showcase for grammar rules, all of which are equally worthy of students' attention, however rare and exceptional they may be.

A true paradigm shift is initiated by the latest RG1 Latin textbook, *Ain tū?* (Nedeljković et al. 2020), which introduced several revolutionary innovations. Inspired in some respects by Ørberg's *Lingua Latina per se illustrata* series (2011), this textbook explicitly subordinates grammar to reading comprehension. The centre of each lesson is a text, typically a dialogue, about a scene in the daily life of a fictitious Roman family (gradually complemented by another, narrative text on a related classical civilization theme). The texts are unrestricted by the grammar that the students already know or learn in that unit but equipped with grammatical and lexical annotations where necessary instead. Besides providing a more natural and interesting reading, this approach sends the message that grammar is only a tool, not an end in itself.

In presenting actual grammar rules, the textbook pioneered the 'spiral progression' method: instead of addressing an entire section of grammar rules at once (e.g., all impersonal verbs, or all uses of infinitives), it opts for supplying students with a carefully measured, steady dose of grammar, progressing from more frequent, relevant and simpler, towards the less frequent, exceptional and complex, all aimed at gradually increasing reading competence. For example, verbal inflection does not start with the first conjugation, which requires a phonetic explanation already in the first person singular, but with the simplest and most regular second conjugation; the third conjugation, being relatively most complex, is taught last, once the students have already got familiar with -*u*- vowel in the third person plural in the fourth conjugation. The fourth declension neuter nouns – the students' all-time 'favourite' *cornu* – are omitted on account of rarity. Likewise, the Imperfect Indicative, being much rarer in ancient sources than its formal regularity might suggest, is taught after the Future. The Pluperfect and Future Perfect are postponed to RG2, which made room for Deponent Verbs. Third declension adjectives begin with the two-nominative type, -*is*, -*e*, as a model for the far less frequent types with one and three nominatives. Since the focus is on usage not on the structure of Latin grammar as a field, related morphology is sometimes introduced or returned to on different occasions for different reasons; one particularly bold move is presenting personal pronouns at first instance without the genitive, because the students have not yet learned the syntax of genitive where the form would appear. In sum, this textbook judiciously sacrifices the conventional order of grammar instruction to focus on reading comprehension.

However, the teacher survey shows that implementation of the *Ain tū?* (Nedeljković et al. 2020) approach has still some way to go. First, a half of respondents have never used the book. Of those who have, less than a quarter (24.1 per cent) approve of its order of grammatical units, while over a half (51.7 per cent) see it as by far the most problematic aspect of the textbook; by contrast, the order of units in Pakiž 1 (and, by extension, Vulićević & Maskareli 1978), is praised by 45 per cent of examinees, and only 4 per cent are dissatisfied with it.

In instructive contrast, these methodological concerns do not apply to Latin for Specific Purposes, quite likely due to the reduced grammar and, especially, the focus on basic understanding of relatively simple technical texts and phrases. BM Latin teachers seem equally satisfied with the new, illustrated textbooks by Vagić and Marković (2007, 2014) and Gemaljević (2007) as they are with their predecessor, which was in use for nearly fifty years (Popović 1961), whose layout is the same as in Vulićević and Maskareli (1978, 1979) for RG Latin. J Latin teachers sometimes use the specialized legal Latin textbook Stanojević and Jovanović (1987) and often, without any difficulty, in combination with any of the RG1 textbooks available, for general grammar instruction.

The situation with Greek is presented in different ways from RG and BM/J Latin. There is no Serbian high school Greek textbook available; for better or for worse, teachers resort to foreign ones, such as Croatia's Martinić-Jerčić and Matković (2013) and the British publications *Reading Greek* (JACT 1978) and *Greek Stories: a GCSE Reader* (Taylor & Waite 2012). Rarely restricting themselves to any one of these from beginning end, Greek teachers generally come up with their own teaching materials as they go alones. A Greek textbook would be welcome, but given the minuscule number of Greek students nationwide (about two new classes each year), there is perhaps little financial incentive for anyone to do so. The optimistic interpretation might be that the lack of a universal resource is arguably less of a problem in courses taught to such a small number of interested students. Indeed, this in turn allows teachers to stay flexible in designing the instruction and adjust the course material to the generation at hand.

Some observations on classroom experience and pedagogy

In addressing the issue of classical languages perception among students, it is the RG Latin that deserves special attention. It is simultaneously by far the most popular national classical language programme, and the only one without either immediately obvious practical application, like BM/J, or a philological justification, like PhG/PhGCl. It is there that the old-school, morphology-centred approach to Latin teaching risks alienating a large portion of high school students.

Survey results (above) show that RG Latin instruction thus remains fairly conservative. There are several possible explanations for this, not mutually exclusive. The vast majority of current teachers have learnt Latin the conventional way. *Ain tū?* (Nedeljković et al. 2020) appeared only recently, just before the Covid-19 lockdown mandated distance learning, when, presumably, some teachers felt uneasy experimenting with a completely new approach.

It is instructive to summarize the distribution of examinees' choices of minimal requirements for a passing grade. Around 75 per cent assign passive recognition of basic morphology, 65 per cent would accept reciting Latin proverbs, 50 per cent basic vocabulary, while 30 per cent assign a classical civilization theme (that is, not a language requirement strictly speaking). Arguably, it is not only teachers who, for reasons mentioned above, give preference to morphology and rote memorization: such tasks are also relatively simple for students. Indeed, close to 30 per cent of teachers report that it is precisely the *regularity* of Latin grammar that students find attractive. On the other hand, 53 per cent report that rote memorization is at the very top of students' complaints (60 per cent objections are at the complexity and 54 per cent at the quantity). One conclusion might be that attractive, and eventually successful Latin teaching highlights that grammar regularity is a benefit and learning aid, but that mastering it is not the sole goal.

Latin teaching has as yet not received the theoretical support it deserves. Among the very few studies on Latin pedagogy, a recent one (Dimitrijević 2019) adduces some survey data for discussing curricula, although the parameters of the study and the conclusion are unclear. The only available handbook of classical languages instruction (Šijački-Manević 1998, followed by an article in 2001) amounts to writing down the traditional practice; it essentially reminds prospective teachers to teach in the way they were going to teach anyway. Significantly, Šijački-Manević is strategically against conversational Latin, on the grounds that it is awkward, embarrassingly funny and doomed to fail. In complete opposition to this view, coining Latin neologisms is favourably presented in Nedeljković 2005 (written in Latin). Indeed, as we shall see, it is precisely oral articulation of Latin that seems to attract younger generations the most.

Cooperation and initiatives

For as long as anyone can remember, the central institution which directly and indirectly services this extensive network of classical languages instruction in Serbia has been the Classics Department (CD) at the University of Belgrade.

The CD faculty members constitute the core of the Serbian Association of Classical Studies (Asocijacija za klasične studije Srbije, AKSS), which among other activities organizes the national competition in classical languages for secondary school students. Around 150 to 200 high school students participate in the competition every year, organized for each programme and grade separately (RG1, RG2, BM, PhG1, PhG2, etc.). Tests for all categories (except BM) have always been designed as a reading comprehension exercise (written translations of passages, with or without a dictionary), in order to discourage reciting the forms as the sole criterion (for an analysis of results for the 2009/13 period, see Pendelj 2014).

AKSS, with CD as headquarters, organizes annual seminars for teachers and students. The teacher meetings typically consist of reports and workshops in sharing experiences and successful practices. Towards the end of the calendar year, the AKSS and CD host winners of the national competitions and their teachers; these events usually feature lectures in classical civilization and various types of workshop activities. During the Covid-19 lockdown period, these events have been placed on hold, and resuming them in full is a work still in progress. In the meantime, the CD faculty organizes smaller bi-monthly meetings with high school teachers, interested in sharing various types of specific classroom activities and instructional practices.

One further example of successful cooperation between the CD and secondary institutions in the past few years has been weekend workshops, playfully titled *Weekendium*. Several times a year, high school and university students take part in various hands-on activities moderated by their teachers and university professors, usually hosted by a volunteering high school. Activities range from indoor educational games (Greek and Latin crossword puzzles, escape rooms, etc.) to various on-site engagement with material remains (e.g., reading and copying inscriptions or clay tablets), where possible. One of the staples of the *Weekendium* is work with comic 'fragments': a comic dialogue is segmented into individual lines on separate slices of paper and the goal is to reassemble the dialogue. Depending on the participants' language level, the original text is sometimes annotated for vocabulary of phrasing, and depending on the available time, volunteers sometimes perform the reassembled text on the spot.

Lastly, in 2018, several CD faculty members and teachers from the two philological *gymnasia* initiated a joint project of revival of the tradition of Latin instruction in the Gymnasium of Sremski Karlovci, under the original, early eighteenth-century name of

Collegium Carolivicanum. The main activities within the *Collegium* project are regular weeklong summer schools. Financially supported by the Municipality and the Gymnasium of Sremski Karlovci, as well as various fundraising and partnerships with businesses, the *Collegium* manages to subsidize the tuition and board costs significantly. The programme regularly includes beginners and intermediate/advanced Latin and Greek, while other courses vary, from Biblical Hebrew, Classical Chinese, Old Slavonic, as well as various indoor or outdoor workshops, e.g., with inscriptions, and visits to archaeological sites. All instruction is in Latin, while the rest of the activities are moderated in Serbian. These include two afternoon sections, which lead to the performance for the closing ceremony. In the music section, those interested and sometimes experienced in vocal or instrumental performance prepare a Latin song selection, mostly medieval. In the drama section, students rehearse an abbreviated prose adaptation of a Roman comedy to perform in the original Latin, with stage solutions created on the spot. Evenings are usually reserved for guest lectures by departmental faculty and researchers from various institutions, with topics ranging from introductions to other historical languages (Sanskrit, Old Persian, Old English, Gothic, etc.) to presentations of the epigraphic heritage on the territory of Serbia.

After the 2018 and 2019 *Collegium Carolivicanum* Summer Schools in Sremski Karlovci, which had a more international profile (2020 and 2021 were skipped due to Covid-19 pandemic measures), the 2022 and 2023 events, hosted in the nearby Sremska Mitrovica, shifted a bit towards local audience, of 30–40 high school and university students from across the country. The town of Sremska Mitrovica is situated on the locality of the Roman imperial capital Sirmium, around the well-preserved imperial palace. Besides impressive archaeological remains, a *lapidarium* with ancient inscriptions in the regional museum provided an excellent opportunity for various activities. The *Collegium* summer schools proved very popular. For classical philology standards, the media coverage was outstanding, and various public institutions and business partners have begun to offer support.

Conclusion

As elsewhere, classical languages in Serbia are cherished by the few and there is really not much new to say about the problems the discipline faces. But Serbia might be atypical in that Latin is omnipresent in secondary education in every corner of the country: every other high school graduate has learnt it at some point. This has enabled establishing a broad, national network of enthusiasts among teachers and students interested in classical languages in whichever aspect. Our experience has been that the best way for Classics to win back the place it deserves is through coordinated individual initiatives in a bottom-up, grassroots movement. Some of the advice to colleagues worldwide might then be the following:

1. Where possible, use local archaeological or archival material as a brand to advertise national relevance. The students will be additionally motivated, local communities will take pride, and educational authorities and sponsors might respond favourably.

2. Alongside raising awareness of the continuing relevance of classical languages for the modern world, do not be embarrassed by the fact that they are at the same time ancient and exotic. A solid portion of students find a particular appeal in that and the broader public is at the very least intrigued. While popular culture has always loved exotic

languages, real or invented, we are now witnessing a growing influx of spoken classical languages on film and TV. Classicists would do well to ride the wave.

3. Rather than panicking over the very real information about small numbers of people in the discipline, try to make use of it. While, of course, advocating that classical languages benefit everyone, one should target those students who might precisely appreciate the implication that their interests and talents are in some way a special privilege. Many students thrive the most in smaller groups.

4. Organize events with concrete, hands-on activities for students and teachers across institutions. High school students will get to discover that there is an entire galaxy of intellectual tradition and effort behind a high school subject that they perhaps knew only through samples designed for uniform programmes. The close-knit, retreat-style gathering of young people with unusual interests, scattered all over the country as a minority in their classroom communities, helps solidify those interests: they realize they are not alone. Schoolteachers who participate receive the necessary boost of motivation to offset the effort of day-to-day teaching in not always optimal conditions. Finally, secondary school and university teachers are reminded that they are on the same mission.

The authors would like to thank their colleagues who helped with advice and firsthand information: Natalija Džakić, Svetlana Marković, Saša Trifunović, Jelena Vukojević, Vojin Nedeljković, Milica Janković, Jelena Savić, Jelena Rudović, Branko Stojkov and Violeta Vlajković Bojić.

References

Dimitrijević, D. (2019), 'Latin Curricula, Attitudes and Achievement: An Empirical Investigation', in V. Dimovska-Janjatova and D. Toševa (eds), *Monumentum aere perennius*, Skopje: Združenie na klasični filolozi Antika, 27–42.

Gemaljević, O. (2007), *Latinski jezik za prvi razred medicinske, veterinarske i poljoprivredne škole*, Beograd: Zavod za udžbenike i nastavna sredstva.

JACT (1978), *Reading Greek*, Joint Association of Classical Teachers' Greek Course, Cambridge: Cambridge University Press.

Martinić-Jerčić, Z. and D. Matković (2013), *Prometej: udžbenik grčkog jezika za 1. i 2. godinu učenja*, Zagreb: Školska knjiga.

Nedeljković, V. (2005), 'De vocabulis novis et mixobarbaris', *Lucida intervalla*, 32: 71–8.

Nedeljković, V., M. Bakić and J. Savić (2020), *Ain tū?: početni udžbenik latinskog jezika za gimnazije*, Beograd: Eduka.

Ørberg, H. (2011), *Lingua Latina per se illustrata*, Indianapolis, IN: Hackett Publishing.

Pakiž, M. and D. Dimitrijević (2003/19), *Latinski jezik I: za I razred gimnazije*, Beograd: Zavod za udžbenike.

Pakiž, M., T. Kiselički Vaš and M. Kisić (2006), *Latinski jezik 2: za II razred gimnazije*, Beograd: Zavod za udžbenike.

Pendelj, B. (2014), 'Srednjoškolsko takmičenje u znanju latinskog, 2009–2013: podaci i pouke', *Lucida intervalla*, 43: 217–25.

Popović, R. (1961), *Latinski jezik za prvi razred zdravstvene, veterinarske i poljoprivredne škole*, Beograd: Zavod za udžbenike i nastavna sredstva i dr.

Stanojević, O. and M. Jovanović (1987), *Latinski za pravnike*, Beograd: Zavod za udžbenike i nastavna sredstva.

Šijački-Manević, B. (1998), *Metodika nastave latinskog jezika*, Beograd: Zavod za udžbenike i nastavna sredstva.

Šijački-Manević, B. (2001), 'Latinski jezik u savremenoj nastavi', *Zbornik Matice srpske za klasične studije*, 3: 87–92.

Taylor, J. and K. Waite (2012), *Greek Stories: A GCSE Reader*, London: Bristol Classical Press.

Vagić, J. and V. Marković (2007), *Latinski jezik za medicinsku školu, prva godina učenja*, Beograd: BIGZ.

Vagić, J. and V. Marković (2014), *Latinski jezik za medicinsku školu, prva godina učenja*, Beograd: Data Status.

Vulićević, Lj. and M. Maskareli (1978), *Latinski jezik za I razred srednjeg usmerenog obrazovanja*, Beograd: Zavod za udžbenike i nastavna sredstva.

Vulićević, Lj. and M. Maskareli (1979), *Latinski jezik za II razred srednjeg usmerenog obrazovanja*, Beograd: Zavod za udžbenike i nastavna sredstva.

SLOVENIA

Miran Sajovic

Introduction

Latin and Greek language teaching, in the form we have today in Slovenia, is the 'successor' of a long-standing process that began in 1849 when the Austrian educational reform became the model and the basis for all schools within the Empire until present-day (Hriberšek 2005: 46–62). After the Second World War, however, grammar schools with Greek and Latin education immediately suffered severe criticism; thus, only two remained in Slovenia: in Ljubljana and in Maribor. The classical curriculum increasingly faced accusations of elitism, impracticality, and tightening social differentiation. Situations started to change with the new (communist) authorities – they took no interest and had no plan or goal in this area. The first signs of a slow turnaround appeared in the mid-1980s: the Gymnasium Poljane (in Ljubljana) introduced Latin into the regular curriculum, and in 1988 a classical humanities course was incorporated into it. After Slovenia declared independence in 1991, schools at different levels showed more interest in teaching classical languages. Today, in primary and secondary schools the students can make a choice about classical languages; Latin remains in medical schools as a subject for medical terminology acquisition (Hriberšek et al. 2019: 140–3).

The present school system in Slovenia is divided into three levels. The first level, also known as 'compulsory basic education', consists of primary and lower secondary education that lasts for nine years in a single-structured public or private school. The second level, or 'upper secondary education', lasts for two to five years, depending on the programmes, which are the *gimnazija* (*gymnasium* of different streams) and *matura* (examination programme for university admission), or vocational and professional. The third level is tertiary education in either public or private institutions, which is in accordance with the Bologna Process.

In compulsory basic education, pupils can learn a foreign language as their second language; in the final three years, they may even opt for a third language as an optional subject. The primary-lower-secondary schools offer English, German, French, Croatian, Italian, Hungarian, Chinese, Latin, Macedonian, Russian, Serbian and Spanish. Latin is taught as a compulsory subject only at two primary-lower-secondary schools in Ljubljana: Alojzij Šuštar Primary

School – St. Stanislav Institute, and Prežihov Voranc Primary School. Several other schools offer Latin as an optional activity.

In upper secondary education, Latin is taught at some schools that follow a general *gymnasium* programme and a classical *gymnasium* programme. On the other hand, Greek is almost absent in Slovenian upper higher education. It can be found only at the Diocesan Classical Gymnasium – St Stanislav's Institution, where Greek is taught in one class each year (around thirty students) of the five or six classes. Several upper secondary schools offer Greek as an optional subject, but the number of students varies greatly.

Latin and Greek are also present in tertiary education. There is a Department of Classical Philology at the Faculty of Arts in the University of Ljubljana. Latin is also taught separately in some other departments, such as History, Romance Languages, and Archaeology. Latin and Biblical Greek are acquired at the Faculty of Theology of the University of Ljubljana. One may find Latin courses in the University of Maribor and the University of Primorska (in Koper), although on a smaller scale.

While official statistics are not available, from interviewing teachers from all three levels, it is said that the number of students enrolling in Latin has been stable in most schools over the last decade and has mostly stayed the same. At the moment, the enrolment of students in Slovenia is slightly higher than in the past, but in the future it will be less.

Status of classical subjects

The subjects of classical studies available in Slovenian school programmes are mainly in the Latin language. These subjects are compulsory only in classical *gymnasia* and in some general gymnasia where the school makes it mandatory. For instance, in the Poljane Gimnazija, there are two streams of *gymnasium*: 'general studies' and 'classical studies'. The 'general studies' stream does not provide Latin or Greek lessons, while in 'classical studies', the students learn Latin as a second foreign language for all four years. The 'classical studies' stream is carried out at five public upper secondary schools in Slovenia: Gimnazija in Škofja Loka, Prva gimnazija in Celju, Gimnazija Poljane in Ljubljana, Prva gimnazija in Maribor, Gimnazija in Novo mesto; in private schools, only the Catholic Diocesan Classical Gymnasium – St Stanislav's Institution offers classical studies.

Classics education in our society is highly generational dependent: while the older people see it with many benefits, the younger emphasize the uselessness of these subjects. The loud opposition against classical language learning in our school system claims that such education is deemed to be of little worth, there are nonetheless arguments defending their presence:

(a) The influence of Latin language is omnipresent in many modern European languages like Italian, French, Spanish, German and English; it is still heavily used in present-day terminology of particular disciplines such as Medicine, Veterinary Science, Pharmacy, Chemistry, Physics, Theology, etc.

(b) Learning Latin, in particular, helps intelligence development and creates good learning habits amongst adolescents.

(c) The study of classical subjects allows an all-round understanding of the roots of European history (through the study of Graeco-Roman civilization).

(d) Latin offers linguistic confidence to the students by instructing them to know general language phenomena.

(e) By knowing the temporal and spatial interconnectedness within Latin language, students are prepared to comprehend the variety of the European cultural landscape and become more objective and tolerant; collaterally the classical studies thus develop students' ability to understand each other.

(f) Latin studies improve students' cognitive skills.

(h) The students obtain good habits - they are more systematic.

Trends in the teaching of classical subjects

The teachers of classical languages in Slovenia tend to keep up with the times and discoveries in didactics of (classical) languages. This is especially evident in textbook selection and classroom interaction. The Latin textbooks that once prevailed mainly contained unrelated sentences in each grammatical chapter with translation exercises from Latin into Slovenian and vice versa; nowadays, the textbooks contain different exercises that focus not only on translation but also on grammar and cultural circumstances. Individual chapters in textbooks often also contain shorter compositions in Latin relating to a particular story. Today in Slovenia, modern classical language teaching is, in principle and in practice, based on a contextual approach (Škerjanc 2000: 6). The approved programme for classical languages by the Ministry of Education assumes that 70 per cent of linguistic content and 30 per cent of cultural and civilization content should be studied.

Teachers mainly use two textbooks in compulsory basic education: *Lingua Latina*, by Aleksandra Pirkmajer Slokan (2022) and a textbook adapted for Slovenian pupils by author Barbara Bell, *Minimus: First Steps in Latin* (Bell 2000). In the following discussion, attention will be given to the textbook of Aleksandra Pirkmajer Slokan. *Lingua Latina* consists of three books. It is adapted to the specific circumstances of primary-lower-secondary school teaching. There is also an *index verborum* containing a glossary of all the words, grammar sheets, an alphabetical list of the authors of the sentences and a list of grammatical expressions and abbreviations. Each chapter is divided into two broad parts: the content and the exercises. The content part always consists first of an introductory text in Latin, which also defines each lesson thematically, and a set of original ancient sentences. This is followed by the *Ars grammatica* section, which, both in the form of explanatory notes and tables, illustrates the grammatical content. The second part of each lesson consists of a separate chapter dedicated to exercises. These are very varied and allow students to consolidate newly acquired material. Of particular interest are the exercises that bring Latin closer to pupils as a living, spoken language and highlight its presence today: in the epigraph corner, pupils can read and analyse surviving ancient inscriptions; in the context of Latin for everyday use, they can learn about etymology and various phrases that are still useful today, the science corner introduces them to specialist terms in chemistry, medicine and botany, thus introducing them to new (modern) Latin words and expanding their general knowledge (Žmavc 2008: 168–73).

In upper-secondary school (*gymnasium*), teachers mainly use textbooks by Slovenian author Robert Čepon: *Usus* 1, 2, 3 (2007) and *Iter* 1 (2022) (this is the new version of *Usus* 1). Čepon, has prepared these textbooks based on his teaching materials at the First Secondary School Maribor (Prva Gimnazija Maribor). With this title, in three years, students can achieve the necessary linguistic competence to read easier passages from original Latin texts. Each unit begins with sentences and quotations from Latin authors, which the teacher uses to introduce the new information. The main text of each unit is, in most cases, short enough to be translated into one lesson with the teacher's guidance. The exercises require filling in the tables, completing sentences and texts, converting and transforming one construction into another, identifying and analysing grammatical constructions and forms, and translating from Latin into Slovene and vice versa. At the end of each unit, a Latin–Slovene dictionary is provided. The unit concludes with a text on *Tolle et lege*, which aims at further consolidating new content through translation from Latin into Slovene. A glossary is unnecessary for the exercises, as words that are not part of the core vocabulary are already translated alongside the text or collected in the glossary at the end of each *Tolle et lege* chapter.

In the Department of Classical Philology at the University of Ljubljana, professors use the Latin-adapted textbook *Latin from Words to Reading* (Keller & Russell 2008), translated by Movrin. *Texts and Exercises for Greek Lessons* (Mihevc-Gabrovec 1978*)* is commonly used for the Greek language. The latter has proven to be very effective. It results from many years of experience teaching the Greek language at the Department of Classical Philology. Its feature is that the author uses original Greek sentences from the first lesson. For ease of understanding, only a few citations are given in the Attic dialect, rather than in their original. The first quote is usually more complex, which the teacher is supposed to explain. All grammatical material, however, is so divided that it can be mastered in two academic years on two hours a week. The text corresponds to the respective level of knowledge; the textbook is intended for young adults, that is, more mature students in tertiary education. In the Faculty of Theology, *Salve, urbs aeterna* by Čop (2012) is used with an auxiliary textbook by Benedik 2013, *In piam memoriam*. It should also be emphasized that some teachers prepare not only textbooks but also their own teaching material, which they usually use only in their classes as internal (auxiliary) material.

In the pedagogical process in recent years, it has been evident that professors tend to adopt more original texts as soon as possible, even if they are adapted according to the level of students. Several modern teaching aids are also used, such as photographs, films, and online material. Distance learning, especially during the Covid-19 pandemic, has proven less effective. This is probably because almost no one was prepared for this form of teaching. But it becomes one of the possibilities for the future to meet students and colleagues worldwide regardless of geographical distance. This is why professors attend seminars online, mainly organized by the Department of Classical Philology of the Faculty of Arts, as scholars there are also trained in digital humanities.

Teachers and professional development

The National Education Institute in Slovenia annually organizes a study group for Latin teachers. Currently, Professor Barbara Damjan is the Latin advisor at the Institute and is in charge of regular contact with teachers outside of the meetings. The teachers collaborate in preparing and implementing the school and national Latin competitions and share additional teaching materials (especially for the Culture and Civilization section of teaching and the preparation of materials for the final exam).

A seminar on the didactics of the Latin language is also organized by the Faculty of Arts in Ljubljana – Department of Classical Philology, every year. This seminar is more theoretical and aims to update teachers' professional skills, especially in classical language teaching. Teachers can also apply for training abroad, given that the schools participate in the Erasmus+ programme.

Collaborative activities

Teachers, if there are several of them, are grouped in their home schools to share their experiences in teaching Latin in particular; they also plan interclass joint programmes, such as visits to museums and excursions. There are collaborations with other organizations, such as museums and universities, occasionally and more ad hoc, with excursions, competitions or special courses.

Perhaps the most tangible is the connection of the Department of Classical Philology of the Faculty of Arts in Ljubljana with other international programmes promoted by Erasmus and Erasmus+. The Department of Classical Philology currently has student and professor exchange agreements with the University of Vienna, Masaryk University in Brno, Charles University in Prague, Aristotle University in Thessaloniki, University of Athens, University of Zagreb, University of Foggia and University of Milan. In July 2023, the Department of Classical Philology participated in the Modern Greek for Classicists project in Athens.

Conclusion

To conclude, here are some thoughts that can help classical language teaching and the passing on of ancient culture to descendants. Firstly, it is irrational to expect a favourable circumstance. In the past, Slovenian teachers, especially during the post-war period, had to face many obstacles and constraints. Still, it is only because of their perseverance, hard work and ingenuity in 'impossible' circumstances that the presence of classical languages in our territory has been guaranteed. This is a vital message for today's world when we are often confronted with a reluctant environment regarding learning classical languages and the main argument for their uselessness.

Another important message is that it is necessary to keep up to date in teaching methodology and not to be afraid of new experiments. Some Slovenian professors have composed new and high-quality textbooks, especially for Latin, and have created a number of private materials which are exchanged and enriched.

The third thought is that it is necessary to connect with each other in creating a network of exchanging ideas and sharing experiences; equally significant is that one should overcome academic jealousy – with the more people you are connected with the more you know.

There is also a good impact on the teachers of Classics when recognized and qualified academic centres, such as the National Education Institute in Slovenia and the Department of Classical Philology, constantly evaluate their teaching performance. These institutions contribute to quality teaching, updating the teaching methodology and personal professional development.

References

Bell, B. (2000), *Minimus: First Steps in Latin,* Cambridge: Cambridge University Press.

Benedik, M. (2013), *In piam memoriam*, Ljubljana: Faculty of Arts.

Čepon, R. (2007), *Usus*, Ljubljana: Modrijan.
Čepon, R. (2022), *Iter*, Ljubljana: Modrijan.
Čop, B. (2012), *Salve, urbs aeterna*, Ljubljana: Faculty of Arts.
Mihevc-Gabrovec, E. (1978), *Texts and Exercises for Greek Lessons*, Ljubljana: Faculty of Arts.
Hriberšek, M. (2005) *klasični jeziki v slovenskom šolstvu: 1848–1945*, Ljubljana: Založba ZRC, ZPC SAZU.
Hriberšek, H., A. Inkret and J. Kavčič (2019), 'Latin and Greek: yesterday, today, tomorrow', in T. Balažic Bulc, J. Kenda, M. Lah and V. Požgaj Hadži (eds), *Paths and Detours of Teaching Foreign Languages in Slovenia*, Ljubljana: Scientific Publishing House of the Faculty of Arts, University of Ljubljana, 139–54.
Keller, A. and S. Russell, trans D. Morvin (2008), *Latin from Words to Reading*, Ljubljana: Scientific publishing House of the Faculty of Arts.
Pirkmajer Slokan, A. (2022), *Lingua Latina* (1st edn 2007), Ljubljana: DZS.
Škerjanc, K. (2000), 'Classical Education in Slovenia', *Keria: Studia Latina et Graeca*, 2 (1), 101–8.
Žmavc, J. (2008), [Review] 'Aleksandra Pirkmajer Slokan: *Lingua Latina*: a textbook for Latin in grades 7–9, class of nine-year primary school education. 3 volumes', *Keria Studia Latina et Graeca*, 10 (1): 168–73.

SPAIN

José Luis Navarro

Introduction

Small changes have occurred in the field of Classics over the last twenty years in Spain. Although three different educational bills were introduced in this time, they were quite ephemeral and did not affect many subjects. In February 2020 a new bill (LOMLOE 2020) was very quickly approved by the new government. At this particular moment it is being developed, but we are able to discern in some detail if the position of Classics in the new curriculum will be improved or seriously damaged or will remain the same. When a new government was appointed in Autumn 2019, after a year of permanent political instability, one of its first decisions was to submit a newly updated educational bill inspired by many of the pedagogical principles that had previously inspired the *Ley de Ordenación General del Sistema Educativo* in the 1980s (LOGSE 1990). All classicists thought that a real catastrophe was about to fall on our subjects, but we were ready to fight, and once again all together we were able to make the Government modify its previous schemes concerning Classics. Consequently, we must confess that, even if we did not get everything we asked for, we are still alive. Of course, the world has changed after the pandemic, concerning mostly the use of new technologies in the classroom and beyond; this means that new subjects have been introduced to the national programme, causing some damage to Classics which was obliged to fight once again against several optional updated technological subjects. Finally, the feared apocalypse never came and, as indicated in previous lines, we are still alive!

Curriculum

Not many changes have occurred in the field of Classics since 2006 (LOE 2006). Some concern both languages, but while in the case of Latin there has been an improvement, in the case of Greek it has caused serious problems.

Latin has not been a compulsory subject at the ESO (Secondary Compulsory Education 12–16) since 1999 when it was abolished, but it has been reintroduced at the age of sixteen as a compulsory subject for students following a non-scientific branch of studies. In fact, the last year of the secondary education allows the students to follow one of three different itineraries: Scientific, Artistic or Humanistic. In this branch Latin is compulsory for three hours a week, covering vocabulary, a general survey of grammar together with lots of etymology, and an outline of Roman History; an introduction to public and private life in Rome completes the syllabus. The main aim is to offer a positive aspect of both Latin language and Roman civilization focusing in their influence on the Spanish language. In fact, more than 15 per cent of pupils have followed this branch successfully for the last ten years.

Latin is still necessary for those who decide to study to the Baccalaureate, following the so-called Humanistic branch for two years (students aged 17–18 years). Students at this stage take four hours a week. Approximately 12 per cent of the students decide to follow this branch, and so they have to take Latin for two years.

Greek by contrast has lost its role inside the Humanistic branch. Until 2006 students following the Humanistic itinerary of study took Greek for two years, hand in hand with Latin. Since 2006 Greek has only been compulsory in the first year. In the last course of the Baccalaureate, Greek is included in a list of at least four subjects, such as Geography, Sociology, History of Art, French, Psychology and others. A high number of pupils prefer easier subjects, dropping Greek instead. Not even 8 per cent of students manage to take it as a subject for the National Examination (LOMLOE 2020).

Cultura Clásica (Classical Civilization) must be offered as an optional subject at any private or public school to all students aged fifteen and sixteen years (the two last years of compulsory secondary education). That means the subject has been growing more and more. However, no more than two hours per week are available. Whether a class can be formed with sufficient members depends quite often on the decision of the direction of the school. Oratory, Debate and Theatre was recently introduced at secondary education as an optional subject, to be taught preferably by Classicists and/or philologists.

The Latin and Greek courses consist mostly of language skills: grammar and quite a lot of vocabulary, together with translation of texts. It is regarded as important that those texts should always be fitted into the frame and context of Latin and Greek civilization and should never be independent of them. *Cultura Clásica*, however, does not deal with grammar at all. A short approach to vocabulary is included into the syllabus of the second year. For Latin and Greek language the official syllabus suggests:

- Latin: Texts from the Republican and Imperial periods focusing on first century BCE and first century CE.
- Greek: Classical prose authors of the fifth and fourth century BCE are the main part of the syllabus, although Pausanias, Plutarch and Apollodorus are especially welcome.

Medieval Latin, Modern Greek (Byzantine or *koine*) and even Vulgar Latin are mostly excluded. A classical pronunciation (*pronuntiatio restituta*) is followed for Latin (not ecclesiastical Latin nor a Spanish pronunciation). For Greek, the so-called Erasmian pronunciation is used.

Methods and text books

Concerning textbooks, there have been no essential changes, in the sense that no real new course books have been produced in the last twenty years but simply some revisions of the old ones. A certain number of teachers have decided to get rid of them, preferring instead to use new materials suitable for computers and screens. There is something to be underlined mostly in the field of Latin: there is still considerable interest in the teachings of Hans Ørberg. Although he died in 2010, his book *Lingua Latina per se illustrata* is still alive. The full book, including culture and civilization approaches, was translated into Spanish for the first time in 2008 (Ørberg et al. 2008). In my previous report (Bulwer 2006) I mentioned *Reading Greek* and *Reading Latin* as very up-to-date course books in the field of non-paradigmatic traditional texts (Jones and Sidwell 1978, 1986). That was in the 1990s. But Ørberg, following in fact the same methodological patterns, has become successful in Spain at least for the last fifteen years. That kind of boom was accompanied by a renewed interest in living Latin, and nowadays also by spoken Greek. I have made detailed criticisms of most of those publications elsewhere. I should simply point out that many teachers, starting with Ørberg or any other spoken methods, change to more traditional methods in the last course at High School before facing the National Examination leading to university. As the students near the National Examination, its demands are such that many teachers feel the need to adopt more traditional teaching approaches.

Most textbooks start off using adapted or invented texts, but they normally move quite quickly into original texts. However, it is not always accepted that the goal of learning Latin and Greek Language is to read texts in their original and authentic state. All teachers move at their own pace, but in the end grammar, vocabulary and syntax are always present in the National Examination, together with classical civilization. It is the way of presenting grammar, vocabulary and syntax that has changed. Of course, nobody would propose that grammar has to be chanted nowadays as it was in the 1960s.

Teachers

The situation for teachers is different depending on which type of school they work in. State schools offered excellent prospects in the past. Greek and Latin departments were separated, and it was compulsory to provide a post in each state school. That privileged situation lasted until 2010. Then teachers from any subject were forced to take twenty hours a week instead of fifteen, and as a result Hellenists had to deal with Latin and Latinists with Greek. One single department was created at each school (called Classics, as expected) and there were lots of problems to make options for Classics efficient. As for the teacher's salary, €2,100 (£1,820 / $2,220) per month (not including a seniority supplement) remains nearly unchanged for the last twenty years. In private schools, however, the situation is harder. In fact, Greek has been abolished in more than 90 per cent of the schools. Classicists must share their work with members of the Spanish Language and Literature department in each school. This teacher will work twenty-five hours a week for a salary of about €1,900 (£1,650 / $2,000) per month.

As for teaching Classical Civilization, a large amount of teaching material using the new technologies is available, and most teachers use it very successfully. On the other hand, for the teaching of Greek and Latin Language, a number of teachers still insist on chalk and blackboard. To underline that, after the Covid-19 pandemic, every tool connected with computers, mobile phones, video games and fascinating modern screens was enthusiastically, though not always successfully, introduced. Replacing the teacher of Latin and Greek by all these technological devices has not been easy; the teacher is still there. However, at the recent examination for entering university, 74 per cent of the students were successful in Greek and 75 per cent were successful in Latin. These results are very similar to the results for the last twenty years.

Activities

Activities both for pupils and teachers have been continuously increasing since 2004: students undertake visits to museums and ancient Roman towns all over Spain. The museums provide a lot of extremely helpful teaching material which is able to be understood and used by any student either at primary or secondary school. Festivals of Ancient Drama are organized all over the ancient Roman theatres of Spain. More than 100,000 students attend the performances every year all through the academic year but mostly from early March to May. In order to learn more about the full event, see *Teatro Total* (Navarro 2005). For teachers the Spanish Association of Classical Teachers (SEEC) organizes instructional tours every year to different locations of the ancient world either at home or abroad (www.estudiosclasicos.org). From 2005 to 2015 some excavations in progress invited small groups of students each summer. They joined the archaeological team for a couple of weeks around the ancient Roman city of Complutum, near Madrid.

But no doubt the most important remarkable event in the field of educational activities for teachers and students is the so called *Domus Baebia Saguntina* (see https://domusbaebia.com). Named after a local Roman family from Saguntum whose members are well documented, it is a local institution run by the enthusiastic group of teachers *Ludere et Discere*. The *Domus* has had its own building since 2008. It is fully equipped with all kinds of resources for learning in a very active, positive and sensitive way about everything concerning the private and public life in the ancient Roman world. Two full-time staff are responsible for the perfect functioning of the project. A few metres beyond this institution is the Museum of the Greek and Roman Stage, established in 2011, which provides a supplement to the full activity at the *Domus* and offers lots of workshops and activities related mostly to Greek Drama. Both institutions have joined their efforts for the last twelve years offering opportunities through Euroclassica to students from any country in Europe, to attend the Academia Saguntina European School in Classical Civilization.

Finally, many students take part in the European project ECCL (European Curriculum for Classical Languages), with tests for Greek (EGEX) and Latin (ELEX), run by Euroclassica at beginners and intermediate level since 2015 until the present. Successful pupils who take the test are rewarded with a certificate and Spain has had the highest number of entries for EGEX for the last three years.

Society and politics

It has been a long time since Franco died in 1975. Franco´s regime always supported Classics: priests and nuns were called to disseminate Greek and Latin texts all over the country hand in hand with the powerful church who influenced the whole educational system for at least thirty years. Once Franco died, the socialists took over for at least fifteen consecutive years from 1982 to 1996. During those years a new educational bill was approved, deleting any vestige of Franco (LOGSE 1990). That caused many problems for our subjects. The Socialist government organized education in a completely different way, trusting faithfully in theoretical pedagogic approaches. As an immediate result Latin (which had been compulsory for three hours a week at the age of fifteen) was removed and Greek was simply mentioned as an optional subject in a long list of other subjects. When the right-wing Popular Party gained control from 2004 to 2008, a big battle took place in order to reintroduce Philosophy, History and Classics. Since 2004 small, detailed changes have occurred and the present situation seems to be becoming worse (LOE 2006). The Ministry of Education allows all regional governments to decide on the allocation of any subject into any regional board. That means that in practice any inspector or any director at any school will decide which subject will be taught any year, depending on the circumstances. Latin and Greek are always ranked on the list, but there will be a footnote advising that a certain number of students is required, or a certain room must be available, or a qualified teacher cannot be available at the moment. The subjects exist, but the real chance of taking them does not exist at all.

Many people today regard Classics as an old-fashioned, useless subject; but there are always, mostly on the most important newspapers, some authoritative voices to be continuously heard, supporting both languages. I am thinking of the big success of Andrea Marcolongo's *The Ingenious Language: Nine Epic Reasons to Love Greek* (2017/19). That small colloquial, sincere book was sold out in a few days, to an audience made up of people not knowing Greek at all. Something similar happened with the very thick book by a young Spanish Classicist, Irene Vallejo, *El infinito en un junco* (2019). It deals with the transmission of ancient classical texts from early times up to the twenty-first century. It has been translated into several languages and reprinted every year.

On the other hand, from SEEC we are in touch with all kinds of associations willing to support humanistic studies. SEEC has existed since 1952 and we are enthusiastically engaged both in FIEC (*Fédération internationale des associations d'études classiques* / International Federation of Associations of Classical Studies) and Euroclassica. At present the president of FIEC is Professor Jesus de la Villa, who has also been President of SEEC. Euroclassica also had a Spanish president José L. Navarro, a member of SEEC, for the period 2011–15.

University

At the beginning of the twenty-first century, more than thirty universities offered specific degrees in Classics. Many of them had a small department with a small budget and a small number of students. For the last twenty years quite a lot of those small departments have been forced to rearrange their curricula in order to survive. Most of them had to join Ancient History and Archaeology in order to rebuild their curricula, offering instead a new degree called Sciences and Languages of Antiquity. This path has been followed by several universities, although Madrid, Barcelona, Salamanca, Santiago, Granada – those who were the pioneers in the teaching of Classics – managed to keep their degree courses as usual. At Madrid Central University, for example, about twenty students get a degree in Classics each year. Even so, there are colloquia, conferences, congresses and seminars throughout the year all over Spain, although there may be more speakers than listeners. Reviews are published in increasing numbers and publications and research on many different topics grow continuously, not to mention in service training courses to introduce innovatory methods. All the major works of Greek and Latin literature have been translated into Spanish and since 2010 Greek has been reintroduced as a subject of the National Examination. Nowadays the requirements for those who enter a Classics degree course consists of a translation from Eutropius, Caesar, Nepos or possibly Livius or Sallustius (Latin) and another from Aesopus, Apollodorus, Lysias or Xenophon (Greek).

Universities which have kept their curricula as usual have maintained high standards of achievement; other universities who had to rearrange their courses made considerable changes to the authors set for study and so instead offered to the students high-level programmes in the field of research. Spoken Latin and Greek methods have been introduced for students at the first or second course of their degree.

The future

To conclude: after an encouraging revival for the last twenty years with the reintroduction of Latin and the important development of Classical Civilization (*Cultura Clásica*), a very black cloud has settled over Greek. As it is now inside the syllabus as a completely optional subject requiring a certain number of students, Greek may well disappear from the Baccalaureate in a few years.

Unfortunately, Classical Civilization will have to share its timetable with some other 'updated subjects', eventually moving from two hours to one hour per week. Nowadays it is demanded by a quite remarkable number of students. At the moment we still manage to keep it at two hours per week; otherwise, it would become meaningless.

Latin miraculously has not been banished from secondary education, as the curriculum scheme has been kept in the recent new bill (LOMLOE 2020). It should keep a quite solid position only in the Humanistic branch inside the high school as an important subject for the National Examination.

Spanish Classicists have managed to get through the hostile atmosphere at the end of the 1990s, but even so the struggle continues if we want to keep Classics alive in our schools and universities

References

Bulwer, J. (2006), *Classics Teaching in Europe*, London: Duckworth.

Jones, P. and K. Sidwell (1978), *Reading Greek*, Cambridge: Cambridge University Press.

Jones, P. and K. Sidwell (1986), *Reading Latin*, Cambridge: Cambridge University Press.

Marcolongo, A. (2017), *The Ingenious Language: Nine Epic Reasons to Love Greek*, trans W. Schutt 2019, London: Europa Editions.

Navarro, J. (2005), *Teatro Total*, Madrid: Ediciones Clásicas.

Ørberg, H., E. Canales and A. Gonzalez Amador (2008), *Lingua Latina per se illustrata*, Guadix: Cultura Clásica.

Vallejo, I. (2019), *El infinito en un junco: La invención de los libros en el mundo antiguo*, Madrid: Ediciones Siruela.

Educational Bills (BOE: *Boletín Oficial del Estado*, the official review edited by the Government to publish laws and decrees and other official documents.)

LOE 2006, *Ley Orgánica de Educación*, BOE 3 May 2006.

LOGSE 1990, *Ley de Ordenación General del Sistema Educativo*, BOE 30 October 1990.
LOMCE 2013, *Ley Orgánica para la mejora de la calidad educativa*, 9 December 2013.
LOMLOE 2020, *Ley Orgánica de Modificación de la LOE*, 29 December 2020.

SWEDEN

Axel Hörstedt

Introduction

Classics, that is, Latin, Greek and Classical Archaeology and Ancient History, are marginalized subjects in Sweden with few students at all levels of education. What until 1970 was the core of one of two possible study programmes at the upper secondary school today must fight for its survival. Classics are only studied at high school (*gymnasiet*) and at universities in Sweden, as well as at some adult study associations.

Secondary education

At the beginning of the 1990s, the responsibility for primary school and upper secondary school implementation was shifted from the state to the municipalities. During the same time, the system was introduced, unique to Sweden, of independent schools (the so-called *friskolor*) financed by the municipalities. However, the school curricula are regulated by the Swedish National Agency for Education's guidelines, which must be followed by all, regardless of whether they are municipal or independent. Grades A-F are given in primary (from the age of twelve) and secondary schools. In the upper secondary school (for students aged 16–19), most courses are one-year and comprise one hundred credits, i.e., one hundred hours distributed over the academic year. In 2011 the latest major reform of primary and secondary education was launched. With this reform the Humanities programme was introduced and is undoubtedly the smallest of the six theoretical study programmes that give access to tertiary education. The Swedish National Agency for Education (skolverket.se) and Swedish Statistics (scb.se) provide statistics concerning upper secondary schools and from these websites are the following figures. During the academic year 2022/23, a total of 221,490 students took a theoretical study programme in upper secondary school in Sweden. Of these, 1,879 students attend the humanities programme, which is less than 1 per cent of the total number. Furthermore, since the above-mentioned reform in 2011, the number of students in humanities has steadily decreased year by year, due to many municipalities not starting the programme or closing it down due to few students applying for the programme. Of Sweden's more than 1,300 upper secondary schools, approximately forty schools offer a humanities programme. Over 90 per cent of those who study humanities programmes attend municipal schools. Schools with a humanistic programme are found above all in the metropolitan regions and in the more densely populated southern parts of Sweden. As already said, Latin is studied in Sweden only in upper secondary school, not in elementary school. With the reform of 2011, the secondary school's humanities study programme was created with two orientations: culture and languages. Of these, the culture orientation is now the most popular: approximately 55 per cent of students choose this orientation without Latin, while 45 per cent study the language orientation with compulsory Latin (for comparison, it should be said that when the programme started in 2011, the language orientation was the most popular). Before 2011, the humanities course of study was part of the social science programme before it was separated as an autonomous programme. Latin is therefore only read as a compulsory subject in the language orientation of this study programme. Common to both orientations, however, is the course Human Languages (*Människans språk*), which is a compulsory introductory course in linguistics.

In this context, it is important to mention the course *Latin – språk och kultur* [Latin – language and culture]. It comes in three courses, 1–3, but most schools offer either just the first or the first two. Looking at the number of students, 432 studied Latin in 2021, which can be compared with 1,541 high school students who studied the subject in 2011 and 2,134 students in 2005. Greek is an even more marginalized school subject that has been taught in two high schools in Sweden for the last ten years, with a total of about twenty students.

Tertiary education

Latin, Greek and Classical Archaeology and Ancient History (in Swedish *Antikens kultur och samhällsliv*) are found at four universities in Sweden: Lund, Gothenburg, Stockholm, and Uppsala. The subjects belong to different departments depending partly on how the respective universities are organized, partly on tradition. For example, in Uppsala Latin and Greek are included in the Department of Linguistics and Philology (including ancient languages and all non-European languages), while they are included in the Department of Languages and Literatures in Gothenburg (which includes all languages except English and Swedish) and in Stockholm in the Department of Romance Studies and Classics and in Lund in the Centre for Languages and Literature. Since 1909, Classical Archaeology and Ancient History has constituted its own academic discipline at Swedish universities, separated from the languages (Siapkas 2017: 16–17 and 163). This subject often shares department with archaeology or history. In terms of the number of students, the universities that offer distance learning at beginner level have a larger influx to their courses. According to figures presented at the Swedish Philology Congress in Stockholm 2022, in 2021 there were a total of roughly 530 students in Latin and roughly 300 students in Greek at Swedish universities, from beginner level to bachelor's level. Orientation courses are also included in these figures. Graduate students and master students, on the other hand, are only a handful in the whole country, as are the number of doctoral students, all universities included.

The Covid pandemic led to an increase in the number of students enrolling in universities in general in 2020 (Berlin Kolm 2021), and the feeling is that Classics also got a share of this increase.

Some state-funded adult study associations also provide courses in Latin and Greek in several parts of the country, but it is difficult to obtain figures on how many studies there are and what level the teaching is. These courses are often held in the evening once a week.

Interest in the Classics

Nowadays, Latin studies, and Classics for that matter, are regarded as a curiosity that in many cases renders surprise and raised eyebrows among the uninitiated. What is the use of studying a supposedly useless and old dead language? What do you get out of it? Latin is only compulsory for students in the language orientation of the Humanities high school programme. Most secondary schools with this programme offer the courses Latin 1 and to some extent also Latin 2 – each course extends over one academic year. At some schools, Latin may also be offered as an optional course for students other than Humanities students. Grades in Latin and Greek are also not required for admission to any tertiary study programme. In upper secondary school, as in society at large, the interest in humanistic subjects is declining, which also applies to Latin. Education in Sweden has moved more and more in the utility-oriented direction, where knowledge in the Classics is not in demand or per se has a given place and is out-competed by the natural and social sciences.

The arguments for studying Latin have also come to include aspects other than purely linguistic. Above all, the usefulness of Latin for the study of other modern European languages, especially as a lender of words, and for language understanding through grammar, is emphasized today. Other arguments for Classics are that these subjects contribute to an understanding of history, culture, and lead to general education. Over the years, the Swedish Classics Association has contributed with brochures and pamphlets to increase the influx of and awareness of high school Humanities courses, preferably Latin and Greek. But it is not just Classics that suffer from disappointing student numbers, other Humanities subjects as well, especially modern languages have a small number of university students in general in Sweden. The independent think-tank HumTank has published a small pamphlet called *Fantastiska ämnen och varför man studerar dem* [Fantastic Subjects and Why One Studies Them, my translation] (2023) and two reports (Degerman et al. 2021; Salö et al. 2022) which analyse the state of humanities subjects in Sweden, including Classics.

Even though the subjects are small and the number of students small, questions related to Classics and ancient history still seem to engage and excite many people. This was not least evident in the autumn of 2019, when the Swedish National Agency for Education proposed to remove the section on Ancient History from the primary school History curriculum, which led to massive criticism and debate in the press and social media in which many leading academics participated. In the end, the proposal to remove the section on Ancient History was withdrawn, although the section still forms only a vanishingly small part of the primary school curriculum.

Sweden also has a small but active number of Classics scholars who frequently write in the daily press, are heard on radio, seen on social media and participate in debates about Classics. These undoubtedly contribute to spreading knowledge about the Classics. Further proof that the interest in classical languages is still living is Tore Janson's nationally as well as internationally successful book *Latin: kulturen, historien, språket* (Janson 2002), published in translation as *A Natural History of Latin* (Oxford 2004).

Teaching practices

In the last thirty years or so, the Swedish curricula for high school Latin have gone from being more focused on the language to embracing to a greater degree also other aspects of Roman culture, history and social life. This is not least noticeable in the upper secondary school courses *Latin – språk och kultur* [*Latin – language and culture*, my translation]; the syllabus description is found on the website for Skolverket (2023). An example can be given from the syllabus which prescribes 'reading and interpretation of very simple Latin texts' [my translation] such as texts from textbooks, simple and edited authentic texts and famous quotations. The focus is not only on classical Latin, but the students must also get a taste of medieval Latin and Latin of later times. The teacher shall cover the basics of Latin pronunciation, basic grammar and syntax and basic vocabulary. The syllabus also emphasizes the role of Latin as a carrier of culture from a historical perspective and its influence on modern languages, including English. Students also learn about the history of the Latin language and about Roman political history. In addition, Roman culture in the form of art, mythology, and family relations is studied, and how these are reflected in literature and art in later times.

In the classroom, this has led to teachers working more interactively and with group work and oral presentations alongside text reading. All this places rather high demands on the materials used in teaching to be comprehensive, with glossaries, explanations and comments, exercises, and texts about, for example, Roman everyday life. Many teachers, therefore, feel the need to supplement the primary teaching material with other material such as films and documentaries, pictures, and reconstructions of ancient monuments, as well as other texts in Swedish or English. In the following section, the most frequently used textbooks in Latin will be briefly presented.

The oldest textbook that is still in use is *Liber primus Latinus* by Erik Tidner (1971) which consists of short Latin texts about Rome's earliest times, to some extent based on stories from Livy's *Ab urbe condita*. This book has recently been republished by Uppsala University where it is used in the beginner's course. However, *Liber primus Latinus* is not adapted to current secondary school courses, which makes it rather difficult for today's high school students to understand. Since the 1990s, new teaching materials for the upper secondary school have been created to meet the students' demands for a more attractive and easy-to-understand structure. The book *Via Nova* by Lars Larsson and Håkan Plith (1990), which was used in several high schools, is an adapted Swedish version of a Dutch book, originally for younger school children, but which was suitable for the basic courses in Swedish high schools. One of the earlier most ubiquitous books is *Vivat lingua Latina!* by Staffan Edmar (1996), which is based on classical Latin texts in edited form. The book also includes chapters on language history and classical morphemes and morpheme formation, as well as sections on Roman history. The sequel by the same author, *Vivat litteratura Latina!* (1999), is an anthology consisting of primarily classical authentic, sometimes lightly edited texts, with commentaries. From the early 2000s comes *Fabula* by Johanna Svensson and Tove Niclasen (2005), which is a Swedish version of an originally Danish textbook. This book consists of a coherent story in which the students follow the adventures of the Roman girl 'Julia' in Ostia, chapter by chapter, in relatively long texts.

A textbook created to fit the demands of the 2011 school reform is *In medias res* by Joanna Engstedt et al. (2012), which is primarily built around easy authentic and newly written texts. As the book aims to be comprehensive, there are also chapters on everyday life, language history and history. A more recent book that is intended to be suitable for high school as well as for self-study is *Latin – en introduktion* by Andreas Nordin (2016), which, like the aforementioned book, contains short and simple edited authentic texts with exercises, a glossary and chapters on morphology, everyday life and history, as well as a fairly comprehensive chunk of grammar. Both these books consist of authentic text from antiquity, the Middle Ages and early modern times. The texts are, for instance, taken from *Etymologia* of Isidore of Seville, the *Carmina Burana*, Comenius' *Orbis Pictus,* and the poets Martial and Catullus.

The Swedish Educational Radio (UR) has in recent years produced short explanatory films that explain certain aspects of classical literature and history such as the *Iliad*, Cleopatra and society in Greece and Rome for use in schools.

The digitization of education is an important political issue in Sweden. This means that most upper secondary schools use digital learning platforms and that students are each assigned a computer by the school. In addition to printed teaching materials, the explosion of digital resources such as YouTube has meant a welcome and refreshing addition of material to teaching. Since Swedish students can be expected to understand English very well, teachers often use clips and videos in English in their teaching. A free Swedish website created for self-study in Latin is www.latinforalla.net ['*Latin for All*', my translation], by the same author of the previously mentioned *Vivat lingua Latina!* The website consists of eight sections with texts, explanations of grammar, and exercises.

Another Swedish-based commercial website whose purpose is to encourage studies in reading and speaking Latin is Latinitium.com. The content of videos and texts on this page is aimed at interested people worldwide but is often too difficult for Swedish high school students. In 2018, Latinitium.com published *Pugio Bruti – A Crime Story in Easy Latin* (Pettersson & Rosengren 2018), something as unusual as a modern easy reader for lower-intermediate learners.

Since the Swedish higher education reform in 2007, which was prompted by the Bologna Process, the universities have revised their curricula. With the Bologna Process, curriculum work in higher education has started to be based more on a socio-cultural perspective than before (Lindberg-Sand 2008: 5–6). Universities also use digital learning platforms in teaching. For the universities, the abolition of compulsory grades in Latin and Greek from upper secondary school has contributed to other types of students looking for these courses. But it has also placed demands on designing new textbooks and course materials. Although there is a national philological congress every three years that aims to bring together teachers and researchers in Latin and Greek from all Swedish universities for discussions on the subject and pedagogical challenges, there is no jointly produced course material for introductory courses in Latin and Greek. Each department therefore uses different materials for their beginner courses, either developed by the department's teachers or already existing books (such as the aforementioned *Liber primus Latinus* and *Vivat lingua Latina!*). On continuing courses, anthologies, and text editions with either Swedish or English commentaries are used.

At university level, the introduction of distance learning has proven particularly fruitful in attracting students, especially to introductory courses in Latin, Greek, Classical Archaeology and Ancient History. As an example, most of the study groups in Lund and Gothenburg are made up of distance-learning students. Master's students in Classical Archaeology and Ancient History have the opportunity to take courses that are located at the Swedish Institutes in Rome and Athens.

To varying extents, the universities also provide orientation courses for people who have not previously studied Classics such as 'Latin for philosophers', 'Latin for natural scientists', 'Latin for choral musicians', 'Greek Mythology', 'Medieval Latin for beginners' and 'Roman Emperors'. In addition, advanced courses in Latin epigraphy and Latin palaeography and codicology can be mentioned, which also attract students from other humanities subjects either with advanced or limited knowledge of Latin.

Teachers and teacher-supply

Since the number of schools offering courses in classical languages is steadily decreasing, the regrowth on the Latin teacher side is not very large either. This is also partly due to schools closing Humanities study programmes, and partly due to retirements.

Only one university in Sweden has the right to graduate for Latin teachers, namely the University of Gothenburg, and a few students are examined there with some regularity. The statistics say that 51 per cent of all active Latin teachers in the country are qualified, which means that almost half of the teachers either lack formal teacher training or sufficient degrees in the subject.

Professional development is not automatically given to secondary teachers of classical languages. Budget restrictions rarely allow teachers to participate in expensive courses at the school's expense, and it is up to each individual school to decide whether teachers can attend courses or not. However, Swedish teachers have a statutory right to a certain number of hours of professional development each school year. Nonetheless, the number of courses offered is limited.

Every other year, the Swedish Institutes either in Rome or in Athens, in collaboration with the Swedish Classics Association, organize free courses for Latin teachers for two weeks, including guided tours and visits to archaeological excavations. The Swedish Classics Association annually holds lectures for the purpose of in-service training on different topics related to the profession as well as the opportunity for Latin teachers to meet and discuss the subject's content and pedagogical issues.

Although there are national guidelines for all teachers to follow, no coordinated national tests for the Latin courses are issued by the Swedish National Agency for Education. Therefore, network meetings are a way to ensure that teaching is uniform throughout the country.

Contacts between schools and other organizations

It depends above all on the individual teacher to create and maintain contacts with colleagues at other schools and with universities and museums. Some teachers organize study trips with their students to *Medelhavsmuseet* (the Mediterranean Museum) in Stockholm, or to *Glyptoteket* (Art Museum) in Copenhagen in Denmark, or to university towns such as Gothenburg, Lund and Uppsala where there are collections of objects from antiquity. Some schools organize trips to Italy (preferably to the city of Rome and its surroundings such as Ostia Antica and Pompeii), but this requires either that the school finances the students' trip or that the teacher seeks external funds such as scholarships, which are labour-intensive activities. The Swedish School Act prohibits schools from having activities where the students must pay for themselves, since the Swedish school must be equal to all, and thus free of charge for parents and students. Such study tours can be used by the schools that organize them for marketing purposes to attract students.

Because responsibility for teaching lies at the municipal level, it is difficult to get a national overview of Classics teachers. One way to reach upper secondary Latin teachers is through the already mentioned Swedish Classics Association's network. Such contacts have led to collaborations between, above all, schools and universities. The Swedish Classics Association appoints regional representatives who have previously arranged local teachers' meetings to discuss the subject and educational issues. But given that the number of Latin teachers has decreased sharply, such meetings no longer occur as often in the various regions. University teachers, in collaboration with schools, sometimes arrange lectures for school classes free of charge because it is part of the universities' so-called 'third task', that is public outreach (apart from research and teaching) to spread and share knowledge to society.

Conclusion

Classics in Sweden's upper secondary schools suffer from decreasing student numbers. Since the subjects are small, in many cases it is up to the individual teacher to enthuse students and to create networks. Contact with other teachers and with universities is thus important for vital discussions and development of the teaching. Due to the focus of Swedish syllabuses not only on linguistic matters, teachers are often prone to be creative in combining traditional textbook teaching and other kinds of teaching methods and materials. Unfortunately, contemporary Classics teaching on the upper secondary level has not yet been explored in research.

References

Berlin Kolm, S. (2021), *Universitetskanslersämbetets pandemiuppdrag – Delrapportering 1, Rapport 2021:9* [The university chancellor's office's pandemic mission – Interim reporting 1, Report 2021:9], Universitetskanslerämbetet.

Degerman, P., K. Dodou, K. Holmqvist-Sten and L. Degerman (2021), *Humaniora i skolan. De humanistiska ämnenas plats och villkor i den svenska gymnasieskolan och i grundskolans högre år* [Humanities in school. The place and conditions of humanities subjects in Swedish upper secondary school and in the upper years of primary school]. Available online: http://humtank.se/wp-content/uploads/2021/06/rapport_6_2021_a5_final.pdf (accessed 15 October 2023).

Edmar, S. (1996), *Vivat lingua Latina!*, Stockholm: Liber.

Edmar, S. (1999), *Vivat litteratura Latina!*, Stockholm: Liber.

Engstedt, J., A. Raab and E. Schough Tarandi (2012), *In medias res*, Stockholm: Sanoma utbildning.

Janson, T. (2002), *Latin: kulturen, historien, språket* [Latin: the culture, the history, the language], Stockholm: Wahlström & Widstrand.

Larsson, L. and H. Plith (1990), *Via Nova 1*, Stockholm: Bonniers.

Lindberg-Sand, Å. (2008), *Läranderesultat som utgångspunkt för högskolans kurs- och utbildningsplaner* [Learning outcomes as a starting point for the university's course and education plans], Lund: Centre for Educational Development.

Nordin, A. (2016), *Latin – en introduktion* [Latin – an introduction], Stockholm: Appell förlag.

Pettersson, D. and E. Rosengren (2018), *Pugio Bruti – A Crime Story in Easy Latin*, Latinitium.com. Available online: https://latinitium.com/ (accessed 15 October 2023).

Salö, L., L. Runefelt, K. Petrov, J. Borgland and C. Johansson (2022), *Humaniorastrategier i Sverige* [Humanities strategies in Sweden]. Available online: http://humtank.se/wp-content/uploads/2022/07/rapport_7_2022_a5_final.pdf (accessed 15 October 2023).

Siapkas, J. (2017), *Från Laokoon till Troja. Antikvetenskapens teoretiska landskap, 1* [From Laocoon to Troy. The theoretical landscape of ancient science, 1], Lund: Nordic Academic Press.

Skolverket (2023), Skolverket [School Board]. Available online: https://www.skolverket.se/ (accessed 15 October 2023).

Svensson, J. and T. Niclasen (2005), *Fabula. En berättelse från romersk kejsartid* [Fabula. A story from Roman imperial times], Stockholm: Liber.

Tidner, E. (1971), *Liber primus Latinus*, Stockholm: Almqvist and Wiksell.

Antje-Marianne Kolde

Introduction

In Switzerland, education is in the hands of the twenty-six cantons. Therefore, there are as many systems of education as there are cantons. Since 1970, several agreements have been established about school coordination for compulsory education on the federal level and also between the different language regions (German-speaking cantons with Graubünden on one hand, and the French-speaking cantons with Ticino on the other). This has led to harmonization at different levels. At present, schools (state, non-religious and free) have the same structure in the whole country. The first three Cycles are compulsory:

Cycle 1: Nursery School (ages 4–6) for two years.

Cycle 2: Primary School (ages 6–12) for six years (five in Ticino).

Cycle 3: Secondary 1 (S1) (9th, 10th, 11th grades/years: ages 13–16) for three years (four in Ticino).

The final Cycle is not obligatory:

Cycle 4:

Secondary 2 (S2) for two to four years at a Post-compulsory School.

General Cultural School for two to four years.

Commercial School for three to four years.

Mature School for three to four years.

The choice of options is introduced at the end of Primary School, but there are many moments where a change in direction is possible within the curriculum. At the end of the Post-compulsory School, studies can be continued at university or in a specialized institution. In spite of the harmonizations on the federal or regional level, the place occupied by some academic subjects in the curriculum and the timetable can vary considerably from one canton to another. This is the case with Classical Studies (Greek and Latin languages and literature). Because of the sovereignty of the cantons, remarks concerning the whole of Switzerland are necessarily approximate; in addition, it is important to take the specificities of each language region and the cantons into consideration.

It is not possible to take Latin or Greek in Primary School in any of the language regions. Both languages enter the curriculum as optional subjects in Secondary 1. The courses can be continued in Secondary 2 and, of course, at university. It is not possible to establish the numbers of students at any level of teaching.

Latin and classical Greek in schools

To encourage pupils to take up and continue their studies of one or both of the ancient languages, the curriculum of the two secondary school cycles (S1 and S2) of the language regions puts forward the following arguments: studying the Greek and Latin languages and civilizations through their vocabularies, grammars, texts and other aspects of their art and daily life allows pupils to have access to the main sources of Western thought, to enrich their cultural capital, to develop positive attitudes towards languages (ancient and modern) and the learning of them, to master their function and practice, and to make critical comparison with the modern world in many different areas. These different links between the lived experience of the pupils and the critical distance that their classical studies allow them to acquire are to be found in the course books that are used. Teachers are careful to draw them out.

Classical Studies in Secondary 1 (S1)

Suisse romande (French-speaking area of Switzerland)

Latin The curriculum for this area (*Plan d'études romand* or PER; CIIP 2022) is a framework for compulsory school and is common to the seven French-speaking cantons and to the French-speaking part of the multilingual cantons. Adopted in 2010, it came into force in 2011 or 2012 and consists of six subject areas, one of which is Languages (French, German, English or Latin). As in the seven French-speaking cantons, francophone Valais does not offer it at S1 level: Latin appears only at a cantonal level as a special option and its teaching depends on each canton. It can be taken in the 9th, 10th and 11th grades in Vaud, Jura and Fribourg (where it is obligatory in the 9th grade in the pre-gymnasium branch), in the 9th and 10th in Berne; the timetable allocations will always vary. Geneva and Neuchâtel offer an introductory course (see below) before proposing a course in Latin for two years in Geneva and one year in Neuchâtel. At the end of compulsory school, the progress of a French-speaking Latinist, if it is possible, will vary according to each canton from two to twelve periods a week (for details, see Specificité Cantonale Latin et Grec 2016)

The curriculum for Latin (*plans d'études* (PE)) in each canton is based on the Latin PE of the PER (see https://portail.ciip.ch/per/disciplines/4). It is divided into three sections - language, literature and culture - and six components: lexis, morphology and syntax (these two components open up the possibility of an integrated teaching approach to other languages), translation of texts into French, research into ancient sources in Latin or in translation, use of documentary resources, and observation of cultural continuity. None of these sections should be privileged over the others. The knowledge acquired at the end of the S1 stage of secondary education depends on the number of teaching periods delivered.

As Latin teaching is specific to each canton, the PER does not prescribe a course book. Several cantons use a course book which was published for use in the PER and which favours an inductive approach (Agocs et al. 2012–14) with materials for teachers.

Classical Greek Classical Greek does not feature in the PER. It is nevertheless taught in several cantons (Berne, Fribourg, Jura and Vaud) for one or two years as an optional course, generally for pupils in the pre-*gymnasium* branch with a timetable allocation of between two and four periods; in Fribourg it cannot be chosen in the 11th year ndependently of Latin. In Neuchâtel a special option in the 11th year that groups Greek and Latin together is available, with two periods for each language.

The curricula of the cantons are based on the Latin programme of the PER and so respect the three sections above.

The most popular course books are *Organon 2000* and *Organon 2005* (Bassin et al. 2000; 2005) often used with others such as *Odysseia* (Charletoux et al. 2018). They favour the inductive approach and the first two demand a great investment on the part of the teacher, as they provide only a slender grammatical content.

Introductory courses In Neuchâtel, all the pupils of the 9th class follow a course of Ancient Languages and Culture (*Langues et Cultures de l'Antiquité*) reserved in the 10th year to pupils who have good results in French. This course of two weekly periods in the 9th year and one in the 10th aims to introduce the pupils to the Greek and Roman world by using an approach which allows them to understand current cultural and linguistic phenomena by going back to their ancient origins and to reflect on their permanence, their transformations and their original appearances. It is based on the coursebook *Langues et cultures de l'Antiquité* (Fidanza & Kolde 2017) which suitably gives pride of place to local Swiss archaeology and to multilingualism. It favours the inductive approach.

In Geneva all the pupils follow in the 9th year the course Latin Language and Culture (*Langue et culture latines*). This course offers a general education in classical culture, which leads to knowledge of the influence of the ancient world of Greece and Rome in the Mediterranean world and its languages. It is based on the course book *Monstrum* (Alvarez et al. 2020), which favours the inductive approach.

Ticino

In Ticino, Latin is taught for the last two years of S1 with two and then four periods weekly. The curriculum consists of three equal parts: language and its evolution in the Romance languages; literary and historical texts; Roman history, culture and society. Teachers have a free choice of course book but agree within the same establishment. There is no Greek in S1 in Ticino.

German-speaking Switzerland

Latin In 2014 the twenty-one Swiss-German cantons (or the German-speaking part of the multilingual cantons) all adopted a curriculum framework (*Lehrplan 21/L21* (Curriculum 21 2014a)) which is divided into eight areas, of which that of Languages includes Latin. Each canton decides whether to offer this and only six do so: Aargau, Appenzell Ausserhoden, Appenzell Innerrhoden, Fribourg, Saint Gall and Zurich, in the 9th and 10th years, with no fixed timetable allowance. Basel-Landschaft, Basel-Stadt and Glarus offer introductory courses (see below).

The cantonal curriculum is based on the Latin curriculum of L21 (Curriculum 21 2014b). It is centred on the language competences of the Common European Framework of Reference for Languages (CEFR) (listening, reading, speaking and writing), and on two areas, one of which is focused on the links between languages, and the other on the links between cultures. Schools have a free choice of course book.

Greek Greek is not a part of L21 but can be offered in the optional courses framework.

Introductory courses Pupils in 10th and 11th years in Basel-Stadt and Basel-Landschaft must choose between two optional courses: *Lingua mit Italienisch* or *Lingua mit Latein*. This is taught for two periods a week and Latin is taught following the principles of integrated language teaching, based on the course book *Aurea Bulla* (Müller et al. 2015–17), which gives a lot of attention to Swiss Roman sites and aims for an introduction to Latin language and culture.

In Glarus the course *Kultur und Sprache der Antike* (Ancient Language and Culture two periods in 10th and 11th years) invites the pupils to examine the ancient origins of modern cultural and linguistic phenomena. There is no suitable course book.

Looking at the teaching of Latin in S1, it could be stated that both curriculum frameworks (PER and L21) put the accent on the same components (language, literature and the link to the pupils' daily lives). But on the other hand, as far as the course books are concerned, although they were created for French-speaking Switzerland (*Suisse romande*), those used in Swiss German schools come from Germany and those in Ticino from Italy. Furthermore, on the level of the language regions and the cantons, teaching is more harmonized in *Suisse romande*, but the Swiss German schools and teachers have greater autonomy.

Classical Studies in Secondary 2 (S2)

General

The curriculum framework of S2 is currently being reformed. Even if certain changes are made, principally concerning the weighting given to transferable skills and interdisciplinarity, it should not result in radical alterations either to the range of subjects taught or to the assessment levels. These are fixed by federal guidance on the recognition of higher secondary school leaving certificates (*certificats de maturité gymnasiale*). In the framework of the current reform of higher secondary schools (*études gymnasiales*) their length will no doubt be made uniform in four years for the whole of Switzerland. As far as the curriculum subjects are concerned, the cantons have a degree of autonomy which is especially evident in the offer (or lack of it) of some of them, including Latin and Greek.

During the higher secondary school (*gymnasium*) three languages are compulsory: the main language of education (French, German, Italian, according to the language region), a second national language (Italian, German, French), and a third language (German, Italian, French, English, Latin, Classical Greek). Each *gymnasium* offers English.

Latin and Greek can be chosen as a special option (*option spécifique* (OS)), with an increased timetable allocation (four periods over three or four years), set against other languages, sciences, art, economics, law, or psychology; or as a foundation subject (*discipline fondamentale* (DF)), with a lower allocation of three periods for three or four years and generally set against English; or finally as an optional subject with a small allocation and mark which does not count for the final leaving certificate.

Suisse romande

Latin The length of the *gymnasium* course varies according to the canton: in Vaud, Neuchâtel, Jura and Berne it is three years; in Geneva and Fribourg it is four; in Valais it is five, the first year being the final year of S1. All offer Latin as OS, except Berne, where it is only available as

DF; Vaud, Fribourg and Geneva also offer it as DF. To choose Latin in S2 the pupil must have followed it in S1.

The cantonal curricula which follow the federal curriculum (under revision, as mentioned above) all aim for the following: to acquire linguistic knowledge sufficient to read basic texts, to establish a dialogue between the ancient and the contemporary world to better understand it, to acquire an advanced level of French, and to deepen knowledge of other European languages. For language learning most schools continue to use the course books from S1; the choice of texts to read is usually made by the teachers.

Greek Two cantons offer Greek as OS (Geneva and Fribourg), two as DF (Valais, Neuchâtel), Vaud offers both; Jura and Berne offer neither. In the cantons where Greek is taught in S1, it is advised to choose it to be able to continue in S2. In Valais, Greek can only be taken in combination with Latin.

The aims of the cantonal curriculums are very close to those of the Latin programme.

Language learning is generally based on the course books already mentioned and also Ἑρμαιον. *Initiation au grec ancien* (Vernhes 2003). The choice of texts is often created by the teachers.

Introductory courses In Vaud, an optional course in ancient culture (two periods a week) is offered to pupils in post compulsory education. From 2025, this course will be given to pupils in the school of general culture (*l'école de culture générale*) which prepares them to be primary school teachers.

Ticino

Ticino offers both languages for the four years of the *Scuola Media Superiore* with a higher timetable allocation for Latin (4+4+4+4 for OS ; 4+3+3+3 for DF) and a normal one for Greek (3+3+3+4). To choose Greek, pupils must have been taking Latin in S1. The aims of the programme are in continuity with those of S1. Reading and translation of texts are at the centre of the teaching of both languages. Each institution has a free choice of course book and often they choose from Ørberg's *Lingua latina per se illustrata* (2006), *Il Tantucci plus* (Tantucci & Roncoroni 2015), *Athenaze* (Balme et al. 1990), *Il nuovo Lingua greca* (Bottin et al. 2002), and Holtermann's *Kantharos* (2018).

German-speaking Switzerland

Latin In German-speaking Switzerland there is a distinction between the *Kurzzeitgymnasium* (four years: the last year of S1 and three of S2) and the *Langzeitgymnasium* (six years: three of S1 and the other three of S2). In several German-speaking cantons, Latin can only be taken in S2. If it is taught in S1, the pupil must have taken it in order to choose it in S2. The Latin courses are offered as either OS (as in Appenzell Innerrhoden), as DF or OS (in Basel-Stadt, Solothurn or Zurich), or as DF (in Glarus), for example. It is excluded from the programme in some cantons (notably Uri and Obwald).

The programmes, individual to each institution, prepare pupils for the *Latinum Helveticum* (SEFRI 2011), the Swiss version of the *Latinum* (lower or upper), an examination well known in the German-speaking world which evaluates linguistic knowledge and the ability to translate. The teachers are free to choose their course book, for example *Prima brevis* (Utz et al. 2014), combined with their own choice of texts.

Greek Greek is offered in about half the cantons, generally as OS (both cantons of Basel where Greek is only taught with Latin, and Solothurn), sometimes as DF (St Gallen). The programmes, again individual to each school, prepare for the *Graecum*, the Greek equivalent to the *Latinum*. As in the case of Latin, the teachers of Greek are free to choose their course book, such as *Xenia* (Kampert et al. 2014), combined with their own choice of texts.

The teachers of S2 are even freer than those of S1. Even if the programmes of each canton indicate a range of authors, texts and themes to teach, the choice and the treatment of the texts is the teacher's responsibility.

Summary

To conclude the section of secondary education, we should emphasize that the new curricula of S1 and those for S2 (currently being drawn up) are intended to establish more connections with other branches of language and literature to reveal links to the *hic et nunc*. The course books, newly created in several cantons to help implement the new curricula, place emphasis on these elements.

Often the new curricula and new course books use new methods. Consequently, teachers often make use of digital technology and incorporate it in many different forms and ways in their lessons. An example which can be given is a project of the *Haute école pédagogique Vaud*, which gets pupils to work on Latin texts generated by artificial intelligence (see LATINIA 2023 and Cavaleri 2022). More and more teachers are including in their classes moments of spoken Latin or Greek, especially in the acting out of short scenes; in the *Kantonsschule* of Solothurn two teachers deliver their lessons almost entirely in Latin and expect their pupils to converse in Latin, as in modern language lessons (Jung & Krebs 2021; Jung 2021; Tárrega 2021).

Classical Studies in universities

Of the ten universities in Switzerland, those of Geneva, Lausanne, Neuchâtel, Fribourg, Berne, Basel and Zurich offer courses in Latin and Greek language and literature at undergraduate and Masters level in the Faculty of Literature and of Theology. Lucerne and the University of Italian-speaking Switzerland in Lugano offer them in the Faculty of Theology. The university of St Gallen, which has an exclusively commercial focus, has no Classics.

Teacher training

In most cantons, teacher training is undertaken by the *Hautes écoles pédagogiques* (HEP). Subject to cantonal and intercantonal regulations, they offer initial, continuing and complementary training, as well as research and development. Most cantons have an HEP, although some have been regrouped into one institution. Qualification for entry to a course in the HEP depends on the chosen level: a leaving certificate from the *gymnasium* for primary school, an undergraduate degree for S1, and a Masters degree for S2 in the chosen subject(s).

As with all professional training, the training of a teacher is a dual one: while following courses at HEP, student teachers also take on classes in school, either alongside a mentor who hands over more and more lessons, or on their own while under the supervision of a mentor who visits them regularly. The teacher-trainers in the HEP are practitioners and academics and regularly visit the lessons given by their student teachers.

A teaching diploma for the appropriate level is awarded at the end of the HEP studies. Cantonal recognition of the teaching diplomas is regulated by the CDIP (*Conférence des directrices et directeurs cantonaux de l'instruction publique* [Conference of the cantonal directors of public education]). For S1 and S2 levels teaching diplomas from different HEPs are not recognized at present on a national level; depending on the institution in which the teacher has trained, it is necessary to take extra training to teach in another canton.

For the training of Classics teachers, it is different according to each canton as Classics training is not available in all HEPs. In *Suisse romande*, if the training is coordinated on the language regional level – future teachers of Classics of the French-speaking cantons are grouped together – the access conditions and the diplomas obtained vary according to the cantons: some separate S1 and S2, while others put them together. Teacher training lasts two semesters but the total length of the training varies from one institution to another. In German speaking Switzerland the outlook is very diverse. In certain cantons the training is done in HEPs (Berne, HEP *Fachhochschule Nordwestschweiz*), and in the others it takes place in universities (Zurich). The entry qualifications (undergraduate degree for S1, Masters degree for S2) and the possibilities (or not) of mobility are the same as for *Suisse romande*. During their careers, and according to the cantons, teachers are offered continuing professional development (academic or didactic) in universities and HEPs, often in collaboration. The possibilities of an internal career within the school are often of an administrative level (head of department in school or in the canton, senior leadership team) and do not depend on the subject taught.

Cultural trips and site visits

In all the cantons teachers organize cultural trips to the theatre, museums and archaeological sites. In different cantons there are open days for all pupils of different stages (S1 or S2) or for both (S1 and S2). Some teachers occasionally use peer teaching as a method (pupils of S2 and S1). The Classics departments of several universities offer initiation days to pupils of S2. In many cantons the pupils can win a competition with final year work – a research piece completed in the penultimate year of their studies at *gymnasium* – if they tackle a topic connected to the ancient world. The prizes are sponsored by the universities, museums or private foundations.

As well as festivals organized by the archaeological sites which are directed to a wide audience, there are other cultural events aimed at schools and an intergenerational and intercantonal school audience, such as the *IXber, Lateinischer Kulturmonat St. Gallen* [St Gallen Latin Cultural Month] or the *Schweizerischer Lateintag* [Swiss Latin Day]. Every year many classes participate in the European Classics Festival in France (*Festival Européen latin grec*), which includes a public participatory reading. It should be noted that these initiatives, which depend on individual efforts and are rarely institutionalized, demand a great deal of engagement on the part of the organizers, generally teachers organized into associations on the cantonal or federal level: the *Association suisse des philologues classiques – Schweizerischer Altphilologenverband – Associazione svizzera dei filologi classici*, all member associations of Euroclassica, brings together S2 Latin and Greek teachers from all over Switzerland.

Occasionally there are political initiatives from the cantons which promote Classics. This is the case in Vaud, where there is a plan of action to support the ancient languages (2021–5). This involves several interventions and measures to reinforce the attraction of studying Classics, notably a biennial cantonal ancient languages competition for S1, the organization of meetings and debates or support for visits to the archaeological heritage of the canton.

Two periodicals regularly publish contributions connected to Classics teaching: the *Bulletin de l'ASPC* [ASPC Bulletin] and *Babylonia, revue suisse consacrée à l'apprentissage et à l'enseignement des langues* [Babylonia, Swiss magazine dedicated to language learning and teaching].

It is not possible to measure the impact of these initiatives on the real delivery of teaching in schools or on the number of pupils who sign up for a Classical course – some give up their study of Latin or Greek at a certain moment, not through dislike or lack of interest, but because there is no place in the already crowded timetable for another challenging subject. Many teachers on the other hand emphasize their unifying and motivating effect and the attention they give to these school subjects.

Conclusion

The diversity of the landscape of Swiss education, which is favourable to personal, local, and targeted initiatives, undoubtedly supports the teaching of Classics in many cantons, and even leaves it in a relatively healthy state, since it allows the discipline to adapt to new situations and to incorporate itself in a number of networks.

References

Agocs, M., M. Baud, V. Durussel, A.-M. Kolde, S. Maréchaux, and A. Rapin (2012–14), *Latin Forum 9ème – 11 ème*, Lausanne: DGEO.

Alvarez, J.-B., S. Blanc, M. Miéville and N. Simon (2022), *Monstrum*, Genvea DGEO.

ASPC (2023), *Bulletin de l'ASPC*. Available online: http://philologia.ch/wordpress/verein/bulletin/ (accessed 17 October 2023).

Babylonia (2023), *Babylonia, revue suisse consacrée à l'apprentissage et à l'enseignement des langues* [Babylonia, Swiss magazine dedicated to language learning and teaching]. Available online: https://babylonia.online/index.php/babylonia (accessed 17 October 2023).

Balme M., G. Lawall and J. Morwood (1990), *Athenaze I-II*, Oxford: Oxford University Press.

Bassin, D., E. Bovet, J.-G. Demont and J.-L. Vial (2000), *Organon 2000*, Lausanne: LEP.

Bassin, D., E. Bovet, J.-G. Demont and J.-L. Vial (2005), *Organon 2005*, Lausanne: LEP.

Bottin, L., S. Quaglia and A. Marchiori (2002), *Il nuovo Lingua greca*, Milan: Minerva italica.

Cavaleri, D. (2022), 'L'enseignement du latin à l'aube de l'intelligence artificielle' [Teaching Latin at the dawn of artificial intelligence], *Bulletin SAV-ASPC-ASFC*, 100: 5–20. Available online: http://philologia.ch/wordpress/wp-content/uploads/2022/10/94d8a841-a1d0-4667-9b39-1d0a7de0dc5f.bulletin_100-2022.pdf (accessed 17 October 2023).

Charletoux, M., E. Lesueur and P.-O. Luet (2018), *Odysseia*, Paris: Hachette.

CIIP (2022), CIP: Conference Intercantonale d'Instruction Publique de la Suisse Romande et du Tessin, Plan d'études romand (PER) [Intercantonal Conference of Public Education of French-speaking Switzerland and Ticino, French-speaking study plan]. Available online: https://www.ciip.ch/

Plans-detudes-romands/Plan-detudes-romand-scolarite-obligatoire-PER/Plan-detudes-romand-PER (accessed 7 November 2023).

Curriculum 21 (2014a), Lehrplan 21. Available online: https://www.lehrplan21.ch (accessed 17 October 2023).

Curriculum 21 (2014b), Lehrplan 21: Latin. Available online: https://v-fe.lehrplan.ch/index.php?code=b 1 45 (accessed 17 October 2023).

Fidanza, C. and A.-M. Kolde (2017), *NEoLCA, Langues et cultures de l'Antiquité, 9e année – 10e année* [NEoLCA, Languages and cultures of Antiquity, 9th grade – 10th grade], Neuchâtel: SEO.

Holtermann, M. (2018), *Kantharos,* Stuttgart: Klett Verlag.

Jung, B. (2021), 'Loquimur et scribimus, quo melius legamus': Latine docere am Gymnasium, *Bulletin SAV-ASPC-ASFC,* 98: 18–23.

Jung, B. and D. Krebs (2021), '"LATINE DOCERE" – Pilotversuch mit dem Lehrmittel LINGUA LATINA PER SE ILLUSTRATA an der Kantonsschule Solothurn' ['LATINE DOCERE' – pilot test with the teaching aid LINGUA LATINA PER SE ILLUSTRATA at the Solothurn Cantonal School],' *Bulletin SAV-ASPC-ASFC* 98: 5–17

Kampert, O., R. Knab and W. Winter (2014), *Xenia,* Bamberg: Buchner.

LATINIA (2023), LATINIA. Générer du latin pour mieux l'acquérir [Generate Latin to better acquire it]. Available online: https://latin-ia.hepl.ch/ (accessed 17 October 2023).

Müller, M., R. Gutierrez, A. Netti, A. and K. Wesselmann (2015–17), *Aurea Bulla: Latein, Mehrsprachigkeit, Kulturgeschicht* [Aurea Bulla: Latin, multilingualism, cultural history], Verbesserter Nachdruck Liestal: Basel-Landschaft.

Ørberg, H. (2006), *Lingua Latina per se illustrata,* Indianapolis, IN: Hackett Publishing.

Specificité Cantonale Latin et Grec (2016), Specificité Cantonale Latin et Grec: année scolaire 2016-2017 [Cantonal Latin and Greek specificity: 2016-2017 school year]. Available online: https://www.irdp.ch/data/secure/2601/document/16latin_et_grec_cycle_3_1617.pdf (accessed 18 October 2023).

SEFRI (2011), Examen complémentaire 'Latinum Helveticum'. Available online: https://www.sbfi.admin.ch/sbfi/fr/home/formation/maturite/maturite-gymnasiale/latinum-helveticum.html (accessed 18 October 2023).

Tantucci, V. and A. Roncoroni (2015), *Il Tantucci plus,* Milan: Posideonia.

Tárrega, J. (2021), VIA LATINA – ein neues Latein-Lehrmittel. *Bulletin SAV-ASPC-ASFC,* 98: 24. Available online: http://philologia.ch/wordpress/wp-content/uploads/2021/10/Bulletin_98-2021.pdf) (accessed 18 October 2023).

Utz, C. and A. Kammerer, M. Biermann, J. Burdich, R. Czimmek, W. Freytag, A. Lücker, B. O'Connor and E. Visser (2014), *Prima brevis,* Bamberg: Buchner.

Vernhes, J.-V. (2003), Ἕρμαιον. *Initiation au grec ancien,* Paris: Éditions Ophrys.

TURKEY

Seda Şen

Introduction

Asia Minor, or Anatolia, has been the setting for many ancient civilizations, and the ongoing excavations in archaeological sites indicate that there is still a need for Turkish people who know classical languages as well as other secondary European languages to establish a bridge of communication. The need for such people, however, does not mean that the teaching of Latin and Greek is available for all students. The education of classical languages and literatures is limited to undergraduate and post-graduate programmes. Students in a variety of undergraduate programmes, including medicine, pharmacy, dentistry, law and history, have compulsory Latin grammar and Latin vocabulary and area-specific terminology courses. Departments of western languages and literatures (i.e. English Studies, American Studies, French Language and Literature, Archaeology etc.) have compulsory Classical Mythology / Western Civilization courses, in addition to some departments teaching Latin as a compulsory language course. In the Classical Mythology and Western Civilization courses, the culture and civilization of the classical world is introduced to students as foundations for future courses through the texts of famous writers, poets and playwrights, which include Sophocles, Euripides, Aristophanes, Aristotle, Plato, Homer, Sappho, Virgil and Ovid.

Apart from such programmes that offer knowledge about the classical world, teaching Latin and Greek languages is limited to a handful of universities. There are a total of 208 universities in Turkey, out of which only three universities with a total of five sub-departments have enrolled students in their BA programmes: Latin and Greek languages and literature are taught at Ankara University, İstanbul University and Akdeniz University.

The Department of Ancient Languages and Cultures at Ankara University is the oldest of all three of the universities, dating back to 1936, founded with the encouragement of Mustafa Kemal Atatürk, the founder of the Turkish Republic. The department is unique in Turkey in that the sub-departments include not only Greek and Latin languages, but also Hittitology and Sumerian which also includes courses on the Assyrian, Akkadian and Urartian languages and how to read cuneiform scripts from civilizations of Asia Minor. Formerly set up in 1936 as a Classical Languages sub-department, it was separated in 1960 into two separate sub-departments: Latin and Classical Greek languages and literatures.

Even though the foundations of İstanbul University date back to the fall of Constantinople in 1453, the department of Ancient Languages and Literatures was founded much later in 1943. After the restructuring of the universities in 1933 by Mustafa Kemal Atatürk, who encouraged universities to be restructured in the model of the new Republic he envisioned, the Faculty of Humanities was founded. The Classical Languages Institute was established with its founding members including Professor Ronald Syme from the University of Oxford, Professor Oliver Davies from Ireland and Professor George Ewart Bean from the University of Cambridge. Clemens Emin Bosch became the inaugural Chair of the Department when the institute was transformed into a department in 1938.

The Department of Ancient Languages and Cultures at Akdeniz University was founded in 1997 by Professor Sencer Şahin, the archaeologist who directed the excavations of the famous Lycean–Pamphylian route in Southern Anatolia. The Greek Language and Literature sub-department started accepting students in 1998, while the Latin Language and Literature sub-department is new since it only began accepting students in 2019 and has no graduates so far. As the department and sub-department web pages clearly state, even though the two sub-departments have been distinguished from one another, the four-year curriculum is designed in a way that allows students to develop in both Greek and Latin languages and cultures. Table 11 shows the number of students currently enrolled in each department, providing insight on the rise and fall of the popularity of these departments.

Ankara University has a Greek Language and Literature sub-department under the Department of Ancient Languages and Literatures, and one under the Western Languages and Literatures department, named Contemporary Greek Language and Literature. Akdeniz University Latin Language and Literature was founded in 2019 and will have its first graduates in the upcoming semesters.

Table 11. Number of students currently enrolled in each department of universities in Turkey

	Ankara University Latin Language and Literature	Ankara University Greek Language and Literature	İstanbul University Latin Language and Literature	İstanbul University Ancient Greek Language and Literature	Akdeniz University Latin Language and Literature	Akdeniz University Ancient Greek Language and Literature
Academic staff	6	3	7	6	7	8
2022 freshmen students	31	21	52	52	31	41
2022 total registered Students	182	110	334	287	111	255
2023 freshmen students	31	22	52	52	31	41
2020 graduates	2	4	8	8	–	10
2021 graduates	6	3	18	5	–	19
2022 graduates	5	5	10	10	–	9

Source: © Seda Şen 2023.

According to the data of 2022, the total number of freshmen students enrolled after the university entrance exam was 207, and in 2023 this number has remained almost the same. According to the Table 11, there are currently a little over 1,200 students who are enrolled on classical languages and literatures undergraduate programmes. Even though the total number of graduates in the past three years has increased, the total graduate number in all three years imply that the number of students who succeed in graduating in the expected four-year spectrum is quite low.

Four-year curricula and course syllabi

For the present study, being an American Studies graduate, I contacted the faculty members of each department, requesting them to fill out a survey that would provide further information about various subjects, including the increase or decrease in the popularity of the department, the use of technology in their classes and the sources they use to teach their courses. Out of the three universities, six undergraduate programmes and thirty-seven academic staff, only two of the faculty members responded, declaring that they used online meeting programs (Zoom, MS Teams etc.) during the Covid-19 lockdowns and have not continued using them afterwards. The rest of the analysis, therefore, is a report of what is available online in the websites of these programmes.

As part of the Bologna Process and the European Higher Education agreements, all universities in Turkey have their syllabi and four-year core curricula available online. An overview of these programmes provides further information on the teaching of classical languages in Turkey. For further information on the four-year curricula of the programmes, the website links to the curricula have been added to the sources, which include hyperlinks to the syllabi for each course.

In the case of teaching Ancient Greek and Latin, the core curricula of the three universities mentioned use similar programmes. The four-year curriculum in teaching Greek involves mainly introductory courses on grammar and civilization/ history in the first year, then advancing into courses on literature, philosophy and genre-based compulsory and elective courses. In all the Greek undergraduate degree programmes electives and compulsory courses on Latin grammar and Roman literature and culture are offered, and in Latin undergraduate degree programmes; likewise, Greek language, literature, and culture courses are available as elective and compulsory courses.

Specifically, in the case of Ankara University, the Faculty of Language, History and Geography, in the sub-department of Greek Literature, offers courses in Greek grammar, an overview of the Classical World and its cultural history, the history of Classical Greek literature, and period courses that provide detailed information on the Archaic, Classical and Hellenistic periods. Courses on writers such as Homer and Hesiod, classical historiography, Greek prose, Latin grammar, texts of Classical drama and the history of Greek philosophy are compulsory. In the Greek Language and Literature sub-department, the four-year programme lists a wide variety of electives, including sculpture, art, numismatics, archaeology, mythology, ancient civilizations and their cultures, art of poetry, and western languages (especially Portuguese and Spanish). In the Latin Language and Literature department, Latin Grammar, Literary Genre courses on Greek and Roman literature, and translation courses are compulsory courses in the first year. From the second year onwards, while grammar courses continue, translation, text analysis, syntax and literary history courses are introduced. In the third year, author based (i.e. Cicero and Ovid) courses and courses on mythology are compulsory. Political and social history of the Roman Empire, and genre-based courses (Roman poetry, drama etc.) are offered only in the final semester and a wide range of electives are offered each semester.

At İstanbul University, in the sub-department of Greek Language and Literature, the four-year curriculum begins with courses on Greek grammar, Greek mythology, Latin grammar and grammar exercises, and proceeds with genre-focused courses on epic Greek poetry, archaic Greek poetry, Greek tragedy and comedy, historiography, and culture courses, such as Greek culture, and advanced language courses, which include Greek language and its dialects. Translation of Greek texts continue for a number of semesters. Additionally, different from the other two programmes in Turkey, İstanbul University offers a compulsory course on classical studies and its relation to critical theory. Apart from this, there are courses on Greek philosophy, Hellenistic culture and literature and Greek epigraphy. In the Latin Language and Literature sub-department, Greek and Roman mythology, literary history, and an introduction to the field of classical languages are offered in the first year, along with grammar courses continuing throughout the four-year programme. In the second year, textual analysis, literary history, social life in the Roman Empire are some of the compulsory courses. In the third and fourth years, genre-based courses (letters, stories, tragedies, comedies) are included.

At Akdeniz University, the curriculum has courses on Greek grammar, mythology, and an overview of Greek literature divided into four semesters. Other courses focus on Greek political history, society and life, governmental institutions and public life of the Archaic, Classical and

Hellenistic periods. In addition to courses on Greek language, literature and culture, the programme offers Latin grammar and Roman literary history courses. In the Latin Language and Literature Department, the four-year curriculum includes courses on Latin grammar and grammar exercises, as well as courses on literary history, the Roman Republic and Empire, courses on social life, politics and institutions in the Roman civilization, general archaeology, and linguistics courses on Latin. In the third and fourth years of the programme, Greek is offered as compulsory courses.

In all these programmes, as one can deduce, the education of Latin and Greek languages and cultures are offered in curricula that intertwine the two. While in some of the programmes Greek and Latin language teaching focus more on linguistics and translation, others include mainly the study of literature and offer textual analysis, cultural studies and genre studies courses in addition to the grammar courses.

After graduation

The Greek and Latin four-year BA programmes that are offered in Turkey all state that their graduates have high employment rates in places like archaeological sites and museums, focusing especially on the translation of ancient texts. As the website of the ancient languages and literatures department in Ankara University informs, some Ottoman texts that were written in Latin are usually also translated by the graduates of Greek and Latin departments. Some other careers available for graduates include working as tourist guides, translating texts found in archaeological sites, or following other career tracks such as history, linguistics or philosophy and applying their expertise in classical languages to these fields, or enrolling into teacher education departments.

Conclusion

In conclusion, even though the education of classical languages is limited to undergraduate and graduate levels, the graduates from these departments have a number of employment opportunities in which they can continue working on classical languages. However, especially in the case of Turkey, the number of graduates seem to be low; in each department it seems that only one tenth of the students who enrol each year into these departments are able to graduate in time from these departments.

YÖK Atlas webpages for statistics

Akdeniz University, Sub-Department of Ancient Greek Language and Literature: https://yokatlas.yok.gov.tr/lisans.php?y=100710066.

Akdeniz University, Sub-Department of Latin Language and Literature: https://yokatlas.yok.gov.tr/lisans.php?y=100790419.

Ankara University, Sub-Department of Greek Language and Literature: https://yokatlas.yok.gov.tr/lisans.php?y=101110351.

Ankara University, Sub-Department of Latin Language and Literature: https://yokatlas.yok.gov.tr/lisans.php?y=101110245.

İstanbul University, Sub-Department of Ancient Greek Language and Literature: https://yokatlas.yok.gov.tr/lisans.php?y=105610131.

İstanbul University, Sub-Department of Latin Language and Literature: https://yokatlas.yok.gov.tr/lisans.php?y=105610219.

Departmental or sub-departmental webpages

Akdeniz University, Department of Ancient Languages and Literatures: https://edkb.akdeniz.edu.tr/.
Ankara University, Department of Ancient Languages and Literatures: http://www.dtcf.ankara.edu.tr/ogrenci-isleri/akademik-birimler/eskicag-dilleri-ve-kulturleri-bolumu-2/.
İstanbul University, Department of Ancient Languages and Literatures, Sub-department of Latin Language and Literature: https://latindili-edebiyat.istanbul.edu.tr/tr/_.
İstanbul University, Department of Ancient Languages and Literatures, Sub-department of Greek Language and Literature: https://eskiyunandili-edebiyat.istanbul.edu.tr/tr/_.

Bologna Process 4-year curricula pages

Akdeniz University, Sub-Department of Ancient Greek Language and Literature: https://obs.akdeniz.edu.tr/oibs/bologna/index.aspx?lang=tr&curOp=showPac&curUnit=33&curSunit=236#.
Akdeniz University, Sub-Department of Latin Language and Literature: https://obs.akdeniz.edu.tr/oibs/bologna/index.aspx?lang=tr&curOp=showPac&curUnit=33&curSunit=10272#.
Ankara University, Sub-Department of Greek Language and Literature: http://bbs.ankara.edu.tr/Ders_Plani.aspx?bno=1404&bot=1.
Ankara University, Sub-Department of Latin Language and Literature: http://bbs.ankara.edu.tr/Ders_Plani.aspx?bno=1657&bot=254.
İstanbul University, Sub-Department of Ancient Greek Language and Literature: https://ebs.istanbul.edu.tr/home/dersprogram/?id=1107&birim=ancient_greek_language_and_literature__undergraduate_program__(formal_education)&yil=2023.
İstanbul University, Sub-Department of Latin Language and Literature: https://ebs.istanbul.edu.tr/home/dersprogram/?id=1123&yil=2023.
Survey conducted by the author: https://docs.google.com/forms/d/e/1FAIpQLSc1OVBAsqJfUof73kYSBa_KS2s3kE-zcuzagG1fLc-XCbnZmQ/viewform?usp=sharing.

UK: ENGLAND

Aisha Khan-Evans

Introduction

Schools in England fall into two categories: state-maintained and private schools. In England classical subjects have often been regarded as the preserve of private schools, that is, schools which charge attendance fees; many within and outside of education assume there is little, or potentially no, Classics in the curriculum of England's state schools.

In the academic year 2022/23, there were 24,442 schools in England, of which 16,783 were state-funded primary schools educating children aged four to eleven, and 3,444 state-funded secondary schools, generally educating children and young people from ages eleven to eighteen. There were also 2,408 independent schools, although many of these educate the primary age range, or only go up to age thirteen.

Within these two categories of schools, there are several different types: the state schools do not charge fees and receive their funding either directly from the government or via their local authority; the 'private' or 'independent schools' charge fees rather than being government-funded. I will use the term 'independent' to include all schools which charge fees. All children in England are entitled to a free place at a state school from the ages of five to sixteen and they all must remain in education or training until age eighteen. Many schools therefore have 'sixth-forms' which educate students between the ages of sixteen and eighteen; in some areas separate 'sixth form colleges' cater for this age group.

The most common types of state schools are academies and free schools. They are independent from the local authority, run as not-for-profit trusts, but receive funding direct from central government. These schools have more freedom in certain areas than other state schools, which are funded via their local authority. For example, they can set their own term-dates (instead of the local authority) and have more freedom within their curriculum. In theory, beyond a core of Mathematics, English and Sciences, academies and free schools do not have to follow the National Curriculum, though in practice most choose to do so. They generally have to follow the same admissions code as other state schools, with exceptions, for example, for faith-based schools (such as Muslim, Greek Orthodox, Catholic or Church of England schools).

Most of England's state schools are not academically selective, but a few are. These are known as 'grammar schools' (the title stemming from their original purpose of educating priests in Latin). In the 1960s and 1970s, the idea of comprehensive secondary schooling, that is inclusive and without academic selection, was introduced. From this point, the number of grammar schools dropped drastically. Of the 3,444 state secondary schools in England, only 163 grammar schools remain (Long et al. 2023) and most are also academies.

In England, the classical subjects offered are Latin, Ancient Greek, Ancient History and Classical Civilization. The Education Reform Act of 1988 (UK Parliament n.d.) introduced a new National Curriculum for England for students up to age sixteen, with no mention of classical subjects (Forrest 1996). This obviously had a huge impact on numbers: 16,023 students were entered for GCSE Latin in 1988, with over half of them educated in state schools (BBC 2008) and by 2000 the number had fallen to 10,561, with just over one-third educated in state schools (BBC 2008). There have, however, been some more favourable changes since then. At primary level, the National Curriculum now requires all state schools to teach a foreign language at Key Stage 2 (ages 7–11) and this can include ancient languages (Department for Education 2013). Biblical Hebrew and Sanskrit are also endorsed for study as ancient languages, but in practice there are little data on their teaching (Holmes-Henderson & Kelly 2022). This inclusion of ancient with modern seems to be unique in Europe, though only a small number of schools, up to 4 per cent, have taken up the option of ancient languages (Bracke 2023). Nevertheless, according to the British Council's recent survey of language trends in England, Latin has made its first appearance in the 'top four' primary languages taught, behind French, German and Spanish (British Council 2023: 7).

Elsewhere in the primary curriculum, the study of Greeks and Romans forms part of the History National Curriculum for Key Stage 2. Beyond this age group, however, there is no reference to the study of any aspect of the ancient world, including its languages, in the National Curriculum (Hunt 2022). Nevertheless, there does seem to be interest in ancient languages (Hunt 2023a). While the British Council survey indicates that Mandarin is the fourth most popular language in state school curricula at Key Stage 3 (students aged 11–14), Latin seems to be on a similar footing to Italian and Japanese amongst those outside the 'big three' (British Council 2023). With relatively small numbers responding, however, it may be difficult to extrapolate from the data. Indeed, the number of state schools teaching Greek at Key Stage 3 is so small that it is not reported.

In spite of their absence in the National Curriculum for secondary age students, learners can take each classical subject up to GCSE (General Certificate of Education, a national examination taken aged fifteen or sixteen, originally introduced in 1986) and at A Level (Advanced Level, taken at age seventeen or eighteen, during the final year of formal schooling, introduced in the 1950s primarily for access to university). In England in 2023, there were 15,592 entries for GCSEs in classical subjects. Although this is less than 1 per cent of the total GCSE entry, that number has changed very little in the last twenty years, suggesting that, in spite of increased pressures on timetables and finances, young people continue to opt for classical subjects where they are offered (Grigsby 2020; Hunt 2023c; Classics for All 2023). For example, although the number of students taking GCSE Latin has fallen since the introduction of the National Curriculum, numbers have remained fairly steady between 10,000 and 12,000 for several years, aside from a slight dip in 2023 to 8,559 (OCR 2023).

Greek, however, has suffered at both GCSE and A Level under timetabling and financial pressure, not to mention staffing. GCSE Greek entries fell to under 1,000 (at 995) for the first time in 2023 (OCR 2023) and A Level enrolment is hovering a little below or above 200 (OCR 2023). There is, however, more positive news for Greek, with the introduction of an Intermediate Certificate in Classical Greek (ICCG), a qualification established by a group of Classics teachers who teach regularly on the JACT Greek Summer School. While the group would like the GCSE itself to be more accessible, their aim is to provide a national qualification which is feasible for a wider range of students and in settings where timetabling precludes, or reduces, the teaching of Greek (Le Hur 2022). The ICCG is a purely linguistic qualification, suitable for all ages and recognized by universities.

Financial pressures have taken a particular toll on the sixth-form curriculum (the A Level year groups), meaning almost no state schools offer Greek at this level. During the 2010s, sixth-form funding per student fell by 28 per cent (Sibieta 2022) and smaller subjects have also been affected by AS and A Level reform. In September 2000 AS (Advanced Subsidiary) qualifications were introduced – the AS was designed as a qualification in itself but also formed the first half of a full A Level course (Dearing 1996). This had a positive effect on 'minority' subjects such as Classical Civilization, often taken by those without prior knowledge of the classical world: entries for AS Classical Civilization increased by nearly 40 per cent from their introduction to 2015 (Khan-Evans 2018). The government's examination reforms, however, 'decoupled' AS and A Levels, so that the AS no longer counts towards the final A Level (Gove 2014) and in practice most schools do not offer AS levels at all. Numbers taking A Level Latin have recently fallen for the first time to fewer than 1,000 (985 in 2023) (OCR 2023).

In 2010, the English Baccalaureate, or EBacc, was introduced as a performance measure for schools. Without being a qualification in itself, it was designed to encourage schools and their students to take at least five of their GCSEs in subjects originally framed as 'core academic' subjects (Department for Education 2017); these include ancient languages and Ancient History but not Classical Civilization. This stance may have had an initial effect on the curriculum in some state schools, as already noted, although numbers taking ancient language

GCSEs do not seem to have changed significantly in that time. For GCSE Ancient History, however, entries have been a little below or a little above 1,000 since 2013, compared with 200 in 2011. The 2023 entry figure of 1,249 (OCR 2023) possibly suggests some effect of the EBacc on school leaders in determining their GCSE offer. As noted, where classical subjects are offered, there seems to be a positive level of interest from students. In 2023 in the UK, for example, classical subjects ranked number five in terms of GCSE enrolment increases for 'titles that cover a range of subjects' (JCQ 2023).

A relatively small number of schools also offer classical subjects via the International Baccalaureate Diploma, or IB, for students aged fifteen to nineteen. Like A Levels, IB qualifications are included for admission to university courses. There are eighteen universities in England offering Classics-related courses at undergraduate level (Bachelors' degree, a level six qualification) and courses have evolved to give access to those applicants with no classical background.

The status of Classics in England

Up to the mid-twentieth century, Classics had been seen as 'the bedrock of an elite education in the UK' (Hodgkinson 2021: 106) until what were seen as two main 'crises' (Culham & Edmunds 1989): firstly, in 1960 the universities of Cambridge and Oxford dropped O Level Latin (an examination taken at age sixteen, later replaced by GCSEs) as a compulsory entry requirement; secondly, the proposal for 'comprehensivization' of secondary schooling, as mentioned above. The Classics community, however, worked hard to evolve and address potential misconceptions about classical subjects, resulting in the establishment of the Joint Association of Classical Teachers (a UK organization for the promotion of Classics in schools and universities, known as JACT), under the impetus of John Sharwood Smith, a lecturer in Classics Education at the London Institute of Education, among others. JACT has since been absorbed into the Classical Association (CA) but they and individuals following in the footsteps of Sharwood Smith continue to work to sustain and expand access to classical subjects.

Attitudes towards Classics, in politics, in schools and in different regions, are varied and complex but 'Classics poverty' in secondary education in the UK has remained with us since the 1970s (Hunt & Holmes-Henderson 2021: 1). Indeed, the government is seeking to address this with the Latin Excellence Programme established in 2022 'to increase the uptake and attainment in Latin in state schools across England' (Centre for Latin Excellence n.d.). Inevitably, factors such as school funding, teacher-training places and education policy have had a significant impact on numbers studying classical subjects up to A Level or IB. The IB organization has recently taken the decision to withdraw its qualification in Classical Greek and Roman Studies, first introduced in 2010, after 2025, for reasons of economic viability. This suggests that important factors in where classical subjects are offered may be financial rather than ideological.

In the Key Stage 3 curriculum, Latin dominates in independent schools as the most commonly taught language after French, German and Spanish, with Greek at a similar level to Mandarin (British Council 2023). In the state sector at this level, it seems that Latin and Greek are more commonly part of an extra-curricular offer (British Council 2023). Nevertheless, similar numbers of state and independent schools currently offer classical subjects at examination level with around 350 schools in each sector (Hunt 2023b). Because of the wide range of curriculum patterns, it is difficult to make any generalizations beyond the fact that in practice classical subjects are optional in many schools and many schools will not offer all four subjects.

Of the four subjects, Classical Civilization has the largest number of examination candidates. In 2023 there were 4,540 entries (OCR 2023) for GCSE Classical Civilization, the highest number since the 1990s, and the picture is similar for A-Level. Interest in promoting non-linguistic classics seems to spread beyond those already involved in Classics education. The Advocating Classics Education (ACE) Project in the UK has gained significant funding from the Arts and Humanities Research Council (AHRC). It aims to promote the teaching of Classical Civilization and Ancient History in state schools and was founded on the premise that these subjects have already proven popular and successful (Hall & Holmes-Henderson 2017). ACE, along with other organizations, of which more below, has done much to offer training and to 'upskill' teachers to introduce classical subjects.

Perceptions by school leaders and others of Latin and Greek as elitist may also vary by region. While non-linguistic Classics remain relatively popular across England, access to A-Level Latin is much more likely in London and the south-east of England (Hunt & Holmes-Henderson 2021). There have been significant moves to address some of the potentially negative perceptions of Classics and it is important to note here the strength of feeling and the tireless work of individuals and groups to challenge inequalities of access, which will be discussed later.

Current trends in Classics teaching

Categorizing language courses with an admittedly blunt instrument, we might say they fall into two camps: reading courses, such as the *Cambridge Latin Course* (*CLC*) (CSCP 2022) and *Suburani* (Hands Up Education 2021), and courses leaning towards a grammar-translation approach, such as *De Romanis* (Radice et al. 2020), Cullen and Taylor's *Latin to GCSE* (2016) and Taylor's *Greek to GCSE* (2016). In England, *CLC*, first published in 1970 by the Cambridge School Classics Project (CSCP) set the tone for what are termed reading courses. It adopts an inductive approach, or 'reading-first' (Clapp 2013: 51), whereby reading is not the same as decoding, nor the same as translating. As such, *CLC* presents a continuing narrative, set in the first century CE, with recurring characters, and an emphasis not only on language but on the culture of the ancient world; the latter is made explicit in the second of the course's aims:

> The course presents the language not as an end in itself, nor as an instrument of general mental training, but rather as a means of gaining access to a literature and the culture from which it springs.
>
> (CSCP 1982: 12)

Although schools rarely use the fifth (and final) volume, and often very little of the fourth, even six years ago the *CLC* was used in some way by 93 per cent of schools (personal communication: Caroline Bristow, Director of CSCP, 13 October 2023) and the lead fictionalized character, Caecilius, had made such an impact that he served as a basis for the 'Fires of Pompeii' episode of the BBC's *Doctor Who* (Hales & Paul 2011).

Nevertheless, an increased awareness of social justice issues has meant that aspects of the course did not meet twenty-first century needs (for example, Churchill 2006; Parodi 2020; Perale 2023). A glance at the CSCP blog is indicative of the project's recognition of the need to support diversity and CSCP has now produced new editions of the first two books (CSCP 2022; 2023) which offer 'improved representation of women, people of colour, those with disabilities and marginalised groups such as enslaved men and women' (Bristow 2022b). The change in gender balance, not least the introduction of a new female character and the shift in perspective on enslavement, has been noted and welcomed (Hayes 2023; Johnson 2023). A number of other characters have been introduced or adapted to show a wider range of diversity. See, for example, the fictionalized character Barbillus, 'redrawn to reflect the Greco-Syrian-Egyptian heritage' of the real Barbillus who inspired the character (Bristow 2022a).

Issues of diversity have also been addressed in a newer reading course, *Suburani*, produced by the not-for-profit organization Hands Up Education (2021). Although it seems, anecdotally, that *CLC* still has the market share, *Suburani* is becoming increasingly popular. Like CSCP, the authors' intention was to create a character-driven narrative course, with 'characters with whom students could identify. . .[to] attract a more diverse set of students' (Delaney et al. 2020: 77). This meant focusing on ordinary people and places, 'with sensitivity to issues that are now so important to students and teachers: enslavement, imperialism, diversity, gender, sexuality' (Tims 2022). The authors were also able to draw on up-to-date evidence, for example, making use of information on the more 'unexpected trades' of women, such as working as a fishmonger' and using archaeological evidence such as skeletons in Londinium of Black African ancestry (Delaney et al. 2020: 78). The narrative arc, which would reach 'all corners of the Empire', also increased the potential diversity of the course and the course hopes to engage students in 'investigat[ing] the more complex and nuanced aspects of Roman civilization' (Delaney et al. 2020: 79–80).

Swallow gives examples of his experiences of teaching 'difficult stories' (2023: 162) using another relatively new Latin course, *De Romanis* (Radice et al. 2020). *De Romanis* is intended to differ from reading courses and 'tends towards grammar-translation' (Wall 2021: 125), specifically explaining new material before practising it, or 'grammar-first' (Clapp 2013: 51). It differs, too, from what are sometimes called 'traditional' grammar-translation courses: like *CLC* and *Suburani*, *De Romanis* emphasizes culture as well as language and the Teacher's Guide suggests that interest in the Roman world should be 'centre-stage', with the cultural theme of each chapter intended to be introduced before looking at the Latin (Bloomsbury n.d.). Each book centres on a theme, firstly Roman religion and secondly Roman history (Radice et al. 2020). The course counters *CLC*'s and *Suburani*'s setting in the late first century CE, noting that most of the literature learners will go on to read predates this period. Instead, it introduces learners to authors such as Virgil and Cicero and includes specific source material in its 'Sources to Study' sections, which are designed to lend themselves to an Ancient History or Classical Civilization approach, so helping to prepare any students who might go on to study either subject at GCSE. The course has other innovative aspects, such as a separation of 'core' and 'additional' language, to allow for adaptive teaching. The additional language sections include opportunities to write from English into Latin, currently an option on the GCSE Latin language paper. (It should be noted that *Suburani* also promotes this option in a way not traditionally associated with reading courses.) Vocabulary is seen as the 'single most important ingredient' (Bloomsbury n.d.) and is introduced before reading.

Bloomsbury also produces other commonly used courses: *Latin to GCSE* (Cullen & Taylor 2016) and its equivalent *Greek to GCSE* (Taylor 2016). In creating their course, Cullen and Taylor make no apology for moving away from the reading course approach (Williams 2023). There is, for example, no paralinguistic ancient civilization material introduced in the first chapter. Nevertheless, in the Latin course book, the passages 'have been selected both for their intrinsic interest . . . and for their importance in Roman history' (Cullen & Taylor 2016: x). The first book of the course focuses initially on the Trojan War and Aeneas's journey, then on the founding of Rome itself and the first kings. The second concentrates on the early Republic and culminates (almost) in the assassination of Julius Caesar, before wider-ranging revision passages.

While Latin teachers increasingly use more than one Latin course, *Greek to GCSE* (Taylor 2016) appears to have cornered the market and it is rare to encounter a school department teaching Greek at this level with anything else. Like its Latin counterpart, it has been revised to prepare students for the GCSE and is endorsed by the examinations board OCR. Many Greek learners already study or have studied Latin and *Greek to GCSE*, taking a 'fairly traditional' approach 'does not eschew comparisons [with Latin]' (Taylor 2016: ix.). Each section 'concentrates on stories with one source or subject' (Taylor 2016: ix) and Book 1 ranges from Aesop to Homer and some Greek history. Book 2 also covers historical topics such as the Persian Wars, as well as philosophy and Greek myths.

Since the introduction of the reformed examinations (first teaching in September 2016 for languages and 2017 for Classical Civilization and Ancient History) publishers Bloomsbury Academic have produced course books endorsed for the examinations in all four classical subjects. Ancient History examinations at GCSE and A-level seek to develop learners' ability to interrogate the past. The two 'period studies' focus on the process of change and the two 'depth studies' on understanding events and historical questions. Each level includes literary and archaeological sources. There is a more explicit focus on themes and ideas in Classical Civilization. At GCSE it is also divided into two strands, a 'Thematic Study' and 'Literature and Culture' and the A-Level is divided into three areas, one of which is purely literary, involving the study of epics. Across 'Culture and the Arts' and 'Beliefs and Ideas', the sources vary: for example, purely visual and material sources for the study of the 'Greek Art' and purely literary sources in the 'Politics of the Late Republic'.

All of the books offer additional online resources, such as videos, quizzes and suggestions for further reading. They give clear instructions on the format of the examinations and examination suggestions such as, for Ancient History GCSE, consideration of 'second order concepts . . . change and continuity; cause; consequence; significance; similarity and difference' (Fowler et al. 2017: 6). The books on both subjects are constructed thematically and usually begin with brief summaries, before outlining the examination format. Perhaps predictably, given the breadth of each subject's specification, it is difficult to highlight any particular pedagogical trends.

One trend which has arisen across classical subjects is the increasing use of online tools for teaching. All the books mentioned have some online resources and/or activities, not least the *CLC* where the material has been developed over two decades; in 2000, the government awarded the Cambridge School Classics Project, then under the leadership of Bob Lister, funding to develop digital materials, beginning with videos, and online activities such as vocabulary testers and online parsing, and moving onto more interactive digital learning

(Colvin & Hay 2020). A similar wealth of resources is available for *Suburani*. This more interactive use of technology in the classroom predates the Covid-19 lockdowns and perhaps exemplifies two recent major shifts in pedagogy identified by Natoli and Hunt (2019): firstly, towards more 'active learning methods that emphasize critical thinking and collaboration', and in Greek and especially Latin

> a growth in the variety of methodological approaches to teaching language, with grammar translation and reading approaches being joined by linguistic, spoken and comprehensible input (CI) methods.
>
> (Natoli & Hunt 2019: 18)

In terms of active learning, teachers are increasingly using technological tools for promoting active participation, for supporting collaboration and for checking learning. They can be used for conveying material, to promote engagement, or to give feedback to teachers. Teachers may be familiar with the SAMR model, where technology is used for task Substitution, Augmentation, Modification or Redefinition. Substitution merely replaces an analogue task without enhancing it pedagogically, such as a worksheet being completed online. For augmentation, the technological possibilities also enhance it: a *Kahoot!* quiz has advantages over pen and paper, for example, in allowing the teacher to see which questions proved challenging. Perhaps the most effective aspects of SAMR are modification, which uses technology to redesign the task or activity, and redefinition, which allows for the creation of new activities which would not have been feasible without the technology. Modification could allow students to collaborate on an activity such as designing a guide to the forum, created online and allowing real time collaboration, as well as timely feedback from the teacher and each other. A redefinition task might involve creating a virtual trip: the Google Arts and Culture website, for example, allows an online exploration of thousands of museums, as well as 'tours' such as a tour of Greece and how it has been shaped by its history, while Hay (2019) suggests a walk-through ancient Alexandria via *Assassin's Creed: Origins* while teaching *CLC* Stage 17. The adaptation of video games for education is perhaps the most widespread use in the redefinition category in Classics. For example, Cannatella (2022) has experimented with the *Rome: Total War* saga to increase motivation in conveying Ancient History content; and Craft (2019) uses *Minecraft* for engagement in language acquisition.

Collaboration and the promotion of student agency in the Classics classroom seem to be the most cited advantages of technology, such as the use of Microsoft OneDrive and OneNote or Google Classroom. It allows live editing during a discussion, for example, of Latin literature (Lewis 2019). The use of technology can also remind us of alternative approaches to student engagement. Moore (2023) found that using the chat function in online learning allowed for more inclusion and participation, something which Lewis (2019) also found. In a similar vein, the use of anonymous posts in apps such as Padlet and Mentimeter seems to encourage greater participation, as Cleary (2022) found, with students feeling better able to take risks in responding, which also provides a platform for peer comments and questions.

Artificial Intelligence, or AI, for education is still in relative infancy. ChatGPT might help teachers to create questions and provide feedback or it might help students to generate responses (see Ross 2023, who notes that it appears to be less reliable for Greek grammar than for Latin). Magic School AI might be used similarly, and to create model answers (exemplar or non-exemplar), to summarize YouTube videos and generally create more personalized learning to assist adaptive teaching. On a larger scale, researchers from the universities of Bristol, Bath and King's College London have established the Virtual Reality Oracle Project to explore the ancient world, designed primarily for supporting A-Level Classical Civilization, using virtual reality to 'elicit higher feelings of presence compared to conventional 2D displays' (Jicol et al. 2023: 2).

Another shift in pedagogy in recent years has been in various forms of Active or Living Latin. This approach has been popular for some time in the USA, led by experts such as Bob Patrick (2019), and has now gathered some support in England, having largely disappeared as a practice in the early twentieth century. Proponents of Active or Living Latin take their inspiration from Krashen's principles of language acquisition (and it is *acquisition* of language rather than language *learning*) and in particular his Comprehensible Input (CI) Hypothesis (Krashen & Terrell 1983). Patrick (2019) gives a clear summary. In the classroom, this has often taken the form of Teaching Proficiency Through Reading and Storytelling, or TPRS, whereby the teacher uses stories and personalized questions and answers (PQA) to provide Comprehensible Input in the target language (Bracey 2019). Whether using TPRS or other versions, the input should be 'comprehensible, compelling, and caring' (Ash 2019: 65).

Teacher training and professional development

There are now significantly more opportunities to train to teach Classics in England than there were some twenty years ago, with eleven institutions (including school-based organizations) on the government teacher training website offering twenty post-graduate routes for the academic year 2024/25. In addition, Classics for All (CfA) a UK charity founded in 2010, has had a profound impact on opportunities for teaching and learning classical subjects in state schools. Much of their work involves training 'non-specialist' teachers (that is, teachers who are qualified in other subjects than Classics) to offer classical subjects in their schools, thereby supporting schools to introduce Classics, in particular in areas of low social mobility. Even so, schools often struggle to recruit Classics teachers, notably in some areas of the country, such as the north and the midlands. Retention is also an issue; in England, teacher recruitment regularly falls below the target number of teachers required to meet rising numbers of pupils and retention is also falling (Fullard & Zuccollo 2021).

My own research has suggested that classicists are often drawn to teaching by an 'attachment' to classical subjects (Khan-Evans 2013: 17) and this might suggest that 'updating knowledge and skills' (Taylor et al. 2021: 215) is a particularly important aspect of continuing professional development. Since the Covid-19 pandemic, there has been a welcome proliferation of online support and training for classicists. The Classical Association hosts a wealth of resources for teaching classical subjects, including podcasts and videos to support exams, and resources for learning enrichment, such as the Panoply Vase Animations Project and the Trojan War Podcasts. A number of active regional Classical Association branches host resources on the website. Many of these also relate to examination material but not all: Dr Ian Goh on Roman Food and Dr Amy Coker on Ancient Greek Swearing look particularly interesting.

Teaching can be a solitary profession and a feeling of isolation might be particularly acute in small Classics departments; the opportunity to meet and exchange ideas with other Classics teachers is a valued aspect of professional development, Taylor's 'collaboration with colleagues' category (Taylor et al. 2021: 215) also providing opportunities for reflection. These numerous opportunities range from hour-long, often online 'teachmeets', to bigger conferences. The Classical Association Teaching Board regularly holds professional development events focused on each of the classical subjects and hosts some of the material from past events on its website. Large conferences are organized annually by the Classical Association, Cambridge School Classics Project, and Hands Up Education, as well as the Association for Latin Teaching, run by practising teachers, which supports classical subjects in schools more broadly. The Classical Association conference has worked hard in recent years to engage with teachers by including more pedagogy-focused papers, along with papers dealing with more inclusive aspects of Classics teaching. Panels for 2023 included 'Pedagogy and Inequalities', which had a focus on gender, 'Growing Classics via Innovative and Inclusive Pedagogies', including the Queering the Past(s) project, and 'Decolonising Classics in the Secondary School Classroom'. Support from the Classical Association and other organizations will be discussed further below.

Joined-up thinking

Perhaps because of its somewhat niche position on the curriculum, Classics education is strongly supported through collaboration between multiple large organizations, such as universities and museums. Lecturers from King's College London, in collaboration with Classics for All (CfA), produced videos to enrich the teaching of Classical Civilization and Ancient History and organized professional development on how to use them. The University of Birmingham has set up a new project entitled Classics in the Classroom which is building up exam-related resources for the classroom, starting with the Late Roman Republic. The Warwick Classics Network also alongside CfA, hosts numerous resources for teachers, including videos for past online professional development events. The University of Oxford's resources include TL;DR animations (Virgil, Cicero, the *Iliad*) and it also supports workshops and classes for children, families and other visitors at the Iris Classics Centre, as part of the Iris Project founded in 2013 by Lorna Robinson (2019). Iris Project activities include 'Literacy through Latin', in association with a number of universities, which offers teaching to schools in disadvantaged urban areas

As already noted, CfA has made a significant contribution to Classics outreach and has supported community-based projects, such as the University of Leicester's Life in the Roman World, an archaeology and Classics-focused project with the aim of 'encourag[ing] life-long engagement in the local community and its history' (Scott et al. 2022: 36). The project includes resources developed from up-to-date research at the university, designed for use in Key Stages 2 and 3 across a range of subjects, including History, English, Art and Design Technology. Design Technology also formed the basis for an Iris Project on Roman mosaics, with students aged twelve and thirteen designing and constructing mosaics (Robinson 2019).

Continuing a focus on material culture, the Attic Inscriptions Online project (originally founded by Professor Stephen Lambert at Cardiff University) has now evolved into other projects using the expertise of researchers to 'foster enthusiasm for the ancient Greek world' (Liddell 2022: 36). The translated Greek inscriptions of the Attic Inscriptions: Education (AI:E) project not only support GCSE and A-Level but provide guidance and resources for teaching Key Stages 1 and 2 History. The collaboration also involves museum colleagues such as the British Museum, which presented a Continuing Professional Education (CPD) day for teachers.

The AI:E project follows in the footsteps of a collaboration between the Ashmolean Museum and the universities of Oxford and Warwick, the Ashmolean Latin Inscriptions Project (AshLI), a three-year collaboration aimed to 'tell stories of Roman life, using inscriptions as a starting point' (Masséglia 2016: 31) and their website provides a multitude of free online resources. Museums, of course, are key sites of community engagement with the ancient world; Advocating Classical Education (ACE) partnered with National Museums Liverpool to create interactive sourcebooks for GCSE Classical Civilization, while the Ure Museum of Archaeology with the University of Reading has developed outreach activities, including the Ancient Schoolroom (Dickey 2015), for example.

As well as the organizations above supporting schools, inter-school collaborations in the form of independent state school partnerships have been successful in not only widening access to classical subjects but in engendering a sense of community. Such has been the success of these approaches that a charity to support them has recently been set up. Although not exclusive to Classics, the School Partnership Alliance aims to support the exchange of pedagogy, ideas and resources between the two sectors and this can often include extending Classics teaching to learners within the local community. This can be particularly important in areas of 'Classics poverty'. There are numerous instances of these, some of which are detailed in publications on the Independent Schools Council website. Collaborators on such projects are not simply looking to create fun ways to teach people about the ancient world; they see the projects as genuine knowledge exchange, using clearly thought out and up-to-date research and pedagogy. This is one of many 'reasons to be cheerful' (Thicknesse 2021) about Classics teaching in England.

Conclusion: reasons to be cheerful

Thanks to those in the Classics community, there are several bright spots. While there is still work to be done, learners have increasing access to classical subjects. The number of Latin learners in schools supported by CfA has increased from 2,241 in 2015 to 23,184 in 2022 (Classics for All 2023); CfA's learners of Classical Civilization are much fewer at 3,982 but have nonetheless also increased more than ten-fold in that time; Greek has risen from ten to 224. Away from the school-setting, summer schools in classical subjects attract high numbers, often being oversubscribed (Robinson 2019; Merali-Smith & Nongbri 2022; Stephenson 2023).

One of the most notable shifts in recent years is perhaps the ever-increasing sense of community, which is so important to Classics educators and is perhaps one of the elements which attracts learners. This extends across sectors and levels of experience and the community is working hard to ensure all learners, educators and researchers feel welcome. Inequality and access are being challenged by multiple groups, including some of those mentioned such as the Classical Association, Classics for All and Advocating Classical Education. The Cambridge School Classics Project's commitment to representing people of colour in its updated course has been noted; but we are also ever more aware of the fact that simply representing different races does not in itself equal inclusivity.

In addition, more specific groups are working on Equality, Diversity and Inclusion. For example, the Network for Working Class Classicists was launched in 2021 to tackle inequality and access issues while Professor Susan Deacy has worked for several years on the potential for classical myth to engage children with autism (Deacy 2019) leading to the project 'Our Mythical

Childhood'. Similarly, Professor Ray Lawrence has helped to make Classics more accessible through his own experience of dyslexia (Lawrence 2021) and in 2021, a group of neurodivergent classicists set up Asterion to raise the profile of, and celebrate, neurodiversity in Classics. The creators also seek to address barriers to inclusion more widely. In their research to establish the website, it became clear to them that women and people of colour are disadvantaged in the processes of diagnosis; poverty and neurodiversity are often linked; and there are often intersections between neurodivergence and LGBTQ+ communities (Fraser 2021).

When a strong argument for the worth of classical subjects includes the potential understanding of what it is to be human and how we communicate and connect with each other, such fora and the plethora of individuals and groups who act as a means of support for Classics educators reinforces our sense of community. Long may it continue to thrive.

References

Ash, R. (2019), 'Untextbooking for the CI Latin class: why and how to begin', *Journal of Classics Teaching*, 20 (39): 65–70.

BBC (2008), Education – school Latin rise 'an illusion', *BBC News* 5 January: http://news.bbc.co.uk/2/hi/uk_news/education/7172077.stm.

Bloomsbury (n.d.), *Notes for the teacher: an introduction to the course*. Available online: https://res.cloudinary.com/bloomsbury-online-resources/image/upload/v1651248773/deRomanisBk1/TG%20page/Notes_20for_20the_20teacher__20an_20introduction_20to_20de_20Romanis1.pdf (accessed 30 September 2023).

Bourne, M. (2017), *Independent State School Partnerships (ISSP): Impact of and Lessons Learnt. Research Report, July 2017*, London: Department for Education.

Bracey, J. (2019), 'TPRS, PQA & circling', *Journal of Classics Teaching* 20 (39): 60–4.

Bracke, E. (2023), *Classics at Primary School: A Tool for Social Justice*, London: Routledge.

Bristow, C. (2022a), [Blog] 'Old friends – Barbillus', Cambridge School Classics Project, 20 May. Available online: https://blog.cambridgescp.com/old-friends-barbillus (accessed 2 October 2023).

Bristow, C. (2022b), [Blog] 'The Story's the Thing', Cambridge School Classics Project, 26 May. Available online: https://blog.cambridgescp.com/the-storys-the-thing (accessed 2 October 2023).

British Council (2023), 'Language Trends 2022–23', London: The British Council. Available online: https://www.britishcouncil.org/sites/default/files/language_trends_england_2023.pdf (accessed 15 August 2023).

British Council (2020), 'Language Trends 2020', London: The British Council. Available online: https://www.britishcouncil.org/sites/default/files/language_trends_2020_0.pdf (accessed 15 August 2023).

British Council (2022), 'Language Trends 2021–22', London: The British Council. Available online: https://www.britishcouncil.org/sites/default/files/language_trends_report_2022.pdf (accessed 15 August 2023).

Cannatella, P. (2022), 'Student and teacher perceptions of the value of Total War: Saga in motivating KS3 students in an all-boys state school', *Journal of Classics Teaching*, 23 (45): 22–32.

Cartledge, P. (1998), 'Classics: from discipline in crisis to (multi-)cultural capital', in Y. Too and N. Livingstone (eds), *Pedagogy and Power: Rhetorics of Classical Learning*, Cambridge: Cambridge University Press, 16–28.

Centre for Latin Excellence (n.d.), *The Programme, Centre for Latin Excellence*. Available online: https://latinexcellence.org/the-programme (accessed 17 November 2023).

Churchill, L. (2006), 'Is There a Woman in This Textbook? Feminist Pedagogy and Elementary Latin', in J. Gruber-Miller (ed.), *When Dead Tongues Speak. Teaching Beginning Greek and Latin*, Oxford: Oxford University Press, 86–109.

Clapp, D. (2013), 'De Lingua Latina Discenda: Five Recent Textbooks for Introductory Latin', *Teaching Classical Languages*, 5 (1): 50–69.

Classics for All (2023), Classics for All Impact Report 2010–2022. Available online: https://classicsforall. org.uk/sites/default/files/uploads/impact%20report/Classics-for-All_Impact-Report_2010-2022_ Digital.pdf (accessed 10 November 2023).

Cleary, C. (2022), 'A Case Study Investigation of Year 8 Students' Experiences with Online Learning Through the Padlet App in a State-Maintained Girls' Grammar School', *Journal of Classics Teaching*, 23 (46): 165–75.

Colvin, I. and L. Hay (2020), 'Ancient Languages and the Modern Learner: The Effective Use of Digital Resources in the Latin Classroom'. Available online: https://macau.uni-kiel.de/servlets/ MCRFileNodeServlet/macau_derivate_00002430/kiel-up_2703-0784_p29.pdf (accessed 17 October 2023).

Craft, J. (2019), 'Bridging the Gap Between Students and Antiquity: Language Acquisition Videos with Minecraft and CI / TPRS', in B. Natoli and S. Hunt (eds), *Teaching Classics with Technology*, London: Bloomsbury, 181–92.

CSCP (1982), Cambridge School Classics Project, *Cambridge Latin Course, 1: Teacher's Handbook*, Cambridge: Cambridge University Press.

CSCP (2020), Cambridge School Classics Project, 'Black Lives Matter: Statement from CSCP'. Available online: https://www.cambridgescp.com/black-lives-matter-statement-cscp (accessed 15 August 2023).

CSCP (2022), Cambridge School Classics Project, *Cambridge Latin Course, Book 1, 5th edition*, Cambridge: Cambridge University Press.

CSCP (2023), Cambridge School Classics Project, *Cambridge Latin Course, Book 2: 5th edition*, Cambridge: Cambridge University Press.

Culham, P. and L. Edmunds, eds (1989), *Classics: A Discipline and Profession in Crisis?* New York and London: University Press of America.

Cullen, H. and J. Taylor (2016), *Latin to GCSE*, London: Bloomsbury Academic.

Deacy, S. (2019), [Blog] 'Autism and classical myth'. Available online: https://ics.blogs.sas.ac. uk/2019/05/09/autism-and-classical-myth/ (accessed 14 August 2023).

Dearing, R. (1996), *Review of Qualifications for 16–19 Year Olds*, Hayes: SCAA Publications.

Delaney, C., W. Griffiths, H. Smith, T. Smith and L. Tims (2020), 'Character-Based Learning in *Suburani*: Why the Who Matters', *The Classical Outlook*, 95 (3): 77–83.

Department for Education (2013), 'National curriculum in England: framework for key stages 1 to 4'. Available online: https://www.gov.uk/government/collections/national-curriculum (accessed 28 September 2023).

Department for Education (2016), 'GCE as an A level classical civilisation'. Available online: https:// www.gov.uk/government/publications/gce-as-and-a-level-classical-civilisation (accessed 28 October 2023).

Department for Education (2017), 'English baccalaureate: Equality analysis.' Available online: https:// www.gov.uk/government/publications/english-baccalaureate-equality-analysis (accessed 28 September 2023).

Dickey, E. (2015), 'An Immersion Class in Ancient Education', *Journal of Classics Teaching*, 16 (31): 38–40.

Forrest, M. (1996), *Modernising the Classics*, Exeter: University of Exeter Press.

Fowler, P., C. Grockock and J. Melville (2017), *OCR Ancient History GCSE Component 2*, London: Bloomsbury Academic.

Fraser, C. (2021), 'Building Asterion: Support for Neurodiversity in Classics', Asterion, Council of University Classics Departments, 31 August. Available online: https://cucdedi.wordpress. com/2021/08/31/building-asterion-support-for-neurodiversity-in-classics/ (accessed 10 October 2023).

Fullard, J. and J. Zuccollo (2021), *Local Pay and Teacher Retention in England*, London: Education Policy Institute.

Gove, M. (2014), [Speech] 'GCSE and A level reform'. Available online: https://www.gov.uk/ government/speeches/gcse-and-a-level-reform (accessed 8 October 2023).

Grigsby, P. (2020), 'Bringing classics to the state schools of the Midlands: A year in the life of the WCN', *Journal of Classics Teaching*, 21 (42): 88–91.

Hales, S. and J. Paul (2011), 'Pompeii and the Cambridge Latin Course', in S. Hales and J. Paul (eds), *Pompeii in the Public Imagination from its Rediscovery to Today*, Oxford: Oxford University Press, 356–66.

Hall, E. and A. Holmes-Henderson (2017), 'Advocating Classics Education – a new national project', *Journal of Classics Teaching*, 18 (36): 25–8.

Hands Up Education (2021), *Suburani*, Haverhill: Hands Up Education.

Hayes, E. (2023), [Blog] 'First Impressions of the new book II'. Cambridge School Classics Project Blog. Available online: https://blog.cambridgescp.com/first-impressions-new-book-ii (accessed 23 August 2023).

Hay, L. (2019), 'In the Classroom with Multi-Modal Teaching', in B. Natoli and S. Hunt (eds), *Teaching Classics with Technology*, London: Bloomsbury, 229–38.

Hodgkinson, D. (2021), 'Classics for the Future: A Time for Reflection', *Journal of Classics Teaching*, 22 (44): 106–8.

Holmes-Henderson, A. and K. Kelly (2022), 'Ancient Languages in Primary Schools in England: A Literature Review', Department for Education. Available online: https://assets.publishing.service.gov. uk/government/uploads/system/uploads/attachment_data/file/1120024/Ancient_languages_in_ primary_schools_in_England_-_A_Literature_Review.pdf (accessed 28 September 2023).

Hunt, S. (2016), 'Teaching Sensitive Topics in the Secondary Classics Classroom', *Journal of Classics Teaching*, 17 (34): 31–43.

Hunt, S. (2022), 'Mind the Classics Gap. Current position of classical studies in English schools from Key Stage 2 to Key Stage 3. Challenges and solutions', *CUCD Bulletin*, 51. Available online: https:// cucd.blogs.sas.ac.uk/files/2022/09/Mind-the-Classics-Gap.pdf (accessed 27 November 2023).

Hunt, S. (2023a), 'Latin and Greek in English Primary Schools – seedlings of a classical education', *Journal of Classics Teaching*, 25 (49): 60–4.

Hunt, S. (2023b), 'Initial teacher education for classics. England, 2023. The current position', *CUCD Bulletin*, 53. Available online: https://cucd.blogs.sas.ac.uk/files/2023/10/Steven-Hunt-Latin-Education-final-2.10.23.pdf (accessed 27 November 2023).

Hunt, S. (2023c), *Starting to Teach Latin, 2nd edition*, London: Bloomsbury Academic.

Hunt, S. and A. Holmes-Henderson (2021), 'A level Classics poverty. Classical subjects in schools in England: access, attainment and progression', *CUCD Bulletin* 50. Available online: https://cucd.blogs. sas.ac.uk/files/2021/02/Holmes-Henderson-and-Hunt-Classics-Poverty.docx.pdf (accessed 2 October 2023).

Independent Schools Council (n.d.), *Independent Schools Council*. Available online: https://www.isc.co. uk/ (accessed 15 November 2023).

Iovino, R. (2019), 'Rethinking the teaching of Latin in the inclusive school', *Journal of Latin Linguistics*, 18 (1–2): 85–99.

JCQ (2023), *Appendix GCSE, Project, and entry level trends – UK, 2023 GCSE full course trends*. Available online: https://www.jcq.org.uk/wp-content/uploads/2023/08/GCSE-Project-and-Entry-Level-Trends-2023.pdf (accessed 6 September 2023).

Jicol, C., C. Clarke, E. Tor, H. Yip, J. Yoon, C. Bevan, H. Bowden, E. Brann, K. Cater, R. Cole and Q. Deeley (2023), 'Imagine That! Imaginative Suggestibility Affects Presence in Virtual Reality', *Proceedings of the 2023 CHI Conference on Human Factors in Computing Systems*, 1–11.

Joffe, B. (2019), 'Teaching the venalicius story in the age of #metoo: a reconsideration', *Classical Outlook*, 94 (3): 125–38.

Johnson, J. (2023), [Blog] 'Teaching the 5th edition: Reflections of a Latin teacher'. Cambridge School Classics Project Blog. Available online: https://blog.cambridgescp.com/teaching-5th-edition-reflections-a-latin-teacher (accessed 23 August 2023).

Khan-Evans, A. (2013), *Why Become a Classics Teacher?* [Ed.D thesis], London: King's College London.

Khan-Evans, A. (2018), 'The Appeal of Non-liguistic Classical Studies among Sixth-form Students', in A. Holmes-Henderson, S. Hunt and M. Musié (eds), Forward with Classics: *Classical Languages in Schools and Communities*, London: Bloomsburry Acadmic, 205–13.

Krashen, S. and T. Terrell (1983), *The Natural Approach Language Acquisition in the Classroom*, Oxford: Pergamon Press.

Lawrence, R. (2021), 'Why do I still weep? Thoughts on. . ', *Asterion: Celebrating Neurodiversity in Classics*, 18 November. Available online: https://asterion.uk/index.php/2021/11/18/learning-and-thriving-with-dyslexia/ (accessed 15 August 2023).

Le Hur, C. (2022), 'A New Classical Greek Qualification', *Journal of Classics Teaching*, 23 (45): 79–80.

Lewis, E. (2019), 'VLEs, Latin Literature, and Student Voice', in B. Natoli and S. Hunt (eds), *Teaching Classics with Technology*, London: Bloomsbury, 53–66.

Liddel, P. (2022), 'The Attic Inscriptions: Education Project', *Journal of Classics Teaching*, 23 (45): 35–9.

Long, R., A. Maisura and S. Danechi (2023), *Grammar schools in England – House of Commons Library*, London: House of Commons Library. Available online: https://commonslibrary.parliament.uk/research-briefings/sn07070/ (accessed 15 September 2023).

McMillan, I. (2015), 'Transformatio Per Complexitatem: The 20th Century Transformation of Latin Teaching in the UK', *Journal of Classics Teaching*, 16 (32): 25–32.

Masséglia, J. (2016), 'Rome's Walking Dead: Resurrecting a Roman Funeral at the Ashmolean Museum', *Journal of Classics Teaching*, 17 (33): 31–4.

Merali-Smith, S. and A. Nongbri (2022), 'The East London Classics Summer School', *Journal of Classics Teaching*, 23 (45): 73–4.

Mitropoulos, A., L. Snook and A. Thorley (2017), *OCR Classical Civilisation a Level: Components 23 and 24: Invention of the Barbarian and Greek Art*, London: Bloomsbury Academic.

Moore, J. (2023), '"Caecilius Est Internet": A Study of Year 7 Latin Beginners' Perspectives on the use of an Online Chat function and Breakout Rooms using the Cambridge Latin Course', *Journal of Classics Teaching*, 24 (48): 127–32.

Natoli, B. and S. Hunt (2019), *Teaching Classics with Technology*, London: Bloomsbury Academic.

OCR (2023), [Paper] 'Statistical Summary' presented at CATB Meeting, London, 6 September 2023.

Ofqual (2018), *Get the facts: AS and A level reform*. Available online: https://www.gov.uk/government/publications/get-the-facts-gcse-and-a-level-reform/get-the-facts-as-and-a-level-reform (accessed 10 September 2023).

Parodi, E. (2020), 'A critical investigation of Y7 students' perceptions of Roman slavery as evidenced in the stories of the Cambridge Latin Course', *Journal of Classics Teaching*, 21 (42): 43–54.

Patrick, R. (2019), 'Comprehensible input and Krashen's theory', *Journal of Classics Teaching*, 20 (39): 37–44.

Perale, M. (2023), '"I Still See the Elitism". Classical languages and the language of class at Liverpool', *Journal of Classics Teaching*, 24 (47): 26–33.

Radice, K., G. Lord, A. Cheetham and S. Kirk (2020), *De Romanis Book 1 dei et deae*, London: Bloomsbury Academic.

Robinson, L. (2019), 'Creation and Impact of Regional Centres of Excellence for Classics: The Iris Classics Centre at Cheney', in A. Holmes-Henderson, S. Hunt and M. Musié (eds), *Forward with Classics. Classical Languages in Schools and Communities*, London: Bloomsbury Academic, 149–60.

Ross, E. (2023), 'A New Frontier: AI and Ancient Language Pedagogy', *Journal of Classics Teaching*, 24 (48): 143–61.

Scott, S., G. Savani, J. Ainsworth, A. Hunt and l. Kuhivchak (2022), 'Roman worlds for diverse communities: Engaging new audiences with archaeology and classics', *Journal of Community Archaeology & Heritage*, 10 (1): 33–50.

Sibieta, L. (2022), 'Skills funding: Where could savings actually come from?', *FE Week*. Available online: https://feweek.co.uk/skills-funding-return-to-austerity/ (accessed 15 October 2023).

Stephenson, D. (2023), '43rd JACT Latin Summer School – 2023 Director's Report', *Journal of Classics Teaching*, 49: 1–5.

Swallow, P. (2023), 'Teaching Difficult Stories: Trauma-Informed Teaching in the Classics Classroom', *Journal of Classics Teaching*, 24 (48): 162–4.

Taylor, B., C. Daly, H. Gandolfi, P. Glegg, M. Hardman, C. Pillinger and B. Stiasny (2021), 'The Early Career Framework – A Guide for Implementation', Centre for Teachers and Teaching Research, UCL Institute of Education. Available online: https://discovery.ucl.ac.uk/id/eprint/10124271/ (accessed 28 January 2022).

Taylor, J. (2016), *Greek to GCSE 1*, London: Bloomsbury Academic.

Thicknesse, O. (2021), 'How can independent schools do Classics outreach effectively?', *Quinquennium*, 31 August. Available online: https://www.quinquennium.com/how-can-independent-schools-do-classics-outreach-effectively/ (accessed 10 October 2023).

Tims, L. (2022), 'Suburani: Writing a New Latin Reading Course', *Antigone*. Available online: https://antigonejournal.com/2022/03/suburani-new-latin-reading-course/ (accessed 20 October 2023).

UK Parliament (n. d.), Education Reform Act 1988. Available online: https://www.parliament.uk/about/living-heritage/transformingsociety/livinglearning/school/overview/educationreformact1988/ (accessed 10 October 2023).

Wall, E. (2021), 'Two New Latin Courses: Suburani and De Romanis', *Journal of Classics Teaching*, 22 (44): 123–5.

Williams, E. (2023), [Podcast] 'Tweaked traditionalism with John Taylor', 27 January 2023. Available online: https://podcasts.apple.com/gb/podcast/the-latin-tutor/id1652150324?i=1000596857234 (accessed 15 May 2023).

Winkley, L. (2022), [Blog] 'HMC Blog – Independent and State Partnerships', School Partnership Alliance. Available online: https://schoolpartnershipsalliance.org.uk/hmc-blog-independent-and-state-partnerships/ (accessed 10 October 2023).

List of organizations

Advocating Classical Education (ACE): https://aceclassics.org.uk/
Ashmolean Latin Inscriptions project: https://latininscriptions.ashmus.ox.ac.uk
Association for Latin Teaching (ARLT): https://www.arlt.co.uk
Asterion: https://asterion.uk
Attic Inscriptions: Education (AI:E): www.atticinscriptions.com/education
Attic Inscriptions Online: www.atticinscriptions.com
Cambridge School Classics Project (CSCP): https://www.cambridgescp.com/
Centre for Latin Excellence / Latin Excellence programme: https://latinexcellence.org/
Classical Association (CA): https://classicalassociation.org
Classics for All (CfA): https://classicsforall.org.uk
Classics in the Classroom (University of Birmingham): https://www.birmingham.ac.uk/schools/historycultures/departments/caha/outreach/classroom/index/aspx
Eduqas examinations: https://www.eduqas.co.uk/qualifications/latin-gcse/#tab_keydocuments
Google arts and culture website: https://artsandculture.google.com
Independent Schools Council: https://www.isc.co.uk
Intermediate Certificate in Classical Greek (ICCG): https://intermediategreekcert.com/
Iris Project: http://irisproject.org.uk/index.php
JACT Greek Summer School: https://www.greeksummerschool.org/
IB: https://ibo.org/
Life in the Roman World (University of Leicester): https://romanleicester.com/
National Museums Liverpool: www.liverpoolmuseums.org.uk
OCR (Oxford, Cambridge and RSA Examinations): https://ocr.org.uk/subjects/classics/
Our Mythical Childhood: http://omc.obta.al.uw.edu.pl/
Panoply Vase Animation Project: www.panoply.org.uk
Queering the Past(s) Project: https://classicalassociation.org/queering-the-past
School Partnerships Alliance: https://schoolpartnershipsalliance.org.uk
TL;DR (University of Oxford): https://www.youtube.com/@facultyofclassicsuniversit1458
Trojan War Podcasts: https://trojanwarpodcast.com
University of Oxford TL;DR: https://www.youtube.com/watch?v=klwQkx9SsSc
Ure Museum (University of Reading): https://collections.reading.ac.uk/ure-museum/
Virtual Reality Oracle Project: http://www.vroracle.co.uk
Warwick Classics Network: https://warwick.ac.uk/fac/arts/classics/classicsnetwork
WJEC examinations: https://www.wjec.co.uk/qualifications/latin-gcse#tab_keydocuments
Working Class Classicists: https://www.workingclassclassics.uk

---

UK: NORTHERN IRELAND

Amber Taylor and Arlene Holmes-Henderson

Introduction

Northern Ireland is home to 1.9 million people, the smallest of the UK's four nations. There are 794 primary schools and 192 post-primary schools (of which 66 are academically selective grammar schools and 126 are non-selective secondary schools) (Collen 2023: 5). The current Northern Ireland Primary Curriculum (NIC) was introduced in 2007 and places an emphasis on developing knowledge, understanding and skills in young people as individuals, as contributors to society, the environment and the economy. It sets out minimum requirements with flexibility of interpretation in a local context.

Hunt and Holmes-Henderson (2021) reported that access to Classics in English schools relied on 'wealth or luck'. In Northern Ireland, access to Classics in schools relies on prior attainment or luck since classical subjects are mostly restricted to academically selective or fee-paying secondary schools. Unlike other parts of the United Kingdom, Northern Ireland has no statutory curricular provision for languages (ancient or modern) in primary school. Language learning in Northern Ireland is compulsory at Key Stage 3 (ages 11–14), however the flexibility of interpretation means it is not compulsory in every year group. Northern Ireland thus has the shortest time for compulsory language learning of any country in the continent of Europe. Further, there is no government guidance on how much time should be spent on language learning; meaning that individual school principals decide on how much time is allocated for language learning (Collen 2023: 6). Most pupils learn a modern, not an ancient, language in the early stages of secondary school in Northern Ireland.

The Humanities curriculum in Northern Ireland exists within the WAU (World Around Us) framework (NIC 2007) which is organized under four interrelated strands: Interdependence; Place; Movement and Energy; and Change Over Time. With a skills-based curriculum, school leaders and teachers are empowered to choose the subject content for teaching and learning. In practice, because there is such scant access to the study of the Greeks and Romans in Northern Ireland, schoolteachers who were educated there (in school, university and teacher training) are unlikely to have learned enough Classics to feel confident in selecting this as a focus for student learning. It is a vicious circle.

Languages education in Northern Ireland

In the 2023 Languages Trends Northern Ireland survey (Collen 2023), no responding schools reported teaching Latin or Greek at Key Stages 3 to 5 (ages 11–18). French was offered at Key Stage 3 in 90 per cent of responding schools, Spanish in 80 per cent, Irish in 35 per cent of schools and German in 17 per cent of schools. At GCSE (national examination at age 16), Spanish attracts most candidates followed by French, Irish then German. At A-Level (national examination at age 17), the order is slightly different, with Irish making strides: Spanish, followed by Irish, then French, and lastly German. Where are the students of Latin and Greek? They do exist: in primary, post-primary and community settings. They are small in number but mighty in spirit, as the following case studies demonstrate.

Classics in primary schools

Language Trends Northern Ireland (Collen 2023) identified that Latin is being taught in the primary sector. While Spanish, French and Irish dominate, it is encouraging to see that 2.4 per cent of responding schools were teaching Latin at Key Stage 2 (ages 7–11).

It should be noted that languages in the primary sector are not compulsory in Northern Irish schools, unlike the curricula of mainland UK (Department for Education 2013). Conceptualizing Classics as an umbrella term, encompassing not only languages but also history, literature and mythology, it is easy to assume that it could fit nicely into the flexible skills-based curriculum Northern Ireland offers. While the NIC (2007) only explicitly mentions The Romans once when suggesting suitable topics for the Movement and Energy section of the Key Stage 2 World Around Us (WAU) specification, The Romans topic is considered by some teachers in NI to promote the cross-curricular framework of NIC (Taylor 2020). One teacher used The Romans to teach subjects such as WAU, Literacy, Numeracy and Personal Development and Mutual Understanding (PDMU) (Taylor 2020). This hints at a promising future; but we cannot escape the fact that many teachers in Northern Ireland are not confident in leading any classical topic at this level due to the lack of opportunity to study the subject during their own school experiences (Taylor et al. 2022; Taylor 2020).

Case study: the Romans in the world around us

Amber Taylor, Hollybank Primary School

I teach in a small primary school in the Greater Belfast area. Our curriculum, as I am sure any teacher in Northern Ireland would say, is jam-packed. I am lucky that my school allows each teacher to run their own club between 2 and 3pm on a Thursday. These clubs have a purpose: each club teaches the pupils a new skill or topic they would not normally experience. I chose to create a Classics club. During this time, we learn some Latin, the Greek alphabet (and we rap it too), we learn about the ancient gods and Socratic debate. All in all, the children who come to the club enjoy it. I find the best reactions come when you reveal something connected to a real-life context, like where we get the names for the planets, or why the alphabet is called the 'alphabet'. Even the revelation as to why some clocks have letters instead of numbers carries a real 'A-HA' moment. Children who have attended my club often come up to me in the corridor to say 'salve!' in Latin or rap the Greek alphabet as quickly as they can. Parents have informed me that some of the greatest memories their child had of primary school were learning about mythology with me. It is a real honour that I get to share my love of Classics and see it grow in children.

Across Northern Ireland, there is growing pressure for teachers to use digital technology to enhance their teaching. I ask the children to create slideshows of a Roman family annotated with some basic Latin sentences. They really enjoy creating digital collages of Roman gods and creating 'Top Trump' cards with the information they collected. Classics is definitely a subject that can be utilized in the modern age. I can stretch and challenge higher ability children with some etymology discussions and I can explore the difference between right and wrong using Socratic debate to settle playground arguments. Classics truly is the cross-curricular topic of any teacher's dreams – it is just a shame that this sentiment is not shared more widely in Northern Ireland.

Case study: ancient philosophy in the Ardoyne

Kevin McArevey, Principal

In Holy Cross Boys' primary school, we see philosophy as a way of life. You might have seen the film about our ancient philosophy teaching, *Young Plato*? It is a multi-award-winning observational documentary film set in post-conflict Ardoyne, which is a working-class Catholic area of north Belfast.

Firstly, let me establish what I believe philosophy to be – it is about making judgements, about what you think is right or wrong, true or false, possible or impossible. Equally, it is thinking about thinking in line with Plato's definition which involves analysing and questioning ideas. Hence, bringing these ideas together to see how they relate. You do philosophy in every aspect of your life. Thinking changes lives so to change the way you feel then change the way you think. Subsequently, it is our hope that the strategies and thinking from philosophy will be a lifeboat that will come along one day and save lives whenever someone is in a dark place and at their lowest ebb. We embrace philosophical themes for discussion with pupils, such as loneliness, bullying, anger, respect, racism, sexism, telling lies to stop you becoming another north Belfast suicide statistic, and realize that life is a gift, and you will be sorely missed by your amazing family. It is my belief that Stoic Philosophy lends itself to soothing generational trauma which will allow the boys to become the victor and not the victim.

Ardoyne is now a marginalized community dealing with poverty, dissident activity, drugs and alcohol problems. You will see many strategies/techniques used by the children in *Young Plato* and many of them are from The Philosophy Foundation (TPF). The TPF trained all of our staff and we are known as a TPF school. We need to respect and celebrate differences – tell me your story, tell me why you think that? You will understand why they disagree if you effectively listen – we do not have to agree. What we must do is learn to disagree with empathy because, 'What stands in the way becomes the way', according to Marcus Aurelius. The staff, community and parents of Ardoyne see that academic philosophy and street philosophy go hand-in-hand to help raise the standards and achievements of pupils, staff and the wider community of Holy Cross Boys.

Over the last ten years, we have seen ancient philosophy make significant impacts on our boys. From an academic perspective, they show improvements in literacy, independence in learning and deeper thinking skills. These skills are identified as priorities in a subsequent policy document to NIC 'Thinking Skills and Personal Capabilities' (CCEA 2019). Socially, students are better at solving problems together, exploring feelings and modelling inclusivity. Behaviourally, they show increased confidence, and self-esteem, greater respect for others, and quieter pupils speak up more. Please watch *Young Plato* online at www.youngplato.com – you will not be disappointed.

Classics in post-primary

The lack of policy support for classical subjects in the NIC makes it difficult to introduce and sustain classical subjects in the post-primary curriculum. Latin and Classical Civilization are taught at a handful of voluntary controlled academically selective grammar schools such as the Royal Belfast Academical Institution, Methodist College Belfast, Victoria College, Regent House Grammar School and Belfast High School.

Case study: Classics provision in a Northern Irish post-primary school

Julian King

This school is a selective grammar school in Northern Ireland. It welcomes 140 pupils per year at age eleven. The Classics department comprises a single member of staff.

Curriculum

Year 9 'Classics' is offered for sixty minutes per week to all pupils. This is designed as an introductory 'foundation' course. September–October: Greek mythology; October–November: Greek language (= alphabet, transliteration) using *Greeks and Romans* (Wright 2011); January–March: Roman legends (Wright 2011); April–June: Latin language, *sum*, *amo* (present tense) and *puella* (all cases), vocabulary × 50 (Zinn 2006).

Year 10 Pupils may choose to study Classical Civilization and/or Latin. Ninety minutes per week each, using *Discovering the Greeks* (Corsar 1977) and *The Legend of Odysseus* (Connolly 1986); and for Latin, *So You Really Want to Learn Latin?* (Oulton 2020).

Year 11 Those who have taken Latin in Year 10 may continue to the Oxford, Cambridge and RSA (OCR) GCSE examination. OCR GCSE Classical Civilization is open to all pupils, regardless of their Year 10 choices: 150 minutes per week each.

Year 13 Those who have taken Latin to GCSE may continue to OCR A-Level; OCR A-Level Classical Civilization is open to all pupils, regardless of their earlier choices (both OCR), 300 minutes per week each.

How does the landscape look for Classics in NI from your perspective?

By accident more than by design, I have little or no contact with any other schools or teachers. In my school, I enjoy the support of senior leadership, at least insofar as I am encouraged to offer the curriculum outlined above. However, when numbers fall below a certain (rather shrouded) total, I am obliged to teach interested students after school. I am willing and able to do this, but, looking to the future, it is obviously not really a viable model.

Barriers

An increasing number of subjects are competing for timetable time. In recent years, for example, extra 'literacy' and 'numeracy' lessons, beyond the standard English and Maths lessons, have been added to the KS3 timetable. 'Classics' comprises two distinct examination subjects: Latin is obliged to compete for potential students against Classical Civilization (and vice versa). It seems reasonable that students will often choose one but not both of the classical subjects. If one subject were to be abandoned, this might increase uptake in the other – but in my opinion, this is not a price worth paying.

We have an increasingly anxious, even fearful, student population. Many of our students crave the familiar, they fear anything unknown, especially if there is any perception of 'difficulty'. Their parents fail to challenge this approach to life. Hence my choice above of what I regard as primary school texts for use with junior classes (Wright 2011; Zinn 2006). Perceived 'irrelevance' is a barrier too. Even amongst students (and, often more importantly, parents) who do value classical subjects, it is difficult to make the case for the liberal arts in the context of constant STEM propaganda, from the Prime Minister down. Money: our school cannot afford to allow a member of staff to teach classes of four pupils, when I could be deployed to teach junior English or History to thirty.

It cannot be denied that, compared with the rest of the curriculum, GCSE and A-Level Latin are difficult. Diligent students can and do succeed – but there are no class discussions; there is no colouring-in. It therefore takes too long (until Year 12) for students to arrive at a standard high enough to allow them to access the most rewarding aspects of any given Latin course, notwithstanding the *Cambridge Latin Course* (Cambridge School Classics Project 2022).

What is going well?

My lessons go well; Classics in Year 9 is popular, often quoted as students' 'best' or 'favourite' subject – until choices have to be made. In recent years, typically thirty-five out of 140 have chosen to continue with Classical Civilization in Year 10; approximately twenty in Latin. The course content as devised by the examinations board OCR is, generally, a 'good thing'. I have minor criticisms, but students who follow any or all of these courses do, I think, receive quite a good classical grounding; they are more or less well prepared for further study. For those who choose to continue to GCSE and/or A-Level in either or both Classical Civilization/Latin, exam results tend to 'go well'.

Priorities for improvement

The perennial problem is, of course, numbers. After over thirty years in the job, I remain mystified as to why sometimes I will reap a crop of, say, twenty students for GCSE Classical Civilization; a year later the number might be eight. At A-Level, the numbers fluctuate between twelve and zero. It is the same story for Latin: at present I have none at sixth form level, one Year 11 and two Year 12 GCSE candidates. But it is perfectly possible that there might be six in next year's Year 11 class, rendering three (or more) for A-Level in 2026–8.

Recommendations

GCSE and A-Level Latin are rightly perceived to be hard. I think this is a virtue, but there is no doubt that it costs candidates. WJEC/Eduqas Latin examinations are, in my opinion, much less demanding – but for this very reason provide a less effective preparation for A-Level study. OCR should look at this. Attractive textbooks have helped in the past, and forty years ago, SUJB (the Southern Universities Joint Board) produced an O Level which tested the course as delivered by the *Cambridge Latin Course* (Cambridge School Classics Project 2022). But the *Cambridge Latin Course* does not adequately prepare students for the OCR examinations. Hence my use of the admittedly less attractive, but definitely more effective Oulton books. Perhaps *De Romanis* (Radice et al. 2020) works better? I don't know: these cost time and money to test.

What technologies do you use? Do you feel they improve your teaching/engagement?

Our school uses Google classroom for communication and document sharing. 'Quizziz' and 'Wordwall' for vocab learning can be said to 'improve engagement' – but for more senior students I consider most technology to be little more than gimmickry. Neither teachers nor students are deceived by bright colours or the use of 'devices' instead of books.

Community Classics

Case study: the Classical Association in Northern Ireland

Amber Taylor, CANI Outreach Officer

Currently, the majority of community outreach is carried out by the Classical Association in Northern Ireland (CANI). CANI's aim is to promote Ancient History and Classical Studies and to support education in these subjects throughout Northern Ireland. The committee consists of volunteers from schools, universities and third sector organizations who give their time and expertise for free. CANI's income derives currently from subscriptions. In the past, they have also enjoyed donations. Events are hosted every semester and are normally academic talks with speakers from universities across the UK and Ireland. As a result, attendees are often those studying or working in higher education.

Every year, CANI hosts an event in the Ulster Museum specifically targeting children of primary and post-primary age. The event is very well attended, with over 100 primary pupils for the morning session. The post-primary session of the event in 2023 saw almost forty pupils in attendance from different grammar schools. While CANI hopes to promote the study of the ancient world at this event, some pupils attending were studying Religious Studies A-Level at the time. They were invited specifically for CANI's talk on Constantine.

For primary age children, CANI focuses on supporting the NIC in a variety of practical activities. There is a presentation on ancient Greek drama with corresponding drama mask making. Additionally, children are invited to experience CANI's handling table. This table has an assortment of objects and items intended to stimulate young people's curiosity. These include coins, maps, board games (some children are lucky enough to get to play these), wax tablets and more. In recent years, CANI has also made use of new technology in 3D printing. Taken straight from scans of busts of emperors from the Louvre, children are allowed first hand experience with objects they may never have access to otherwise. Teachers remark every year on the joy and excitement exhibited by primary children during this event – a clear indication that Classics is a suitable topic for WAU.

The post-primary section of the event, while well-attended in 2023, is more difficult to get right. With rising bus costs, increased pressure on school attendance and fewer schools teaching classical subjects, it means that the scope of talks required to draw in more pupils becomes ever wider. CANI's talks in 2023 were entitled *From Rubicon to Actium* and *Christian Persecution from Paul and Constantine*.

To add in a practical element for post-primary children and primary children alike, CANI often invites the re-enactment group Legion Ireland to set up camp in the main hall of the

Ulster Museum throughout the day. This group is a living history and re-enactment society who aim to portray the Roman Army in the first and second centuries AD They cause quite a stir amongst all attendees and are a key component to the day's success.

Public engagement is also a key focus for CANI. The organization frequently posts short educational videos onto their Instagram and TikTok social media channels. These whirlwind tours take viewers through many of Rome's emperors – the good, the bad and the ugly. In 2022, CANI held a competition for primary pupils to write a short poem on something they learned that day, or were inspired by. The winner was a pupil of St Joseph's Primary in Belfast. They recorded themselves reading their poem and CANI posted it to their social media accounts. In adding this feature to the conference, CANI proved that Classics in Northern Ireland are not only engaging for young children but can be taken into the modern age to promote cross-curricular ICT skills. CANI committee members frequently visit schools to deliver short curriculum-supporting talks. Examples include *20 Things Every Latin Student should know about Rome* and *Understanding the Oracle of Delphi*.

Case study: teaching Classics from Belfast to the rest of the world

Helen McVeigh, Classics Academy

During the pandemic, it was not possible for the Belfast Summer School to meet in-person in July 2020 and instead we held classes online. That summer, over 100 people from around the world joined online classes in Greek and Latin.

My business niche is quite unique and when I began teaching students, in person, I did so in the evenings while I worked at the day-job. There are not enough students in Northern Ireland to justify a full-time business, but by extending into offering Greek and Latin online, my customer base has grown to incorporate students around the world. Having gained confidence in online teaching from the Belfast summer school, I began to offer weekly classes, scheduled on Saturdays, at times which take account of time differences as best as possible. This term alone, we have students from the UK, Ireland, Netherlands, Switzerland, Czech Republic, Georgia, Romania, USA, Canada, Mexico, Ecuador, Hong Kong, Japan, South Korea, Australia and New Zealand. The system allows students to register termly. Classes at all levels are offered each term, so it is possible for students to continue throughout the academic year, or to take a break and jump back in when they need to. In addition, each term we offer stand-alone courses, six to ten weeks in duration, on a variety of subjects connected to the ancient world. These are designed to complement the UK Classical Civilization and Ancient History exam specifications.

Intensive one to two week courses take place in July/August and a one-day refresher in January.

All classes are online, with the exception of one week of intensive classes in the summer. Online learning offers the flexibility and accessibility that in-person classes cannot provide. For example, we provide recordings of classes on request. These can be for a variety of reasons, such as student accessibility, and time differences. Classics Academy students are mostly adults but we have a small number of post-primary age students in the classes. Our classes are conducted on Zoom. Some tutors create a group chat for discussion between lessons, others use Zoom break-out rooms for class activities. When teaching Greek, I use a Smartpen and notebook as a form of whiteboard to complement my teaching. Notebook pages can be saved as pdf and are shared with students. By being able to share the pages from the notebook, students have a record of what we have discussed. They do not need to worry about copying something from a whiteboard before it is erased, rather they can listen to the explanation, in the knowledge that they will receive my notes in an email shortly after the class has concluded.

In Northern Ireland, the provision of opportunities to raise the profile of the ancient world in primary schools is key. Once young people have moved to post-primary school, the decision to study, or not to study, is largely already made, and depends entirely on whether the subject is on the curriculum. The Classics Academy provides a crucial service. We provide teaching not only to students worldwide who either have not had the opportunity to study classics, or were unaware of its existence, but also to our local young people. When I was a student, and talked to people outside the university environment about what I was studying, their reactions were weird and wonderful. Often I was asked outright 'What is Classics?' but sometimes the questions veered towards English literature or even classical music! I add this is a means of highlighting a widespread unfamiliarity with the subject in our part of the world.

Recommendations

Representatives for ancient languages need to have a seat at the policy-making table. This has been instrumental in securing parity of esteem for ancient languages in both Scotland and England (Holmes-Henderson & Kelly 2022) where they enjoy equal curricular status with modern languages. In autumn 2021, the Council for the Curriculum, Examinations and Assessment convened a Modern Languages Programme Board (MLPB) with representatives from business, higher education institutions, primary and post-primary schools. The MLPB currently has four key streams of work: (i) primary languages; (ii) languages at Key Stage 3; (iii) qualifications; and (iv) an exploratory group specifically for Irish. If it is planned that this group will shape future directions for language learning policy in Northern Ireland, there must be a representative for Latin and Greek. We would suggest that the Classical Association of Northern Ireland is ideally placed to source such a group member.

Teacher training is essential if Classics Education is to expand in Northern Ireland. Taylor et al. (2022) recommended that training should be available in the forms of Initial Teacher Education modules and workshops for qualified teachers. Online training courses remove barriers to access for busy teachers and ought to be explored for the Northern Ireland-specific curricular context. Any training, while useful for post-primary teachers, should first be prioritized for primary teachers as they are least likely to have experienced Classics in their own education, causing a natural lack of awareness of the subject (Taylor et al. 2022). We remain hopeful about what is possible: Holmes-Henderson (2016) noted that 70 per cent of those who attended a primary Classics training day in Belfast stated they would be likely to implement Latin into their classroom as a result.

References

Cambridge School Classics Project (2022), *Cambridge Latin Course, 5th edition*, Cambridge: Cambridge University Press.

CCEA (2019), Council for the Curriculum, Examinations and Assessment, 'Thinking Skills and Personal Capabilities at Key Stages 1 & 2'. Available online: http://ccea.org.uk/curriculum/key_stage_1_2/skills_and_capabilities/thinking_skills_and_personal_capabilities (accessed 19 November 2023).

Collen, I. (2023), 'Language Trends Northern Ireland: Language Teaching in Primary and Post-Primary Schools', *British Council Northern Ireland*. Available online: https://nireland.britishcouncil.org/sites/default/files/language_trends_2023_report.pdf (accessed 1 December 2023).

Connolly, P. (1986), *The Legend of Odysseus*, Oxford: Oxford University Press.

Corsar, K. (1977), *Discovering the Greeks*, London: Hodder.

Department for Education (2013), 'The National Curriculum in England: key stages 1 and 2 framework document', Government UK. Available online: https://assets.publishing.service.gov.uk/media/5a81a9abe5274a2e8ab55319/PRIMARY_national_curriculum.pdf (accessed: 19 November 2023).

Holmes-Henderson, A. (2016), 'Teaching Latin and Greek in primary classrooms: the Classics in Communities Project', *Journal of Classics Teaching*, 17 (33): 50–3.

Holmes-Henderson, A. and K. Kelly (2022), *Ancient Languages in Primary Schools in England: a Literature Review*. London: Department for Education, His Majesty's Government. Available online: https://assets.publishing.service.gov.uk/government/uploads/system/uploads/attachment_data/file/1120024/Ancient_languages_in_primary_schools_in_England_-_A_Literature_Review.pdf (accessed 1 February 2024).

Hunt, S. and A. Holmes-Henderson (2021), 'A level Classics poverty. Classical subjects in schools in England: access, attainment and progression', *CUCD Bulletin*, 50: 1–26. Available online: https://cucd.blogs.sas.ac.uk/files/2021/02/Holmes-Henderson-and-Hunt-Classics-Poverty.docx.pdf (accessed 1 December 2023).

NIC (2007), 'The Northern Ireland Curriculum Primary'. Available online: http://www.nicurriculum.org.uk/docs/key_stages_1_and_2/northern_ireland_curriculum_primary.pdf (accessed 19 November 2023).

Oulton, N. (2020), *So You Really Want To Learn Latin?*, London: Galore Park Publishing.

Radice, K., G. Lord, A. Cheetham and S. Kirk (2020), *De Romanis*, London: Bloomsbury Academic.

Taylor, A. (2020), [Dissertation] 'Classics in the Primary Classroom: An Exploration of Teacher and Pupil Perspectives on the Benefits, Challenges and Future Development of Classics Education in the Context of Primary Schools in Northern Ireland'. Unpublished.

Taylor, A., A. Holmes-Henderson and S. Jones (2022), 'Classics education in Northern Irish primary schools; curriculum policy and classroom practice', *Journal of Classics Teaching*, 24: 52–8.

Wright, A. (2011), *Greeks and Romans*, London: Galore Park Publishing.

Zinn, T. (2006), *Latin Prep*, London: Galore Park Publishing.

Organizations

CANI (Classical Association of Northern Ireland): https://classicalassociationni.wordpress.com/

Helen McVeigh: Classics Academy: https://helenmcveigh.co.uk/

Legion Ireland: http://www.romanarmy.ie/

The Philosophy Foundation: https://www.philosophy-foundation.org/

Young Plato: www.youngplato.com

UK: SCOTLAND

Alex Imrie

Scotland is proud of its links to antiquity. In the Scottish National Portrait Gallery, the Processional Frieze recounts key moments in Scotland's history. It features several Roman emperors and generals alongside Calgacus (the great resister of Rome in Tacitus' *Agricola*), as if claiming both the indigenous population and imperial invaders as direct ancestors (NGS

2021). Edinburgh is known as the 'Athens of the North', with the Town College (now University of Edinburgh) carrying the oldest known Greek inscription in the city (Brown 2022: 55–6).

Knowledge of antiquity can also be observed beyond Scotland's university cities. We must be careful not to exaggerate the semi-mythicized 'lad o'pairts' phenomenon (of a lowly born individual transcending class limitations through learning), but comparatively wide access to Classics among people from diverse backgrounds existed, through a network of parish schools. This was grounded in the principles of the Reformation, which emphasized the importance of producing literate as well as devout citizens (Hall & Stead 2020: 235–8). This history speaks to a nation which valued classical subjects, but the more recent reality is that teachers have battled against a systemic decline in Classics, resulting in its near annihilation in state schools (Imrie 2019: 111). There remains optimism today, though, with many people working together to revive the subject.

Education in Scotland

Scotland's education system differs from that of England. As part of the devolutionary settlement accompanying the re-establishment of the Scottish Parliament, the Scotland Act 1998 devolved education policy to the Scottish Government. Scotland has not been subject to the modifications or projects launched in England, such as the reforms of the Westminster coalition government, 2010–15 (Hunt 2018: 9–11).

The Scottish education system has around 800,000 pupils aged 3–18 in local authority operated schools. These include Gaelic Medium delivery and special schools assisting pupils outside the mainstream (Scottish Government 2021). The system begins with Early Learning and Childcare (ages 3–4) and primary education (ages 5–12). Secondary education is divided into a lower level (ages 12–15), referred to as the Broad General Education (BGE), and an upper level (ages 16–18) referred to as the Senior Phase. These stages form components of a holistic model known as the Curriculum for Excellence, a future-oriented programme designed to encourage pupils to become successful learners, confident individuals, responsible citizens and effective contributors – the so-called 'four capacities' (OECD 2021).

Senior Phase examinations begin with the National 5 (N5) exams, equivalent to the English GCSE (ages 15+), with scaled down options available for lower attaining pupils: the National 3 (N3) and National 4 (N4). The Higher is comparable to the English AS-Level (ages 16–17), with an option for pupils to study Advanced Highers (equivalent of the English A-Level; ages 17–18). Highers are used to determine university entrance in Scotland. Scottish courses are only a year in length (unlike the two-year A-Level). There is less time to develop foundational knowledge, and each individual result accrues fewer tariff points with the Universities and Colleges Admissions Service, which is used by UK universities to assess whether students meet course entry requirements. All exams in Scotland are currently overseen by the Scottish Qualifications Authority (SQA), although this organization will be replaced with a new body, Qualifications Scotland, in Autumn 2025, following controversy surrounding assessment during the Covid-19 pandemic (Imrie 2020). For the time being, if the exam board does not support the subject, it is nearly impossible to introduce it.

Classics in the Scottish curriculum

In primary schools, many have chosen to offer a unit on the Romans at Primary 5 (ages 9–10). Without a pre-set syllabus, this unit depends on the teacher's knowledge and interest. Recently, the Classical Association of Scotland (CAS) created a stand-alone unit deliverable at the same stage, focused on the Olympian deities. This unit capitalizes on the enduring popularity of Greek mythology spurred by Rick Riordan's *Percy Jackson* novel series (Ramaswamy 2023). However, the provision of classical subjects in the primary phase remains sporadic.

Until 2018, Latin was not taught at primary level. Attempts by university student-led groups to offer lessons through the Iris Project (www.irisproject.org.uk) failed to develop into a more sustainable national strategy (Denholm 2015). From 2018, Latin was introduced into the primary curriculum predominantly in the City of Glasgow (Scotland's largest single local authority) and in Aberdeenshire. A collaborative effort by council officers, teachers, and the charity Classics for All (CfA) developed a unit of Latin based on the *Minimus* coursebook (Bell 1999), offered in partial fulfilment of the Scottish Government's Languages 1+2 policy (where pupils learn two additional languages before completing primary education). The lack of Latin teacher training has made it difficult to expand any programme, but it has embedded in several locations (Peebles 2023). Glasgow City Council has included Latin in its teachers' professional development programme, and Scotland's National Centre for Languages supports Latin.

At secondary education, a distinction must be made between the Broad General Education (BGE) and the Senior Phase. At BGE, access to classical subjects is severely lacking and there is no Classics curriculum prescribed by Education Scotland, the executive agency responsible for quality and improvement within education nationally. This is partly because Classics is a minority subject in the Senior Phase (since BGE classes are typically used to prepare pupils for senior qualifications) and partly because of a timetable overcrowded with other subjects. Some schools opt to offer stand-alone units during the second or third years of BGE, or adapt units in bigger subjects (e.g. English or History) to include ancient material, but this remains an individualized approach. Many classes at BGE are taught by non-subject specialists.

At Senior Phase, provision is split into Latin and Classical Studies. Greek is no longer supported by SQA and is not taught in state-maintained schools, although some independent schools offer short courses or the English GCSE/A-Level curriculum. Latin is supported by SQA from N3 to Advanced Higher. The course is comprised of two components (Translating and Literary Appreciation) with a dissertation at Advanced Higher. In the Translating paper, students do not need to memorise vocabulary: the focus is knowledge and understanding of accidence and syntax (Holmes-Henderson 2020). Students should remember Latin terminology, however, for the Literary Appreciation exam.

Classical Studies is similarly distinct. At N3–5: students study three topic areas: Life in Classical Greece, Life in the Roman World, and Classical Literature (texts in translation). At Higher, themes are Power and Freedom and Religion and Belief. At Advanced Higher, the themes deepen, with History and Historiography, Individual and Community, Heroes and Heroism, and Comedy, Satire and Society. Assessment is by coursework and examination, differing from Latin, where there is coursework at Advanced Higher only.

As in other areas of the UK, there is a perennial debate on the value of Classics (particularly Latin) in the curriculum (Golding 2021). As in Wales, considerable political appetite exists to nurture indigenous languages. For Scotland, that means Gaelic. Gaelic is also a minority subject (in 2022, for example, 205 pupils sat the N5 exam, compared to 415 in Latin) and tension arises whenever alternative languages are championed publicly. The notion that Latin is the preserve of a privileged fee-paying minority is persistent. This issue may be concentrated in Scotland owing to the entrenchment of political lines between the ruling Scottish National

Party and the Conservative opposition. With the controversial former Conservative UK Prime Minister Boris Johnson representing a high-profile classicist in British media (Higgins 2019), Classics has become something of a political football for a commentariat often entirely detached from the subject, or who oppose private education wholesale. The supposed elitism of Latin is difficult to dispel. Additionally, some parents or grandparents remember their own Latin lessons prior to the 1980s, recalling it as a difficult subject, taught archaically, and lacking contemporary relevance for them (Boyd 2021). Teachers have sought to tackle this problem head on, by focusing on accessibility and the cultural capital that can be gained. This message of inclusivity has been increasingly successful. Historically, two state-maintained schools (Kirkcaldy High School and the Nicolson Institute in Stornoway) regularly put forward the largest cohorts for Latin examinations. Latin's success in reaching a diverse pupil body is proven by the fact that Latin was often the *only* senior qualification achieved by some of the less academic pupils (Shearer 2019). As a result, some schools with Classical Studies are also considering Latin.

The marginal nature of Classics in Scottish schools has ironically allowed teachers freedom to promote it in ways that respond to local requirements. The last decade has seen a worrying narrowing of the curriculum at secondary level. This has exacerbated pre-existing social inequalities and may be linked with less positive student performance, especially concerning progression to higher education (Shapira & Priestly 2023). Classical Studies can diversify a school's programme and gives pupils the opportunity to add a new subject to their grade transcript. It also offers an outlet for pupils who do not undertake other subjects at Advanced Higher level. The results speak for themselves. Latin is still found predominantly in the private sector, but interest in offering the subject is increasing among state-maintained schools and the majority of pupils sitting Classical Studies at N5 and Higher are in the state-maintained sector. There has been a significant increase of exam entries in recent years: 490 pupils at Higher in 2022-23, compared to 400 in 2018; 245 at N5, compared to 78.

Delivering Classics in Scottish schools

There is no dedicated set of Latin resources for the Scottish curriculum, a surprising fact given that the *Ecce Romani* Latin series was developed by the Scottish Classics Group (SCG 1971). Latin teachers tend to favour the *Cambridge Latin Course* (CSCP 1998) or *Suburani* (Hands Up Education 2020) to anchor their courses. In a survey of the Scottish National Teachers' Network conducted in Summer 2023, the grammar-translation method is not popular among teachers who wish to appeal to a broad spectrum of learners. Reading courses are a more popular option, but are difficult to match to the SQA requirements. The struggle with Latin's image as a difficult subject has prompted a two-pronged approach: hard points of grammar and vocabulary are often instructed directly, but teachers also diversify the range of topics and the types of learning activities. Jennifer Shearer, a retired teacher from Kirkcaldy High School, noted that a customized programme offers teachers greater control and flexibility, and can make the course more exciting for a pupil base which is far from homogeneous in academic ability and ambition. Teachers therefore adapt resources and share abridged samples of original Latin. This allows them to control the pace of classes more effectively, while also aligning with the SQA.

Classical Studies similarly lacks published, curriculum-specific materials. The lack of resources makes it difficult to orientate new teachers, but it allows some freedom for those with the time to develop materials. Teachers consult a variety of sourcebooks on antiquity for their own development, often dictated by personal taste (e.g. Boatwright et al. 2011).

At BGE, Education Scotland mandates no curriculum. Teachers must develop their own units to fulfil the expectations and outcomes of the Curriculum for Excellence. In the Senior Phase, the content of courses is outlined more rigidly by the SQA. But without an accompanying textbook or publicly accessible resources, teachers must again innovate and share. While this affords a level of freedom, certain topics are better served by the collective effort. Sophocles' *Antigone* is a perennial favourite study, for example, and is well-supported by teacher-made resources and shared via the national network. By contrast, materials on religious topics are harder to find: information in school books is too brief or generic, while undergraduate textbooks are too complex.

Given the minority nature of Classics in Scotland, teachers must defend their timetable allocation. The 2023 survey revealed concerns about maintaining a high profile within school and the local community. Departments are often small, single-person, and promoting Classics via initiatives which reach the entire pupil body and stress its interdisciplinarity is important. At Buckie Community High School, for example, teacher Susan Rowley held an event which showcased connections between Classics, Religious Education, English and Science, culminating in a physical recreation of haruspicy involving the Biology department and a local butcher's produce! A sense of community and identity counteracts precarity. Classics activities can be advertised via posters outside the classroom, for example, to advertise the subject beyond those already enrolled. Teacher George Connor of Monifieth High School (MHS) offers 'Classicist' badges to new students. His response to the 2023 Survey: 'Pupils leave MHS and consider themselves Classicists. It's a big deal.'

Engagement with local media is growing. Jennifer Shearer was adept at raising awareness of the success of her Latin classes, taking every opportunity to emphasize their inclusivity and thus recruiting more students in a manner out of proportion to a single-person department (Robertson 2012). George Connor has enjoyed considerable success in boosting the profile of Classical Studies in local and national media, detailing the growth of his department as an example of the potential for Classics to engage a diverse range of students (Devlin 2021).

There has been some opposition from school leadership teams, but an upward trend in interest surrounding Classics is incontrovertible. Since 2018, not only has there been a steady increase in examination entries for Classical Studies, numbers in Latin have also remained stable against a backdrop of decline in other languages. This trend is in both the state-maintained and the independent sectors. Teacher Mary O'Reilly (Hamilton College) reported that Latin enjoyed high uptake as an optional BGE course, and outperformed French in the Higher. It should also be stressed, however, that the general picture is affected by national teacher shortages across all subjects as much as by localized pupil preferences (Learmonth 2023).

Teacher training in Scotland

There is currently no straightforward avenue for anyone to qualify as a Classics teacher at any of the nine Scottish universities which currently offer the Professional Graduate Diploma in Education (PGDE). Latin and Classical Studies ceased to be options for teacher training when the University of Glasgow closed their programme in 2011. Since then, Classics teachers have qualified with a PGCE gained in England or an international equivalent, and gain further accreditation by the General Teaching Council of Scotland (GTCS). Teachers are required to demonstrate a minimum engagement with the subject (80 credits at university level) before being authorized to teach Senior Phase classes. This usually represents at least one year of formal study unless the GTCS chooses to recognize some of the teacher's existing qualifications.

This situation currently represents the most significant obstacle to expanding Classics. In 2019/20, there was a concerted effort by academics and teachers to re-introduce classical PGDE options at Moray House School of Education at the University of Edinburgh, but without institutional support these plans fell through. Discussions elsewhere have proven equally difficult owing to the current distraction of a crisis in recruitment and retention across the teaching profession. University leadership seems unwilling to trial new options for teacher training in Latin or Classical Studies when the intake would likely be low for now, especially when even more established subjects struggle to enrol trainees (Hepburn 2023).

Collaboration in Scottish Classics

The survival of Classics in Scotland has relied on collaboration between schools in the independent and state-maintained sectors, and between schools and universities. Since 2018, CAS maintains contact with all groups, supported by the charity Classics for All. CAS has an active mailing list, engages with the SQA and collaborates with the Scottish Network of Classics Teachers to hold two meetings a year. The network began in 1996 as the South Lanarkshire Council Classics Network, a council-run group to which teachers from the private and state-maintained sectors joined, to discuss delivery and examination. When the local authority withdrew its support in 2016/17, St Aloysius' College in Glasgow took over. Thanks to the energy and collegiality of staff there, notably the current network chair, teacher Lee Baker, it continues to grow and add teachers from schools across Scotland's thirty-two local authorities. It now counts around ninety members. National networking activity was essential. Many Classics teachers represent single-person departments and require support for materials and coursework moderation. It is a first port of call for new Classics teachers and can offer rapid responses to teacher requirements as well as fostering a community.

Historically, there has been little contact between schools and the Scottish universities which currently offer Classics degrees (Edinburgh, Glasgow and St Andrews). This can be explained partly by a general contraction in the number of Scots attending Scottish universities, and partly by the vicious cycle of fewer schools offering Classics resulting in fewer pupils entering higher education to study it. University Classics departments recruit most of their UK intake from England, with the majority from independent schools (Canevaro 2021). This led to an environment where both sides were ignorant of the other's practices, and an atmosphere of distrust. Schoolteachers voiced concern that universities only showed interest when it benefitted themselves. CAS has bridged this divide by harnessing the enthusiasm of university academics but channelling it to the needs of the school community. CAS means to focus the resources and personnel of universities to serve the wider community in ways that play to each group's strength, providing teachers access to universities to disseminate cutting-edge research to their pupils.

Instrumental in shaping these efforts into a coherent national programme has been Classics for All (CfA). Since 2017, it has funded a regional organizer based in CAS to oversee efforts to nurture and protect the subject across the country. CfA supports initiatives to expand Classics provision, financially backing every new centre to commence Classics in Scotland. It funds a programme of mentoring for teachers offering Latin/Classical Studies for the first time. This is doubly beneficial because it links members of the community and develops consistency across a wide area. The most significant contribution of CfA is its commitment to supporting already-qualified teachers in other subject areas to gain training credit in Classical Studies. CfA provides financial support, while CAS facilitates networking. This is undoubtedly a demanding and time-consuming process, but it is sustainable. Six teachers have gained accreditation in this way so far.

Conclusion

Classics in Scotland faced a near-existential threat, but prevailed and is now on the path to re-establishment. Its survival has been thanks to the perseverance of teachers, committed to seeing it flourish. Through collaboration, we have bolstered existing departments and recruited new ones. By developing Classics sustainably, we are introducing the subject to children of all abilities and backgrounds, something inconceivable only a decade ago. Classicists in Scotland make no claims to our discipline being the panacea to pupils' academic needs, but instead advocate for opening doors to a diverse world, familiar and yet radically different, enriching learners' intellectual wellbeing as much as their final examination transcripts.

Pupils in South Ayrshire are now studying the Roman Republic; those in Angus are taking first steps in Latin; pupils in Aberdeenshire are taught by a teacher completing her own Master's in Classics; and so many pupils in Moray enrolled, that one school offered full classes from N5 to Higher in Latin and Classical Studies only a year after introducing the subjects. Our community is increasingly able to respond to that hunger for Classics as it spreads to all corners of *auld Scotia*.

References

Bell, B. (1999), *Minimus: Starting out with Latin*, Cambridge: Cambridge University Press.

Boatwright, M., D. Gargola, N. Lenski and R. Talbert (2011), *The Romans: from Village to Empire (A history of Rome from its earliest times to the end of the Western Empire)*, Oxford: Oxford University Press.

Boyd, B. (2021), 'Letter: Time to accept that the game is over for the teaching of Latin in our schools', *The Herald*, 9 March. Available online: https://www.heraldscotland.com/news/19145265.letters-time-accept-game-teaching-latin-schools/ (accessed 18 September 2023).

Brown, I. (2022), *Auld Greekie: Edinburgh as the Athens of the North*, Stroud: Fonthill Media Ltd.

Canevaro, M. (2021), 'Working-Class Classics: myths, stories and experiences', *Network for Working-Class Classicists*, 27 October. Available online: https://www.workingclassclassics.uk/2021/10/27/working-class-classics-myths-stories-and-experiences/ (accessed 18 September 2023).

CSCP (1998), Cambridge School Classics Project, *Cambridge Latin Course*, Cambridge: Cambridge University Press.

Denholm, A. (2015), 'Scottish pupils to be taught Latin to boost literacy', *The Herald*, 26 May. Available online: https://www.heraldscotland.com/news/13215399.scottish-pupils-taught-latin-boost-literacy/ (accessed 18 September 2023).

Devlin, L. (2021), 'Angus teacher backs Classics', *The Courier*, 15 July, 18.

Golding, J. (2021), 'Plan to teach Latin in state schools 'utterly misconceived', says former head', *Independent Education Today*, 5 August. Available online: https://ie-today.co.uk/news/plan-to-teach-latin-in-state-schools-utterly-misconceived-says-former-head/ (accessed 18 September 2023).

Hall, E. and H. Stead (2020), *A People's History of Classics*, London: Routledge.

Hands Up Education (2020), *Suburani*, Haverhill: Hands Up Education.

Hepburn, H. (2023), 'Teacher recruitment in Scotland: "missed opportunities" condemned', *TES Magazine*, 13 May. Available online: https://www.tes.com/magazine/news/general/teacher-recruitment-scotland-missed-opportunities-condemned (accessed 18 September 2023).

Higgins, C. (2019), 'Boris Johnson's love of Classics is about just one thing: himself', *The Guardian*, 6 October. Available online: https://www.theguardian.com/commentisfree/2019/oct/06/boris-johnson-classics-prime-minister-latin-greek (accessed 18 September 2023).

Holmes-Henderson, A. (2020), 'What's it like training in England but teaching in Scotland?', *Quinquennium*, 8 January. Available online: https://www.quinquennium.com/whats-it-like-training-in-england-but-teaching-in-scotland/ (accessed 18 September 2023).

Hunt, S. (2018), 'Getting Classics into Schools? Classics and the Social Justice Agenda of the UK Coalition Government, 2010–2015', in A. Holmes-Henderson, S. Hunt and M. Musié (eds), *Forward with Classics: Classical Languages in Schools and Communities*, London: Bloomsbury Academic, 9–26.

Imrie, A. (2020), 'The Coronavirus Pandemic, Exams Crisis and Classics in Scottish Schools', *Journal of Classics Teaching*, 21 (42): 55–9.

Imrie, A. (2019), 'Caledonia resurgens: reflections on the campaign to revive Classics teaching in Scotland', *Journal of Classics Teaching*, 20 (39): 111–16.

Learmonth, A. (2023), 'Rural schools disproportionately affected by lack of language teachers', *The Herald*, 17 July. Available online: https://www.heraldscotland.com/news/23658905.rural-schools-disproportionately-affected-lack-language-teachers/ (accessed 18 September 2023).

NGS (2021), National Galleries of Scotland, *William Brassey Hole: Processional Frieze in the Great Hall of the Scottish National Portrait Gallery* [Website, updated 2021]: Available online: https://www.nationalgalleries.org/art-and-artists/159703/processional-frieze-great-hall-scottish-national-portrait-gallery (accessed 18 September 2023).

OECD (2021), Organization for Economic Co-operation and Development, *Scotland's Curriculum for Excellence: Into the Future*, Implementing Education Policies, Paris: OECD.

Peebles, C. (2023), 'It's a dead language and I want to bring it back: Rebirth of Latin at Monifieth High', *The Courier*, 12 September. Available online: https://www.thecourier.co.uk/fp/education/schools/4709683/latin-state-schools-scotland-monifieth-high/?utm_source=twitter (accessed 18 September 2023).

Ramaswamy, R. (2023), 'Why learn mythology?', *The Michigan Daily*, 14 March. Available online: https://www.michigandaily.com/opinion/why-learn-mythology/ (accessed 18 September 2023).

Roberston, A. (2012), 'Beatus homo qui invenit sapientiam' [Blessed is the man who finds wisdom], *The Courier*, 31 January.

SCG (1971), The Scottish Classics Group. *Ecce Romani: a Latin Reading Course*, Edinburgh: Blackie.

Scottish Government (2021), *Curriculum for Excellence 2020–2021 – OECD review: initial evidence pack*. Available online: https://www.gov.scot/publications/oecd-independent-review-curriculum-excellence-2020-2021-initial-evidence-pack/ (accessed 18 September 2023).

Shapira, M. and M. Priestley (2023), 'Sobering report card for Scotland's Curriculum for Excellence', *The Herald*, 20 February. Available online: https://www.heraldscotland.com/news/23328350.cfe-failing-pupils-teachers/ (accessed 18 September 2023).

Shearer, J. (2019), 'Just what are they teaching in schools nowadays?' [paper presentation], Classical Association of Scotland: Edinburgh & South-East Centre Seminar Series (25 September), Edinburgh.

UK: WALES

Danny Pucknell

Introduction

Wales is imbued with references to its own historical and, indeed, classical past. Dotted around its landscape are reminders of the ancient world. For example, Caerleon, the site of a Roman fort near Newport, remains a powerful reminder of the presence of the Romans in Wales. The site contains the remains of the Roman fortress, bathhouse and amphitheatre, and has become a popular site for both schools, colleges and tourists (Cadw 2023). Welsh schoolchildren were once raised with an understanding and appreciation of the history of the British tribes who resisted the Roman invasion. Hall and Stead describe the impact of the story of Caractacus and how he, a figure of which relatively little is known, helped forge a Welsh national identity around the time of the First World War (Hall & Stead 2020: 255). Despite this, references to the classical world have appeared less frequently in recent decades on the curricula of Welsh schools and colleges. As Bracke has commented 'educational and socio-political contexts in Wales differ significantly from the rest of the UK' (Bracke 2015: 35) and this leads to a very particular set of circumstances.

I will outline the situation in schools and colleges in Wales. I will then detail some of the challenges Classics faces in Wales and focus on the grassroots work of teachers and educational bodies to revive the fortunes of classical subjects. Finally, I will turn to the opportunity presented by the New Welsh Curriculum in 2025.

Education in Wales: students 11–18

Census data record that in 2021 there were 588,000 students and schoolchildren in Wales, ranging from age five to those studying for a post-16 qualification (Welsh Government data from the census of 2021). As of August 2022, the Joint Council for Qualifications (JCQ, the exam governing body) noted that there was a total of 311,072 entries at GCSE across all subjects for that academic year (JCQ 2022). It is worth noting that although the Welsh education system is structurally similar to England's, there are some curricula and examination differences, such as the compulsory Welsh Baccalaureate qualification and the fact that Wales has distinct first- and second-year qualifications, which have made the study of Classics more challenging in Wales.

All students up to the age of eighteen have to complete the Welsh Baccalaureate qualification as one of their A-Level options. Despite the academic benefits of the Baccalaureate (such as asking students to research and write an extended piece on a topic of their choice), it does take the place of a traditional A-Level subject in the list of options. Most students take three subjects at AS (the first year of an A-Level) and the Welsh Baccalaureate. Very few students can take four. This limits the number of students who can take Classics as the fourth subject and few do so. A similar pattern has emerged in England, where Hunt has noted that 'the marginalisation of AS levels means many schools only allow their students three A-Level subjects, which has affected the number of students choosing to study Classics' (Hunt 2018). In Wales the compulsory Baccalaureate qualification has produced a similar effect for Classics to that which the marginalization of AS has done in England.

The provision and structure of exams are other limiting factors. A state-maintained school must only use the WJEC (Welsh Joint Education Committee) examination board's subject qualifications. This poses a challenge as WJEC does not offer any classical subject in Wales (although Eduqas, its sister examination board, does offer a Latin examination at age 16, but this is only taught in England). Therefore, teachers in Wales have to use an English examination board such as OCR (Oxford, Cambridge and RSA examinations) in order to teach classical subjects for assessment at A-Level. This may not seem a large issue to those who do not teach in Wales, but as A-Level provision in Wales is different to that in England, it can pose logistical challenges. Wales still maintains a system of modular examinations, set at AS and A-Level, whereas England has linear end-of-course examinations (Bristow 2021; DfE 2020). The change in the structure of A-Levels in England has created a challenge for students who opt to take Classics or Ancient History, because they will be working to a different academic timetable for their other subjects.

Situational challenges and issues at A-Level

It is not a lack of enthusiasm for the subject, but several logistical issues which hold back the study of the ancient world. They appear to fall into three broad categories: the lack of a nationwide qualification for Classics in Wales; the compulsory nature of the Welsh Baccalaureate; and the lack of available teacher training. Below I shall detail how each of these factors has limited the teaching of Classical subjects in Wales.

Classics is a subject which exists on the fringes of the National Curriculum. Mainly the preserve of private schools, it has seen little growth in state-maintained schools for decades. However, despite the challenging landscape, enthusiasm for the subject has begun to grow. Much Classics teaching goes on as an off-timetable lesson or enrichment session, put on by staff members who value and appreciate the subject. In order to aid them, Classics for All, a charity founded in 2010 to encourage more state-maintained schools to offer classical subjects, is helping to provide both funding and teacher-training and to encourage schools to provide timetable space for classical subjects.

At a presentation in the Cambridge School Classics Project Conference in 2021 I discussed the challenges of setting up a Classics A-Level cohort. Holmes-Henderson and Hunt's report had indicated the true extent of the scarcity of classical subjects in schools outside London and the south-east corner of England, describing it as a kind of 'Classics poverty' (Hunt & Holmes-Henderson 2021). At the time, the number of centres teaching Classics in Wales was in an even worse condition. In general, in Wales the number of students sitting exams for Classical Civilization, Ancient History, Latin and Greek is decreasing, with centres keeping the subjects on the curriculum an exception rather than the norm.

One example of a particular college may help to reveal the extent of decline in the subject. Gower College, a college for students aged 16–19 near Swansea, boasts a curriculum of forty A-Level subjects and a cohort of 2,000 full-time learners. It highlights the issue. In the 2013/14 academic year, Gower College enrolled thirty-two students for Classical Civilization and thirty-five for Ancient History. These numbers showed a healthy take up for the subjects. However, in recent years, schools and colleges have seen a decline. In 2020/21 the number had dropped to a total of seventeen for Classical Civilization and eleven for Ancient History. This reflects a decline across Wales. In fact, the Welsh examination database lists no entries in 'Classical Studies' for either the 2021/22 or 2022/23 academic years under the WJEC (Welsh Examination Database 2022). It does not account for students who are sitting Eduqas, OCR or Pearson examinations: these will not show up within the database because they are not provided by WJEC. This is the major issue currently impacting the study of the ancient world in Wales. It is not merely a lack of enthusiasm for the subject that has produced a total of zero exam entries, but the fact that there remains a lack of Welsh provision for the subjects.

Classics for All and grassroots Classics

The excellent and vital work done by Classics for All (CfA) on a UK wide level has seen numbers of students studying Classics and related subjects grow since the charity's founding in

2010. The largest area of growth has been seen in primary schools, with 638 schools having introduced or developed the study of a Classical subject with the support of CfA. Numbers across the UK for secondary schools and colleges are not quite as high, with 553 secondary schools taking up a Classical subject since the charity's foundation. Much of this vital work is conducted through CfA's regional hubs. Dedicated to contacting schools in their designated area of the UK, these hubs act as a contact point for schools who want to place Classical subjects on their curriculum. As of 2021, CfA have relaunched its hub in Wales.

This CfA hub in Wales was first founded in 2015 by Dr Evelien Bracke of Swansea University, to promote the teaching of classical subjects in state schools in Wales. In 2016/17 the Hwb (Welsh for 'Hub') made a solid start, and in its first year of operation in Wales, CfA helped 2,625 Welsh students study the ancient world. CfA achieved this both by working with schools already teaching Classics to increase numbers, and by working with schools with no history of Classics teaching. CfA trained non-specialist teachers in Classics, Latin or Greek and helped them integrate the ancient world into the curriculum. CfA also seeks to grow the number of students by using its fifteen regional network hubs across the UK which coordinate training and ensure that teachers have ongoing support. These hubs provide training, support and host events to encourage the sustainable growth of Classics. The approach has clearly found success, as by the end of 2022, CfA recorded 150,000 pupils studying the ancient world. The Classics for All 2010–2022 Impact Report notes that Wales is amongst the most under-represented region in the UK, with only nineteen schools with any kind of study of the ancient world (Classics for All 2023: 3). This highlights the challenge, but also recognizes the work achieved by CfA in Wales.

The excellent work undertaken by Bracke, as the coordinator of CfA's Welsh Hwb, resulted in sixty-four new teachers and thirty schools trained across Wales. At the height of the Hwb's outreach activities, thirty-seven institutions were receiving help. In what was a substantial setback for progress, Bracke took up a post in Belgium and left CfA in 2017. In 2019, attempts were made to revive the network under Lucy Roberts at Wyedean School, but this was curtailed by the Covid-19 pandemic. As many classical subjects were run as twilight hours or lunchtime clubs, many of these were curtailed during the move to remote learning. The number of students learning Classics is difficult to calculate, as the Welsh Hwb suffered a period of abeyance for three years. The Hwb was revived in 2021. This has only underlined how much the teaching of Classical subjects in Wales has nearly always relied on individuals for sustainability.

The Welsh network was re-established by CfA under the guidance of Hwb coordinator, Leigh-Rowan Herring. In the first year of operation (2022), Herring, a Latin teacher at Gyfun Gywr, has made a major contribution to the growth of the subject, particularly at primary level, with the inclusion of Latin in new and existing partner schools across Wales. According to Herring in the 2022/23 academic year there were approximately eleven schools in Wales that teach Classics on the curriculum. In the past year, however, the Hwb has created new links with eight new secondary schools. In addition, ten more are planning to introduce Classics in some form in the 2023/24 academic year. Two secondary schools, Ysgol Aberconwy and Croesyceiliog, received grants for the training to put Classics on their curriculum in 2022 (Herring, 2023). Not only has the Hwb made significant progress at grassroots level but it has also gained the support and cooperation of the universities of Cardiff and Swansea, under the guidance of Maria Oikonomou.

The New Welsh Curriculum

The Welsh Government has long been resistant to the concept of a Classics A-Level created and run by the Welsh examination board. Despite the challenges of the educational landscape in regard to the study of the ancient world in Wales, the arrival of the New Welsh Curriculum in January 2025 provides an opportunity to change the current situation.

The Curriculum is designed to be fluid, and so will allow teachers to make decisions on what will be on their own schemes of work. The best way to include Classics as a subject within the new curriculum is to embed it in existing subjects. Looking at the specification for some subjects already on the curriculum, there are some Classics texts already being studied. In Drama, *Medea* is one of the texts offered at A-Level. This means that there are a significant number of students already gaining knowledge of classical texts without Classics being named as a distinct subject.

However, as well as the possible integration of classical influences on the curriculum, there is also the opportunity for study of the ancient world as unique subjects. The study of Latin and Greek has been marginalized in schools since the 1960s and the reforms of the late 1980s have left little curriculum space for the study of classical languages (Holmes-Henderson & Hunt 2021: 1). The situation in Wales has found itself facing even more profound challenges due to a desire to protect the Welsh language. Since the devolution of education in 1999 to the constituent parts of the UK, Welsh state-maintained schools have been required to teach the Welsh language at all levels. Welsh has become the second language option for many students. Data gathered by Drury in 2022 noted that independent schools are not bound by the same constraints, which explains the strength of Latin in the private sector (Drury, personal communication, June 2022). Table 12 below presents a comparison of where Latin and Welsh feature on the curricula of twenty-six independent schools in Wales. This table shows that, unlike the state-maintained schools where Welsh language is compulsory up to GCSE, of the twenty-six independent schools, only one makes Welsh compulsory at GCSE, and fewer than half make it an option. This frees up curriculum space for other languages, including Latin. Nine of these schools have Latin as a compulsory language up to Key Stage 3 (age 11–14). While no independent school has Latin as compulsory beyond that, eleven schools do have it as an option at GCSE and four up to A-Level. Until the reforms of the 2025 New Curriculum come into action, state-maintained schools do not have the same freedom of choice with their curriculum.

Table 12. Provision of Welsh language and Latin in Welsh independent schools

	Number of schools at each Key Stage		
	Key Stage 3	Key Stage 4	Key Stage 5
Welsh (compulsory)	7	1	0
Welsh (optional)	5	11	4
Latin (compulsory)	9	0	0
Latin (optional)	2	11	4

Source: © S. Drury 2023.

From 2025, schools will have to teach English, Welsh and one other language. Originally this had been specified as a 'modern foreign language', but now the wording reads 'additional language'. This creates an opportunity for Latin to become the third language in state-maintained schools in Wales and is being discussed by members of the Welsh Government and members of the Classics for All team (Hwb10 2022). In addition, we are beginning to see progress at the grassroots level. Ysgol Gyfun Gwyr (a CfA-supported school) has introduced A-Level Latin and the first student sat their AS-Level exams this year (Herring 2023).

Teacher training

At present, there are no specific teacher training courses in Wales for those who wish to teach Classics. It is more likely that someone who teaches History or English will have to learn to teach Classics while currently employed at a school. From 2024, however, Swansea University and the CfA Hwb will enter into discussion about how Classics can be incorporated in the Initial Teacher Education programme for the Postgraduate Certificate in Education (PGCE) module at the university. Not only is this a promising development for the training of teachers at Swansea but is an initiative which will dovetail well with the work which Herring has done as the Hwb co-ordinator. Herring has created a curriculum which for the moment centres around teaching at primary level. The Hwb has already seen some success with this as Classics has been introduced at Ty Trafle School and discussions are ongoing with several other primary schools. The primary curriculum allows lessons on the ancient world to work alongside the objectives of the New Curriculum for Wales (Herring 2023). During the 2023/24 academic year, Herring will facilitate training on the school syllabus she has created, in order to allow more teachers to teach the ancient world with greater confidence.

Future ambitions

The UK's Classical Association (CA) aims to make Classical subjects more widely accessible and has developed links with schools, colleges, universities and other charities. Its twenty-seven local branches aim to reach as wide an audience as possible. In Autumn 2023 Cardiff University relaunched their CA branch with the aim of making it a greater part of the wider community by partnering with local schools and colleges. Both the CA and CfA have a role in improving public engagement with Classics and are working closely to foster the teaching of Classics in schools and colleges.

Conclusion

Although Classics teaching faces unique challenges in Wales, this should not downplay the many positives for the subjects' continued growth. The picture for Classics in Wales is as bright as it has been for many years. The future trend for the number of students studying the ancient world in Wales is undoubtedly upward, helped by the unceasing work of the Welsh Hwb. The study of Classics in Wales is beginning to gain some traction, enough perhaps to shift the attention of educational policy-makers towards having classical subjects on the curriculum at a national level. The option to add Latin to the curriculum at primary level must be seen as a breakthrough moment for the subject. It will not only allow study of the ancient world in Wales but will also create a love for the subject amongst many more students, one which is likely to endure through their time in compulsory education. This is an opportunity which the Welsh government should not fail to capitalize on during the rollout of the New Curriculum. If policy begins to shift in a positive direction for the study of the ancient world, then there is one other area that is of critical importance. If Classics is to grow, an established course for the training of teachers specifically for classical subjects is vital. With Swansea looking at introducing a Classics specific module on their PGCE, the most influential stakeholders, such as CfA and the CA, should add their voices to call for more educational institutions in Wales to follow suit. Only then will Classics be able to establish its former position in Wales.

References

Bracke, E. (2015), 'Bringing Ancient Languages into a Modern Classroom: Some Reflections', *Journal of Classics Teaching*, 16: 35–9.

Bristow, C. (2021), 'Reforming Qualifications: the how, the why and the who', *Journal of Classics Teaching*, 22: 60–3.

Cadw (2023), Caerleon Roman Fortress and Baths. Available online: https://cadw.gov.wales/visit/places-to-visit/caerleon-roman-fortress-and-baths (accessed 6 August 2023).

Classics for All (2023), *Impact Report, 2010–2022*, London: Classics for All.

DfE (2020), Department for Education. Secondary accountability measures (including Progress 8 and Attainment 8). Available online: https:// www.gov.uk/government/publications/progress-8-school-performancemeasure (accessed 6 August 2023).

Hall, E. and H. Stead (2020), *A People's History of Classics*, Routledge: London.

Herring, L.-R. (2023), *Progress report for 2022–23 – Welsh Hwb*, London: Classics for All.

Hunt, S. (2018), 'Getting Classics into Schools? Classics and the Social Justice Agenda of the UK Coalition Government, 2010–2015', in A. Holmes-Henderson, S. Hunt and M. Musié (eds), *Forward with Classics: Classical Languages in Schools and Communities*, London: Bloomsbury Academic.

Hunt, S. and A. Holmes-Henderson (2021), 'A level Classics poverty. Classical subjects in schools in England: access, attainment and progression', *CUCD Bulletin*, 50.

Hwb10 (2022), *Developing a Vision for Curriculum Design*, Welsh Government. Available online at https://hwb.gov.wales/curriculum-for-wales/designing-your-curriculum/developing-a-vision-for-curriculum-design/#curriculum-design-and-the-four-purposes (accessed 6 August 2023).

JCQ (2022), *GCSE results reflect planned grading arrangements for first summer exams in three years*, Joint Council for Qualifications: 2–3. Available online at https://www.jcq.org.uk/wp-content/uploads/2022/08/Wales-GCSE-JCQ-Media-Release-25-August-2022.pdf (accessed 6 August 2023).

Pucknell, D. (2021), *From the Ground Up: Founding a Classics Cohort in Wales*. Advocating Classical Education. Available online: https://aceclassics.org.uk/founding-a-classics-cohort-in-wales/ (accessed 6 August 2023).

Welsh Examination Database (2022), *WJEC Examination Date*. Available online at https://statswales.gov.wales/Catalogue/Education-and-Skills/Schools-and-Teachers/Examinations-and-Assessments/Key-Stage-4/gcseentriesandresultspupilsaged15only-by-subjectgroup (accessed 7 August 2023).

EUROPE AND RUSSIA: FURTHER READING

Steven Hunt and John Bulwer

In Albania, the communist dictator Enver Hoxha (1908–85) effectively banned the teaching of 'Classics' as he sought to develop a national spirit which looked back to its Illyrian tribal roots rather than to the period of Roman occupation (Hodges 2009). The contemporary education system does not seem to support Classics; however, the University of Tirana offers a BA in Greek languages, Literature and Civilization, of which a small part includes Ancient Greek language and history (University of Tirana 2023). There appears to be no classical education in Moldova or Montenegro, whose education systems have other priorities.

In Ukraine, classical languages have not been taught in schools for a generation, although they survive in university-level courses in philology (A. Grablevsky, personal communication, 2 June 2023). A recent article in the *Guardian* newspaper noted continuing efforts to preserve the country's archaeological heritage during the current war (Higgins 2023).

In the Vatican City, Latin remains in official use, although the development of a Latin Academy sponsored by Pope Benedict XVI seems to have come to nothing (Lucie-Smith 2013). The most famous Latin teacher there in recent times, Father Reginald Foster (known colloquially as 'the Pope's Latinist') passed away in 2020. His energetic and unconventional teaching style can be discerned in Mistretta and Pedicone (2021). *Radio Vaticana* continues to provide the news *Latine* and users of the Vatican bank machines can choose Latin for transactions if they wish. In San Marino, the Scuola Secondaria Superior, founded in 1883, is the single secondary school. It follows the Italian education system and offers Latin and Greek through its Gymnasium and Scuola Linguistica programmes. In Andorra, schools follow Spanish (Catalan), French or Andorran education programmes. The authors could find only one school – the Spanish-run Colegio España María Moliner – which offered Latin.

An international conference 'Monsters in the Classroom' on the teaching of Classics in primary schools across Europe took place in 2022 online. Contributions may be found here, for Belgium (Bracke 2023), England (Hunt 2023c), France (Duchemin et al. 2023), Greece (Manolidou & Goula 2023), Italy (Di Donato & Taddei 2023) and the Netherlands (Van Gils 2023). In Belgium, Bracke studies the positive impact of learning Ancient Greek on primary age students and provides a thought-provoking commentary on classroom practice and learning outcomes (Bracke 2022).

In Greece, Manolidou et al. (2023) describe the Eliniki Agogi institute which teaches Ancient Greek to primary age school students, using active methodologies (speaking, singing, drawing, acting). Manolidou's children's book *Wisdom Tour* springs from her institute's experiences of collaboration with an international school in Beijing, China (Manolidou 2023). Concern at the inadaquacy of teaching Ancient Greek can be detected in Zekas' crticism of the methodology espoused by course materials used in Greek schools (Zekas 2014). Seranis (2008) explores the place of Latin in the modern Greek curriculum and Fountanopoulou and Kostara (2023) describe efforts to improve the training of teachers at the National and Kapodistrian University in Athens. A similar disquiet about the ineffectiveness of the teaching methodology employed in Dutch *gymnasia* can be seen in Crump (2008).

A fascinating glimpse of the neo-Greek epic *Astronautilia*, composed 1993–4 by the Czech academic and writer Václav Pinkav (under the pen name of Jan Křesadlo) can be read in *Antigone Journal* (Broadbent 2023).

Gonzalez et al. (forthcoming) describes teaching and learning practices with college students and researchers at the Antioch Recovery Project – an ongoing research lab dedicated to the study of mosaics from the city of Antioch-on-the-Orontes and its surroundings in Turkey.

Classics and Class (Morvin & Olechowska 2016) provides details about the teaching of Classics in schools and universities in Communist Europe. The book includes chapters on Britain, Soviet Russia, Ukraine, Czechoslovakia, Democratic Republic of Germany, Slovenia, Bosnia and Herzegovina, Bulgaria, Croatia and Poland. For further reading about the roles that Greco-Roman antiquity played in the development of national identity and politics in Russia and Bulgaria, see Torlone (2009) and Kirin (2010). Similary for Russia and Ukraine, see Grablevsky (2023). Péter Hajdu's *Modern Hungarian Culture and the Classics* (forthcoming 2024) promises to provide a fascinating exploration of the continuing impact of the Classics in that country.

Euroclassica is the federation of European associations of teachers of Classics in schools; see Navarro and Martinez (2021) for an account of the first thirty years of its existence. It meets annually in a diferent country each time to bring together teacher representatives of their national associations to exchange ideas and resources, and to offer mutual support. It has also published *Europatria* (De Oliveira 2013) and *Europatrida* (De Oliveira 2019), volumes with chapters from many European countries discussing which Latin and Greek texts are in some way fundamental for their nations. In a similar way, *European Symbols* (Glatz & Thiel 2015) is a Euroclassica book for European students to use in class, with a chapter devoted to many different European countries and their classical heritage. It contains texts in Latin and Greek with plenty of vocabulary help for reading about the importance of ancient culture for each nation; it is in English but is designed for class use in any language. The website (www.euroclassica.eu/portale/euroclassica.html) contains a section of reviews of recent books about Classics pedagogy. For an overview of the education systems of the twenty-seven Member States of the European Union, as well as Albania, Bosnia and Herzegovina, North Macedonia, Iceland, Liechtenstein, Montenegro, Norway, Serbia, Switzerland and Türkeye (but not the UK) see *Eurydice* (2023).

Readers may be interested to read historical articles about Classics teaching in a number of countries, published between the 1960s and early 2000s by the Joint Association of Classical Teachers. These include Belgium (Constant 1964), Denmark (Jacobsen 1968), France (Schilling 1963), Germany (Hornig 1966; Kaudewitz 2008; Matthiesson 1988; Olschewski 1990), Italy (Cernuta 2008), Malta (Borg 1990), Poland (Korzeniowski & West 1991) and Russia (Buriachko 2004; Muravlev 1991). Wülfing (1986) reported on an international conference of Classics teachers held at Tübingen to discuss changes in the aims, access and pedagogy for classical languages, in response to more general educational reforms across Europe. For a similar overview, see Bulwer (2006, 2018). For an overview of Classics in Portuguese schools and the challenge for teachers there, see Pereira (2018) and elsewhere in this book. Delord (2019) gives a personal view of what it is like to be a teacher of Latin in France at present in the face of reforms and other current issues.

The career of the remarkable W. H. D. Rouse, co-developer of the Loeb series of simultaneous translations of Greek and Roman authors, and his espousal of the Direct Method of Latin teaching, which was popular in England at the turn of the last century, can be read in Stray (1992). Rouse's legacy lives on in the Association for Latin Teaching. The changes in ways of teaching in British schools since the 1960s can be discerned through reading Morris (1966), Sharwood Smith (1977), Morwood (2003) and Lister (2007). The increase in non-linguistic courses of classical civilization and ancient history at the school level is a particularly noteworthy feature of these times, as well as the development and widespread use of digital resources. For reading about the development of the world-leading *Cambridge Latin Course* and its impact on classics education in the UK and beyond, see Forrest (1996) and Lister (2007, 2015). Lister's edited volume *Meeting the Challenge: International Perspectives on the Teaching of Latin* (2008) draws together contributions from several European states, including the use of interactive media, linear reading and increasing access to Latin. Neville Morley's *Classics. Why it matters* (2018) makes a brief but lively case for the study of the ancient world not as one which supposedly develops the acuity of the mind but as one which provides insight and lessons from the past, through the present and to the future.

For a brief resumé of the most recent developments of Classics teaching in UK schools, see Hunt (2023a). Hunt explores the paradox of the British Government's harnessing of Classics to its socio-economic 'levelling up' agenda of the 2010s (Hunt 2019) and public responses to the development of the Latin Excellence Programme in England (Hunt 2020a). Hunt provides contextual information about qualfications in classical subjects in the UK (2020b), teacher training (2023b) and classical studies at Key Stages 2 and 3 (2021). He has also written about non-specialist teachers' experiences of teaching Classics (2020c) and about problems of access and inclusion to Classics (Hunt & Holmes-Henderson 2021).

The theme of elitism in Classics has also been taken up by Perale (2023) and the authors of the web-blog Working Class Classicists. A recent national survey in the UK showed the depth of the problem at the Higher Education stage: the further one goes up the academic scale, the less representation there is of working-class people (Canevaro et al. 2024). At the other end of the scale, a national survey carried out on behalf of the Classical Association showed a very strong desire from teachers for revitalized assessments in Latin, Greek, Ancient History and Classical Civilization at all levels (Hunt 2024). These reports may perhaps overlap. A series of working groups for each subject area has been set up by the Classical Asscociation, working with the examination boards, to make recommendations for future changes to the examinations system. Holmes-Henderson (2023) draws on several case studies from schools in England to show how teaching classical languages, literature and material culture can benefit students in historically socio-economically disadvantaged communities. She maintains the Advocating Classical Education website along with Edith Hall (https://aceclassics.org.uk/). James Robson's and Mair Lloyd's studies of *ab initio* classical languages courses in British universities reveal insights into practices and methodologies which are mostly traditional grammar-focused (Robson & Lloyd 2018; Lloyd & Robson 2018). However, shifts towards a wider variety of language teaching approaches, including active approaches, are also indicated (Lloyd & Robson 2023). Some of this is in response to a recognition of the changing experiences and needs of students, inclduing those that have come to classics through non-traditional routes (Wuk 2022), or who may be neurodiverse (Fraser 2021); some is due to an increase in interest in alternative methods of teaching, learning and assessment which has derived from the experiences of online teaching during the Covid-19 lockdowns (Lovatt 2020).

References

Beveridge, M. (2000), 'Reflections on a Year in England', *JACT Review*, 27: 5–6.

Borg, S. (1990), 'The Classical Scene in Malta: 1979–89', *JACT Review*, 8: 10–12.

Bracke, E. (2022), *Classics at Primary School. A Tool for Social Justice,* London: Routledge.

Bracke, E. (2023), 'Teaching Latin and ancient Greek in the 21st-century Primary School: Framing local approaches to international challenges', *Journal of Classics Teaching*, 25 (49): 33–8.

Broadbent, B. (2023), 'The Last of the Greek Aoidoi: Jan Kresadlo's Astronautilia', *Antigone Journal*, 17 October. Available online: https://antigonejournal.com/2023/10/jan-kresadlo-astronautilia/ (accessed 7 November 2023).

Bulwer, J., ed. (2006), *Classics Teaching in Europe*, London: Duckworth.

Bulwer, J. (2018), 'Changing Priorities in Classics Education in Mainland Europe', in A. Holmes-Henderson, S. Hunt and M. Musié (eds), *Forward with Classics. Classical Languages in Schools and Communities*, London: Bloomsbury Academic, 67–88.

Buriachko, S. (2004), 'Classics at St Petersburg Classical High School (1989–2003)', *Journal of Classics Teaching*, 3: 14–15.

Canevaro, L., M. Canevaro, B. Mazzinghi Gori, H. Stead and E. Williams Reed (2024), *Class in Classics*, Edinburgh: University of Edinburgh.

Cernuta, B. (2008), 'The Teaching of Classics Abroad: Italy', *Jounral of Classics Teaching*, 15: 2.

Constant, P. (1964), 'L'Association des Classiques sortis de l'Universite de Liege', *Didaskalos*, 2: 96–105.

Crump, L. (2008), 'A contemporary subject for contemporary Europe: the much-disputed role and relevance of Latin at Dutch gymnasia', in B. Lister (ed.), *Meeting the Challenge. International Perspectives on the Teaching of Latin*, Cambridge: Cambridge University Press, 31–43.

Davies, R. (2000), 'A Year in New Orleans', *JACT Review*, 27: 4.

De Oliveira, F., ed. (2013), *Europatria*, University of Coimbra.

De Oliveira, F., ed. (2019), *Europatrida*, University of Coimbra.

Delord, R. (2019), *Mordicus. Ne perdons pas notre latin!*, Paris: Les Belles Lettres.

Di Donato, R. and A. Taddei (2023), '"Educare all'Antico". Teaching Classical Civilisation in Italian primary and lower secondary schools', *Journal of Classics Teaching*, 25 (49): 48–51.

Duchemin, L., A. Durand and B. Franceschetti (2023), 'The Nausicaa experience: Teaching Ancient Greek in French preschools and primary schools', *Journal of Classics Teaching*, 25 (49): 39–42.

Eurydice (2023), 'National Education Systems', European Commission. Available online: https://eurydice.eacea.ec.europa.eu/national-education-systems (accessed 30 November 2023).

Forrest, M. (1996), *Modernising the Classics. A study in curriculum development*, Exeter: University of Exeter Press.

Fountanopoulou, M. and E. Kostara (2023), 'Embedding Diversity in Classics Teachers' Training. A case study at a Greek university', in D. Libatique and F. McHardy (eds), *Diversity and the Study of Antiquity in Higher Education*, London: Routledge, 130–41.

Fraser, C. B. (2021), Introducing Asterion: a new initiative celebrating Neurodiversity in Classics, *CUCD Bulletin*, 50: 1–5. Available online: https://cucd.blogs.sas.ac.uk/bulletin/ (accessed 22 February 2024).

Glatz, P. and A. Thiel (2015), *European Symbols*, Horn, Austria: Euroclassica.

Gonzalez, E., D. Ortiz and J. Stager (forthcoming), 'Research-driven Pedagogy and Public-Facing Outcomes: The Antioch Recovery Project', in C. Gardner and S. Higgins (eds), *Ancient Pasts for Modern Audiences*, London: Routledge.

Grablevsky, A. (2023), 'Barbarism and its Discontents in Ancient and Modern Ukraine', *Antigone Journal*. Available online: https://antigonejournal.com/2023/05/barbarism-ancient-modern-ukraine/ (accessed 2 December 2023).

Hajdu, P. (forthcoming 2024), *Modern Hungarian Culture and the Classics*, London: Bloomsbury Academic.

Higgins, C. (2023), 'Battle for the past: the Ukrainians trying to save their archaeological treasure amid war', *The Guardian,* 26 December. Available online: https://www.theguardian.com/science/2023/

dec/26/battle-for-the-past-the-ukrainians-trying-to-save-their-archaeological-treasure-amid-war (accessed 28 December 2023).

Hodges, R. (2009), 'Nikita Khrushchev's visit to Butrint', *Expedition*, 51 (3): 24–6.

Holmes-Henderson, A., ed. (2023), *Expanding Classics: Practitioner Persepctives from Museums and Schools*, London: Routledge.

Hornig, G. (1966), 'Die Situation des altsprachlichen Unterrichts in Westdeutschland', *Didaskalos*, 2 (1): 127–38.

Hunt, S. (2019), 'Getting Classics into Schools? Classics and the Social Justice Agenda of the UK Coalition Government, 2010–2015', in A. Holmes-Henderson, S. Hunt and M. Musié (eds), *Forward with Classics. Classical Languages in Schools and Communities*, London: Bloomsbury, 9–26.

Hunt, S. (2020a), 'The Latin Excellence Programme (England 2021). The Story So far', *The Classical Outlook*, 97: 2.

Hunt, S. (2020b), 'School Qualifications in Classical Subjects in the UK. A Brief Overview', *CUCD Bulletin*, 49. Available online: https://cucd.blogs.sas.ac.uk/files/2020/01/HUNT-School-qualifications-in-classical-subjects-in-the-UK-3.pdf (accessed 2 December 2023).

Hunt, S. (2020c), 'Introducing Latin. Non-specialist Latin teachers talk', *Journal of Classics Teaching*, 21 (42): 36–42.

Hunt, S. (2021), 'Mind the Classics Gap. Current position of classical studies in English schools from Key Stage 2 to Key Stage 3. Challenges and solutions', *CUCD Bulletin*, 51. Available online: https://cucd.blogs.sas.ac.uk/files/2022/09/Mind-the-Classics-Gap.pdf (accessed 2 December 2023).

Hunt, S. (2023a), *Starting to Teach Latin*, 2nd edition, London: Bloomsbury Academic.

Hunt, S. (2023b), 'Initial Teacher Education for Classics. England, 2023. The current position', *CUCD Bulletin*, 53. Available online: https://cucd.blogs.sas.ac.uk/files/2023/10/Steven-Hunt-Latin-Education-final-2.10.23.pdf (accessed 2 December 2023).

Hunt, S. (2023c), 'Latin and Greek in English Primary Schools – seedlings of a classical education', *Journal of Classics Teaching*, 25 (49): 60–4.

Hunt, S. (2024), 'Classical Studies Trends: teaching Classics in secondary schools in the UK', *Journal of Classics Teaching*, 25 (50): 1–17.

Hunt, S. and A. Holmes-Henderson (2021), 'A level Classics poverty. Classical subjects in schools in England: access, attainment and progression', *CUCD Bulletin*, 50. Available online: https://cucd.blogs.sas.ac.uk/files/2021/02/Holmes-Henderson-and-Hunt-Classics-Poverty.docx.pdf (accessed 2 December 2023).

Jacobsen, B. (1968), 'The General Classics course in Danish secondary schools', *Didaskalos*, 2 (3): 36–45.

Kaudewitz, R. (2008), 'The Teaching of Classics Abroad: Germany', *Journal of Classics Teaching*, 15: 3–4.

Kirin, A. (2010), 'Eastern European Nations, Western Culture, and the Classical Tradition', in S. Stephens and P. Vasumia (eds), *Classics and National Cultures*, Oxford: Oxford University Press, 141–62.

Korzeniowski, G. and S. West (1991), 'Classics Teaching in Poland', *JACT Review*, 10: 13–14.

Lister, B. (2007), *Changing Classics in Schools*, Cambridge: Cambridge University Press.

Lister, B., ed. (2008), *Meeting the Challenge: International Perspectives on the Teaching of Latin*, Cambridge, Cambridge University Press.

Lister, B. (2015), 'Exclusively for everyone – to what extent has the *Cambridge Latin Course* widened access to Latin?', in E. Archibald, W. Brockliss and J. Gnoza (eds), *Learning Latin and Greek from Antiquity to the Present*, Cambridge, Cambridge University Press / Yale Classical Studies, 184–97.

Lloyd, M. and J. Robson (2018), 'A Survey of Beginner's Language Teaching in UK Classics Departments: Latin', *CUCD Bulletin*, 47: 1–25. Available online: https://cucd.blogs.sas.ac.uk/files/2018/05/LLOYD-ROBSON-CUCD-Latin-Survey.pdf (accessed 22 February 2024).

Lloyd, M. and Robson, J. (2023), 'A Survey of Beginners' Latin Teaching in UK Classics Departments (2019)', *CUCD Bulletin*, 52: 1–33. Available online: https://cucd.blogs.sas.ac.uk/files/2023/06/LLOYD-ROBSON-CUCD-Digest-Report.pdf (accessed 22 February 2024).

Lovatt, H. (2020), [Blog] 'Language and Other Assessments in the Time of Covid-19', CUCD Education Committee Blog. Available online: https://cucdeducation.wordpress.com/2020/04/03/language-and-other-assessments-in-the-time-of-covid-19/ (accessed 22 February 2024).

Lucie-Smith, A. (2013), 'The Pope's New Academy for Latin', *Journal of Classics Teaching*, 27: 78–9.

Manolidou, E. (2023), *Wisdom Tour, Book 1: Athens*, Athens: Helleniko Ekdotiki.

Manolidou, E. and S. Goula (2023), 'In Greek we trust! Παίζοντες μανθάνομεν', *Journal of Classics Teaching*, 25 (49): 56–9.

Manolidou, E., S. Goula, S. and V. Sakka (2023), 'Ancient Greek for Kids: From Theory to Praxis', *Journal of Classics Teaching*, 24 (47): 3–11.

Matthiesson, K. (1988), 'On the Position of Classical Languages in the Federal Republic of Germany', *JACT Review*, 4: 5–8.

Mistretta, M. and J. Pedicone (2021), 'New Approaches to Ancient Languages: The Paedeia Institute's Pedagogy', in M. Lloyd and S. Hunt (eds), *Communicative Approaches for Ancient Languages*, London: Bloomsbury Academic, 189–94.

Morley, N. (2018), *Classics. Why it matters*, Cambridge: Polity Press.

Morris, S. (1966), *Viae Novae: New Techniques in Latin Teaching*, London: Hulton Educational Publications.

Morwood, J., ed. (2003), *The Teaching of Classics*, Cambridge: Cambridge University Press.

Movrin, D. and E. Olechowska (2016), *Classics and Class*, Ljubljana: Univerza v Ljubljana Filozofska fakulteta.

Muravlev, A. (1991), 'Classics Teaching in Russia', *JACT Review*, 12: 11–12.

Navarro, J. and R. Martinez (2021), *Euroclassica 1991–2021, Thirty Years Defending and Promoting Classical Languages in Europe*, Madrid: Ediciones Clásicas.

Olechowska, E. and D. Movrin, eds (2016), *Classics and Class: Greek and Latin Classics and Communism at School*, Ljubljana: DiG publishing house. Available online: https://www.academia.edu/42748876/Classics_and_Class_Greek_and_Latin_Classics_and_Communism_at_School (accessed 30 November 2023).

Olschewski, B. (1990), 'Classical Education and Society in Engtand in the First Half of This Century: Comparison with Germany', *JACT Review*, 7: 4–8.

Perale, M. (2023). "I Still See the Elitism". Classical languages and the language of class at Liverpool', *Journal of Classics Teaching*, 24 (47): 26–33.

Pereira, S. (2018), 'The Status of Latin in Portugal: Resilience and Resistance', *Journal of Classics Teaching*, 37: 30–4.

Robson, J. and M. Lloyd (2018), 'A Survey of Beginner's Language Teaching in UK Classics Departments: Ancient Greek', *CUCD Bulletin*, 47: 1–25. Available online: https://cucd.blogs.sas.ac.uk/files/2018/04/ROBSON-LLOYD-CUCD-Greek-Survey.pdf (accessed 22 February 2024).

Schilling, R. (1963), 'La situation des langues classiques dand l'enseignement francais', *Didaskalos*, 1: 27–36.

Seranis, P. (2008), 'Poor relation or necesary evil? The place of Latin in the Greek curriculum', in B. Lister (ed.), *Meeting the Challenge. International Perspectives on the Teaching of Latin*, Cambridge: Cambridge University Press, 21–30.

Sharwood Smith, J. (1977), *On Teaching Classics*, London: Routledge and Kegan Paul.

Stray, C. (1992), *The Living Word. W. H. D. Rouse and the Crisis in Classics in Edwardian England*, Bristol: Bristol Classical Press.

Torlone, Z. (2009), *Russia and the Classics*, London: Duckworth.

University of Tirana (2023), Faculty of Languages: Greek. Available online: https://fgjh.edu.al/departamenti-i-gjuhes-greke/ (accessed 8 January 2024).

Van Gils, L. (2023), 'At the gymnasium through your football buddy's aunt. Accessibility of classical education in the Netherlands', *Journal of Classics Teaching*, 25 (49): 52–5.

Wuk, M. (2022), 'Teaching Latin ab initio at Lincoln: Reflections from a Post-1992 University', *CUCD Bulletin*, 51: 7–12. Available online: https://cucd.blogs.sas.ac.uk/files/2022/09/Perspectives-on-Classics-2.pdf (accessed 22 February 2024).

Wülfing, P. (1986), 'Latin and Greek in Europe: the present situation', *JACT Review*, 4: 9–12.

Zekas, C. (2014), 'In the Shadow of Diachrony: Ancient Greek Language in the Contemporary Greek Gymnasio', *Journal of Classics Teaching*, 30: 22–9.

PART 2
THE AMERICAS

CANADA

Margaret-Anne Gillis

Introduction

When most people think of Canada, they think of a vast landscape hidden beneath a blanket of snow. Some may envision pods of orcas playfully breaking the crest of Pacific waves or the majestic Rockies reaching to the heavens. Some may hear the song, 'Wheat Kings', about the golden wheatfields of the Prairies stretching to infinity. Others may think of the CN Tower scraping the clouds or perhaps *les petites maisons* of Quebec City. Fans of the pandemic sensation, the shanty, may chant like the sou'wester-clad fishers aboard a schooner, pulling in nets laden with cod. Invariably, no one thinks of classicists toiling away in an ivy-covered library, translating some tome of Virgil, even though Canada has produced some notable classicists, such as Alexander McKay, one of the founders of the Virgilian Society and the Villa Virgiliana in Bacoli, Italy. However, the state of Latin, Greek and Classical Civilization courses in the schools and universities of Canada, which will be referred to as 'Classics', currently is not what it once was; it primarily results from the disastrous Royal Commission Report (Warren 1967–8), but there are a host of other reasons. The modern challenges faced by Classics are perplexing mostly because they emerge from Canada's evolution as a nation, its political system, geographic scale, historical conflicts, economic pragmatism, a change in the post-secondary educational system and a lack of teacher training and certification, all of which might erroneously seem to signal a slow march towards obscurity. In just half a century, Classics has nearly disappeared from the secondary school system across the country as qualified classicists retired and provincial curricula shifted to meet the modern demands. In turn, this has affected the Classics programme at every university in the country. In short, it is a Canadian thing, certainly worthy of investigation. It is not a long story, and it certainly is not over.

Canada is a country of ten provinces and three territories which spans the continent of North America. It occupies four-and-a-half time zones. Geographically massive, Canada is home to forty million people, who have descended from immigrants and First Nations, Canada's indigenous population, and who together created the nation over nearly six centuries. As home to a host of people from around the globe, enriching the country in myriad ways, the linguistic and cultural diversity simultaneously merged a unique set of opportunities with challenges alike for governments at all levels. Canada has three levels of government: municipal, provincial and federal. Unlike most countries around the world, where education is a national concern, Canada boasts no federal, centralized education policy. Education is entirely a provincial purview. When the founders of Canada signed the British North America Act in 1867, the powers of the federal and provincial governments were delineated and powers which the colonies (now provinces) possessed prior to Confederation would remain. Canada's motto itself: *a mari usque ad mare* (which we now translate as 'From Sea, to Sea, to Sea' as an expression of northern sovereignty) indicates how Canada's early federal government was binding together a nation which spans a continent metaphorically and literally. The only way to administer such a huge geographic area was to support strong provincial governments. Since education existed prior to the Canadian Confederation, it remained the responsibility of the provinces and each province's Ministry of Education sets the curriculum for its constituents. Despite this autonomy, the educational systems are remarkably similar.

Firstly, this is the result of the work of Methodist Minister Egerton Ryerson, who devised the system of education in Ontario (which other provinces later adapted) long before Confederation. In addition, an interprovincial collaboration exists between Ministries of Education to share curriculum documents as a result of agreements which emerged from discussions about labour mobility and professional certification. Since Canada is a country of immigrants to this day, the challenges and opportunities it faced a century ago in trying to integrate newcomers into the fabric of Canadian communities remain. This is very much visible in the current language curricula across the country. For instance, in Saskatchewan (in the Prairies), which welcomed the greatest number of Ukrainian immigrants a century ago, students can study the Ukrainian language, not just in a single grade, but also as an immersion course from Grades 1 to 12 (Saskatchewan Curriculum n.d.), similar to that which exists for French immersion programmes across the country. It is possible for students in Nova Scotia (on Canada's east coast) to study Gaelic, because such a large Scottish community immigrated there (Government of Nova Scotia n.d.). On the west coast, high school students can study Japanese, Mandarin, Cantonese and Punjabi, among other languages, owing to the immigrants from Pacific rim nations who settled there (BC's Curriculum n.d.). In every province, students can study First Nations' languages (such as Ojibway, Cree, Mi'kmaq and many more, depending on the First Nations residing within that province) in recognition of the key relationships between indigenous and non-indigenous peoples in Canada (Bellefontaine 2021). French is a compulsory subject in every province, either through immersion, or regular core programming over multiple grades. However, it is important to note that not every Canadian is bilingual and this will be discussed in greater detail later.

Classics in schools

In Canada today, the only province which maintains Classics in its high school curriculum policy is Ontario, though the curriculum of Alberta does list Latin in an appendix document dating to 1986 (Alberta updated the curriculum policy documents for its high school diploma in 2010 but did not include Latin). Sadly, despite the long educational tradition, Quebec deleted Latin from its curriculum in 2009 (Peritz 2009). At first glance, what stands out is the respect for heritage languages as a homage to the immigration which built the country. On closer inspection, Classics is almost absent. It is important to note that each province does allow a provision for 'locally-developed' courses and this accounts for the sparse provision of Latin in some private schools in British Columbia and Alberta (Alberta Education 2023). The strongest Classics enrolments are in Ontario in both publicly-funded and private schools because there is curriculum policy to support it (Government of Ontario 2023).

The most significant blow to the proud tradition of Classics across Canada came amidst the social and political turmoil of the 1960s. In 1968 the Ontario government released its Royal Commission Report called Living and Learning, most 'affectionately' called the Hall–Dennis Report (Hall & Dennis 1968). The document raised legitimate concerns about outdated curriculum, student disengagement, the need for greater access to educational opportunities, the need to teach skills appropriate to the modern world, appropriate integration of technology, along with dozens of other recommendations. The key recommendation, which would forever change the course of history for Classics in Canada, was that the committee recommended that greater access to more elective courses be offered in order to meet the needs and interests of students better – education had to move with the times. Many, from students, to teachers, to school board officials, read that as a recommendation to remove Classics from the curriculum, which it was not (and that is why the official Ontario Ministry of Education policy documents for Classical Studies survive today). The damage was done, and, almost overnight, Latin enrolments dropped to critically low numbers. Classics teachers who retired were not replaced. Classics departments were amalgamated with other language departments. The need for faculties of Education to produce Classics teachers declined to the point where they completely stopped offering a Bachelor of Education in that specialty. By extension, that dealt a severe blow to the Classics departments at many universities as their Classics majors no longer had a direct path to employment as teachers (although the huge variety of other employment benefits and options remained). Classics' troubles had just begun, because other provinces soon followed suit.

The study of languages remained an important topic for both Ministries of Education and the federal government. A cursory glance at any Canadian history text outlines the historical conflicts between England and France during the colonization of North America. The question, from before Confederation, has been: how can the two be united into one country? The federal government has struggled for more than a century to address this. Amidst the social turmoil of the 1960s, language rights and cultural identity became crucial and complex political forces. The recognition of official bilingualism, accompanying the ever-growing cultural mosaic, brought a new respect for the languages and cultures of every citizen of the country. In 1969 Trudeau's Liberal government introduced the Official Languages Act. Canada became officially bilingual, protecting the rights of its French citizens no matter which province they inhabited. At this point, education became the primary tool by which to achieve these goals, and again, with lightning speed, each Ministry of Education across the country introduced compulsory French language education beginning in the elementary schools and extending to middle and high schools. In 1984 Ontario introduced a compulsory French credit for graduation from high school. Funds within each language department were dedicated to French. French language education at the universities' Departments of French increased as the demand for teachers grew. Faculties of Education increased access to a Bachelor of Education in French. In schools, timetable space, classrooms and classroom resources became dedicated to French language education. And, instead of educators seeing opportunities for classical languages to support and contribute to multicultural and multilingual initiatives because the changes came too rapidly, Classics languished.

As Classics programmes vanished from the high schools across the country, Classics departments at universities remained relatively stable, though every single university dropped Latin or Greek as an admission requirement to the university overall, and to their Classics departments in particular. Certainly, the numbers of students seeking a Bachelor of Arts in Latin or Greek dwindled. University after university began to remove the BA in Latin and replace it with a BA in Classics or Classical Studies. Departments began to shrink as new professors were not hired to replace retiring ones. By the 1980s, the only Faculty of Education in the country to maintain a Bachelor of Education in Classics (Latin) was at the University of Toronto (FEUT). This merged with the Ontario Institute for Studies in Education (OISE) in 1996. A BEd in Latin was on the books, but inactive. In 1987/88, for one year only, Queen's

University in Kingston, Ontario offered a Bachelor of Education in Latin, but the applications of possible candidates were too few to make the degree sustainable. In 1997, after four years of intensive negotiating by the Ontario Classical Association, OISE offered an Additional Qualification Course (preliminary) and an Honour Specialist Course in Classical Studies: Latin (advanced training) for practising teachers for the first time since the 1970s. Among those teachers was one student who was entering OISE in the fall to complete her BEd for certification at the high school level. She was given special permission to enrol in this AQ/HS class in July and her degree, conferred in May 1998, was in Classical Studies: Latin. This was some proof of concept that a Bachelor of Education could be possible. After years of lobbying by the Ontario Classical Association, in 2000 OISE offered the Bachelor of Education in Classical Studies: Latin until 2005. It drew students from across Ontario and beyond. However, in 2005 it was clear that the enrolment in the course was too low to be economically viable and the university closed the programme. It did allow one more AQ/HS course to operate in the summer of 2006 in which sixteen candidates enrolled – eight received an Honour Specialist designation, four received an Additional Qualification course and four received pre-service course work towards their Bachelor of Education, conferred in 2007. This was a great success and indicated a wonderful untapped potential, even if it might not generate huge financial recompense for the institution.

A very short-lived Bachelor of Education in Classical Studies: Latin existed at York University from 2009 to 2014, training a handful of candidates, but it too fell to the axe of budgetary restrictions. No jurisdiction in Canada has been able to offer a Bachelor of Education in Classical Studies: Latin ever since. That is related entirely to the numbers of university Classics majors not enrolling in sufficient numbers of Latin or Greek credits, because teaching credentials are tied to the classical languages. The Ontario College of Teachers confers accreditation – a licence – to all teachers in the province after they have completed their Bachelor of Education degrees, as well as to anyone from an extra-provincial training facility, Canadian or international. The college recognizes training in Classical Studies: Latin, though it also accepts Greek credits; Classical Civilization courses are not recognized in this tally. And herein lies the rub. Teachers who seek accreditation to teach Classics must complete some post-secondary classical languages credits. And, for Classics at the secondary level to survive, teacher training and accreditation are critical.

Classics in universities

Classics programmes at the post-secondary level have undergone some structural changes out of necessity. Budgetary cutbacks, curriculum streamlining and job preparedness, among other pressures, have taken their toll on Classics departments. Of the ninety-seven publicly-funded universities in Canada, only forty-three (sixteen of which are in Ontario) offer any kind of Classics degrees. As mentioned previously, school boards closed Classics programmes, and the need for teachers with specialist training in the Classical languages decreased so rapidly that universities stopped granting degrees in the classical languages alone, offering instead 'Classics' or 'Classical Studies'. Classics departments began to shift away from an emphasis on the languages to the more broadly appealing half-credit courses (no need to invest an entire year) in Classical Civilization. Importantly, students were no longer reading Latin and Greek texts in the original language; they were encountering Greek and Roman art and archaeology, religion, etymology, including scientific terminology, but not Latin or Greek *per se*. (It is worth noting that McMaster University in Hamilton, Ontario, offers a course called 'Latin for Medical School' which attracts some 2,000 students per year.) Today, those early offerings have been expanded to include courses on Pompeii and Herculaneum, Women in the Ancient World, Classics in Film, and the list goes on.

As part of the universities' initiatives demonstrating employment opportunities for all arts degrees, on practically every webpage, a list of possible careers such as editor, scholar, lawyer, journalist, diplomat, to name but a few, appears (although there are even more which could be added). On Classics departments' webpages, few actually list 'teacher', and no one lists a job as a 'Classics Teacher' among students' options. Prior to 1968 every university boasted a healthy Classics department; today, few are autonomous. A website search for a 'Department of Classics' yields a Department of Classical Studies, Ancient Studies, Greek and Roman Studies, History and Classics, Classics and Religious Studies, Classics and Archaeology, Classics and Medieval Studies, and the list continues. In one case, Classical Studies was found in and course-coded as Humanities.

Amalgamation, either enforced or freely embraced, brings with it a host of challenges, most notably because a Classics department loses its identity. (That loss of autonomy and identity is exactly what happened to the high schools in the 1970s.) There can be a blurring of the subject areas and in some cases, Classics courses are hidden, a challenge for attracting potential classicists from the student body. At a handful of universities, it is possible to major in Latin and/or Greek; most universities, on average, offer approximately 4–8 half-credit courses in each language; some offer far fewer and a couple offer more. Few universities make Latin or Greek a requirement for a degree in Classical Studies, which renders that degree terminal, meaning there is no path to pursue Classics at graduate school. Approximately half of the Classics departments do advise students that pursuit of a Master's degree in Classics requires credits in Latin and/or Greek, and strongly recommend taking the languages. Some universities offer Classical Studies as a 'Minor' for a Bachelor of Arts only. This landscape makes it difficult to attract students destined to be Classics teachers. While students who have taken one of more years of Latin at high school may take courses in Latin (or, perhaps, Greek), and/or Classical Civilization at the post-secondary level, only a small number continue as majors because they assume that job prospects are non-existent. But while it is not as direct a path as it once was, and it may be a bit overgrown, in Ontario, the path is there. Without a Bachelor of Education in Classical Studies: Latin being offered, potential teachers must be content to pursue an education degree where their Classics credits count as history or humanities courses for admission to a BEd generally.

In Ontario, currently, there are teachers in schools, certified to teach a variety of subjects, but who have in their academic background Classics courses; these are the 'hidden classicists'. This is very likely the case in other provinces too. If students drawn to Classics departments enrol in a Latin or Greek course, they are starting from scratch. Often, students who studied Latin all the way through high school do not continue past the first or second year, even if they have access to more courses. Some cite their degree path has too many compulsory components or they are interested in pursuing graduate work in another field. The main reason: pedagogical approach (a discussion of which will follow). The lack of students taking courses in the classical languages is a problem for the universities because it puts extraordinary pressure on graduate programmes. Of the existing Classics programmes, only nine offer study to the PhD level (two may be completed *en français*) and it is possible to gain admission to a PhD with as few as four

Latin and/or Greek credits, in the hopes that the student will acquire competency during tenure in the degree. Interestingly, most graduate programmes in Classics suggest that a student demonstrate reading proficiency in one modern language, and only one programme demands German as well as a fourth language, in addition to the Latin and Greek required. Invariably, most graduate candidates come from other provinces or outside the country. Job prospects in Canada for post-doctoral students are few and far between, relegating many to the training grounds of sessional work or leaving the country for employment. It appears, at this point, that the state of Classics in high school has impacted programming at the university level. Without the obvious career path of teaching for graduates holding a BA in Classics, the universities have seen their departments reduced because the two are inextricably linked.

Ontario figures prominently in the discussion because that is where curriculum policy at the high school level exists, and where the vast number of programmes reside. The correlation between high school programmes supporting Classics at university in this province is tenuous but statistically relevant. In 1998, thirty years after the release of the Hall–Dennis Report (1968), Ontario completely revised its curriculum as part of Progressive Conservative Premier Mike Harris's 'Common Sense Revolution'. Subjects were forcibly amalgamated, often with a great deal of angst among teachers. Classical Studies was amalgamated with international languages, supporting then some ninety languages in the city of Toronto alone. This merging of non-conversational Latin and Greek with the international languages, which focus half of their expectations on oral/aural communication, posed great challenges in devising a unified set of teaching expectations. It was not an easy marriage. There was great discussion about the title of the document: *Classical and International Languages* (Ontario Ministry of Education and Training 1999). The editors decided that all the documents would be organized alphabetically, and this worked out well for classical languages because administrators, teachers, parents and members of the public saw that 'Classical' languages still exist in the curriculum.

There were other struggles though. Latin and Greek offered courses consecutively for three years, while international languages offered credits from Grade 9 to Grade 12. In the end, this three-year sequence worked in the favour of classical languages because it retained more students. By the time the document was revised in 2016, the international languages sought alignment with Classical Studies' shorter sequence (Government of Ontario 2023). Sadly, the three credits of Classical Civilization in the previous document released in 1984 were reduced to one credit at Grade 12; that was a blow to Classics teachers. At the present time, enrolments in all languages across the province are suffering for a number of reasons. The sheer number of compulsory credits (18 of 30) completed in the four years of high school often forces students to make hard choices (Graduation Requirements n.d.). The focus on STEM subjects consumes even those limited option credit spaces. The emphasis on technological training to encourage students to embrace careers in the trades further competes for students' attention. But perhaps the biggest challenge is students' impoverished reading and writing abilities in English as a result of the Whole Language approach introduced in the 1980s. This has diminished a student's ability to understand the fundamentals of a phonetic language like Latin or Greek and often influences them not to continue past the first year, even though continued study in either language could develop those skills. Finally, Covid-19 pandemic learning has affected all languages. Despite Canada's support of multilingualism, many students shy away from further language study (ICEF 2022).

At the secondary school level in Ontario, Latin is the main 'Classics' subject taught, whereas at the post-secondary level, it is clearly Classical Civilization. There is a divide between the high schools and the universities. In Ontario, post-1968, Latin survived in pockets around the province where there were already strong programmes because the teachers embraced a new approach to teaching introduced by the reading method found in the *Cambridge Latin Course* (CSCP 1998). Those teachers already heard the call to action in the Hall–Dennis Report (1968) about adapting their teaching styles to meet the interests and needs of their audience. Gone are the days of rote memorization of endless verb and noun paradigms. Now, discussions focus on Roman culture, and the Latin stories which students read reflect that. Students learn about mythology, clothing, food, entertainment and elements of culture which parallel their own life experiences. This is the primary difference between high school and university approaches to language instruction. University professors most often focus on traditional pedagogical methods in order to move students into translating original source texts often too quickly, and without recognizing the gaps in their students' English language background. Few students are willing to allocate the time and energy needed to learn a language *ab initio*. And so, university classical language courses languish beyond the first year. Departments compensate by creating exceptionally intriguing Classical Studies courses. The great irony is that it is the scholars' own abilities to read and translate the original Latin and Greek sources which allow them to apply their research in designing the suite of classical civilization courses on offer. In high school, teachers must adapt constantly, using every pedagogical trick in their arsenal to make Latin and Greek palatable to their audience. And it is the pedagogical approach when teaching the classical languages which is the principal difference between the two panels. If classical languages are to survive at both levels, this is where the conversation between high school teachers and professors must begin.

Subject associations and the promotion of Classics

No teacher, at any level, can be effective without opportunities to advance their academic and pedagogical repertoire of skills. Therefore, subject associations are absolutely vital to any teacher, in any subject, because they allow for collaboration and sharing pedagogical approaches and resources. They build allies in a world where teachers in all panels may need to reach out for help from time to time. For Classics, in particular, association provides important support, alleviating the professional isolation the lone Latin teacher in a school, or a school board, experiences. By 1969, after the Hall–Dennis Report (1968) was released, in the northern region of Ontario a group of Latin teachers met at Korah Collegiate in Sault Ste Marie, three hours north of Toronto, on the first Saturday of May to hold a series of events which would allow them to give their students a chance to see Latin in an entirely new way. They offered a history contest, a Latin translation contest, a Latin vocabulary and derivative contest, and *Quaerite Summa*, a series of rapid-fire questions about elements of Roman life where students signalled their answers by 'buzzing in' on a machine. There was a simulated archaeological dig, some running events and even a chariot race. The students 'ad libbed' a short skit on an ancient theme and held a fashion show just ahead of the banquet where toga-clad participants enjoyed a feast worthy of the Romans. The night concluded with a dance to celebrate. That single event was a resounding success and the Ontario Student Classics Conference was born.

By 1988 teachers realized that they needed a longer conference and a larger venue to host the 500 Classics students attending. In 1989 Queen's University in Kingston hosted the hordes of Classics enthusiasts which descended upon it from across the province. Despite a brief hiatus during the Covid-19 pandemic when the event moved online, it has resurrected itself at Brock University. The Classics Conference energizes Latin classrooms in unanticipated ways. The event encourages teachers and students to apply their knowledge of the ancient world in unique and creative ways; it builds a rapport and relationship with the teacher in a way the regular day's teaching does not; it extends students' social contacts, often providing a safe place for the student who has limited social outlets; it encourages and builds leadership skills through fundraising and intramural events; it provides the Classics Club, which accompanies any conference-bound class, a prominence in the school by allowing students to contribute to its overall student life.

The Classics Conference often retains students who might have chosen a different elective subject, other than Latin, in the next academic year. The excitement and enthusiasm of the students promotes not only the Classics Club but Latin in magical ways. It allows for interaction between the Classics Conference participants and university officials who attend the event. It introduces students to Classics professors, demystifying post-secondary education, and even assists students in refining their post-secondary destination and course choices. The Classics Conference provides opportunities to promote Classics in the wider community when the media publicizes the event (the chariot race is always popular with the media), as part of the university's community engagement, which promotes it. It also allows teachers and professors to engage in critical dialogue about trends in the classroom, challenges and successes; it increases teachers' professional contacts beyond their subject associations and unions with the professional community which affects them most directly. This event is the reason why many students have gone on to study Classics at university and then teach it. All the necessary elements required to build Classics in both panels come together at this conference – there is no other event of its kind in Canada. It bears repeating: without Classics majors, who also enrol in classical languages courses, seeking a Bachelor of Education with an eye to teaching Latin, there is no future for the subject at the high school level.

A number of classical organizations across Canada support professors and their students as well by providing conferences at which they can deliver academic papers and engage in important discussions about the state of the profession. The Classical Association of Canada West rotates its meetings through the participating universities from British Columbia to Manitoba. The Atlantic Classical Association provides the same opportunities for the professors within New Brunswick, Nova Scotia, Prince Edward Island and Newfoundland to meet in the same way. The professors of Quebec enjoy opportunities to meet via *La Société d'études anciennes du Québec*. The Classical Association of Canada (CAC) is a national organization which meets annually in a rotating schedule so that classicists from across the country can convene. Its focus is primarily on providing professional opportunities to the professoriate, and graduate students who will one day be a part of that professoriate. Its Board of Directors established a 'pre-university teacher' role in 2000 to encourage dialogue with Classics teachers at the secondary level. The association offers the Grace Irwin Memorial Scholarship, a homage to a beloved teacher of Latin and Greek in Toronto. The CAC holds an annual translation contest for high school students across the country. But that is the extent of its engagement with high school teachers, and conversations about effective pedagogical strategies to support Classics or encourage teaching as a career infrequently occur. Finally, the Ontario Classical Association provides regular engagement between teachers and professors; both panels meet each October or November and share papers and discussions of common interest in the provision of classical education in Ontario. The mission is for teachers and professors to work side-by-side on initiatives to support the subject. The time has come for the various classical associations to begin the larger conversation of ways by which to close the gap between the panels and work towards promoting teaching Classics as a viable career option for graduates in order to rejuvenate programmes at all levels in all provinces.

The future

On first glance, the state of Classics in Canada may seem grim. Canada is vast, so vast that its provincial educational systems may seem too rigid to accommodate the possibility of Classics returning to the curriculum, but there is a mechanism in the over-arching curriculum policies via the 'locally developed course' so that communities can meet the interests of their students. This is one place to start. The wonderful diversity in languages and cultures ranging from the First Nations to a host of heritage languages may seem to contain educational challenges too great for provincial governments, such that small subjects like Classics continue to be relegated to the shadows, but in fact these create enormous opportunities for Classics to support acquisition of all languages. The overwhelming focus on STEM as a result of the perceived shift in the Canadian economic landscape affects student choices of subjects, but here again is another opportunity for teachers of Latin and Greek to demonstrate their ability to support students in learning specialized terminologies and to hone their critical thinking skills. The Covid-19 pandemic negatively impacted all subjects in every jurisdiction around the globe, but here too is a chance for Classics to help in the recovery of students' language skills. In response to directives by the Ontario Human Rights Commission's Right to Read (2022), a new Language Arts curriculum is replacing the Whole Language system with Phonics in the elementary schools in Ontario and this is an ideal place for Classics teachers to provide support.

However, one critical challenge remains: the accelerated retirement rate of teachers. Not only does this jeopardize the continued presence of Classics in the curriculum, but it also inhibits such outreach and public engagement. Most critically, the lack of a Bachelor of Education in Classical Studies: Latin, which would encourage undergraduates to continue to study Latin and Greek, is a seemingly insurmountable difficulty. Or is it? Classics is still a viable programme at university and for students studying Bachelor of Arts degrees, who are choosing to enrol in Classics courses: there is some very rich earth in which to sow some seeds. The British charity Classics for All has generated hundreds of new Latin, Greek and Classical Civilization programmes across England by offering training to practising teachers in other subject disciplines. Classics for All has demonstrated that where students are introduced to Classics early in their academic development, they improve their language and critical thinking skills, and often these successes prompt students to proceed to study Classics at university. If these students receive a degree in Classics from a university, or even just enrol in Classics courses including the languages, then these could be the teachers of the future who can rejuvenate Classics in the school system overall. At the very least, they are allies of the subject. Such a bold undertaking on the part of Classics for All took some vision to see the potential, some effort to establish the groundwork, some cooperation between the high schools and universities, some ingenuity to find the means and personnel, and some luck; but there is no reason why that cannot happen on this side of the Atlantic. That slow march to obscurity does not have to be the final destination for Classics programmes in Canada. Perhaps those images of pods of orcas, the majestic Rockies, the Prairies' golden wheatfields, the lofty CN Tower, *les petites maisons*, the fishers hauling in their nets can be accompanied by images of thousands of students sitting in classrooms discussing the House of Caecilius in Pompeii and pointing out some English words derived from Latin as they prepare for the Classics Conference. That is not giving up on a 'lost cause', because Classics in Canada is not one. That is optimism. In short, it is a Canadian thing.

References

Alberta Education (2023), 'Programs of Study'. Available online: www.education.alberta.ca/international-languages-10-12/programs-of-study/ (accessed 14 August 2023).

BC's Curriculum (n.d.), 'Languages. Building Student Success'. Available online: https://curriculum.gov.bc.ca/curriculum/languages/courses (accessed 14 August 2023).

Bellefontaine, M. (2021), 'Northwest Territories Drops Alberta K-12 Curriculum after at Least 40 Years of Use', *CBC*, 17 December. Available online: www.cbc.ca/news/canada/edmonton/nwt-alberta-kindergarten-grade-12-school-curriculum -1.6289214#:~:text=Edmonton- (accessed 14 August 2023).

CSCP (1998), *Cambridge Latin Course* (4th edition), Cambridge: Cambridge University Press.

Government of Nova Scotia (n.d.), 'High School Full Course List. Education & Early Childhood Development'. Available online: https://curriculum.novascotia.ca/english-programs/high-school/full-course-list (accessed 15 August 2023).

Government of Ontario (2023), 'Classical Studies and International Languages'. Available online: www.dcp.edu.gov.on.ca/en/curriculum/classical-studies-intl-languages (accessed 14 August 2023).

Graduation Requirements (n.d.), 'Graduation Requirements for the English Program'. Available online: https://www.edu.gov.mb.ca/k12/policy/gradreq/docs/grad_req_en.pdf (accessed 17 August 2023).

Hall, B. and E. Dennis (1968) 'Living and Learning: The Report of the Provincial Committee on Aims and Objectives of Education in the Schools of Ontario'. Available online: www.connexions.org/CxLibrary/Docs/CX5636-HallDennis.htm. (accessed 1 September 2023).

ICEF (2022), 'Canadian language schools weather another decline in 2021 but emerge with "optimism for recovery and growth"', *ICEF Monitor*, 3 August. Available online: https://monitor.icef.com/2022/08/canadian-language-schools-weather-another-decline-in-2021-but-emerge-with-optimism-for-recovery-and-growth-in-2022/ (accessed 19 December 2023).

Ontario Human Rights Commission (2022), 'Executive Summary'. Available online: www.ohrc.on.ca/en/right-to-read-inquiry-report/executive-summary (accessed 2 September 2023).

Ontario Ministry of Education and Training (1999), *Classical and International Languages*. Available online: https://www.uwindsor.ca/education/sites/uwindsor.ca.education/files/curriculum_classical_studies_and_international_languages_9-10.pdf (accessed 19 December 2023).

Peritz, I. (2009), 'Cogito, Ergo Latin', *The Globe and Mail*, 15 September. Available online: www.theglobeandmail.com/news/national/cogito-ergo-latin/article4214730/ (accessed 17 August 2023).

Saskatchewan Curriculum (n.d.), 'Blackboard Learn'. Available online: https://curriculum.gov.sk.ca/ (accessed 14 August 2023).

Warren (1967–8), 'Royal Commission Report'. Available online: https://www.heritage.nf.ca/articles/society/royal-commission-education-1968.php (accessed 19 December 2023).

Organizations

Brock University: https://brocku.ca/
Classical Association of Canada: https://www.cac-scec.ca/
Classics for All: https://classicsforall.org.uk/
Classical Association of the Canadian West (CACW): www.sfu.ca/classics/cacw/index.html

La Société des Études Anciennes du Québec: https://www.laseaq.org/
McMaster University: https://www.mcmaster.ca/
Ontario Classical Association: www.ontarioclassicalassociation.ca/
Ontario College for Teachers: https://www.oct.ca/
Ontario Institute for Studies in Education: https://www.oise.utoronto.ca/home
Queen's University, Kingston: https://www.queensu.ca/
Vergilian Society: https://www.vergiliansociety.org/
York University: https://www.yorku.ca/

UNITED STATES OF AMERICA

Teresa Ramsby

Introduction

Elementary and secondary education in the United States is a complicated patchwork of public schools, publicly funded magnet and charter schools, privately funded schools, and home-schooling environments. Each type of school manifests many variations in its educational environment: a public, magnet or charter school will follow a state-approved curriculum but can also feature a wide variety of thematic and academic structures (college-preparatory, vocational, a focus on the arts, STEM (Science, Technology, Engineering and Mathematics), language immersion, etc.). Private (or independent) schools can take any number of forms, such as highly subsidized, religious schools in urban centres or expensive, boarding-option schools that may feature an international student body. Home-schooling can take place within a single family or within a community of neighbours or among online subscribers with similar learning goals. In addition, there are increasing opportunities for students to take online courses through various platforms to augment or replace courses taken at brick-and-mortar schools. In some locations, high school juniors and seniors may take courses at their own schools or at local colleges that can then be applied towards college-credit.

Funding for public schools comes from federal, state and local governments, and the formula that determines school funding differs for each of the fifty states within the US. On average, local funding provides 45 per cent of the budget for schools, and since most of that support comes from property taxes, public schools are highly dependent on regional property values (Hanson 2023). All students are entitled, by law, to enter their district's public schools unless punitive measures have expelled them. Admission into charter and magnet schools may depend on a qualifying application or exam, or a lottery system. In some states, parents can apply for vouchers to send their students to private schools using state funds. 'School choice', the option of selecting a public school outside one's residential area or district, is also available in most states. The educational choices available to US parents and their children, therefore, often depends on where they live.

Each of the US fifty states and five territories (American Samoa, Guam, the Northern Mariana Islands, Puerto Rico, and the US Virgin Islands) has a department of education that determines the overall structure of the curriculum to be used by publicly funded schools within the state or territory. 'World Languages' is the title given by most departments of education to the discipline of second language learning. The standards of learning the various world languages, including classical languages, are periodically updated by the American Council for the Teaching of Foreign Languages (ACTFL) and cooperating disciplinary organizations. The American Classical League (ACL) cooperates in applying the standards to Latin and Greek. The standards are widely known as the 'Five Cs' (Communication, Cultures, Connections, Comparisons and Communities), with many constituent elements and benchmarks that are indicative of student proficiency in the language at different learning levels. These standards and benchmarks are then typically adapted by each state's Department of Education to match the learning goals of that region.

The specific languages taught vary from district to district and school to school, depending on parental and student interest and enrolments and, naturally, on the availability of teachers. Requirements for taking courses in World Languages vary widely across the US. According to a 2017 report published by the American Council for International Education (ACIE), only sixteen states have language requirements for all publicly educated students and the remaining states treat languages as electives (ACIE Report 2017: 6). Perhaps not surprisingly, a Pew Research Center study indicates that when schools do not implement language requirements, US high school students take far fewer courses in World Languages (Devlin 2018). Since 2011, there has been increasing encouragement from groups promoting language learning for states to grant a 'global seal of biliteracy', a certification that recognizes a student's proficiency in a second language and that may count towards language requirements at a college or university. At this stage, only a small percentage of US colleges currently recognize this certification. There are two significant assessments of Latin, provided annually, whose scores are generally recognized at the college level for credit towards language requirements: the College Board's Advanced Placement Latin exam and the Latin exam offered by the International Baccalaureate programme. Success in these assessments typically requires three to four Latin courses in high school, which serves as an incentive for some students to continue taking the language.

Classical languages and subjects in US schools and perceptions of Classics

Latin is still widely taught in the US, and in 2017 was ranked the fifth most popular language, with an estimated 210,306 students in grades 9–12 taking Latin, and roughly 2,000 in grades 3–8 (ACIE Report 2017). Ancient Greek is taught far less frequently, and in most cases is merely introduced to students in units within existing Latin courses or in extra-curricular 'Latin clubs'. Most students do not have access to Latin until the seventh, eighth, or, more typically, ninth grade (ages 12–15), and it is rare to see Latin offered before the seventh grade. The length of time a student takes Latin depends on the language requirement, a student's interest or success in the courses, and a student's schedule. Most schools that offer Latin also offer other language study options, and so Latin is typically a course that students select from available options. There are some (though not many) public, charter and magnet schools that require years of Latin study, as do many private or independent schools.

Courses on Greek and Roman histories and cultures, ideal complements to or preparation for Latin learning, are taught as units within Social Studies courses in many US schools, but a cursory look at state curricular guidelines reveals a wide range of grade-levels in which the subject appears, with some schools offering Graeco-Roman history only in elementary grades and others only in high school. The amount of time spent on this topic varies considerably by district and school, with some schools teaching the subject only once for a few weeks, and other schools repeating instruction about the ancient world at various levels. Greek mythology may be presented to elementary or middle school students, and ancient literature in translation, such as Homer's *Odyssey* or Sophocles' *Oedipus Tyrannus*, may be presented in high school English Language Arts classes. Even so, there are no consistent, nationwide expectations that students will learn about these topics, and it is difficult to find statistics on how many students learn about the Greek and Roman world or its literature.

Since the presentation of such information about the Graeco-Roman world is often not provided to students at the same time as Latin instruction is offered, Latin teachers typically provide historical and cultural information to contextualize the ancient Mediterranean world as they teach Latin. Indeed, they are encouraged to do so by the 'cultures', 'comparisons' and 'connections' standards for classical language learning (among the 'Five C's' mentioned above). Latin teachers typically have a broad understanding of the history, material culture and cultural practices of the classical world, and they frequently bring elements of this into their classrooms. For example, teachers host Roman banquets, introduce stories from myth, show images pertinent to the ancient world (artistic works from a wide variety of periods, archaeological sites and reconstructions of ancient sites are very popular), and encourage students to make comparisons between the ancient world and their own, as attested by countless online video posts. These pedagogical practices are bolstered by conferences, online blogs and social media groups where teachers share ideas with each other about effective ways to facilitate a connection between their students and the ancient world. There are likewise events designed for Latin students that feature and assess (in games and activities) contextual understandings of the ancient world as well as linguistic skills, such as the National Junior Classical League convention that occurs annually in the summer and is attended by more than a thousand Latin students. Regional and local events also occur throughout the US for Latin students.

It is difficult to address the value or perception of Classics in American education without delving into the complicated history of class, race and regional attitudes that pertain to educational access. Since the founding of the North American colonies, the study of classical languages was deemed necessary only for those seeking post-secondary education and planning to enter vocational and professional life in the clergy and the law, a life designed almost exclusively for young white men (LaFleur 2000: 8–11). As a result, Latin was made available in elite schools or through private tutors for the sons of wealthy Americans, with a few notable exceptions, such as the still extant Boston Latin School, founded a year before Harvard College to educate students regardless of family income (Wright 1889). America's engagement in the slave trade and the deep-seated and bitter racism inflicted upon all those of African heritage, and, by extension, many other immigrant groups living in the US, are relevant to educational access and, thus, the perception of classical languages. After 1740, until President Abraham Lincoln signed the Emancipation Proclamation in 1863, it was illegal in most southern slave-states for Black people to be taught to read (Span 2005; Span & Sanya 2019). After 1863, millions of newly freed persons sought an education that had long been denied them and their ancestors, and for some this education included study of the classical languages that might open doors to post-secondary education and professional careers (Ronnick 2012; McPherson 2014: 154–71).

In 1918, W. E. B. Du Bois, the well-known Black writer, theorist and activist, and accomplished student and instructor of classical literature, harshly criticized an education report's suggestion that classical languages be removed from the education of Black students (Jones 1916; Ravitch 2000: 107–12). Du Bois wrote that any who denied Black students access to courses of higher learning like Greek and Latin 'make it absolutely impossible for Negro students to be thoroughly trained according to modern standards' (Du Bois 1918: 2). Even so, the ongoing debate between Du Bois and other Black leaders, like Booker T. Washington, who favoured vocational training over liberal arts education for Black students, demonstrates that the study of classical languages has long been perceived both as an unnecessary hurdle for those seeking education and as a benefit that could lift marginalized people into the echelons of higher learning and, thereby, standing and affluence within American society (Span & Sanya 2019; Withun 2022).

Additionally, persistent racial segregation of schools in the post-bellum years in the United States had a profoundly negative effect on the access that many students of colour had to a well-resourced education and the kinds of schools where Latin and Greek might be offered (Ravitch 2000: 371–7). In the ensuing seventy years since *Brown v. Board of Education*, the US Supreme Court decision in 1954 that rendered school segregation unconstitutional, there have been many shifting perspectives on what school curricula should offer. All this has certainly affected the perception of classical languages in schools. In the late 1960s and early 1970s, the period of the civil rights movement, many schools rejected the study of classical languages as an irrelevant discipline inherited from outdated educational models that catered to the interests of established elites (Kitchell 1998; Adler 2016). As a result, the number of students taking Latin in US high schools plunged from half a million in 1965 to roughly 150,000 in 1976, a drop of nearly 75 per cent (LaFleur 2000; Kitchell 2020).

The efforts of K-12 [school-level] and college Latin instructors and many national and regional organizations dedicated to the study of classical languages, brought renewed attention to the potential benefits of taking Latin. The Sub-Committee on National Latin Guidelines, formed in 1986 to compile data on the study of Latin in US schools, describes compelling reasons that communities choose to feature Latin in their schools' curricula, including: 'the improvement of English vocabulary, an increased awareness of language structures, [and] the broadening of cultural horizons' (Davis 1991: 8). Other benefits often cited were improvements in literacy and in reading and writing scores on the Scholastic Aptitude Test (SAT), an exam that assesses general academic proficiencies of college applicants in the US. These efforts improved perceptions of Latin study in K-12 schools, and enrolments in Latin rose again gradually, landing in the range 200,000 to 220,000 students from 2010 to 2023, yet still well below the numbers of the early 1960s.

Despite this return to some stability in the number of students taking Latin, there persist concerns about what the study of classical languages achieves, whom it serves, and to what extent it benefits students, particularly students of colour. As Eric Adler points out, despite great disagreement among scholars in the American 'culture wars' of the 1980s and 1990s about the future of humanities and what should constitute the canon literature, there was general agreement that Classics the discipline, with its focus on Greek and Latin, was 'stodgy and elitist' (Adler 2016: 140). Some have declared Classics inherently elitist and racist in the way it is taught and in the cultural and historical hegemonies associated with it (Pearcy 2005; Bracey 2017; Poser 2021; Umachandran and Ward 2024). These arguments are met, in turn, with concerns that students, and particularly students of colour, are being underestimated in their ability to take on the rigours of learning classical languages (e.g. McWhorter 2021). There are others who promote alternative methods of teaching classical languages to make them more accessible to a greater population of students, an issue that will be featured at greater length in the next section. A definitive study in the United States is still needed to discern what skills and to what extent the identified skills benefit from Latin language learning, though some limited studies do exist (Haag & Stern 2003; Crosson et al. 2018).

For many decades, one idea used to promote the study of Latin has been that it facilitates students' understanding of the foundations of 'Western civilization'. There are connections, of course, between the ancient Mediterranean world and many political and social aspects of Western cultures and of non-Western cultures, whether through colonialism or self-determination. Yet some groups have demonstrated an interest in privileging 'the foundations of Western civilization' through the study of Latin to promote historical perspectives that focus on the achievements of European settlers of North America and their descendants, achievements that are sometimes sanitized and ahistorical, at the expense of a wider understanding of global, cultural achievement (Adler 2016: 196–200; Zuckerberg 2018: 22–39, 185–90; Francisco & Burris 2023). An unfortunate result of this privileging of European history and culture is an implicit message broadcast to students of colour that they would do well to avoid an entire humanities discipline and its hundreds of volumes of literary sources, that this branch of study is not for them. To the contrary, these ancient sources unlock a dimension of historical perspectives and literary creativity to any who engage with them, offering myriad opportunities for examining the ancient world and assumptions made about it, assumptions that can only be questioned and rewritten if studied through multiple perspectives.

In response to this problem, there have been considerable efforts among many Classics organizations to disassociate the study of Latin from any such privileging of Western civilization, as seen, for example in the 'What Is Classics' statement on the website of the international Society for Classical Studies (see https://classicalstudies.org/about#WhatisClassics). Many people have presented papers at conferences and in teaching journals on the value of learning about the ancient world in ways that eschew the notion Greek and Roman 'whiteness' and that feature the achievements and perspectives of a multicultural ancient world, bringing the long-overlooked voices of, for example, women and enslaved people into focus (e.g. Dugan 2019; He 2022; Das 2022; Kennedy 2022). Many instructors now use Latin and Greek texts as tools for examining complicated and problematic cultural realities throughout history. When encouraged to study Latin in an environment where the ancient world offers modes of open discovery, rather than tools of politicized propaganda, many students of colour take interest (Stringer 2019; Patrick 2020; Taylor 2021; Vanderpool 2021a, 2021b).

The perception of the study of classical languages in the United States, therefore, is not just a story of the discipline itself and any concomitant effects or benefits of taking Latin, but of its perception as a tool wielded for differing social and political purposes. As Classics is redefined and reassessed by new generations through the dedicated work of informed teachers, it remains relevant and engaging to young people throughout the United States.

Trends in Classics teaching in the US

The *Standards for Classical Language Learning*, first published in 1997 and revised in 2017, is the major document that outlines the overall objectives and benchmarks for students learning classical languages, principally Latin, and is available on the website of the American Classical League (*Standards* 2017). The standards for language learning, the 'Five Cs' and their constituent parts, present the purposes of learning languages: so students can use and share, comprehend and interpret, and present information in the language (Communication), understand the cultural products and practices of the ancient world (Cultures); compare Latin to other languages (Comparisons); find intersections between Latin and other disciplines (Connections); and find fellowship through the process of learning Latin in extra-curricular activities and in the broader world (Communities). For each standard, levels of proficiency are established, so that student abilities, when assessed, can be assigned to a particular level and, thus, progress can be demonstrated over time. These proficiency levels are labeled novice, intermediate, advanced, and superior, and the first three levels are sub-divided into low, mid and high. This rubric is accompanied by helpful narrative descriptions so that teachers can match and identify students' abilities as they assess them. Latin teachers often refer to these standards in their own curriculum planning and use their benchmarks in assessing student progress.

The specific methods that US teachers use to instruct students in the Latin language are quite various but tend to coalesce around three major approaches to teaching Latin: grammar-translation, reading comprehension, and communicative Latin (also called 'active Latin'). This volume's co-editor, Steven Hunt, cogently and elaborately describes and evaluates each of these three styles of teaching in his 2022 book, *Teaching Latin: Contexts, Theories and Practices*, and I point the reader there for immensely helpful details and bibliography regarding the development and practice of each method. What follows is a brief summary of each approach.

Throughout much of the twentieth century, the primary method of teaching Latin in US schools has been 'grammar-translation', where each unit of learning conveys one or more aspects of Latin grammar matched with sentence-length exercises and readings, typically from brief, un-adapted or lightly adapted Roman sources that feature those grammatical aspects. Grammatical knowledge, therefore, precedes the reading of texts, a method of learning Latin that privileges grammatical structures, paradigms and terminologies, and that necessitates the ability to memorize these and apply them to short passages of text, typically taken out of their literary context, for the purposes of translation into English. Textbooks used in association with this method include *Wheelock's Latin* by LaFleur and Wheelock (2011) and the *Jenney's* Latin textbooks by Jenney, Baade and Burgess (1990).

In the early 1990s, Latin teachers acted upon their increasing observations that many students struggled with the rote memorization of grammatical concepts and became bored, having minimal access to compelling texts appropriate to their level (Gruber-Miller 2006). This led to many teachers adopting the method referred to as 'reading comprehension', in which teachers offer their students texts newly created or heavily adapted from Roman sources. These texts feature, typically, a sequential narrative that begins with shorter sentences and simpler syntactical structures and more limited vocabulary, and then builds gradually to longer, more complicated syntactical structures and a richer vocabulary. When approaching a reading, the teacher asks students to first read for comprehension, with copious vocabulary aids provided. Students are then asked questions about the text so they can demonstrate their understanding of it and are asked to speculate how a word's form makes it function in the sentence. Only then, ideally, are students introduced to the relevant grammatical concepts. This approach allows students to read longer passages of text and develop greater confidence in their reading ability (Craib 1992; McCaffrey 2006). The emergence of textbooks with engaging narratives or heavily adapted stories from Latin texts like the *Cambridge Latin Course* (CSCP 2016) (the most popular Latin textbook in the US), *Ecce Romani* by Gilbert Lawall

(2005), the all-Latin reader *Lingua Latina per se illustrata* by Hans Ørberg (2003), *Latin for the New Millennium* by Milena Minkova and Terence Tunberg (2008), and *Suburani* by Hands Up Education (2020), make this approach viable in the Latin classroom. Teachers also use 'tiered' texts, featuring successively more complicated adaptations of a Latin text until the original is supplied, or 'embedded' readings, featuring simplified, but not adapted, texts with phrases successively added back in until the original is restored. Due to the abundant resources developed for this method, it remains a highly popular pedagogical style.

Around 2010, the method sometimes referred to as 'communicative Latin' emerged in the US, in which Latin is introduced to students through its frequent, spoken use in the classroom. At the same time, there was growing awareness among Latin teachers regarding the research of linguist Stephen Krashen and his theories on methods of second language acquisition, namely that (similar to the way infants learn their first language) students must be exposed to a great deal of 'comprehensible input', whereby the language is spoken comprehensibly in their presence so that they mentally absorb vocabulary and syntax as they listen and respond using the same words and constructions they hear used repeatedly (Krashen 1982; Patrick 2011). Students are then asked to read the language in texts that use the forms they have already heard and used in the classroom. The language is very gradually complicated, and as this happens, students are asked to link grammatical inflections to meaning, and, with targeted and explicit exposure to grammatical principles, they read the language more proficiently over time using gradually more advanced texts (Carlon 2013, 2023). A key aspect of this method is its focus on vocabulary: students are repeatedly familiarized with Latin vocabulary through spoken Latin until they have internalized the meaning of 90 to 95 per cent of the words they are expected to read in a text, the amount recognized as the key to proficient reading (Schmitt et al. 2011; Carlon 2016). Students exposed to Latin in this way become better able to read, listen to and use Latin as a spoken language, increasing the kinds of activities that occur in the classroom and, potentially, making Latin classes more engaging. New assessments have developed to capture the skills of students taught by this method, such as the ACTFL Latin Interpretive Reading Assessment (ALIRA) available through Language Testing International. Many proponents of this method also credit it with enlarging and diversifying the student population taking Latin in their schools (Stringer 2019; Patrick 2011, 2015, 2020). At least one recent survey has demonstrated that this method has grown in popularity since 2010 within the US (Ramsby 2020).

Due to a growing need for Latin texts that match the linguistic level and reading proficiency of a student, a cottage industry of Latin readers that present stories in Latin at various reading levels, dubbed 'Latin novellas', has exploded in the United States (Ramsby 2022; Vanderpool 2021b). Some Latin teachers who prefer this method use established textbooks, like *Lingua Latina* or the *Cambridge Latin Course* as a textual source for the spoken Latin activities they do in class, while some do not use established textbooks, but rather provide texts they have created or Latin novellas for students to read on their own or with the rest of the class. Students in classes using the communicative Latin method, proponents claim, are given more Latin texts to read, thus corroborating their mental map of the language and its vocabulary as they gradually increase their ability to read syntactically more challenging works in Latin.

No definitive study has yet been done to prove which of these three methods is more effective in teaching Latin. Indeed, the parameters and meaning of the phrase 'teaching Latin effectively' can be configured very differently from one Latin classroom to another, depending on its goals and benchmarks. Some assume that the goal of taking Latin in high school is to read classical

Roman authors, yet in a survey sent to Latin teachers in 1989, only 33 per cent of responding teachers reported that 'the reading of Latin literature in the original language was a very important reason to students for studying Latin', while 82 per cent of teachers reported that the most important reason students took Latin 'was to boost their SAT scores' (Davis 1991: 6). In a 2015 survey, 45 per cent of Latin students reported that their number one reason for taking Latin was to learn about ancient mythology (Goodman 2015). These results are a reminder that Latin classes in the US serve many important functions, only one of which is the reading of classical Roman authors. The elective nature of Latin courses within most schools grants most teachers the freedom to select the methods that they deem effective within their school community.

Digital technology plays an ever-increasing role in the Latin classroom, regardless of the methodology pursued. Students in many schools receive designated laptops which they use, for example, to do exercises and assessments that their teachers create for them on digital platforms, play interactive games on sites with multimodal applications for various disciplines, and watch videos about Latin and the ancient world. There are also numerous textual resources online where teachers can access classical, medieval, Renaissance and legal texts, and thus broaden their students' exposure to Latin works. Digital technology was crucial to the operation of all classes throughout the Covid pandemic and continues to be a useful partner to Latin teachers as they engage their students, who increasingly enjoy online activities, in studying this ancient language.

Latin teacher preparation in the US

Opportunities for Latin teacher training, or educator preparation, exist primarily through graduate-level programmes within Classics departments at several universities in the US. The degree offered is usually at the Master's degree level and is often conferred with teaching licensure, or certification, obtained from the same university's department or school of education, a cooperative venture that successfully produces teachers every year. Licensure granted through these educator preparation programmes is typically a level higher than preliminary licensure which ensures that educators with this certification begin their careers without pursuing additional coursework in education. Most states also offer a third level of licensure, often referred to as 'professional licensure', obtained after years of teaching experience and with additional subject matter coursework and/or evidence of professional development (such as attendance at conferences and workshops). Licensure is required in most states for teachers working in public schools, but not necessarily at publicly-funded charter or magnet schools. Licensure is usually not required for teachers working in private or independent schools. In general, certified teachers in public schools, typically also represented by labour unions, tend to earn more than uncertified teachers in charter, magnet, or private/independent schools.

Graduate Latin programmes that provide teaching licensure tend to offer courses featuring Roman or medieval Latin authors so that students gain a broad understanding of the content of the discipline. Some programmes offer pedagogy courses designed specifically to explain methods of teaching Latin and allow students to practise them among their peers. The challenge for many Classics programmes that offer licensure is that university departments of education often demand that many courses be taken in education for the granting of licensure. Classics departments would do well to insist to schools of education, state departments of education, and even to legislators, if necessary, that pedagogy courses be granted by their own faculty so that more Latin teachers enter the field prepared to teach Latin in ways that are informed, effective and engaging. This also requires interest among Classics faculty in teaching pedagogical methods, an interest that has increased in recent years, as seen in numerous publications by college faculty on methods and teacher preparation (e.g. Dugdale 2012; Keeline 2019; Pistone & Ker 2023). Moreover, effective pedagogy is not linked only to subject matter knowledge; a holistic system of instruction accounts for behavioural management as well, such that successful teachers develop strategies within their instructional methods that meet the challenges of behavioural and interest variabilities within the classroom. A teacher who only knows how to teach out of a textbook using modes of reading, translation, and grammatical analysis, for example, is less likely to succeed in the modern classroom than a teacher who understands ways to implement various styles of learning and differentiated instruction, whereby students may be allowed to have choices about modes of learning or be given different tasks or responsibilities in the learning process (Ramsby & Spencer-Bunch 2020).

There are some undergraduate Classics departments that offer coursework in pedagogy for the benefit of their majors intending to pursue a teaching career, but this is not common. Most students who identify in their undergraduate years that they wish to teach after college will minor or double-major in education while pursuing a Classics major. Education courses, however, do not provide expertise in teaching Latin, and it is thus to be encouraged that Classics faculty offer pedagogy courses periodically to students interested in teaching Latin. Students who are able to meet the required coursework and field experience (such as pre-practicum and practicum) while double majoring in Classics and Education will receive licensure with their undergraduate degree.

Students leaving a Classics programme, whether at undergraduate or graduate level, without licensure often find it challenging to obtain certification while pursuing a career in K-12 teaching. The means of obtaining licensure vary from state to state and the process by which licensure is obtained can be time consuming. It is therefore highly recommended that Classics majors interested in teaching in US public schools make plans to seek out undergraduate licensure opportunities or apply to one of the many graduate-level programmes offering an MA in Classics with educational licensure. A complete list of these programmes exists on the SCS website (https://classicalstudies.org/education/graduate-programs-north-america).

The preparation of Latin teachers going into the field is addressed in the 2023 *Guidelines for Latin Teacher Preparation*, a revision of the 2010 *Standards for Latin Teacher Preparation*. The *Guidelines* is the work of an ACL-SCS committee and is now available on the websites of the two organizations. The four guidelines are: Content Knowledge; Pedagogical Knowledge, Skills, and Understanding; Other Areas of Responsibility; and Professional Development and Lifelong Learning. Each guideline explains the various expectations for teachers of Latin and the appropriate skills that teachers will need to effectively teach in the modern classroom. As is made clear in the *Guidelines*, Latin teachers are expected to be more than competent readers and interpreters of Latin. They are expected to be aware of the available literature in Latin from many historical periods, to understand the cultural practices and products of the Romans and the wider ancient Mediterranean world, and to be informed about methods of student assessment, classroom management and professional development. In addition, Latin teachers need to be aware of the major pedagogical methodologies of the discipline so that they can implement curricula and methods that work best for their students or that are expected at their place of employment.

Professional development opportunities for Latin teachers in the US are readily available. ACL offers an annual institute that features workshops, paper presentations and other events designed to inform and inspire Latin teachers. Regional Classics organizations – the Classical Association of New England (CANE), the Classical Association of the Atlantic States (CAAS), the Classical Association of the Middle West and South (CAMWS), and the Classical Association of the Pacific Northwest (CAPN) – offer annual conferences that regularly feature panels and presentations designed for K-12 teachers interested in learning new methods, honing their skills in particular areas, or learning about recent research. State Classics organizations also offer annual meetings where pedagogical ideas and scholarship are shared. The international Society for Classical Studies features panels for K-12 teachers at its annual meeting and offers a reduced rate of membership for K-12 teachers. In addition, there are *conventicula* hosted by a number of institutions and organizations where Latin teachers can gather and immerse themselves in spoken Latin for a few days or a week or more, thus building the skills they will need to implement communicative Latin methods in their classrooms. Many organizations, such as the Vergilian Society, the American Academy in Rome and the American School of Classical Studies at Athens, offer summer tours designed for teachers (as well as university-level students and lifelong learners) who wish to gain familiarity with the sites and topography of the ancient Mediterranean world. The principal obstacle to attending these events is often funding. There are several disciplinary organizations that offer prizes and scholarships for travel annually, and with a bit of online research, teachers may find a scholarship offered for a programme they wish to attend.

The principal challenge to Latin teacher preparation in the twenty-first century will be the availability of teaching positions within the discipline. There has been damage to the wellbeing of Latin programmes in the US since the 2017 survey mentioned above. The debilitating blows of economic turmoil and a global pandemic have caused many school districts to cut programmes like Latin in response to calls for greater investment in STEM courses, modern languages, and vocational preparation programmes in K-12 schools (e.g. Gordon 2019). Latin teachers and Classics faculty in the US have done good work promoting the study of Latin, but the discipline must continue to examine its goals and practices in order to safely secure its place within publicly funded education.

Cooperation between organizations and schools

There are many fruitful associations between schools and Classics organizations in the US. The American Classical League is the primary organization for Latin teachers in the US and has thousands of members and many intersections with other groups like SCS and state organizations. When teachers learn their schools may be dropping their programmes, they reach out to ACL for help in advocating for the continuation of Latin at their school – sometimes effectively. Additionally, most Classics organizations offer travel grants, scholarships for licensure programmes, and support for classroom resources to K-12 teachers. Also, as mentioned above, there are many meetings and conferences throughout the year, hosted by Classics organizations and other entities, like ACTFL and its state subsidiaries, that provide professional development opportunities for Latin teachers.

Latin teachers in the US are highly creative planners, and they take ample opportunity of the cultural resources within their regions. Teachers plan field trips to museums that feature ancient art and other products of the ancient world, and museums often provide ready-made activities for students visiting their collections. Teachers take their students to performances of Greek and Roman plays in their areas, and they get involved with theatrical productions of ancient plays within their own schools. Many Latin teachers plan trips abroad with their students, taking advantage of the many travel companies and Classics organizations that offer student tours of sites from the ancient Mediterranean world.

There are also several publications dedicated to pedagogy in the US from which Latin teachers derive the benefits of information and a sense of community. One of the most widely-read Classics journal in the US is *The Classical Outlook*, a quarterly journal supported by ACL that features articles on pedagogical practices, theoretical perspectives on teaching, scholarship relevant to teaching, and reviews of recent books that teachers may find useful. CAMWS offers the journal *Teaching Classical Languages*, a free access, online publication, that also features articles relevant to pedagogy. CANE also offers a free access, online publication, *The New England Classical Journal* with content often directed to K-12 teachers. Many other classics-related journals that regularly present scholarly research also feature pedagogical articles, such as *Classical World*. The future of Latin in US schools remains promising due, in part, to the fact that the organizations that exist to serve the Latin instructional community are dynamic and motivated to meet the needs of Latin teachers throughout the nation.

Conclusion

Latin pedagogy in the United States demonstrates consistent re-examination and creative innovation, thanks to the immense interest and dedication of thousands of K-12 and college instructors who consider ways to make Latin more engaging to the US student population. When I ask students in my Latin courses at the University of Massachusetts Amherst about their high school Latin teachers, I often hear superlative praises from them about the creativity and ingenuity of their teachers who 'reached' them as a student and taught them to care about ancient history and cultures. I see this energy and drive to improve the field, its teaching methods, and its impact when I attend conferences, like CANE and ACL and SCS, and speak with those engaged with pedagogy and with those creating resources for students of Classics. Latin as a subject of study has a resilience and allure that continues to attract K-12 students, and that is good news for the future of Latin in US schools.

Even so, there are challenges that the discipline must continue to consider, and one is the loss of interest in K-12 Latin students in continuing their studies at the college level. In the 2019/20 academic year, while roughly 200,000 students were taking Latin in high school, only 736 undergraduate degrees in classics were conferred (Basken 2021). That gap, between the allure of Latin to K-12 students and the interest in college majors in pursuing Latin, is one that continues to confound the discipline, perhaps even more acutely so in recent years when humanities courses in general have lost popularity. If even 1 per cent of high school Latin students pursued a classics degree in college, two thousand students would major or double major in classics, more than doubling the current number. Yet it seems that for many students the high school experience with Latin is a sufficient endpoint.

One solution to this problem may be greater idea sharing and problem solving between instructional faculties of the K-12 and collegiate institutions to increase the alignment between college expectations for classical language majors and the goals and methods of K-12 Latin teachers. This may mean incremental or even radical change in the way Latin is taught at the college level, perhaps one more attuned to the reading method or the communicative methods, as some have already proposed (e.g. Keeline 2019; Keeline & Kirby 2023). Such change would mean increasing opportunities for college faculty to learn new methodologies, granting them time and funding to pursue that knowledge. This may mean greater collaboration between colleges, particularly state and publicly funded colleges, and their regional schools so that K-12 Latin students know about the programmes and opportunities available to them at the college level. This is not an insoluble problem, but it requires many agents of change. There are organizations that can facilitate that process, and their collaboration is to be encouraged.

Another challenge that the discipline faces is need for greater support for those who wish to prepare to become Latin teachers. The programmes that exist to train Latin teachers, typically at the graduate level, are increasingly fully funded, and this is good news. Yet more of the courses offered to future Latin teachers need to be taught by experienced and innovative Latin teachers. Education courses serve useful purposes, but they do not always pertain to the holistic nature of teaching Latin that requires not only subject matter knowledge, but also understanding of ways to make the Latin classroom welcoming and accessible to all students. It is one thing to learn about the importance and needs of a diverse student population in general, it is quite another thing to build a Latin programme that attracts diverse students to its courses. The frequent appearance of pedagogical suggestions and solutions in publications and among conference presentations in the US make it clear that Latin instructors care that their courses are perceived as available to all students. College faculty in Classics departments might consider contributing their pedagogical expertise more frequently to ensure that their students who are considering a teaching career receive information about ways to make their Latin classroom a welcoming and engaging place.

Despite the challenges outlined above and pointed to earlier in this chapter, there is much to celebrate regarding the wellbeing of Latin pedagogy and programmes within US schools, as this chapter has also shown. To learn more about the teaching of classical languages in the United States, Steven Hunt's recent volume, *Teaching Latin: Contexts, Theories and Practices* (2022) provides excellent explanations of the major pedagogical methods used in the United States (as well as the UK) and delves into topics such as diversity and inclusion in the Latin classroom and digital resources for Latin teachers. The bibliographies (one for each chapter) that Hunt offers are extremely useful and up-to-date. I also point the reader to the recently revised *Guidelines for Latin Teacher Preparation*, now available on the Society for Classical Studies and American Classical League websites, that includes an *Addendum of Resources* one can access that contains a lengthy bibliography of pedagogical resources. I also point the reader to the revised *Standards for Classical Language Learning*, available currently only in draft form on the ACL website. The websites of ACL, SCS, and the many regional Classics-related organizations are also useful places to see the work and dedication of Latin teachers in the US on display and the many resources available to support the teaching of Latin in the US.

References

Adler, E. (2016), *Classics, the Culture Wars, and Beyond*, Ann Arbor: University of Michigan Press.
ACIE (2017), American Council for International Education, 'The National K-12 Foreign Language Enrollment Survey Report', ACIE. Available online: https://www.americancouncils.org/sites/default/files/FLE-report-June17.pdf (accessed 31 October 2023).

Basken, P. (2021), 'Is Classics' empire in terminal decline?', *Times Higher Education*, 14 October. Available online: https://www.goacta.org/2021/10/is-classics-empire-in-terminal-decline/ (accessed 31 October 2023).

Bracey, J. (2017), 'Why Students of Color Don't Take Latin: Dispatches from the Front Lines', *Eidolon*, 12 October. Available online: https://eidolon.pub/why-students-of-color-dont-take-latin-4ddee3144934 (accessed 31 October 2023).

Carlon, J. (2013), 'The Implications of SLA Research for Latin Pedagogy: Modernizing Latin Instruction and Securing its Place in Curricula', *Teaching Classical Languages*, 4 (2): 106–22.

Carlon, J. (2016), 'Quomodo Dicitur? The Importance of Memory in Language Learning', *Teaching Classical Languages*, 7 (2): 109–35.

Carlon, J. (2023), 'Mind the Gaps: Between Theory, Goals, and Practice in Teaching Latin Students to Read', *The Classical Outlook*, 98 (1): 6–9.

Craib, C. (1992), 'Putting the Reading Method into Practice', *The Classical Outlook*, 69 (4): 117–19.

Crosson, A., M. McKeown, D. Moore and F. Ye (2018), 'Extending the bounds of morphology instruction: teaching Latin roots facilitates academic word learning for English Learner adolescents', *Reading and Writing*, 32 (3): 689–727.

CSCP (2016), Cambridge Latin Course (US 5th edition), New York: Cambridge University Press.

Das, A. (2022), 'Contagious: Covid, Cheating, and the Need for Diversity, Equity, and Inclusion in Classics', *The Classical Outlook*, 97 (2): 41–5.

Davis, S. (1991), *Latin in American Schools: Teaching the Ancient World*, Atlanta: Scholars Press.

Devlin, K. (2018), 'Pew Research Study: Most European students are learning a foreign language in school while Americans lag', *Pew Research Center*, 6 August. Available online: https://www.pewresearch.org/short-reads/2018/08/06/most-european-students-are-learning-a-foreign-language-in-school-while-americans-lag/ (accessed 31 October 2023).

Du Bois, W. (1918), 'Negro Education'. *Crisis*, 15 (4): 173–8.

Dugan, K. (2019), 'The "Happy Slave" Narrative and Classics Pedagogy: A Verbal and Visual Analysis of Beginning Greek and Latin Textbooks', *New England Classical Journal*, 46 (1): 62–87.

Dugdale, E. (2012), 'Classics Pedagogy for Teaching in a Liberal Arts College', *The Classical World*, 106 (1): 124–9.

Francisco, K. and C. Burris (2023), *A Sharp Turn Right: A New Breed of Charter Schools Delivers the Conservative Agenda*, New York: Network for Public Education. Available online: https://networkforpubliceducation.org/topics/reports/ (accessed 31 October 2023).

Goodman, E. (2015), *The National Latin Survey: Latin in Secondary Schools Needs Analysis*, Thesis for Applied Linguistics, Teachers College, Columbia University. Available online: http://www.nationallatinsurvey.com/about.html (accessed 31 October 2023).

Gordon, B. (2019), 'Carpe teach 'em: What is Latin's modern value to high school students?', *The Citizen-Times*, 23 September. Available online: https://www.citizen-times.com/story/news/local/2019/09/23/latin-classes-high-schools-teach-english-history-and-grammar-skill/2340433001/ (accessed 31 October 2023).

Gruber-Miller, J. (2006), 'Communication, Context, and Community: Integrating the *Standards* in the Greek and Latin Classroom', in J. Gruber-Miller (ed.), *When Dead Tongues Speak: Teaching Beginning Greek and Latin*, Oxford: Oxford University Press, 9–23.

Guidelines for Latin Teacher Preparation (2023). Available online: https://classicalstudies.org/education/guidelines-latin-teacher-preparation.

Haag, L. and E. Stern (2003), 'In Search of the Benefits of Learning Latin', *Journal of Educational Psychology*, 95 (1): 174–78.

Hands Up Education (2020), *Suburani*, Haverhill: Hands Up Education.

Hanson, M. (2023), 'U.S. Public Education Spending Statistics', *EducationData.org*, 8 September. Available online: https://educationdata.org/public-education-spending-statistics (accessed 31 October 2023).

He, F. (2022), 'Project Nota: Amplifying the Voices of Female Authors in Latin Classrooms', *The Classical Outlook*, 97 (4): 159–61.

Hunt, S. (2022), *Teaching Latin: Context, Theories and Practices*, London: Bloomsbury Academic.

Jenney, C., E. Baade and T. Burgess (1990), *Jenney's First Year Latin*, Englewood Cliffs: Prentice-Hall.

Jones, T. (1916), *Negro education: a study of the private and higher schools for colored people in the United States*, 2 vols, Education Resources Information Center. Available online: https://eric.ed.gov/?id=ED542635 (accessed 31 October 2023).

Keeline, T. (2019), '*Aut Latine aut Nihil*? A Middle Way', *The Classical Outlook*, 94 (2): 57–65.

Keeline, T. and T. Kirby (2023), 'Latin Vocabulary and Reading Latin: Challenges and Opportunities', *Transactions of the American Philological Association*, 153 (2): 531–59.

Kennedy, R. F. (2022), 'Teaching Race in Greco-Roman Antiquity: Some Considerations and Resources', *The Classical Outlook*, 97 (1): 2–8.

Kitchell, K. (1998), 'The Great Latin Debate: The Futility of Utility', in R. A. LaFleur (ed.), *Latin for the Twenty-First Century: From Concept to Classroom*, Glenview, IL: Addison-Wesley Educational Publishers, 1–14.

Kitchell, K. (2020), 'The Future of Our Past: The Repeating Cycle of Pedagogical Complaint', *The Classical Outlook*, 95 (1): 1–7.

Krashen, S. (1982), *Principles and Practice in Second Language Acquisition*, Oxford: Pergamon Press. Available online: https://www.sdkrashen.com/content/books/principles_and_practice.pdf (accessed 31 October 2023).

LaFleur, R. (2000), 'Latin and Greek Enrollments in America's Schools and Colleges', *Association of Departments of Foreign Languages Bulletin*, 31 (3): 53–8.

LaFleur, R. and F. Wheelock (2011), *Wheelock's Latin* (7th edition), New York: Harper Collins.

Lawall, G. (2005), *Ecce Romani*, Hoboken, NJ: Prentice Hall.

McCaffrey, D. (2006), 'Reading Latin Efficiently and the Need for Cognitive Strategies', in J. Gruber-Miller (ed.), *When Dead Tongues Speak: Teaching Beginning Greek and Latin*, Oxford: Oxford University Press, 113–33.

McPherson, J. (2014), *The Struggle for Equality: Abolitionists and the Negro in the Civil War and Reconstruction*, Princeton: Princeton University Press.

McWhorter, J. (2021), 'The Problem With Dropping Standards in the Name of Racial Equity', *The Atlantic*, 7 June. Available online: https://www.theatlantic.com/ideas/archive/2021/06/princeton-classics-major-latin-greek/619110/ (accessed 31 October 2023).

Minkova, M. and T. Tunberg (2008), *Latin for the New Millennium*, Wauconda, IL: Bolchazy-Carducci Publishers.

Ørberg, H. (2003), *Lingua Latin per se illustrata*, Newburyport, MA: Focus Publishing.

Patrick, R. (2011), 'TPRS and Latin in the Classroom: Experiences of a US Latin Teacher', *Journal of Classics Teaching*, 22: 10–11.

Patrick, R. (2015), 'Making Sense of Comprehensible Input in the Latin Classroom', *Teaching Classical Languages*, 6 (1): 108–36.

Patrick, R. (2020), 'Teaching Latin Through the Back Door', *The Classical Outlook*, 95 (1): 15–19.

Pearcy, L. (2005), *The Grammar of Our Civility: Classical Education in America*, Waco, TX: Baylor University Press.

Pistone, A. and J. Ker (2023), 'The *CO* Interview: A College Educator Reflects Publicly on Classics Teaching', *The Classical Outlook*, 98 (3): 101–6.

Poser, R. (2021), 'He Wants to Save Classics from Whiteness. Can the Field Survive?', *The New York Times Magazine*, 2 February. Available online: https://www.nytimes.com/2021/02/02/magazine/classics-greece-rome-whiteness.html (accessed 31 October 2023).

Ramsby, T. (2020), 'Changing Methods in Latin Teaching: Highlights of a Survey', *The Classical Outlook*, 95 (1): 20–7.

Ramsby, T. (2022), 'The Utility and Representational Opportunity of Latin Novellas', *New England Classical Journal*, 49 (1): 102–11.

Ramsby, T. and A. Spencer-Bunch (2020), 'Differentiated Instruction in the Latin Classroom: Feasibility and Best Practices', *The Classical Outlook*, 95 (2): 45–54.

Ravitch, D. (2000), *Left Back: A Century of Failed School Reforms*, New York: Simon and Schuster.

Ronnick, M. (2012), '"Saintly Souls": White Teachers' Advocacy and Instruction of Greek and Latin to African American Freedmen', in S. Bell and T. Ramsby (eds), *Free at Last: The Impact of Freed Slaves on the Roman Empire*, London: Bristol Classical Press/Bloomsbury, 177–95.

Schmitt, N., X. Jiang and W. Grabe (2011), 'The Percentage of Words Known in a Text and Reading Comprehension', *Modern Language Journal*, 95 (1): 26–43.

Span, C. (2005), 'Learning in Spite of Opposition: African Americans and their History of Educational Exclusion in Antebellum America', *Counterpoints*, 131: 26–53.

Span, C. and B. Sanya (2019), 'Education and the African Diaspora', in J. Rury and E. Tamura (eds), *The Oxford Handbook of the History of Education*, Oxford: Oxford University Press, 399–412.

Standards for Classical Language Learning (2017), Draft. Available online: https://www.aclclassics.org/Portals/0/Site%20Documents/Publications/Standards_for_Classical_Language_Learning_2017%20FINAL.pdf (accessed 31 October 2023).

Stringer, G. (2019), 'What Can Active Latin Accomplish? Well Let Me Just Show You', *The Classical Outlook*, 94 (2): 81–93.

Taylor, R. (2021), 'Marginalized: Black Students and Latin in Independent Schools (New York City)', *The Classical Outlook*, 96 (1): 7–12.

Umachandran, M. and M. Ward (2024), *Critical Ancient World Studies: The Case for Forgetting Classics*, Abingdon and New York: Routledge Press.

Vanderpool, E. (2021a), 'Recreating the Voice of the Gladiator for the Secondary School Latin Classroom', *The Classical Outlook*, 96 (2): 60–6.

Vanderpool, E. (2021b), 'Novellas as a Bridge to Authentic Latin Literature', *The Classical Outlook*, 96 (3): 108–13.

Withun, D. (2022), 'W.E.B. Du Bois's Enduring Education Debate with Booker T. Washington', *Real Clear Education*, 18 February. Available online: https://www.realcleareducation.com/articles/2022/02/18/web_du_boiss_enduring_education_debate_with_booker_t_washington_110703.html (accessed 31 October 2023).

Wright, J. (1889), 'Classical Education in the United States', *The Classical Review*, 3: 77–80.

Zuckerberg, D. (2018), *Not All Dead White Men: Classics and Misogyny in the Digital Age*, Cambridge, MA: Harvard University Press.

Websites

American Council on the Teaching of Foreign Languages (ACTFL): https://www.actfl.org/
American Classical League (ACL): https://www.aclclassics.org/
Society for Classical Studies (SCS): https://classicalstudies.org/

HAWAII

Arlene Holmes-Henderson

Introduction

Hawaii is, perhaps, not an obvious location for the learning and teaching of classical languages and literatures. There has been, however, a consistently high number of students studying classical subjects at both high school and university levels in recent decades. I propose five reasons why classical education is blossoming in the Aloha state's high schools and at the University of Hawaii.

High schools in Hawaii

Classical Greek is not taught at high school level in Hawaii. Latin, however, is taught in two fee-paying schools in Honolulu, on the island of Oahu. At Iolani High School in Honolulu, students can choose to study five languages: Japanese, Latin, Chinese, Spanish or French. With 2,200 students across the school, Japanese is the most popular language enrolment option (40 per cent) but Latin comes a close second (35 per cent). The five dynamic and creative teachers in the Classics department prepare students to sit the National Latin Exam (an informal qualification, 'recognition for accomplishments in the classroom', run by the American Classical League) and Advanced Placement (AP) Latin (a formal qualification offered by the US College Board). Classes contain keen, motivated and industrious pupils who seek to deepen and broaden their familiarity with the language, literature and culture of the ancient world. The AP classes are particularly spritely with promising classical scholars keen to engage critically with original literature. Nearby, Punahou School (*alma mater* of former President Obama) offers Latin only in Grades 8 and 9 (students aged 13–15) but an annual trip to Italy ensures that the legacy of learning Latin is treasured. Inspired by the teaching they enjoyed in Hawaii, some students from these private schools further their study of Classics on the US mainland.

The University of Hawaii at Manoa

Without feeder public high schools and community colleges to provide a stream of classically educated freshmen, the University of Hawaii seems an unlikely location for a centre of excellence in the study of classical languages, literatures and civilizations. It is also some 7,000 miles distant from the outer reaches of the territories inhabited by the Greeks and Romans. These factors, however, act as little deterrent to large numbers of students who, year after year, exhibit intellectual hunger for Classics courses.

This 'postcard from Hawaii' provides an outline of the Classics courses at the University of Hawaii and suggests that the textbooks which are used for language instruction there are partly responsible for high student recruitment and retention. I offer an overview of the varied series of enrichment lectures delivered by visiting academics and archaeologists and give five reasons for these positive trends in Classics education in this region of the Pacific.

The Classics BA programme is part of the Department of Religions and Ancient Civilizations within the College of Arts, Languages and Letters, and has been offered at the university since its foundation in 1907. The one full professor, one associate professor and four instructors deliver language courses at 100, 200, 300 and 400 levels, as well as reading courses on Greek and Roman historians, Roman Studies (including epic poetry), Egyptian Hieroglyphics, and seminar classes on Greek and Roman mythology. A new pathway for Classics majors has resulted in a ten-fold increase in Classics majors, by allowing students to combine courses in Language, Historical Studies and Cultural Studies, and offering inter-disciplinary courses which contribute to general education requirements such as 'World Myth'. These courses, organized by the Classics department, draw on the expertise of staff across the university, including the Department of History, the Department of Philosophy, and the Hawaiʻinuiākea School of Hawaiian knowledge. The creativity of the Classics staff means that there are always new opportunities for students to further their classical learning formally and informally. This is the first of five reasons why the study of Classics is blossoming in the Aloha state.

Secondly, undergraduates at the University of Hawaii must fulfil a language requirement. Before graduation, students must show competence at the 202 (or equivalent) level in Hawaiian or a second language by completing a four-semester sequence (usually 101, 102, 201 and 202) in a single language. This is good news for the study of classical languages since Latin, Classical Greek and Egyptian Hieroglyphics count. Latin is taught using *Reading Classical Latin: a reasonable approach* (Ball 2010). This textbook teaches Latin using stories from Greek and Roman mythology and has been written by the ex-Chair of the Classics department, Robert Ball. Classical Greek is taught using *Homeric Greek – a book for beginners* (Pharr 2007) which uses excerpts from Homer's *Iliad* and *Odyssey*. These teaching texts might differ from the ones used for teaching ancient languages in other parts of the USA, but they were chosen to engage students' interest from the outset and place the learning of grammar and vocabulary in a wider narrative context.

Perhaps the most positive feedback comes from those students who have chosen to study Latin or Greek based on the promotion of the language courses through the large and popular seminar course 'Greek and Roman Mythology'. This course attracts several hundred students per semester and, having read multiple classical texts in translation, a healthy proportion of these students make the choice to enrol on beginners' Greek and Latin courses. The familiarity with previously-met subject matter boosts students' engagement and motivation. They can build on prior learning and deepen engagement with the themes and concepts already explored. This is the third reason why the study of Classics is blossoming in the Aloha state.

Fourthly, students in Hawaii may be 2,500 miles from the nearest branch of the American Classical League, but they are exposed to many extra-curricular opportunities to extend and enrich their study of the classical world. Here, just two are highlighted. The Archaeological Institute of America assists in bringing speakers from the mainland to the University of Hawaii. These experts in various fields of classical studies give lively, entertaining and informative lectures to the students and staff of the university, and to the public. Students of the University of Hawaii are also given the opportunity to take part in archaeological digs twice a year. The Director of Excavations at Tell Timai in Egypt is the Chair of the Classics department and is able to take a group of students for practical archaeological training every digging season. For many students, the visit to Tell Timai is their first international trip and first 'hands-on' experience of archaeology. The positive experiences not only encourage them to take further courses in Classics but also initiates a ripple effect – they report back to their peers, which keeps a steady stream of students interested in studying Classics.

The fifth reason that the study of Classics is blossoming in Hawaii is the perpetual embrace of the 'aloha spirit' and 'fun factor'. Students at the University of Hawaii have formed a student Classics Club and arrange a number of classical themed events every term including movie evenings and toga parties. The instructors promote the activities of the student club in seminars, lectures and classes and attend where possible. The opportunity for students to explore their interest in the classical world informally has contributed greatly to enrolment in classical courses and the vibrancy of learning and teaching in the department.

The Classics department at the University of Hawaii has visions of expansion and it is bucking many trends in the study of humanities, even within the budgetary confines of a state university with limited resources. Passion, enthusiasm and creativity are, however, in plentiful supply and the forecast for Classics in the Aloha state is bright.

References

Ball, R. (2010), *Reading Classical Latin: a reasonable approach*, Burr Ridge, IL: Learning Solutions/ McGraw Hill.
Pharr, C. (2007), *Homeric Greek – a book for beginners*, Whitefish, MT: Kessinger Publishing.

ARGENTINA

Álvaro Matías Moreno Leoni, Diego Alexander Olivera and Natalia María Ruiz de los Llanos

Classical Studies and Ancient History at the universities

Resulting from a complex history beginning in colonial times with the foundation of a rudimentary Jesuit *Colegio Máximo* in Córdoba – later recognized as a university – where Latin, Arts (Philosophy) and Theology were taught to priests, the Argentine university system had 132 universities in 2022. In the late nineteenth century, once the Argentinian federal state was organized, only the National Universities of Córdoba and Buenos Aires existed, joined later by La Plata (1905), Litoral (1919), Tucumán (1921), Cuyo (1939), Nordeste, and Sur (1956) after their nationalization, while private universities were authorized only in 1959. In the early 1970s, the so-called Taquini Plan implied the territorial expansion and relative decentralization of the university system, which was initially developed to control the growing student opposition to dictatorship. Since the late 1980s, university expansion has resumed (Buchbinder 2010: 191–234).

In Classical Studies, currently, there are only two specific undergraduate programmes: a degree in teaching and a Bachelor's degree in *Letras Clásicas* in Córdoba since 1968. However, other undergraduate programmes in Literature and History offer various mandatory courses in Latin, Greek, Classical Literature or Ancient History in their curriculum. In Buenos Aires, La Plata or the Sur, there are specific orientations within the Literature major, with specialized courses during the final two years of undergraduate studies. Since the early 1970s, echoing the criticism of Eurocentrism, national curricula in Literature and History have increasingly focused on national and Latin American Studies. In several national universities established in the 1970s, and especially in those founded later, the classical curriculum has nearly disappeared. The National Pedagogical University (2017) is an exception, as it offers highly specific courses in Classical Studies and Ancient History within the Literature and History programmes.

In postgraduate studies, the field of Humanities has been modestly growing since the Federal Education Law (1993). There is a Master's programme in Classical Studies in Buenos Aires (2006) and a Postgraduate Diploma in Society and Culture in the Ancient Mediterranean in Salta (2021). Furthermore, most doctoral programmes in Literature and History at major universities (Buenos Aires, La Plata, Córdoba, Rosario, Cuyo) include the possibility of writing a thesis on Classical Studies or Ancient History.

Despite being currently fragmented and increasingly excluded from undergraduate curricula, Classical Studies and Ancient History in Argentina have had one of the best performances in Latin America during the twentieth century, particularly in terms of scholars, research institutes and publications. Fuelled by national political, cultural and economic centralism, the bulk of these academic achievements were centred, however, in Buenos Aires, whose experience in the humanities was ground-breaking.

After the Battle of Caseros in 1852, which paved the way for the organization of the national state on a federal basis, the Department of Preparatory Studies at Buenos Aires was reorganized and two Latin chairs were incorporated. Optional courses were introduced in 1854 in Ancient Literature and also in Ancient History and the Middle Ages (Piñero & Bidau 125–6 1889). After the nationalization in 1881, there was an unsuccessful attempt to establish a Faculty of Humanities and Philosophy, including undergraduate courses on Ancient Greek, Near Eastern History, Roman and Medieval History, Greek and Latin Literature, and even Elements of Sanskrit and Germanic languages (Piñero & Bidau 270 1889). Behind this classical humanist plan was the classical philologist Mattia Calandrelli, who had arrived in Argentina in 1871 having studied linguistics and oriental literatures in Naples under eminent scholars such as Giacomo Lignana and Michele Kerbaker. He held the Chair of History in the Department of Preparatory Studies, Ancient History at the *Colegio Nacional*, and from 1874, the newly created Chair of Classical Philology at the university. His efforts foreshadowed those of other Italian scholars who arrived in Buenos Aires in the late nineteenth century, such as Francesco Capello or Clemente Ricci. Additionally, through his teaching, Calandrelli inspired the first academic book on Ancient History written by an Argentinian, *La sociedad romana en el primer siglo de nuestra era. Estudio crítico sobre Persio y Juvenal* (1878) by Ernesto Quesada.

The Faculty of Philosophy and Letters was finally established in 1896, playing a crucial role in the institutionalization of Classical Studies. With modest beginnings, there were significant changes from 1920 onwards. Firstly, there was a shift from amateur professors to professionals. Secondly, the classical orientation was deepened, increasing the number of mandatory Latin and Greek courses for all undergraduate students of Literature, Philosophy and History. Thirdly, this period witnessed the establishment of the first research institutes (Buchbinder 1997: 113–28). In 1927, the *Instituto de Literaturas Clásicas* was founded, currently *Instituto de Filología Clásica*. Additionally, in 1939, the journal *Anales del Instituto de Literaturas Clásicas* appeared, renamed to *Anales de Filología Clásica* ten years later.

In 1921, Ricci was appointed to the Chair of Civilization History, later renamed Ancient and Medieval History, which has now evolved into Ancient History I, Ancient History II and Medieval History. The Italian scholar had arrived in 1893. While in Italy he had already published a short essay on the Battle of Ticinus, but in Argentina he became a celebrity in the early twentieth century, regularly contributing to cultural journals and periodicals, in addition to his notable book *La historia de Europa y la segunda Roma. La significación histórica del cristianismo* (1909). In 1924, the *Gabinete de Historia de la Civilización* emerged under his direction, though later renamed as the *Instituto de Historia Antigua y Medieval* (1927). Since 1995, its new name is *Instituto de Historia Antigua, Medieval y Moderna* 'Prof. José Luis Romero'. A specialized library was developed, focusing on editions of classical authors and facsimile reproductions of manuscripts to train undergraduate students. Alberto Freixas, Ricci's successor in the chair and the institute, created the journal *Anales de Historia Antigua y Medieval* (1948). A monographic series was also significant in the early decades, being published in several volumes by Ricci and his seminar undergraduate students on by then atypical historical sources such as the *Hellenica Oxyrhynchia* or the *Monumentum Ancyranum*.

Classical Studies later extended to other university institutions. In La Plata, by 1918, there was a course on Ancient Civilizations within the History section. There José L. Romero defended his doctoral thesis *Los Gracos y la formación de la idea imperial* (1937). However, the institutionalization of Ancient History did not occur until the 1990s, following the establishment of the *Centro para el Estudio de las Sociedades Precapitalistas* and its journal *Sociedades Precapitalistas* (2019), which continues the short-lived *Boletín de Historia de Europa*. There was no specific degree programme for Classical Studies, although between the 1930s and 1950s notable exiled German scholars like Eilhard Schlesinger and Guillermo Thiele were teaching there. In terms of institutional development, we should highlight the current *Centro de Estudios Helénicos* (2004), successor to the *Centro de Estudios de Lenguas Clásicas – Área Filología Griega*, as well as the *Centro de Estudios Latinos* (1993). These centres publish two journals: *Synthesis* (1994) and *Auster* (1996).

In Córdoba, at the *Instituto de Humanidades* (1940–6), the exiled Italian scholar Rodolfo Mondolfo taught History of Philosophy, as well as Greek I and II. Following the establishment of the Faculty of Philosophy and Humanities in 1947, the Departments of History and Classical Languages (1957) were formed. In 1968, the School of Modern Literature was created, which included the aforementioned undergraduate programme in Classical Literature (Coria 2015: 99). However, there were no specialized journals after the *Boletín del Instituto de Filosofía* (1934–9) until the *Ordia Prima* Group initiated their eponymous journal in 2002. Two years later, they also began the monographic collection *Ordia Prima Studia*. In contrast, in History, undergraduate studies emerged from the former *Instituto de Estudios Americanistas* (1936), where initially there was no place for universal history, and ancient history vanished until its development in the late 1990s.

In Tucumán, the *Instituto de Lenguas y Literaturas Clásicas* (1947) was created under the direction of the Spanish exile Clemente Hernando Balmori, with Schlesinger as the head of the Classical Linguistics Section. In the following year was added the *Gymnasium* University Institute, a humanist school affiliated with the university. Both institutions were enhanced with an important specialized library and the publication of several translations of classical authors and textbooks. For a while, there was a specific BA programme in Classical Literature, but similar to the situation in Córdoba, Ancient History did not experience significant development.

In Cuyo, Ireneo Cruz, Professor of Greek I and II, as well as Ancient History, established the *Instituto de Lenguas y Literaturas Clásicas* (1943) and launched the journal *Revista de Estudios Clásicos* (1944). However, in Ancient History, the *Instituto de Historia Universal* is a relatively recent development (1992), preceded by the journal *Revista de Historia Universal* (1988). Additionally, there was a short-lived *Boletín Argentino de Historia de Europa* (1989–1995), published by the former Association of University Professors of European History, which organized the European History Conferences between the 1980s and 1990s.

The *Simposio Nacional de Estudios Clásicos*, organized by the *Asociación Argentina de Estudios Clásicos*, holds significant importance in the national academic landscape, convening every two years. The inaugural conference took place in Mendoza in 1970 and the association's Board of Directors was elected the following year in Córdoba, with Alberto J. Vaccaro serving as the first president. In the first volume of the *Argos* journal (1977), it was mentioned that at that time the association had 500 members spread across nine regional chapters: Buenos Aires, Mendoza, La Plata, Bahía Blanca, Paraná, Córdoba, Rosario, Resistencia and Tucumán. This showcases the widespread interest and participation in Classical Studies across different regions of Argentina fifty years ago.

Greek and Latin in secondary school

There are very few secondary educational institutions that currently include the teaching of Greek and Latin languages and cultures in their curricula. These institutions can be primarily grouped into: (a) secondary schools (pre-university) affiliated with public national or private universities, (b) bilingual schools (Italian, French and English); (c) humanistic schools. They do not share a single curriculum since each institution determines which subjects to offer (Latin, Greek, Classical Literature, Classical Culture, Civilization and Literature, Mythology), along with the specific content and allocated hours for these academic subjects.

Among the secondary schools affiliated with public national universities, we have the *Colegio Nacional Buenos Aires* (CNB, University of Buenos Aires), the *Instituto Libre de Segunda Enseñanza* (ILSE, privately managed and endorsed by UBA), the *Colegio Nacional de Monserrat* (CNM, National University of Córdoba), and the *Gymnasium* (National University of Tucumán). The CNB, the ILSE and the *Gymnasium* include only Latin as a curriculum subject, with three to four hours per week. In the first two named, Latin is taught from the first to the fourth year, covering topics of civilization, literature and morphosyntax. In the *Gymnasium*, Latin is taught throughout the five years of high school, focusing on cultural content in the first two years and morphology and syntax in the last three years. On the other hand, the curriculum in CNM was reformulated in 2022, reducing Latin and Greek hours in almost all years. In 2001, the plan had thirty-three hours for classical languages and cultures from the first to the seventh grade, and it transitioned to a plan with twenty-five hours distributed between both curriculum areas. At the private Catholic school Santo Tomás de Aquino, in Buenos Aires and affiliated with the Pontifical Catholic University of Argentina, Latin language, syntax and culture are studied for the first three years.

Among private bilingual institutions, for example, the Italian School 'Cristoforo Colombo' in Buenos Aires offers Latin for four years with three to four hours weekly. However, in recent years, several bilingual schools have removed Latin from their curricula, as was the case with the Italo-Argentinian School 'Dante Alighieri' in Salta.

Finally, there are institutions that follow the Modern Humanistic Plan of Study. In 1952, Archbishop Roberto J. Tavella of Salta, taking German and Italian schools as a model, founded the first Modern Humanistic High School in Salta Capital. The goal was to educate young men and women in the values of classical and Christian humanism. Decree No. 9508 (1958) approved the curriculum. His plan structured secondary education over seven years, encompassing the final two years of primary school and the standard five years of secondary education. Several hours are dedicated to the study of Latin and Greek, allowing for the exploration of morphosyntactic elements, literary, philosophical and cultural aspects of the classical world, though experimental sciences or modern languages are not neglected. Over seven years, thirty-nine hours of Latin and twenty-nine of Greek are taught, with more hours during the initial years, as the last two years retain only three weekly hours for each subject. Starting from the 1960s and onwards, numerous humanistic schools were established in different Argentine provinces following Tavella's plan: Catamarca, Santiago del Estero, Tucumán, Salta, Misiones, Entre Ríos, Córdoba, San Juan, Mendoza, Buenos Aires.

Nevertheless, the enactment of Federal Education Law No. 24.195 (1993) and National Education Law No. 26.206 (2006) had a negative impact on these institutions. They were forced to adjust their curricula, reducing the hours dedicated to classical studies in favour of more utilitarian subjects. Years later, given the strong humanistic tradition in Salta, the Modern Humanistic Plan was updated to meet the demands of a new society while maintaining the same number of hours for classical languages and cultures, through Provincial Education Law No. 7546.

Today, there are still humanistic high schools with curricula adapted to the jurisdictional requirements of each province. In many of these institutions, the teaching of the Greek language has disappeared, with only two or three years of Greek literature or culture remaining. As for Latin, it has fared better, as it is still part of the curriculum throughout the six or seven years of humanistic education, although with a considerable reduction in the number of hours compared to the original plan. Some schools incorporate the teaching of Latin from the fourth or fifth grade in primary education. These humanistic schools are:

- In the Litoral: the *Bachillerato Humanista 'Monseñor Jorge Kemerer'* (Posadas, Misiones) and the *Bachillerato Humanista Moderno 'Monseñor Dr. Roberto J. Tavella'* (Concordia, Entre Ríos).

- In Cuyo: the *Colegio Secundario 'Santo Domingo'* (San Juan), the *Colegio 'Isabel La Católica'*, the *Colegio 'Tomás Moro'*; the *Instituto Bachillerato Humanista 'Alfredo Bufano'* (Mendoza); and the *Instituto 'San Francisco Javier'* (San Rafael, Mendoza).

- In the Central region: the *Colegio Jesús María* and the *Colegio León XIII* (Córdoba).

- In Argentine Northwest region (NOA): the *Instituto 'San Pedro Nolasco'* (Santiago del Estero) and the *Colegio Privado Nuestra Señora del Valle* (Catamarca).

Its worth noting the seven humanistic schools in Salta, six of which are private Catholic institutions, and one is a public and secular school with a large number of students. All of these institutions follow a single humanistic plan that has preserved the same amount of Latin and Greek hours proposed in 1952. These are: *Bachillerato Humanista Moderno de Salta, Colegio Mayor 'Monseñor Roberto J. Tavella'* (Metán), *Escuela Parroquial 'Nuestra Señora de la Merced', Instituto Humanista de la Santísima Trinidad, Instituto Bicentenario 'María Reina', Colegio 'San Buenaventura',* and *Colegio Secundario N° 5095 'General Manuel Belgrano'* (a public school).

Ancient History in secondary school

Since the organization of the national educational system with the creation of National Colleges from 1863 onwards, secondary education in Argentina has held the idea of the country's integration into the world through a shared cultural heritage, which made it a part of Western civilization (Dell'Elicine 2019). This has been changing in the present century. Nationalist rhetoric now suggests a spatial focus centred on the American continent and national history. As a result, among the three antiquities – Eastern, Classical and Pre-Columbian – the last has gained greater significance, especially in regions with stronger cultural influences from indigenous peoples.

The decline of classical Ancient History in provincial states curricular designs is evident. With exceptions like the province of Córdoba, related topics are taught only in the first year of the Common Basic Cycle (CBC) of secondary school. This subject covers a wide historical period, starting with Palaeolithic and Neolithic communities and concluding with classical civilization. Consequently, the content of classical Ancient History is covered in a single unit within the first year. Furthermore, in most provincial states, History is not a separate subject within the CBC. Instead, it is combined with Geography and Ethical Formation to form a subject called Social Sciences. In other words, teachers are required to cover History, Geography and Citizenship content, limiting the exploration of Greek and Roman history sometimes to just one or two classes.

The situation is different in public schools affiliated with national universities. For example, at the *Colegio 'Carlos Pellegrini'* of the University of Buenos Aires, History is taught as an independent subject. In the CNM, affiliated with the National University of Córdoba, Classical Ancient History is taught during the first three years, allowing for the exceptional teaching of atypical contents like the Hellenistic World. In schools affiliated with universities, therefore, Classical Ancient History has more space within the curriculum design.

Returning to provincial state schools, a brief overview of the various curriculum designs can help us understand the limited incorporation of classical Ancient History in Argentine federal secondary education.

In the Pampas region, both in the Autonomous City of Buenos Aires (CABA) and the Province of Buenos Aires, the curriculum designs include various aspects of classical society. In CABA, there is even a unit on the concept of Late Antiquity. In La Pampa, on the other hand, the curriculum covers the development of the first states, and teachers must choose two case studies from among them, with Greece being an optional content. The same does not apply to Rome.

In the NOA, Catamarca has a traditional curriculum focused on the city-state, including Athens, Sparta, the Roman Empire, and its disintegration. In Jujuy, the emphasis is on political forms, philosophical and religious ideas, and the legacy of antiquity. In Salta, once again, we find the study of early states, including the Greek *polis* as an optional content for teachers. For Rome, the High Empire is omitted in favour of the crisis of the third century CE and the imperial disintegration. Finally, in Tucumán, classical Ancient History is not part of the curriculum, as after covering the Neolithic period, teachers move directly to the Spanish colonization in the Americas.

In the Northeast region (NEA), an area with a significant presence of indigenous peoples, Classical Antiquity is absent from the curriculum in Chaco. In Formosa, ancient Greek history is optional and is taught when studying the formation of states, similar to the approaches in La Pampa and Salta. In Corrientes, there is an ideological position that recognizes Greek history as the origin of Western civilization, with more space dedicated to it compared to the curriculum designs of neighbouring provinces.

The curriculum designs in the central region, a region with a strong European immigration between the late nineteenth and early twentieth centuries, there are variations. In Santa Fe, classical Ancient History is not included in the curriculum. In Córdoba, more emphasis is placed on the Roman case than the Greek. Teachers are expected to deal with the state formation process with a comparative approach between the ancient Near East, Greece and pre-Columbian America, although the curriculum goes into much more detail about the Roman Empire. Entre Ríos stands out among these three provinces for allocating more space to Classical Antiquity. However, it is important to remember the gap between the theoretical curriculum and its practical implementation in the classrooms, where the content is rarely taught in its entirety.

In the Cuyo region, classical Ancient History is taught in San Luis. Spartan, Athenian, and Roman societies are studied together under the strange label 'thalassocrat societies'. On the other hand, Mendoza does not include Classical Antiquity in its curriculum.

Finally, in the Patagonia region, where we were only able to check the curriculum designs of Neuquén and Río Negro, pre-Columbian history is prioritized, and Classical Antiquity is ignored. However, in Neuquén, the topic of various modes of production could allow the discussion of ancient slavery. All three provinces – Neuquén, Río Negro and Mendoza – have recently experienced conflicts related to claims by indigenous peoples. In this context, the recovery of pre-Columbian cultures as an integral part of local identities explains the preferences.

In summary, the teaching of classical Ancient History in Argentine secondary schools is disparate and its importance has been diminishing. The ideological tension between a Eurocentric view that positions Argentina as a Western country and an Americanist perspective emphasizing pre-Columbian cultures and the uniqueness of the American continent has been leaning towards the latter. National educational policies aim to strengthen a national and regional view of the country's global integration. In this context, the antiquity that matters is the antiquity of the Americas, as it is considered the origin of the Argentine nation.

For this work, provincial curriculum designs and the study plans of schools and universities across the country have been reviewed, accessible on the websites of each institution. Interviews have also been conducted with professors, teachers and administrators at various levels of education.

References

Buchbinder, P. (1997), *Historia de la Facultad de Filosofía y Letras*, Buenos Aires: Eudeba.

Buchbinder, P. (2010), *Historia de las Universidades Argentinas*, Buenos Aires: Sudamericana.

Coria, A. (2015), *Tejer un destino. La formación de pedagogos en la Universidad Nacional de Córdoba, Argentina, 1955–1976*, Buenos Aires: Miño y Dávila.

Del'Ellicine, E. (2019), 'La Antigüedad clásica se recibe en las escuelas. República, valores cívicos y nacionalismo en los manuales de escuela media argentina (1920–1955)', *Veleia*, 36: 137–46.

Piñero, N. and E. Bidau (1889), *Historia de la Universidad de Buenos Aires*, Buenos Aires: Martín Biedma.

Quesada, E. (1878), *La sociedad romana en el primer siglo de nuestra era. Estudio crítico sobre Persio y Juvenal*, Buenos Aires: Martín Biedma.

Ricci, C. (1909), *La historia de Europa y la segunda Roma. La significación histórica del cristianismo*, Buenos Aires: Kidd.

BOLIVIA

Tatiana Alvarado Teodorika

The difficulty and complexity of presenting an overview of classical studies in Bolivia lies primarily in what is meant by 'Bolivia'. Often, the history of education, as well as the history of literature or even literary criticism, has considered intellectual production in Bolivia only from

1825, the year of the founding of the Republic, reducing to silence, and thus oblivion, the previous period, which geographically corresponds to a part of the viceroyalty of Peru: specifically, the Real Audiencia de Charcas. Intellectual production in this geographical space, which has barely aroused the interest or curiosity of scholars, has only begun to generate serious and rigorous studies in the last four decades, but there is still much to be done in this respect.

That said, these pages will provide an overview of the presence of Latin (essentially) and Greek (when possible), from the sixteenth century to the present day, and from the area covered by the Real Audiencia de Charcas to present-day Bolivia. This panoramic view will make it possible, to a certain extent, to understand the convoluted paths that classical languages have taken in this territory, whether in education or in research.

By way of introduction, for a continental view, the learned study by Juan Gil (2008–12) should be taken into account; for a point of view concerning the viceroyalty of Peru, Teodoro Hampe Martínez's book (1999) is worthy of note; and for the geographical area of the Real Audiencia de Charcas in particular: Andrés Eichmann Oehrli (2001), who reviews the teaching and use of Latin and also presents an anthology of texts produced in Charcas; and Josep Barnadas (2005), who, through 329 bibliographical entries, compiles the Latin production in the Audiencia de Charcas and present-day Bolivia. Barnadas' (2005) contributions are indispensable as regards the history of Latin. His insistence on the need to recover its study for a better understanding of history and of texts in Charcas was tireless. We owe him great advances in this field.

The history of the teaching of Latin in the territory is closely related to the founding of colleges and universities, although it should not be forgotten that, prior to this, classes were taught in church settings (seminaries and convents, for example). Latin was taught in the seminary and in the colleges, and early on it came to be taught by the Society of Jesus, so that, in keeping with the Western tradition of the time, it was not only the language of the religious sphere, but also of the arts and sciences.

The city of La Plata (today known as Sucre, in the department of Chuquisaca), the current capital of Bolivia (La Paz being the seat of government) was founded in 1538, and by the early 1560s a school of first level instruction for *mestizo* children was established in the city's San Francisco convent, with Francisco Perero, a former slave, as its first tutor. In 1580, a chair of indigenous languages was established, run by lay priests, and subsequently passed to the Colegio de Santiago, run by the Society of Jesus. In 1591, the Jesuits, who had recently settled in the city, established a chair of Latin in their own house (perhaps one of the first references to the teaching of Latin in the territory of actual Bolivia). In 1595 the Seminary of San Cristóbal was founded (run by the archbishops) and in 1600 the convent of San Agustín opened a chair of Arts in its own house. That same year, in view of the need to open a college for ecclesiastics and laymen, Bishop Alonso Ramírez de Vergara, in agreement with the *Audiencia* and the town council, submitted a proposal to the king to found a university with chairs of Latin, Arts, Theology and Canons. In 1608, the cantor of the Cathedral of La Plata, Don Diego Felipe de Molina, died and left a bequest of his house for the university to be founded, as well as his library, with 515 volumes. This bequest prompted the Real Audiencia de Charcas to make a new request to the king in 1613 (ABNB, GML 223, 4–6; Barnadas 1995: 51, 76).

On 8 August 1621, at the demand of King Philip III, Pope Gregory X issued the apostolic bull in favour of the Society of Jesus so that students who had studied in the colleges of the Society where there was no university would receive from the 'archbishops and bishops of the

Metropolitan Church and Cathedrals' the degrees of 'bachiller', 'maestro' and 'doctor' in the faculties where they were studying, and on 20 March 1622 he ordered the same to viceroys and *Audiencias*. Thus the bull and the royal decrees reached the viceroy Marquis of Guadalcázar and he ordered them to be put into practice on 22 March 1623. By this time the Royal University of San Marcos had already been founded in Lima in 1551, but the journey from La Plata to Lima was too long and, considering not only the distance but also the expenses and dangers, the Society acted as mediator in the request for the foundation of a university in La Plata. On 27 March 1624, the Jesuit Juan Frías de Herrán, on the very same place occupied by the Colegio de Santiago de la Ciudad de La Plata and under the patronage of Saint Francis Xavier, founded the Real y Pontificia Universidad de san Francisco Xavier (Royal and Pontifical University of San Francisco Xavier – USFX). The Jesuit Ignacio de Arbieto, who had taught Theology at the college in Lima, was appointed as the first Dean of the University, and the following professorships were established: that of *Prima* by Father Ignacio de Arbieto; the Vespers chair by Father Francisco Lupercio Zurbano; Miguel de Salazar in charge of Moral Theology; the Arts Department under the direction of Father Ferdinando Reiman; the *Latinidad de Mayores y Humanidad* by Father Federico Fornabona; the *Latinidad de Medianos y Menores* under the direction of Father Francisco de Morales; and an Aymara-speaking one.

The grammarian collegians applied to the chair of *Latinidad* in the Colegio de San Juan. The professors of *Latinidad* were to receive in their classrooms the collegiate and secular students who presented themselves, and free of charge (ABNB, U 68, 8r–11v). The first lesson in *Humanidad* was given in Latin by Father Federico Fornabona, in praise of Virgil and his works. Later, Juan Rodríguez de León, a graduate of the University of Lima, and Antonio Salazar, a graduate of the University of Osuna, among others, joined the teaching staff. In the 1580s, the chairs of Sacred Scripture and Canons were added, which, as might be expected, were also taught in Latin.

Having said this about teaching, it seems relevant to point out that in this period, as Josep Barnadas (1992: 45) has already stated, the 'Bolivian' neo-Latin tradition is rather marginal in relation to other geographical spaces of the continent and in relation to literature written in Spanish itself.

In the following century, the achievements that had been made (always humble in the field of education) in the growth of the university and the inclusion of new teachers ceased to be a reality by 1771. Once Charles III had expelled the Society of Jesus from his overseas dominions in 1767, the university was in a sorry state, with the absence of the Jesuits leaving many positions vacant. As Eichmann Oehrli (2020: 19) argues, the expulsion mainly affected education. Some professors kept their classes in the colleges, but only the professor of Latinity kept his at the university, thanks to the endowment of the chair of languages. After the expulsion, class hours and exam time were also reduced. In order to reestablish teaching, and with 'the most urgent need', they appealed to the crown for help, arguing: 'how much splendour and glory the education of youth and the progress of letters brings to the monarchy' (Eichmann Oehrli 2020: 19) The Royal University of San Francisco Xavier had a certain degree of dependence on that of San Marcos in Lima, whose constitutions had to be observed at the opening of each academic year in Chuquisaca. In this period, the chairs of *Latinidad* were still considered indispensable, which was not the case with the chair of language (i.e. 'indigenous language') which, due to the lack of professors, was extinguished and replaced by the chair of Medicine. Worthy of note is the manifest change in the use and coexistence of languages in these early decades of the reign of the Bourbons, which evidenced a series of transformations both overseas and in the metropolis. In fact, in a decree of May 1770, proposed by the Archbishop of Mexico, the bishops were ordered to stop taking into account the use of the language when proposing curates, and to take into account only merit so that 'the different languages used in these dominions would be banished and only Castilian would be spoken', an order contrary to the decree of 9 July 1769 (ABNB, U 39, ff. 59r–78v, 216–221r, 235–242v).

A few decades later, on 6 August 1825, when the area comprising the territories of the Audiencia became independent under the name of the República del Alto Perú (Republic of Upper Peru) and shortly afterwards under that of the Republic of Bolivia, it was enacted in the Law of 9 January that in the departmental capitals there should be a college in which Spanish, Latin, French, English; poetry, rhetoric, philosophy, jurisprudence and medicine (all in Spanish) would be taught (*Colección oficial de leyes y decretos* 1834: 78–9). The regulations of 28 October, under the presidency of Antonio José de Sucre, specify the exams for Latin studies (three exams every six months).

The first one:

– of the declensions and conjugations; of the chapters of *genere nominum*, of *nominum declinatione*, of *verborum preteritis et supinis* of Sánchez's grammar (this was probably the *Principios de la gramática latina* de Juan Sánchez, Seville: Alonso de la Barrera, 1589); of the analysis and study of the first book of the *Fables* of Phaedrus.

The second:

– of prosody and syntax of Sánchez; analysis and study of the second book of the *Fables* of Phaedrus; translation of the third book of Quintus Curtius and the exercise of some versions from Spanish into Latin; the general rules of Latin orthography.

The third:

– translation and analysis of the *Aeneid* and the first book of Horace's *Odes* and *Poetical Art*; the study from memory and declamation of the most interesting passages of the *Aeneid*; some Latin compositions in prose and verse.

(*Colección oficial de leyes y decretos* 1834: 200–1)

In November 1830, the Universidad Mayor de San Andrés (UMSA) was founded in the city of La Paz. Juan de la Cruz Cisneros, one of its founders, wrote in a letter to the city prefect in November 1831 that the university taught only *Latinidad* and Modern Philosophy (ABNB, MI34-13, 6); on 27 October Juan Velasco was approved for the chair of *Latinidad*. The UMSA made Latin a requirement for admission to the faculty of Philosophy, and for the explanation of Latin authors (part of the Theology programme). With the founding of the Republic, the USFX introduced a competitive examination for the chairs of Spanish and Latin grammar, which consisted of reading a half-hour 'oration' in the respective language (ABNB, MI69-10, 98r–98v). Years later, in October 1849, permission was granted to found, in La Paz, the Colegio Ayacucho de instrucción secundaria de pensión particular (ABNB, MIP38-11, 8r–8v), and among the subjects lectured related to classical languages were Latin Etymology, Latin Syntax and Orthography, and Translation of Latin texts. A year later, in November 1850, it was agreed that for the final examination for the degree of *Licenciado*, a half-hour dissertation in Spanish and a composition in Latin and another in Spanish would be required (ABNB, MIP38-11, 41r).

A decade later, in 1860, the decree of 18 November was promulgated detailing the classes of secondary instruction, where one finds: Latin Grammar from 6th to 3rd grades, and then Recitation and Explanation of Authors in 2nd and 1st grades. In higher instruction, the decree promulgates the study of four years of 'high Latinity' through versions, recitations, textual analysis and dissertations (*Resoluciones Supremas* 1860, 321–4).

In January 1895, during the presidency of Mariano Baptista (1892–6), it was decreed, among other articles on secondary education, that the seven existing chairs could be found in the following six areas of knowledge: National Language; Geography and History; Mathematics; Physical and Natural Sciences; Latin, Religion and Philosophy; Modern Languages (French and English) (*Instrucción pública* 1896: 279). In the analytical plan of studies, its content is thus described: Latin and Religion, with four hours per week (*Instrucción pública* 1896: 351–2). This information, however, contradicts a provision of the Council of Instruction of La Paz which, in 1874, determined that the teaching of Latin would be voluntary in secondary education, replaced by French (Romero Pittari 1999: 211). The optional nature of Latin mentioned here is a glimpse of the first steps towards its disappearance in education.

However, although the first period of the Republic had important plans for the regular urban school system (1825, 1845 and 1874), they were not duly implemented, no doubt due to the organizational and political instability of the nascent country. Furthermore, the quality of Latin teaching was considered to be too advanced for the national context (Castro Torres 2017: 212, 259). Of particular note in this period is the *Método fácil y sencillo para aprender a un tiempo los rudimentos de ambas gramáticas española y latina* [Easy and simple method to learn the rudiments of both Spanish and Latin grammar at the same time] (1836), by the jurist Francisco Ignacio Medeiros, a sort of grammatical method composed of questions and answers that give a parallel account of grammatical elements for both languages, very useful if one considers that Latin was a compulsory subject according to the statute of 1874. One of the private colleges where Latin and Greek were taught was the Liceo América del Sur, in the city of La Paz (Castro Torres 2017: 185). It could be said that Latin was still, at that time, the language of a literate circle, including the author of the *Opúsculos poético-latinos* (1850), the historian and poet José Manuel Loza (1801–62). It should be noted that by the year 1873, the Sucre Library housed 1,434 works (2,267 tomes) in Latin (Castro Torres 2017: 363).

Given the limitations of public education, from the middle of the century onwards, notable actions were taken to promote private education. Examples of these are: the Hospital de Cochabamba of D. Francisco de Viedma, which maintained an asylum-school around 1845; and the San Calixto school in La Paz, founded in 1882, run by the Jesuits, thanks to the fact that Monsignor Calixto Clavijo bought the former house of Field Marshall Andrés de Santa Cruz and donated it for the use of the institution (Castro Torres 2019: 211). The following also made their property available for the foundation of schools in Sucre: Don Francisco and Doña Clotilde Urioste de Argandoña, princes of La Glorieta; Don Gregorio Pacheco; Don Belisario Boeto; Doña Isabel Urriolagoitia de Lazúrtegui; Doña Julia Urriolagoitia de Saavedra; and Monsignor Francisco Pierini, Archbishop of La Plata. Don Gregorio Pacheco, elected to the presidency of the Republic (1884–8), also gave up his salary and invested his fortune in founding schools. These praiseworthy and laudable efforts were not enough to achieve an education that would benefit more people. Let us consider, for example, what in the 1870s

Minister Daniel Calvo stated: 'Taking as a basis the population of 2,200,000 inhabitants of Bolivia, those educated by the *fisco* correspond to a proportion of six per cent, leaving the remaining ninety-four per cent condemned to ignorance, since the interest of private initiative in education is not felt' (Grigoriu 1975: 281, quoted in Castro Torres 2019: 207).

With these data, it becomes apparent that, if education was a kind of privilege, the study of Latin was even more so. Although its teaching was still compulsory in the syllabus drawn up by the minister Jenaro Sanjinés in 1888, it was definitively replaced by modern languages in the National Education Plan of December 1903, when, for political rather than pedagogical reasons, the liberal government constrained religious establishments to adopt the fashionable teaching system (the concentric) and to lower the academic level (Castro Torres 2019: 208–41).

By 1964 and by decree, 23 per cent of the national budget was earmarked for education; and by decree 6798 the granting of the Bachelor's degree to students of minor seminaries, who studied Humanities, Latin, Greek and Human Sciences and Letters, was authorized (Suárez Arnéz 1986: 123, 255). It is very likely that the study of Latin and Greek was relegated to private spaces and, despite having been initially intended for public education, was not implemented in the curriculum. In the 1940s, in La Paz, Latin and Greek were taught as compulsory subjects in the degree course in Philosophy and Letters (the only one in the country) at the Universidad Mayor de San Andrés. The latter for three years, with three classes a week, and the former for four years, with three classes a week. In the 1950s, there was a Greek teacher who came from Italy and used the Fontoynont method, translated from French; the Latin teacher, Walter Navia, used a grammar method translated from Italian. Very quickly the number of years of study was reduced. Mario Frías Infante was also a teacher of Greek and used his own method, which he developed in a rudimentary way, even manually, and added to this the Spanish method of the publications of Jaime Berenguer Amenós; Carlo Pianese was also a teacher of Latin in these years. Latin and Greek did not remain in the syllabus for long and disappeared as compulsory subjects at the UMSA. From the 1970s onwards they became optional and in the 1980s they disappeared.

In the last decades of the twentieth century and the first decades of the present century, the Universidad Mayor de San Andrés, the Universidad Católica Boliviana in La Paz, the Universidad Nuestra Señora de La Paz and the Universidad de San Simón in Cochabamba, have offered optional classes and have relied on the contribution of people who have dedicated themselves and all their time to the study of the Classics and their teaching, despite the fact that neither Latin nor Greek were any longer subjects in school or university curricula.

Let us consider the foremost scholars in this regard. First of all, Mario Frías Infante (1934–) (see BPB at https://www.boliviabpb.org/), teacher of Latin and Greek, but also author of works for secondary education such as the collaborative work *Iniciación literaria* (1976), *Lenguaje y literatura* (1979), *Diccionario de sinónimos* (1987), and of translations: Horace's *Epistle to the Pisones*; Cicero's *On Friendship* and *On Old Age* (1985); Plato's *Crito* (1965 and 2009), Homer's *Odyssey* (1981), Sophocles' *Oedipus Rex* (1985), Sophocles' *Antigone* (1986) and, in a bilingual critical edition, Socrates' *Apology* (1999), *The Didache* (2016), Plato's *Ion* (2017), and Homer's *Iliad* (2021). And, as a result of one of the Greek classes he taught at the Universidad Católica Boliviana: the *Hymn to Demeter* (2017), translated by Libardo Tristancho and Marcelo Villena Alvarado, was published. Currently, two of his students, Boris Chamaní and Pamela Valdéz, teach the optional course in Greek at Universidad Mayor de San Andrés.

Another well-known Greek scholar in the country was Juan Araos Úzqueda (1952–2022). He studied Philosophy and Classical Languages at the University of Chile, taught at the Universidad Mayor de San Simón, and at the Universidad Católica Boliviana in Cochabamba (optional subject). In the latter, he taught Latin and, at the beginning of the 1990s, Greek (which was outside the curriculum), free of charge. Amongst his students the most notable disciple is Ramiro Salazar. Juan Araos Úzqueda is the author of more than sixty studies published in Bolivia and abroad on various subjects, including Homer, Aristotle, Heraclitus, Parmenides, Plato, Protagoras and others. He has also translated Heraclitus (1993), Parmenides (1994) and the biblical *The Song of Songs* (1999). His translation of Plato's *Ion* has remained unrevised for publication and unpublished by decision of the Fates.

Last but not least, Andrés Eichmann Oehrli. He taught Latin during the last decade of the twentieth century at the Universidad Nuestra Señora de La Paz using French methods (Gason Baudiffier and Thomas for the second and third years). His students included Estela Alarcón, Carmen Solíz, Sergio Sánchez and Marianela Wayar, as well as the Bolivian historian Teresa Gisbert. He also taught Latin in the Philosophy course at the Universidad Mayor de San Andrés. During these years, he published with Carlos Seoane *Melos damos vocibus. Códices cantorales platenses* (Seoane 2000), two volumes that represent the first complete cataloguing, in Latin America, of a collection of choral codices from a cathedral.

Andrés Eichmann Oehrli, founder of the Bolivian Society of Classical Studies (1998), is currently president of the institution. He is also the promoter and organizer of the Classical Studies colloquia in Bolivia, and the promoter and director of the journal *Classica Boliviana*, which has published twelve issues to date. His works deal mainly with the classical tradition in the Real Audiencia de Charcas during the sixteenth to eighteenth centuries; he is the author of the *De boliviana latinitate* (Eichmann Oehrli 2001); he has translated the Latin letter of Calvo de la Vanda to Pedro Frasso (Eichmann Oehrli 2007); the letter of Pedro Sarmiento de Gamboa to Lord Burghley (Eichmann Oehrli and Zuleta Carrandi 2016a); the Latin letter of Manuel de Peñalosa y Mansilla, in his article 'Ingenio y erudición en una carta latina de Charcas' (Eichmann Oehrli 2016b); and in 'Iniciativas indígenas en el culto católico colonial' (Eichmann Oehrli 2020) he discovers the Latin of the so-called 'reziris' who, today, sing songs for the dead, in the cemetery, and part of their chant is a reproduction worn out by memory and time of the *Rituale Romanum*. He received formal recognition for his work concerning the recovery of texts with the translation of abundant Latin epigraphs in the paintings of the church of Carabuco.

With this brief overview, we can conclude by saying that the classical languages (especially Latin), after having been incorporated into studies in the sixteenth century, with the scope they could have had at that time, remained in force for approximately two centuries, despite their marginality. The turn that took place in the eighteenth century confined Latin mainly to higher education, and the nineteenth century witnessed the limitations of the public system, which left the possibilities of progress in terms of education in the hands of the private sector, while keeping a watchful eye on the evaluation of content and level. The teaching of both languages since the twentieth century has been possible thanks to the generosity of certain scholars who have given and shared their time and knowledge. They have convinced others of the need to study classical languages and culture for a better understanding of the past and a necessary key for the reading of the future. May they find others of like mind on this path.

References

Manuscripts

ABNB, Archivo y Biblioteca Nacionales de Bolivia, Ministerio del Interior (MI), expediente 34-13.

ABNB, Archivo y Biblioteca Nacionales de Bolivia, Ministerio del Interior (MI), expediente 69-10 (ff. 72r–72v, 98r–98v, 101v–102).

ABNB, Archivo y Biblioteca Nacionales de Bolivia, Fondo documental Universidad San Francisco Xavier de Chuquisaca (U), expediente 68 (ff. 8r–11v).

ABNB, Archivo y Biblioteca Nacionales de Bolivia, Fondo documental Universidad San Francisco Xavier de Chuquisaca (U), expediente 39 (ff. 59r–78v).

ABNB, Archivo y Biblioteca Nacionales de Bolivia, Fondo documental Ministerio de Instrucción Pública (MIP), expediente 38-11 (ff. 8r–8v, 41r–41v).

ABNB, Archivo y Biblioteca Nacionales de Bolivia, Fondo documental Gunnar Mendoza Loza (GML), documento 223 (pp. 4–6).

Documentary fonds

Centro Bibliográfico y cultural Histórico de la Universidad de Chuquisaca:

Colección oficial de leyes, decretos, órdenes, resoluciones que se han expedido para el régimen de la república boliviana, t. 1, vol. 2. Paz de Ayacucho: Imprenta del colegio de artes de Bernardino Palacios, 1834.

Colección oficial de leyes, decretos, órdenes. Resoluciones supremas de la república de Bolivia, 1860.

Revista de Instrucción pública de Bolivia, t. 2. Sucre: Imprenta 'Bolivar' de M. Pizarro, 1896.

Articles and books

Barnadas, J. (1992), '¿Cuán "neolatina" ha sido Bolivia?', *Revista Unitas*, 8: 42–8.

Barnadas, J. (1995), *El seminario conciliar de san Cristóbal de La Plata – Sucre (1595–1995)*, Sucre: Archivo-Biblioteca Arquidiocesanos 'Monseñor Taborga'.

Barnadas, J. (2005), *Ensayo bibliográfico sobre el latín en Bolivia (siglos XVI–XXI)*, La Paz: Cuadernos de Classica Boliviana I, Sociedad Boliviana de Estudios Clásicos-Centro de Estudios Bolivianos Avanzados-Plural.

Castro Torres, M. (2017), *El sueño y la realidad: historia de la educación en Bolivia (1800–1874)*, La Paz: Instituto Internacional de Integración Convenio Andrés Bello.

Castro Torres, M. (2019), 'Un hito de la educación boliviana: los primeros 25 años del colegio San Calixto de La Paz (1881–1906)', *Anuario de Estudios Bolivianos Archivísticos*, 26 (1): 203–52.

Eichmann Oehrli, A. (2001), *De boliviana latinitate. Breve studium cum varium auctorum antologia desumpta*, La Paz: Plural.

Eichmann Oehrli, A. (2007), 'Textos encomiásticos latinos en Charcas', *Classica Boliviana*, IV: 29–55.

Eichmann Oehrli, A. (2010), 'Pronunciación del latín en América: testimonios de Charcas (siglos XVIII–XIX)', *Classica Boliviana*, V: 191–206.

Eichmann Oehrli, A. and J. Zuleta Carrandi (2016a), 'Edición y traducción de la "Carta a lord Burghley" de Pedro Sarmiento de Gamboa', *Hipogrifo*, 4 (1): 23–42.

Eichmann Oehrli, A. (2016b), 'Ingenio y erudición en una carta latina de Charcas: Manuel de Peñalosa y Mansilla escribe a Pedro Frasso en 1678', *Classica Boliviana*, VII: 97–134.

Eichmann Oehrli, A. (2020), 'Iniciativas indígenas en el culto católico colonial', *Anuario de la Academia Boliviana de Historia Eclesiástica*, 26: 113–26.

Gil, J. (2008–12), 'Escribir en latín: ventajas e inconvenientes', in *Res publica Litterarum. Suplemento monográfico 'Tradición Clásica y Universidad'*, 3–34.

Hampe Martínez, T. (1999) *La Tradición Clásica en el Perú Virreinal*, Lima: Universidad Nacional Mayor de San Marcos.

Romero Pittari, S. (1999), 'El latín en la literatura boliviana finisecular', *Classica Boliviana*, I: 211–14.

Seoane, C. (2000), *Melos damus vocibus. Codices cantorales Platenses*, La Paz: Programa de Coparticipación, Organización de los Estados Americanos (OEA), Viceministerio de Cultura, Universidad Nuestra Señora de La Paz.

Suárez Arnéz, C. (1986), *Historia de la educación boliviana*, La Paz: Don Bosco.

Website

BPB: Biblioteca del Parnaso Boliviano: www.boliviabpb.org

BRAZIL

Paula da Cunha Corrêa

Interdisciplinary *Minimus* Project (Greek, Latin, Archaeology and Philosophy), and Classics in Brazilian schools

Greek and Latin ceased to be mandatory in Brazilian school curricula in the 1960s and this, among other factors, led to the gradual exclusion of the classical languages from practically all schools across the country. Today, besides the university courses, Greek and/or Latin are only regularly taught at a single private international school in São Paulo (the Lycée Pasteur School prepares students for the Baccalaureate, with classes taught in French, while German, Spanish, Greek and Latin are offered as electives in middle and high school) and in a few seminaries and monasteries (Sobrinho 2013).

In this scenario and inspired by a 'Classics for All' promotional video, a group of Greek and Latin faculty members of the University of São Paulo (Paulo Martins, Marcos Martinho dos Santos, João Angelo Oliva Neto, Alexandre P. Hasegawa and Paula da Cunha Corrêa) created in 2013 a local 'Projeto *Minimus*' to reintroduce Greek and Latin in a public school. The main objective of the project was to teach Greek and Latin languages through materials that also present various aspects of classical culture (mythology, history, politics, theatre, poetry, music, art and architecture), to broaden their horizons and to introduce elementary and middle school students to the institutions, concepts and forms that are part of our world and still manifest in our daily lives. In the first years, the project was funded by the Onassis Foundation USA (2013–14), and after by the Faculty of Philosophy, Letters, and Human Sciences (FFLCH/USP) and the Universities' Protectorates (PrG and PrCEU/USP). Since 2018 all Greek and Latin monitors are undergraduate students that receive bursaries from the university for participating in the project (Bolsa PUB), while the Archaeology and Philosophy monitors are graduates with faculty bursaries.

Since an important part of the pedagogical project of the Desembargador Amorim Lima Municipal Public School in which the project was implemented is that each student's pace is respected, the students are taught in small tutorial groups of five to seven students, and their results in terms of language proficiency has always varied greatly, for while some only manage to go as far as the Greek alphabet and the first chapters of *Minimus – Conhecendo o Latim* (Bell & Forte 2015), others finish Book 1 of *Minimus* and the initial chapters of *Athenaze* (Balme &

Lawall 2011), being able to read small texts in Greek and Latin. It would be interesting to determine to what extent the Greek and Latin classes at Amorim Lima make a difference in students' language and maths skills. As all students have Greek and Latin as mandatory, there is no way for us to ascertain their progress with a control group for comparison. However, students have constantly told us how Latin has helped them in their Portuguese classes, especially in grammar.

The success of 'Projeto *Minimus*' at Amorim Lima was recognized when the Principal invited the programme to remain in the school after a semester, and the community chose as their theme for the 2013 Culture Festival 'Greece and Rome in Classical Antiquity'. For the event, students exhibited Pythagoras' theorem and geometric figures, made labyrinths in which they re-enacted the myth of Theseus and the Minotaur, created comic books and photo-novels about the *Odyssey*, demonstrated wool dyeing, played with toys that existed two thousand years ago, wrote fanzines with the Twelve Labours of Hercules, built a model of Troy and a 1.8-metre tall paper-mâché Trojan Horse, prepared Roman food, designed an installation about Procrustes, demonstrated a Roman classroom with wax tablets and writing instruments, and explained the democratic institutions of the polis. The seventh-grade students performed Sophocles' *Antigone*, while fourth-grade students presented a ten-minute 'pocket *Aeneid*' (Corrêa 2018).

From the perspective of our undergraduate and graduate students, the project provides a unique didactic experience since it is practically the only means of teaching Greek and Latin language courses in Brazilian schools. Teaching these classes requires the monitors not only to review and to further develop their proficiency in Greek and Latin, but it also presents them with the challenge of adapting the existing methods and creating additional teaching materials for these students whose education, general culture and environment differ considerably from that of those for whom *Minimus* and *Athenaze* (or JACT's *Reading Greek* (2007), in its Brazilian translation) were originally designed.

Now, moving forward, this chapter aims to update information not only on the following years of the 'Projeto *Minimus*' at the University of São Paulo (2017–23), transformed in 2018 into the 'Projeto *Minimus* Interdisciplinar', but also to give an account of other outreach projects in Classics that have been developed by state and federal universities in schools across the country.

Interdisciplinary *Minimus* Project (2018–)

In 2018 'Projeto *Minimus*' became interdisciplinary at the Amorim Lima school, through the addition of morning and afternoon alternating semesters of mandatory Classical Archaeology and Ancient Philosophy classes for 8th grade students from the morning and afternoon shifts, coordinated respectively by Maria Cristina N. Kormikiari, from the University of São Paulo's Museum of Archeology and Ethnology (MAE), and Roberto Bolzani, from the Philosophy Department (FFLCH/USP). During 2017 Alexandre P. Hasegawa (FFLCH/USP) coordinated the projects' Greek and Latin courses.

Archaeology

Since their inclusion in the project, the archaeology classes have been divided basically into two modules: the first addresses Archaeology as a scientific discipline, its history, practices, theory, major schools of thought, etc., and the second discusses the History and Archaeology of Mediterranean Antiquity, focusing on Greece and Rome. Through this division, it is possible to explore different issues related to both the discipline, from a general perspective, and to the Ancient Mediterranean – such as the social role of archaeology, its potential for expanding knowledge of the history of human societies, and more specifically, imperialism; colonization and resistance; Hellenization/Romanization; otherness/identity; identity and discourse; religion and politics; urbanism/urbanization; transformation of public spaces; monuments; iconography; domestic space; technology, production and consumption; territory and landscape; and contacts and borders.

The main objective of these classes is, on one hand, to demystify the work of an archaeologist, as it is generally conveyed by popular culture (movies, series, comics, games, etc.), as romantic and adventurous. On the other hand, the aim is to critically enhance and expand the students' previously acquired knowledge of the Ancient Mediterranean (especially Greece and Rome), and to foster reflection on ancient societies through the study of material culture.

So that students may visually engage with the materiality, PowerPoint presentations are used, and activities include the analysis of material culture through images of various objects, buildings/monuments, and landscapes, prompting discussions on their possible uses, appropriations, and reappropriations, and simulating archaeological analysis. Pre-research activities are also assigned ahead of a new topic to stimulate students' curiosity and research experience.

In addition to these presentations and activities, students also study through the use of materials, images, and audio-visual and digital resources produced by the educational sector of the Museum of Archaeology and Ethnology of the University of São Paulo (MAE/USP), the Laboratory of Provincial Roman Archaeology (LARP/MAE/USP), the CNPq research group of Interactive Archaeology and Electronic Simulations (ARISE), and the Laboratory of Study on the Ancient City (LABECA/MAE/USP). Examples include the video 'What is Archaeology?' (LABECA/MAE n.d.), digital models of a Greek house, temple, and harbour, available at LABECA; the digital game 'Sambaquis – A history before Brazil', at ARISE; and the simulation 'DOMUS', the 'Rome Touch' App and the digital game 'The Last Banquet in Herculaneum', from LARP (see below for URLs). In addition, replicas of archaeological objects, such as those in the didactic kit on the Ancient Mediterranean designed by MAE/USP, are brought to the classes to increase students' proximity and engagement with the materiality of these ancient societies. The contextualized use of these resources provides a great stimulus for learning, due to their entertaining and scientific nature.

As for student assessment, not only traditional activities such as essays and seminar presentations are requested, but also activities such as artistic productions (paintings, drawings, cartoons) on abstract elements of the Greek and Roman religions, and even a simulated trial on a fictitious case of repatriation of archaeological material. In this case, students have to present well-founded arguments based on current legislation on heritage protection and on the deliberations established by the Convention Concerning the Protection of the World Cultural and Natural Heritage, adopted in 1972 by UNESCO.

This section derives from a report on the classes by Matheus Morais Cruz, a graduate student at MAE/USP who has taught the Archaeology classes at Amorim Lima since 2021. For an article on the first years, see Kormichiari et al. (2020).

Philosophy

The aim of the Philosophy classes at the Amorim Lima School, proposed at first by the 'Projeto *Minimus*' Philosophy Programme coordinator, was to add to the study of the Greek language some knowledge specific to Greek culture, from the standpoint of philosophical themes, as well as to show the students how the language itself provides elements for the formulation of philosophical concepts. Thus, the students would examine, at an introductory level, the following themes:

1. Myths as a way of understanding nature, humans, and gods;
2. The philosophical question *par excellence*: 'what is. . .', found in the everyday use of language and reformulated by Philosophy;
3. The creation, by philosophers, of a philosophical vocabulary based on the basic vocabulary of the language, such as the terms/concepts for 'matter' and 'quality', through their Latin versions.

However, as the Archaeology and Philosophy monitors are graduate students, and are frequently encouraged to develop their own course programmes, Antonio L. Kerstenetzky proposed an introduction to philosophy structured according to two principles: The first, to discuss certain aspects of Greek philosophy – the different kinds of problems Greek philosophers faced and the solutions they presented; and the sectond, using both this historical background and other motivating elements to stimulate discussions in which students participated in a philosophical debate.

The main objective of Antônio's course plan was to foster the moral deliberation of students – in other words, to motivate them to reflect on what kinds of knowledge, beliefs and justifications are mobilized when we are faced with a difficult decision. Thus, issues such as the following were discussed: Is it more important to consider the consequences of one's actions, or if the actions, in themselves, are correct? Are there universal principles that should regulate our actions, or are they specific to each culture? This type of discussion naturally led to political discussions (especially because 2018 was a year of presidential elections in which the two leading candidates polarized the whole society), which focused on decision-making. Issues such as the legitimacy of votes were discussed; whether decisions made unanimously are fairer than those made by the majority; how political representation works in our democracy and if it is fair; and whether there is any room for violence in politics. There were also discussions on how human nature influences these debates, whether human beings are naturally violent, just, and/or unjust.

These classes were inspired by the Philosophy for Children methodology developed by the American philosopher Matthew Lipman (2003). All discussions started from a motivating 'case', real or hypothetical situations that were analysed to address each theme. Students were encouraged not only to voice their opinions, but also to justify them. The monitor's role was therefore not only that of a moderator, but also to advance the students' arguments by showing them the possible consequences of their opinions and to prompt those who agreed or disagreed to manifest their own thoughts. The moments when a student convinced another to change his/her opinion through argumentative skills were especially valued. To enrich the discussions, a broad philosophical repertoire was presented, which often went beyond the Greek context:

in addition to Plato and Aristotle, concepts were drawn from Montaigne, John Rawls, David Estlund, Mary Beard, Philippa Foot, Steven Lukes, Immanuel Kant, Ruth Benedict, David Hume, Nancy Holstrom, John Locke, John Stuart Mill, Thomas Hobbes and Machiavelli, among others. Since Antonio Kerstenetzky was admitted at Princeton to read for a PhD, Silvia Anderson, a former graduate student and 'Projeto *Minimus*' monitor, filled in as a volunteer to teach the Philosophy classes in 2022.

Greek and Latin (2017–23)

Expanding 'Projeto Minimus' to other schools

One the goals of 'Projeto *Minimus*' was to expand Greek and Latin to other public or private schools, besides the Amorim Lima School. In 2017 it was introduced in two private schools in São Paulo. At the Colégio Equipe, Márcio Mauá Chaves Ferreira (a graduate student at the time) taught Greek as part of the Elementary and Middle School extra-curricular activities, and it is worth noting that these became the school's most popular extra-curriculars, while Silvia Anderson, then a graduate student, started to teach Greek to 7th and 8th grade students as a curricular elective at the Colégio Oswald de Andrade. These were very successful during their duration but, unfortunately, short-lived experiences.

The weekly classes at Colégio Oswald de Andrade took place during the second semester of 2017. The students were very interested, and as a result, good progress was made. At the end of the year, there was a celebration, and the class created a board game with themes from Greek mythology to showcase the course to those who did not take part in it. However, in 2018, although the students were enthusiastic about the classes, the school usually has their own staff teach the elective courses and, after a semester, they returned to this practice.

At Colégio Equipe, ancient Greek classes were also taught weekly, but as extra-curricular courses for different groups: one, for second- to fifth-grade students, and the other for high school students and external participants. The course's objective was to introduce the students to ancient Greek by means of the initial chapters of *Athenaze* (translated by the 'Projeto *Minimus*' team), and to present classical culture through its iconographic, historical and mythological manifestations. The course for the younger students lasted one semester and, despite its brief duration, it seems to have achieved some of its main objectives. The students gained some knowledge of the Greek verbal system, and, due to *Athenaze*'s use of texts that, although adapted, reflect historical and social conditions of ancient Greece, they examined some aspects of classical culture. The same may be said for the second course, which allowed for a deeper exploration in both language and the other cultural aspects, due to the students' greater maturity. The school offers these courses through an institute, and, after a semester, other courses in different fields of knowledge were offered.

At the beginning of 2018 'Projeto *Minimus*' introduced Latin classes at the Professora Nilce Cruz Figueiredo Municipal Public School as elective courses for 5th and 6th grade students. Sixty-eight students were enrolled. This school is in the Lauzane Paulista neighbourhood, on the outskirts of northern São Paulo and approximately two hours from the University of São Paulo by public transport. The contact was made by Amanda Oliveira, a former student of the Professora Nilce Cruz Figueiredo school, who at the time was a Latin undergraduate at USP participating in 'Projeto *Minimus*'. Amanda planned and taught the classes, proud to be now introducing Latin in her former school, close to where she still lived. However, in 2019 a new full-day curriculum was implemented at the school, and the new management unfortunately chose to discontinue the project, opting for other subjects for its electives.

In 2022 'Projeto *Minimus*' began three workshops at the Escola de Aplicação (EA) of the University of São Paulo. This is a public school that lies within the São Paulo/Butantã campus and is administered by the University's Faculty of Education. On his experience as monitor during the first year of the project at the Escola de Aplicação, Johnny Dotta reported:

During the second semester of 2022, I conducted three workshops at the Escola de Aplicação offered by 'Projeto *Minimus*' as extra-curricular activities: Latin (for 4th and 5th grade students), Greek, and a Workshop on text production based on fables (the latter two for Middle School). I already had experience with the first two courses, as I had been a monitor for Latin and Greek at the Amorim Lima school. However, the structure of the classes in each of these schools is quite different: at Amorim Lima, a school that favours alternative methodologies, monitors allow students to work independently and at their own pace, while encouraging them, answering questions, and explaining specific topics. On the other hand, at the Escola de Aplicação classes are more traditional, and lecture based. Despite the seemingly more rigid nature of this second type of class, I felt that the workshops at the Escola de Aplicação were as interactive as those at Amorim, especially among younger students.

The fable workshop was the continuation of a project started in the previous semester at the Amorim Lima school. With the aim of using Classical texts for conflict resolution in schools, Professor Marcos Martinho dos Santos developed reading and text production exercises (similar to those of ancient *progymnasmata*) based on fables – a genre that generally depicts characters in conflict and competing against each other (Santos 2022a,b). This material was brought to 'Projeto *Minimus*' by Professor Paula da Cunha Corrêa, and I was responsible for applying it in a Middle School workshop. Despite some challenges and the fact that not a single student managed to complete the programmed exercises, I consider the results positive. The workshop proved capable of aiding the students in acquiring the resources and using them in their re-elaborated and original texts, in which the characters should try to resolve the conflicts through cooperation, not competition. It would be great to use this material for an entire semester at the Escola de Aplicação, with a dedicated class.

It is important to detail how each of the workshops at the Escola de Aplicação progressed, as each had very different developments throughout the semester. The Latin workshop was undoubtedly the most successful, with great participation, a constant number of students throughout the semester, active student engagement, and a positive verification of the knowledge acquired at the end of the course. Perhaps because they were younger, I observed a more emotional involvement with what they were learning and with their enjoyment of the Latin class as a learning space outside their school routine. Additionally, many of them had knowledge of other Romance languages, learned at school or at home. Being native speakers of a Romance language, they progressed quickly and without difficulty through the initial lessons.

A clear example of this was a day when a student, with minimal explanation from me, deduced on his own that *gratias tibi ago* was a way of saying 'thank you' in Latin. In one of the last classes, I conducted a review in which I simply guided the students through the lessons we had covered, and they themselves explained all the topics we had seen. This was sufficient proof for me that they had truly benefited from the semester.

The Greek workshop was a middle ground. It had a significant initial enrolment, but the number of students did not remain the same from the beginning to the end of the semester. Unfortunately, many dropped out. However, my guess is that the reason for this was less of a difficulty with the content of the workshop, and more of a mismatch of expectations. In the initial class, for example, I noticed that many students were there because they were avid readers of the Percy Jackson books (Riordan 2005–23), and all were very excited to talk about mythology in class. As the semester progressed, I believe many lost their interest when they understood that what they would learn in class was not mythology but reading and writing Greek. Many told me they had other commitments outside of school (such as sports), and since the workshop was an extra-curricular and the students were a bit older, it seems that many of them simply preferred to spend their time on other things. In spite of this, a reasonable number of students remained until the end, and the workshop yielded good moments, such as when they read a Greek text for the first time after learning the alphabet. They realised that, even with difficulty, they could read it and didn't want the class to end before finishing the text. The main problem with the Greek workshop, in my opinion, had nothing to do with the class itself but resulted from the fact that I had only one semester with them. Greek requires an extended study time, as it involves learning another alphabet and is more distant for Portuguese speakers. In one semester, I could only teach the alphabet, practise reading some words, and translate a short text. The students who stayed until the end would certainly benefit from at least one more semester, which unfortunately was not possible.

The Fable Workshop had the lowest enrolment. If I remember correctly, I had only three or four students, and only one attended the classes from the beginning to the end of the semester. I had some hypotheses for the low enrolment: the workshop was held bit later in the day, and on the same day as the Greek workshop. The fable is a genre with which students are familiar and thus it may generate less interest than themes such Latin and Greek that are not taught in our schools. Besides, fables may be considered by these older students as stories for young children, but I did not have the opportunity to verify if any of these alternatives were correct. Besides, the student who attended all the classes already wrote very well, something I could perceive early in the semester. Thus, I couldn't really assess the real impact that this workshop had on her learning since she finished the semester at the same high level at which she started. However, I must reiterate that the material is excellent, and its positive results have been verified at the Amorim Lima school. Therefore, it would be interesting to try using it again at the Escola de Aplicação, adapting the workshop as needed to attract a larger number of students.

In 2023 the Greek and Latin Workshops at the Escola de Aplicação, taught by Clara Sperb (a voluntary graduate) and Maria Vitória Cuin de Souza (undergraduate), faced some difficulties. Although in our experience it is necessary for students to have at least a full year of classes to achieve results in Greek and Latin, the school's regular workshops last only from six to twelve sessions, and therefore the scheduling of year-long workshops (with four sessions per month) is not simple. Besides, despite the manifest interest of the students in the previous year, another workshop, that offers support for students in Maths and that is very popular, due to difficulties in the monitors' and school's scheduling, was held at the same time as the Latin Workshop. However, since the Escola de Aplicação is directed by colleagues of the Faculty of Education and maintained by the university, there has been a firm interest in the continuity of the project at the school, and we hope that it will be as long-lived and as successful as it has been at the Amorim Lima School.

Continuity of Greek and Latin at the Desembargador Amorim Lima Municipal Public School

Greek and Latin classes continue strong at Amorim Lima, having completed ten years in August 2023. There have been periods in which there were more (ten) or less (seven) monitors, due to the number of bursaries made available by the university, but the Greek and Latin programmes have not altered much during these years. Concerning the teaching methods, while the Brazilian translation of Barbara Bell's *Minimus* (Bell & Forte 2015) with minor adaptations and additional exercises, has always worked very well, Greek monitors generally use *Athenaze* (Balme & Lawall 2011) although some have lately preferred *Aprendendo Grego* (the Brazilian translation of JACT's *Reading Greek* (2007)), and for a more engaging introduction to the Greek alphabet, project members translated and published a free online version of *Basil Batrakhos and the Mystery Letter* (Andrew et al. 2020).

Covid-19 and the long quarantines did not interrupt 'Projeto *Minimus*', but required a great effort from all in order to create the online synchronous classes that were held via Google Meet. The remote classes were important not only to guarantee the continuity of the students' learning, but also to keep them occupied and in contact with their classmates during such a challenging period in which they were confined to their homes. Despite the limitations of access (many did not have a satisfactory internet connection at home) and interaction, resulting from the abrupt adoption of the online sessions, there was noticeable interest and participation of the students, and the classes also provided a stimulus for the monitors to search for and employ other educational tools, such as digital games, visual and audio-visual materials.

Among other activities of 'Projeto *Minimus*' at Amorim Lima during this period, noteworthy was the participation of students and monitors in the *Festival Européen Latin-Grec*, with a public reading of the *Iliad* on 22 March 2019 (see YouTube URL below) as well as in the Harvard Centre of Hellenic Studies' 'Odyssey "Round the World"', on 9 December 2019, when Amorim Lima school students, monitors and faculty took part in this 24-hour event featuring readings of the *Odyssey* by various universities and actors. Still in 2019, the above-mentioned two-month Workshop on Fables at the Amorim Lima School was organized for 7th grade students, and later developed into the Fable Workshop at the Escola de Aplicação. This year (2023) at Amorim Lima's culture fair, students and monitors created activities related to the theme of 'Fear' in Antiquity, ten years after the school celebrated Classical Antiquity in their annual culture fair, in honour of 'Projeto *Minimus*' first year at the school.

Other outreach programmes in Classics in Brazilian schools

There have been other relatively recent Greek and/or Latin outreach programmes in public schools across the country, but none of which are now active. The objective of *Paideia: Ensinando grego antigo*, a year-long project coordinated by Dominique Vieira Coelho dos Santos and Dyel Gedhay da Silva, was the introduction of Greek in the community of Itajaí, Blumenau (Santos & Silva 2020). In the southernmost state, Rafael Brunhara, who participated in the 'Projeto *Minimus*' as a graduate monitor in 2013, years later, as a faculty member at the University of Rio Grande do Sul (UFRGS), developed a similar project in collaboration with the university's Escola de Aplicação called '*Minimus*-Sul' in 2018. It was an initiative linked to two courses offered in the Greek language programme at UFRGS (Teaching Practice in Greek I and II), involving two students: Clara Sperb and Bruno Palavro (both currently graduate students, Clara is now a volunteer at the USP 'Projeto *Minimus*').

Another '*Minimus* Project – Latin for Children' was developed in the north, in Manaus, from 2016 to 2018, at the Professor, Tereza Rosa Aguiar Abtibol Municipal Public School, as part of the Institutional Scholarship Programme for Teaching (PIBID), and coordinated by Carlos Renato Rosário de Jesus, from the State University of Amazonas. Nine undergraduate monitors taught 3rd and 4th grade students a weekly two-hour class, by means of the Brazilian translation of *Minimus* (Bell & Forte 2015), and extra materials such as games and exercises, with a focus on the relations between Portuguese and Latin, in order to develop the student vocabulary and understanding of their native language. The results were very beneficial, for the students enjoyed the activities, were highly participative, and appeared to have grasped well the proposed course contents. There was an observable improvement in their performance and interest in their regular Portuguese classes, and the project also expanded their cultural horizons. Unfortunately, the project ended from the lack of subsequent funding.

Also at the State University of Amazonas, but at a different Campus, that of Parintins, Weberson Fernandes Grizoste developed two outreach projects at the São Francisco de Assis Municipal Public School: the 'Classical Latin Language Course' (with an emphasis on translation) which consisted of classes taught on Saturday mornings, from August 2017 to July 2018, by three Latin undergraduates to four university students, three graduate students, and nine 8th-grade school students, and the project 'Latin in School: Notions of Classical Philology' (from August 2022 to July 2023), that aimed at providing school students with basic notions of Romance philology, from the origins of classical and vulgar Latin up to the present day, with a focus on Portuguese. For two other projects recently developed by Fernandes Grizoste, 'Latin in Sign-Language' and 'Ludi Insulae', see YouTube URLs below.

Simone Cordeiro Oliveira Pinheiro, at the Federal University of Acre (Floresta Campus), in the Amazon region, coordinated in 2019 the 'Latine' outreach project, at the Irmã Diana Municipal Public School in the city of Cruzeiro do Sul, for twenty-nine students (aged 8–10). The project introduced the students to the Latin language and culture, by means of the Brazilian translation of *Minimus* (Bell & Forte 2015) with reflections on the linguistic, social and cultural elements that contributed to the formation of Romance languages, especially Portuguese (UFAC 2022; Albano 2019).

There are numerous Greek and Latin extra-curricular and outreach language courses offered in federal and state universities for the public at large, but these are not in schools, nor are they designed for school students, but for adults and other university students. However, there are university outreach projects for school students in other fields of Classical Studies, such as Mythology, Literature, History, Archaeology and Philosophy. These have been organized by university museums and/or by faculty members such as 'Contos de Mitologia' (Mythology Tales), conceived by Tereza Virgínia Ribeiro Barbosa and Neiva Ferreira Pinto twenty years ago, when both were colleagues at the Federal University of Minas Gerais. In 2003, this outreach project then began at the Federal University of Juiz de Fora with Neiva Ferreira Pinto and is today coordinated by Fernanda Cunha Sousa and Charlene Martins Miotti (Zanirato & Sousa 2015). Its objective is to promote classical culture in schools, developing the student's creativity and a love for reading through the storytelling of the myths narrated by Greek and Latin poets. The project has been currently developed at the Presidente Tancredo Neves Municipal Public School for the 5th and 6th grade students, and Charlene Miotti's proposal for this year (2023) encompassed a selection of myths on catasterisms, aiming to arouse the student's imagination and, at the same time, to divert their attention from screens, addressing the teachers' concerns regarding the extreme difficulty of expression and interaction found among their students in the post-pandemic return to school (Miotti 2023).

At the Federal University of Rio de Janeiro, 'Mitologando' ('Mythologizing'), was created in 2019 and coordinated by Katia Teonia Costa de Azevedo of the Federal University of Rio de Janeiro. The programme is designed to expand student's knowledge of classical antiquity and to stimulate the interest in the study of these cultures, developing readers, improving their oral communication skills, and promoting textual interpretation. Additionally, the project seeks to encourage a critical reflection on social, cultural, and human values from antiquity to the present day, analysing, for example, how certain aspects of classical antiquity persist or not in our contemporary society. To achieve these purposes,' Mitologando' is based on a literary repertoire of Greek and Latin classical culture, as well as children and youth literature related to classical antiquity. It practices storytelling, literary mediation and dramatic reading, in public schools, cultural facilities and at the Faculty of Letters of UFRJ. The works are selected in collaboration with the FABULA Research Group, that enriches the content of the activities and ensures a well-founded approach. The combination of ancient narratives and contemporary literature provides a comprehensive and engaging educational experience for the project's target public, establishing a meaningful connection with classical culture.

Also, at the Federal University of Rio de Janeiro, Pedro Ribeiro Martins coordinates the Anima-Mito project in partnership with the Multimedia Education Group. Created for public schools, the project starts with readings and reinterpretations of myths from which the students build narratives and produce audio-visual animations. Pedro Martins is also part of the Centre for Documentation in Classical Languages (NDLC), which cooperates with the National Library Foundation to improve the cataloguing of rare books in Greek and Latin. The NDLC and the National Library Foundation promote school essay contests on themes from classical antiquity, the Ramiz Galvão Prize, and has held Greek typography workshops to present the history of books and the emergence of the press during the Renaissance period. This workshop focuses on the National Library Foundation's collection of rare books and enables students to learn, in practice, book printing processes by means of handmade rubber Greek and Latin types.

In the Midwest, at the Federal University of Mato Grosso do Sul, through a partnership of the Atrivm Research Group and the Pedagogical Residency Program (Philosophy Subproject, UFMS/CAPES), Carlos Eduardo da Costa Campos and Cristina de Souza Agostini developed in various of the state schools 'A Day at the Museum', to make the collection of the National Historical Museum in Rio de Janeiro more widely known, and to disseminate the science of numismatics as an essential tool for a more profound understanding of the history of currency and its relationship with the societies' ideologies. And by means of these efforts, Classical Studies are beginning to gain prominence at the Federal University of Mato Grosso do Sul, as well as in the state's public schools.

Conclusions

As always and everywhere, funding is a decisive factor for the development and survival of any project. However, in Classics, and especially in the case of classical languages in Brazil, since the 1960s, much depends on the interest of the school directors. The availability of adequate teaching resources is also fundamental, as the publication of the Brazilian version of *Minimus* (Bell & Forte 2015) has shown, through the success of the University of São Paulo's 'Projeto *Minimus*' and the emergence of similar projects throughout the country that rely on this translation of Barbara Bell's students' and teachers' books. Although we have a Brazilian version of JACT's *Reading Greek*, it is mostly used in the first semesters of undergraduate Greek courses, since students rarely arrive at Brazilian universities with any prior knowledge of the language, and it is usually considered difficult and graphically less appealing for elementary and middle school students. Perhaps the next step should be to provide a more appropriate and entertaining Greek learning method for our school students.

Although the focus of outreach projects lies in the benefits these may offer the school students or the wider community, in Brazil, because university outreach programmes are generally created and coordinated by faculty, but executed by students, there is an extra gain for these, as Pedro Henrique da Silva Sousa, a 'Projeto *Minimus*' monitor at the University of São Paulo, observes:

I still remember my first class. It was the first week of college, and we read the proem of the *Iliad*. I, who had never been exposed to classical literature before, was deeply enthralled; it was, so to speak, love at the first reading, a passion that persists today. However, I also remember that, even at that time, I felt a certain regret for not having encountered this literature earlier in my life.

When I joined the 'Projeto *Minimus*', the process of teaching something I love to children contributed and still contributes immensely to my education. In a way, it's a manner of providing them with what I myself did not have access to. What pleases me the most is seeing how this knowledge aids in the understanding of other areas, especially in the comprehension of our own language and culture. Furthermore, contact with literature is always a positive experience for them. I specifically recall a class when, after teaching them the alphabet, I showed them Archilochus' Fr. 2W and asked them to read it aloud. The students found the sound amusing and spent the rest of the class repeating, amidst laughter, the word μεμαγμένη.

The benefits of the project in the education of children are quite evident. However, I consider that the project's mission is not necessarily to form Hellenists and Latinists, but to offer them the possibility of knowing and engaging with classics in their youth; and to create a context of freedom in which they can look at themselves and decide whether they like it or not. And within this diverse group of students, there are those with a sparkle in their eyes, one that reminds me of my first class.

I thank the 'Projeto *Minimus*' undergraduate and graduate monitors – Antonio L. Kerstenetzky, Clara Sperb, Johnny Dotta, Márcio Mauá Chaves Ferreira, Maria Vitória Cuin de Souza, Matheus Morais Cruz, Pedro Henrique da Silva Sousa, Silvia M. M. G. Anderson – who allowed me to quote or summarize their activity reports, as well as the colleagues that shared information on their outreach projects: Carlos Renato Rosário de Jesus (Universidade Estadual do Amazonas), Charlene Miotti (Universidade Federal de Juiz de Fora), Cristina de Souza Agostini (Universidade Federal do Mato Grosso do Sul), Katia Teonia Costa de Azevedo (Universidade Federal do Rio de Janeiro), Pedro Ribeiro Martins (Universidade Federal do Rio de Janeiro), Rafael Brunhara (Universidade Federal do Rio Grande do Sul), Simone Cordeiro de Oliveira (Universidade Federal do Acre) and Weberson Fernandes Grizoste (Universidade Estadual do Amazonas).

References

Albano, G. (2019), Ufac ensina latim a crianças em projeto de extensão que aborda aspectos linguísticos e culturais. Available online: https://g1.globo.com/ac/cruzeiro-do-sul-regiao/noticia/2019/08/01/ufac-ensina-latim-a-criancas-em-projeto-de-extensao-que-aborda-aspectos-linguisticos-e-culturais.ghtml (accessed 20 December 2023).

Andrew, C., P. Jones, P. C. Corrêa, I. V. Rokiskei and J. S. Matos (2020), *Basílio Bátrakhos e a carta misteriosa: grego clássico para jovens,* Universidade de São Paulo: Faculdade de Filosofia, Letras e Ciências Humanas. Available online: www.livrosabertos.sibi.usp.br/portaldelivrosUSP/catalog/book/612 (accessed 20 December 2023).

Balme, M. and G. Lawall (2011), *Athenaze: An Introduction to Ancient Greek*, Oxford: Oxford University Press.

Bell, B. and H. Forte (2015), *Minimus – Conhecendo o Latim* (livros do aluno e do professor), transl. F. Alvim, São Paulo: Filocalia

Corrêa, P. C. (2018), 'Reintroducing Classics in a Brazilian Public School: Project Minimus in São Paulo', in A. Holmes-Henderson, S. Hunt and M. Musié (eds), *Forward with Classics. Classical Languages in Schools and Communities,* London: Bloomsbury, 55–66.

JACT (2007), [Book series] *Reading Greek,* Cambridge: Joint Association of Classical Teachers / Cambridge University Press.

JACT (2014), [Book series] *Aprendendo grego. Texto e vocabulário, gramática e exercícios*, trans. C. Bartalotti and L. Cabral, São Paulo: Odysseus.

Kormichiari, M., F. Perissato and F. Ferreira (2020), 'Saberes arqueológicos na escola pública: ações educativas do Labeca aplicadas ao "Projeto Minimus Interdisciplinar"', *Perspectivas e Diálogos: Revista de História Social e Práticas de Ensino*, Caetité, 2 (6): 35–65.

LABECA/MAE (n.d.), [Video] What is Archaeology? Available online: https://youtu.be/lxwBBP_sNcg (accessed 20 December 2023).

Lipman, M. (2003), *Thinking in education,* Cambridge: Cambridge University Press.

Miotti, C. (2023), [Conference presentation] 'Desafios para a segunda década do CirceA – Círculo de Estudos da Antiguidade', SBEC 2023 International Conference in Belém, Pará.

Riordan, R. (2005–23), [Book Series] *Percy Jackson and the Olympians*, London: Penguin.

Santos, D. V. C. dos and D. G. da Silva (2020), 'O projeto Paideia: Ensinando grego antigo no município de Blumenau (SC)', *Nuntius Antiquus*, 16 (1): 193–218.

Santos, M. M. (2022a), *Componha uma Fábula, Resolva um Conflito – livro do aluno*. Available online: https://drive.google.com/file/d/1_KvMzhqAisKoMPCWoT75KQp0WJgbrCeG/view (accessed 20 December 2023).

Santos, M. M. (2022b), *Componha uma Fábula, Resolva um Conflito – livro do professor*. Available online: https://drive.google.com/file/d/1ah4ezDozHRxua8EkvHw0mdRb4I9wsm3t/view (accessed 20 December 2023).

Sobrinho, J. (2013), 'O Latim no Brasil na primeira metade do século XX: entre leis, discursos e disputas, uma disciplina em permanência', *Phaos: Revista De Estudos Clássicos*, 13: 39–63.

UFAC (2022), Proyecto Campus Floresta enseña latín a estudiantes de escuelas públicas. Available online: https://www.ufac.br/site/noticias/2019/projeto-do-campus-floresta-ensina-latim-para-alunos-de-escola-publica-em-cruzeiro-do-sul (accessed 20 December 2023).

Zanirato, T. F. and F. C. Sousa (2015), 'Universidade: escola para a sociedade – um relato sobre experiências de pesquisa e extensão', *Phaos: Revista De Estudos Clássicos,* 13: 137–52.

Organizations

Anima-Mito project: https://www.youtube.com/@anima-mitoufrj8143

Atrivm Research Group: https://www.atrivmufms.com/

Conflict Resolution through Classical literature: https://sites.google.com/view/conflictandclassics/abstracts-workshop-1 and https://sites.google.com/view/conflictandclassics/poster-and-programme-workshop-2

Desembargador Amorim Lima Municipal Public School: https://amorimlima.org.br/institucional/

Fabula Research Group: www.fabula.letras.ufrj.br and @fabula.ufrj

Festival Européen Latin-Grec: https://www.youtube.com/watch?v=mN4OiEkf35o

Grizoste, F. YouTube videos. Latin in Sign-Language: https://www.youtube.com/playlist?list=PL9sjq7YRMZv0xvmXGbsJj8dWNBrkGcdV1 and Ludi Insulae: https://www.youtube.com/watch?v=dvB6dtTfkCU

Harvard Centre of Hellenic Studies' 'Odyssey "Round the World"': https://chs.harvard.edu/event/odyssey-round-the-world/

Interactive Archaeology and Electronic Simulations (ARISE): http://www.arise.mae.usp.br/

Laboratory of Provincial Roman Archaeology (LARP/MAE/USP): http://www.larp.mae.usp.br/

Laboratory of Study on the Ancient City (LABECA/MAE/USP): https://labeca.mae.usp.br/

Lycée Pasteur School, São Paulo: https://lyceepasteur.com

Mitologando: www.mitologando.letras.ufrj.br and @mitologando

Museum of Archaeology and Ethnology of the University of São Paulo (MAE/USP): Museu de Arqueologia e Etnologia (usp.br)

Projeto Minimus Interdisciplinar: https://minimus.fflch.usp.br/

Ramiz Galvão Prize: https://www.gov.br/bn/pt-br/central-de-conteudos/noticias/premio-ramiz-galvao-de-redacoes-cerimonia-de-premiacao-da-1a-edicao-na-biblioteca-nacional

Sambaquis – A history before Brazil: http://www.arise.mae.usp.br/sambaquis/

CHILE

Paulo Donoso, Leslie Lagos and Néstor Urrutia

Introduction

This chapter will introduce a general view of the current situation of classical studies in Chile. This view will introduce different educational stages and other instances where classical studies have taken place. The narrative involves historical aspects and a critical overview of Chile's actual state of humanities.

Chile is located far away from the Greek *poleis* or what was the Roman Empire, both in terms of time and space. However, the classical world is the foundation of our culture and civilization. Examples of this include the investigations of Professors Gazmuri (2017), Huidobro (2021) and Viveros (2019). Our republican basis, educational models, and even aesthetic points of view are inspired by the Graeco-Roman past. However, how current is knowledge about the Classics in our educational system? This chapter consists of a short review on different levels to share a view of the field in Chile.

Education system

Let us begin by reviewing the educational system. In the primary school curriculum, on a national level, from the third to the seventh year, some units allow students to identify the Graeco-Roman legacy as an essential contributor to Western culture, as an introduction to comparative history. It is usually used as an example of elements related to cultural value, law, religion, art, institutions and others or as an excuse to develop activities in physical geography with particular attention to Rome (MINEDUC 2012). Our education system only refers to Graeco-Roman culture in a general, almost casual way, focusing only on political and daily life aspects. Classical languages are not included in the curriculum, but some schools teach them only because of tradition and without following the designated plan. Some examples are Colegio Santa Úrsula of Vitacura, Colegio San Francisco of Las Condes, Colegio Francisco Encina of Ñuñoa and Colegio La Maisonnette of Vitacura.

During the nineteenth century, places were created where Greek and Latin were taught because the academy needed to align with republican standards. Andrés Bello, a Latinist and politician, motivated the studies of classic languages. However, after 1880, they became optional, which explains the present situation (Castillo 1996). As a result of that decision, there are nowadays only a few places dedicated to studying these languages at the college level. Among the universities of CRUCH (Consejo de Rectores de Universidades de Chile), only nine of the twenty-six institutions have Greek and Latin as actual courses in their curriculum maps (see Table 13).

Table 13. Universities in Chile which offer Greek or Latin languages

University	Programmes
Pontificia Universidad Católica de Chile	Philosophy – Theology
Pontificia Universidad Católica de Valparaíso	Philosophy – Theology
Universidad Alberto Hurtado	Philosophy
Universidad Católica de Temuco	Philosophy
Universidad de Chile	Philosophy – Linguistics
Universidad de Los Andes	Philosophy – History – Literature
Universidad de Santiago	Philosophy
Universidad de Valparaíso	Philosophy
Universidad Metropolitana de Ciencias de la Educación	Philosophy – Castilian

Source © P. Donoso 2003.

If we amplify the criteria to degrees that involve classical studies rather than just languages, then the number of courses multiplies (see Table 14).

In Chile, classical studies training at the postgraduate level has been reduced to only one programme, taught by the Centro de Estudios Clásicos of the Universidad Metropolitana de Ciencias de la Educación. This programme was created in 1996 under the title of *Magister en Lengua y Cultura Clásica*; in 1999, it was renamed *Magister en Estudios Clásicos,* with a degree in *Lengua y Cultura Clásica* [Classical Language and Culture] or with a degree in *Cultura Grecorromana* [Graeco-Roman Culture] (Bustos & Soaje, 2022). In the Centro de Estudios Clásicos from the beginning of the programme in 1996 until 2019, nineteen theses were defended in both degrees (there have been no registrations since 2019).

In other universities, there are doctoral and Master's programmes with expert staff in Ancient History, Classical Philosophy and Literature. This group of academics has allowed

Table 14. Universities in Chile which offer Classical Studies

University	Programmes
Pontificia Universidad Católica de Chile	History – Philosophy – Aesthetic – Theology
Pontificia Universidad Católica de Valparaíso	History – Philosophy – Theology
Universidad Alberto Hurtado	History – Philosophy – Languages – Bachillerato
Universidad Austral de Chile	History – Language
Universidad Católica de Temuco	History – Philosophy – Language
Universidad Católica del Norte	Philosophy – Religion
Universidad Católica Silva Henríquez	History
Universidad de Chile	History – Philosophy – Linguistics
Universidad de Concepción	History – Philosophy – Bachillerato
Universidad de la Frontera	History
Universidad de la Serena	History – Philosophy – Castilian
Universidad de Los Andes	History – Philosophy – Literature
Universidad de Magallanes	History
Universidad de Playa Ancha	History – Philosophy
Universidad de Santiago	History – Philosophy
Universidad de Talca	Historia – Philosophy – Religion – Castilian
Universidad de Tarapacá	History
Universidad de Valparaíso	History – Philosophy
Universidad Diego Portales	History
Universidad Metropolitana de Ciencias de la Educación	History – Philosophy – Castilian

Source © P. Donoso 2023.

some staff to mentor doctoral and Master's theses in this field. There are seven of these universities. The first groups were founded between 1842 and 1928: Universidad de Chile, Pontificia Universidad Católica de Chile, Universidad de Concepción and Pontificia Universidad Católica de Valparaíso. The second group are private universities, founded in the 1980s: Universidad Adolfo Ibañez, Universidad Andrés Bello and Universidad de los Andes. All of these universities have developed doctoral and master's programmes in Ancient History, although the postgraduate programmes are centred on the humanities in general.

Classical conferences

Chile has a solid tradition in academic meetings and is internationally renowned in classical studies. These meetings started taking place in the second half of the twentieth century. In 1953, The Departamento de Extensión Cultural of Universidad de Chile organized conferences about Byzantium, the Renaissance and its influence on the American discovery to commemorate the 500th anniversary of The Fall of Constantinople (Donoso 2018; Cruz 2023: 134–5). The central coordinator was Fotios Malleros Kasimatis, a Greek citizen who arrived in Chile in 1947. On the same subject, the Pontificia Universidad Católica de Valparaíso pioneered in meetings an ancient history theme with the *Semana Bizantina* [Byzantium Week] in 1958, celebrated once. Then, in June 1973, the first *Semana de Estudios Romanos* [Roman Studies Week] took place, which is still celebrated today. This initiative has become the main reference point for Roman Studies in History, Law and Philosophy for the last fifty years. Its creator was history professor Héctor Herrera Cajas (1988a). In these meetings, many experts, such as William W. Harris, Paul B. Harvey, Gabriella Albanese, Maria Antonieta Giua, Cesare Letta, Lucio Troiani, Umberto Laffi, Michel Roddaz, Giuliano Crifó and Jorg Rüpke have attended through the years. Another example of similar activities is the *Encuentro Internacional de Centro de Estudios Clásicos* [International Meeting for the Centre of Classical Studies] by Universidad Metropolitana de Ciencias de la Educación. All started with a meeting called *Paideia y Humanitas* in 1989, hosted by Héctor Herrera Cajas, Giuseppina Grammatico Amari and Francisco Rodríguez Adrados. This meeting was the only time Spanish philologist Adrados visited the country. The seventeenth meeting occurred in 2022 under the title 'The ultimate goal for mortals is health'.

In 1961, the Greek consuls in Valparaíso and Santiago donated the Pabellón Griego to the Universidad de Chile (Castillo 1998–9). The pavilion is a one-floor building with an entrance inspired by a two-column ionic temple, where the Centro de Estudios Griegos, Bizantinos y Neohelénicos was founded in 1968. This Centre was born under the initiative of Fotios Malleros Kasimatis, who was the director until 1986. Since 1997, the Centre has offered a Diploma en Estudios Griegos programme. The library has over 8,000 volumes, including a collection of Greek classics and mainly Byzantine and Modern Greek collections.

In 1988, the Centro de Estudios Clásicos was founded in the Universidad Metropolitana de Ciencias de la Educación. In the inaugural speech, Dean Héctor Herrera Cajas said:

> We have to return to the Acropolis, but the Acropolis is a ruin, and it will continue to be ruined if we cannot rescue from them the essence that every period requires. The Acropolis has been an inspiration for centuries to great poets and thinkers. The Acropolis is an eternal symbol of ancient people who burst with life vibrancy and nourished

different periods of Western history with variable intensity. On the same note, we offer this gift to our homeland's culture for the young and youthfully spirited. We are convinced that the first group involved in the classical world will be an example to others of our legacy as a university. We want to be at the centre of the biggest problems of the modern world in the educational field. We are convinced that it cannot only be studies of methodology or instrumentality but also establish solid concepts, creativity and elegance, which are abundant in the sources of the classics [...]

(Herrera Cajas, 1988b: 17)

Academic publications

Academic journals are a great way to show the results of the diversity of research and academic studies. In Chile, researchers of the classic world can publish in various journals. Although we have a strong tradition of meetings about the classical world, relatively few journals are open to publications related to the field since the majority are focused on contemporary, Chilean and Latin-American studies. On the other hand, law journals have much to say because they address themes such as Roman Law or the relation between the jurisprudence of Rome and local norms in the Roman Empire. A similar situation happens with literature and philosophy journals, as they are heterogeneous and pave the way for researchers of the Graeco-Roman world, mainly if they focus on studies of the present era. History journals have been a significant support for classical world studies. Many were set up in the last twenty years and provide opportunities for classical scholars: the *Revista de Historia* of the Universidad de Concepción (since 1991), the *Revista Intus-Legere Historia* of the Universidad Adolfo Ibañez (since 2007) and the *Revista Historia 396* of the Instituto de Historia of Pontificia Universidad Católica de Valparaíso (since 2011). All of them are dedicated to historical studies and have significant diffusion.

Founded in 1970, the annual journal *Byzantiun Nea Hellás* focuses on Greek, Byzantine and Neohellenic studies; it is published by the Centro de Estudios Fotios Malleros of Universidad de Chile mentioned above. The section *Vetera Graeca* is dedicated to historical, philosophical, literary and linguistic studies related to Greece, and is interdisciplinary by nature.

Among all the classical studies related journals, the most senior one is the *Semanas de Estudios Romanos,* which takes the name of the meeting that started in 1973 in the Pontificia Universidad Católica de Valparaíso. This journal is focused on Roman studies of all kinds and is well known for its academic excellence.

The *Limes* journal was founded in 1988 by the Centro de Estudios Clásicos of Universidad Metropolitana de Ciencias de la Educación. According to Bustos and Soaje (2002):

[*Limes*] had the objective of stimulating and organising the studies, analysis and interdisciplinary debate of Classic themed related, among which the Greek and Latin languages can be found, as well as literature, history, philosophy, religion, mythology, art and tradition, becoming at the same time a tool of diffusion and motivation for the readers to discover the Greek-Latin world, learn from it and appreciate it.

(Bustos & Soaje, 2022: 109)

It also became a showcase for researchers at the time. On the other hand, the Centro de Estudios Clásicos has another journal called *Iter*, which is a summary of monographs (see UMCE, n.d.). Bustos and Soaje again: '[*Iter*] collects works presented in meetings, colloquiums and symposiums, as well as analysis, critical studies, essays, investigations, and project results presented in seminaries or inspired by them' (Bustos & Soaje, 2002: 111–12).

In 2009, the interdisciplinary journal *Historias del Orbis Terrarum – Estudios Clásicos, Medievales y Renacentistas* was created as part of the programme of Revistas Científicas Chilenas. In 2022, issue 28 published the dossier 'Los Estudios Clásicos en Chile' with five papers that showed the history of the classical presence in Chilean education. Donoso and Sáez reported: 'In this way, Greek-Roman classics have been present in Chile since the colonial era as part of the political, social, cultural, religious and mental structures of society, diving into a long-term tradition of integration of a more significant cultural corpus' (Donoso & Sáez 2022: 9–10).

The creation of *Grecorromana. Revista Chilena de Estudios Clásicos* in 2019 has been a transcendental milestone for classical studies in Chile (Cruz 2023: 151). Annually published and interdisciplinary, the journal is affiliated with the Departamento de Humanidades of Universidad Andrés Bello and has published four volumes.

Support for Classics

In Chile, there are no public policies to support classical language departments. This situation was criticized by the Latin scholar Antonio Cussen in a publication in the newspaper *El Mercurio* in 2015:

> Our country is the only one in the OCDE (. . .) that has not even one university with a classical philology department - a centre where teaching and cultivating Latin and Greek is the main purpose. This is truly a shame. The Universidad Católica closed down its Departamento de Filología Clásica during the 1970s; the Universidad de Chile closed down its Departamento de Lenguas Clásicas in the 1980s; the Universidad Metropolitana de Ciencias de la Educación (. . .) has suspended its Centro de Estudios Clásicos. The Centro de Estudios Griegos, Bizantinos y Neohelenicos is the only academic link with the ancient world nowadays, by the hand of a great and humble man called Miguel Castillo Didier, besides other exceptional people such as Antonio Arbea and Oscar Velásquez.

(Cussen 2015)

Promoting Classics for the future

Nowadays, the teaching of classical languages takes place in other departments. However, some educative environments have advocated the interest in learning Greek and Latin languages. The *Circulus Latinus Iacobopolitanos*, founded in 2015 by Lilí Saavedra and Antonio Cussen, has developed a dynamic activity around teaching and promoting the Latin language among universities and schools. Their last project was the *Schola Aestiva Chiliensis*, an immersive Latin summer school held in January 2023. Publicity for the summer school noted:

Considering that Latin has been spoken and written uninterruptedly for the last 25 centuries, the *Schola Aestiva Chilensis* offers a moment of dialogue inspired by the desire to step into the present with all its deep roots [in the past]. Therefore, not only will it provide the participants with personal improvement, but it will also mean being part of a community of people with a literary heritage given by the Latin language.

(AdPrensa 2023)

In recent times, the main focus of research on Greece and Rome belongs to historians, second to philosophers and researchers of classical literature and languages. In 2019, the Grupo de Estudios Interuniversitario del Mediterráneo Antiguo (GEIMA) was inaugurated by Paulo Donoso Johnson, Leslie Lagos Aburto, Andrés Sáez Geoffroy and Néstor Urrutia Muñoz, academics and researchers from different Chilean universities (Cruz, 2023: 150). The initiative of GEIMA is

to create a space for emergent researchers in the field of ancient history in Chile [. . .]. This group looks forward to building potential and strengthening ancient world studies from a broad point of view through themes linked to the Greco-Roman past and other ancient Mediterranean civilisations in a political, strategic and cultural way. It is also essential to decentralise studies and investigations in this field, spreading and creating connections between universities constantly and fluidly and sharing results beyond the academy, which is a real challenge in a country with a geography like ours.

(GEIMA 2019)

During the Covid pandemic between 2020 and 2021, GEIMA gathered foreign and local researchers from Europe and Latin America in a virtual meeting and invited them to discuss the classical world and its issues. This project also created *GEIMA Historia Antigua Ediciones* (registered in Camara Chilena del Libro ISBN 956-09579) to respond to the lack of an edition focused on ancient history publishing. GEIMA has published three books: *Geografía, política y pensamiento en época antonina. Una visión del imperio romano en el siglo II* (Sáez 2021), *Alejandro Magno. Propuestas de estudio, investigación y reflexión* (Lagos 2023) and *Limites II: Redes, movimientos y contactos en el mundo antiguo* (Sáez 2022). We are looking forward to continuing to add titles.

General conclusions

In Chile, there have been various attempts to involve classical studies in training plans, but this has faded through time in the local universities. There are notable attempts to keep classical languages alive in degrees that are not mainly focused on them. Moreover, they often offer content related to the classical world, usually in the earliest semesters of their courses, which clarifies that the classical past is fundamental to constructing the West.

There have been attempts, such as the Centro de Estudios Griegos, Bizantinos y Neohelénicos under Fotios Malleros and the Centro de Estudios Clásicos under Giuseppina Grammatico Amari to keep places dedicated to the field. However, despite the large number of publications and different promotional activities, it has been left behind by the academy. Even so, Chile keeps a great tradition of academic meetings about the classical world as a central theme, allowing us to keep in touch with the rest of the world to share interests. Some of the most recent projects – the *Schola Aestiva Chiliensis* and the *Grupo de Estudios Interuniversitario del Mediterráneo Antiguo* – have raised the importance of classical studies through different approaches.

References

AdPrensa (2023), UDP inicia escuela de latín y lleva el idioma a espacios tradicionales de Santiago. Available online: UDP inicia escuela de latín y lleva el idioma a espacios tradicionales de Santiago – AdPrensa – agenda de prensa (accessed 11 October 2023).

Bustos, C. and R. Soaje (2022), 'Historia del Centro de Estudios Clásicos y su aporte al estudio de la cultura grecorromana en Chile', *Historias del Orbis Terrarum*, 28: 96–130.

Castillo, M. (1996), 'Los estudios clásicos en Chile: retrospectiva y perspectiva', *Anales de la Universidad de Chile, Sexta serie*, 3: 35–49.

Castillo, M. (1998–9), 'Treinta años del Centro de Estudios Griegos (1968–1998)', *Byzantion Nea Hellás*, 17–18: 11–12.

Cruz, N. (2023), 'Estudiar e Investigar Historia Romana Antigua en Chile: Siglo XX–XXI', *Grecorromana*, V: 133–58.

Cussen, A. (2015), 'El latín, lengua viva', *El Mercurio*, 21 September. Available online: http://www.economiaynegocios.cl/noticias/noticias.asp?id=185128 (accessed 11 October 2023).

Donoso, P. and A. Sáez (2022), 'Presentación del Dossier Los Estudios Clásicos en Chile', *Historias del Orbis Terrarum*, 28: 9–11.

Donoso, P. (2018), *Recepción histórica y política de las Historias de Tucídides. Algunos casos en lengua hispana*, Valparaíso: Ediciones Universitarias de Valparaíso.

Gazmuri, S. (2017), 'Los modelos políticos de la antigüedad clásica y su papel en los discursos republicanos en Chile (1810–1833)', *Revista de Estudios Avanzados*, 27: 37–53.

GEIMA (2019), Grupo de Estudios Interuniversitario del Mediterráneo Antiguo. Available online: https://www.facebook.com/geima.historia.3/about_details (accessed 11 October 2023).

Grammatico, G. (1988), 'Palabras introductorias al acto inaugural del Centro de Estudios Clásicos', *Limes*, 1: 20–32.

Herrera Cajas, H. (1988a), 'Dimensiones de la responsabilidad educacional', Editorial Universitaria.

Herrera Cajas, H. (1988b), 'Discurso de inauguración del Centro de Estudios Clásicos', *Limes*, 1: 14–18

Huidobro, M. and E. Calderón (2021), 'Continuidades, Cambios y Relecturas en la Enseñanza del Latín en Chile durante un Periodo de Transición (1800–1830)', *Historia 396*, 11 (1): 203–40.

Lagos, L., ed. (2023), 'Alejandro Magno. Propuestas de estudio, investigación y reflexión', *Colección GEIMA Historia Antigua. Serie Historia Helenística Nº1*, Chile: GEIMA Ediciones.

MINEDUC (2012), *Programas de Estudio*, Santiago de Chile.

Sáez, A. (2021), 'Geografía, política y pensamiento en época antonina. Una visión del imperio romano en el siglo II', *Colección GEIMA Historia Antigua. Serie Historia de Roma Nº1*, Chile: GEIMA Ediciones.

Sáez, A., ed. (2022), *Limites II: Redes, movimientos y contactos en el mundo antiguo. Colección GEIMA Historia Antigua. Serie Historia Antigua Nº1*, Chile: GEIMA Ediciones.

UMCE (n.d.), Index, *Iter* Journal. Available online: http://revistas.umce.cl/index.php/iter/about (accessed 11 October 2023).

Viveros, A. (2019), 'Representaciones clásicas en la arquitectura y la escultura de Santiago y Buenos Aires entre 1870 y 1920', Presentaciones y autores del Congreso Internacional: El modelo Beaux-Arts y la Arquitectura en América Latina, 1870–1930, Universidad Nacional de la Plata.

VENEZUELA

Mariano Nava

A short historical introduction and current status

As in most of the colonies during Spanish domination (sixteenth to early nineteenth centuries), knowledge of Latin was essential to the educational system in the territories that later formed Venezuela. If Spanish was the language of domination that guaranteed the unity and the administration of the empire, knowledge of Latin was essential as an instrument of religious unity. Latin was taught primarily in religious seminaries, but also in 'Latinity Schools' established by the ecclesiastical authorities. In the second half of the eithteenth century, nine of these schools were founded in the Province of Venezuela. Classical grammar and rhetoric were taught there, but fragments of main authors, like Cicero, Horace, Virgil or Seneca were also read.

Along with the founding of the first colleges and universities, Latin continued to be considered the language of knowledge. Between the years 1629 and 1767, when Jesuits were expelled from the Spanish colonies, the school of San Francisco Javier, which can be considered the first major Venezuelan school, operated in Mérida, a little city in western Venezuela. Latin humanities were taught there according to the *Ratio Studiorum*, the pedagogical system of the Jesuits, based on the reading and the study of the classics. In 1721 the 'Real y Pontificia' University of Caracas was founded. As for all universities in Spain and its colonies, mastery of Latin was essential at this university, especially for degrees such as Philosophy, Law or Theology, the most important by then (Nava 2010).

At the beginning of the nineteenth century, with the Hispanic American revolution and independence, the situation of Latin studies in Venezuela barely changed. In 1828, Bolivar and the renowned Venezuelan doctor José María Vargas made important changes to the regulations of the University of Caracas (which would no longer be called 'Royal and Pontifical'). The study of the Greek language was introduced, but the predominant role of Latin remained. However, the state of poverty in which the Venezuelan Government was left after the Independence War precluded the implementation of these dispositions (Leal 1981). The first major Venezuelan school where both Latin and Greek language and literature were taught in Caracas was founded in 1848 by the liberal writer and politician Juan Vicente González (Fernández Heres 1968). The foundation of the 'El Salvador del Mundo' school represents a true starting point of the non-religious classical studies in Venezuela. In 1870, President Antonio Guzmán Blanco issued a decree establishing public, free and mandatory education, but without any provision regarding teaching of Greek or Latin (Bruni Celli 2006). Since then, the Venezuelan national government establishes curricula for primary and secondary education.

Currently, the Organic Law of Education No. 5929 from year 2009 regulates the National Education System. According to it, secondary education is mandatory, and it is aimed at adolescents from 12 to 17–18 years old (Unesco 2019). The secondary education syllabuses are established by the Curriculum for Secondary Education, introduced by the national government in 2017. According to this plan, the subject World History, taught at the second year of secondary education (students aged around 14 years) encompasses content related to the history of Greece and Rome. Literary studies are carried out during the fourth and fifth years of secondary education (16–18 years). These literary studies are organized by genres (epic poetry, lyric poetry, theatre and narrative genres) and are presented chronologically. At the fourth year, genres of Venezuelan and Latin American literature are studied, and at the fifth year, Universal Literature is studied. The *Odyssey* and *Oedipus the King* are studied on chapters of epic poetry and theatre (AA.VV. 2017).

As for university education, there are only four major universities offering literature studies as a degree, namely the Central University of Venezuela in Caracas; the 'Andrés Bello' Catholic University, also in Caracas; the University of Zulia, in Maracaibo, and the University of Los Andes, in Mérida. All of them have introductory courses related to classical Graeco-Latin literature. The University of Los Andes is the only one among them offering a specialization in Classical Languages and Literatures. Furthermore, the History major encompasses subjects related to Ancient History, and a specialization in Literature is also offered for the Education major.

As mentioned before, the University of Los Andes in Mérida is the only university in the country offering Classical Studies as a degree and it is part of the School of Letters at the Faculty of Humanities and Education. As part of their curriculum, students must take five semesters of Greek and Latin languages, as well as courses and seminars on aspects of classical culture and civilization. The Department of Classics also supports with mandatory Greek and Latin general courses for Arts degree students.

While at the secondary education level, courses on Classical Literature and Culture have massive attendance, since they are part of the general curriculum, the number of students at university courses has progressively decreased, due to the general crisis that Venezuela is going through (Pérez Hernaiz 2018; Pérez Hernaiz & Smilde 2017). It is also noteworthy that there are no Master's or doctorate degrees in Classical Studies in the country.

From optional to almost non-existent

Given that secondary education syllabuses are established by the national government, literature courses, like many others, are mandatory. The system in force until 2017 had two modalities for secondary education: Sciences and Humanities. The Humanities option included basic studies of Greek and Latin, as well as French. This plan was repealed in 2017.

As previously mentioned, the World History course in the second year of secondary education is on the ancient history of Greece and Rome (AA.VV. 2013: 49–83, 85–97). Part III deals with Greece and Part IV with Rome. In the textbook there are titles such as 'Greece introduces slavery in Europe' (p. 59, it is noteworthy that there is no mention of slavery in other civilizations such as Egypt, for example); 'Formation of a class-based society with private property' (p. 62); or 'When Greece was a colonizing power' (p. 73). The Language and Literature course at the fourth year focuses on the genres that are most cultivated in Venezuela and Latin America, such as the narrative ones (story, novel), lyric, theatre and essay. There is no mention of Greek literature (AA.VV. 2012a).

Literary genres in universal literature are studied in the fifth-year Language and Literature course. Two works of Greek literature are studied: in the chapter on epic poetry and in that of theatre. The *Odyssey* is studied in epic poetry (pp. 201–21). A plot synopsis of the poem, a selection of fragments and a short biography of Homer are presented. At the end, there are some questions about the poem. Sophocles' *Oedipus the King* is studied in the theatre section (pp. 246–53). Likewise, a plot synopsis of the work, a selection of fragments and a short biography of Sophocles are presented, as well as some final questions. There is no other reference to Greek or Roman literature, even on topics such as lyric poetry.

On the other hand, universities create their own syllabuses for their courses. Unfortunately, due to a widespread prejudice against humanistic careers, classical studies are perceived by most students as useless. This situation is exacerbated by the lack of training of teachers on the best strategies to encourage literary studies, as well as a lack of effective reading incentives by the national government. It is common knowledge in Venezuela that a professional degree in Literature is more disadvantageous than an engineering degree, for instance, in terms of salaries and wages.

Current trends of classical teaching

At the moment, topics related to culture and classical literature have been significantly reduced from the syllabuses at the secondary education level, and their remnants are related to the cultivation of genres in national literature. That is to say, there is neither universal approach, nor an interest in classical themes by themselves, but rather in relation to Venezuelan literature. Consequently, if a classic genre is not related to Venezuelan literature, it remains unstudied. In this regard, it is noteworthy that the Venezuelan works and authors to be studied are approved by the government, particularly those with appropriate political affinity. In short, the study of the classics is reduced, mediated and politically manipulated.

The main teaching tool continues to be the book, where contents and texts to be read are organized. However, the teacher is free to suggest some specific websites for students to do research about certain authors or works. This stimulates the search for information through the Internet. Many of these strategies gained prominence following the Covid pandemic in Venezuela, which was officially declared in February 2020. Thereafter, students had only virtual classes for more than a year. Perhaps the most valuable experience from this situation was the possibility of training students on Internet research.

To be a Professor of 'Lengua y Literatura'

At present, there are three ways to work as a Language and Literature teacher certified by the Venezuelan Government. The first is by pursuing a degree as a Professor of Language and Literature at the 'Libertador' Experimental Pedagogical University (UPEL), a university aimed at training secondary education teaching staff and which has campuses in the main cities of the country. The second one is by studying for the 'Education' degree, with a specialization in Literature, which can be found in almost all the major universities in the country. These options offer training in pedagogical techniques and general information on literature, but not specialized in classics. The third option is by studying for a university degree in Literature and then taking the Teaching Update Programme (*PAD* in Spanish), a kind of postgraduate teaching training.

Currently, it is not difficult for graduates to get a job in the education sector. However, significant challenges regarding salaries and working conditions still remain.

No outdoor activities

Unfortunately, the economic crisis and the slow recovery after the Covid pandemic have dramatically reduced schools' outdoor teaching activities. Before the pandemic, middle school students frequently visited universities and museums. It should be noted that in Venezuela there are no museums or associations focused on ancient classical culture.

Conclusion

Although the new teaching curricula for literature and history apparently show an intention to relate the contents to a time and a cultural environment closer and more closely related to the student's personal experience, the contents in force since 2017 show the dangers of ideologization and political bias that seek to indoctrinate students. Nowadays, Venezuela has a socialist government with an anti-Western ideology. However, historical events, as well as literary and artistic processes, should be studied according to their intrinsic value, as essential elements of Western culture and identity, from which Latin America cannot be excluded. This should lead to a more complete understanding of Venezuelan culture. The teaching of Classics should depend more on highly qualified teachers than on the ideological orientation of governments.

References

AA.VV. (2012a), *Palabra creadora. Lenguaje y Literatura. Cuarto Año, Educación Media*, Caracas: Ministerio del Poder Popular para la Educación.

AA.VV. (2012b), *Palabra universal. Lenguaje y Literatura. Quinto Año, Educación Media*, Caracas: Ministerio del Poder Popular para la Educación.

AA.VV. (2013), *Historia de la Humanidad. Segundo Año, Educación Media*, Caracas: Ministerio del Poder Popular para la Educación.

AA.VV. (2017), *Áreas de formación en Educación Media General*, Caracas: Ministerio del Poder Popular para la Educación.

Bruni Celli, B. (2006), 'Situación de los estudios clásicos en Venezuela', in C. Ponce Hernández and L. Rojas Álvarez (eds), *Estudios Clásicos en América en el Tercer Milenio*, México: Universidad Nacional autónoma de México, 177–206.

Fernández Heres, R. (1968), *La enseñanza del griego en Venezuela*, Caracas: Universidad Central de Venezuela.

Leal, I. (1981), *Historia de la UCV*, Caracas: Universidad Central de Venezuela.

Nava, M. (2010), *Envuelto en el manto de Iris. Humanismo clásico y literatura de la independencia en Venezuela*, Mérida: Universidad de Los Andes.

Pérez Hernáiz, H. (2018), Higher Education in Venezuela: Faculty Exodus from Public Universities, *Venezuelan Politics and Human Rights*, 18 June. Available online: www.venezuelablog.org/higher-education-faculty-exodus-venezuelas-public-universities/ (accessed 10 October 2023).

Pérez Hernáiz, H. and D. Smilde (2017), Venezuela's Higher Education Crisis Worsens, *Venezuelan Politics and Human Rights*, 27 November. Available online: www.venezuelablog.org/venezuelas-higher-education-crisis-worsens/ (accessed 10 October 2023).

Unesco (2019), *Sistema de información de tendencias educativas en América Latina. Venezuela*. Buenos Aires, May 2019. Available online: https://siteal.iiep.unesco.org/sites/default/files/sit_informe_pdfs/siteal_ed_venezuela_20190520.pdf (accessed 10 October 2023).

THE AMERICAS: FURTHER READING

Steven Hunt

The editors have not been able to ascertain the provision of classical languages in state schools in much of Central America and the Caribbean that have not been mentioned earlier. It is likely to be scanty.

In Peru, no classical languages are taught at the high school level. At the Pontifical Catholic University of Peru in Lima, only one Latin course is taught in the specialties of Linguistics and Literature and three courses of Classical Greek are taught in the specialty of Philosophy (S. Reisz, personal communication, 6 June 2023). Classics is taught at the university level in Ecuador.

For the Caribbean, Greenwood (2010) names schools in Trinidad, Barbados, British Guiana (now Guyana), St Lucia and the Leeward Islands which, under the British colonial educational system, used to offer Latin and Greek, along with Cambridge School Certificate examinations and so-called classical 'Island Scholarships' for successful candidates to attend British or Canadian universities.

The CF School in Georgetown, Grand Cayman, has been offering Latin for some years. The Head Teacher Steph Rasmussen, an ex-Classics teacher from England, says,

> I do believe I am the only Latin teacher here in the West Indies at the moment. I [...] have implemented [Latin] through Key Stage 3 and Key Stage 4. There are students who come to our after-school programme to learn Latin from other schools and successfully completed a GCSE and A level outside of their own academic school studies with me. I have also taken 2 students from another school in our after-school programme through a Classical Civilisation A level. Additionally, I run an adult Latin programme after school with 6 members who regularly attend weekly, and have introduced Greek to Key Stage 3 curriculum last year.
>
> (S. Rasmussen, personal communication, 2 October 2023)

The owner of CF is currently planning a sister school, which will also have classical studies, including Latin, on the curriculum (Connolly 2023). The new school will have 225 Latin students in the first year.

In 2023 one student (the first for several years) took A-Level Latin in St Ignatius Catholic School in Grand Cayman. Elsewhere, individual tuition of Latin in the Caymans has been provided online (M. Beer, personal communication, 23 September 2023). Queen's College, the last state secondary school in Barbados to offer Latin, stopped doing so in the 1990s (K. Watson, personal communication, 2 June 2023). Some international schools may offer classical languages where they offer American AP courses, but examination of online curricula shows nothing.

For the impact of the classical tradition in Latin America, see Laird and Miller (2018), Cruz and Huidobro (2018) and Campos Muñoz (2021). For further reading about the roles that Graeco-Roman antiquity played in political thinking in Mexico, after the execution of Emperor Maximilian in 1911, see Laird (2010).

The University College of the West Indies, originally set up with a Classics department, never issued a degree in Classics (Greenwood 2010). It no longer offers a Classics programme. Latin survives only in its motto: '*oriens ex occidente lux*'. For further reading about Classics in the Caribbean, see Greenwood (2005, 2010) and Bopari (2022).

Readers may be interested to read historical articles about Classics teaching in a number of countries in the Amercian continent, published between the 1960s and early 2000s by the Joint Association of Classical Teachers. These include the USA (Connor 1973; Kelly 1969; Kirk 1971; Little 2008; MacDonald 1966; Phinney 1985; Ryder 1968) and Canada (Whalen 1985). An 'exchange trip' between teachers in the UK and the USA is described in a matched pair of reminiscences by Davies (2000) and Beveridge (2000).

More recent publications which detail the teaching of Latin in schools in the USA can be found in LaFleur (1998), Gruber-Miller (2006) and Kitchell (2015). For thought-provoking studies of the teaching of Classics in USA prisons, see Capettini and Rabinowitz (2021), and for developments in Classics education in USA Higher Education Institutions, see Libatique and McHardy (2023). A recent article by Richardi (2023) describes the growth of the Christian classical schools in the USA, in which Latin is often a foundational subject. Forthcoming chapters by Craig Williams about the impact of Graeco-Roman culture on indigenous writers from North America promise to be worth reading.

Finally (and this might seem gratutitous, but it is not easily resisted) Latin has appeared on the Moon. The Apollo XI mission requested messages from every country which could be left in a capsule there. Pope Paul VI asked that the following message be written from the Vatican:

Domine, Dominus noster, quam admirabile est nomen tuum in universa terra! quoniam elevata est magnificentia tua super caelos. Ex ore infantium et lactentium perfecisti laudem propter inimicos tuos, ut destruas inimicum et ultorem. Quoniam videbo caelos tuos, opera digitorum tuorum, lunam et stellas quae tu fundasti. Quid est homo, quod memor es ejus? aut filius hominis, quoniam visitas eum? Minuisti eum paulominus ab angelis; gloria et honore coronasti eum; et constituisti eum super opera manuum tuarum. Omnia subjecisti sub pedibus ejus, oves et boves universas, insuper et pecora campi, volucres caeli, et pisces maris qui perambulant semitas maris. Domine, Dominus noster, quam admirabile est nomen tuum in universa terra!

Psalmus 8.

Ad Dei nominis gloriam, qui tantam praestat hominibus virtutem, miro huic incepto bene precamur.

Paulus PP. VI. A.D. 1969

It should be remembered that Father Reginald Foster (1939–2020), the Latinist responsible for much of the output from the Vatican at this period, also told the story of man's first landing on the Moon, in Latin (Fleming 1971, quoted in Kuhner n.d.).

References

Beveridge, M. (2000), 'Reflections on a Year in England', *JACT Review*, 27: 5–6.
Bopari, J. (2022), 'V.S. NaipauL, Latin Literature and Ancient Rome', *Antigone Journal*. Available online: https://antigonejournal.com/2022/11/naipaul-latin-part-1/ (accessed 14 December 2023).

Campos Muñoz, G. (2021), *The Classics in South America*, London: Bloomsbury.

Capettini, E. and N. Rabinowitz, eds (2021), *Classics and Prison Education in the US*, London: Routledge.

Connolly, N. (2023), 'New Private High School Planned for George Town', *Cayman Compass*, 28 September. Available online: https://www.caymancompass.com/2023/09/28/new-private-high-school-planned-for-george-town/ (accessed 7 November 2023).

Connor, W. (1973), 'Some recent changes in the state of the Classics in the United States', *Didaskalos*, 4 (2): 347–59.

Cruz, N. and M. G. Huidobro, eds (2018), *América Latina y lo clásico: lo clásico y América Latina*, Santiago, Chile: Ril Editores.

Davies, R. (2000), 'A Year in New Orleans', *JACT Review*, 27: 4.

Greenwood, E. (2005), '"We speak Latin in Trinidad": Uses of Classics in Caribbean Literature', in B. Goff (ed.), *Classics and Colonisalism*, London: Gerald Duckworth & Co. Ltd., 65–91.

Greenwood, E. (2010), *Afro-Greeks: Dialogues between Anglophone Caribbean Literature and Classics in the Twentieth Century*, Oxford: Oxford University Press.

Gruber-Miller, J. (2006), *When Dead Tongues Speak. Teaching Beginning Greek and Latin*, Oxford: Oxford University Press.

Kelly, D. (1969), 'Teaching Latin in America: some recent developments', *Didaskalos*, 3 (1): 100–9.

Kirk, G. (1971), 'Impressions from America', *Didaskalos*, 3 (3): 600–13.

Kitchell, K. (2015), '"Solitary perfection?" The past, present, and future of elitism in Latin education', in E. Archibald, W. Brockliss and J. Gnoza (eds), *Learning Latin and Greek from Antiquity to the Present*, Cambridge, Cambridge University Press / Yale Classical Studies, 166–83.

Kuhner, J. B. (n.d.), [Blog] The first press profile of Fr. Reginald Foster. Available online: http://www.johnbyronkuhner.com/2021/02/the-first-press-profile-of-fr-reginald-foster/ (accessed 27 February 2024).

LaFleur, R. (1998), *Latin for the 21st Century. From Concept to Classroom*, Glenview, IL: Scott Foresman-Addison Wesley.

Laird, A. (2010), 'The Cosmic Race and a Heap of Broken Images: Mexico's Classical Past and the Modern Creole Imagination', in S. Stephens and P. Vasumia (eds), *Classics and National Cultures*, Oxford: Oxford University Press, 163–81.

Laird, A. and N. Miller, eds (2018), *Antiquities and Classical Traditions in Latin America*, Chichester: Society for Latin American Studies.

Libatique, D. and F. McHardy, eds (2023), *Diversity and the Study of Antiquity in Higher Education*, London: Routledge.

Little, S. (2008), 'The Teaching of Classics Abroad: USA', *Journal of Classics Teaching*, 15: 5.

MacDonald, J. (1966), 'On teaching Classics at Groton', *Didaskalos*, 2 (1): 48–56.

Phinney, E. (1985), 'The Current Classical Scene in Arnerica', *JACT Review*, 2: 2–5.

Richardi, J. (2023), '"Neither Orthodox Nor Enlightened": Dorothy Sayers and Classical Education in America', *New England Classical Journal*, 50 (2): 9–28.

Ryder, T. (1968), 'A glimpse at the American scene: under-specialization and Classics in translation', *Didaskalos*, 2 (3): 46–52.

Whalen, P. (1985), 'Classics in Canadian Schools', *JACT Review*, 13: 2–4.

Williams, C. (forthcoming), 'Greece, Rome, Antiquity: Some Indigenous Voices from North America, in M. Formisano and G. Sissa (eds), *Classics: What Next?*, Berlin: de Gruyter.

Williams, C. (forthcoming), 'Indigenous Writers of North America and Greco-Roman Antiquity: Postcolonialism without the Post?', in B. Akrigg and K. Blouin (eds), *The Routledge Handbook of Classics, Colonialism, and Postcolonial Theory*, London: Routledge.

PART 3
AUSTRALASIA

Louella Perrett

Introduction

Education in Australia is primarily the responsibility of the individual state and territory governments, although policy direction, regulation and funding are shared to a degree with the Australian Federal Government. Each state has its own education regulatory authority which provides infrastructure and oversees curriculum, assessment and reporting. The Australian Curriculum, Assessment and Reporting Authority (ACARA) is an independent statutory body which developed the National Curriculum. As ACARA does not have the authority to mandate, however, implementation is at the discretion of the individual states and territories, allowing for individual contextualization. ACARA's Framework for Classical Languages offers language specific curricula in Latin and Greek for Years 7–10 and has been adopted by the states and territories where the classical languages are offered. New South Wales (NSW) has taken an 'adopt and adapt' approach to the Australian Curriculum, developing its own syllabi (NSW Education Standards Authority 2023a). Latin is taught in NSW, Victoria, Queensland, South Australia and the Australian Capital Territory (ACT). Greek survives only in NSW and Victoria. Sanskrit is taught in one primary and one secondary school in NSW and is listed as a senior secondary course in the ACT. Classical Studies is only offered in Victoria as a senior certification subject. The independent school sector in Australia is very strong and it is in these private schools that the classical languages are primarily taught, with academically selective government schools coming second.

It is difficult to ascertain the number of students studying the classical languages in the junior secondary years as the data released by the different states are inconsistent and reporting on school achievement at the end of the compulsory years in most states is decentralized. NSW, however, provides course candidature numbers for the Record of School Achievement which is attained at the end of Year 10 (NSW Education Standards Authority 2023c). Between 2012 and 2022, the number of students studying Latin has been mostly above 400, with 475 being the highest enrolment. Statistics for Greek are less reliable, the most recent recorded being 42 for 2021. Data relating to course completion for the senior secondary certifications are more readily available. In NSW there are no beginner courses for Latin and Greek at senior level. Students who have studied Latin or Greek to Year 10 undertake the 2 Unit Continuers Course for the Higher School Certificate (HSC) examination and have the option of adding a third unit with the Extension Course. The number of HSC students studying the Latin Continuers course over the last twenty years has fluctuated between 140 and 195, with a low 131 registered for 2019. Since then, numbers have risen steadily, reaching 160 in 2023. Approximately 57 to 70 per cent of Continuers students choose to do the Extension Course each year, a relatively high proportion compared to other disciplines which offer an extension unit, but not surprising given the high calibre of the candidature. Greek numbers have fluctuated between nine and twenty-seven, averaging nineteen for the Continuers course and between six and nineteen (averaging nine) for the Extension course (NSW Education Standards Authority 2023b, 2023d).

There has been a steady rise in Latin enrolments for the Victorian Certificate of Education (VCE). While only sixty-nine students were reported studying Latin in 1995, in 2014 the number had risen to 194 (Kemp 2016: 86). Since then, there has been a mostly steady increase with 278 students taking the subject in 2022 (Victorian Curriculum and Assessment Authority 2023). There are no prerequisites for entry into the first three units but Unit 3 is a prerequisite for entry into Unit 4. In the ACT, the Board of Senior Secondary Studies offers Beginning and Continuing Latin, Beginning and Continuing Sanskrit and Continuing Classical Greek; there are no data available yet relating to student numbers.

Small candidatures in the classical languages are problematic in some states in terms of economic viability and the infrastructure required to manage course delivery. There is an agreement between the states, however, which allows students to access the curriculum of other states for senior certification. Victorian students sit for the NSW HSC examination in Greek, and both Queensland and South Australia students sit for the NSW HSC in Latin. Thus in addition to the NSW numbers reported above, Victoria has been contributing on average ten Greek students per year, South Australia between three and six Latin students, and QLD between fourteen and seventeen Latin students. Queensland adopted the NSW HSC curriculum after an evaluation of the senior syllabus at a time when only two schools offered Latin (Queensland Curriculum and Assessment Authority 2016). The number has now risen to five. In South Australia there is only one school, founded on the Jesuit tradition of a classical education, offering the subject. In addition to the numbers listed above, there are eleven schools in Australia which offer Latin for the International Baccalaureate (IB) and Middle Years Programme and one school with IB Classical Greek (International Baccalaureate 2023).

Status of classical subjects

The inclusion of classical languages in the curriculum is dependent on the type of school and the language provision requirements regulated by each state's education authority. The latter vary significantly from state to state and across each stage of learning. Whilst in Victoria primary schools have to provide a languages programme, in NSW language study is optional. In 2018 NSW embarked on an ambitious curriculum reform; the final report recommended 'every student to commence learning a second language during their primary years, making use of technology where possible' (NSW Education Standards Authority 2020: xvii). Unfortunately, this was not supported in the government response. Primary school Latin is found in only a few schools: schools with both a primary and secondary campus, which can avail themselves of the services of the secondary Latin teacher(s); independent schools which espouse the ethos of a classical education (one of these schools also offers Sanskrit); and primary-only schools where the Latin programme has been driven by a staff member or parent with a strong passion for the Classics.

All schools have to provide a languages programme in the secondary years. Victoria has a decentralized approach, mandating the content of the curriculum, but leaving the responsibility for structure to individual schools. To remain compliant with official registration requirements, schools need to demonstrate how the key learning area will be 'substantially addressed' (Victoria Registration and Qualifications Authority 2022: 20). The NSW Standards and Education Authority (NESA) takes a more prescriptive approach, mandating 100 hours of study in one language over one continuous twelve-month period between Years 7 and 10. Students can then continue their study as an elective. Study at senior level is also optional.

The status of the classical languages is frequently challenged. Concerns include different perceptions about the worth or relevance of classical languages in general and, in more practical terms, their contribution to tertiary entrance scores; the economic viability of small classes; the restricted number of subjects that can be presented for senior certification; timetable structures which affect the continuity of learning; students being asked to make subject choices with little or no exposure to the languages; parental, sibling or peer pressure, particularly when it results from a negative experience with the Classics. An exciting research project undertaken by Kate Edwards, a PhD student from the University of New England, may soon provide a better picture of the current landscape, at least for Latin. Edwards is examining quantitative and qualitative data collected from over 1,800 survey and interview participants to determine the place, purpose and potential of the teaching of Latin in Australian secondary schools.

Course rationales give insight into the perceived benefits of studying the classical languages and constitute a ready-made advocacy tool for teachers. The classical languages were not part of the original scoping of the Australian Curriculum. Their inclusion was achieved through a persistent campaign on the part of the Classics teaching community. ACARA's Framework for Classical Languages presents a very robust rationale for their inclusion in the curriculum, recognizing their distinct nature (ACARA 2023). Its key points emerge in the curriculum documents of other jurisdictions and echo the sentiments that teachers have been using to promote their subjects at local school level:

1. An appreciation of the enduring legacy of the ancient world on our modern institutions, arts, literature, thought and values, including the influence on the development of other languages.
2. The linguistic benefits: how a knowledge of the classical languages can expand students' vocabulary and instil an awareness of how language works.
3. The effect on the learner, stimulating curiosity, an openness to ideas and enjoyment of the learning process.
4. The development of transferable skills in literacy, communication, critical and creative thinking, analysis and problem solving.

The last argument has acquired greater weight with the growing emphasis in modern curricula on the connection between subject-specific knowledge, skills and understanding, and the development of general capabilities. Intercultural understanding, ethical understanding and twenty-first-century skills are appearing more explicitly in our curriculum, as is the alignment with cross-curriculum priorities. Whilst their integration places greater demands on the teachers, it also offers opportunities for further justification of our subjects. For example, the meaningful and respectful integration of civics and citizenship, diversity and difference, and Aboriginal and Torres Strait Islander Histories and Cultures can be a persuasive reminder of how studying a classical language can contribute to the formation of young minds and, hopefully, more aware, responsible global citizens. Embracing a broader purpose for the Classics curriculum can go some way towards dispelling the myth of irrelevance.

Beyond advocacy, teachers have been willing to adopt creative, practical solutions to make the introduction or retention of a classical language more appealing to school authorities. Acceleration and course compression provide a way around the restricted number of units or subjects that can be studied at senior level. For example, in South Australia Latin is studied only through an accelerated programme, as students can present only four subjects for the senior certification, one of them being a mandatory research project. In NSW students may study more than the minimum ten units (most subjects comprise two units, with extension courses equating to one), though this is often discouraged. Furthermore, pragmatic considerations often prevail when students make their subject selections. Completing the senior certification course in a classical language in Year 11 provides a solution. Measures to counter the obstacle of economic viability are holding classes outside the timetable, before and after school, delivering the course with less face-to-face period allocations, or combining multiple courses or levels in the one class, for example, HSC and IB. The latter is particularly challenging, but a testament to the teachers' commitment to keeping the subjects going. More recently, some schools have offered courses online, sharing teachers from other schools. Lunchtime clubs have also been used to expose students to unfamiliar subjects such as Greek.

Trends in the teaching of classical subjects

Neither the Australian Curriculum nor the NSW Classical Languages K-10 syllabus prescribe a pedagogical approach. It is clear, however, that the emphases of these curricula have implications for programme design at school level. At the core of both lies the focus on engaging with, understanding and interpreting the classical world through texts. The study of systems of language is not carried out in isolation, but is subservient to the goal of interpreting meaning, texts and the ancient world. Other common curriculum elements are translating (into English), responding to texts and intercultural understanding. The NSW Classical Languages K-10 syllabus is new, 2024 being the first year of implementation. Although not vastly different from its predecessor in content, its alignment with the Australian Curriculum has been strengthened and it presents as a generic framework for the classical languages, supported by language specific examples. The design of the syllabus has taken into consideration the different educational contexts, timetabling structures, time allocations and entry points. The previously mandated list of vocabulary and grammatical structures has been replaced by a suggested list of structures students should become familiar with by the end of Year 10 to access more easily the content of the senior courses. The Australian Curriculum has a similar approach. Across the different stages, students move through a progression of texts of increasing complexity, from simple to predictable to moderately complex texts. Although Year 10 has been traditionally seen as a pathway to the study of authentic texts at senior level, teachers are free to select synthetic and/or original texts, depending on the needs and competence of their students. Students are encouraged to respond to texts in a variety of ways and can exercise the option of writing in English or the target language. The syllabus requires teachers to view translation as a meaningful activity that goes beyond the traditional purpose of accessing texts, reinforcing grammar structures and assessment. Students explore the translation process, becoming more aware of the nuances of language, and how culture is expressed through language. They are encouraged to become more discerning in their selection of structures and vocabulary to reflect the emphasis, tone and register of the original text. Through this process, they develop their literacy skills in English.

Both curricula have a more nuanced approach to intercultural understanding, requiring students not only to study classical civilization, but to reflect on the role of language and culture, and in particular the relationship between language, culture and identity. The learner is challenged to take on a more prominent and personal role in this process, as he/she moves from being an observer of other cultures to considering how learning the classical language shapes his/her own values, attitudes and identity. This requires teachers to become more imaginative as they search for strategies to assist students in making deeper connections with the content.

The senior secondary courses in all states focus on the reading of original texts, deepening understanding of their underlying ideas in their social, cultural and historical context, and developing skills in literary analysis. A point of difference is found in the ACT curriculum, a generic languages framework from which both the modern and classical languages curricula derive. There are implications for pedagogy, as alongside understanding texts, students are also assessed on their ability to communicate and create texts in the language. Assessment must include an inquiry-based learning task. The active use of the target language has also entered the IB programme with the new composition element.

Reading-based methods, *Athenaze* (Balme et al. 2016), the *Cambridge Latin Course* (CSCP 2022) and the *Oxford Latin Course* (Balme & Morwood 1996) are the most widely used materials, with *Suburani* (Hands Up Education 2020) beginning to make some inroads into the market. The provision of online resources accompanying both the *Cambridge* and *Suburani* courses is an attractive feature. Apart from its engaging activities, it addresses the use of technology and differentiation, which are mandatory elements of the Australian Professional Standards for Teachers. Both courses, with their commitment to a more realistic view of society in ancient Rome and a more sensitive approach to cultural issues, offer plenty of scope for developing intercultural understanding. *Eureka! An introduction to Classical Greek for Young Australians* (Matters & Kerrison 2017) is an inductive reading course which models an authentic approach to intercultural understanding. It can be used as a stand-alone course, as an adjunct to *Athenaze*, or as the basis for a Greek club. The stories are drawn from mythology and frequent connections are made with stories from Australian Indigenous cultures. Each chapter presents an interaction between four young Australians from different ethnic backgrounds, reflecting on their learning experience, and the role of language and culture in shaping identity. Other methods include Ørberg's *Lingua Latina per se illustrata* (2011), and for those who prefer a more traditional approach to teaching grammar, the *Greek to GCSE* (Taylor 2016) and *Latin to GCSE* (Cullen & Taylor 2016) series. There is an emerging interest in the communicative method, but at this stage schools seem to be integrating elements of it into their pedagogy rather than fully embracing it as their dominant method.

Teachers have always supplemented course books with their own materials but this is becoming more of a trend. Apart from any personal dissatisfaction with available textbooks, factors which have spurred teachers to become more proactive in material production are time allocated to a subject and the year of entry. Year 9 entry equates to two fewer years to attain the proficiency levels required to cope with senior work compared with entry in Year 7. Teachers are selective in the way they use commercial course books designed to be covered in four or more years: using only some of the course levels or abandoning it altogether in favour of writing their own are some of the options. Another factor is the ever-growing expectation for teachers to be responsive to the learning needs of their students, designing programmes that best fit their educational context. At senior level, teachers may use commercially available readers or anthologies, as well as the prescribed editions of texts set for study, but it is not unheard of them editing their own text selections, supplying vocabulary and glossed notes.

The lockdown Covid-19 experiences have unwittingly resulted in some long-term benefits as regards teaching practice because they forced teachers to experiment with and embrace new tools and strategies. Some of these are:

1. Exploiting the functionalities of the school's online learning management system.

2. Online vocabulary learning tools, particularly those which enable tracking.

3. Discussion boards, chat forums and online surveys to promote discussion on cultural topics.

4. Turning online quizzes into language consolidation drills and not limiting them to assessment.

5. Shared Google Docs and Google Slides for group or pair work, not limited to culture tasks, but also used for language work such as the collaborative editing of translations, compiling a shared word bank, or flipped classroom activities where students take charge of grammar instruction.

6. Use of technology for lesson exit tickets, for example, completing a quick online survey, or adding a reflection to a shared Google Doc.

7. Teaching dictionary skills through online glossaries.

Having to manage online assessments without compromising validity made teachers more comfortable with the use of LockDown Browser (an app used for student assessments). Teachers have discovered that some tasks can be administered and marked online much more efficiently: morphology, vocabulary, English derivations and basic cultural knowledge lend themselves to discrete item testing. Teachers have also become more adept at open-book tasks, designing questions that assess higher order thinking and the student's ability to apply knowledge. Other strategies have been oral translations, personal written evaluations of different translations of a text, and interviews eliciting critical analysis of prescribed text.

Teachers and professional development

A significant challenge facing schools wishing to retain or reintroduce the Classics is the shortage of teachers. The most common pathway to becoming a teacher in Australia is completing a four-year teaching degree such as a Bachelor of Education or an undergraduate degree in the related teaching language followed by a postgraduate teaching degree such as a Master of Teaching. An obstacle that is faced by prospective Classics teachers is that, depending on the institution attended, a classical language teaching method is not always available and students may be asked to complete instead a modern language method. Teachers need to apply for initial accreditation or registration with the statutory authority and then maintain their accreditation by fulfilling professional development requirements which are mapped against the Australian Professional Standards for Teachers. Each state's education authority provides professional development opportunities, but these tend to be on topics related to teaching practice in general; subject specific professional development is offered when there are changes to syllabi or assessment requirements. More targeted support comes from the Classical Languages Teachers' Association (CLTA) and the teachers' wing of the Classical Association of Victoria through conferences, workshops and the dissemination of resources. Teachers also benefit from attending lectures and conferences organized by the various universities and through memberships with other Classics organizations such as the Classical Association of NSW and the Australasian Society for Classical Studies. The Sydney University Teaching Classical Languages Symposium is a biennial conference which has been very successful in bringing together Classics educators from the primary, secondary and tertiary sectors.

Collaborative activities

The teaching associations organize an array of student activities: HSC/IB/VCE seminars and dinners for senior students; reading, classical design and Classics trivia competitions; a Classics camp for Year 8. Teachers share resources through the association websites and participate in the exchange of examination papers. Some schools combine to take students on overseas Classics trips. The CLTA also provides a yearly scholarship for prospective Classics teachers, an award for students studying classical languages at university, and funds for teachers to support Classics projects. There is a high degree of interaction with the universities: summer and winter schools are open to school students, and lecturers regularly present on prescribed texts to both teachers and students and are involved in the setting of certification examinations alongside teachers.

Conclusion

The Australian Classics teaching community is vibrant and dynamic, unswerving in its commitment to promote Classics. The teaching associations work closely with education authorities on the drafting of examinations and curriculum development and have a voice in the process. Although numbers of Classics school students are relatively small, the overall outlook is promising. The last three years have seen intense syllabus reform, with even the Australian Curriculum undergoing a process of decluttering. It is hoped that these curriculum measures will have a positive impact on the growth of our subjects.

References

ACARA, Australian Curriculum, Assessment and Reporting Authority (2023), 'Framework for Classical Languages'. Available online: https://www.australiancurriculum.edu.au/f-10-curriculum/languages/framework-for-classical-languages/rationale/ (accessed 21 August 2023).

Balme, M. and J. Morwood (1996), *Oxford Latin Course*, Oxford: Oxford University Press.

Balme, M., G. Lawall and J. Morwood (2016), *Athenaze*, Oxford: Oxford University Press.

CSCP (2022), *Cambridge Latin Course*, Cambridge: Cambridge University Press.

Cullen, H. and J. Taylor (2016), *Latin to GCSE* [Book Series], London: Bloomsbury Academic.

Hands Up Education (2020), *Suburani*, Haverhill: Hands Up Education.

International Baccalaureate (2023), 'Find an IB World School'. Available online: https://www.ibo.org/programmes/find-an-ib-school/?SearchFields.Region=&SearchFields.Country=AU&SearchFields.State=&SearchFields.Keywords=Latin&SearchFields.Language=&SearchFields.BoardingFacilities=&SearchFields.SchoolGender= (accessed 23 November 2023).

Kemp, A. (2016), 'O Tempora. . . The Change in Year 12 Latin Unseen Translation', *Iris: Journal of the Classical Association of Victoria*, 29: 86–101. Available online: https://classicsvic.files.wordpress.com/2018/05/kemp.pdf (accessed 4 October 2023).

Matters, E. and E. Kerrison (2017), *Eureka! An Introduction to Classical Greek for Young Australians*, Sydney: First edition.

NSW Education Standards Authority (2020), 'Nurturing wonder and igniting passion: Designs for a new school curriculum'. Available online: https://www.nsw.gov.au/education-and-training/nesa/about/strategies-and-reforms/curriculum-reform/final-report (accessed 4 October 2023).

NSW Education Standards Authority (2023a), 'NSW and the Australian Curriculum'. Available online: https://curriculum.nsw.edu.au/about-the-curriculum/introduction (accessed 23 November 2023).

NSW Education Standards Authority (2023b), 'Complete Board of Studies NSW Statistics Archive'. Available online: https://www.boardofstudies.nsw.edu.au/ebos/static/ebos_stats.html (accessed 3 October 2023).

NSW Education Standards Authority (2023c), 'School Certificate, Stage 5 and Preliminary Grade Distributions'. Available online: https://www.boardofstudies.nsw.edu.au/bos_stats/sc-grade-distributions.html, (accessed 3 October 2023).

NSW Education Standards Authority (2023d), 'HSC Facts and Figures'. Available online: https://educationstandards.nsw.edu.au/wps/portal/nesa/11-12/hsc/about-HSC/HSC-facts-figures (accessed 25 November 2023).

Ørberg, H. (2011), *Lingua Latina per se illustrata*, London: Hackett.

Queensland Curriculum and Assessment Authority (2016), 'Latin literature review: Senior syllabus'. Available online: https://www.qcaa.qld.edu.au/downloads/senior/snr_syll_redev_latin_lit_review.pdf, (accessed 21 August 2023).

Queensland Curriculum and Assessment Authority (2023), 'Statistics'. Available online: https://www.qcaa.qld.edu.au/news-data/statistics (accessed 27 September 2023).

South Australian Certificate of Education (2023), 'Stage 1 and Stage 2 subject enrolments in the SACE'. Availabe online: https://www.sace.sa.edu.au/web/sace-data/subject-enrolments (accessed 27 September 2023).

Taylor, J. (2016), *Greek to GCSE* [Book Series], London: Bloomsbury Academic.

Victoria Registration and Qualifications Authority (2022), 'Government Guidelines to the Minimum Standards and Requirements for School Registration'. Available online: https://www.vrqa.vic.gov.au/schools/Pages/standards-guidelines-requirements-for-schools.aspx (accessed 13 November 2023).

Victorian Curriculum and Assessment Authority (2023), 'Research and statistics'. Available online: https://www.vcaa.vic.edu.au/administration/research-and-statistics/Pages/Index.aspx (accessed 27 September 2023).

NEW ZEALAND (AOTEAROA)

John Hayden

Aotearoa is a unique nation. Geographically isolated, sparsely populated, yet endowed with a vast cultural heritage all its own. The first settlers probably arrived from Polynesia between 1200 and 1300 CE, having discovered New Zealand as they explored the Pacific, which they navigated by the ocean currents, winds, and stars. Europeans first visited in 1642, before a steady stream of whalers, sealers, and traders settled in the late 1820s. On 6 February 1840, our founding document, Te Tiriti o Waitangi (The Treaty of Waitangi), was signed by representatives of the Crown and Indigenous Māori iwi (tribes) and hapū (sub-tribes). As a constitutional document established to guide the relationship between the Crown and Māori, Te Tiriti still resonates today, nowhere more obviously than in our education system.

The tyranny of distance –18,500 kilometres from Rome, and a paltry 17,518 from Athens – has done little to dampen Antipodean enthusiasm for Classics. Aotearoa's Indigenous population has customs and traditions which echo those of the ancients, and much ink has been spilled on the parallels between these seemingly disparate cultures. Māori and the Greeks have rich mythologies – the similarities between Maui, the Māori trickster god, and his Greek counterpart Prometheus are striking: both strive to improve humanity (Maui slows the sun, giving his people enough daylight hours, while Prometheus gives humans fire) and suffer severe consequences for it – Maui is crushed to death, and Prometheus is chained to a rock as his liver is pecked out daily by an eagle. Alongside such stirring tales of creation and demigods, there is no shortage of conflict across these mythologies. The Trojan War, which is told in a combination of poetic and historic style in Homer's *Iliad,* and the *Aeneid* of Virgil, are epics of violent conquest helmed by the gods. In Māori mythology, the god of war (Tūmatauenga) is also the god of mankind. The abuse of Nīwareka by Mataora or the death and destruction wrought by Achilles and Rome's divinely-sanctioned yet oh-so-bloody empire show the *faiblesse* of mankind for violence across these cultures.

Such oral histories were passed down through iwi long before the arrival of European colonists, while the concept of *manaakitanga* (hospitality, kindness, generosity, support) has an almost uncanny connection to ancient Greek *xenia*. Indeed, oral traditions play an integral role across both cultures, brilliantly articulated by the late Agathe Thornton in her book *Māori Oral Literature – As Seen by a Classicist* (1986). Alongside Thornton and her essential treatise, a number of other titans of classical scholarship have connections down under. The gargantuan legacy of Ronald Syme – our most eminent classicist – casts the largest shadow; Emeritus Professor George Cawkwell – a Rhodes Scholar and Praelector in Ancient History at University College, Oxford, who taught Ernst Badian – also called this country home. Curiously, Badian himself had moved with his family to New Zealand in 1938, before attending Oxford after completing a BA at Canterbury University in 1945. Richard F. Thomas, the George Martin Lane Professor of the Classics at Harvard, was brought up in New Zealand and educated at the University of Auckland, while the efforts of Emeritus Professors John Barsby and Chris Dearden, who fought hard for the subject to be integrated into our secondary school system, can and must not be understated; certainly, their Herculean undertaking nearly fifty years ago is deserving of its own volume. Latterly, artist Marian Maguire, whose etchings and lithographs combine Greek vase imagery with colonial New Zealand subjects, has gained international recognition, and in doing so has raised the profile of the subject in Aotearoa.

National Certificate of Educational Achievement (NCEA)

Much like the country we call home, our secondary education system is a fledgling one. Since 2002, NCEA (the National Certificate of Educational Achievement) has been the most common assessment programme in secondary schools throughout Aotearoa. According to Ministry of Education statistics, as at September 2023 around 160,000 students per year study towards their NCEA certificates. For comparison, in 2021 there were 6,385 IB (International Baccalaureate) students receiving schooling in New Zealand (960 at primary and intermediate schools and 5,435 in secondary education), while 9,750 were enrolled in the Cambridge examinations system. For the sake of brevity, attention is paid to NCEA as the predominant system in the country. Likewise, the focus here is on secondary Classics education in Aotearoa, given that primary and intermediate school Classics are largely foundational, focusing mainly on myths and oral traditions, while the subject at early-secondary level falls under the aegis of the Social Sciences curriculum.

NCEA is divided into three levels, imaginatively titled Level 1, Level 2 and Level 3, with Level 1 commencing for ākonga (students, learners) around age fifteen, and Level 3 providing the necessary ballast and rigour for those heading onto tertiary education at eighteen years of age.

The key ingredients in NCEA are standards and credits, with one leading to the other. Each NCEA subject (as of October 2023 there are sixty-seven) is composed of standards, with each standard having a credit weighting, and it is these credits which count towards the final qualification. In order to obtain the NCEA, ākonga need a minimum of eighty credits at each level, which must include a minimum number of literacy (writing, speaking and listening) and numeracy (number, measurement and statistical skills) credits, which can be gained across a number of different subjects. These standards are assessed both internally (in-class, usually research-based, and with the opportunity for students to receive written and verbal feedback) and externally (in a formal examination setting)

Credits can be built up throughout the academic year, or in some cases across multiple years, which is a strength of the system as it allows flexibility for individual ākonga. Within each standard are four possible levels of attainment – Not Achieved (N), Achieved (A), Merit (M), or Excellence (E) – designed, again, so that individual learners can strive for the level of which they are capable. 'Not Achieved' is the only grade where no credits are awarded, while A, M, and E give indications as to how well ākonga did in each standard. Though students will not gain more credits for Merit or Excellence grades, there still remain good reasons for aiming high – if 50 or more credits at Merit or Excellence are accrued across subjects, the qualification will gain a Certificate Endorsement; if 14 credits are achieved at Merit or Excellence level within a single subject, that results in a Subject Endorsement, which comes in handy as ākonga move onto tertiary education or a particular vocational field. Students know that if they aim for a particular job or university course, they need credits in the standards that will be useful to that end goal – universities in Aotearoa (or worldwide, for that matter) want to see lots of Es in a student's NCEA transcript.

The content

It is worthwhile noting that New Zealand introduced Classical Studies as a senior option in schools when the teaching of Latin – a staple since colonial times – began its decline in the 1980s. For many years now, it has been an incredibly popular and successful course aimed at exploring key topics from the ancient world (without a language requirement). Originally it was introduced only at Level 2 and 3 (or the previous equivalent) and then very recently a Level 1 course was introduced, to allow for younger students to experience a longer time in the course.

Prior to NCEA, Secondary Classics in Aotearoa was assessed under the Sixth Form Certificate, Bursary and Scholarship models, where the following topics/contexts were offered:

Alexander the Great
Art and Architecture of the Roman Empire
Athenian Art and Architecture
Athenian Democracy
Athenian Vase Painting
Attic Comedy
Augustus
Greek Drama

Greek Science
Greek Social Life
Homer's *Odyssey*
Juvenal's Satires
Politics in the time of Caesar and Cicero
Pompeii
Roman Religion
Roman Social Life
Socrates
Virgil's *Aeneid*

From the inception of the subject until 2005, students were required in the external examination to answer short questions on a range of extracts for three of the above contexts. For instance, a question from the Virgil context may be based on an extract from Book 1 (let us say, Venus appealing to Jupiter, then Jupiter giving his prophecy) and might ask questions along the lines of:

A. Who is speaking in this passage?

B. What is the relationship of the speaker to Aeneas?

C. What happened in the part immediately preceding this passage?

D. Where else throughout the poem are similar ideas expressed?

Art standards had a visual component, with particularly vexing questions showing a plate from Exekias' masterpiece (Achilles and Ajax intently playing a board game) and asking ākonga to describe the other side of the vase, or requiring description of the *interior* of the Ara Pacis Augustae.

This short-answer mode of assessment was changed in 2006 to short essays of around one-and-a-half pages – one prompt, for example, is 'Analyse, using evidence, ways in which the Niobid Painter successfully depicted the human form' – NCEA Level 3 2008. The assessment was refined again in 2009 to the mode used at present, where ākonga now answer up to three essays in long-form across a three-hour examination. Examples of these essay prompts presently include 'Explain how one or more characters behaved or did not behave according to the expectations of a classical society' (Ideas and Values, Level 2 2023) and 'Discuss the extent to which mood was effectively conveyed in one or more classical artworks' (Art and Architecture, Level 3 2023). Significantly, the art standards now combine the contexts – Roman Art and Architecture, Greek Vase Painting, Athenian Sculpture, and Art of Pompeii, so that students have a broader than ever palette from upon which to draw.

At Scholarship level – a one-off three-hour examination, designed for more intensive study – ākonga are asked to write essays on two of the above contexts of their choosing, and to write a third essay interpreting a range of (often unseen) primary source material – both written and visual. This is designed to display a wide breadth of knowledge of the classical world. Questions in 2021 included, for instance, in the Augustus context (Section A):

'Their personalities had always been diametrically opposed. Octavian planned and schemed; Antony reacted more spontaneously to events. Octavian often broke his agreements; Antony fulfilled his promises.' – Anthony Everitt.

> Given their personalities, was the breakdown in the relationship between Octavian and Antony inevitable?

While the source analysis section (Section B) runs:

> Choose EITHER Resources A to D (Ancient Greece) OR Resources E to H (Ancient Rome), which provide evidence about gender and society in the classical world.

> Discuss at least THREE of the resources and the insight they give into relationships between men and women.

For this source analysis section, study can focus on either Greek or Roman contexts, and includes a choice of concepts: either Culture and Identity, with specific focus on gender and society, or Empire and Power, with specific focus on authority and freedom. Also of note in 2021 was the inclusion of Homer's *Iliad* in the Scholarship exam, which was particularly pleasing to those kaiako (teacher/s, educator/s) who focus on epic poetry for NCEA Levels 1–3. Generally speaking, those who sit the scholarship examination often have designs on pursuing Classical Studies at tertiary level; should a candidate successfully gain a scholarship, there is a monetary award – this ranges from a one-off $500 payment for a single subject award to $10,000 per year for up to three years for premier award winners.

Across NCEA Levels 1, 2 and 3, the framework remains strikingly similar (see below for a link to in-depth details of standard titles, modes of assessment and credit weighting).

At Level 1 the key assessment word is 'demonstrate' (e.g., Demonstrate understanding of ideas and values of the classical world – External, 4 credits); Level 2 encourages students to 'examine' (e.g., Examine a significant event in the classical world – Internal, 4 credits), while 'analyse' (e.g., Analyse the impact of a significant historical figure on the classical world – External, 6 credits) is what is expected of Level 3 students.

The external standards at all three levels focus on core ideas – Ideas and Values, Art, and Historical/Socio-Political life. The internally assessed standards cover similar ground, but given that these are often attempted in-class, and with a range of source material on-hand, these are the assessments that ākonga are particularly drawn to. The beauty of the NCEA system is that there is scope for kaiako and ākonga alike to pursue their proclivities, without making the subject seem rigid and impenetrable – a widely-held misconception, particularly in this part of the world, owing to the subject's perceived 'elitism' and erroneous labelling as the domain of the high-brow.

Though traditionally assessment has taken the form of literary essays, the mode of internal assessment has changed to cater for the ever-growing number of ākonga with learning differences. Certainly, in the NZQA external examinations, students are required to write up to three long-form essays – depending on which standards they have been entered for, and how many credits they need to gain their NCEA certificate – in a three-hour timeframe. Internal assessment, however, which usually takes on the form of a research assignment, can be presented either as a written report, a PowerPoint presentation, an oral presentation, or even a poster. As long as a clear thesis and primary source material is present, ākonga may choose their own mode of delivery, as well as their context.

Anecdotally, the 'lasting influences' standards are the ones which ākonga find most enjoyable, as they are able to make connections between their own world and experiences with those of the ancients. These standards see students attempting to trace ancient influence through to modern times, be it the presentation of a particular figure in mythology, and how that may have morphed to fit modern ideals (for instance, the ways in which the tales of Helen, Medea, Medusa and Penelope have been repurposed as feminist icons); the way in which Graeco-Roman architecture has inspired contemporary building, such as sports stadiums or monuments to victory; or even how heroes such as Achilles and Aeneas have shaped the crafting of Hollywood blockbusters, from *Star Wars* through to *Moana* and beyond.

Another standard which encourages classical reception (that is, the ways in which ancient ideas and ideals are presented and absorbed by us) is Level 2's 'Examine a significant event in the classical world', where learners choose an event, describe it (using primary source evidence), then reflect upon why and how it has influenced post-classical society. With a seemingly infinite list of such events to choose from, ākonga and kaiako are generally encouraged to follow their own interests. The eruption of Vesuvius leads ākonga to the conclusion that, in spite of the devastation, what remains gives valuable insight into the daily lives of those in the empire, as well as humanizing one of the ancient world's most destructive natural disasters. Likewise, Caesar's assassination enables learners to question and come to grips with the notion of tyranny, with no shortage of post-classical examples from upon which to draw.

The Battle of Thermopylae is another excellent context for this standard, with a proven success rate. Not only does it allow students to indulge in a session or two of watching Zack Snyder's *300* (for context, of course!), but it also gets them thinking critically about the differences between primary source material and modern adaptations, and looking beyond the ostensible impact of the battle – in this case, how the seeds of democracy were sown, which lead to eventual Greek victory. Many ākonga ponder the influence the battle has had worldwide, which includes a rise in Islamophobia and railing against 'otherness', due to Herodotus' depiction of the 'barbarian' invaders. Also, in a local sense, the idea that the Greek defeat was turned into a metaphorical victory rings true when they think of the ANZAC (Australian and New Zealand Army Corps) forces, roundly routed at Gallipoli in 1915, yet whose sacrifice indelibly stamped us with a sense of national identity, for better or worse.

Ākonga are able to draw upon the rich vein of Aotearoa's history – while fulfilling our obligation to Te Tiriti – with Level 1's 'Demonstrate understanding of links between aspects of the classical world and another culture'. One task for this standard involves learners comparing ancient/Homeric Greek guest friendship (*xenia*) with tikanga o te marae (protocols in the meeting place/household) in relation to manaakitanga (hospitality, kindness, generosity, support), and explaining the links between these seemingly disparate contexts. Not only does this task draw upon Thornton's prescient scholarship, but it also acquaints learners with the mores and codes of the ancients while enlivening an aspect of Classics unique to Aotearoa, giving precious opportunity to display the prior knowledge and lived experiences of our ākonga.

All told, the width and breadth of contexts, tasks, and modes of assessment helps keep ākonga engaged and enthused in the subject. Even though such a world seems so remote, opportunities abound through initiatives such as university open days, inter-school classics quizzes, and guest lectures from academics. Given our geographical proximity to such expertise, networking is both essential and effortless, and tertiary institutions are all too happy to assist future classicists any way they can. Likewise, there are generous professional development opportunities courtesy of our subject association NZACT (New Zealand Association of Classics Teachers: https://www.nzact.org.nz/), with regular conferences, nationwide Best Practice Workshops, and scholarships for new kaiako, alongside an active, vigorous, and most importantly, encouraging online presence.

The future

Controversially, 2024 will see yet another overhaul for NCEA, with this particular iteration set to impact Classical Studies more keenly than ever. In late 2020, NZQA (New Zealand Qualifications Authority), alongside the Ministry of Education, announced sweeping changes to Level 1, which will have taken effect by the time this volume goes to print. The number of subjects offered for assessment will be reduced by ten to thirty-two, with Classical Studies, Art History, Media Studies, and Psychology no longer being offered at Level 1. The Ministry claims reducing the number of standards from 41 to 16 would provide for more coherent learning; the then Minister of Education Chris Hipkins noted in a press release:

> 'These subject changes are carefully designed to give students a broader foundation at the start of NCEA and more pathways for their learning, as well as reducing workload for teachers and students' (Chris Hipkins, in *School News* 2020).

Among the more egregious ways the Ministry has broadened student pathways is to abolish Latin at all NCEA levels, meaning Aotearoa will become the only English-speaking country where Latin is not offered at secondary school level. Though fewer than 200 students from around ten schools study Latin per year, with only twenty-five students continuing through to Level 3, New Zealand Association of Classical Teachers president Rob Griffiths noted in a Radio New Zealand interview: 'Latin is essentially the base of the English language, but more importantly, it's a subject which teaches the skills of mental processing, analytical reasoning, critical thinking – it's exactly what we try to develop in our students' (Rob Griffiths, in RNZ 2020). What makes this decision even harder to fathom is that for decades our politicians have decried the falling rates of literacy in our country – which could probably be graphed against the decline in interest in Latin. Learning second languages can be incredibly important for the development of children, and there are few people who have learned Latin that would deny it gives you a much greater understanding of your own language.

Alongside this short-sighted decision, Classical Studies at Level 1 will only be supported as a possible context within Level 1 History. This will narrow student subject choice, and it also decreases the opportunity for specialization in the humanities, as both subjects will be diluted. Likewise, some of the considerations the Ministry says it gave to the changes were whether the subjects provided broad, foundational learning, and preparation for advanced study. This is utterly contradictory, as Level 1 Classics covers a range of areas, including literature, arts, religion, philosophy and politics. It is unlike any other historical subject, as students have to learn how to make sense of fragmentary, sometimes contradictory, information from multiple different sources (literature, art, mythology, language, all three sciences, architecture and numismatics). These critical analytical skills cannot just be ticked off and absorbed in other subjects.

In spite of such alarming Antipodean developments, if we Classics kaiako, continue to channel trailblazers such as Syme, Thornton, Barsby and Dearden, while looking to the ancients on how to persevere when times are tough, we will no doubt find that, irrespective of boundaries of space or time, this whakataukī (proverb) rings true:

He aha te mea nui o te ao? He tangata, he tangata, he tangata!

What is the most important thing in the world? It is people, it is people, it is people!

References

RNZ (2020), '"Disappointment and frustration" over NCEA Level 1 subject changes', *Radio New Zealand*, 4 December. Available online: https://www.rnz.co.nz/news/national/432101/disappointment-and-frustration-over-ncea-level-1-subject-changes (accessed 12 December 2023).

School News (2020), 'NCEA Level 1 changes announced', *School News*, 8 December. Available online: https://www.schoolnews.co.nz/2020/12/ncea-level-1-changes-announced/ (accessed 12 December 2023).

Thornton, A. (1986), *Māori Oral Literature, As Seen by a Classicist*, Dunedin, New Zealand: University of Otago Press.

Organizations

NCEA (National Certificate of Educational Achievement): https://www2.nzqa.govt.nz/ncea/subjects/subject/classical-studies/
NZQA (New Zealand Qualifications Authority): https://www2.nzqa.govt.nz/ncea/
NZACT (New Zealand Association of Classics Teachers): https://www.nzact.org.nz/
For further information, go to https://www2.nzqa.govt.nz/ncea/subjects/subject/classical-studies/

AUSTRALASIA: FURTHER READING

Steven Hunt

Readers may be interested to read historical articles about Classics teaching published by the Joint Association of Classical Teachers in Australia (Martyn 1970; Matters 2008) and New Zealand (Barsby 1974; 1975; 1984). A more recent commentary than these can be found in Matters (2018). Peddar (2023) describes his experiences as a teacher of Latin in Australia, taking into consideration the needs of a diverse and multi-cultural intake. For surveys of classical reception in Australia and New Zeland, see Johnson (2019) and Burton et al. (2017). The latter publication includes a chapter by Holmes-Henderson in which she compares how Classics is included in the education systems of New Zealand and the UK. The influence of Classics on senior Māori statesman Sir Apirana Turupa Ngata (1874–1950) can be read in Perris (2022). For an interview with the New Zealand artist Marian Maguire, best known for her lithographs and etchings which combine ancient Greek vase painting with New Zealand colonial history, and whose work adorns the cover of this volume, see Hughes (2012).

The website www.legonium.com ('Where Latin meets Lego'), run by Sydney Classics teacher Anthony Gibbins, contans much advice on teaching Latin, including a guide to the Latin course book *Lingua Latina per se illustrata* and many other Lego-brick-based Classical topics.

While there is (unsurpisngly) no regular provision of Latin teaching in Antarctica, the American Latin teacher Trevor Layman provided lessons to what must have been a small group of enthusiasts when he visited the McMurdo Station in 2013–14 (Gowing 2015).

References

Barsby, J. (1974), 'The Classics in New Zealand – Part 1: in the schools', *Didaskalos*, 4 (3): 470–81.

Barsby, J. (1975), 'The Classics in New Zealand – Part 2: in the universities', *Didaskalos*, 5 (1): 147–55.

Barsby, J. (1984), 'The Classics in New Zealand', *JACT Review*, 1: 13–15.

Burton, D., S. Perris and J. Tatum, eds (2017), *Athens to Aotearoa: Greece and Rome in New Zealand Literature and Society*, Wellington, New Zealand: Victoria University Press.

Gowing, A. (2015), [Blog] Trevor Layman's New Book! Department of Classics, University of Washington. Available online: https://classics.washington.edu/news/2015/05/05/trevor-laymans-new-book (accessed 20 February 2024).

Hughes, J. (2012), 'Practitioners' Voices in Classical Reception Studies: Marian Maguire', *Open University*. Available online: https://www5.open.ac.uk/arts/research/pvcrs/2012/maguire (accessed 1 December 2023).

Johnson, M., ed. (2019), *Antipodean Antiquities: Classical Reception Down Under*, London: Bloomsbury.

Martyn, J. (1970), 'New wine in old bottles: Classics at Melbourne University', *Didaskalos*, 3 (2): 240–50.

Matters, E. (2008), 'The Teaching of Classics Abroad: Australia', *Journal of Classics Teaching*, 15: 5–7.

Matters, E. (2018), 'Classics in Australia. On Surer Ground?', in A. Holmes-Henderson, S. Hunt and M. Musié (eds), *Forward with Classics. Classical Languages in Schools and Communities*, London: Bloomsbury Academic, 47–54.

Peddar, D. (2023), 'Steps towards inclusivity: Modifying challenging content, navigating pedagogical materials and initiating student reflection within the Classics classroom', *Journal of Classics Teaching*, 48.

Perris, S. (2022), 'Classics and Māori Culture in New Zealand: Sir Apirana Ngata', *Antigone*. Available online: https://antigonejournal.com/2022/11/classics-maori-new-zealand-ngata/ (accessed 1 December 2023).

PART 4
MIDDLE EAST AND ASIA

CHINA

Li Qiang, Liu Jianchang and Li Hui

Introduction

Although there has been a long history of connections and possible interactions between the people of the regions of the Mediterranean Sea and China, especially since kinds of ancient Greek and Roman-Byzantine culture and objects have been found or traced in China (Kordosis 1992; Li 2015a, b), Classical language education in China originated in the Mongolian Yuan Dynasty (1279–1368), as Latin education began to spread with Christianity. In 1305, Giovanni da Montecorvino (1247–1328), the bishop of Khanbaliq, in a letter to a friend in Europe, mentioned he had brought forty boys to teach them Latin, and the Bible in order to translate it from Latin into Chinese so as to spread Christianity. He and his students translated the New Testament and Psalms, which was a pioneering contribution to Latin education in China. However, with the collapse of the Yuan Dynasty, Christians also disappeared from China, which led to the end of Latin teaching. Then, from the sixteenth century, Western navigators, explorers and missionaries started to travel to China, and the Portuguese occupied Macau. Later, many Jesuits came and set up a primary school to teach Latin. It was the first Western-style school in China. In 1594, Alessandro Valignano S.J. (1539–1606) opened a seminary in Macau, where students from China and Japan could learn Latin; it became the St Paul School, and the first university in Macau and China. Latin was the basic course of the curriculum. During this period, the Jesuits translated many Classical works, such as Euclid's *Elements*, *Aesop's Fables* and Aristotle's philosophical works. They also published the *Wonder of Western Writing* (西字奇蹟, *Xizi Qiji*) and *Aid to the Eyes and Ears of Western Literati* (西儒耳目資, *Xiru Ermuzi*), the latter of which has the first Romanized Chinese character glossary to help Westerners learn Chinese. Thus, classical knowledge was not only important in spreading classical culture, but also contributed greatly to the Chinese language. Their contributions opened the era of 'Eastward spread of Western learning' (西学东渐) and brought classical knowledge into traditional Chinese society. Another important symbolic event for Latin in China happened in 1605 when China's most famous Western library at Nantang in Beijing was set up. In the early Qing Dynasty (1644–1912), Latin education flourished at the court due to its diplomatic use and cultural attributes. Greek also started to be taught due to the influence of the Russian Orthodox church. In 1780, the French priest Hamel Lep laid the foundations for a Latin seminary in Yunnan. As we can see, though there are lots of evidence for classical education before the late nineteenth century, they were not systematic and mostly used for Christian proselytising and politics, and Greek was less important than Latin. In fact, the classical education for its own justification only took root in China after the late Qing Dynasty and truly developed after the Reform and Opening-up policy in 1978 (X. Zhang 2017; Leeb 2002, 2019; Mutschler 2019).

Classical education before the 1980s

After the Second Opium War (1856–60), the Qing Dynasty finally began to open its mind to reach the world and gradually launched the Self-Strengthening Movement (自强运动/洋务运动),

absorbing advanced Western science and technology. The failure of the first Sino-Japanese War (1894–1895) aroused the Qing Dynasty's interest in political reform and the enlightenment, and revolutionary thoughts became popular in China. With this background, the intellectuals began to seek classical culture from Western knowledge at that time, and Western classical works were gradually translated into Chinese. At first, Liang Qichao, Yan Fu and other intellectuals, great reformers or scholars in China, introduced and translated many works about the history and politics of ancient Greece and Rome concerning Western constitutionalism, like the *Little Book of Athenian History* (雅典小史), *The Soul of Sparta* (斯巴达之魂) and so on. There were also many translations of Greek tragedies. Zhou Zuoren, studying Greek in Japan, translated many works of Greek literature and myth, including all Euripides' tragedies. The active translation and transmission of classical culture by these intellectuals has laid a foundation for classical education in China. Meanwhile, with the development of the Chinese Revolution, Marxism was introduced into China and quickly became mainstream. The importance of the classical tradition in Marxism was also valued by people at that time. Additionally, the Christian Church schools and universities in China also provided education in Classics, especially the teaching of the ancient languages (Liu 1960: 71–8). In short, In China at that time a rudimentary framework for classical education had been established, but it was still limited to the circle of intellectuals. After the founding of the People's Republic of China, the Soviet education system was introduced. In 1952, the reorganization of Chinese higher education was carried out. The Chinese Government divided the teaching staff of higher education into different subjects and banned church schools. This left Western Classics in different faculties such as literature, history, philosophy and others. But even so, classical scholars emerged between the 1950s and 1980s, such as Professors Lin Zhichun (Ancient History), Luo Niansheng (Greek Literature) and Miao Litian (Greek Philosophy). They made persistent efforts in researching and translating Greek history, literature and philosophy. Therefore, Western Classics in China continued to move forward amidst setbacks.

Classical education from the 1980s to now

After the Reform and Opening-up policy (1978) was put forward, Chinese academia began to boom and flourish. However, due to the limits of ancient languages teaching, the lack of institutions, experience and other reasons, no department of Classics had been established. Instead, classical studies were just divided into classical literature, ancient history, Greek philosophy and so on. Therefore, the systematic establishment of classical education in China was put on the agenda.

In 1985, Professors Lin Zhichun, Zhou Gucheng and Wu Yujin collaborated on a paper of research on ancient civilizations in China (Lin et al. 1985: 1–3). Then, in the same year, with Lin himself as its director, the Institute for the History of Ancient Civilizations (IHAC) was established at Northeast Normal University, becoming the first educational institution for Classics in China. It also provided a programme in Egyptology, Assyriology, Byzantinology and Hittitology at both BA and MA level. From the beginning, Lin invited scholars in Classics from North America and Western Europe to provide courses in classical languages and related subjects. Among the earliest foreign scholars, William Brashear (Egyptian Museum in Charlottenburg) and Fritz-Heiner Mutschler (Technische Universität Dresden).

Among the earliest foreign scholars were the representatives. For the first time, students were introduced to ancient languages learning in a systematic way (Brashear 1990: 71–8; 1997: 81–5; Huang 2019: 371).

After 2000, universities which were enthusiastic for Classics, ancient civilizations, Western culture and liberal arts education started to establish their institutions for classical education gradually and systematically. For example, the school of Liberal Arts, Renmin University of China, started to train BA students totally in Classics from 2010. Peking University also established the Research Centre for Western Classics in 2011. In 2011, Beijing Foreign Studies University (BFSU) received approval from the Ministry of Education to establish a Latin language and literature major. In September 2015, BFSU established China's first Latin department. In 2018, the Latin Department enrolled its first undergraduate students. In a word, in recent years there has been an upsurge in Classics, as more and more students choose to study Classics and to study abroad.

We will first discuss the official education for Classics at universities, and secondly the extra-curricular activities. Then we will also mention the Classics in elementary education.

Universities

IHAC, the first authority focusing on Western civilizations, was set up in 1985 at Northeast Normal University. It provides courses at both BA level and MA level in Classics, including languages, history and archaeology, and it is the only institution in China that employs three to five foreign scholars (Classics, Egyptology, Assyriology and Byzantinology) per year for teaching. For BA study, besides some courses about classical languages, ancient history and classical historiography, there are also many seminars at BA level, such as Introduction on Ancient Greek History, Seminar on Ancient Roman History, History of Byzantium, European Cultural History, Appreciation of Ancient Greek Art and the History of Sino-Roman Relationship. All the seminars are two credits for one semester. As for the MA level, courses are offered by IHAC. In IHAC's educational system, there are courses for ancient and modern languages, ancient history, ancient text reading, seminars on various topics and other many interesting courses. Ancient Greek here is taught by using Wilding's *Greek for Beginners* (1973) and Latin is by using *Wheelock's Latin* (Wheelock & LaFleur 2011). All the courses for language learning are four credits for one year and courses for reading are four or two credits per year. The reading materials are offered by teachers and they change every year or semester, giving students a broad prospective (Günther 2019: 115–25).

Next are two major centres of Classics in China: Peking University (PKU) and Fudan University (FDU). PKU has had a Classical Philology programme at the BA level since 2010, covering Western Classics, Asian and African Classics (i.e., Assyriology, Hittitology and Egyptology), Chinese Pre-Qin History and Tunhuangology, and is linked to the three departments of history, foreign languages and philosophy. As for Western Classics, students who are freshmen at humanities departments can apply to study Greek (including ancient Greek, New Testament Greek and Modern Greek) and Latin, with two credits for one language per semester for two years. Students can choose to study two languages for one year or choose one course for two years. At the same time, there are two four-credits classical language reading courses and a course for the introduction to Western Classics and Medieval Studies. It also pays attention to comprehensive training in Chinese Classics, Egyptology and Assyriology.

The MA level curriculum is broadly consistent with the BA programme, taking into account both language and reading courses.

Peking University also conducts joint training for the Latin major with Beijing Foreign Studies University. Students here may access Classics without much difficulty and they are very eager to study it. Their interest for Classics mostly arises from the courses of ancient history and myths, which attract lots of students to apply for this programme. Then, Fudan University, another centre for Classics, also has a programme for Western Classics at BA level to encourage students to study it. Western Classics at Fudan University has elementary and intermediate stages. In the elementary stage, students learn Greek and Latin for three credits, and also take the Introduction to Classics, Greek and Roman History, and Greek Philosophy. The advanced stage continues to study Greek and Latin for one year, and conducts seminars on Greek and Latin literature, Greek and Roman history and historiography, and comparison between Chinese Classics and Western Classics. It is worth mentioning that Fudan University also offers visiting and exchange programmes, involving well-known Western universities such as Oxford University, lasting for one semester or one year. There is also a cooperation with Harvard University's 'Olympia Summer School', for which outstanding students may apply. At the same time, Fudan University actively invites well-known scholars to give lectures and holds related summer schools for Classical philology, numismatics and epigraphy.

Thirdly, Renmin University of China is famous for its Strauss Research Centre and its emphasis on the integration of Chinese and Western Classics. Western Classics education mainly covers three departments: the School of Liberal Arts, the School of History and the School of Philosophy. The courses of the School of Liberal Arts are presided over by Professor Liu Xiaofeng. They offer courses for language learning, reading and even some courses of classical music. For language learning, they use *From Alpha to Omega* (Groton 2013) and *Wheelock's Latin* (Wheelock and LaFleur 2011) to teach and their language courses are five credits for one language per semester. They also have their own textbooks called *Janus* and *Cairus* for reading courses, which include Homer, Plato and Thucydides. They also use *The Cambridge Grammar of Classical Greek* (Boas et al. 2021) and Greenough and Allen's *New Latin Grammar* (2017) both in the original and in Chinese translation by Gu Zhiying. In the School of Liberal Arts, the Austrian scholar Leopold Leeb has been teaching classical languages since 2004 (Zhang 2017). He works at the Department of Comparative Literature with his own textbooks, which I will fully discuss later. As for the School of History, they use *Elementary Greek* (Burgess and Bonner [1868] 2022) and *First Year Latin* (Collar and Daniell [1918] 2022) based on students' own interests. And for the School of Philosophy, teachers there teach Latin with their own handouts and Greek by *Ancient Greek: a New Approach* (Ruck 1971).

It is also worth mentioning the Latin major of Beijing Foreign Studies University (BFSU), which is based on the systematic and intensive study of the Latin and Greek languages and literature. In 2011 the Ministry of Education gave permission for the creation of the first complete Latin department, as well as the only current Latin major in the PRC, and in 2015 the Latin department was formally founded at BFSU. In 2016 the major programme of studies was set up and the first twelve majors were enrolled in 2018. It only enrols every four years and since 2022 it has begun to enrol students for a Master's programme. They adopt the 'Nature' method by introducing Ørberg's *Lingua Latina per se illustra* (Ørberg 2019, 2021) and the Italian edition of *Athenaze* (Miraglia and Borri 2013) to teach Greek. As with many Chinese undergraduate majors, the first two years of courses are predetermined: first Year: Latin 1,

Latin Poetry, Elements of Latin Civilization, Latin II, Roman History, History of Classical Latin literature; second year: Latin III, Greek I and II, Latin Translating and Writing I and II, Greek History and Culture, Selected Reading from the Latin Classics I and II. In the third year, students will go abroad for an exchange year. In 2020/21 at La Sapienza University in Rome, the students took courses in Western Art and Archaeology, the History of Early Christianity and Late Antiquity, History of Greek Literature, Selected Readings from Greek Literature, Greek and Latin Philology, Medieval Latin Literature. On top of this, students must have mastered Italian! In the fourth year, majors will take seminars at BFSU in Research Methods, Philosophy, Renaissance Latin Literature, Linguistics, Sinological Latin Reading etc. The department has established a partnership with the Centre for Western Classics at Peking University, where students from both institutions can take courses from each other (Alvares and Li 2020)

In addition, there are many universities that include Greek and Latin as the core of Western classical education. We will list them briefly here:

- Nankai University offers courses in ancient Greek, Latin and Modern Greek (Leeb 2014d). All three are for two credits and last for one semester.

- The University of Chinese Academy of Social Sciences offers three credits for seminars of Greek and Roman History, and also three credits of elementary and advanced Greek, which takes one year to study.

- Beijing Normal University offers BA level courses for Greek and Roman History, Western Culture, and Christianity, with two or three credits for MA level.

- Sun Yat-sen University in Guangzhou and Zhuhai, both offer classical education of Classical Language for four credits and seminars of Classics for two credits. They use Luschnig's *An Introduction to Ancient Greek: A Literary Approach* (2007) for teaching, with one course every week for two credits. Sun Yat-sen University (Zhuhai) could also offer courses for epigraphy according to the needs of students. The Liberal Arts Academy at Sun Yat-sen University also provides courses of classical languages.

- Students at Southwest University could take Greek first at BA level to learn basic grammars, using *Reading Greek* (JACT 2007) and in the next semester they will take the course 'Research on Ancient Greek Literature' for four credits by using Wilding's *Greek for Beginners* (1993) and *A Primer of Greek Grammar* (Abbott & Mansfield [1867] 2001). They can also participate in the Latin course with the textbook *Wheelock's Latin* (Wheelock and LaFleur 2011) at MA level, with thirty-six hours learning for one semester. The School of Law and the School of Philosophy there also could provide courses for Latin in Law, and Greek.

- Central China Normal University offers Greek and Latin at the MA level, four credits for one year, by using the textbook *Learn to Read Greek* (Keller and Russell 2011) and *Learn to Read Latin* (Keller & Russell 2014).

- Shanghai Normal University offers many courses for BA students. Besides courses of classical languages for two credits, it also provides reading courses for Thucydides, Tacitus and Homer, even E. Gibbon is included. And it also offers courses for Classical literature and political culture. As for the MA level, it offers Classical languages for one year, one course per week. As for textbooks, Greek use, *Greek: An Intensive Course* by

Hansen and Quinn (1992) and *A Primer of Greek Grammar* by Abbott and Mansfield ([1867] 2001) and for Latin it uses teachers' own handouts.

- Capital Normal University offers courses for Medieval Latin and Classical Greek for four semesters and teaching in both English and Chinese. It also offers seminars about ancient history and civilizations.

- Sichuan University offers three credits of Greek and Latin with reading courses for two credits, and also a Modern Greek course. (All the information for the courses in these and other universities were collected through private interviews.)

Classical languages and their medieval forms are also taught to the students in Medieval Studies. Tianjin Normal University is an important centre for Medieval Studies in China. It offers Latin for two semesters to BA students, three hours per week and one semester for MA students, using *Wheelock's Latin* (Wheelock and LaFleur 2011). Professor Li Yongyi, from Chongqing University, has translated and provided a commentary for Ovid, Horace and Catullus. He offers 'Basic Latin (1)' and 'Basic Latin (2)' in the School of Foreign Languages and Cultures, two hours per week, using the *Cambridge Latin Course* (CSCP 2022). In the same university Professor Huang Ruicheng also offers Latin and Greek courses. Jinan University is a centre for Carolingian studies, and it offers eight credits of Medieval Latin in two semesters for BA and MA students, using *Wheelock's Latin*. South China Normal University is well-known for its research in French history from the early period to modern times, and it offers one year of two hours per week for seventeen weeks for MA students, using *Wheelock's Latin*. In addition, there are other universities which have scholars in Medieval Studies which also offer Latin. Shanghai University offers eight credits of Latin to MA students for one year. Zhejiang University offers Medieval Latin for MA students, three hours per week for one semester, using *Wheelock's Latin*. Anhui Normal University offers courses for one academic year teaching Latin, using *Learn to Read Latin* (Keller and Russell 2014). Wuhan University and Nanjing University also offer courses of Greek.

The Departments of Philosophy in China also provide related courses for Classical languages, which are very similar to the courses we have mentioned, but their speciality is reading selected texts from Greek or Latin philosophers, especially focusing on Plato and Aristotle. In addition to Peking University and Fudan University, Sichuan University, Sun Yat-sen University, Shandong University and Southwest University can provide related courses. Meanwhile, Latin in Law (in Departments of Law, especially Xiamen University, Southwest University of Political Science and Law, and China University of Political Science and Law) is taught at basic level for students majoring in Law and at advanced level for those who study Roman Law and Legal History. Medical Latin is attracting students' interests nowadays in medical education (Du 2008; Zhan and Tan 2011; Ye and Shi 2012).

Extra-curricular activities

Publications of textbooks

Chinese scholars believe that access to Classics should be through philological methods. Therefore, they pay much attention to language learning and have written, introduced and translated many textbooks, including some famous textbooks, to teach classical languages, as well as using original books. Most of them are for Latin, such as *Wheelock's Latin* (Wheelock and LaFleur 2017, trs Zhang), *Lingua Latina per se illustra* (Ørberg 2021, trs Li), *Lawyers' Latin, a Vade-Mecum* (Gray 2009, trs Zhang), *Standardwortschatz Latein* (Mader & Siemer 2015 trs Zhang) and *Vocabulaire Latin* (Zhang and Yan 2018). As for the written books, Professor Leopold Leeb, an Austrian scholar at Renmin University, has published a series of his own textbooks in Chinese: *Initia Linguae Latinae: Grammatica* (Leeb 2014a), *Initia Linguae Latinae: Scripta Collecta* (Leeb 2014b) and *Basic Vocabulary for Latin* (Leeb 2014c). There are also two ancient Greek textbooks in the same series (Leeb 2014d; 2015). He has also written a Latin textbook called *Cursus Brevis Linguae Latinae* (Leeb 2010c), published by the Commercial Press. He wrote not only a Latin-Sino dictionary, but also a dictionary for sayings and idioms in Chinese (Leeb 2006a; 2006b; 2011). He also wrote some books about classical reception in China (Leeb 2012). In sum, Professor Leeb has made a great contribution to classical education in China (Leeb 2010a; 2010b; 2019; 2021). Also, recent years have witnessed publications about the phonetics of classical languages, translated by Professor Huang Ruicheng of Chongqing University (Allen 2023a,b,c). Another foreign expert is Professor Michele Ferrero, who has taught Latin and Greek optional courses at the Beijing Foreign Studies University and at other institutions in Beijing from 2009, and who published the textbook *Lingua Latina ad Sinenses discipulos accomodata* (Ferrero 2014).

Professor Liu Xiaofeng published his own handouts as textbooks as well, but they are less popular today (Liu 2005). Other books like Liu Xun's *Cicero Dixit* (2018), Xin Delin's textbook *Latin and Greek* (2007), and other teachers' textbooks: for Latin *Basic Latin* (Xiao 1983), *Latin Grammar* (Xin 2015), and for Greek *Introduction to Ancient Greek Language, Literature and Grammar* (Liu 2006), *Textbook to Classical Greek* (Zhou 2009) and *Brief Textbook for Koiné Greek* (Fu 2009) are also very important. Chinese Christians need to learn Greek for the New Testament and there are two books written by famous scholars: Yang's *Textbook for New Testament Greek* (Yang 2010) and Huang's *Textbook of Ancient Greek for New Testament* (Huang 2008). People also use *Brief Textbook for Ancient Greek* (Sun 2010) and *Textbook for New Testament Greek* (Yang 2010). For Latin in Roman religion, there is *Selected Texts for Roman Religion* (Vermander and Wu 2012). Greek and Latin dictionaries with Chinese are also very popular for beginners: *Dictionarium Latino-Sinicum* (Xie et al. 1988a), *Dictionarium Parvum Latino Sinicum* (Xie et al. 1988b) and *Dictionary of Greek-Sino Language* (Shui and Luo 2004). In Latin for law, a type of book used in China is *Latin-Chinese Dictionary of Legal Terms and Maxims* (Chen 2009). Finally, there are four books as introductions for Classics: *An Introductory Research Guide to Greek History* (Huang and Yan 2021), *An Introductory Research Guide to Roman History* (Liu 2021), *An Introduction to Byzantine Study* (Chen 2012) and *An Introduction to Classical Studies* (Zhang 2022).

Lectures and seminars

Universities and other research centres organize discussions, lectures, seminars and other series of educational activities. They invite scholars from China and foreign countries. For example, IHAC at Northeast Normal University has three lecture series: Rizhi Classics, common lectures and the International Byzantine Seminar Lecture Series; Peking University organizes lectures mostly for Classics, and there is a lecture series at Nankai University for Byzantine studies.

Students who have learned the basic grammar of Greek, Latin and Sanskrit can apply for the summer school held at Shanghai Normal University. This lasts nearly one week and students read selected texts from various authors. It is organized for free every year in July, with ten students for every language, most of whom are MA students. It also offers funding for students to encourage them to improve their classical languages. Fudan University organized a summer school for Roman History recently, attracting many Chinese student participators. Professor Michele Ferrero has run short-term summer Latin courses at Beijing Foreign Studies University and organized summer camps in Rome for Latin language and culture.

Having learned and read lots of ancient texts, students in China can also take part in the Standard Exam organized by Peking University with IHAC and Fudan University. This standard exam is the only one in China for classical languages and it is set every year. The exam is divided into beginner and intermediate levels. Students at the beginner level will read Plato and Xenophon's philosophical texts for the Greek exam and Caesar and Nepos for Latin. Students at the intermediate level will read Herodotus and Isocrates for Greek and Cicero and Sallust for Latin. Students who take this exam will read a paragraph of about 200 words, for three hours, doing an English translation. They are examined by Western scholars and are expected to receive the certification in about one month.

Primary and secondary schools

Classical education has not been included in the teaching syllabus of the Ministry of Education in today's China. Nonetheless, some classical knowledge has been inserted into education at primary and secondary schools. Students at that level will learn some Greek literature translated into Chinese, such as the *Iliad*, *Oedipus the King* and *Aesop's Fables*; and Greek and Roman history, mostly for democracy in Athens and Roman law. Although it is clear that classical education has not grown up at that level, there are still some schools offering language courses. Leopold Leeb, who works at Renmin University, provides Latin to high school students at Beijing No.11 School. American scholar David Quentin Dauthier used to provide Latin in the high school attached to Beijing Normal University. In addition, some private high schools (No. 8 and No. 101) in Beijing, Shenzhen and Shanghai also provided courses in Latin for students' preparation in entering universities in the US or Europe. Meanwhile, some alumni from IHAC, who are teachers in different high schools, also express their passion and will open some selective courses in Latin and Greek for high school students. (This information comes from personal communication with teachers.)

We have found a case of teaching Latin in primary school. In Anhui, Culver Academies first-year student, Ashley (Yuqi) Zheng leads third graders at her former elementary school in Hefei, Anhui, in an exploratory Latin course based on the Paideia Institute's *Aequora* Curriculum (James 2021).

Private classical education

Out of all the universities in China, there are only a few universities that can offer language courses for Classics. Many students therefore participate in courses provided by private teachers or other institutions.

Private teaching

Chen Qing, an Associate Professor at Southwest University, received his PhD at Jilin University and was a visiting scholar at Thomas-Institut der Universität zu Köln in 2015. He established an online private school for classical education and translation. He offers courses of Greek, Latin and logic. His Greek course is for fifteen days, which takes place during summer or winter holidays in China. He uses *Athenaze* (Balme et al. 2016) to teach ancient Greek and each round of courses can progress for five chapters. He also offers advanced courses by reading Thucydides and others. As for Latin, the time and learning intensity are the same as Greek. He uses *Lingua Latin per se illustrata* (Ørberg 2019) with the help of *Wheelock's Latin* (Wheelock & LaFleur 2011), *Reading Latin* (Jones 2016) and his own handouts. His advanced Latin course is to read Caesar. More information could be found on his personal website https://www.conf-aris.com.

Liu Xun, also called Paulus, received his MA at Pontificium Institutum Altioris Latinitatis of the Pontifical Salesian University. He provides online teaching of Latin at different levels, using *Wheelock's Latin* or *Lingua Latina per se illustrata*, and he also wrote a book called *Cicero Dixit* (Liu 2018) which is a book for Latin grammar. For Paulus' public account on Wechat, see 保禄学堂, and for his online courses, see http://www.yicir.com/.

Institutions

Compared with private teachers, language courses in institutions can provide more systematic education to help students enhance their classical languages. The first institution is Bolanguages, which is an online teaching group organized by Chinese students studying abroad. The class there is a small group of four to six people or one-to-one/two teaching. One course is thirty-six hours of learning and will take two processes to finish one textbook. For Greek, they use *Greek to GCSE* (Taylor 2016). They also provide prose and verse reading courses and writing courses. For these, students study the *Latin Prose Composition* (North and Hillard [1913] 1997) and *Learn Latin from the Romans* (Dickey 2018). The dialect courses they provided use Stephen Colvin's *A Historical Greek Reader: Mycenean to the Koiné* (2007) and will be based on students' interests in different Greek dialects. For Latin teaching they use *Lingua Latina per se illustrata* (Ørberg 2019; 2021) to learn the basics and also read texts from Latin writers like Caesar, Virgil, Horace, Livy and Cicero. They also provide courses for Medieval Latin and the American AP and British A-Level Latin examinations.

Another institution for classical education is called 'Scholars'. It provides a series of courses online called 'The Wisdom of the Tower of Babel'. It offers Greek and Latin courses. For Greek, they use *Reading Greek* (JACT 2007) for ten weeks for three hours every week. For Latin, they use *Lingua Latina per se illustrata* (Øberg 2019; 2021) with three level stages, focusing on fully developing language skill. Every week is six hours for Latin over twelve weeks. It also provides tutors after class to help students learn Greek and Latin.

In China there are currently a lot of students who are preparing to go to high school or college abroad, and so many study-abroad organisations have been created to help them, including Latin programmes. They hire part-time college or middle-school teachers to provide one-on-one classes to help students prepare for examinations such as the American NLE (National Latin Exam) and AP Latin examination.

Since the reorganization of Chinese higher education in the 1950s, church schools and universities mostly went separately, with many of the former abolished or merged. But some of the remaining church schools nowadays also have their own importance in classical education as they provide Latin and Greek education for ecclesiastical use.

Private teaching for secondary school

As mentioned above, students cannot get a systematic education of Classics. Therefore, some parents employ private teachers for classical education. They think that there are five reasons that classical education could benefit their children. Honestly speaking, classical language learning from their point of view could not only be helpful for the studying of Classics, law and even science and engineering, but could also aid students in their application to some international universities. Then, as for the languages themselves, they think learning classical languages could help their children master other European languages and understand the thinking patterns of classical languages. Finally, those benefits could be said in sum to broaden the horizon and to improve patience and perseverance (see, for example, https://mp.weixin.qq.com/s/TMZhrGhz0kYu_MZ8eaJxig and https://mp.weixin.qq.com/s/2Bn9da4GrcBy3B2SnJ6fKA).

In addition to language learning, children who are still young may also get some cultural impression about classical literature, myth and other attractive information. Many academic groups for children, such as Museion, Stonecity and Nova Alexandria are organized by students at higher level to teach and introduce them into the world of Classics.

Conclusion

Classical education in China can be traced back to the fourteenth century with the coming of Christianity, though not on a large scale. Its intermittent further development between the sixteenth and nineteenth centuries was also due to Christianity, especially under the Jesuits. In the twentieth century, especially the first half, Chinese scholars with a background of studying in Europe, the US and Japan, promoted translations of classical works, while schools and universities sponsored by the Western Christian Church also played an important role.

Since the 1980s, with the establishment of IHAC, classical education started regular development in universities, offering programmes in classical languages, history, philosophy and literature at BA, MA and PhD level. Since 2011, with World History becoming a main discipline along with Chinese History, and in 2013, with 'the Belt and Road Initiative', much attention has been given to world history and foreign languages and cultures, and Chinese universities have opened more courses in classical education. Elementary education has also noticed its importance, and even people outside of universities have become interested in classical education, studying classical languages in private ways (online course, Wechat app and so on) for all kinds of reasons.

Now, we predict a prosperous future for classical education in China.

References

Abbott, E. and E. Mansfield ([1887] 2001), *A Primer of Greek Grammar,* London: Focus Classical Reprint.

Allen, W. (2023a), *Vox Latina: A Guide to the Pronunciation of Classical Latin* (古典拉丁语语音), trans. R. Huang, Xi'an: Northwest University Press.

Allen, W. (2023b), *Vox Graeca: A Guide to the Pronunciation of Classical Greek* (古典希腊语语音), trans. R. Huang, Xi'an: Northwest University Press.

Allen, W. (2023c), *Accent and Rhythm: Prosodic Features of Latin and Greek* (重音与节奏：拉丁语和希腊语的韵律特点), trans. R. Huang, Xi'an: Northwest University Press.

Alvares, J. and H. Li (2020), 'The First Full Latin and Greek Program at a University in the People's Republic of China (PRC)', *The Classical Outlook Journal of the American Classical League* 59 (2): 56–62.

Balme, M., G. Lawall and J. Morwood (2016), *Athenaze*, Oxford: Oxford University Press.

Boas, E., A. Rijksbaron, L. Huitink and M. de Bakker (2021), *The Cambridge Grammar of Classical Greek* (剑桥古典希腊语语法), trans. Z. Gu and Z. Yang, Shanghai: East China Normal University Press.

Brashear, W. (1990), 'Classics in China', *The Classical Journal*, 86 (1): 73–8.

Brashear, W. (1997), 'China Update 1997', *The Classical Journal*, 94 (1): 81–5.

Burgess, T. and R. Bonner ([1868] 2022), *Elementary Greek*, Unknown: Legare Street Press.

Chen, W. (2009), *Latin-Chinese Dictionary of Legal Terms and Maxims* (拉丁语法律用语和法律格言词典), Beijing: Law Press.

Chen, Z. (2012), *An Introduction to Byzantine Studies* (拜占庭学研究入门), Beijing: Peking University Press.

Collar, M. and M. Daniell ([1918] 2022), *First Year Latin*, Unknown: Legare Street Press.

Colvin, S. (2007), *A Historical Greek Reader: Myecnaean to the Koiné*, Oxford: Oxford University Press.

CSCP (2022), *Cambridge Latin Course*, Cambridge: Cambridge University Press.

Dickey, E. (2018), *Learn Latin from the Romans*, Cambridge: Cambridge University Press.

Du, Q., ed. (2008), *Latin for Chinese Medicine* (中医药拉丁语), Beijing: Science Press.

Ferrero, M. (2014), *Lingua Latina ad Sinenses discipulos accomodata* (拉丁语基础教程), Beijing: The Commercial Press.

Fu, Y. (2009), *Brief Textbook for Koiné Greek* (简明共通希腊文教程—词法、语法、句法), Shanghai: Shanghai Jiao Tong University Press.

Gray, J. (2009), *Lawyers' Latin, a Vade-Mecum* (律师拉丁语：一个流行语), trans. L. Zhang, Beijing: Law Press.

Greenough, J. and J. Allen (2017), *Allen and Greenough's New Latin Grammar* (拉丁语语法新编), trans. Z. Gu and Z. Yang, Shanghai: East China Normal University Press.

Groton, A. (2013), *From Alpha to Omega: A Beginning Course in Ancient Greek*, Newburyport, MA: Focus Publishing.

Günther, S. (2019), 'Teaching and Learning Latin and Roman History in Reading Course in IHAC', *Journal of Latin Language and Culture*, 7: 115–25.

Hansen, H. and G. Quinn (1992), *Greek: An Intensive Course*, New York: Fordham University Press.

Huang, X. (2008), *Textbook of Ancient Greek for New Testament* (古希腊（新约）教程), Shanghai: East China Normal University Press.

Huang, Y. (2019), 'Classical Studies in China', in A.-B. Renger and F. Xin (eds), *Receptions of Greek and Roman Antiquity in East Asia*, Leiden: Brill, 363–75.

Huang, Y. and S. Yan (2021), *An Introductory Research Guide to Greek History* (希腊史研究入门), Beijing: Peking University Press.

JACT (2007), *Reading Greek*, London: Joint Association of Classical Teachers.

James, V. (2021), Classical Studies in Mainland China. Available online: https://ics.blogs.sas.ac.uk/2021/08/23/Classical-studies-in-mainland-china/ (accessed 6 November 2023).

Jones, P. (2016), *Reading Latin*, London: Bloomsbury.

Keller, A. and S. Russell (2011), *Learn to Read Greek*, New Haven, CT: Yale University Press.

Keller, A. and S. Russell (2014), *Learn to Read Latin*, New Haven, CT: Yale University Press.

Kordosis, M. (1992), 'China and the Greek world. An introduction to Greek-Chinese studies with special reference to the Chinese sources, in Hellenistic-Roman-Early Byzantine period (2nd c. B.C. – 6th c. A.D.)', *Historicogeographica Meletemata* 2: 143–254.

Leeb, L. (2006a), *Dictionary for Sayings in Ancient Greek, Roman, and the Period of Church Fathers* (古希腊罗马及教父时期名著名言辞典), Beijing: Religion Culture Publishing House.

Leeb, L. (2006b), *Dictionary of Latin Idioms* (拉丁成语词典), Beijing: Religion Culture Publishing House.

Leeb, L. (2010), *English-Chinese Summaries of Western Classics Volume I 100 Classics of Ancient Greece and Rome* (西方经典英汉提要 • 卷一：古代经典100部), Beijing: World Publishing Corporation.

Leeb, L. (2010a), *English-Chinese Summaries of Western Classics Volume II: 100 Classics of Late Antiquity* (西方经典英汉提要 • 卷二：古代晚期经典100部), Beijing: World Publishing Corporation.

Leeb, L. (2010b), *English-Chinese Summaries of Western Classics Volume III: 100 Classics of the Middle Ages* (西方经典英汉提要 • 卷三：中世纪经典 100 部), Beijing: World Publishing Corporation.

Leeb, L. (2010c), *Cursus Brevis Linguae Latinae* (简明拉丁语教程), Beijing: Commercial Press.

Leeb, L. (2011), *Dictionarium Parvum Latino-Sinicum* (拉丁语汉语简明词典), Beijing: World Publishing Corporation.

Leeb, L. (2012), *Pons Latinus* (拉丁语桥 • 拉丁语/英语/汉语修辞学词典), Beijing: China Book Press.

Leeb, L. (2014a), *Initia Linguae Latinae: Grammatica* (拉丁语入门教程I：语法篇), Beijing: Beijing United Publishing.

Leeb, L. (2014b), *Initia Linguae Latinae: Scripta Collecta* (拉丁语入门教程II：文献篇), Beijing: Beijing United Publishing.

Leeb, L. (2014c), *Basic Vocabulary for Latin* (拉丁语基本词汇手册), Beijing: Beijing United Publishing.

Leeb, L. (2014d), *Education of the Greek Language* (ΔΙΔΑΣΚΑΛΙΚΟΝ ΤΗΣ ΕΛΛΗΝΙΚΗΣ ΓΛΩΣΣΗΣ) (古希腊语入门教程), Beijing: Beijing United Publishing.

Leeb, L. (2015), *Basic Vocabulary for Ancient Greek* (古希腊语基本词汇手册), Beijing: Beijing United Publishing.

Leeb, L. (2019), 'Latin in China between the 20th and 21st Centuries' (拉丁语在中国，20–21世纪), *Journal of Latin Language and Culture*, 7: 126–80.

Leeb, L. (2021), *Latina in Beijing: Libellus Pupillorum Sinensium* (中国学生简明拉丁语入门), Shantou: Shantou University Press.

Leeb, L. (2022), 'Latin Schools in China between the 16th and 20th Centuries', *Journal of Latin Language and Culture*, 10: 137–63.

Li, H. (2018), 'The Status of Latin Language Teaching in China', *Latinitas*, 1: 137–52.

Li, H. (2020), 'Grammatical Translation Method, "Natural" Method and Latin Teaching in China' (语法翻译法、 "自然" 教学法与中国的拉丁语教学), in G. Zhao (ed.), *Studies on European Languages and Cultures* (欧洲语言文化研究), No. 10, Beijing: UNESCO Literature Press, 82–98.

Li, Q. (2015a), 'Roman Coins Discovered in China and Their Research', *Eirene. Studia Graeca et Latina*, 1–2: 279–99.

Li, Q. (2015b), 'The Image of the Roman Empire (Byzantine Empire) in Chinese Sources: 1st–7th Centuries', PhD Dissertation, University of Ioannina, Greece.

Lin, Z., G. Zhou and Y. Wu (1985), 'The Bank Left by the Classical Civilizations in China Must be Made up' (典文明研究在我国的空白必须填补" > "古典文明研究在我国的空白必须填补), *World History*, 11: 1–3.

Liu, J. (2021), *An Introductory Research Guide to Roman History* (罗马史研究入门), Beijing: Peking University Press.

Liu, K.-C. (1960), 'Early Christian Colleges in China', *Journal of Asian Studies*, 20 (1): 71–8.

Liu, X. (2005), *Kairos: Textbook for Ancient Greek Language* (古希腊语文教程), Shanghai: East China University Press.

Liu, X. (2018), *Cicero Dixit* (西塞罗曰：古典拉丁语基础语法及英语单词前后缀的「前世今生」), Beijing: Tsinghua University Press.

Liu, Y. (2006), *Introduction to Ancient Greek Language, Literature and Grammar* (古希腊语言文字语法简说), Shanghai: Shanghai People Publishing.

Luschnig, C. (2007), *An Introduction to Ancient Greek: A Literary Approach*, Indianapolis, IN: Hackett Publishing Co. Inc.

Mader, M. and J. Siemer (2015), *Standardwortschatz Latein* (拉丁语标准词汇学习手册), trans. Y. Zhan, Beijing: Peking University Press.

Miraglia, L. and Borri, T. (2013), *Athenaze*, Frascati: Accademia Vivarium Novum.

Mutschler, F.-H. (2019), 'Western Classics at Chinese Universities – and Beyond: Some Subjective Observations', in A.-B. Renger and F. Xin (eds), *Receptions of Greek and Roman Antiquity in East Asia*, Leiden: Brill, 430–44.

North, M. and A. Hillard ([1913] 1997), *Latin Prose Composition*, London: Duckworth.

Ørberg, H. (2019), *Lingua Latina per se illustrata: Pars I Familia Romana* (拉丁语综合教程 1), trans. H. Li, Beijing: Foreign Language Teaching and Research Press.

Ørberg, H. (2021), *Lingua Latina per se illustrata: Pars II Roma Aeterna* (拉丁语综合教程2), trans. H. Li, Beijing: Foreign Language Teaching and Research Press.

Ruck, C. (1971), *Ancient Greek: a New Approach,* Cambridge, MA: MIT Press.

Shui, J. and N. Luo (2004), *Dictionary of Greek-Sino Language* (古希腊语汉语词典), Beijing: The Commercial Press.

Sun, Z., ed. (2010), *Brief Textbook for Ancient Greek* (古希腊语简明教程), Shanghai: Shanghai People Press.

Taylor, J. (2016), *Greek to GCSE*, London: Bloomsbury.

Vermander, B. and Y. Wu (2012), *Selected Texts for Roman Religion* (古罗马宗教读本), Beijing: The Commercial Press.

Wheelock, F. and R. LaFleur (2011), *Wheelock's Latin*, 7th edition, New York: Collins Reference.

Wheelock, F. and R. LaFleur (2017), *Wheelock's Latin* (韦洛克拉丁语), trans. B. Zhang, Beijing: Beijing United Publishing Corporation.

Wilding, L. (1973), *Greek for Beginners*, 2nd edition, London: Faber and Faber Limited.

Xiao, Y. (1983), *Basic Latin* (拉丁语基础), Shanghai: The Commercial Press.

Xie, D., Y. Ma and W. Li, eds (1988a), *Dictionarium Latino-Sinicum* (拉丁语汉语词典), Beijing: The Commercial Press.

Xie, D., T. Zhang and W. Li, eds (1988b), *Dictonarium Parvum Latino Sincum* (拉丁语汉语小词典). Shanghai: Shanghai Foreign Language Education Press.

Xin, D. (2007), *Latin and Greek* (拉丁语和希腊语), Beijing: Foreign Language Teaching and Research Press.

Xin, D. (2015), *Latin Grammar* (拉丁语语法), Beijing: Foreign Language Teaching and Research Press.

Yang, J. (2010), *Textbook for New Testament Greek* (新约圣经古希腊语教程), Chengdu: Sichuan University Press.

Ye, C. and X. Shi (2012), *Lingua Latine, Botanices* (植物拉丁文教程), Beijing: Higher Education Press.

Zhan, Y. and X. Tan, eds (2011), *Latin for Medicine* (医药拉丁语), Beijing: China Medical Science Press.

Zhang, H. (2017), 'Leopold Leeb: Teaching Classics in China', *China Today*. Available online: http://www.chinatoday.com.cn/english/life/2017-10/10/content_747915.htm (accessed 10 October 2023).

Zhang, L. and Q. Yan, eds (2018), *Vocabulaire Latin* (拉丁语3000词), Beijing: The Commercial Press.

Zhang, W. (2022), *An Introduction to Classical Studies* (西方古典学研究入门), Beijing: Peking University Press.

Zhang, X. (2017), 'Latin in the End of Ming and the Beginning of Qing of China' (明末清初拉丁语在中国), *Journal of Latin Language and Culture*, 7: 112–14.

Zhou, Z. (2009), *Textbook to Classical Greek* (古典希腊语教程), Hangzhou: Zhejiang University Press.

Online resources

Bilibili (https://www.bilibili.com/), one of the most well-known websites for videos among Chinese younger generations, has various video uploaders, including videos about classical language learning (see, for example, Androcles: https://space.bilibili.com/36512122; BrightRivers: https://space.bilibili.com/31530534; and qammus: https://space.bilibili.com/476217023). Many famous scholars also have accounts at this website offering online courses for languages and culture, like Professor Li Yongyi at Chongqing University and Professor Ruan Wei at Hunan Normal University (see, for example, https://space.bilibili.com/52678543, http://latinedu.net/, https://space.bilibili.com/1026501026 and https://space.bilibili.com/301156993). Additionally, there are many interesting videos for children (see, for example, https://space.bilibili.com/1099355471, https://space.bilibili.com/10272827 and https://space.bilibili.com/514051666).

There are many public accounts on Wechat (a Chinses chatting app with multi functions) as well. They are for language learning, literature reading, academic information spreading and even palaeography. One of the most important public accounts is the urbs_animi (拉丁语灵都), which is supervised by Professor Leeb. This public account provides some Latin sayings, proverbs and phrases for Latin writing for about three days a week. Other public accounts for classical languages like Hodgepodge of Classics (古典乱炖), Athenaion (尔苑古语), Xiangbo Culture (相伯文化), Xuanjie (悬解), and Mirror of Toynbee offers information for Greek and Latin courses. Other public accounts offer academic information for Classics such as GRpocketbook, Database of I Love Classics (爱古典数据库), Classics and Interpretation (经典与解释) and Research on Medieval Palaeography. Public accounts like Latin Language and Literature and the Jiangan Academic Society for Platonism give information about Classics in a more general way.

INDIA

Mali Skotheim

Introduction

With over 265 million children enrolled in nearly 1.5 million schools across the country, the educational system in India is vast (Department of School Education and Literacy 2023). Education is compulsory in India through age fourteen, with optional upper secondary education through age seventeen. The National Education Policy (NEP) of 2020 moves away from the NEP 1986 10+2 system (ten years primary and secondary education, and two years higher secondary education) to a 5+3+3+4 model (five years foundational, three years preparatory, three years middle, four years secondary), which expands early childhood education. The higher secondary participation rate is about 29 per cent (OECD 2019).

Private institutions are an important part of the educational landscape in India, both at the school level and among higher education institutions (HEIs). In 2014/15, 29.6 per cent of primary and secondary students in India attended private institutions, although this proportion varied widely by state (Kingdon 2022: 1,798). Among the private secondary institutions are several Jesuit schools, some of which have a history of teaching Greek and Latin, but no longer offer these subjects. Private colleges and universities attract approximately 40 per cent of the BA student population (OECD 2019). Ashoka University is one such private university, founded in 2014 on a liberal arts model.

Any discussion of the place of Greek and Roman studies in India must be put into the larger context of the study of the classical languages and cultures of India, which is what 'Classics' is far more likely to be understood to refer to in India today. Notably, a central goal of the NEP 2020 is the re-invigoration of classical Indian languages and knowledge traditions, and a call for Sanskrit to be far more widely available at the secondary and tertiary levels.

Requirements

There are no requirements for students to learn Greek or Latin in Indian schools, and neither language is recognized as an academic subject in the Central Board of Secondary Education secondary school curriculum (CBSE 2020/21). Classical languages, however, are at the centre of current policies and debates around education in India. The NEP 2020 set as a central priority the revamping of the Indian educational system to prioritize classical education, by which they mean primarily Sanskrit and other Indian knowledge traditions. In the introduction to the policy, the NEP states 'The rich heritage of ancient and eternal Indian knowledge and thought has been a guiding light for this Policy' (NEP 2020, Introduction). The NEP 2020 characterizes this new aim of Indian education as deriving from the ancient and medieval university centres of India, being Takshashila, Nalanda, Vikramshila and Vallabhi (NEP 2020, Introduction). A major ramification of the NEP 2020 concerns language instruction. The NEP requires instruction in three languages, with choice given to regions, schools and students 'so long as at least two of the three languages are native to India' (NEP 2020, 4.13). Classical languages are a central component of the plan:

> The importance, relevance, and beauty of the classical languages and literatures of India also cannot be overlooked. Sanskrit, while also an important modern language mentioned in the Eighth Schedule of the Constitution of India, possesses a classical literature that is greater in volume than that of Latin and Greek put together, containing vast treasures of mathematics, philosophy, grammar, music, politics, medicine, architecture, metallurgy, drama, poetry, storytelling, and more (known as 'Sanskrit Knowledge Systems'), written by people of various religions as well as non-religious people, and by people from all walks of life and a wide range of socio-economic backgrounds over thousands of years. Sanskrit will thus be offered at all levels of school and higher education as an important, enriching option for students, including as an option in the three language formula.
>
> (NEP 2020, 4.17).

While the NEP acknowledges that 'India also has an extremely rich literature in other classical languages, including classical Tamil, Telugu, Kannada, Malayalam, Odia. In addition to these classical languages Pali, Persian, and Prakrit [. . .]' (NEP 2020, 4.18), the policy directs resources towards Sanskrit above all other classical languages. The policy sets as a goal two years of instruction in a classical language, in public or private schools (NEP 2020, 4.19).

In addition to classical language instruction, the NEP aims to integrate 'Indian Knowledge Systems' (IKS) into all fields of study, from science and mathematics to philosophy, art and architecture, and literature (NEP 2020, 4.27). Teacher training guidelines lay out the IKS approach to chemistry, metallurgy, economics, mathematics and astronomy. For instance, the IKS teacher induction programme for chemistry and metallurgy incorporates archaeological artefacts and Sanskrit alchemical texts, and a refresher course titled 'Mathematics in India: from Vedic period to modern times' includes extensive coverage of Sanskrit mathematical treatises, with only one of nineteen units devoted to modern Indian mathematics (University Grants Commission 2023, Annexure 1A, course 2; Annexure 1B, course 5). A closer look at the subject matter reveals some of the attitudes regarding the place of Greek knowledge in relation to IKS. Indian and Greek mathematical thinkers are introduced together, at certain points, and compared, but the Greek presence is very slight. One unit includes 'The Bodhāyana Theorem (so called Pythagoras Theorem)' and in the same course, Pāṇini, the *circa* fifth-century BCE Sanskrit grammarian, is compared with Euclid (University Grants Commission 2023,

Annexure 1B, course 5). The strategy seems to be to occasionally point out corresponding concepts in Greek and Indian mathematics, while presenting the IKS as the most legitimate.

The IKS teacher training guidelines suggest that this incorporation of classical knowledge will involve discussion of ancient civilizations beyond India, but do not specify which ones, or how precisely this will work. In their induction programme, one unit of the introductory course is listed as 'India and the World: Influence of IKS on the world, knowledge exchanges with other classical civilizations, and inter-civilizational exchanges' (University Grants Commission 2023, Annexure 1A, course 1). No further details are specified. In theory, knowledge exchange between India and other classical civilizations could involve any number of topics of relevance to Greek studies, including connections and comparisons between Indian and Greek philosophy; the promulgation of Buddhist tenets in several languages, including Greek, by the Mauryan king Ashoka in the third century BCE; the Indo-Greek kingdoms; Gandharan art, and commerce between India and the Mediterranean world.

Trends in Classics teaching

Historically, Greek and Latin was taught at Jesuit institutions, and later in the British Indian school system. The Jesuit presence in India began with Francis Xavier's arrival in Goa in 1542, only two years after the founding of the order. As elsewhere, education was a central component of the Jesuit mission, and Xavier founded a Jesuit college in Goa the following year, with instruction in Latin.

Under the British Raj (1858–1947), Greek and Latin was taught, but not widely available in India, leading to controversy over the use of these languages in civil service exams. In the 1840s, the civil service exams in Madras were boycotted due to the inclusion of questions about Christianity, and prizes in Greek and Latin – 'languages that could only be learned at the private grammar school run by John Anderson' (Frykenberg 2008: 329). Phiroze Vasunia has demonstrated how the Indian Civil Service at this time privileged Greek and Latin rather than classical Indian subjects in order to exclude Indians from the service (Vasunia 2013: 193–235). In this context, he argues, Indians gravitated more towards Homer than Virgil, as Virgil was more closely aligned with British imperialism (Vasunia 2013: 239–78). Similarly interested in Greek, the nineteenth-century poet Dalpatram Dahyabhai produced a Gujarati translation of Aristophanes' *Wealth* (Vasunia 2013: 279–99).

In their study of Jesuit education in Ranchi, Athreya and co-workers note that while the number of Jesuit primary schools in Ranchi shrank after India's independence in 1947, Jesuit secondary schools expanded (Athreya et al. 2020: 97). As of 2012, there were 124 Jesuit secondary schools in India (Pinto SJ 2014: 27), including some of the most elite secondary schools in the country, such as St Xavier's Collegiate School in Kolkata (founded 1860). Since 1947, Jesuit schools have turned more towards the democratization of education, and education for social good (Pinto SJ 2014: 27). This shift in mission may explain why Greek and Latin is not a current priority at Indian Jesuit schools.

The preference for Greek myth, literature and history over Roman studies persists in India today. There are several possible reasons for this. One is the perception that Greek and Indian literature are more closely linked through Indo-European literature. Another is the historical presence of Greeks in India, as well as Central Asia, from the time of Alexander onward. For example, Greeks (*yavanas,* 'Ionians', though a broader range of Westerners) are mentioned in

Tamil and Sanskrit literature. The journal *Yavanika* (https://elinepa.org/yavanika/) is devoted to the topic of Greeks in ancient India, and Indo-Mediterranean trade is a burgeoning subject of academic research.

Foreign relations also have a part to play in Indo-Greek studies. The prime ministers of Greece and India respectively, Kyriakos Mitsotakis and Narendra Modi, have recently announced a strategic partnership between Greece and India (Goswami 2023). While there are various political and economic reasons for such a relationship, it is based in part on claims to the ancient heritage of each country, and their historical ties. In Athens, the Hellenic-Indian Society for Culture and Development, with the Athens Centre for Indian and Indo-Hellenic Studies, seeks to develop business ties between Greece and India via cultural activities, including the promotion of Indo-Greek studies.

Speaking from my own experience teaching in the English department at Ashoka, many students have previously been exposed to Greek and Latin literature and culture through other subjects in secondary school, for instance in English and History, as well as through popular culture (especially through Rick Riordan's *Percy Jackson* series, and Madeline Miller's *Song of Achilles*). It is not uncommon for students to arrive at Ashoka with knowledge of Aristotle's *Poetics* from high school English classes, and awareness of Alexander the Great from History. Faculty in the English department at Ashoka regularly incorporate Greek and Latin literature in translation into their classes, particularly works with close relationships to English literature, such as Homer's *Odyssey* and Ovid's *Metamorphoses*. My own classes focused on Greek and Latin literature in a global context, for example, comparing Aristotle's *Poetics* with the *Nāṭyaśāstra*, and reading Greek, Sanskrit and Japanese Noh dramas in translation. Students at the undergraduate and graduate level frequently engage in research with a comparative angle. One of my thesis students, Dhruvan Nair, compared Greek and Malayalam literary cultures surrounding athletics, while another, Brinda Sarma, wrote about writings attributed to Neopythagorean women and early Buddhist nuns. Greek dramatic reception in the modern world is also a topic of interest to English students at Ashoka.

Sanskrit and Old Persian are regularly offered languages at Ashoka. Although Greek and Latin language is not offered as part of the regular curriculum, six students signed up for an independent study on introductory Greek language, which I offered in Spring 2021, and over thirty attended an extra-curricular Latin reading group in Spring 2022 (though a much smaller group stuck with it over the course of the semester). Their reasons for wanting to study these languages are worth considering. In the Greek class, one student said that he wanted to study Greek in order to read the Greek edicts of Ashoka. One was interested in philology and etymology in Renaissance English literature, another had started studying Greek at a university in the US and wanted to continue, while others were driven by general curiosity. Reasons for joining the Latin reading group were similarly diverse. One graduate student wanted to read a Jesuit Latin text about Tamil Nadu, which had not been translated into English. Undergraduates expressed interest in reading Ovid in the original, and learning more about etymology and English vocabulary.

Teacher training and professional development

As discussed above, one of the stated aims of the NEP 2020 teacher training guidelines is on the inclusion of knowledge exchange between India and other classical civilizations (of which

Greece and Rome would surely be a part). The plan for training in IKS involves three programmes, master teaching training, an induction programme, and refresher courses, all with a significant focus on classical Indian knowledge.

There are a few opportunities to study Greek and Latin at the tertiary level in India. Since 1998, Jawaharlal Nehru University (JNU) in New Delhi has had a Chair in Greek, supported by the A.G. Leventis Foundation with several grants, and covering courses in Greek civilization, comparative study of India and Greece, and modern Greek language (Leventis Foundation 2023). The position is held by Vasileios Syros, a Byzantine and Ottoman historian. Anil Kumar Singh also teaches Greek language, culture, and Graeco-Indian studies in the School of Language, Literature and Culture Studies at JNU. Together with the Indo-Hellenic Research Centre in New Delhi, JNU organized a ten-day summer school in August 2023 on 'Greek Language, Culture and Civilization', open to undergraduate and graduate students, educators and professionals. Topics included Greek language, culture, history, literature and philosophy.

In Uttar Pradesh, at the Mahatma Jyotiba Phule Rohilkhand University, Bareilly, the Department of Ancient History and Culture (founded 1985) organizes conferences with the Indian Society for Greek and Roman Studies, collaborates with Greek institutions, and publishes the journal *Yavanika* on Indo-Greek topics. They also engage in teaching and research on Indo-Iranian studies, suggesting that their engagement with Greek is part of a larger conception of India in a global context.

Neighbouring countries have programmes in Greek and Roman Studies, including Greek and Latin language, at the college level. In Sri Lanka, the University of Peradeniya offers a full slate of Greek and Roman studies at the undergraduate and graduate level, covering Greek and Roman literature, philosophy, art, and history, as well as Greek and Latin language (BA through PhD), as part of their Department of Classical Languages. Weerakoddy (2010) sketches the history of Greek and Latin education in Sri Lanka, and notes that in 1978, the government encouraged classical language study, leading to the formation of the Department of Classical Languages at the University of Peradeniya in 1980. He suggests three reasons for the decline in classical studies since the independence of Sri Lanka in 1948: a shift to the sciences, a rise in interest in national culture, and the use of Tamil and Sinhala rather than English as the language of instruction. Translations from Greek and Latin into Tamil and Sinhala increase access to Graeco-Roman texts (Weerakoddy 2010: 12).

The Faculty of Classical Languages at Peradeniya advised the National Institute of Education in Sri Lanka on the creation of a secondary school curriculum in Greek and Roman Civilization, introduced in 2009 (Weerakoddy 2010: 12; National Institute of Education 2009). The teacher training manual includes a detailed curriculum, covering Hesiod's *Works and Days*, Sophocles' *Philoctetes*, Euripides' *Alcestis*, Greek history from the eighth to the fifth centuries BCE (including Greek colonization), the constitutions of Athens and Sparta, and the Graeco-Persian War (Roman civilization is not mentioned, despite the title). [Ed. See also Wickramasinghe (Sri Lanka) in this book.]

In Pakistan, the Institute of Language and Linguistics at the University of the Punjab, in Lahore, offers certificates in Greek and Latin, taught by Zechariah Qamar, who also produces interlinear translations in Greek and Urdu. The Forman Christian College in Lahore offers a certificate in Biblical Language, with training in koiné Greek and Hebrew, as a prerequisite for their MPhil in Biblical Studies.

Partnerships

The NEP 2020 emphasizes experiential learning, including taking students on field trips to historical sites and museums. Sites visited will naturally depend on where the school is located, but in some areas of the country, could certainly involve seeing Greek and Roman artefacts. A museum is being constructed in Kerala, for example, which will house the finds from Pattanam (Muziris), which include Mediterranean amphorae, glass, coins and other trade goods. Students in West Bengal might visit the Gandharan art collections at the Indian Museum Kolkata, with its fusion of Greek artistic style and Buddhist themes. A few examples of Gandharan art are on display at the National Museum in New Delhi.

There are some opportunities for students to take extra-curricular courses on topics relating to Greek studies. The Indo-Hellenic Research Centre in New Delhi organizes courses in Greek literature, history, and culture, as well as modern Greek language, which are open to learners at any stage. The Greek Club Kyklos, in Kolkata, founded by Asit Chakraborty in 1988, offers weekly Greek classes, and publishes Bengali translations of Greek texts and other works on Greek topics, including on the Greek presence in Bengal in antiquity.

Ashoka University regularly offers classes for advanced secondary school students, on a wide range of topics. These are classes of approximately three weeks duration, which are meant to give students a glimpse of the types of activities they might do in a college class, and exposure to the liberal arts model of Ashoka. In the summer of 2022, I taught one of these classes, on women in Greek myth and literature, focusing on Helen of Troy.

Conclusion

The disappearance of Greek and Latin education in India is not indicative of an absence of interest in these topics, but rather shifting goals in educational policy. The NEP 2020 makes it quite clear that the classical languages of India will see greater investment over the coming years, and that millions of school children will learn about classical Indian literatures, philosophies, civilizations and scientific accomplishments. If this plan is executed in the way that it is described in the NEP, it would surely be the largest Classics-based education system in the world. In the current political climate, it is highly unlikely that Greek and Roman studies will form a significant part of this curriculum.

Training opportunities at the college level are essential for supporting wider access to Greek and Roman studies. The distinct difference between Sri Lanka and India in this regard is surely due to the faculty of Peradeniya, who provided their expertise for the development of the Greek and Roman Civilization secondary school curriculum. I have had students at Ashoka University who are seriously interested in the study of Greek and Roman literature and history, and have engaged in fascinating research on comparative ancient literature and history, connections between India and the Mediterranean, and classical reception. Many students have asked me how they can study Greek and Latin. Realistically, in order to gain competency in these languages, they must go abroad, but for most students, this is only possible with a graduate scholarship. This puts them in a bind, as MA and PhD programmes in Classics in the UK or the US require prior study of the languages. This funnels them into English or Comparative Literature instead. Lastly, Greek and Roman studies belong not only to accredited educational institutions, but also to organizations like the Kyklos Club; in a context in which access to Greek and Latin is limited, these organizations are an essential part of the ecosystem.

References

Athreya, A., R. d'Souza and I. Goddeeris (2020), 'The Postcolonial Expansion of a Mission: Jesuit Education in Ranchi, India, after 1950', in K. Christiaens et al. (eds), *Missionary Education*. Leuven: Leuven University Press, 80–117.

Central Board of Secondary Education (2020/21), *Senior School Curriculum Class IX–X 2020–21*. New Delhi. Available online: https://cbseacademic.nic.in/curriculum_2021.html (accessed 16 October 2023).

Christiaens, K., I. Goddeeris, and P. Verstraete, eds (2020), *Missionary Education: Historical Approaches and Global Perspectives*, Leuven: Leuven University Press.

Department of School Education and Literacy, Ministry of Education, Government of India (2023), *UDISE+*. Available online: https://udiseplus.gov.in/#/home (accessed 16 October 2023).

Frykenberg, R. (2008), *Christianity in India: From Beginnings to the Present*, Oxford: Oxford University Press.

Goswami, A. (2023), 'Greece and India Become Strategic Partners', *Greek Reporter*, September 3. Available online: https://greekreporter.com/2023/09/03/strategic-partners-greece-india/ (accessed 4 October 2023).

Kingdon, G. (2022), 'The Private Schooling Phenomenon in India: A Review', *Journal of Development Studies*, 56 (10): 1795–1817.

Leventis Foundation (2023), 'Greek Chair, Jawaharlal Nehru University, New Delhi'. Available online: https://www.leventisfoundation.org/universities-institutions/greek-chair-jawaharlal-nehru-university-new-delhi (accessed 5 September 2023).

National Institute of Education, Faculty of Languages, Humanities and Social Sciences (2009), 'Greek and Roman Civilization. G.C.E. A/L. Grade 12. Teacher's Instruction Manual.' Maharagama, Sri Lanka: National Institute of Education. Available online: https://govdoc.lk/category/teacher-guides/greek-and-roman-civilization (accessed 16 October 2023).

OECD (2019), *Education at a Glance 2019: OECD indicators*, Paris: OECD Publishing.

Pinto SJ, A. (2014), 'The achievements of the Jesuit educational mission in India and the contemporary challenges it faces', *International Studies in Catholic Education*, 6 (1): 14–32.

University Grants Commission (2023), *Guidelines for Training/ Orientation of Faculty on Indian Knowledge System*, New Delhi: University Grants Commission. Available online: https://www.ugc.gov.in/pdfnews/3746302_Guidelines-for-TrainingOrientation-of-Faculty-on-Indian-Knowledge-System-(IKS).pdf (accessed 1 October 2023).

Vasunia, P. (2013), *The Classics and Colonial India*, Oxford: Oxford University Press.

Weerakoddy, D. (2010), 'Classics in Sri Lanka', *CA News*, 43: 11–13.

ISRAEL

Lisa Maurice

The Israeli Education System

Education in Israel is compulsory from kindergarten to twelfth grade, with the school programme divided into three stages: primary education (grades one to six, approximately ages six to twelve), middle school (grades seven to eight, approximately ages twelve to fourteen) and high school (grades nine to twelve, approximately ages fifteen to eighteen). Within this system there are two separate streams, for the Jewish and Arab populations respectively. The former is divided between religious and secular schools, as well a third category of ultra-orthodox independent religious schools. The latter is subdivided into two more groups: Arab and Bedouin schools, and Druze and Circassian schools. Christian children study in different streams based upon the majority population of their area. In addition, a very small number of private schools exist; these tend to reflect the philosophies of specific groups of parents (e.g. Democratic Schools), or are based on the curriculum of a foreign country (e.g. The American International School in Israel) (Maurice 2021: 468–9).

Nevertheless, the vast majority of Israeli children attend state schools, going through an educational programme that culminates in the *bagrut* matriculation examination in the final years of high school. The *bagrut* certificate is a requirement for entry into higher education and one of the criteria used for selection of applicants to elite military units. Grades are heavily based on national examinations administered by the ministry of education, although a recent reform has introduced a larger component that is examined internally by the school. The *bagrut* encompasses many subjects at different levels of difficulty, with the 2-unit level being the lowest and the 5-unit level the highest. To qualify for the certificate a minimum grade of 55 per cent must be achieved in each of the exams, which include a number of compulsory core subjects: English language (written and oral) and literature (3–5 units), Mathematics (3–5 units), Civics (2 units), History (2 units) Hebrew or Arabic (2 units) and literature (2 units) (Jewish philosophy is also compulsory in state religious schools). Biblical and religious texts are also examined in varying amounts of units according to the nature of the school. In addition, at least one 5-unit elective must be taken, while 2-unit disciplines can be expanded to up to five units, to reach a total of a minimum of twenty-one units required for certification, although many students complete thirty or more. In addition to these examinations, students must complete 180 hours of physical education, thirty hours each of two 'general education' subjects, ninety hours introduction to science and 180 hours volunteer work (Decalo 2016). Classics does not form any part of the compulsory curriculum but does appear peripherally in a few subjects.

The history of Classics in Israeli education

In Jewish tradition, the classical world, in the form of the Hellenistic and Roman conquering powers, have always been the enemy (Maurice 2016: 310–11). As a result of this opposition, and despite the treasure trove of classical remains that fill the country, the ancient world has always had a negligible presence in the modern State of Israel, where the Biblical tales have greatly taken precedence over those of Graeco-Roman culture. There is none of the common heritage identification that is found in the United Kingdom, for example, despite the fact that the Graeco-Roman culture played perhaps an even more pivotal role in this geographic region than it did in the UK. Not only did religious Jews feel no need to include the classical tradition in their education systems but even secular Zionists regarded the Bible, upon which their ideology was based, as paramount (Maurice 2021: 465).

As a result of this lack of identification with Greece and Rome, Classics plays only a marginal role in the Israeli education system. This is despite the dreams of some of the early founders of what would become modern Israel; David Ben-Gurion, first Prime Minister, was an admirer of Graeco-Roman culture who founded a national project intended to translate into Hebrew great books from all nations and generations, and in particular classical works (Baratz 2023: 11). Similarly, the ideology of those who established the education system was that the new state should become a 'civilized', educated place, on a par with Europe, where most of them had grown up and been educated. Thus, for instance, when the first Hebrew language high school was founded in Tel Aviv in 1905, it was modelled on the European system, and given the title of *Gymnasia*. Latin was on the curriculum as a matter of course, since the stated aim of the *Gymnasia* was to provide an education which was the same as at 'every high school in Europe and America – Bible and Talmud; past language and its literature; languages: French, German, English, and Latin; geometry and algebra, [...] physics and chemistry, zoology and botany, main geology and mineralogy; history, drawing, etc.' Similarly, when the first university, the Hebrew University, was founded in 1925, Greek and Latin were among the first subjects taught at that institution, although, again, the justification for this was that it was argued that these languages were necessary for the understanding of, and participation in, Bible Studies (Maurice 2016: 311–12).

Nevertheless, other classical texts soon began to be taught, a process especially stimulated by the immigration of some superb classical scholars who had fled persecution in Europe: Victor (Avigdor) Tcherikover, Hans (Yohanan) Lewy and Max Schwabe were the founding fathers of classical studies in Israel, and all were products of the high-level German scholarship of the beginning of the twentieth century, and students of the great names of that scholarship – Ulrich von Wilamowitz-Moellendorff, Eduard Norden and others. The influence and approach of these three men coloured classical studies in Israel during its inception and development, and classical philology was, therefore, the focus of Israeli scholarship. From these beginnings, classical studies in Israel expanded, as these scholars were joined by others, and the founding of more universities in the 1950s and 1960s (Bar-Ilan University in 1955, Tel Aviv University in 1956, Haifa University in 1963 and Ben-Gurion University of the Negev in 1969) provided more scope for the teaching of Classics. The Israel Society for the Promotion of Classical Studies (ISPCS) was founded in 1971 in order 'to promote the study of Classics in Israel and to foster relations between Israeli classicists and colleagues from abroad'. Three years later, the journal *Scripta Classica Israelica* appeared for the first time (Maurice 2021: 467–8).

Despite these developments, Classics remained – and remains – marginal in Israeli society, and in particular in Israeli education. In neither of the Jewish streams of Israeli education was the study of the arts that underlie Western civilization seen as important. For the secular education track, the ideals of settling the land and socialism, as exemplified by the kibbutz system, meant that Western humanities were regarded as irrelevant at best, and dangerously elitist at worst (Gazi'el 1996, 42). Thus, the State Education Law of 1953 aimed to base the foundations of elementary education on, 'the values of Jewish culture and the achievements of science, on love of the homeland and loyalty to the state of Israel, on work in agriculture and in the crafts, on Halutzic [pioneering] preparation, on a society based on freedom, equality and tolerance, mutual aid and love for one's fellow man' (Gazi'el 1996: 39).

No mention of the arts or humanities features in this description. On the other hand, for the religious track, the Jewish texts and culture were central, to the exclusion of those of Western civilization. It should also be noted that the mass immigration of Sephardic Jews (of North African and Asian origin) in the 1950s, and Ethiopian Jews in the 1980s and 1990s, neither of which groups had roots in the Western classical tradition, meant that this tradition was unknown and irrelevant to a large proportion of the population. This led to clashes of ideology between the immigrants and the Ministry of Education, whose employees hailed from Europe, and ultimately, decades later to the founding of the Sephardic Ultra-Orthodox (Shas) school system, in which the humanities are even more insignificant (Maurice 2016: 314–15).

Classics within the formal curriculum

History

As a result, schoolchildren will encounter the Greeks or the Romans within only very limited contexts within the school curriculum. One of these contexts is as part of the history curriculum. At pre-high school level, there are two units within the history syllabi for sixth to ninth grades that deal with the ancient world. One, entitled 'The Graeco-Roman world and the Jews', covers classical and Hellenistic Greece and the Hellenistic encounter with Judaism. The second, 'The Roman world and the Jews', focuses on Rome, Judea and the rise of Christianity (Maurice 2021). Some of the topics included in these units are: the characteristics of Hellenism; Israel in the struggle between the Seleucid and Ptolemy kingdoms; Hellenism in Judea; Antiochus' decree; the Maccabean Revolt; Judas Maccabaeus; the Great Jewish Revolt, The Uprising of the Jewish Diaspora (116–117 CE) and Bar Kokhba (Baratz 2023: 14). Within the history curriculum, both Greece and Rome, therefore, are taught mainly in a Jewish context, that of the 'Second Temple Period', where the impact – almost entirely negative – of these cultures upon the Jews is stressed.

Literature

The other area of the general curriculum in which students may be exposed to the classical world is literature. The ninth grade syllabus features as an option in the form of four stories from classical myth: Echo and Narcissus, Orpheus and Eurydice, Daedalus and Icarus, and Midas' Golden Touch. This is only one option out of a whole range of texts that constitute each category, so the number of students who study them is probably limited, but two of the stories, Daedalus and Icarus and Orpheus and Eurydice, are also included as part of the selection of world literature for the *bagrut* syllabus, within the category of 'short stories' (the other genres studied are drama, poetry and novels). In addition to the short stories, a selection from the *Odyssey* has been chosen as an option on occasion. In the summer of 2014, for example, the fourth unit of the literature course, for those choosing literature as a specialization elective, and taking a full five units of literature, included this. Perhaps surprisingly, the text selected, in prose translation by Ahuvia Kahana from 1996, was not that of Odysseus' adventures on his wanderings – the Cyclops, the Lotus Eaters, the Sirens, Scylla and Charybdis – but rather Book 23, in which the reunion of Penelope and Odysseus, and the hero's subsequent departure for Laertes' orchard, are recounted (Maurice 2021: 471–2).

Within the drama section of the course, students study two plays, one of which is modern, and the other a tragedy, either by Shakespeare or Sophocles. A very limited amount of time is therefore devoted to the plays, only one option of which is of classical content. The situation has also been exacerbated by the new programme introduced in 2015, which mandated the removal of the listing of specific material on which students would be tested in each matriculation examination, thus leading to more open questions to allow for the wider variation in texts now studied. The reform also reduced the content of the syllabus by 30 per cent. Despite these alterations, the presence of the Greek play was maintained, since, according to Shlomo Hertzig, the central subject supervisor for literature of the Education Ministry, Greek tragedy was felt to be an essential core element in the study of literature. Each of the two dramas (one either classical or Shakespearian, one modern) is then examined either internally by the teacher, through course work, or externally via written exam, but the choice as to which is examined in each way is left to the teacher (Maurice 2021: 472).

Theatre studies

In addition to the literature elective, there is also a theatre studies elective, in which the role of classical drama is more notable than in the literature elective. Of the three units that comprise the course, the first is centred on dramatic theory ('The language of the theatre'), and the third on twentieth- and twenty-first-century Western and Israeli drama. The second, however, provides a choice between the study of either classical drama or of Shakespeare, with students being examined on either a Shakespearian tragedy and comedy, or a Greek tragedy and a new comedy. Thus, it is possible to spend one-third of the entire course on classical drama. Reliable information, however, about how many students have chosen these options is not available.

Those choosing to teach a Greek tragedy may choose either Sophocles' *Antigone* or the *Oedipus Rex*, both of which are, of course, taught in Hebrew translation. The *Antigone* is available in six different translations in Hebrew: one by Shlomo Dykman, originally from 1966 but reprinted in 1971 and 1980, one by Carmi Charny (from English translations rather than from the original Greek) from 1970, one by Aharon Shabtai from 1990, another by Shimon Buzaglo from 2007, and the most recent by Devorah Gilulah (2014). The *Oedipus Rex* was also translated by Dykman (1964), Shabtai (1981), Buzaglo (2012) and Gilulah (2015), as well as by Tchernokovsky (1929). Only those translations by Dykman, Carmi and Shabtai are listed in the *bagrut* syllabus, however, rather than the more recent versions, in itself a reflection of the fact that the texts included in the syllabus have remained more or less unchanged for the past decade (Maurice 2021: 472–3).

Philosophy

One further area within which the classical world plays a role is a further *bagrut* elective, namely Philosophy, taught in relatively few schools, but in which Greek philosophy plays a prominent role. Compulsory texts of this elective include Plato's *Apology* or a section from *Gorgias*, the allegory of the cave from the *Republic*, and some selections from Aristotle's *Nicomachean Ethics 1–2*. In addition, there are a number of optional texts by classical authors, including Plato (extracts from the *Meno*, *Theaetetus*, *Phaedo* and the *Symposium*), Aristotle (excerpts from *Politics*, *Poetics*, *On Interpretation*, further chapters of the *Nicomachean Ethics*), Longinus (extracts from *On the Sublime*), and Arrian (a selection of the *Enchiridion of Epictetus*) (Baratz 2023: 15).

Classical civilization and Latin

Finally, there is one small area in which school students may now truly undertake what is regarded in many parts of the world as Classical Studies. The Israel Arts and Science Academy, a school aimed at gifted students, has a unique Humanities Department which accepts about fifteen pupils per year. Within this department, students follow a three-year programme that focuses on the central texts and ideas of Western culture, with three hours a week in the first year dedicated to Classical Civilization and Ancient History. In addition, all students in the programme must study either Latin or Arabic. The Latin course, which has been in existence for nine years and has produced dozens of graduates, lasts for the entire three years, covering the same material as university level elementary Latin. Completion of the course earns the student an exemption from this study at university should they go on to study Classics. As a development of this programme, Ella Kaplan and Amit Baratz developed a full five-unit Latin *bagrut* elective which received official ministry approval in 2022, and around ten students have taken up this option in 2023. While this number is tiny, it is a start and it remains to be seen how, and if, it will develop (Baratz 2023: 15–16).

Trends in the Israeli teaching of Classics

While the presence of Classical Studies within the Israeli education system is minimal, the choices made with regard to material selected is illuminating. It is notable and striking, for example, that none of the four mythological tales that feature in the literature curriculum feature the Greek gods centrally; although this is a syllabus for both religious and secular schools, the conservative nature of the wider Israeli society perhaps makes the use of explicitly pagan deities uncomfortable enough that such tales are not a natural choice. Secondly, the selected stories are predominantly didactic, stressing moral lessons in some way. Again, the uneasiness with mythology in general and paganism in particular may well have led to an, albeit subconscious, choice of myths whose usage could be justified by such elements. Similarly, the choice of Book 23 of the *Odyssey* may be the result of the fact that in this book the emphasis is upon the human rather than the divine. As such, the interaction between husband and wife is the main focus of the teaching of this unit (Maurice 2021: 472).

In the study of drama, whether in the Theatre Studies or Literature electives, although the teacher can choose between *Antigone* and *Oedipus Rex*, the former is by far the more popular of the two. This is particularly the case within the religious educational stream, where *Antigone* is not only more popular than the *Oedipus*, but also chosen more than other modern playwrights, such as Ibsen and Brecht. The reason for this popularity, especially among the religious education stream, according to Tali Yaniv, the Chief Supervisor for literature in the religious stream, is that the students connect more with the *Antigone* (Maurice 2021: 473–4). This is due both to the strong female protagonist on which the plays centres but also to the conflict inherent in the play between the compulsions of religion (in the form of the laws of the gods) and those of the state (in the form of the king). Religious pupils living in the wider secular world identify strongly with this dilemma, seeing great relevance in the themes of the play.

An indication of both the popularity of *Antigone* and the identification with the play for religious students is reflected by a set of lesson plans for teachers, produced by the Lev Lada'at organization, founded by the Department of Religious Education in cooperation with Herzog College (www.levladaat.org/data/upl/UFCK/10955_Lev_ladaat_A4.pdf). This supports 'Educational Subject Supervisors in the National Religious stream, promoting learning in different fields of knowledge, [and] acting as partners in the development of teaching and learning materials'. Among these materials is an extensive page on the teaching of *Antigone*, specifically targeted for this audience. On this page, in addition to traditional materials analysing the play, its themes are compared to classic Jewish texts, with Maimonides' Aristotelian-influenced principle of the golden mean compared with Antigone and Creon's excesses and hubris, with the humility of Moses. Finally, a modern Hebrew song is shown, through a YouTube clip and the written lyrics, and students are invited to make comparisons between the messages of the ancient drama and the modern product of popular culture (Maurice 2021: 475–6).

In fact, the popularity of the *Antigone* is not confined to the religious sector, as is demonstrated by the wide range of Hebrew language resources created for those studying the play. Multiple online lesson plans and audio-visual aids are available, and many of these are highly imaginative and well produced. Some are the product of professional educational websites, supported by the Ministry of Education, such as the Lev Lada'at site mentioned above. Others are devised or collected by individual teachers or schools, or by subject coordinators. Yet more are found on websites aimed at children, which include educational aids for students, and cover a range of subjects. Although there is no supervision or regulation of these items, which are submitted by individuals who contribute them unsolicited, the standard is generally high. In a clear bid to ease the difficulties, and appeal to students through audio-visual resources, all the websites link to YouTube, which contains parts of the play in the only video version that contains Hebrew subtitles. This is, however, the rather dated 1986 BBC production of *The Theban Plays* directed by Don Taylor. Despite the age of the film, it seems still to be in demand, judging by the dozen or so comments attached by those wanting clips of more of the play, although this may be as much from an inability to understand it purely from a written text as from appreciation of the production itself (Maurice 2021: 476–8).

A final point that should be made as somewhat of a counterweight to the absence of Classics in the formal education system is the enthusiasm for classical mythology within Israeli youth, which sometimes creeps into pedagogy (Maurice 2020). One such area is in the programmes for gifted children which exist either in schools or as after-school courses (Vidergor & Reiter 2008: 39–40), where classical mythology often appears, although no official or organized syllabus for the subject exists, with everything being left up to the individual teachers (Maurice 2021: 478–9). Another example is the programme developed by myself and Ayelet Peer for autistic youth, which focuses on helping them understand and cope with complex emotions (Maurice 2021: 479–82).

Conclusion

Classics has never played more than a very marginal role in the Israeli education system, featuring only tangentially in the history curriculum at 6th grade, and minimally in the literature syllabus in the final grades of high school. Where Classics does appear in these contexts, it is flavoured with a local slant that interprets the Graeco-Roman presence through the eyes of Jewish tradition and in keeping with the sensibilities of modern Jewish Orthodoxy. Nevertheless, there is interest and enthusiasm for the ancient world both among students and teachers, and indeed more widely, and it is to be hoped that this will continue and perhaps even grow, especially in light of new programmes such as the Latin elective in the *bagrut* matriculation.

References

Baratz, A. (2023), 'Greece and Rome in Israeli Schools', *Scripta Classica Israelica*, 42: 9–18.

Decalo, M. (March 2016), 'Graduation in The Israeli Education System' (https://meyda.education.gov.il/files/KishreiChutz/theisraelieducatinsystem30032016.ppt).

Gazi'el, Ḥ. (1996), *Politics and Policy-making in Israel's Education System*, Brighton, UK: Sussex Academic Press.

Maurice, L. (2016), 'The Reception of Classical Mythology in Israeli Children's Fiction', in K. Marciniak (ed.), *Our Mythical Childhood*, Leiden: Brill, 309–32.

Maurice, L. (2020), 'Percy Jackson and Israeli Fanfiction: A Case Study', in K. Marciniak (ed.), *Our Mythical Hope*, Warsaw: University of Warsaw Press.

Maurice, L. (2021), 'Classical Mythology and the Israeli Education System', in L. Maurice (ed.), *Our Mythical Education: The Reception of Classical Myth Worldwide in Schools, 1900–2019*, Warsaw: University of Warsaw Press, 465–83.

Vidergor, H. and S. Reiter (2008), 'Satisfaction with school among gifted Israeli students studying in various frameworks', *Gifted and Talented International*, 23 (1): 39–40.

JAPAN

Shiro Kawashima

Introduction

In Japan, classical studies are addressed in higher education: they include languages, literature, philosophy, history, and art from ancient Greece and Rome. Some universities offer specialized programmes and courses in classical studies to provide students with a comprehensive understanding of the cultural and intellectual heritage of the classical world. In addition, non-formal educational institutions offer education in classical studies as part of lifelong education.

The education system in Japan is divided into three main parts. Compulsory education consists of six years of elementary school and three years of junior high school. After that, high school lasts three years, and undergraduate university programmes commonly span four years.

Ancient history and some basic information about classical literature are studied during this educational path. Generally speaking, classical languages are not taught in elementary and junior high school, while some high schools included Latin in their curriculum. However, according to a survey in 2014, there were thirty-nine students in four schools, which decreased to twenty students in one school by 2017, and as of 2021, no schools were offering these courses (Ministry of Education 2021). Greek and Latin are little or none in Japan's high school education.

On the other hand, classical studies education at the university level encompasses a wide range of subjects. Despite the lack of exact statistical data, it is worth noting that more than 130 universities have full-time academic positions in classical studies. This can be estimated by looking at the information about the members of the Classical Society of Japan (CSJ), which was established in 1950 and currently boasts around 400 members, serving as the core of academic societies in Japan focused on classical studies. Moreover, many more universities offer courses in these disciplines taught by part-time lecturers. Such universities provide at least some form of classical studies education.

Most Japanese students approach Greek and Latin at university for the first time. Students specializing in classical studies and those pursuing related studies, such as Western literature, need to take classes in Greek and Latin languages. Moreover, even if unrelated to their majors, students who have developed an interest in the Classics through manga, movies, video games, etc., are also often motivated to take these courses.

At Kyoto University, several courses focus solely on introductory grammar. Approximately ninety students enrol in introductory Greek grammar each year, and around 160 students choose to study Latin grammar in total. Generally, there is a tendency among students to choose Latin over Greek. Consequently, several universities offer only Latin without providing Greek courses.

Furthermore, there is a concept of lifelong education in Japan, and many institutions facilitate non-formal learning besides the formal education system. Universities offer various courses in the form of open seminars and Extension Programmes. In addition, large and small companies provide non-formal learning opportunities. Unlike civic education, typically conducted in community centres, these institutions are commercial entities and provide courses as part of their business operations. According to market research, such institutions' market size in 2022 amounted to ¥33 billion (£182 million / $220 million).

Formal education in classical studies within schools is limited in Japan and classical education typically begins at the university level. On the other hand, even after graduating from university, individuals can begin or continue studying classical subjects through non-formal educational institutions. This chapter presents an insight into Japan's classical studies education in situations like these.

Opportunity and motivation to study classical subjects

University students of Classics are expected to enrol in Greek and Latin language courses. However, classical subjects are commonly offered as optional courses. At some time, Latin was mandatory in majors such as English Literature and Italian Literature, but it gradually shifted to an elective in many universities. Moreover, even if students are delving into ancient history or philosophy, studying ancient languages remains optional at some universities.

Not all universities offer Greek or Latin. Therefore, whether students can take classical language courses or not depends on the university they attend. Nonetheless, in universities with relatively comprehensive humanities programmes, these courses are offered, and some students may even choose their university based on the presence of classical studies. However, there is a growing tendency for practical subjects such as science, computer studies, or business English conversation to be considered more important than humanities and to reduce the emphasis on classical languages.

In the realm of education, similar issues have emerged in the teaching of Japanese Classics, sparking debates. The instruction of Japanese classical literature (*Kobun*) and classical Chinese (*Kanbun*), both mandatory subjects, has gradually declined in prioritization across all levels of public education, from elementary to high school. The requirement of Japanese classical education has elicited divergent opinions, with some advocating for their complete removal from the curriculum.

The Science Council of Japan (2020) compiled recommendations for high school language education, expressing concerns about the current state of education and emphasizing the significance of Japanese Classics. Additionally, they proposed curriculum revisions that promote an awareness of the continuity between ancient and contemporary language and culture. In formulating these recommendations, reference was made to Greek and Latin language education status in Western countries. Some people believe studying Japanese Classics is essential for understanding modern cultures. Similarly, Western classical knowledge is considered indispensable to fully understanding European history and culture.

Furthermore, the ancient civilizations of the West are generally well-known in Japan. Classical studies began in the sixteenth century, and the teaching of Latin also began in mission schools (cf. Taida 2017 and 2018). Despite intermittent periods, the history of classical studies in Japan is long.

Consequently, books on ancient history, philosophy and literature are prevalent, and numerous publications are released yearly. Children read Aesop's fables and Greek mythology in picture books. There is continuous availability of manga, movies, games, and other forms of media that revolve around themes such as ancient history and mythology, as Kawana (2018) and Scilabra (2018) demonstrate in several examples. In addition, Greek tragedies and comedies are often performed on stage. Japanese translations of Greek and Roman works are also published constantly. For instance, Kyoto University Press's *KUP Greek and Latin Classics* [*Seiyo Koten Sousyo*] has published over 160 volumes, aiming to translate the entire collection of classical works into Japanese.

Even for those interested in learning Greek and Latin, the opportunity is typically limited to a few years after entering university. Despite these constraints, the importance of Classics is acknowledged, and its popularity drives an active publication of materials related to Classics. People who wish to study Classics often pursue self-directed learning through non-formal educational institutions.

For instance, NHK Culture Center and Asahi Culture Center offer various courses of lifelong learning and organize nationwide classes as a business. These learning organizations can serve multiple purposes, including obtaining certifications, addressing educational gaps, and striving for skill enhancement in hobbies. Furthermore, many people take humanities classes to enrich their lives. In these institutions, alongside hobby classes such as dance lessons and flower arrangements, some courses offer the study of classical languages, ancient history, and Plato's philosophy. Moreover, some classes focus on the reading of Homeric Greek. Each class follows a progressive learning programme and has a minimum of twenty participants of various ages in each class.

There are also informal educational institutions, such as Ludus Collinus [*Yamano Gakko*], the Tokyo School of Classics [*Tokyo Koten Gakusya*], and KUNILABO, specializing in classical studies and humanities. They offer a curriculum that begins with introductory grammar and progresses to systematic mastery of classical languages. Additionally, they provide courses in philological studies or reading original texts. For instance, students learn to read Sophocles' tragedies and Virgil's epics in their original languages. Although they are small organizations, it is noteworthy that such institutions specializing in the Classics, like the Tokyo School of Classics, have been successful as a business.

These non-formal educational institutions provide opportunities for individuals who want to study classical studies and many instructors in these institutions hold academic positions, such as university professors. Many classical scholars recognize that one of their responsibilities is to promote classical knowledge to the broader Japanese public.

Teaching Classics

When it comes to education in classical studies, disciplines such as philosophy, history, literature and language each have their distinct methodologies. University courses come in various forms, with classes designed for specialized students in classical studies that involve reading and interpreting Greek or Latin texts and lectures for non-specialized students that utilize translations. Moreover, the approach can vary depending on the teacher.

Classical language education in Japan tends to be relatively conservative. The primary emphasis lies in acquiring a solid foundation in grammar by using textbooks as a principal resource. Classes typically begin with introductory grammar and progress to the intermediate level for enhanced reading comprehension. Occasionally, exercises such as Latin writing are also conducted. In beginner reading classes, students read relatively learner-friendly texts, such as works by Caesar and Plato, referring to straightforward commentaries. Students delve into more specialized and intricate textual materials as the curriculum advances.

Texts in Japanese catering to classical language learners come in various forms, ranging from beginner-level textbooks to specialized and detailed grammar books. Older textbooks, such as the Greek grammar written by Tanaka and Matsudaira (1951) and the Latin textbook by Nakayama (1987), are typically structured for students aiming to study Classics at the university. These books often omit detailed explanations because professors are supposed to provide them verbally. However, in recent years, the interest in classical languages has grown among those taking it up due to cultural interest, and opportunities to learn classical languages are increasingly available beyond universities. As a result, relatively new textbooks exhibit more attentive considerations.

For example, the Latin elementary textbook by Yamashita (2013) contains detailed explanations of learning how to read classical languages. These explanations provide careful guidance to beginners. This textbook extensively employs classical sentences in its examples and exercises, and this approach aims to embrace the needs of people interested in Classics as part of their cultural education. The Greek language textbook by Horikawa (2021) follows a comparable approach. Instead of simply listing conjugation tables, it offers detailed grammar explanations that readers can easily understand.

The Latin textbook by Kawashima (2016) offers careful and straightforward explanations by incorporating easily comprehensible examples and exercises. Thanks to its colourful layout, this book makes studying Latin easy and enjoyable by structuring it as a contemporary foreign language and including explanations of Roman culture. On the other hand, there are texts aimed at specialized learners, such as the comprehensive and detailed Greek language textbook by Ciesko (2016).

It must be said that older textbooks remain beneficial, especially in university classes, thanks to teachers' ingenuity. Several reading texts with beginner-friendly commentary are written in Japanese for beginner reading classes, but more are needed. Thus, many classes use texts written in English. A significant problem in classical language education is the scarcity of comprehensive and easily accessible dictionaries. Many textbooks include vocabulary lists that cover the words used in those textbooks. However, when examining a word's usage or attempting to read at a more advanced level, learners often must use Latin and Greek dictionaries in English, French or German. Fortunately, this gap is close to being filled by the forthcoming publication of extensive dictionaries in Japanese.

Some students also study classical subjects through studying abroad. Universities offer various programmes that students can relatively easily access, but their economic circumstances strongly influence these opportunities. University tuition fees are high, and Japan's scholarship system is insufficient. The issue of students' socio-economic status causing educational inequality is severe and requires improvement.

Recent advancements in digital technology have changed the approach to education. Online classes became familiar in universities and non-formal educational institutions during the Covid-19 era. Equipment, technology, and skills for online education became widespread, and especially in non-formal educational institutions, the impact was significant. Previously, the main users were people who had plenty of free time, but thanks to the realization of online courses, participation of working students in their twenties and thirties has increased. They are free from the constraints of location and time. Moreover, accessing recorded classes has become possible, in case one misses a session. Having gained these new participants, non-formal educational institutions have continued with online courses, and more flexible participation methods are becoming increasingly popular.

The forum 'Classical Studies and Digital Humanities' took place at the annual conference of the Classical Society of Japan in 2023. While discussing the use of digital technology in classical education, a programme for using manuscripts during original text reading was introduced. For instance, while reading Ovid's *Metamorphoses*, digital images of related manuscripts were projected onto a monitor alongside the critical edition of Oxford Classical Texts, allowing for comparing different versions. This initiative aids in acquiring manuscript reading skills and enhancing skills of textual critique. Furthermore, it led to an expansion of curiosity among participants about ancient and medieval times.

At this forum, the attempt to create practice exercises for classical Greek language learners by using generative Artificial Intelligence (AI) tools was demonstrated. This activity aims to provide supplementary teaching materials for textbooks. For instance, by instructing a generative AI, it becomes possible to make examples of sentences suitable for demonstrating the grammatical concept of relative pronouns based on text in the style of Plato's dialogues, even if those sentences actually do not exist. Various sentences can be composed by using specific words and different cases, allowing the creation of fill-in-the-blank questions where students can input the appropriate words easily. Alternatively, it might be enjoyable to devise examples of sentences that depict unrealistic scenarios, which would have been impossible in ancient times. While AI-generated sentences require occasional instructor adjustments to ensure accuracy and coherence at this current stage, they can be valuable and distinctive teaching tools.

Teacher training and professional development opportunities

It must be said that Japan's training system for future teachers of Classics needs to improve. On one hand, the government trains teachers from elementary to high school in general subjects. On the other hand, teaching at universities requires the qualities of researchers, but it does not necessarily demand teaching methods or educational skills. Therefore, there is no special teacher training to teach Latin and Greek. Educational approaches can vary across classrooms depending on each educator's creativity, aptitude and effort.

In contrast to the extensive research on modern foreign language teaching methodologies, comprehensive educational studies of teaching methodologies for Greek and Latin need to evolve more, with an apparent need for scholarly monographs or instructional manuals in these domains. Considering this situation, especially targeting young researchers and post-doctoral fellows, lectures on teaching methods at the university level are increasingly being organized under the leadership of various academic societies. Such teacher training aims to improve by sharing appropriate teaching techniques for each discipline.

In the already mentioned 'Classical Studies and Digital Humanities' forum, discussions about the application of digital technology in classical education highlighted notable merits and incredible potential but also underscored some anxiety. For instance, there was a lively debate about the new digital technologies that should be incorporated into didactical methods. Participants discussed the usefulness of digital tools that automatically identify the conjugations of verbs and the meanings of each word. Digital technology can relieve the suffering of memorizing conjugations and looking up words. However, grappling with dictionaries and conjugation tables remains crucial for organizing information into a cohesive understanding beyond acquiring discrete pieces of information. The melding of tradition and new technology in classical education calls for re-examining educational perspectives.

Collaboration between schools and classical organizations

There is no systematic connection between schools and organizations related to classical studies, such as universities and associations in Japan. Generally speaking, reducing the distance between the quality of high school and university programmes has become a pressing issue. Therefore, collaboration between these two institutions is recognized as necessary, and various efforts are underway.

Classical studies, in particular, are rarely taught in schools, and even the academic field of classical studies has yet to be widely recognized. Indeed, even in universities, only some departments use the label 'Classics' and scholars in this field are often affiliated with various other departments. For example, ancient history falls under the History or Western History Department, while ancient philosophy is part of the Philosophy Department. At Kyoto University, Classics, Ancient Philosophy and Ancient History are each categorized separately within the Faculty of Letters. Furthermore, researchers in Roman law belong to the Faculty of Law, while ancient architecture is studied in the Faculty of Engineering.

To make it more accessible, the Classical Society of Japan (https://clsoc.jp/csj.html) utilizes its website to promote classical studies and facilitate communication with non-specialists. On their website, they publish general essays on classical studies and have a Q&A section where non-experts, including school students, can ask questions about classical topics, and researchers from the Classical Society of Japan provide answers.

Non-formal educational institutions, which anyone can access, also expand opportunities for classical education. Furthermore, teaching at non-formal educational institutions provides young researchers with valuable experience and a meaningful career development avenue, or it suggests an alternative way to engage with classical studies. Teachers in these institutions are often classical scholars, including university professors and post-doctoral researchers, associated with the Classical Society of Japan. Therefore, non-formal educational institutions can smoothly collaborate with academic societies and universities. Considering the current situation in Japan, cooperative relationships between the three will be essential to developing classical studies.

Conclusion

In Japan, classical education primarily revolves around universities. The development of classical studies at the school level is not highly anticipated. However, there is a growing interest in Classics among Japanese people, and classical studies often become a pursuit after schooling or university education.

In addition to Open Courses or Community Education affiliated with universities, non-formal educational institutions also cater to the aspirations of those who wish to study classical subjects. The fact that these institutions operate as viable businesses underscores the demand for classical education beyond traditional academic settings. Classical studies are not limited to formal education but extend to lifelong learning. These perspectives prompt a re-evaluation of the role of classical education in Japan and open up new possibilities.

References

Ciesko, M. (2016), *ΓΡΑΜΜΑΤΙΚΗ ΤΗΣ ΑΤΤΙΚΗΣ ΔΙΑΛΕΚΤΟΥ* (古典ギリシア語文典), trans. K. Hirayama, Tokyo: Hakusuisya.

Horikawa, H. (2021), *Elementary Ancient Greek: Basic Language Learning Series* (しっかり学ぶ初級古典ギリシャ語), Tokyo: Beret Publishing.

Kawana, S. (2018), 'Cool Rome and Warm Japan: *Thermae Romae* and the Promotion of Japanese Everyday Culture', in A. Renger and F. Xin (eds), *Receptions of Greek and Roman Antiquity in East Asia*, Leiden: Brill, 259–86.

Kawashima, S. (2016), *Learning Basic Latin* (基本から学ぶラテン語), Tokyo: Natsumesha.

Ministry of Education (2021), *Report on International Exchange and More at High Schools* (高等学校等における国際交流等の状況について), Available online: https://www.mext.go.jp/a_menu/koutou/ryugaku/koukousei/1323946.htm (accessed 10 September 2023).

Nakayama, T. (1987), *Classica Grammatica Latina*, Tokyo: Hakusuisha.

Science Council of Japan (2020), *Improvement of High School Japanese Language Education* (高校国語教育の改善に向けて), Available online: https://www.scj.go.jp/ja/info/kohyo/kohyo-24-t290-7-abstract.html (accessed 10 September 2023).

Scilabra, C. (2018), 'Back to the Future: Reviving Classical Figures in Japanese Comics', in A. Renger and F. Xin (eds), *Receptions of Greek and Roman Antiquity in East Asia*, Leiden: Brill, 287–309.

Taida, I. (2017), 'The earliest history of European language education in Japan: Focusing on Latin education by Jesuit missionaries', *Classical Receptions Journal*, 9 (4): 566–86.

Taida, I. (2018), 'History and Reception of Greek and Latin Studies in Japan 73', in A. Renger and F. Xin (eds), *Receptions of Greek and Roman Antiquity in East Asia*, Leiden: Brill, 73–88.

Tanaka, M. and C. Matsudaira (1951), *Introduction to Ancient Greek* (ギリシア語入門), Tokyo: Iwanami Shoten.

Yamashita, T. (2013), *Elementary Latin: Basic Language Learning Series* (しっかり学ぶ初級ラテン語), Tokyo: Beret Publishing.

KURDISTAN (IRAQ)

Botan Maghdid

Classical history within the Kurdistan Regional-Iraq (KRI) curricula is required but is an ancillary facet of the region's educational framework. Spanning twelve years, after kindergarten, pupils at the age six go to primary school then up to secondary school. The Kurdistan school system mandates the inclusion of history at various developmental stages: Circle 2 (ages 10–12), Circle 3 (ages 13–15), and within the Literary branch during secondary school (ages 16–18).

The establishment of the Kurdistan Regional Government (KRG) in 1992 marked a pivotal juncture in the educational landscape of KRI, particularly concerning the treatment of history as a subject in schools. Preceding this milestone, the historical narrative of Kurdistan had consistently suffered marginalization under successive Iraqi governments, where the Kurdish history was subsumed within the broader Iraqi historical context, resulting in its effective omission from the curricula. After the establishment of the KRG, history as a subject in the school curricula has become a vital component of endeavours to cultivate and disseminate a unified Kurdish identity, integral to an overarching nation-building project.

This intentional emphasis on 'Our' history, juxtaposed with 'Other' histories, has led to the notable prioritization of Kurdistan's history, concurrently marginalizing other historical periods, including classical history. It is imperative to underscore, however, that this emphasis does not seek to engage in contentious discourse with modern Iraqi historiography and representations of classical history, particularly that of the Romans, who are often equated with modern Western imperialism. Quite the opposite, despite its rare discussion in the curriculum, the history of the Greeks or Romans is not depicted as that of occupiers, imperialists or oppressors, which is a departure from the narrative that may have been prevalent in the former Iraqi school curriculum.

In the curriculum for Circles 2 and 3, the exploration of classical history is markedly rare. Mere paragraphs in the *social subjects* book, in Circle 3, is dedicated to this subject, homing in on Alexander of Macedon's conquests in the East and the subsequent division of his empire among military officers. The ensuing Hellenistic culture, emerging from the dynamic interplay between the 'West' and 'East', is cursorily presented in these paragraphs (Sharif et al. 2023: 74).

A subsequent discussion of the classical history appears in the 'History of [world] Civilisations' in Circle 4 (Pshdary et al. 2021), a comprehensive guide to world history civilizations. Despite its 224 pages, a meagre eleven (pages 87–97) are earmarked for Greek civilization, with an additional eight pages allocated to Roman civilization (pages 98–105). Notably, the Greek segment enjoys a more profound exploration, delving into political systems, religion, the Olympic games, and philosophical thought.

While the portrayal of Greek culture and civilization remains unequivocally positive, the authors exhibit a discernible lack of zeal for Roman history. It argues that the Roman ways took their civilization and lifestyle from the Greeks, relegating their contributions to human civilization only to the realm of laws (Justinian's law reforms are presented as an example) and buildings, such as the Colosseum in Rome (Pshdary et al. 2021: 100). This could cautiously be interpreted as a reflection of the common understanding perceived in the region that the most significant Roman contributions to the world civilization were only in the realms of military and politics which was thought not relevant to the subject of a book on world civilization. Throughout the narrative, the authors consistently weave in the history of ancient Kurdistan, underscoring its relevance within the broader tapestry of world history (Sharif et al. 2023: 94). For instance, in the section of Greek historiography, it mentions that Herodotus visited Egypt, Iran and Kurdistan (Pshdary et al. 2021: 94), in a way that perceives Kurdistan as a political entity.

Each chapter concludes with probing questions designed to illuminate pivotal areas deemed indispensable for students to grasp. In the section devoted to Greek civilization, four incisive questions prompt reflection, including an exploration of the rise of democratic systems in Athens and the profound significance of the Olympic games (Pshdary et al. 2021: 97). Artfully responding to these inquiries inevitably fosters a resoundingly positive perception of Greek contributions to humanity. In contrast, the section pertaining to Roman civilization is succeeded by three questions. The initial query prompts students to elucidate the motivations behind and mechanisms through which the Romans emulated Greek civilizations. Addressing this question may foster an understanding that the contributions of Roman civilization to global heritage were comparatively limited.

Remarkably, the General Directorate of Curricula and Publications under the Ministry of Education of the KRI provides a teacher guide for the Art subject in Circle 3, featuring two chapters dedicated to the history of Greek arts (Abdulla et al. 2019: 45–51) and the history of Roman arts (Abdulla et al. 2019: 52–60). This guide distinguishes itself by initially outlining the inherent benefits of the subject. Beyond acquainting students with the history of ancient Greece and its profound heritage, it fervently urges educators to impart the 'greatness of the Greeks' (Abdulla et al. 2019: 46) and their unwavering pursuit of perfection, as is evident in the remnants they left behind.

What distinguishes this guide is its departure from conventional approaches. Unlike other curricula, it refrains from presenting human civilization as a linear progression starting from the ancient Middle East, particularly in ancient Mesopotamia. Instead, it steadfastly focuses on extolling the greatness of the Greeks and how their enduring contributions defy the sands of time (Abdulla et al. 2019: 45–51). The guide contends that Greek architectural styles persist in modern cities, Greek philosophers remain subjects of contemporary discourse, and the echoes of figures like Hippocrates resound in the oaths of aspiring doctors. Furthermore, it boldly asserts that modern astronomers and mathematicians stand on the shoulders of the foundational discoveries made by the Greeks. This emphasis on Greece as a perennial fount of civilization, coupled with a restrained mention of the impact of Middle Eastern civilizations, marks a distinct departure from other curricula, even those tailored for undergraduate study.

In summary, classical history receives minimal attention in the Kurdistan school curriculum. Within this constrained focus, the primary emphasis lies on elucidating the cultural and civilizational contributions of the classical period to humanity, with specific emphasis on Greek history over Roman in the fields of democracy, philosophy and law more than the poetical issues.

References

Abdulla, K., A. Abas, A. Hussin, S. Khoshnaw, Q. Salih and M. Abdullah (2019), *Art Education: a teacher guide for Year Eight*, Erbil: Ministry of Education Press.

Pshdary, Q., M. Zebary and Z. Tofiq (2021), 'History of Civilisations: for the secondary stage, Year Ten Literary Branche', *Edit 16*, trans a Committee from the Ministry of Education, Erbil: Dara Printing Company.

Sharif, O., O. Fathulla, A. Ottman and K. Omer (2023), *Social Subjects: For Year Seven*, A Joint Committee from Kurdistan Universities and Ministry of Education, Erbil: Dara Printing Company.

SINGAPORE AND MALAYSIA

Steven Hunt

In Singapore, the private Tanglin Trust School and the International French School offer classical subjects. The French School offers different language streams which follow the French national curriculum. Latin is taught only in the middle school, for one to three hours per week depending on the curriculum pathway chosen, leading to the *Diplôme National du Brevet International* qualification.

At the Tanglin Trust School, Head of Classics Hannah Dech provides the following information. Latin is a curriculum subject for the first two years, with 200 students in Years 7 and 8 (ages 11–12), studying the *Cambridge Latin Course* on an hour per week. In Year 9 (age 13), Latin becomes optional: forty students continue. Other options include a bespoke Classical Civilization course which covers Heroes, the Trojan War and Sparta/Athens. Around forty students take this. Both Latin and Classical Civilization courses in Year 9 are for an hour per week. In Years 10–11 (ages 14–15), Latin is again optional. Around fifteen students take the International General Certificate of Education (IGCSE), with five hours per fortnight study time. In Years 12–13 (ages 16–17) around five students choose Latin for the International Baccalaureate examination.

Hannah Dech also runs a Greek co-curricular where she aims to complete the Intermediate Certificate in Classical Greek. She reports:

> We have previously offered the Ancient Greek GCSE as a [co-curricular] to the most able keen beans before OCR pulled their qualifications from international schools, but lost the time to run it by the time they reinstated qualifications for schools that didn't have access to any other board. This actually crippled our department, as we used to offer Classical Civilisation GCSE and A Level, then had to stop when they pulled the exams so lost a teacher, then weren't allowed to increase the size of the department again when we were able to offer it again.
>
> (Hannah Dech, personal communication, 28 June 2023)

There seems to be no opportunity to study the classical world in state schools in Singapore.

At the university level in Singapore, provision is small. I am indebted to Professor Steven Green for the following information.

> Latin has been offered for a number of years at Yale-NUS. All students take the Common Curriculum before choosing their major at the end of the second year. Key components of the Common Curriculum are the courses 'Literature and Humanities 1' and 'Philosophy and Thought 1' which 'seek to offer a selection of texts that put regional South East Asian culture into meaningful dialogue with a range of global traditions' (Chia & Green 2022: 211). The reading of the whole of Homer's *Odyssey* and the study of texts by Aristotle and Plato has led to student demands for language teaching to enable them to read the originals. Latin and Greek were thus provided from beginners to advanced levels. With the closure of Yale-NUS in 2025, once the remaining cohorts have completed their courses, faculty staff are transitioning into NUS departments, from which they hope to launch a Minor in Global Antiquity in due course, with Latin.

The Nanyang Technological University offers some Latin tuition, not as extensive as that offered by Yale-NUS.

(Steven Green, personal communication, 12 May 2023)

In Malaysia, Epsom College, a British-style private international school, entered a candidate for Classical Civilization A-Level in 2016. The school's website does not show any current provision for learning classical languages or literature. There are many other international schools across Malaysia, which offer an American or British-style curriculum. None of their websites, however, indicate the provision of any classical subjects.

Reference

Chia, P. and S. Green (2022), 'Liberal Arts and Face Cosmetics: Ovid's Medicamina into Mandarin', in T. Sienkewicz and J. Liu, *Ovid in China: Translation, Reception, and Comparison*, Leiden: Brill, 210–22.

SOUTH KOREA

Steven Hunt and Margaret Baird

For most children in South Korea, there is no formal teaching about the ancient Graeco-Roman world in schools. Korea has a rich mythological tradition and it is through this many children and adults also come into contact with Greek Mythology. South Korea has its own tradition of *Manwha* (*manga*) comics. One of the most popular is Hong Eun Young's 'Greek and Roman Myths in Comics' series, with thirty-nine to read. They spawned their own twenty-episode TV cartoon series *Olympus Guardian* in 2002, and an animated film *Olympus Guardian: Gigantes Counterattack* in 2005. In South Korea's ambitious, literate society, these often casual encounters can be easily followed up. In a discussion about her research for the 'Our Mythical Childhood' project, Elizabeth Hale noted: 'One of the things I learned [. . .] was the extent to which the books I read as a kid alluded to Classical mythology. I didn't notice then, because I wasn't looking for it, but mythological themes are everywhere' (Hale, quoted in Connect 2023).

In South Korea, mythology crops up in surprising places. K-Pop, a quintessentially Korean fusion of popular music, dance routines and sharp clothing, has spread internationally and grown into a subculture that has amassed huge numbers of teenagers and young adults. BTS is perhaps the most well-known K-Pop band, well-documented (by classicists) for their song 'Dionysus' (2019), which references the god's wild, partying, festive characteristics (Hale 2020; Chae 2020). But other bands have also explored mythological themes, such as the story of Narcissus, the Labyrinth, the Muses and many others (Davis 2020).

Another place for more physical encounters with Greek mythology is the Greek Mythology Museum in Jeju. Students come face-to-face with the Olympian gods, dress as an ancient Greek, visit the Oracle and meet the heroes and monsters of the past, in a series of Greek-effect galleries. According to the museum's website, the educational aim that 'Knowing Greek mythology will equip you with the global cultural literacy is that will enable you to understand the root of Western Civilisation' (Greek Mythology Museum 2023). To take interest further, the National Museum of Korea has recently mounted an exhibition of Greek and Roman artefacts on loan from the Kunsthistorisches Museum in Vienna (Park 2023).

On a different cultural plane, a 2012 performance of Kim Yong-geol's modern ballet *Orpheus and Eurydice* mixed the traditional plot with Korea's shamanic, traditional images of the after life (Lee 2012). In 2018 the director Ong Keng Sen put on a version of *Trojan Women*, in a fusion of traditional Korean pansori singing, K-Pop and Euripides (Tan 2018). All of this tells us that exploring the Classics on one's own terms is fine: Berlatsky (2023), an academic writing about how young adult fiction often forms a gateway to further reading and study of the worlds in which they are set, notes, with reference to books set in the classical past, that 'It doesn't *have* to lead to the real thing.'

If a student *does* want the real thing, the private North London Collegiate School Jeju seems to be one of the few places which offer a full British-style Classics education. Latin is taught all through the school, from beginners, through the International General Certificate of Education (IGCSE), to the International Baccalaureate (IB) examination. Students start in Year 7 (age 11), with the study of two of Latin, Mandarin, French or Spanish as a foreign language. In Year 8 they choose one of these two and Latin is a popular option. Numbers for IGCSE are in the region of seventeen, with an increasing uptake; for the IB, there are regularly five to seven candidates. To encourage involvement, teachers provide wider Classics activities: a Latin Society, participation in the British ARLT Reading Competitions, and visits to the Greek Mythology Museum. Several students have gone on to universities in the USA.

There are several other schools in South Korea which teach Latin: Korean Minjok Leadership Academy, Cheongshim International Academy and Hankuk Academy of Foreign Studies, among others.

The Interdisciplinary Programme of Classical Studies is at Seoul National University, in the capital city Seoul. The programme is a graduate programme offering MA and PhD degrees in Classics. It also offers undergraduate courses in Mythology and Civilization, Greek Tragedy, and Classical Literature as well as Greek and Latin at all levels (https://humanities.snu.ac.kr/en/academics/Interdisciplinary-Programs). Seoul National University is one of the most active research centres for the study of the humanities in Korea and provides a base for the Institute of Graeco-Roman Studies. Now working in the University of Arts in Berlin, Korean-born Byung-Chul Han has translated several classical authors into Korean.

References

Berlatsky, N. (2023), 'Young Adult Fiction Doesn't Need to Be a "Gateway" to the Classics', *The Atlantic*, 27 October. Available online: https://www.theatlantic.com/national/archive/2014/10/young-adult-fiction-doesnt-need-to-be-a-gateway-to-the-classics/381959/ (accessed 7 November 2023).

Chae, L. (2020), 'Like Dionysus. BTS, Classics in K-Pop, and the Narcissism of the West', *Eidolon*, 29 October. Available online: https://eidolon.pub/like-dionysus-1d1b8fb428e1 (accessed 7 November 2023).

Connect (2023), 'A deep, discursive dive into Classical mythology', *University of New England: Connect*, 28 July. Available online: https://www.une.edu.au/connect/news/2023/07/a-deep-discursive-dive-into-classical-mythology (accessed 7 November 2023).

Davis, J. (2020), '10 K-Pop Group Comebacks That Were Inspired By Greek Mythology', *Koreaboo*, 20 July. Available online: https://www.koreaboo.com/lists/10-kpop-group-comeback-inspired-greek-mythology/ (accessed 7 November 2023).

Greek Mythology Museum (2023), Greek Mythology Museum. Available online: http://www.greekmythology.co.kr/english/ (accessed 7 November 2023).

Hale, E. (2020), [Blog] 'BTS, Dionysus, and the agonies and ecstasies of art', *Antipodean Odyssey*. Available online: https://antipodeanodyssey.wordpress.com/category/k-pop/ (accessed 7 November 2023).

Lee, C. (2012), 'Greek mythology meets Jeju folktale in modern ballet', *The Korea Herald*, 1 August. Available online: https://m.koreaherald.com/view.php?ud=20120801001155 (accessed 7 November 2023).

Park, Y. (2023), 'National Museum of Korea shows legacy of ancient Greek, Roman civilizations', *The Korea Herald*, 18 June. Available online: https://www.koreaherald.com/view.php?ud=20230615000787 (accessed 7 November 2023).

Tan, C. (2018), 'Trojan Women: the Greek tragedy that became a queer Korean opera'. *The Guardian*, 16 May. Available online: https://www.theguardian.com/stage/2018/may/16/trojan-women-ong-keng-sen-euripedes-korea-southbank-centre (accessed 7 November 2023).

SRI LANKA

Chandima Wickramasinghe

Classics has been taught in the University of Peradeniya, Faculty of Arts, since its founding in 1942. It is one of the oldest departments. Ever since then Classics has been taught in schools (at grades 12 and 13) with Greek (and Latin) languages being part of the syllabus for the General Certificate of Education Advanced Level examination (GCE A-Level).

After some time (perhaps in the 1970s) besides teaching ancient languages, a subject titled 'Greek and Roman Civilization' (now popularly known as GRC) was also introduced to the A-Level syllabus, for the same grades (12 and 13). For GRC, a selection of Greek and Roman texts in translation and Greek and Roman history have been taught to this very day. This was to attract more students for the subject as the number of students opting to learn the ancient languages began to dwindle over time.

When no students had been taking Greek as a subject for A-Level for a few decades, the Department of Examinations removed Greek from the syllabus for the A-Level. As of now, only GRC is offered at A-Level examination.

The syllabus of GRC is revised periodically by the University Department of Classical Languages that offers undergraduate and postgraduate programmes in Greek and Roman Studies. Previously the degree programmes were called Western Classical Culture to distinguish it from Eastern cultures such as Sanskrit, but the subject title was simplified to Greek and Roman Studies to make it more familiar and attractive to those who studied GRC at school.

The Greek and Roman Literature section contains both prose and verse, including Greek and Roman epic poetry, tragedy and comedy. The current GRC syllabus contains:

- Literature. Hesiod's *Works and Days*, Sophocles' *Philoctetes*, Euripides' *Alcestis*, Aristophanes' *Wasps*, Terence's *Mother-in-law*, Apollonius' *Voyage of Argo*, Cicero's *On Old Age*.

- History. Greek history: from the eighth century to the death of Alexander the Great in 323 BCE; Roman history: from the beginning of Rome to the death of Augustus Caesar in 14 CE.

Generally, we have about 270–280 school candidates annually sitting for GRC at A-Level examination (this is compared to some thousands of school candidates sitting for popular subjects). However, Classics is still alive in the school system in Sri Lanka being a part of the A-Level syllabus, although it is taught only in a few leading schools as currently it is taught in English language medium.

In this situation, the Sri Lankan University Grants Commission has been persuaded by the academics of the Faculty of Arts at the University of Peradeniya to select an additional number of fifteen to thirty students each from among the students eligible to enter the university system, but with a high score for endangered subjects such as GRC (which is not very popular among the general school population). When selected for high performance at GRC, for example, they are expected to follow all through their university career the courses from the degree programme to which they have been assigned (e.g. Greek and Roman Studies).

In addition to GRC, another subject offered for A-Level is 'Drama and Theatre' which also contains numerous aspects of Greek drama, such as genre, dramatists and their style. This is taught in all three media (Sinhala, Tamil and English).

MIDDLE EAST AND ASIA: FURTHER READING

Steven Hunt

In Vietnam, Laos and Cambodia, Greek and Latin are not taught in schools (N. Pairaudeau, personal communication, 12 May 2023). For a discussion about the role Graeco-Roman antiquity played in the French Empire's colonial schools in Vietnam in the recent past, see Nguyen (2020). In Thailand, Bromsgrove International School in Bangkok used to offer Classical Civilization, with a candidate entered at A-Level in 2015. The school's website shows no current provision for classical subjects.

In Taiwan, the Taipei American School offers courses in Latin and Greek to International Baccalaureate (IB) and Advanced Placement (AP) levels (Taipei American School 2023). Edward Nolan teaches at the National Taiwan University. He writes:

> The study of Greek and Roman Classics in Taiwan takes multiple forms but is mostly concentrated in higher education, although some international schools offer Latin and even Greek. Many freshman or sophomore students pursuing undergraduate degrees in Foreign Language or English departments in Taiwan are required to take courses with titles like 'Introduction to Western Literature' (西洋文學概論) that cover Greek and Latin literature (mostly Epic and Greek Tragedy) alongside the Bible and some medieval literature such as Dante's Divine Comedy in English translation. These courses are meant to prepare students for later studies in foreign literature. In addition, Greek and Latin language courses are available to students at some select universities, such National Taiwan University, National Taiwan Normal University, and Fu Jen Catholic University. Latin is more available and frequently studied than Greek. Study beyond basic language and introductory courses is highly dependent on the faculty available at a particular university, as it is not the norm for Taiwanese Universities to have (Western) Classics departments, but rather for such faculty to teach as part of History, Philosophy, Anthropology, Foreign Languages and Literatures, or even English departments.
>
> I have taught Greek and Roman Classics in Taiwan for a little over a year. Teaching first-year Latin and Introduction to Western Literature at National Taiwan University, my own experience has been overwhelmingly positive. My Latin students at National Taiwan University take the course primarily out of pure interest and a desire to be challenged, and it is sometimes difficult to find the right balance in finding material that is both challenging and appropriate for beginners. As always, teaching students in required courses is a trickier affair, but I find that the fascination students in the West might have with the perceived oddness of the Greeks and Romans is only magnified for students who have had less previous exposure.
>
> (Edward Nolan, personal communication, 14 October 2023)

For a description of Classics teaching in the private ISF Academy in Hong Kong, see Christou (2017). She describes a thriving Classics department following an international British curriculum. Classical Studies are also taught at the Korean International School in

Hong Kong. For further reading about how the Greek Classics are being pressed into use in contemporary Chinese politics, see Bartsch (2023). Bartsch (2022) also alludes to the reasoning behind the closure of the Yale-NSU Classics programme in Singapore. For a description of Latin classes at Beijing's Renmin University taught by the Austrian Leopold Leeb, a pioneer of classics education in China, see Che (2022). A description of the full classical studies programme at Beijing Foreign Studies University can be found in Alvares and Li (2020). Representatives of the Italian *Accademia Vivarium Novum* have made several cultural exchange visits to China, including Wenli College (Wenli College 2018) and Yenching Academy of Beijing University (Yenching Academy 2019). See also Bouuaert (2018) for a description and reasoning for such cultural events. Wentao Zhai (2023) gives an account of the challenge of translating Virgil into Chinese. The Janus Project, recently inaugurated in Oxford University, broadly aims 'to facilitate scholarly conversation and collaboration on Classics between East Asia and ancient Greece and Rome' (https://janus-project.org/).

For further reading about the roles that Graeco-Roman antiquity has played in the development of modern Japan, see Takada (2010). A cultural cross-over, Yamazaki Mari's manga cartoon *Thermae Romae* (テルマエ・ロマエ) has popularized the ancient Roman world in Japan (Alecci 2010).

Classical history and Latin are taught at the Virginia Commonwealth University in Qatar. Determann (2023) describes how he encourages students to see connections between local classically-styled buildings and the ancient world, as well as through the Latin language. At the British International School in Riyadh, Saudi Arabia, the UK education system is followed, which includes a study of Rome for 11-year-old students. Dubai College in the UAE regularly puts forward several candidates for GCSE and A-Level Latin each year. In the state education systems of the Gulf States, however, there is no provision for the study of the Graeco-Roman world.

In Lebanon, Jordan and Syria immense ruins still stand as testament to the power of Rome, Palmyra and others. Classics, however, does not feature in schools. Nevertheless, in Syria the legacy of Queen Zenobia of Palmyra, who held out against the Roman Empire in the third century CE, lives on in the popular imagination as a liberator from Western oppression. For an exploration of the survival of her legacy, despite political exploitation by President Assad and widespread destruction of sites by ISIS, see Andrade (2018: 215–30). For a discussion on the symbolism of the destruction and abuse of pagan sites in the Middle East, see Morgan (2023). The destruction of classical and other cultural heritage sites in the current conflict in Gaza can be read in Adams (2024).

Graeco-Roman antiquity has played almost no part in the education system of Iran. In the early twentieth century Reza Shah's curriculum was intended to enable the country to catch up with the modern world. It was over-centralized and prescriptive; Persian only was allowed; national pride in the country's pre-Islamic history lent a strong emphasis on the Achaemenids (Mathee 1993). After the overthrow of the regime in 1979, the Islamic Revolution put paid to all that, in schools at least. But generations of Iranians continue to look back to the Achaemenid empire, and to Darius and Xerxes and Cyrus the Great especially (Llewellyn-Jones 2022: 376–97).

Similarly, the Iraqi education system does not, as far as the authors have been able to ascertain, teach about the Graeco-Roman world. However, the country does have an impressive record of scholarship and the display of its archaeological finds (for full details of the work of the Iraq Museum and the vicissitudes of its collections and staff after the 2003 war, see https://en.wikipedia.org/wiki/Iraq_Museum). The work of the Iraqi-American artist, Michael Rakowitz, highlights the history of colonialism and the extraction of Iraqi artefacts into museum collections across the world. He reconstructs artefacts looted from the Iraq Museum and excavation sites from ephemeral materials, such as sweet wrappers and newspapers. His sculpture 'The invisible enemy should not exist' adorned the fourth plinth in Trafalgar Square, London, as a reminder of the destruction by ISIS in 2015 of the original Lamassu figure which had stood at the Nergal Gate of Nineveh since *c.* 700 BCE (Collier 2019).

For reports of the looting of sites in Syria and Iraq, see Ananda (2015). A more recent report on the current state of the site of Apamea in Syria can be found on the Unusual Traveler website (Unusual Traveler 2021). In October 2023, the excavation near the city of Khorsabad by a joint Iraqi-French archaeological team of a Lamassu statue, strategically reburied after its original discovery for protection against ISIS, was widely reported in the news (see, for example, Lucente 2023).

As an overview of classical reception in the Middle East, through the lens of Greek Tragedy, Donizeau et al. (forthcoming), promises to be an excellent source.

Classical languages are not a part of the education systems of the former Central Asian soviet republics of Uzbekistan, Kyrgyzstan, Tajikistan, Turkmenistan and Kazakhstan. A recent exhibition at the Staatliche Museen zu Berlin brought together artefacts from Uzbekistan dating from the fourth century BCE to the fourth century CE (Lendering 2023).

Instead, if we take history teaching in the Kazakh education system as an example, the emphasis in recent years has been on de-Russification and de-Sovietification of the curriculum, to something that more aligns with Kazakh national identity (Kissane 2005; Mynbayeva & Pogosian 2014). The 2012 education reform programme carried out by Nazarbayev University, together with the Universities of Cambridge (UK) and Pennsylvania (USA) does not mention the presence of any Graeco-Roman classical history or literature in the curriculum (University of Cambridge 2020).

The authors are reliably informed that Graeco-Roman antiquity has never formed a part of the education system of Afghanistan (L. Morgan, personal communication, 1 June 2023). However, archaeological exploration in that devastated country has proceeded sporadically, with extensive investigations in southwest Afghanistan before the Soviet invasion of 1979 by the Helmand Sistan Project (2023). The chaos that followed the fall of the Taliban in 2001 and the 'rediscovery' of the 'Bactrian Hoard' is graphically told by Dupree (2005). For more on the classical legacy in Afghanistan, see Omrani (2021), Morgan (2021) and chapter one of Bromberg (2021). Analysis of satellite photos by researchers at the University of Chicago suggests that archaeological sites are being systematically bulldozed to facilitate looting (Khamoosh 2024). Since 2021 Taliban rule has taken a terrible toll on the education system, especially for girls.

Mali Skotheim's chapter on India in this book also mentions the current state of Classics in Pakistan, and some historical references to Sri Lanka. For accounts of the relationship between classical antiquity and the British colonial presence in India, see Mantena (2010), Vasunia (2013) and Bopari (2023). For a short discussion on how archaeology in Pakistan, particularly in respect of Gandharan Buddhist artefacts, has been (mis)used as a way of 'articulating and espousing the politics of nation states as also erstwhile empires', see Datta (2023). Wouters (2023) provides an account of the influence of ideas and beliefs about ancient Greece in Bhutan.

References

Adams, G. K. (2024), 'Widescale destruction of cultural heritage in Gaza', *Museum News*, 30 January. Available online: https://www.museumsassociation.org/museums-journal/news/2024/01/widescale-destruction-of-cultural-heritage-in-gaza/ (accessed 28 February 2024).

Alecci, S. (2010), 'Japan: An ancient Roman at the Japanese public bath', *Global Voices,* 9 August. Available online: https://globalvoices.org/2010/08/09/japan-an-ancient-roman-at-the-japanese-public-bath/ (accessed 22 January 2024).

Alvares, J. and H. Li (2020), 'The First Full Latin and Greek Program at a University in the People's Republic of China', *The Classical Outlook*, 95 (2): 56–63.

Ananda, R. (2015), 'The History and Culture I Saw in Syria Is Now Scarred by War', *HuffPost*, 26 May. Available online: https://www.huffpost.com/archive/ca/entry/the-history-and-culture-i-saw-in-syria-is-now-scarred-by-war_b_7439046 (accessed 7 November 2023).

Andrade, N. (2018), *Zenobia: Shooting Star of Palmyra,* New York: Oxford University Press.

Bartsch, S. (2022), 'Global Classics', *TAPA*, 152 (1): 33–42.

Bartsch, S. (2023), *Plato Goes to China. The Greek Classics and Chinese Nationalism*, Princeton, NJ: Princeton University Press.

Bopari, J. (2023), 'Classical Culture in British India: the Bengal "Renaissance"', *Antigone Journal*. Available online: https://antigonejournal.com/2023/02/classical-culture-british-india-i/ (accessed 18 November 2023).

Bouuaert, J. (2018), 'Quand les Chinois craquent pour le latin', *La Libre*, 17 January. Available online: https://www.lalibre.be/debats/opinions/2018/01/17/quand-les-chinois-craquent-pour-le-latin-opinion-AHM4FKEQNFBERBOEAAJFWN6VPM/ (accessed 7 November 2023).

Bromberg, J. (2021), *Global Classics*, London: Routledge.

Che, C. (2022), 'China looks to the Western classics', *The China Project*, 13 January. Available online: https://thechinaproject.com/2022/01/13/china-looks-to-the-western-classics/ (accessed 7 November 2023).

Christou, A. (2017), 'Hong Kong: Home to the Star Ferry, the Peak Tram and @ShuyuanClassics!', *Journal of Classics Teaching,* 36: 29–36.

Collier, L. (2019), 'Exposing Ghosts of the Past, Michael Rakowitz Pulls Back the Curtain', *Hyperallergic*, 13 August. Available online: https://hyperallergic.com/512711/michael-rakowitz-whitechapel-gallery/ (accessed 7 November 2023).

Datta, D. (2023), [Blog] 'Their Civilization—Whose Archaeology?', *Journal of the History of Ideas*. Available online: https://www.jhiblog.org/2023/11/14/their-civilization-whose-archaeology/ (accessed 8 January 2024).

Determann, J. (2023), 'How to Make Ancient History Relevant to Students in the Gulf Today', *Al-Fanar media*, 20 June. Available online: https://www.al-fanarmedia.org/2023/06/how-to-make-ancient-history-relevant-to-students-in-the-gulf-today/ (accessed 7 November 2023).

Donizeau, P., Y. Khajehi and D. Potenza (forthcoming), *Greek Tragedy and the Middle East*, London: Bloomsbury.

Dupree, N. (2005), 'Cultural Update from Afghanistan', in B. Omrani and M. Leeming (eds), *Afghanistan. A companion and guide*, Hong Kong: Odyssey Publications, 655–8.

Helmand Sistan Project (2023), 'The Helmand Sistan Project'. Available online: https://sistanarchaeology.org/ (accessed 7 November 2023).

Khamoosh, K. (2024), 'Afghanistan: Archaeological sites "bulldozed for looting"', *BBC World News*, 22 February. Available online: https://www.bbc.co.uk/news/world-asia-68311913?fbclid=IwAR3Y6u2xgvSFdiimGxwTCAcGuMb7EFb5KqL0_p4EvUsALMIzgY353o5WcrI_aem_AWtRJ9WL9x0p_xZ4uAUyMPew5S9lPXX87NNd1abgAm5nO8r3T0owZKIR4TP4yfGpa6I (accessed 27 February 2024).

Kissane, C. (2005), 'History Education in Transit: Where to for Kazakhstan?', *Comparative Education*, 41 (1): 45–69.

Lendering, J. (2023), [Blog] 'Oezbekistan in Berlijn', *Mainzer Beobachter*. Available online: https://mainzerbeobachter.com/2023/08/27/oezbekistan-in-berlijn/ (accessed 8 January 2024).

Llewellyn-Jones, L. (2022), *Persians. The Age of the Great Kings*, London: Headline.

Lucente, A. (2023), 'Iraq unveils ancient Assyrian lamassu statue in Nineveh province', *Al-Monitor*, 24 October. Available online: https://www.al-monitor.com/originals/2023/10/iraq-unveils-ancient-assyrian-lamassu-statue-nineveh-province (accessed 7 November 2023).

Mantena, R. (2010), 'Imperial Ideology and the Uses of Rome in Discourses on Britain's Indian Empire', in M. Bradley (ed.), *Classics and Imperialism in the British Empire*, Oxford: Oxford University Press, 54–74.

Mathee, R. (1993), 'Transforming Dangerous Nomads into Useful Artisans, Technicians, Agriculturists: Education in the Reza Shah Period', *Iranian Studies*, 26 (3/4): 313–36.

Morgan, L. (2021), 'Afghanistan, its Pasts and Futures', *Antigone Journal*. Available online: https://antigonejournal.com/2021/08/afghanistan-past-future/ (accessed 7 November 2023).

Morgan, L. (2023), 'Opinion: Civilization in ruins: Bamiyan after Bamiyan', *Kabul Now*, 1 March. Available online: https://kabulnow.com/2023/03/civilization-in-ruins-bhuddas-of-bamiyan/ (accessed 7 November 2023).

Mynbayeva, A. and V. Pogosian (2014), 'Kazakhstani School Education Development from the 1930s: History and Current Trends', *Italian Journal of Sociology of Education*, 6 (2): 144–72.

Nguyen, K. (2020), [Blog] '"Vercingetorix in Vietnam": Addressing the Intersection of Classics and Vietnamese Culture', Society for Classical Studies, 23 September. Available online: https://classicalstudies.org/scs-blog/kn4/blog-%E2%80%98vercingetorix-vietnam%E2%80%99-addressing-intersection-classics-and-vietnamese-culture (accessed 7 November 2023).

Omrani, B. (2021), 'The Greeks, Afghanistan, and the Buddha', *Antigone Journal*. Available online: https://antigonejournal.com/2021/03/greeks-afghanistan-buddha/ (accessed 7 November 2023).

Taipei American School (2023), 'Greek and Latin. Taipei American School'. Available online: https://www.tas.edu.tw/academics/upper-school/departments/classics (accessed 7 November 2023).

Takada, Y. (2010), 'Translation and Difference: Western Classics in Modern Japan', in S. Stephens and P. Vasumia (eds), *Classics and National Cultures*, Oxford: Oxford University Press, 285–301.

University of Cambridge (2020), 'Educational reform and internationalisation: the case of Kazakhstan', University of Cambridge. Available online: https://www.educ.cam.ac.uk/networks/eri/casestudies/kazakhstan/researching/ (accessed 7 November 2023).

Unusual Traveler (2021), 'Apamea Ancient Ruins updated July 2021, first visit since before the war | Syria', *Unusual Traveler*, 10 August. Available online: https://www.unusualtraveler.com/apamea-roman-ruins-syria/ (accessed 7 November 2023).

Vasunia, P. (2013), *The Classics and Colonial India*, Oxford: Oxford University Press.

Wenli College (2018), 'The Millennium Meeting, Classics Endure', Wenli College. Available online: https://mp.weixin.qq.com/s/hPjL9PsN7nuuGsN8um6mkA (accessed 7 November 2023).

Wouters, J. (2023), [Blog] 'Athenian and Naga Hillsides – Ancient Greeks and Contemporary Nagas, Classical Reception Studies Network'. Available online: https://classicalreception.org/athenian-and-naga-hillsides-ancient-greeks-and-contemporary-nagas/ (accessed 26 January 2024).

Yenching Academy (2019), 'Dean Luigi Miraglia of Accademia Vivarium Novum Visits Yenching Academy of Peking University', Yenching Academy of Peking University, 20 September. Available online: https://yenchingacademy.pku.edu.cn/info/1039/2908.htm (accessed 7 November 2023).

Zhai, W. (2022), 'How Would Virgil Speak in Chinese?', *Antigone Journal*. Available online: https://antigonejournal.com/2023/11/virgil-chinese-poetry/ (accessed 18 November 2023).

PART 5
AFRICA

EGYPT, TUNISIA, LIBYA AND MOROCCO

Leslie F. Ivings

The teaching of Classics in these countries has proved the point about subjects having to be versatile, flexible and be able to endure the ravages of even prolonged civil war. This part of North Africa has a rich historical tradition that connects it directly to the field of Classics teaching. They were part of that same Mediterranean world, the *mare nostrum* of Classical Greece, the Roman Republic and Empire, and the Byzantine world. These countries saw and experienced the tumult and change, like the shifting sands of the Sahara, of every major civilization in North Africa from the Carthaginians to the conquering Caliphates. That is why it is so important in the context of this book that we investigate what remains of the teaching of Latin, Greek and classical civilizations in this part of North Africa. Ultimately the lessons that can be learned here can be applied to many types of institutions facing reduction or termination of their Classics Departments.

Egypt

With regard to teaching in Egypt, we must first understand the long-standing tradition of the study of Egyptology. After all, the civilization of Ancient Egypt predates that of our teaching interlocutors of Greece and Rome by more than 1,500 years. Hence with such a rich cultural tradition already in place, there would be a natural bias in the study of Ancient Egypt from a linguistic, historical and archaeological perspective. The exploits of people like Howard Carter and the discovery of the tomb of Tutankhamun that popularized the study of Ancient Egypt in the West also must be considered when we look at modern teaching practices of the Classics.

The most important point of reference in the study of Classics is Cairo University itself. They have designed an excellent programme that solves some unique issues that belong to Egypt alone, namely the influences of the different civilizations on each other and how a student might go and differentiate them all. The BA degree in Graeco-Roman Antiquities neatly solves this question. As a degree it falls into the Department of Graeco-Roman Antiquities, but it is also connected to the Departments of Islamic History, Egyptian History, and Archaeology. It thus creates a four-year degree course that blends all the elements of Egyptian study with those of the study of the Graeco-Roman world. It creates a holistic teaching programme for education in Egypt.

The university requires of the students only proficiency in Arabic and English. During the four years of study, the student is introduced to and trained in the other major languages pertaining to the course, namely Classical Greek, Latin, the Ancient Egyptian Language, Demotic Script and Coptic. As any modern language scholar will tell you, the combination of these specific languages to learn and use professionally is no easy feat, and so during the study towards the BA degree a modicum of specialization is allowed by the choice of elective subjects in any of the major languages mentioned. This is also undertaken for the preparation of the student for postgraduate work. The transfer from undergraduate to postgraduate students is particularly high with this degree course, which is extremely heartening for the training of skilled professionals not only for Egypt but also for the rest of Africa.

With regards to the teaching of classical history, this degree starts with the study of Ancient Egypt and then the History of Islamic Egypt. Both subjects are introductory and are taken in the first semester of study. Thereafter the histories of Greece, Rome and Byzantium are completed. From the second to the fourth years, they are not simplistic courses that last only a semester but are expanded in each year of study. This is achieved by adding subjects in Greek architecture, followed by Roman and Byzantine architecture, balancing it off with a comparative study on the influences of Ancient Egyptian architecture. The same is carried out with subjects on Greek, Roman and Byzantine statues and pottery. Papyrology and numismatics of Ptolemaic and Roman Egypt are also studied at third- and fourth-year level. Graeco-Roman mythology and religious beliefs are also studied in the second year, alongside the cosmology and mythology of Pharaonic Egypt. From the above it is very clear that the course designers had the unique Egyptian situation in mind throughout the creation and design of the degree.

Graeco-Roman sources of history are also studied first in translated form, and later students can elect to study source material by the major Greek or Roman historians in the original Greek and Latin. Special attention is given to those texts that have a specific bearing on Ancient, Ptolemaic and Roman Egypt. With the source studies in Graeco-Roman, socio-economic life is also included. An interesting feature with this socio-economic study is the comparison between Graeco-Roman cities and those existing in Egypt at the time, most notably Alexandria and Thebes. Hieroglyphic texts from the Ptolemaic period are also included in this section. These are given either in translation or according to the language specialization of the student. The reasoning behind this textual and source inclusion is one of differentiation between contextual approaches of writers in the Graeco-Roman world and those writing within the Egyptian context.

Within this degree framework an archaeological component is added. The study is also a synthesis between traditional Ancient Egyptian archaeology and that of the Graeco-Roman period. The subject, called Egyptian Civilization and Archaeology in the Graeco-Roman Period, is taken in the first semester of the first year and starts with an introduction on why these are distinct fields and the differing archaeological methodologies that are applied to them. It again is expanded throughout the four-year programme to include other aspects that are period specific such as Museology and Excavation Sciences. The study of Graeco-Roman monuments in the Nile Delta, Alexandria and in the rest of North Africa is also offered within the framework of the BA degree, as an elective. Also core in this curriculum is the study of Mutual Influences in the Mediterranean Basin, which highlights the desire to put the Graeco-Roman world on par with the Egyptian world.

The study of Classics at Cairo University shows very clearly that the *modus* of teaching is synthesis. It precludes any idea of a cultural hegemony existing over the current philosophy of education behind the Graeco-Roman Antiquities degree, with even the possibility of the study of Christian Monasticism as an option. For those readers wondering about the teaching of sources in translation or later in original languages, they need not be concerned. Professor Adel El-Nahas from the Faculty of Arts has produced three exemplary works that are studied alongside Western material: Greek and Latin Philology, Greek Language I and a Latin Grammar. It should also be noted that since the disturbances after the Arab Spring in 2011 and subsequent attention to stolen antiquities, additional compulsory subjects in the form of Human Rights Law and Caring for a National Heritage have been added.

Tunisia

The teaching of Classics in Tunisia is currently limited to two universities: the University of Tunis El Manar and the University of Sfax. But by no means should this indicate the relative unimportance of the classical field in Tunisia. Like Egypt, Tunisia realizes the importance of study into the Mediterranean civilizations not only because of regional influences but also because of the special position that Tunisia had as a province in Roman North Africa.

The University of Tunis El Manar was founded in 2000. This makes it a relatively young institution, but already, in 1999 when the university was formed by presidential proclamation, a collection of International Higher Institutes was created. The Institute of Human Sciences is chief among these and under its recent reconstitution includes the following departments for advanced study: the Department of Philosophy, the Department of Applied Languages and the Department of Ancient Languages and Civilizations. They joined the already very successful Department of Archaeology and History. The aim of this incorporation was the promotion of the study of the Roman world and the connected languages and thought schools that went with it. In effect this was intended to enhance the archaeology programme that was already in existence.

The study of the Roman world is through a Tunisian lens, with the emphasis of broadening cultural exposure to other Mediterranean nations that have a similar background. The language of instruction is mainly in French and Arabic but, through the language component of the Institute, Greek and Latin are also offered to those students that wish to follow a postgraduate degree in any of the incorporated fields as well as existing historical fields. Roman and Greek history is also offered up to third-year level in the Archaeology Department, the institute wanting understanding of all aspects of the archaeological field and not just the preservation and excavation side. Understanding and analysis have become ever more important after the Arabic Spring. By 2020, the university already constituted a student body of over forty thousand. Islamic history is also offered in the Institute as part of Historical Studies. It does touch upon the history of Byzantium, although not in great detail past that of a first-year first semester course.

At the University of Sfax the position is rather different. The main language of instruction remains Arabic, and its ethos is by far more Arab-centric. Its History Department, for instance, focuses more on Arab Liberation Studies and the History of the Middle East than it does on Ancient History. The core components are divided into three sections: History as a Core Module, Modern History and then History, Archaeology and Heritage Studies. Roman and Greek studies fall into the last section. They are incorporated into the BA Archaeology degree much as you would have expected with Egypt, but removed of those components of Egyptology I have discussed above. Stand-alone modules on Roman Civilization are offered, but only in respect of the Core Module Italian. This module includes both modern Italian and also the Civilization of Italy, which to a large part includes the Roman Empire and some elements of Byzantine history and brings the course right through to the modern Italian Republic.

The University of Sfax was established in 1986. It does not have instruction in either Latin or Greek, but Greek philosophical texts are studied in translation. The translation department mostly focuses on Arabic translation and language. The following European languages are offered: French, English, Italian and Spanish. Uniquely the civilizations of these European countries alongside their languages are also studied, and it is only through them that any history of the Graeco-Roman world is touched upon. On the cultural heritage side of the BA programme, the heritage component also touches upon Phoenician and Carthaginian influences on the surrounding region. The Punic wars are mentioned, but without great detail. The actual effect of the combined studies is rather more profound than the reading would suggest as the sum total projects a Tunisia and humanities in Tunisia that would not have been possible without the influence of the classical world.

Libya

Probably the most unlikely of experiments in research into Classics teaching would be those in Libya. Khaled El Mezughi, a doctoral student at the University of Denver, recently pointed out in their thesis that even some of the greatest private schools in cities like Benghazi are still being used as shelter for people affected by the civil war (El Mezughi 2021). El Mezughi laments that the current education system is woefully inadequate. Prior to the Arab Spring in 2011, the Ghaddafi regime had all but eliminated those subjects that had links to so-called Western imperialism. This action was not limited to the teaching of English but also included Western history and philosophy as well. A curious addition to secondary schools was Jihad Studies, which even boasted quite a few professors at the University of Tripoli.

But here in 2023 at the very same University of Tripoli we find in the Department of History no less than three faculty members who are dedicated to the study of Classical if not Ancient History. And given the uniquely difficult situation I think they deserve a very honourable mention for the work that they are carrying out. To quote the Head of the History Department, Professor Jamal Mohamed Salem Khalifa: 'The Department of History includes the best staff. They have scientific experience and scientific work in all disciplines: Antiquities, the ancient, the mediate, the modern, and the contemporary.' Currently the Faculty of Arts and the Department of History also publish the following in-house journals: the *Journal of the Faculty of Arts*, and the *Arts and Sciences Journal*. Both are actively publishing historical articles from 2015. Courses that are offered start from a BA in Ancient History to a fully-fledged PhD in the same subject.

I want to mention three faculty members in particular. Dr Adel Omran Mohammed Zayed who has research interests in Phoenician-Carthaginian, Greek, Hellenistic and Roman studies; Dr Samira Al-Jarani Ali Al-Sahili focuses on research and teaching pertaining to the relationship between Roman and Carthaginian societies and the ancient inhabitants of Libya and Morocco; and lastly, Dr Ayman Hussein Masoud Al-Tawib studies the mythologies of the Graeco-Roman world and the Levant. These three colleagues have featured in academic journals of Egypt and other Middle-Eastern countries. Their articles are very broad, ranging from Carthaginian–Greek relations in the fifth to third centuries BCE to Ptolemaic–Roman relations from 323 BCE to 31 BCE. If the Libyan example of classical scholarship does not prove the resilience of study and research amid chaos and adversity, then I think nothing will.

Morocco

In Morocco, the only university that offers anything by way of Classics is the University of Mohammed V (UM5) in Rabat, founded by the then King of Morocco in 1957. The languages of instruction were primarily Arabic and French, but have significantly branched out to include Spanish, German and Italian. Classics are studied as a component of the departments of History and at the School for Languages. The Roman history of Morocco is taught from a Moroccan perspective. It delves into the greater influence into the shaping of modern Morocco and French attitudes during the colonial period. The result is that former French pedagogical philosophies are no longer favoured and have been replaced by authentic Moroccan research and discoveries. This is further studied in the Islamic History of Morocco as the rightful heirs to the former Roman Province.

UM5 is also responsible for the training of most of the secondary school teachers in the country; thus the history component of Roman Morocco is briefly touched on for those students in secondary education taking History. Morocco deserves more than just a mention with regards to Classics teaching. Although dismissive of most of the colonial past, they have managed to study the Roman influence in a uniquely Moroccan way and this can be of enormous help to those who study Roman North Africa. Currently the university offers both undergraduate and postgraduate degrees in History but it is only in the undergraduate offerings that Rome and Greece are touched upon. In the school of Languages, Classical Hebrew is also studied and offered. The Faculty of Letters and Human Sciences also created a new Centre for Doctoral Studies, the SEDoc or 'Man and Space in the Mediterranean World'. Although this centre is now fully decolonized, the ability to continue research into Roman North Africa still remains.

Conclusion

After research into the study of Classics teaching in North Africa in this chapter, one cannot but come away with a certain awe. Not just for the dexterity of the courses that are presented or the degrees that are offered, but for the teachers, lecturers and professors that are doing this amazing feat. Add to that the students who, despite poor economic and social conditions, still want to study Classics. In a world of uncertainty they continue, in a land of adversity they thrive. Let us then set our minds to this attitude of doing and continuing the work. To paraphrase Aristotle a little, it is not so important that they may be not obviously useful or necessary, but because it is noble and undertaken for their own sake or for the betterment of self, that we continue to teach Classics.

References

El Mezughi, K. (2021), 'Understanding Libyan Teachers' Intentions and Classroom Practises in Teaching a Foreign Language'. Doctoral thesis, University of Denver, CO.

Universities mentioned

University of Cairo: https://cu.edu.eg/Home
University of Sfax: http://www.univ-sfax.tn/
University of Tripoli: https://uot.edu.ly/
University of Tunis El Manar, Higher Institute of Human Sciences of Tunis: http://www.utm.rnu.tn/utm/fr/establissements-institut-superieur-des-sciences-humaines-de-tunis
UM5 Faculté des Lettres et des Sciences Humaines de Rabat: http://www.um5.ac.ma/um5/faculte-des-lettres-et-des-humaines-de-rabat

Gifty Etornam Katahena

Introduction

In Ghana, there is a general decline in students' interest in classical studies. Michael Okyere Asante (2022) has explored this assertion by discussing various factors that have contributed to the decline and has highlighted Africanization in politics and education in Ghana as the main reason. However, this decline is more evident in the study of classical languages. The study of classical languages in tertiary schools in Ghana began with the establishment of the Department of Classics at the University of Ghana in 1948. Prior to the establishment of the University of Ghana, Ghanaian students had the opportunity to study some aspects of classical history, Latin, or Greek during their educational journey at the pre-tertiary level of education (Goff 2022). During the colonial era in Ghana, Greek and Latin formed part of the educational curriculum, which continued into the post-colonial educational system until the later part of the twentieth century. The introduction of the new junior and senior secondary school structure in 1987 and the final A-Level exams written in 1996 marked the end of the inclusion of classical languages in Ghanaian schools' curriculum at the pre-tertiary stage (Okyere Asante 2022). This change has not only challenged the relevance of studying classical languages at the pre-tertiary level in Ghana, but it has also challenged its relevance at the tertiary level and rendered its study at the tertiary level unnecessary to the progress and development of Ghanaian society. Currently, students who study classical languages do not have prior knowledge and no clear understanding of why they should study Greek and Latin. The University of Ghana remains the only tertiary institution that offers Greek and Latin in Ghana although the University of Cape Coast also offers courses in Classical Studies. As a corollary, this research focuses on the nature of the study of Greek and Latin at the University of Ghana and interrogates the decision of students (both undergraduate and postgraduate) to study classical languages at the tertiary level. By this means, the study aims to explore the challenges and relevance of studying classical languages at the tertiary level by Ghanaian students.

Method and materials

This study employs both qualitative and quantitative methodologies through the analysis of both primary and secondary data. Primary data was collected through a survey of twenty-five former students and brief interviews of some of the former students who studied the classical languages at the University of Ghana. The working sample of the interviewed consists of ten former students currently in various work fields from politics, industrial/business, postgraduate students, and teachers/lecturers. These former students have studied Greek or Latin or both either at the undergraduate or postgraduate level. The questions asked include their interest in the language(s), their learning experience, parental/family support, and the relevance of ancient language study to their current field of employment. The motive for the line of questioning is to expand the discussion of the choice of course of study and the relevance of studying classical languages to them. It is anticipated that a conclusion could be drawn as well on what inspires students to study classical languages and most importantly, the reasons for the decline or loss of interest in the study of classical languages among tertiary students at the University of Ghana. This study further engages secondary data of students retrieved from the Institutional Research and Planning Office (IRPO) of the University of Ghana to provide statistical data to support the analysis and conclusion drawn for this study.

Studying Greek and Latin: the challenges and experiences

Greek

Before studying Greek at the University of Ghana, students had only been exposed to the Greek alphabet used in mathematics in pre-tertiary education. However, it is interesting to note that classical languages are elective courses that students could opt for. In 2010, the Department of Classics was merged with the Department of Philosophy due to the problem of the declining number of teaching staff. The Classics Department at the time had only one full-time lecturer and two part-time lecturers. The course structure at the Classics Department, now the Department of Philosophy and Classics, starts from the foundational/beginners' level (Reading Greek I) which focuses on phonology, punctuation, morphology, declension of nouns, pronouns and adjectives, and the conjugation of verbs, with exercises in transliteration and pronunciation (University of Ghana, Undergraduate Handbook 2015–17). The course continues at the intermediate level (Reading Greek II) where the focus is on basic syntax, with exercises in reading and translation, covering word order: positioning clitic particles, and pronouns; using the definite article to attribute, predict or nominalize adjectives, participles, infinitives and whole sentences; and constructing simple sentences. Both beginners and intermediate levels of the course are offered in the third year and the advanced level is offered in the fourth year in twofold: Reading Greek III and Reading Greek IV. At the advanced level 1 (Reading Greek III), the studies focus on translation and practice in the construction of sentences, both simple and complex, and the advanced level 2 (Reading Greek IV) consolidates the lessons of the previous studies towards the acquisition of a working proficiency through translation and the reading of prescribed primary texts in philosophy, fiction, history and various genres of poetry. Unfortunately, not many students get to study Greek from I to IV. Quite a few were able to study up to Greek III and this is only possible because, from the data retrieved from IRPO, those who got to this stage were graduate students except for one undergraduate student in 2011. No student has chosen to study Reading Greek IV (see Table 15). Some factors would account for this and why the study of Greek is not so appealing to students.

In the survey conducted, out of the twenty-five responses, twenty had studied Greek I. Greek II was widely studied by graduate students as a requirement and not as an elective. The conclusion then is that Greek was not ideally an option for students as compared to Latin (see Table 16). Respondents gave a few pointers on why studying Greek was less appealing. First was the problem with easily identifying the alphabet; it is easier for any English-speaking person to learn Latin than Greek. In an African society with diverse languages, the construction of the English language itself is a problem; however, since the English alphabet is similar to the Latin alphabet, studying Latin is easier according to them. The Greek alphabet is different. In the survey conducted, students who studied Greek indicated the difficulty they faced in pronouncing words and reading simple sentences. In my quest to inquire about why they

Table 15. Students who enrolled in Greek from 2009 to 2023

Programme	2009	2010	2011	2012	2013	2014	2015	2016	2017	2018	2019	2020	2021	2022	2023
Bachelor of Arts															
READING GREEK					4										
READING GREEK I	1	9	6	8	1	4	4	3	2	2	2	2	3	2	2
READING GREEK II	1	1	1												
READING GREEK III			1												
Doctor of Philosophy in Classics															
READING GREEK I															1
Master of Philosophy in Classics															
READING GREEK I	3	2	2	2	2	3	3		1		2		2		1
READING GREEK II		2	1	3	2	2	4	3		1					
READING GREEK III			1	3											
Visiting Studentship															
READING GREEK I									1						
TOTAL	5	14	12	16	9	9	11	6	4	3	4	2	5	2	4

Source: Institutional Research and Planning Office (IRPO), University of Ghana. © Giffy Etornam Katahena 2023.

415

opted for Greek, it was revealed that students who were interested in reading Greek wanted to pursue a master's programme in Classics. Secondly, five students said they needed an additional course to make up for the number of credits required in the third year of their studies. Interestingly, they did not opt for Reading Greek II because, according to them, they completely lost interest due to their experience with the way the course was taught. According to three of them, the lecturer always made the study of Greek I 'scary' and they always did not have the enthusiasm to be in class. Further, they complained of the unavailability of enough material for study apart from the lecturer's recommended book. One student who utilized resources online said some of the lecturer's pronunciations were different from what he found online and that got him more confused.

When asked about their experience and whether they would study Greek again if given the opportunity, the responses were that 'it was fun', 'it was interesting', and 'it was exciting', however, out of the twenty-five respondents, five would want to try again with another lecturer and the rest commented with a 'No'. A follow-up question was whether learning Greek has been relevant or useful to them in any way, especially in their respective careers. Those who are in academia and aspiring to be academics responded positively while those in the industry/business and politics responded negatively.

Latin

Like Greek, not much is known about the Latin language prior to tertiary education. Some senior high schools in Ghana have their motto or slogan in Latin. At best, some students who opt for Latin are intrigued and want to know more. One student interviewed said, 'he thought it was so cool and would like to occasionally say Latin words while speaking English'. Others opted for it because they wanted to pursue law after their first degree and, hence, found it expedient to know Latin as it is not a course officially taught at Law school. Like Greek, the department offers Latin in both the third and fourth years and the focus is on Classical Latin. There are two courses in the third year: Reading Latin I and Reading Latin II. Reading Latin I is considered a foundational or beginner's course. The course focuses on morphology which covers the various verb types and their conjugations, plus the declensions of nouns, pronouns and adjectives, with exercises in reading and translation of basic sentences. Reading Latin II is considered an intermediate course and, at this stage, the focus is on the introduction of basic syntax: word order, comparative constructions, constructions showing agreement; and the construction of questions (single, double, deliberative), commands, and wishes. Reading Latin III focuses on translation and practice in the construction of complex sentences that build reading proficiency. Reading Latin IV focuses on the consolidation of the lessons of the previous studies and on acquiring a working proficiency and comprehension through the translation and the reading of prescribed primary texts in various classical literary genres (University of Ghana, Undergraduate Handbook 2015–17).

From the survey conducted, all twenty-five respondents have studied Latin and only five out of the twenty-five have not studied Greek. Unlike responses from those who studied Greek, those who studied Latin gave positive responses. However, like Greek, a few were able to study up to Latin III and no one since 2009 has studied Latin IV (see Table 16). In addition to responses provided for why some preferred Latin, others felt it would help them improve their vocabulary. Nonetheless, after studying Latin, a respondent said he is yet to find its usefulness.

Table 16. Students who enrolled in Latin from 2009 to 2023

Programme	2009	2010	2011	2012	2013	2014	2015	2016	2017	2018	2019	2020	2021	2022	2023
Bachelor of Arts															
READING LATIN I	1	11	3	11	12	21	21	7	5	11	1	4	4	5	3
READING LATIN II	1	2	2	2					2						3
READING LATIN III			4	1											
Bachelor of Laws															
READING LATIN I										1				1	
Doctor of Philosophy in Classics															
READING LATIN I												2			1
Master of Philosophy in Classics															
READING LATIN I	3	2	2	2	1	2	1		1				1		
READING LATIN II		2	1	2	1	1	5				1				1
READING LATIN III			1	3											
Visiting Studentship															
READING LATIN I											1				
READING LATIN II			1												
TOTAL	5	17	14	21	14	24	27	7	8	12	3	6	5	6	9

Source: Institutional Research and Planning Office (IRPO), University of Ghana. © Gifty Etornam Katahena 2023.

For those in graduate studies, it has helped in translations and understanding of concepts, close reading, and analyses of texts. Unfortunately, I was unable to get in touch with those who studied Latin and went to the law school for feedback on its usefulness. For those in politics, industries/business, they responded that it has no impact on what they are doing professionally.

Like Greek, the learning experience of some was discouraging while others could not hide their excitement. And for those who studied both Greek and Latin, Latin was, as usual, a better learning experience than Greek was. When asked if they would study Latin again should they be given the opportunity, out of the twenty-five respondents, ten commented 'No', ten commented 'Yes', and five said it would depend on who is teaching the course.

Support system

There was a discussion on support or encouragement from family and friends and support in terms of course materials for studies. Respondents who studied classical languages more than five years ago said they relied on course materials from the course instructor only. However, respondents who recently (from five years ago until now) took the course, responded that they had various materials they could rely on including both online sources and the course instructor's prescribed texts. This shows the extent of improvement in the teaching and learning space. In the survey and interview that discussed whether students had some support or encouragement from their family or friends, responses indicated that most of them did not have parental or family support. Two respondents commented that their parents asked how they would get jobs after school after studying the classical languages. Four respondents said their friends thought they were weird for choosing to study classical languages. That notwithstanding, two respondents said their parents encouraged the study of classical languages because their parents had studied Latin as part of their pre-tertiary education. Familial support and encouragement in education are important in Ghana, as in perhaps most parts of Africa. What a child aspires to be is driven sometimes by familial support and sometimes by influences from friends. It was therefore important to get past students' views and experiences on family and friends' support.

Conclusion

From the survey conducted, twenty people studied both Greek and Latin and all twenty concluded that they found it easier studying Latin than Greek. The preference for Latin has probably been the trend since the inception of the department in 1948. A University of Ghana Annual Report (1973–4) by the Vice Chancellor about the Classics Department states, 'The number of students taking various courses in the Department continued to increase and for the first time in many years, a student was admitted to read Greek, and the intake for Latin was the largest for the past four years' (University of Ghana 1975: 54). It is also evident from the survey, interview, and data that students over the years find Latin more appealing and easier as compared to Greek. The challenges discussed have been centred around the availability and accessibility of resources and the professionalism of the course instructors. My interview with some past students highlighted the fact that understanding and appreciating classical languages depends on who is teaching the course and their level of knowledge in the classical languages. And this affects one's experience in one way or another.

The reaction from people around the respondents and the uncertainty of an economic future where supposedly 'dead languages' were studied redirect the question of relevance. From survey to interview, respondents thought studying Greek and Latin could only be beneficial to people who wanted to pursue a career in them, that is, in academia. To the rest of them, it was for fun and the pride that one knows something others do not know. They found it prestigious to be able to embellish their English with Latin phrases but concluded it could not help them economically or in terms of societal development.

References

Goff, B. (2022), 'Decolonizing Classics in Africa: the work of Alexander Kwapong', *Bulletin of the Institute of Classical Studies*, 65: 32–41.

Okyere Asante, M. (2022), 'Classics and the politics of Africanization in Ghana', *Bulletin of the Institute of Classical Studies*, 65: 18–31.

University of Ghana (2015–17), *Handbook for the Bachelor's Degree and Course Description for Programmes in the Humanities*, 2 September, 2015–July 2017.

University of Ghana (1975), *Annual Report: 1973–1974*, Accra: University of Ghana.

NIGERIA, MALAWI, UGANDA, TANZANIA AND IVORY COAST

Leslie F. Ivings

The study and the teaching of Classics are fairly well known in the larger African countries, especially those with either a large European population or those that belonged to the general archaeology or expanse of the classical empires, most notably Rome. In this chapter I examine what remains of Classics teaching in some of the other parts of Africa and the sometimes-surprising results that are found. However, this chapter also will show the shift away from the thinking of former colonial masters and a move towards new interpretations of the impact of language and the history of the ancient world.

Nigeria

Classics is only studied at the University of Ibadan in Nigeria, where the Department of Classics was first established in 1948. Enrolment has been greatly enhanced by the study of legal Latin for all prospective legal practitioners in Nigeria. In 1998, two new courses were added for the study of Roman law, which increased the number of students even more. As of 2018, the Department had a staff complement of ten. This was made possible by assistance from the Leventis Foundation. The Foundation also helped to start a vigorous programme of staff development to make sure that the Department has the best possibly trained staff to accommodate the needs of all students involved with Classics.

The courses that the Department offers remain primarily focused on the study of the Greek and Roman civilizations. The Department believes that despite the colonial history of Nigeria the civilization of the Romans played the greatest part in forming Africa and especially what is today North Africa. Additional emphasis on the study of Roman North Africa and the influence of Greek myth and poetry on Yoruba storytelling has been added to the curriculum with great success. Students who major in Classics now have to take two compulsory modules on Ancient History and Archaeology of North and North-East Africa. This does not mean that classical philosophy and plays are neglected. Students are given the same access to core modules on Greek Philosophy, most notably on Plato and Aristotle. Core and selective modules on the great dramatists of antiquity are also offered, giving students first-hand experience of Aeschylus, Sophocles and Euripides. It should be noted that this is in translated form as introductory courses in Greek and Latin are not available to students in secondary education.

Historiography is also not neglected, with students being exposed to the writings of Herodotus, Thucydides, Suetonius and Tacitus in their undergraduate studies. The political philosophy of Cicero and the great epics of Homer and Virgil are not forgotten either. On the linguistic front within the Faculty of the Humanities, those students studying either English or French Literature are also taught the classical tradition behind these disciplines. Another area of growth for the Department of Classics has been the introduction of courses around the history of the New Testament in the Christian Bible, with many students from theological disciplines wanting a deeper understanding of the times of the early Christian canon. The Department of Classics at Ibadan is very proud of its achievements and regularly reminds all prospective and current students of all of their distinguished alumni. The Department of Classics is also very proud of its Departmental Journal, founded in 1957, *Nigeria and the Classics*, which remains in publication and attracts authors from other Classics faculties in Africa to publish scholarly articles and reviews therein.

One of the most notable achievements of the teaching of Classics at Ibadan University has been the advancement of women in academic roles and the nurturing of talent within its female student corps. Probably the greatest success story of this policy is that of Professor Folake Onayemi. She was the first woman to be awarded a PhD in Classics in Nigeria, and the first Black woman to be Professor of Classics in sub-Saharan Africa. Her specialities were comparative Graeco-Roman, Nigerian Literature and comparative literature / Religious Studies. In a 2023 interview Professor Onayemi acknowledged that Classics faced challenges in Nigeria, most notably on how it remains relevant in an African post-colonial world: students would rather focus on degrees and majors that would ensure financial success (Punch Nigeria 2023). But Professor Onayemi pointed out that in the modern complex world of AI and politics, the ability for African / Nigerian students to study the complex political situations of the First and Second Triumvirates in an African context could prove vital in solving some of the most complex problems in the areas of Africa that are currently experiencing the greatest amounts of civil unrest. Olakunbi Ojuolape Olasope is currently Professor in the Department of Classics at the University of Ibadan. She is an expert on Roman social history, Greek and Roman theatre, and Yoruba classical performance culture (O. Olasope, personal communication, June 2024).

Nigeria, in this uniquely Afro-centric approach to the teaching of Classics, will in all likelihood remain a star on the academic map. And with innovative young heads of department, they will continue to attract students – even if it is only students that take Classics courses to fill up their degrees. There have been many times that these most unlikely of all Classics students end up making some of the greatest contributions to the field of Classics in general. In this case Nigeria is very smart, it uses the best of both worlds approach. Students recognize the contributions that Classics has made, like that of Roman law, and they take those aspects and assimilate them into their own unique circumstances of cultures and beliefs to create something useful and new thus ensuring their relevance and future existence (Olaopa 2021).

Malawi

In the teaching of Classics in Africa, one school stands out. In 1987, in a BBC documentary, it was called 'The Eton of Africa'. Kamuzu Academy was founded in 1981, by Malawi's first President, Dr Hastings Kamuzu Banda. In the most extraordinary shift in post-colonial Africa, Kamuzu Academy was created with the sole ethos of teaching Classics in a very Oxbridge and Ivy League sense. Banda wanted the school to rival the best that Europe could offer: the Academy would be more than a mere British grammar school. Banda is recorded as saying: 'This place is for Classical Education, Greek, Latin, particularly Latin. I want that to be clearly understood by everybody. If you don't like Latin, don't come here!' Latin was thus made a compulsory subject from the beginning of the Academy and even today it is taught up to IGCSE level.

Usually when one deals with projects or schools that are started by dictators, when the dictator dies or is removed from office, those projects or schools that bear his name are just as quickly removed or changed to fit the ideology of the new regime. But not so with Kamuzu Academy. It continued on through the difficult economic times in Malawi in the late 1990s. The Academy also continued a process where more female students were admitted, not only to increase the number of students at the Academy, but also to continue the process of improving its academic performance. As the Headmaster, Mr A. Lambert-Knott said of the Academy in 2018, quoting the Roman poet Horace and referring to the late President Banda: 'Exegi monumentum aere perennius. I have built a legacy more lasting than bronze.'

According to the Deputy Headmaster for Academics, the wide-ranging curriculum covers English (Language and Literature), Mathematics, Latin, Classical Greek, History, Biology, Chemistry, Physics, ICT, French, Music and Art, and Design (Kamuzu Academy 2018). The Classics form the most important part of the ethos of the Academy and one classical subject is compulsory. During the fortieth anniversary celebrations of the school in November 2021, Malawian President Lazarus Chakwera was a guest of honour, which shows that despite the seemingly anachronistic character of the school and its connection to the former president, the Academy remains an influential force in Malawian society and politics (Nkungula 2021). There can be no doubt that the importance that the Classics play at Kamuzu is why it has stayed so influential.

The Malawian experience in teaching Classics is not limited to the Academy and its age range from eleven to eighteen. Indeed, the University of Malawi has recently restructured its Classics Faculty. At Chancellor College, the Department of Languages and Linguistics was reconstituted by the merger of French and Classical Studies with the African Languages department. In this new structure there will be two language sections, one focusing on languages and linguistics, the other section focusing on languages, culture and history of the civilizations of France, Greece and Rome. This is undertaken in a post-colonial context as well as with the more traditional forms of study. The department thus moves on, with analyses of the Classics and the great impact that they have had on shaping Europe and Africa not merely in the past but in modern contexts as well.

Currently the university offers the following graduate and post-graduate degree choices in the newly reconstituted department: BA in Linguistics, MA in Pure Linguistics, MA in Applied

Linguistics, MA in Translation Studies and a PhD in either Pure Linguistics or Applied Linguistics. The department also offers courses in Classical Studies (Language, History, and Philosophy) which can be taken in the following degrees: BA in Humanities and a BEd in Language Education. The longest running concern for the University of Malawi was the availability of suitably qualified language instructors. This concern is also one that was prevalent with the Board of Governors at Kamuzu Academy during the early 2000s. But with the continued existence of theological colleges throughout Malawi, where at least the basics of koiné Greek translation and study are taught along with Introductory Latin, the fears at a basic foundational level have been mitigated to some extent. For at least the near future, Classics and Classics teaching in Malawi seem secure.

Uganda

Classics is still taught at the oldest and largest university in Uganda. Makerere University in Kampala was founded in 1922 and currently boasts a student population of over 30,000. Classics teaching has been restricted to the following fields: Philosophy, Creative Writing / Drama and Theology / Linguistics. Although not as prolific as in Malawi, Makerere University still offers these courses as part of wider degree curriculums in the field of Humanities.

The College of Humanities and Social Sciences offers a course in History of Ancient Philosophy. This is a second-year undergraduate study unit that focuses on the origin of Greek philosophy, starting with the period of naturalism that addresses the cosmological questions on the origin and the end of things, beginning with Thales and working its way past the Pythagoreans and Epicureans to eventually ending with Socrates, Plato and Aristotle. The course also covers Roman philosophy and pays special attention to what extent African philosophies like those of Egypt might have had on those of Ancient Greece. The course wants to equip the student with knowledge and the ability to critically analyse ancient texts in translation.

The College of the Performing Arts offers courses in Ancient Greek Drama, focusing on Sophocles, Euripides and Aristophanes. The plays are offered in translated texts and also focusing on the Neo-Classical revival of Greek Tragedy up to 1700. Makerere is one of the only universities in Africa to study Ancient Greek Comedy and Drama in such a broad context. This is offered in a BA programme in either Creative Writing or Performing Arts. Students can also study these aspects of the development of classical drama within the African writing experience in the twenty-first century. This is another excellent example of a post-colonial course in Classics being used to keep the traditional works alive. The positive impacts of this reception can already be seen in modern Ugandan theatre and creative writing: the acclaimed novelist and Nobel Prize-winning author V. S. Naipaul spent part of his academic career at Makerere University.

Makerere University also offers New Testament Greek (koiné Greek) in their Department of Religion and Peace Studies. Koiné Greek is offered both in an introductory first-year programme with basic vocabulary and translation of short pieces, to a more Advanced Course in the third year that focuses on all aspects from vocabulary to greater emphasis on translation studies. Makerere University also offers a course in Islamic History in the same department. Although not strictly a classical teaching subject, Islamic History does touch on the Eastern / Byzantine Empire from the perspective of conquest and the eventual decline and fall of Constantinople in 1453 CE.

The greatest concerns about the teaching of all the above subjects at Makerere University is political uncertainty, rather than student numbers. As recently as 2017, the campus has been shut down because of student protests wanting democratic change within Uganda. Where you have thinking about democracy, you will inevitably be drawn to the classical examples, such as that of Athens. Thus, even in a climate of political uncertainty, Classics has a way of surviving the turmoil that might surround the world or country that it inhabits, regardless of fashion.

Tanzania

Tanzania currently has no formal programmes for the study of Classics either at school or university level; however, there still exist some notable courses where Classics remains a part.

The University of Dar Es Salaam, instituted in 1970, currently offers the BA (Philosophy and Ethics) and the BA (Philosophy and Literature) courses. Within these two degrees, in the second year, students are introduced to Classical Thought in Translation through a History of Ancient and Medieval Philosophy module. This subject contains philosophical readings from Plato to St Augustine, and the Medieval Islamic thinkers such Averroes. Students can also take a selective course in their second year called Selective Readings in Philosophical Classics. In this elective, more Platonic dialogues and selected works by Aristotle are added.

The University of Dar Es Salaam also offers a degree course in Archaeology and History. Although the archaeological aspect of the course does not focus on any classical archaeology in the Mediterranean, it does teach students concepts and research methodologies in the archaeological field. The primary focus of this is the study of Tanzanian pre-history and the hunter-gatherer communities that lived there. Again, in this degree course, there are two subjects which incorporate elements of Classics. Both are second year courses. The first is A Survey of World History to AD 1500, which makes reference to both Greek and Roman civilizations, although not in any great detail. The basics are covered in a broad sweeping manner. The second subject is African Civilizations, which covers Ancient Egypt, Roman North Africa to the Songhai Empire in Mali. Again, this course does not give great detailed discussions of Roman North Africa, but deserves a mention here. The ultimate idea is that certain periods or civilizations should not be forgotten or erased as they made the expansion of other empires and civilizations possible.

Ivory Coast

Another very honourable mention should go to the University of Abidjan. Within their graduate School of Management, they offer a BA (Law) degree. It is in the first semester of the first year of study that a prospective student will find ENGL181: Western Civilization. This six-month course starts with the Ancient Greeks, moves through the Roman Empire, and ends with the colonial powers of the twentieth century – most notably Britain and France. This should come as no surprise as the Ivory Coast was part of the French colonial possessions prior to its independence. What is encouraging is that Graeco-Roman antiquity is even taught at all. Given the recent civil war in the Ivory Coast, we can assume that some members of the university thought it important enough to teach, even if it is only as a reminder or a warning to the students taking the course.

Currently there are no classical courses on offer in Namibia, Botswana and Zambia. However, each of them places great emphasis on the offering of archaeology up to postgraduate level. Again, the archaeology courses which are offered are not geared to classical archaeology, but focus more on the history of the indigenous peoples and the pre-colonial history of those nations. With regards the teaching of history, their universities mainly focus on liberation movements and the history of Post-Colonial Africa and Globalization. A very interesting phenomenon has, however, started at the history departments at many of the universities within these countries; the study of Chinese history, which includes the history of dynastic, nationalist and Communist China. Even many of the universities that I mentioned in preceding discussions have such subjects in place in general degree practice. This would seem to be a clear reflection of the importance of Chinese influence on the current African context, not only with regards financial support but more importantly with regards intellectual thought.

Conclusion

Earlier in this chapter, while writing about Malawi, I mentioned the quote by Horace. In full, it reads:

> exegi monumentum aere perennius regalique situ pyramidum altius, quod non imber edax, non Aquilo impotens possit diruere....[I have built a legacy more lasting than bronze, taller in stature than the royal pyramids, which neither the biting rain nor the North Wind have the power to destroy. . .].

(Horace, *Odes* III: XXX, lines 1–4, published 23 BCE)

Horace wrote this about his own writings standing the test of time, rather than looking on his works and despairing, as in Shelley's *Ozymandias*. And that pretty well sums up the future of Classics teaching in Africa: many things may be transitory, things go in and out of fashion, but neither the great winds around Africa's southern tip nor the great high monuments of other men will influence the enduring legacy that the Classics bring. Its value is a very human thing: it is a discovery of self, an ultimate acknowledgement of the individual that through any type of learning they can strive for more and to do better. Ignorance of their own past can no longer be a millstone around the new generation's neck and it is with them that the continued teaching of all aspects of Classics will endure.

References

Kamuzu Academy (2018), 'Messages from School Management'. No date. Available online: https://kamuzuacademy.com/senior%20management.html (accessed 3 October 2023).

Nkungula, C. (2021), 'Kamuzu Academy Celebrates 40 Year Anniversary', *Nyasa Times*, 20 November. Available online: https://www.nyasatimes.com/kamuzu-academy-celebrates-40-years-anniversary/ (accessed 3 October 2023).

Olaopa, T. (2021), 'What future for classical studies in Nigeria'?, *The Guardian*, 11 March. Available online: https://guardian.ng/opinion/what-future-for-classical-studies-in-nigeria/ (accessed 3 October 2023).

Punch Nigeria (2023), 'Some students see classics as outdated, immaterial in modern world – UI prof', *Punch Nigeria*, 17 May. Available online: https://punchng.com/some-students-see-classics-as-outdated-immaterial-in-modern-world-ui-prof/ (accessed 3 October 2023).

Universities named

Makerere University: https://chuss.mak.ac.ug/en/
University of Abidjan: https://uniabidjan.com/
University of Dar Es Salaam: https://udsm.ac.tz
University of Ibadan: https://ui.edu.ng/
University of Malawi: https://www.unima.ac.mw/departments/language-linguistics-and-classical-studies

---

SENEGAL

John Bulwer

The Faculty of Letters and Human Sciences of the Cheikh Anta Diop University of Dakar in Senegal maintains the study of classical languages, literature and civilizations. It publishes the journal *Afrosciences Antiquity 'Sunu-Xalaat'*, has an active classical studies society and has recently undertaken a public engagement exercise about the value of a classical education, along with the Senegalese Association of Classical Teachers. Full details can be found at https://afrosciences-antiquity.com/actualite-et-evenement/.

A recent article (Mayoro Dia and Bouré Diouf 2023) gives an overview of the current state of the teaching of Classics (*lettres classiques*) in Senegal. The authors begin by saying that in a context of a general decline in numbers of those studying Classics worldwide, Senegal is no exception. However, it was at the heart of teaching in colonial times and in the first years of independence, thanks to the influence of the first president Léopold Sédar Senghor. He did much to establish the teaching of Classics and many students had the benefit of scholarships in Senegal and France (Senghor 1974, 1979). After he left power, however, numbers dropped in schools and universities as more utilitarian subjects became more popular. The study is arranged in two parts: first, an historical analysis of the methods and problems of teaching the subject in Senegal, and then some proposals for possible solutions.

History

The study of Latin and Greek owed much to the system of teachers sent from France for a period instead of national military service (*en coopération*). Education in Senegal was based on the methods brought by the colonial powers. This was how Senghor himself learnt French as well as Latin and Greek. In this way he sought to replicate the excellence of this education at the university Cheikh Anta Diop (UCAD) in Dakar. Teaching was delivered by *coopérants* in all the branches of the linguistic curriculum for Latin and Greek. From 1979 Senegalese teachers who had studied in France became responsible for the teaching. The poet-president Senghor gave much support to the subject, but new methods began to be introduced, including *Africani Latine discunt*, using new audio-visual technology. Greek was not included in this new method, but work was done to link African civilization with Greek civilization. Teaching concentrated on language learning with a variety of exercises, translation and commentary. After establishing the basics in lower classes by different techniques, in advanced classes new reading and discovery methods allowed the pupils to explore more historical and philosophical themes and elements of ancient civilization. Another more recent active approach concentrates on the languages not only for training in translation but also for interpretative reading and writing. However, there continue to be problems with the uptake and retention of pupils primarily because of the perceived difficulty of the languages, the attractions of scientific subjects, and the association of Latin with the Catholic Church. In addition, there are the demands of modern international languages and general lack of up to date resources.

The teaching of Latin and Greek today

Latin continues to be studied in a number of middle and secondary schools (secular and Catholic) but there is very little Greek. Learning, as reflected in the final examinations, concentrates on texts for translation and grammatical analysis and a further text for comprehension and interpretation instead of prose composition. In the Petit Séminaire de Saint Joseph de Ngazobil, for example, the emphasis is on mythology and civilization using modern technology for motivation. However, many pupils who begin Latin choose not to continue with their studies to the final examinations but choose other subjects mainly for the career opportunities. There have been some official measures on the part of the education department to support Classics, including interventions from the Greek ambassador to Senegal and the Catholic diocese. Other initiatives include school exchanges, academic cooperation, and teaching courses; in addition, the links between Classical languages and other subjects are emphasized to show the connections and to give pupils a solid base from which to advance. Teachers should also be able to give lessons in other subjects in order to integrate Classics in other subject areas. This practical application was already foreseen by the former president (Senghor 1979): 'Loin de négliger les grands auteurs classiques, on cherche (...) à montrer par-delà les différences, le caractère immuable du comportement des hommes. Surtout, on explore la romanité et l'hellénité réelles.' In summary, classical studies in Senegal are encountering real difficulties because of the rise of other subjects. Many who have not taken Classics do not understand what is involved in the subject, or in other cases have been put off by the way they are taught. Many see scientific or economic subjects as more useful. This account of the state of Classics teaching sets out the problems in an attempt to see how humanities subjects can support each other and how new methods and thinking can be used. Rather than reduce the hours available and make uptake of classes more difficult, the authors argue that it would be better to see how Classics can play a part and be an equal partner with other subjects in a modern educational programme.

References

Mayoro Dia and Bouré Diouf (2023), 'État des lieux de l'enseignement des Lettres classiques au Sénégal', ὁ λύχνος 166, November 2023.

Senghor, Léopold Sédar (1974), 'Le Sénégal, le latin et les humanités classiques', *Bulletin de l'Association Guillaume Budé*, 1: 47–61.

Senghor, Léopold Sédar (1979), 'La place des humanités classiques', *Bulletin de l'Association Guillaume Budé*, 2: 154–70.

Simon Idema

The teaching of Classics in South Africa happens primarily at the university level and overall interest in the field has declined considerably in the last few decades. While many Classics departments find themselves under constant threat of downsizing or even closure, a few have managed to achieve some level of stability in spite of a political climate that increasingly values utility and relevance in education. The classical tradition in South Africa is, nonetheless, viewed with a measure of suspicion, and its role as an instrument of colonization and identity construction is well attested (Masters et al. 2022: 1). In this regard, South Africa shares many commonalities with its neighbour to the north, and I refer readers to Obert Bernard Mlambo's chapter in this volume on Zimbabwe for a more in-depth analysis of the classical tradition in post-colonial Africa. Although socio-political factors that are particularly relevant to the South African context will be discussed, the primary aim of this chapter is to present an overview of the current state of Classics within the South African education system.

The South African education system

Education in South Africa is split into three stages: General Education and Training (GET), Further Education and Training (FET), and Higher Education and Training (HET). While Pre-Primary Education (ages birth–5) does exist, these schools are normally run by private individuals or institutions. General Education and Training commences around the age of six when learners enter Grade 0 (also called Grade R, or 'Reception'). This stage of education is compulsory for all learners in South Africa and is divided into three phases: the Foundation Phase (Grades 0–3), the Intermediate Phase (Grades 4–6), and the Senior Phase (Grades 7–9). After completing Grade 9, learners receive a General Education and Training Certificate. Further Education and Training (Grades 10–12) normally happens between the ages of fifteen and eighteen and is not compulsory. Students are required to pass two languages: one at first language level and another at second language level, one of which needs to be an official language (South Africa has twelve official languages including South African Sign Language). Upon completion of the FET phase, learners receive the National Senior Certificate (NSC). This is referred to as matriculation and Grade 12 learners are often called 'matriculants' or 'matrics' for this reason. Primary schools tend to offer Grades 0–7 while high schools offer Grades 8–12. The concept of a middle school is relatively uncommon. From about the age of eighteen, learners who have achieved sufficient scores in their NSC examinations are admitted into Higher Education and Training. This usually involves attending a traditional university or a university of technology. While some vocations may require four or more years to attain a basic degree, the majority of Bachelor's degrees typically span three years. A postgraduate diploma or honours degree can be completed after a basic undergraduate degree, and this is generally required before a student may apply for a Master's and, subsequently, a Doctoral degree. University courses are curated to allow only for a selection of elective modules in a chosen specialization, which may prevent students from taking modules that are deemed outside of their field. This selection can differ drastically from one university to the next, since the structure of these degrees are determined by the departments which offer them and are subject to ratification by internal faculty committees (here faculty denotes an overarching field such as the Faculty of Humanities, the Faculty of Science, and so forth).

The state of Classics in South Africa

Classical languages are not taught at any primary schools in the country and there are now only two high schools (all private schools) that still offer Latin at the secondary level. As previously mentioned, learners are required to pass two languages as part of the NSC examinations. Since English is widely used as the Language of Learning and Teaching (LoLT), many schools offer it as the first language along with another official language, like Afrikaans, isiZulu or Sesotho. As a result, there is little incentive for public schools, particularly in less affluent communities, to offer non-official language subjects. In fact, very few schools require a third language at all. At St Mary's School, Waverley (the author's school), one of the three schools that still offer Latin, learners are required to choose between Latin and French as a third language in Grades 8–9. They can then continue with Latin in Grades 10–12 as one of their three electives, a choice that presents some difficulty for many learners who are under a lot of pressure to take STEM (Science, Technology, Engineering and Maths) subjects. Latin classes are normally quite small, ranging between five and twenty learners in Grade 8 and shrinking to about one to five in Grade 12. As fewer and fewer schools offer Latin, overall numbers have dropped quite drastically, however, the number of matriculants in the country have remained steady at five to ten over the past few years.

At the tertiary level, Latin and Greek, as well as Ancient or Classical Cultures, are still taught at seven of the twenty-six public universities. Although Latin used to be a requirement for the study of Law in South Africa, this has not been the case since 1994, and Classics courses are now generally studied as part of a general Bachelor of Arts or BA Humanities degree. As of 2015, the North West University offers the only BA in Ancient Languages in the country. Language modules generally follow the Oxbridge system, which involves teaching most aspects of language and grammar during the first year, followed by more advanced grammar, readings, translations and literary analyses of advanced texts in the second and third years. At many of the former Afrikaans universities, Koiné Greek is offered instead of Ancient Greek to accommodate theology students, and some universities have been forced to merge Latin and Greek into a single course. Student intake for language modules is generally quite low across all universities and can range from roughly ten to thirty students in the first year. The North West University has seen spikes of over 100 students, although fewer than ten generally continue into the second year. This sort of drop in student numbers occurs at nearly all the universities. In addition to the language modules, universities also usually offer Ancient or Classical Culture courses, as well as Latin or Greek terminology courses geared towards other subjects such as medicine, botany and law. These are generally more popular and can include anything from fifty to eighty students, if not more. Across all Classics courses, it is not uncommon to have fewer than five students reach third year level but, while these numbers are small, they seem to stay consistent.

The perceived utility of Classics

Perhaps the biggest hurdle facing Classics in South Africa today is its perceived lack of utility. While Latin is still touted for helping with English language and for its ability to 'train the mind' to think logically, analytically and critically, classical subjects in general are not seen to have much value. Furthermore, the proposed benefits of Latin are too abstract and intangible for many first-generation South African students who are often incentivized to pursue lucrative careers in order to provide for their families and their communities. Careers in medicine, engineering, and business management are consequently favoured far above language and literature. In addition, many first-generation students know very little, if anything, about the Romans and the Greeks, and therefore have very little motivation to study Classics. An upside of this is that these students do not have strong objections to classical languages and cultures, which are still seen by some as being representative of Western dominance and colonialism. There is a strong need then to reframe Classics in a southern African context and a number of books have been published in the last few years that aim to do just that. *South Africa, Greece, Rome: Classical Confrontations* (Parker 2018) includes chapters by a number of local and international scholars on manifestations of classical reception in South Africa while *(u)Mzantsi Classics: Dialogues in Decolonisation from Southern Africa* (Masters et al. 2022) explores some of the conversations around decolonizing Classics in southern Africa. Decolonization is a somewhat loaded term that is, at its core, an appeal to challenge the systemic values of colonial, and particularly European, institutions. What this means for the study of Classics in South Africa is still being hotly debated.

The teaching of Classics

When it comes to the actual teaching of Latin and Greek, classical language courses are often allotted little teaching time, and since they aim to cover a large amount of grammar in a short period of time, methods for teaching classical languages have changed little in past decades. Moreover, the absence of Latin and Greek at primary and secondary levels has led to a further lack of scholars focused on pedagogy and contemporary methods of language instruction. The majority of institutions that still offer Latin and Greek make use of the grammar-translation method, reading method, or a combination of the two. The *Oxford Latin Course* (Balme & Morwood 1999) is by far the most popular series for teaching Latin at universities, while *Athenaze* (Balme et al. 2016) and the Joint Association of Classical Teachers' *Reading Greek* course (JACT 2007) are used for teaching Classical Greek. At universities where Greek is primarily aimed at theology students, textbooks such as Croy's *Primer of Biblical Greek* (2012) are used. At both secondary and tertiary levels, assessments normally include seen and unseen translations, comprehension, and grammar questions (primarily the naming and explaining of cases and moods). Very few institutions still teach prose composition, and Ancient and Classical Cultures are taught using notes or in-house textbooks. In 2020, the Covid-19 pandemic forced teachers and lecturers to reconsider the way in which they taught and assessed their subjects, yet little good has come out of this as far as Classics is concerned. Many universities simply resorted to uploading lesson plans and recordings, and while these resources are still made available to students now, teaching has largely returned to the way it was. Outside of online dictionaries and concordance tools, I am not aware of digital technologies being extensively used at any other schools or universities, so I can only speak of my own experience. The following is a list of digital tools that I have found particularly useful:

1 *Pear Deck* is a tool that allows for questions and prompts to be added to Google Slides or PowerPoint presentations. The types of questions include drawing, multiple-choice questions, fill-in answers, moving pins, true or false questions and several others. Some of

these features are unfortunately locked behind a paywall and waiting for students to answer questions can take up quite a bit of time. However, *Pear Deck* is a great way to increase student engagement, particularly in online lessons. It also allows teachers to see individual responses.

- *Kahoot!* is a game-based learning platform for creating quizzes using a variety of question types. It is truly one of the best platforms to 'gamify' learning and I have seen students who struggle in standard assessments perform consistently well in Kahoots. A scoreboard is shown between questions which is not ideal for students who are less competitive, and the majority of useful features are locked behind a paywall. This includes a feature to create self-contained courses as well as the option to track student progress.

- *Legentibus* is a digital library of Latin texts which range from beginner level to advanced. In addition to many public domain texts, such as Richie's *Fabulae Faciles*, *Legentibus* also includes Ørberg's *Lingua Latina per se illustrata* series along with many short stories that were written specifically for the platform. *Legentibus* recently launched an educator suite which allows teachers to select texts and chapters as reading assignments and to track student progress. While the stand-alone app is rather expensive, the educator suite makes it a much more viable tool to use with an entire class.

- Other tools that may be useful to teachers are the Digital Atlas of the Roman Empire, a Google maps for Ancient Rome, and the ORBIS geospatial network model, which allows for the calculation of duration and financial costs of travelling between points in the Roman Empire.

Teacher training and professional development

Training opportunities do not exist for teachers of Latin, Greek, and Ancient or Classical Cultures in South Africa, and classical subjects are not considered valid school subjects when enrolling for a Post Graduate Certificate in Education (PGCE), a minimum qualification for teaching at primary and secondary level. Some universities do offer general language-teaching modules; however, candidates are required to have studied official languages in order to register for these. Lecturers at universities are generally not required to have any formal teaching qualifications. While few professional development opportunities currently exist, there has been a renewed interest in organizing teaching and learning *indabas* (meetings) for classical languages in recent years.

The Classical Association of South Africa

Contact between institutions usually occurs under the umbrella of the Classical Association of South Africa (CASA) which, according to its website, has been in existence from as early as 1908. CASA aims to promote the study and appreciation of classical antiquity and produces a regular journal called *Acta Classica* which is recognized internationally. While the membership of CASA predominantly consists of academic staff and students, anyone with an interest in Classics is welcome to join. Regional meetings are held annually and a national conference is organized every two years. In November 2023, it was decided that a stand-alone panel for the teaching of classical languages would be introduced as part of the biennial national conference. In general, there is little contact among the high schools and they have not been associated with CASA for many years, however, it is my hope that this will change moving forward.

The teaching of Classics in South Africa is by no means without its challenges and demands for relevance in a society that is increasingly concerned with utility in education has placed many departments under constant threat of being downsized or closed. In spite of this, some have managed to carve out a comfortable space for themselves by offering supplementary classical culture and terminology courses. The last few years have also seen a growing number of young and diverse attendees at the biennial CASA conference and previously neglected topics, such as women in antiquity, race and culture, decolonization, and Neo-Latin poetry are being studied with renewed interest and vigour. Institutional changes may occur overnight, and no one can predict what the situation will be in a few years' time, but as a teacher of classical languages in South Africa, I am filled with hope for the future.

References

Balme, M. and J. Morwood (1999), *Oxford Latin Course*, Oxford: Oxford University Press.

Balme, M., G. Lawall and J. Morwood (2016), *Athenaze*, Oxford: Oxford University Press.

Croy, N. (2012), *A Primer of Biblical Greek*, Grand Rapids, MI and Cambridge: Wm. B. Eerdmans Publishing Company.

JACT (2007), *Reading Greek*, Cambridge: Cambridge University Press.

Masters, S., I. Nzungu and G. Parker (2022), 'Nothing about us? Reflections on classics in southern Africa', in S. Masters, I. Nzungu and G. Parker (eds), *(u)Mzantsi Classics: Dialogues in Decolonisation from Southern Africa*, Cape Town: African Minds, 1–18.

Masters, S., I. Nzungu and G. Parker, eds (2022), *(u)Mzantsi Classics: Dialogues in Decolonisation from Southern Africa*, Cape Town: African Minds.

Parker, G., ed. (2018), *South Africa, Greece, Rome: Classical Confrontations*, Cambridge: Cambridge University Press.

Websites

Acta Classica: https://journals.co.za/journal/classic

Classical Association of South Africa (CASA): https://casa-kvsa.org.za/

Digital Atlas of the Roman Empire: https://imperium.ahlfeldt.se/

Kahoot!: https://kahoot.it/

Legentibus: https://latinitium.com/legentibus/

ORBIS – The Stanford Geospatial Network Model of the Roman World: https://orbis.stanford.edu/

Peardeck: https://www.peardeck.com/learning-resources

ZIMBABWE

Obert Bernard Mlambo

Introduction

This chapter explores the provenance, history and status of Classics in colonial and post-colonial Zimbabwe. A post-colonial account of Classics in Zimbabwe that excludes the historical and social relations that were fostered by classical education and the appropriation of the Classics into the administration of the colony by the British would imply an odd omission of the important cultural aspects of race relations between Black and white people both in colonial and post-colonial Zimbabwe (see Jeater 2005; Mlambo 2022; Mlambo & McClymont 2022). The academic discipline of Classics is both a product of and longtime accomplice in violent societal structures, including white supremacy, colonialism, classism and misogyny (Konstan 2023). Thus, this chapter shows how colonial and post-colonial Zimbabwe has interacted with Classics in its manifestation to the Black African, both as an academic discipline of study and as a cultural and political front of Western imperialism.

Jo-Marie Claassen (1999) asked a very critical question which suits the context of post-colonial Zimbabwe: 'What is the role of the classics in decolonialized Africa?' This question has perhaps played out much more in Zimbabwe's education system than in any other African country. This is so because the term 'decolonization' in post-independence-war Zimbabwe was understood by the revolutionary government as the process of eliminating colonial legacies, such as unequitable land ownership structures, racism, and the problems of a colonial type of education (Mlambo 2018). The latter was construed more as a political problem by the post-Mugabe government (from 2017 to the time of writing of this chapter) whose relations with the West have not been particularly warm on account of differences over issues to do with human rights abuses, issues of government accountability to its citizens, and issues of corruption in government.

Thus, political considerations of the place of Classics in a decolonized Zimbabwe dwarf analysis of its occurrence and status as an academic discipline of study. Such a bias is necessitated by the terrain of the politics at play in Zimbabwe through which prism the discipline of Classics was conceived and construed by the powers that be. This provides the default scenario for the analysis and framing of the present chapter. The chapter, thus, essentially looks at how Zimbabwe's specific politico-historical context has determined the existence of Classics in a bumpy post-colonial landscape, in which the discipline met with more enemies than friends.

Classics and Zimbabwe's cultural and political milieu

The entanglement of Classics with Zimbabwe's cultural and political milieu, past and present, is part and parcel of current debates in the country's post-colonial education and politics. By current debates, I refer to the broader discourses on decolonizing knowledge in African universities that border on critical race theory, particularly in the Zimbabwean context where the study of the Greek and Roman Classics is seen as part of the scaffolding of white supremacy. Drawing on Achille Mbembe's (2001) concept of the 'post-colony', one can clearly visualize Zimbabwe's historical trajectory from the experience of colonialism and the involvement of Classics in the country's relationship with its former colonial master, Britain. Since the concept of 'post-colony' makes perceptible the colonial relationships and configuration of politics past and present, between the colonizer and the colonized (Mbembe 2001: 14), I will in this chapter show how the politics of the post-colony mirror the precarious position of Classics, in which it is construed as a relic of colonial education in a country on an extreme and often violent decolonization trajectory.

I call this extreme because I believe a valid decolonization drive would be more about minimizing the oppressive use of a foreign culture as represented by Classics, rather than a too radical alienation from classical culture, that is inconsiderate of the context of the global milieu within which Black Zimbabweans have become citizens of the world (see McClymont 2018: 240–2; Bromberg 2021). Classics in Zimbabwe is accused of having served as a handmaid of colonialism, and to have been deployed as a colonial method of political improvization to maintain social, economic and political differences between races. It is further charged with having entrenched, institutionalized and legitimized racial categories that were skewed in favour of the colonizer at the expense of Blacks. There is hostility, in fact, associated with Western culture in general. The association with racism of the figure of Cecil John Rhodes is not forgotten, as southern Africa's post-war political language casts Rhodes as the one who paved the way for apartheid, by working to alter laws on voting and land ownership (Greene 2020; Mugabe 2001).

What is more, Classics' association with the colonial practices of domination and racial discrimination has led the government to raise questions concerning its relevance in a 'free' country. The nature of the questions we might ask ourselves could be construed or framed as follows: Is Classics politically correct in Zimbabwe? Why are the educational authorities in Zimbabwe apprehensive about Classics? What do they resent about Classics? Several answers and explanations may be given to these questions, but the situation as it has turned out in Zimbabwe is such that the government has taken some action that manifests in a collision of forces at the intersection of the politics of the post-colony and the many legacies of colonialism, and has resulted, as I shall explain in detail, in the marginalization of Classics at the University of Zimbabwe. Classics has effectively been treated as a relic of colonialism rather than as a mere academic discipline such as Mathematics.

I will start by giving a detailed account of two facets of Classics' occurrence in Zimbabwe, namely its occurrence and status and position as a cultural tool of the British Empire, and later on, as an academic discipline of study in Zimbabwe. I thus proffer a survey of the history of Classics in colonial Zimbabwe with the aim of further examining the function of education and culture within colonial and post-colonial designs. The foregoing analysis more broadly explores a cultural history of classics in colonial Zimbabwe. The interaction during the colonial period of Whites and of a Black African culture with the classical tradition justifies the foregoing analysis that zooms in on the politics of the post-colony and the consequences such politics have had on Classics at the University of Zimbabwe.

Classics as a culture

For me Classics is not entirely framed in the sense in which it has traditionally been narrowly understood, as the study of the cultures of Greece and Rome, principally with a focus on the great works of Greek and Latin literature, including the political history of Greece and Rome (Konstan 2023). Rather, I look upon Classics in its aspect as, broadly speaking, a condition which has survived colonialism, maintained alive in books, in academic performance, in the criteria for career advancement (Guite 1965), in cultural patterns, in the self-image and aspirations of people (see Claassen 1999; Lambert 2011), and many other aspects of modern experiences of Africans (cf. Ndlovu-Gatsheni 2013). This kind of understanding of the Classics can be further discerned in Frederick Lugard's (1926: 618) description and typology of Roman imperialism as a civilizing force for barbarian Britons, whose imperialism, and whose cultural tool, Classics, he regarded as the torch of culture and progress among the uncivilized world of the African continent.

Classics is in some way a cultural front of the British Empire. I mention this idea in the context of European framings of the Mediterranean as a source of modern Western identity –

in which conception the white race regarded itself as exclusively privileged to help an ailing, weak, and barbaric Black race to civilized ways of life (Lambert 2011; Hilton 2017; Konstan 2023). Barbara Goff aptly captured this idea through her analysis of the concept of the colonial library and its relation to a discourse of classics. In her words: 'A "colonial library" would use classical texts and metaphors as weapons for the subjection of the colonized and to consolidate their cultural dependency' (Goff 2013: 9). I may mention here the appropriation and deployment of classical metaphors by the British colonialists in their explanation of African societal phenomena, as well as a means of justifying their conduct and administration (Jeater 2005: 1). As Diana Jeater puts it: 'Speaking with Southern Rhodesian Africans in the 1920s, administrators, farmers and missionaries did not clearly hear the local voices, but heard echoes from somewhere in the Mediterranean, sometimes between the birth of Homer and the death of Christ' (Jeater 2005: 8). We should note that, as Jeater pointed out, there was an attempt not so much to demonstrate genuine connection between Africans and 'Classical' peoples as to justify direct rule and a superior position in dealing with the natives.

Jeater's context can further be clarified if we relate to the logic of placing Africans in the classical age by the native administrators. Their knowledge about the locals was derived from white ethnographic accounts. White ethnographers such as Bullock (1927) constructed an image of the Black African informed by knowledge of classical literature. Pilossof (2009) has noted how such twentieth-century ideas have persisted in the twenty-first-century white writings about Africans and land expropriation. Jeater (2005: 9) has noted how the African was depicted by the colonialists as the barbarian at the gate and also as similar to the nymphs and shepherds of the classical pastoral ideal. The 'barbarians' metaphor placed the white men as civilizers, bringing Africans into modernity, while the pastoral metaphor placed the burden of preserving all that was best of the old world upon the shoulders of the white men (Jeater 2005: 9; cf. Barker 2007).

Such was the role of Classics in shaping race relations between whites and Blacks in colonial Zimbabwe. In the next section, I examine the place of Classics in Zimbabwean law and politics.

Classics, law and politics in Zimbabwe

Politically, Classics was also involved in the administration of Black Africans. British colonialists, it appears, administered colonies by mirroring the classical Roman political administrative model as they understood it (Mlambo & McClymont 2022). This was quite evident in Southern Rhodesia where the Roman system of co-opting the indigenous elite as collaborators in ruling the local inhabitants was the system particularly encouraged by Cecil John Rhodes (Haigh 1985; Braman 2011). It should be noted that the mirroring of Rome in Rhodesian politics was not a matter of uncritical imitation by Cecil John Rhodes (Mlambo 2022: 39). It is quite true that Rhodes admired Roman achievements, but he was not oblivious to some defects of the Roman Empire, as shown by his appreciation of the improvements brought by the modernity of his time.

Nevertheless, the influence of Roman habits of rule are arguably discernible in the colonization of Africa. It has been argued by a number of scholars that the Roman system of political administration in ancient Britain was used as the standard for the nature of British colonial politics in Southern Rhodesia (Hilton 2017). Mlambo and McClymont further noted that:

This is manifest in other areas too. For example, the institution of Roman-Dutch law as the *locus standi* of jurisprudence in Southern Rhodesia calls to mind the Roman law itself, to which ancient Britons had also been subjected... Yet Roman-Dutch law was applied here, but not necessarily elsewhere, because Britain had taken this legal system over from the Dutch in the South African Cape Province when they annexed it in 1805 – at the time essentially to keep Napoleon out of southern Africa, and to safeguard for Britain the sea route for trade to and from the more lucrative East.

(Mlambo & McClymont 2022: 57)

Zimbabwe itself, of course, has been influenced by the above-mentioned Roman-Dutch law, to such a degree that legal jargon in Zimbabwe is heavily framed and conceptualized in Latin phrases. The 2018 presidential legal challenge made the opposition lawyer Advocate Thabani Mpofu famous for the use of Latin jargon in his submissions to the panel of Zimbabwe's Constitutional Court Judges. One such Latin phrase that he quoted was *Qui facit per alium facit per se* [He who acts through another acts through himself]. He was arguing that the winning presidential candidate, Emmerson Mnangagwa, had benefited from a messy and mathematically unverifiable vote-tally announcement by the Zimbabwe Electoral Commission Chairperson Justice Priscilla Chigumba. This was one moment when the whole nation listened to a legal principle being spoken live in Latin on Zimbabwe's National Television Station. Many ordinary Zimbabweans memorized the phrase, which made quite a wave around the country. In this case the Latin language livened up and added some interest and impetus to Zimbabwean politics. Political temperatures were at such a boiling point that Advocate Thabani Mpofu's deployment of the Latin jargon during the hearing of the petition loosened the mood of the people and allowed for a brief moment of fun during and after the hearing, regardless of the fact that the Constitutional Court of Zimbabwe went on to validate Emmerson Mnangagwa as the winner of the presidential vote.

There has, then, been some classical influence on Zimbabwean politics. In addition to its political influence, then Classics has formed a significant part of the Zimbabwean cultural environment. We may note that its manifestations can be traced to some extent among classically educated persons in Zimbabwe, as indicated below.

The classically educated

Classics in Zimbabwe is not only limited to the classroom or the lecture room. It exists in many forms, and may be discerned among the generation of retired men and women in Zimbabwe who received a classical education, and among the current generation of men and women who have graduated with degrees in Classical Studies, or have taken the subject as a major or as a minor in their university education. It is through the former group of old learners that Classics has existed in village conversations in Zimbabwe. Barbara Goff noted that in West Africa the missionaries 'perceived the classical languages as a sine qua non for a minister of religion, and selected converts were thoroughly trained in Greek and Latin' (Goff 2017: 1). This held true also in colonial Zimbabwe.

This author in 2012 witnessed a conversation between his mother and a member of a local Catholic congregation in his home village, in which the latter wanted to know about a title of Mary, the mother of Jesus, in a song which had the Shona words *Maria muvirigo,* which can be translated in English as 'Virgin Mary'. The second Shona word is derived from the Latin word *virgo*.

Now the author's mother had taken Latin at school. Although this instruction would have barely sufficed for the requirements of a university Latin course, it would have been enough for pupils to understand basic conjugations of verbs and declensions of nouns, as well as master a considerable amount of vocabulary. The classical heritage of the Greek and Latin languages, among other things, were introduced to Africans as part of colonialism's educational tools (cf. Lenel 2002). My mother correctly explained to her fellow villager that *muvirigo* was a Shona word derived from the Latin word *virgo*. This is just one of the many examples of the occurrence of Latin in rural Zimbabwe – demonstrating some remote effects of colonial classicism and the sociology of the Latin language (cf. Pasch 2008).

There is also in post-colonial Zimbabwe a return to classical themes by some Zimbabwean writers (see also Greenwood (2009: 2, 49) on this theme). Most poets who studied in the tertiary institutions of Zimbabwe are influenced by their native oral traditions as well as the literary traditions of Europe. A close look at Musayemura Zimunya's poems (1982) reveals classical influences: in the poem 'Humiliated' he refers to the 'hand of Caesar' (1.7), and his poem 'Monstrous' contains the phrase 'blind as a Cyclops shot in the eye' (l. 11). In 'Roads' is found the phrase 'Black Icarus' (1.18) and in the poem 'Mountain' is found the phrase 'compel us to roll the stone up dzimbabwe' (l. 20) with its suggestion of Sisyphus.

We also find classical influence in the writer Dambudzo Marechera's 'Primal Vision' ('And from Olympus Zeus flew to / rape Fair Leda and Helpless Io' (l.12): see Veit-Wild 1989: 141). In Marechera's *House of Hunger* (Marechera 1978) there are references to, *inter alia*, *Lysistrata*, *The Satyricon, The Golden Ass*, Demosthenes, Battus, Hippocrates, Greek vases, the Trojan Horse, and Pandora's Box. Classical literature cannot be separated from the writings of the aforementioned Zimbabwean writers.

Marechera, especially, experienced the universality of the Classics. He says: 'The ghosts which hover over Great Zimbabwe are the same as those which tormented Troy, those which overwhelmed Carthage, those which watched over Aeneas' (Marechera, in Wild 1989: 136–7). He justifies his own work thus: 'The poetry, though, when it is good, is immortal. Hence the self-consciousness of the structure, the form. And the selective use of myth and legend – the refusal to be bound by any period of human history' (Marechera, in Wild 1989: 136–7).

Such are some of the manifestations of Classics among the classically educated in post-colonial Zimbabwe. In the following section I explore the position of Classics in the context of a decolonization discourse in Zimbabwe.

Classics and decolonization in Zimbabwe

Having traced some of the pro-classical elements influencing Zimbabwean culture, I now consider the process of decolonization and its attended negative association with Classics in Zimbabwe.

Pre-colonial Zimbabwe was dominated by indigenous culture and non-exotic ways of livelihood and knowledge; yet British colonialism brought an end to the supreme power of governance by locals. It brought with it Western culture which inevitably got entangled with indigenous culture, and to a large degree, dwarfed local culture. And this is where Classics may be found to have negative associations in Zimbabwe. As I have noted earlier, relations between Africans and the colonizers were to some degree shaped by the Classics (Jeater 2005; Mlambo 2022; Mlambo & McClymont 2022). In her informative study, Greenwood (2009) has shown how Classics played a part in the control and mediation over power and the intellectual and material-cultural life of the African. Put differently, classical culture played a role in the colonial and post-colonial oppression and appropriation of Blacks by whites (of African land, culture and power) in which images of white domination informed by the issues of civilization and race are manifest (Jeater 2005; Mlambo 2022). Relations between the current government of Zimbabwe and the West are partly defined by the impact of that very colonialism in which the Classical heritage played a part.

The introduction of Western civilization and racial prejudice against Africans through colonization has had a significant impact on the political landscape of Zimbabwe – resulting in the re-evaluation of the manner in which the classical heritage was viewed by the Communist-linked ruling ZANU-PF (Zimbabwe African National Union Patriotic Front) government. This historical baggage of colonialism caused the post-independence government of Zimbabwe to speed up decolonial measures, which as I shall highlight, have been simplified and sometimes radicalized to the detriment of the teaching of Classics in Zimbabwe.

The said decolonial measures taken by the government of Zimbabwe after independence as an attempt to break free from Western cultural hegemony have had implications for the status of a classical education at the University of Zimbabwe. This resulted in a scenario where the fate of the discipline of Classics was influenced by post-colonial politics in Zimbabwe. Classics was involved in the context of two struggles in post-independence Zimbabwe. The first was a struggle in which the government of Zimbabwe attempted to decolonize education. In doing so, the government was mainly driven by racial arguments, which spilled over to some degree from the violent land redistribution exercise that witnessed white farmers being ejected from their farms, and even killed (see Mlambo 2022). The hostile racial attitude to the white farmers was reflected in the sphere of education. A second struggle involved Black academics and learners who were in support of a liberal education and yet have called for the removal of Classics as a discipline of learning at the University of Zimbabwe.

Since the latter struggle was conceived in terms of the liberation of Zimbabwe from Western cultural hegemony, the response of the government was through implementing a heritage-based university curriculum. This had serious implications for the teaching of Classics at the University of Zimbabwe. And, since the latter struggle was concerned with the issues of human rights and academic freedom, it opened up re-evaluation of the role of humanistic disciplines in Africa and their contribution to the Zimbabwean economy.

In the era of radical decolonization in Zimbabwe, Classical Studies has always been under threat (cf. Claassen 2022). The threat of decolonization to the study of Classics in Zimbabwe is real and extreme. At the behest of the new government after the long reign of former president Robert Mugabe, the new government promulgated a new mantra *nyika inovakwa nevene vayo* [a nation is built by its owners]. This philosophy drives a new heritage-based education which jettisons forms of knowledge and ways of knowing that are deemed foreign. It must be stated that the new government does not have any particular hostility towards Asian or East European culture and educational philosophy, but is rather averse to Euro-American knowledge systems, which it views as a threat to the country's intellectual and cultural freedom, sovereignty and independence.

As a result, the new degree programmes that were introduced at the University of Zimbabwe in the post-Mugabe era were construed in terms of the political struggle for freedom from colonial rule by the Liberation War political party, ZANU-PF. In a very subjective and partisan process induced by arguments reminiscent of critical race theory (cf. McCoy & Rodricks 2015; McCabe 2019), the government was clearly determined to change the university curriculum. This was conceived in terms of efforts to break free from Western cultural hegemony. This has ultimately affected the teaching and study of Classics at the University of Zimbabwe. Under a new education policy known as Education 5.0, a large-scale reorganization of the University curriculum has been undertaken, emphasizing indigenous rather than Western priorities. These include an emphasis on innovation and industrialization. Under this regime Classics staff have been forced to come up with new modules that are compliant with the new thrust (Apostolou et al. 2022). To put it in more specific terms, classicists have been challenged to invoke their discipline to help solve the country's problems, such as inflation, unemployment, poor road infrastructure, climate change challenges etc. If Classics has nothing to say in these areas, it means the discipline is irrelevant and must die! This command approach to education is a manifestation of determinist Marxism (cf. Maimela 1989: 29) also at play in Zimbabwe's agriculture sector through the government driven 'command agriculture' – a shoving-down-one's-throat element of industrialization reminiscent of Communist countries.

One of the characteristics of Education 5.0 is a strong emphasis on STEM [Science, Technology, Engineering and Mathematics] which is likely to have been influenced by the Chinese approach to education.

It may be argued that the Zimbabwean government's 'Look-East-Policy' opens up Zimbabwean education to Chinese Marxist and materialist influence. The recent rise of STEM-centrism in Zimbabwean education may be a result of this. For Marxism, science is the only valid form of knowledge, and thus a Marxist Chinese view of education is likely to be strongly STEM-centric. This Marxist-influenced STEM-centrism is likely to be one of the facets reflected if there is an attempt on Zimbabwe's part to emulate China's education system. Hence the recent renewal of STEM-emphasis in Zimbabwean education possibly is influenced by the materialist Marxism of the Chinese system which the Zimbabwean's Look-East-Policy aims to emulate.

Zimbabwean STEM-centrism in recent years has affected the teaching of the humanities in universities in the country. This has had serious implications for teachers of Classics as they could no longer be left free to teach Classics according to their own disciplinary priorities, as they had hitherto always done, but were required to reinterpret their teaching goals in line with the national economic blueprint. This blueprint laid particular emphasis on the production of goods and services, a goal harder for the humanities to contribute towards in comparison with more STEM-centred subjects.

From Zimbabwe's independence to the present, classical education has had to struggle for survival, to the extent, I am afraid, of almost dying. As we look at the history of Classics at the University of Zimbabwe itself, an interaction of pro-classical and anti-classical attitudes can be traced, which has led to the less than ideal situation that exists at present.

Classics in higher education in colonial Zimbabwe

Classical education in pre-independent Zimbabwe dates back to the era of the Federation of Rhodesia and Nyasaland. The Federation, which was an amalgamation of the three former colonies of Northern Rhodesia, Southern Rhodesia and Nyasaland, came into existence on the 1 August 1953. The formal teaching and learning of Classics started in 1958 when the Classics Department was established with the support of the then University College London. Classical education was to continue its widespread dominance beyond the dissolution of the Federation government in December 1963. The discipline was founded on the British educational system, flourished throughout the colonial period during which it enjoyed unfettered dominance, as it was well supplied with huge numbers of students in a colony well-modelled on the traditions of the British public school system (Callinicos 1997: 7).

The transformation of the University College of Rhodesia and Nyasaland in the 1970s into a fully-fledged university was further enhanced by the symbiotic relationship which existed between the school system and the university which, with regard to classical education, was well balanced. Schools within the colonies modelled on the British system supplied the University College of Rhodesia and Nyasaland with mostly white students and a few Blacks who had adequate Latin and Greek to take up degrees in Classics. This status quo remained for many years until after Zimbabwe's independence in 1980.

Enter the University of Zimbabwe!

After Zimbabwean independence, the new Black majority government started an ambitious school-building project with the overarching objective of making education accessible to the Black majority population in the country. Important to note are the risks which independence brought in for a classical education in an African context.

Classical education in the view of some does not integrate easily with the ideas of Negritude, as a result of the involvement of colonialism in epistemic violence, a charge brought forward by Cabral (1980) when he accused colonialism of taking Africans out of their history into the history of Europe. Furthermore, imperial domination has been seen as responsible for stifling the organic and historical development of the culture of a subject people and for liquidating its very essence (Cabral 1980).

Hostility towards Classics in view of colonial associations was to have serious implications for the Classics in independent Zimbabwe. In 1985, Walter Kamba, the first Black Vice-Chancellor of the University of Zimbabwe, attempted to close the Classics Department, which he considered an unimportant relic symbolizing the Eurocentric attitudes of colonialism. Kamba and the idea of an independent University of Zimbabwe must be located in the history of the University and the philosophy of its administration to date (see Katsamudanga & Mujere 2015).

Kamba belonged to the nationalist class (though he carried himself with the air of a British aristocrat). He sought 'the University OF Zimbabwe', and not, 'a University IN Zimbabwe', that is, like his fellow nationalists, he was preoccupied with the 'development agenda', fired up by a spirit of scientistic problem-solving, pigeonholed and superimposed on all disciplines of academic study. This approach to university education is still being pursued by the current university administration, four decades after independence. He propounded his philosophy of university education in a lecture he gave in 1985 at the Institute of Southern African Studies at the University of Lesotho (Kamba 1985). Ironically, he buttressed his argument for a complete change in university business by heavily quoting from the Classics as follows:

Heraclitus of Ancient Greece in the fourth century B.C. maintained that even those things that appeared to be stable were actually in a constant 'state of flux'. Plato examined what he perceived to be ever-changing appearances; Aristotle saw change, interestingly, as the transaction of potentiality to actuality. Augustine in the fourth century and Aquinas in the 13th century tried to understand how change fitted into the divine plan.

(Kamba 1985: 1).

However, the change which Kamba meant involved having to destroy some of the university disciplines, including Classics. So, he was effectively quoting from the Classics in order to destroy the same discipline whose wisdom he drew upon to present his change-argument. Kamba argued that the most important government priorities were the Sciences and Commerce. Salvation for the Classics came from Professor Hastings, who had been the Chairman of the Department of Theology and Philosophy in 1984. He combined Classics with Religious Studies and Philosophy under one department, citing the relevance of Classics in the understanding of Religious Studies and Philosophy.

Since that time, Classics was to face uncertainty under different university administrative regimes, though sometimes doing well in terms of student numbers. This was particularly the case in the late 1980s when student numbers dramatically increased to 7,500 for the whole university. This caused a lot of pressure on major subjects, as it became impossible to absorb everyone, providing an opportunity for Classical Studies to acquire students, as it did not require special qualifications for admission (Callinicos 1997). This trend continued throughout the decades up until 2015, when new demands were made to allow students to choose their preferred subjects.

The Classics section of the Department of Religious Studies, Classics and Philosophy, in the course of its existence, offered courses in Classical Studies, Classics, Latin and Greek at BA General and Honours levels, and Classics at Master's level. Higher degrees, the MPhil, and PhD, were also available. The Classical Studies courses began in the first year with two introductory surveys, one of Greek and Latin literature, and the other of ancient history. In the second and third years, topics relating to literature, philosophy, history and art history could be studied, such as comedy, historiography, didactic poetry and the novel, the Pre-Socratics, Plato, the Roman contribution to philosophy, Early Christian Philosophy, Athens in the fifth and fourth centuries, the Roman Republic and Empire, sculpture, public architecture, pictorial art and numismatics. The Classics section also assisted in the teaching of New Testament Greek in the department, and thus Classics operated as a handmaid to theology at the University of Zimbabwe.

The incorporation of Classics graduates from the University of Zimbabwe into Teachers' Colleges around Zimbabwe also helped a long way in complementing the work that was being done by the Faculty of Education of the University of Zimbabwe. Many theological colleges affiliated with the University of Zimbabwe were the direct beneficiaries of Greek experts trained by the Classics section.

Yet even when the Classics section had adequate numbers of students, there were many challenges faced in the teaching of Classical Studies at the university. Most of the students come from the rural areas, where there was a paucity of resources. The schools rarely possessed any variety of reading matter, and subjects were taught strictly in accordance with the syllabus. Students came to Classical Studies with absolutely no idea of what the subject was about. This contributed in a way to the unpopularity of Classics, leading to fewer and fewer students enrolled. There was little presence of classical language study in the Zimbabwe school system, except for a few elite schools. At the time of writing of this chapter, with the exception of the Hellenic Academy in Zimbabwe, which is interested in Greek culture, and of which the Hellenic Primary School is part (Ioannou 2021), we are not aware of any school offering explicitly Greece-related or Rome-related education in Zimbabwe.

Because there were only three schools left, at least in Harare, which offered Latin up to A-Level, it became increasingly difficult to attract students interested in specializing in Classics. The BA General Degree programme which was made up of two major subjects which was followed for all three years, and one major subject which students could study for two years, or could change in the second year, was scrapped in 2015.

Insofar as Classics was concerned, a very ambitious degree programme, Honours in Comparative History, Culture and Literature, was drawn up, and a Dual Honours Degree Programme in Classical Studies and Philosophy was offered. The former programme had many new modules developed by this author and his colleague Dr John Douglas McClymont. The modules, among many others, were as follows: Classical and English Drama: From Aeschylus to the Present; Comparative Civilizations: Graeco-Roman and Ancient African Civilizations; African and Chinese Civilization and Culture; Western Literature and the Classics; Classical and African Thought; Classical Views of Africa; Grammar and Syntax of English and Classical Languages; History of the English Language and Classical Influence; Classics and Colonial Administration in Africa; Christian Theology and the Classics; Classical Religion and African Traditional Religion; Comparative Mythology; Classics in the Modern World.

However, the above programme was discontinued in 2019, when completely new programmes were further introduced.

Under the influence of the policy of Education 5.0, mentioned above, attempts were made to fashion modules more in conformity with the Zimbabwean Government's new strategy of education. The Department of Religious Studies, Classics and Philosophy was renamed the Department of Philosophy, Religion and Ethics. Distinct Classical Studies programmes no longer exist under the new regime of modules, although the former Classics staff have been offered modules within degree programmes related to Religious Studies (Apostolou et al. 2022). Classical learning under this new regime survives in the form of modules on 'Classical Thinking and Social Transformation', 'Classical Perspectives on Innovation', and 'Classical Approaches to Development'. The Greek and Latin Language courses still exist as elective courses which could be offered to students willing to pursue them.

The present author and his colleague, Dr John Douglas McClymont, in trying to fulfil the new requirements of the heritage-based Education 5.0, drafted for consideration a module which might respond to modern problems that could be faced by students of agricultural disciplines at the University of Zimbabwe whether they be students of plant or animal life or any other agricultural discipline. The module sought to accomplish the following: (a) to answer the question of what agriculture is and how it is linked with society; (b) to help situate agriculture in the larger context of pursuit of happiness, and encourage students to think morally about agricultural issues and realize advantages and dangers; and (c) to help sensitize agricultural students to the issue of property (private versus common), and to realize that property ethics and labour ethics were things farmers or farm workers cannot ignore.

With regard to the discipline of agriculture, the module sought to assist in the following ways:

- To explore ways students of agricultural mechanics would benefit from knowing how geometry is not abstract in origin but since ancient times has related concretely to problems of land measurement.
- To assist students of agricultural economics to realize the connection of domestic economy and the wider kind of economy, and see how agriculture is related to their responsibilities as citizens.

The module also sought to give students of agricultural sciences in the faculty of agriculture a general exposure to agrarian thought through the study of relevant classical material.

To date, however, this module, though discussed, has not yet been implemented. So far, the future of Classics at the University of Zimbabwe would appear to be tied to its contribution as part of Religious Studies.

Conclusion

This chapter has sought to give the reader some understanding of the cultural politics of Classics in colonial and post-colonial Zimbabwe. The existence of Classics in Zimbabwe as a cultural tool of the British Empire and as an academic discipline of study has been to some degree politicized and turbulent. Classics in Zimbabwe is a combat zone for the politics of the post-colony.

Nevertheless, the heritage of Greece and Rome is still cherished even in some remote rural villages of Zimbabwe by old men and women in whose minds the imprint of the Latin language is experienced in some rare conversation. For many years after independence, the University of Zimbabwe has churned out graduates, some with Classical Studies as a major and some studying it as a minor. The country's premier university has done so, it must be stressed, amidst very constraining conditions that intermittently threatened the existence of Classics as an educational subject. Classics has needed to find new ways to survive under a different governmental environment with different educational priorities. Zimbabwean Classics has indeed a unique story worth writing about, and it is still unfinished. Hopefully there will be better times ahead.

References

Apostolou, S., M. Pagkalos and O. Mlambo (2022), *An Interview with Obert Bernard Mlambo on the Occasion of the Monograph, Land Expropriation in Ancient Rome and Contemporary Zimbabwe: Veterans, Masculinity and War (London: Bloomsbury, 2022)*, Isegoria Publishing, 9 September 2023. Available online: https://isegoriapublishing.co.uk/author-profiles/f/mlambo-obert (accessed 19 October 2023).

Barker, J. (2007), *Paradise Plundered: The Story of a Zimbabwean Farm*, Harare: Jim Barker.

Braman, N. (2011), 'Caesar's invasion of Britain', Unpublished Master of Arts thesis, History Department, University of Lethbridge.

Bromberg, J. (2021), *Global Classics*, London: Routledge.

Buckle, C. (2011), *African Tears: The Zimbabwe Land Invasions*, Johannesburg and London: Covos Day.

Buckle, C. (2002), *Beyond Tears: Zimbabwe's Tragedy*, Johannesburg: Jonathan Ball.

Bullock, C. (1927), *The Mashona. The Indigenous Natives of S. Rhodesia*, Cape Town.

Cabral, A. (1980), *A Return to the Source: Selected Speeches by Amilcar Cabral*, New York: Monthly Review Press.

Callinicos, A. (1997), 'Classics in Zimbabwe', *Epistula Zimbabweana*, 10–15.

Claassen, J. M. (1999), 'Classics for the Next Millennium: African Options', *Classical Outlook*, 76: 1–8.

Claassen, J. M. (2022), 'Classics for the third millennium: African options after the Fall', in S. Masters, I. Nzungu and G. Parker (eds), *(u)Mzansi Classics: Dialogues from Southern Africa*, Cape Town: African Minds and Liverpool University Press, 85–118.

Goff, B. (2013), *Your Secret Language: Classics in the British Colonies of West Africa*, London: Bloomsbury.

Goff, B. (2017), 'Classics in West African Education: The Rhetoric of Colonial Commissions', in L. Hardwick and S. Harrison (eds), *Classics in the Modern World: A Democratic Turn?*, Cambridge: Cambridge University Press.

Greene, R. (2020), 'Who is Cecil Rhodes and why are UK demonstrators protesting at his statue'? *CNN*. Available online: https://edition.cnn.com/2020/06/09/uk/cecil-rhodes-protest-oxford-intl/index.html (accessed 20 September 2021).

Greenwood, E. (2009), *Afro-Greeks: Dialogues Between Anglophone Caribbean Literature and Classics in the Twentieth Century*, New York: Oxford University Press.

Guite, H. F. (1965), *What Kind of Classics? An Inaugural Lecture Given in the University College of Rhodesia and Nyasaland on 7 August 1964*, Oxford: Oxford University Press.

Haigh, C. (1985), *The Cambridge Historical Encyclopedia of Great Britain and Ireland*, Cambridge: Cambridge University Press.

Hilton, J. (2017), 'Cecil John Rhodes, the Classics and Imperialism', in G. Parker (ed.), *South Africa, Greece, Rome: Classical Confrontations*, Cambridge: Cambridge University Press, 88–113.

Ioannou, T. (2021), 'Zimbabwe's Greek Primary School's OXI Day Celebration', *GreekReporter.com*, 29 October. Available online: https://greekreporter.com/2021/10/29/greek-school-zimbabwe-oxi-day/ (accessed 25 September 2023).

Jeater, D. (2005), 'Imagining Africans: Scholarship, Fantasy, and Science in Colonial Administration. 1920s Southern Rhodesia', *The International Journal of African Historical Studies*, 38 (1): 1–26.

Kamba, W. (1985), 'The Response of Institutions of Higher Learning to Africa's Rapidly Deteriorating Social and Economic Conditions'. ISAS Occasional Paper No. 2, 30 September 1985: 1–8.

Katsamudanga, S. and J. Mujere, eds (2015), *The University of Zimbabwe at Sixty: Historical Reflections*, Harare: University of Zimbabwe Publications.

Konstan, D. (2023), 'Mapping New Directions in the Humanities: The Case of Classical Studies'. Lecture Delivered at Universidade Do Estado Do Amazonas, Brazil, 6 August 2023.

Lambert, M. (2011), *The Classics and South African Identities*, London: Bloomsbury.

Lenel, B. (2002), *The History of South African Law and its Roman-Dutch Roots*. Available online: https://lenel.ch/downloads/history-of-sa-law-en.pdf (accessed 19 October 2023).

Lugard, F. (1926), *The Dual Mandate in British Tropical Africa*, Edinburgh: Blackwood.

Maimela, S. (1989), 'The Marxist Theory of Human Nature', in S. S. Maimela and A. König, *Systematic Theology: Study Guide 2 for THB-200-T (Anthropology)*, Pretoria: UNISA, 23–9.

Marechera, D. (1978), *House of Hunger*, London: Heinemann.

Mbembe, A. (2001), *On the Postcolony*, Berkeley: University of California Press.

McCabe, D. (2019), 'Kant was a Racist: Now What?' *APA Newsletter on Teaching Philosophy*, 18 (2): 2–9. Available online: https://cdn.ymaws.com/www.apaonline.org/resource/collection/808CBF9D-D8E6-44A7-AE13-41A70645A525/TeachingV18n2.pdf (accessed 19 October 2023).

McClymont, J. (2018), 'Some Misconceptions About Culture: Views from a Zimbabwean Classical Thinker', in F. Mangena and J. D. McClymont (eds), *Philosophy, Race and Multiculturalism in Southern Africa: Zimbabwean Philosophical Studies, III*, Washington, DC: The Council for Research in Values and Philosophy, 233–50.

McCoy, D. and D. Rodricks (2015), 'Critical Race Theory in Higher Education: 20 Years of Theoretical and Research Innovations', *ASHE Higher Education Report*, 41: 1–117.

Mlambo, O. (2011), 'Resurrecting the Teaching of Classics in Zimbabwe's Secondary Schools: The Imperative for a New Paradigm in Zimbabwe's Education Approach', *Zimbabwe Journal of Educational Research*, 23 (1): 44–60.

Mlambo, O. (2018), 'Veterans, Decolonization and Land Expropriation in Post-Independence Zimbabwe', in Á. Alcalde and X. M. Núñez Seixas (eds), *War Veterans and the World after 1945: Cold War Politics, Decolonization, Memory*, New York: Routledge, 167–83.

Mlambo, O. (2022), *Land Expropriation in Ancient Rome and Contemporary Zimbabwe: Veterans, Masculinity and War*, London: Bloomsbury Academic.

Mlambo, O. and J. McClymont (2022), 'Imagining Africans through the Lens of a Classical Education: The Politics of Colonial Administration in Southern Rhodesia', in S. Masters, I. Nzungu and G. Parker (eds), *(u)Mzansi Classics: Dialogues from Southern Africa*, Cape Town: Liverpool University Press, 50–74.

Mugabe, R. (2001), *Inside the Third Chimurenga*, Harare: Department of Information and Publicity.

Ndlovu-Gatsheni, S. (2013), *Coloniality of Power in Postcolonial Africa: Myths of Decolonization*, Dakar: CODESRIA (Council for the Development of Social Science Research in Africa).

Pasch, H. (2008), 'Competing scripts: The introduction of the Roman alphabet in Africa', *International Journal of the Sociology of Language*, 191: 65–109.

Pilossof, R. (2009), 'The Unbearable Whiteness of Being: Land, Race and Belonging in the Memoirs of White Zimbabweans', *South African Historical Journal*, 61 (3): 621–38.

Veit-Wild, F. (1989), *Dambudzo Marechera: A Source Book on His Life and Work*, Trenton, NJ: Africa World Press.

Wikipedia (2022), *Hellenic Academy*. Available online: https://en.wikipedia.org/wiki/Hellenic_Academy (accessed 25 September 2023).

Zimunya, M. (1982), *Thought Tracks*, London: Longmans.

AFRICA: FURTHER READING
Steven Hunt

The authors have found scanty evidence for the study of Classics in schools in other African countries than the ones described earlier in this book. However, the classical tradition has found new outlets, often in combination with local traditions. The book *(u)Mzantsi Classics* (Masters et al. 2022) is well worth reading for contemporary accounts of interactions with the classical legacy and its futures for the peoples of southern Africa. We quote:

> [*(u)Mzantsi Classics*] aims to spur debate about decolonising, transformative praxis by reimagining classics in Africa, on the one hand, and, on the other, turning the spotlight on pedagogies and experiences of students and scholars at different stages of their careers. The chapters present an attempt to identify and even redress some of the damage caused by exclusionary systems of knowledge production which the field of classics may have been used to justify, as well as combat the often paternalistic approaches of the Global North towards African classics. *(u)Mzantsi Classics* captures many voices of southern African classics today, crossing past, present and future haunts and harbours, and bringing something of our ourselves to the conversation.
>
> (Masters et al. 2022: 21)

The University of Ghana held an International Classics Conference in 2018. Full details with further inks can be found at https://www.eosafricana.org/collaborations/ghana-international-classics-conference-2019. In 2021 the Classical Reception Studies Network invited contributions from African teachers and students of Classics. The twenty blogs in the series which resulted from the 'African Takeover' are worth reading for contemporary experiences of Classics in Ghana, Nigeria and South Africa (Classical Reception Studies Network 2021). See also Budelmann (2006) for insight into the appropriation of Greek tragedy by West African dramatists. The recently-formed African Classics Network is a forum to 'facilitate networking between Classical scholars working in African countries or scholars interested in Classics in Africa' (https://african-classics-network.mailchimpsites.com/).

The Our Mythical Childhood project has links with Cameroon. In 2017, Professors Divine Che Neba (University of Yaoundé 1) and Daniel Nkemleke (University of Maroua) enrolled students and student teachers from Cameroon and neighbouring Chad to collect local myths (Dasi 2017). These have been made available on the project's website (Our Mythical Childhood 2023).

In Kenya, currently three private preparatory schools, which follow the British curriculum, teach Latin: Pembroke House, Peponi Prep and Kenton College. Hillcrest Secondary School no longer offers Latin, although the motto of its parent company still survives: '*summum appeto*' (L. Pollock, personal communication, 16 October 2023).

For a personal view of the teaching at Kamuzu Academy in Malawi, see *Goodbye, Dr Banda* by Alexander Chula (2023). For a slightly humorous view of the same school, from the perspective of one its students, see *The Jive Talker* by Samson Kambalu (2022). The school's motto remains '*honor deo et patriae*'. The recently-published *A Monument More Lasting than Bronze: Classics in the University of Malawi, 1982–2019* (McKechnie et al. 2023) promises to be an outstanding guide. For more on Malawi, see Ivings in this book.

Readers may be interested to note, for historical comparison with chapters elsewhere in this book, articles on Classics teaching in Africa by Esan (1966) and Ferguson (1966). Both have their focus on Classics in Nigeria and the Univerity of Ibadan in particular (the university had an active Classics Society 'Hoi Phrontistai'). Lambert (2014) notes that although no school offers classical subjects in Nigeria, the University of Ibadan maintains a healthy department through local outreach. For an understanding of the role of Classics in the colonial period, see Lambert (2011) and Goff (2013).

More recently, Schumann and Theron wrote about the Academia Latina, based at the University of Pretoria in South Africa, and its efforts to promote Latin and classical studies through community projects, including work with schools, and in prisons (Schumann & Theron 2018). The challenge of making the case for Latin in schools and universities at a time when it was becoming near-extinct there continues to resonate today.

The French conquest of Algeria (1830–1903) led to much interest in the Roman ruins by the soldiers and colonisers, who, through the study and memorialization of Roman antiquity, began to see themselves as the true inheritors of ancient Rome (Lorcin 2002). However, it is unlikely that the teaching of Classics was widespread under the French colonial period and any trace of it since Algerian independence in 1962 has long gone. In similar vein, the great sites of El Jem, Dougga and Carthage in Tunisia attract huge archaeological and casual tourist interest today, but there is little notice of this at the school level, as Ivings explains elsewhere in this book. In 2003, when Libya's President Gaddafi started to issue tourist visas, the sites of Leptis Magna and Sabratha temporarily joined the tourist round, until civil unrest following the revolutions of the 'Arab Spring' made visits too dangerous. The sites currently lie abandoned (Aljazeera 2021). However, an exhibition in Tripoli is preparing the way for future fieldwork, rekindling an old Italo-Libyan partnership in which archaeology will act as a bridge to renew economic ties between the two countries (Imam 2022). There are a number of international schools in Libya which offer a British curriculum: their websites do not indicate any classical subjects. See also Ivings in this book.

In Egypt, classical education is not provided in state secondary schools (A. Fahmy, personal communication, 21 January 2024). However, the ancient world has been enlisted in support of the Egyptian Government's plan to kickstart the tourist economy. In 2021 a 'Golden Parade' took place of twenty-two mummies to the new National Museum of Egyptian Civilization, televised for an international audience (Hussein 2021). The Museum itself, planned to open in 2023, has been described as representing a 'symbolic cultural victory' over colonial powers and foreign excavators and is intended to reassemble (amongst many other things) the 5,400 artefacts from Tutankhamun's tomb, many of which have been on continual tour since their discovery by Howard Carter in 1922 (Gornall 2023). Similarly, in 2002 the building of the Bibliotheca Alexandrina (a modern version of the Library at Alexandria, lost around 1,500 years ago) was another heavily politicized act to reclaim Egyptian heritage for the Egyptians (Stephens 2010). Usama Ali Gad (2023) blogs news items and publications related to Egyptian / Arabic scholarship in the field of Graeco-Roman studies, challenging prevailing Eurocentric viewpoints. A news article by Dardir (2023) attests to the continuing power of Greek tragedy in the current politics of Egypt (and Syria). For more details about Classics education in Egypt, see Ivings in this book.

School students in Ethiopia and Eretria learn very little about the Classical ancient world as part of the school curriculum; there is much more focus on the development of the modern states from the Nubian and Aksum kingdoms (see, for example, Julla & Melko n.d.) and the appropriation of the Solomonic tradition (see, for example, Simmons 2022) (personal communication, Mai Musié and Yoseph Araya, 23 October 2023). Reception of the ancient past can be seen in Yatreda : ያትሬዳ, a family of artists in Ethiopia 'making art in the style of tizita-nostalgia and longing for the past' whose YouTube channel presents videos based on mythological heroes, including Andromeda (Yatreda 2023). The recent online workshop 'Memnon, Andromeda, and Chariclea: Exploring Migration and Blackness', organized by Mai Musié, Awet Araya, Yoseph Araya and Sarah Derbew, explored classical mythological stories that centre 'Aithiopian' voices and the impact these stories have had on modern Ethiopian-Eritrean diaspora communities. It promises to be a fruitful collaboration and one can hope for a future publication (https://ics.sas.ac.uk/events/memnon-andromeda-and-chariclea-exploring-migration-and-blackness).

Recent excavations carried out by British archaeologists in Ethiopia have shown links between the Aksumite kingdom and the Roman Empire (Alberge 2015). The renewal of interest in the archaeology of Sudan can be summed up in the words of Sudanese archaeologist Sabrine al-Sadiq of Khartoum University: 'It is very important that Africans do African archaeology . . . because then we will have our own archaeological cultures. There is a lot we understand because we are from here. The idea that people from the west know best is changing' (al-Sadiq, quoted in Burke & Salih 2022).

The *Routledge Handbook of Classics, Colonialism and Postcolonial Theory* (Blouin & Akrigg 2024) promises to be a valuable contribution to the experience of 'Classics' in Africa, as well as in other parts of the world.

References

Alberge, D. (2015), 'Dazzling jewels from an Ethiopian grave reveal 2,000-year-old link to Rome', *The Guardian*, 7 June. Available online: https://www.theguardian.com/world/2015/jun/07/ancient-ethiopia-gravesite-treasure-rome (accessed 20 February 2024).

Aljazeera (2021), 'Jewel of Roman Empire lies neglected in Libya chaos', *Aljazeera*, 28 September. Available online: https://www.aljazeera.com/gallery/2021/9/28/libya-roman-empire-ancient-city-leptis-magna-tourism (accessed 7 November 2023).

Blouin, K. and B. Akrigg (2024), *Routledge Handbook of Classics, Colonialism and Postcolonial Theory*, London: Routledge.

Budelmann, F. (2006), 'Greek Tragedies in West African Adaptations', in B. Goff (ed.), *Classics and Colonialism*, London: Duckworth, 118–46.

Burke, J. and Z. M. Salih (2022), 'Young Sudanese Archaeologists Dig Up History as West Knows Best Era Ends', *The Guardian*, 27 December. Available online: https://www.theguardian.com/world/2022/dec/27/young-sudanese-archaeologists-dig-up-history-as-west-knows-best-era-ends (accessed 8 January 2023).

Chula, A. (2023), *Goodbye, Dr Banda. Lessons for the West from a Small African Country*, Edinburgh: Polygon.

Classical Reception Studies Network (2021), 'African Takeover'. Available online: https://classicalreception.org/category/blog-takeover/african-takeover/page/3/ (accessed 7 November 2023).

Dardir, A. (2023), 'Antigone: Classical Greek tragedy offers lessons for the modern Middle East', *Middle East Eye*, 18 August. Available online: https://www.middleeasteye.net/opinion/antigone-classical-greek-tragedy-offers-lessons-modern-middle-eastt (accessed 8 January 2024).

Dasi, E. (2017), 'Mythical Childhood Class at the Ecole Normale Supérieure: Introducing a New Batch of Students to OMC Project'. Available online: http://omc.obta.al.uw.edu.pl/Cameroon-November-20-2017 (accessed 7 November 2023).

Esan, O. (1966), 'The Classics in Africa', *Didaskalos*, 2 (1): 119–26.

Ferguson, J. (1966), 'Some aspects of the Classics at Ibadan', *Didaskalos*, 2 (1): 111–18.

Gad, U. A. (2023), [Blog] 'Greco-Roman Legacy in Egypt'. Available online: http://classicsinarabic.blogspot.com/ (accessed 7 November 2023).

Goff, B. (2013), *'Your Secret Language'. Classics in the British Colonies of West Africa,* London: Bloomsbury.

Gornall, J. (2023), 'Look ahead 2023: How the Grand Egyptian Museum aims to reclaim the country's ancient past'. *Arab News*, 7 January. Available online: https://www.arabnews.com/node/2225266/middle-east (accessed 7 November 2023).

Hussein, W. (2021), 'Egypt mummies pass through Cairo in ancient rulers' parade', *BBC*, 3 April. Available online: https://www.bbc.co.uk/news/world-middle-east-56508475 (accessed 7 November 2023).

Imam, J. (2022), 'Major exhibition in Libya aims to prepare for a surge of archaeological activity once political stability returns', *The Art Newspaper*, 17 February. Available online: https://www.theartnewspaper.com/2022/02/17/exhibition-explores-italys-role-in-unearthing-libyas-heritage (accessed 7 November 2023).

Julla, D. and T. Melko (n.d.), *History. Student Textbook, Grade 9,* Addis Ababa: Federal Democratic Republic of Ethiopia.

Kambalu, S. (2022), *The Jive Talker, or How to get a British Passport,* London: September Publishing.

Lambert, M. (2011), *The Classics and South African Identities*, London: Bloomsbury.

Lambert, M. (2014), 'On Rainbows and Butterflies: the Classics, the Humanities and Africa', *Acta Classica*, 57: 1–15.

Lorcin, P. (2002), 'Rome and France in Africa: Recovering Colonial Algeria's Latin Past', *French Historical Studies*, 25 (2): 295–329.

Masters, S., I. Uzungu and G. Parker, eds (2022), *(u)Mzantsi Classics. Dialogues in Decolonization from Southern Africa,* Cape Town: African Minds and Liverpool University Press.

McKechnie, P., S. Nyamilandu and S. Kambalu (2023), *A Monument More Lasting than Bronze: Classics in the University of Malawi, 1982–2019,* Washington DC: Center for Hellenic Studies.

Our Mythical Childhood (2023), 'Our Mythical Childhood Survey'. Available online: http://www.omc.obta.al.uw.edu.pl/myth-survey/category/oral (accessed 7 November 2023).

Schumann, C. and L. Theron (2018), 'Academia Latina: Working in South African Schools and Prisons', in A. Holmes-Henderson, S. Hunt and M. Musié (eds), *Forward with Classics. Classical Languages in Schools and Communities,* London: Bloomsbury Academic, 171–85.

Simmons, A. (2022), *Nubia, Ethiopia, and the Crusading World 1095–1402*, London: Routledge.

Stephens, S. (2010), 'The New Alexandrian Library', in S. Stephens and P. Vasumia (eds), *Classics and National Cultures,* Oxford: Oxford University Press, 267–84.

Yatreda (2023), [YouTube] Yatreda : ያትሬዳ. Available online: https://www.youtube.com/@yatreda6413 (accessed 18 November 2023).

PART 6
OTHER

INTERNATIONAL SCHOOLS

John Bulwer

There exists a network of schools around the world that cater for the children of parents who have travelled for their work to a new country. There are many such children who often have a school career that may span several different locations. Some continuity is clearly desirable in their education, and the local system may not be suitable for them unless they were to be certain to spend their whole time in school there and to continue to live there afterwards. These schools often operate in English (sometimes French or other languages) and either follow a national system or one that crosses borders such as the International Baccalaureate (IB), or in the case of the European Schools the European Baccalaureate. In an international city such as Brussels in Belgium, there are four European Schools (for children of families working for the EU) an International School offering a variety of qualifications, an American School following the US curriculum, a British School following the UK system with GCSEs and A-Levels, a *Lycée Français*, a German school and others. The assumption is that the pupils of these schools will move around in their lives and the education they offer will fit them for their future lives wherever they choose to settle down. Such children may choose to stay in the country where they grew up, or return to the original home country of the family, or even move on to a new country in their adult lives. International education is designed to enable this to happen equipping its pupils with enough languages and essential knowledge for their future lives. Even schools following a national curriculum from abroad will adapt their curriculum to fit in with this.

International Baccalaureate

Classical Studies with Latin and Classical Greek does exist in some of these institutions and systems. The International Baccalaureate (IB) has a full Classics programme. The IB is a final certificate for the last two or three years of school and was developed alongside the creation of the United World Colleges (uwc.org) in the Cold War period, but can now be taken in many international schools, and even in some national or independent schools which see it as an alternative to the national system of their own country. Two recent articles (Trafford 2017a and 2017b) highlight the advantages of the IB curriculum for creating Latin and Classics courses in independent schools. The main focus is on the UK, but the principle can be applied worldwide. As the programme has to cater for international schools anywhere in the world there are opportunities for more flexible approaches to teaching and learning and in the final assessment. The IB programme permits the use of a dictionary in final examinations, unlike the UK GCSE and Advanced levels. There is also the requirement for the submission for assessment of a research dossier, where the pupils choose a topic and collect and reflect a number of relevant ancient sources. The IB programme and the Middle Years Programme (outlined in Trafford 2017b), with their emphasis on thematic reading, global contexts and common humanity, can provide models for reforming and renewing Classical Studies programmes in many situations and countries without being dependent on a national system.

National systems abroad

National systems with Latin or Classics on their national curriculum (such as the French *lycées*) will offer it in the usual way in their international schools, and the European Schools have Latin as an optional subject up to the European Baccalaureate. A number of British schools in Cyprus and in European cities such as Madrid, Athens and Alicante were able to offer a full Classics programme up to UK Advanced level until the UK examination board (OCR) withdrew the ability of international schools to enter UK national examinations. Beyond Europe some schools in Hong Kong, Singapore and the Cayman Islands have also been able to offer a similar provision (see Hunt in this book). Some of these schools were set up in the colonial period and owe their continued existence to it, although they have evolved in the post-colonial period into rather different institutions (see Mlambo this volume). An example of this is the Kamuzu Academy in Malawi which has offered a special programme of Classics (McKechnie et al. 2023).

European Schools

A different kind of multilingual and multicultural education is offered by the European Schools (www.eursc.eu). They were initially set up for the education of the children of families who moved country to work for the European Union, first of all to Brussels and Luxembourg and then to other European towns and cities. It seemed the obvious solution to second teachers along with the civil servants working for the (then) European Community so that the different languages and subjects taught in those languages could be delivered by native speakers. Pupils are grouped into language sections according to their first language of education in which they take most of their subjects. In this way no pupil is disadvantaged in their first language and has the opportunity to learn a second and third language in a mixed class with a native-speaker teacher. In the secondary school pupils begin to take some subjects in their second language, particularly History and Geography from third year secondary.

The curriculum offers a broad range of subjects among which is Latin. It is offered in the pupil's first language in principle, but in practice mixed classes are often formed with pupils of different first languages but who are able to take Latin in one of their other languages (usually French, English, Italian or German). Pupils begin in the second year of secondary school (European Schools 2019) and can continue up to the European Baccalaureate (the final school leaving and university entrance certificate). The Latin department of a single school will consist of teachers from as many as seven or eight different countries each teaching in their own language. After four years of Latin pupils take the *Latinum Europaeum,* a harmonized examination for all schools and all language sections. This is equivalent to *Latinum* certificated tests which take place in Germany, Switzerland and Luxembourg (see chapters in this book). At the European Baccalaureate candidates study a thematic selection of texts (or *pensum*) for examination. They have to do an unprepared translation (with the use of a dictionary), analyse an extract from the set texts including a comparison of translations from different languages, and write a critical essay on the literature studied for the theme. Recent set themes have been *Roma et Africa, Feminae Romanae, de Natura* and *Homo et Animal.* Greek is a possible option but is usually taken only by pupils from the Greek section and a group is rarely formed in another language. There is the possibility of a Classical Studies course in the last two years of secondary as a complementary subject (accredited but not for examination in the European Baccalaureate) which offers a course on civilization (mythology, sociology, art and archaeology of antiquity) delivered in one of the vehicular languages but without a Latin or Greek language component.

European Schools provide a truly European education for their pupils who finish their studies fluent in at least two European languages and with a wide-ranging education in other areas. The programmes for all subjects, including Latin, are drawn up in collaboration with representatives of all member states; the Latin programme (available in English, French and German) is an example of a European syllabus not dependent on any one particular national educational system. There is a regular good uptake for the beginners' classes in many language sections, but the numbers decrease further up the school as other options become available; some pupils in mixed classes continue with Latin to the European Baccalaureate. As is often the case, an enthusiastic teacher can make a difference to the creation of classes and their popularity, but Latin continues to be available in this uniquely collaborative education system.

References

European Schools (2019), Programme de Latin – S2 – S7. Available online: www.eursc.eu/Syllabuses/2014-01-D-35-fr-4.pdf (accessed 7 November 2023).

McKechnie, P., S. Nyamilandu and S. Kambalu (2023), *A Monument More Lasting than Bronze: Classics in the University of Malawi, 1982–2019*, Washington DC: Center for Hellenic Studies.

Trafford, S. (2017a), 'The benefits of the International Baccalaureate Diploma for Latin and Classics in the Sixth Form', *Journal of Classics Teaching*, 18 (35): 26–7.

Trafford, S. (2017b), 'Latin and Classical Languages on the International Baccalaureate Middle Years Programme', *Journal of Classics Teaching*, 18 (36): 17–19.

INFORMAL AND ONLINE LEARNING

Steven Hunt

Many of the chapters in this book describe the more formal locations of learning classical subjects in schools, colleges and universities. There are other places to learn. Home schooling is one, of course, of which so-called 'Christian Classical Education' is an increasingly large subsection (Wright 2022; Richardi 2023), often complete with its own course book materials, such as those published by the Memoria Press. For more mature students, opportunities are widespread across the world. In the UK, for instance, places such as the Camden Working Men's College and the City Lit in London have been providing access to classical subjects for adults who, for various reasons, 'missed out' from Classics at school. The Open University and London's Birkbeck College ('*in nocte consilium*') do the same for university degrees. The 'University of the 3rd Age' puts people of more mature years together to read and discuss classical texts.

There are also less formal places which offer classical education to those who are interested but who cannot or do not want to attend classes which necessarily lead to assessment and qualifications. Clubs attached to schools and other institutions provide opportunities for small numbers of students to study subjects which would otherwise be financially unviable in the mainstream school curriculum. In the UK, this is especially the case with teaching Greek, which rarely attracts sufficient numbers to justify full curriculum time, but is often taught off-timetable by a single dedicated teacher (McMenamin 2022; Wright 2016). On a larger scale, the UK charity Classics for All set up Greek courses on Saturday mornings for students from across Liverpool and Cambridgeshire, attracting several dozen students of all ages (Classics for All 2023). These now account for nearly a quarter of students in the UK taking the Intermediate Certificate in Classical Greek – a teacher-designed assessment born out of demand for a more achievable certification than the traditional national examination (LeHur 2022). Elsewhere, students in schools which have no curricular provision for Latin gain input by dedicated individuals such as retired Classics teacher Jane Treasure in Crickhowell (Treasure 2016) or Watford-based peripatetic Classicist Clare Harvey (Harvey 2020).

Outside schools, since the 1990s the Elliniki Agogi has provided an introduction to Classical Greek to 3–12-year-olds in Greece and beyond (Manolidou et al. 2023a). The Nausicaa Association has been providing extra-curricular classical education for primary-aged students in the South of France (Duchemin et al. 2023). The University of Florida provided a successful Classics outreach programme for young people in Gainsville (Bozia et al. 2023), as have the Universities of Swansea (Bracke 2018) and Oxford (Searle 2018) in their localities. Elsewhere numerous *conventicula* and summer schools operate, for people of all ages, ranging from local get-togethers (Parga Ormelas & Parker 2021); the well-known JSST Summer Schools in classical subjects (Stephenson 2023); and the London Summer Schools in Classics, Byzantine History and Homer.

In the past, mass access to Classics has *always* been available, up to a point. People who did not go to the 'right' sort of school have always found ways to nurture their interest in the classical world, whether it be through visits to museums and art galleries, to the archaeological sites themselves, by reading books about the ancients, watching films and TV, or attending performances and shows. Roberts and Petrelli's 2024 study of exhibits at Hadrian's Wall show how multi-sensory and other embodied learning experiences can appeal to a wider range of visitors than before. Meanwhile, Gabriel Zuchtriegel's directorship of the archaeological park of Pompeii continues to update the narrative of the 'dead city' drawing in the public with frequent details of the excavation, conservation and display of new finds, engaging with local schools and communities, and providing snapshots of archaeologists in action (Giuffrida 2021).

There is not enough space to note the huge amount of literature describing the impact of learning about the ancient world through such informal contexts; but, if I were to pick out one book, it would be Hall and Stead's *A People's History of Classics* (2020), which gives a magisterial overview of the multiple ways in which working-class Britons enjoyed their experiences of the ancient world (and for a snapshot, see Henry Stead's (2023) article about auto-didact working-class pit men in the Durham coalfields).

Twenty years ago, the Hollywood film *Gladiator* (Scott 2000) drove enormous interest in the ancient world, and its sequel in 2025 is likely to do the same. Today, videogaming seems to possess similar powers of attraction, as evidenced by the increasing literature on the topic (see, for example, Rollinger 2020; Cannatella 2021; Champion & Hiriart 2023; Vandewalle & Cole 2023; Oulitskaia 2024). The study of table-top games with ancient world themes has recently become a serious field of interest (Cameron 2022); and a number of designers have been busy with 'choose your own adventure' games (Slota & Ballestrini 2019; Salapata et al. 2023; Moser & Thomas 2024). In the UK, the irreverent humour of the children's TV series *Horrible Histories*

(Deary et al. 2009) has usurped *Monty-Python's Life of Brian* (Jones 1979) in every school-child's imagination. Most recently, a TikTok trend, supposedly about how many times men thought about the Romans, went viral (Mitchell 2023), causing huge media interest and spawning a satirical musical number on *Saturday Night Live* (SNL 2023). There are numerous ancient world podcasts, like *History Hit!*, *The Rest is History*, *The Partial Historians*, *History Hack*, *Let's Talk About Myths, Baby!* and *Against the Lore*. Across the world are YouTube videos and webinars and online presentations, group chats and affinity social groups for every topic you can think of. Ray Laurence's animations about life in Rome and Pompeii have reached millions of viewers (Bond 2018; Laurence 2019). 3D reconstructions of the ancient world allow viewers to walk the streets of a virtual Rome, Athens, Ephesus, Silchester. . . .

In the last five or six years the numbers of access points to information about the ancient world and pathways to learn about it have hugely proliferated. From the early days of 'snail-mail' correspondence courses, distance learning has segued into highly efficient and well-run online programmes. The 1990s digitization of resources began to prise open the gateway to the classical world, and, with the improvement in reliability of the internet and Wi-Fi have been able to deliver a classical education to the masses. The ubiquity of the personal computer and smart phones has blurred the boundaries between classroom and home. The internet has democratized Classics. The Cambridge School Classics Project (CSCP) developed video-conferencing early for Latin and Greek teaching: students 'tuned in' for classes and turned in their translations and exercises to be marked and returned to them. Practitioners began to note particular pedagogical features: the advantages and disadvantages of synchronous and asynchronous learning, the importance (or not) of the visibility of the teacher, the motivation of students, the management of a class at distance, and the professional relationship between teacher and students in the virtual classroom (Mead 2004; Seranis 2004; Nightingale 2004; Mullany 2007; Lister 2007; Walden 2019; Hunt 2022a). CSCP developed digital resources in the form of a DVD for the *Cambridge Latin Course* in 2000 and online resources followed (Lister 2007). They became widely used. Apps and commercial computer programmes started to infiltrate classroom practices (Adams et al. 2014). The onset of the Covid-19 lockdowns caused everything to go online almost overnight. The necessity of lockdown teaching hugely accelerated teachers' use of technology, such that it became embedded in everyday learning and strongly impacted on pedagogical thinking and classroom practice in classical education both at school (Hunt 2020; Lamb 2020; Baddeley 2021) and university (Moore 2020). To CSCP's online provision has been added multiple other commercial resources: barely no course book published today comes without its own digital presence.

Online resources and apps are ubiquitous. Wherever they are, students can test themselves with drill apps such as *Kahoot!*, *Quizlet*, *Memrise* and *Blooket*. More focused on classical languages: *Latinitium* provides easily audio Latin texts; *Duolingo* has a Latin version. Little research has been undertaken on the effectiveness of these tools for learning Latin, except for *Memrise* (Walker 2015) and *Duolingo* (Hunt 2022a); nevertheless, they do keep students language-focused and provide masses of language input. Digital platforms such as Zoom, Microsoft Teams, Canva and Google Classroom are now classroom staples: opening a programme is as easy as opening a book.

At the moment, however, national examinations tend to act as a drag on pedagogical choices and teaching practices. For example, in the UK, the examinations boards endorse specific course books: these then govern the examinations for the next twenty years or more. In the USA, the

AP Latin examination is course-book 'blind', but it supports a traditional canon of literature and the style of questions would be familiar to a child from the 1970s (although the examination itself is currently under review). Readers of this volume will find similar tales of traditional examinations determining traditional grammar-translation course materials, and those same materials determining those examinations. It goes around in circles. To be fair, in some chapters in this volume, you will hear no complaints from teachers; but in others, you will detect not a little dissatisfaction about the way in which traditional-style examinations and nationally-prescribed course materials disincentivize pedagogical experimentation or modernization (see Vidović and Pendelj in this volume, for example). Some Classics teachers (see, for example, Claughton 2021 and Nesbit 2021) maintain the painstaking, patient, philological approach. Others describe this as an 'autopsy', with all that this word implies (Gottschalck and Klarskov Jensen in this volume). Some make only occasional forays into online quizzes and vocabulary testers, an approach which is, to me, merely 'old wine in new bottles'. That is only a digitized Victorian classroom experience put in front of Gen Z students who have long started to experiment in other classes with Augmented Reality (AR), Virtual Reality (VR) and Generative Artificial Intelligence (AI) – and in their own homes too. As *Guardian* journalist Simon Jenkins says, complaining about the stultifying nature of the English education system:

> From the age of 11 – by when they should have acquired essential literacy and numeracy – they are afflicted with what is at root an archaic academic traditionalism. They must devote fixed blocs of time to memorising material of minimal future use, and on which they are constantly tested – as if data digitisation and computing had never been invented.
>
> (Jenkins 2024)

Classics teachers too know this. And to Jenkins' point we might draw attention to the way traditional grammar-translation continues to influence contemporary Latin examinations and thereby examination preparation. See, for example, how Baty (1962) and Piantaggini (2020), nearly sixty years apart, describe many of the same problems inherent in this method for student enrolment and retention. It might produce outstanding philologists *in the end*, but with an alarming attrition rate and almost unbearable financial cost for the small classes which it typically engenders, as Kitchell (2015) has noted. Similar debates continue, for example, whether students should be allowed to use online dictionaries and digital parsing tools. As Berthele and Udry state:

> Many teachers would like to use digital translators and online dictionaries in their classroom, but they express uncertainty about how to do so meaningfully. Teachers voice concerns over certain student practices, namely the lack of cognitive involvement when simply translating text without considering the output. Teachers also highlight the gap between curricular/institutional prescriptions and the way the tools are commonly used, a mismatch that can affect their teaching.
>
> (Berthele & Udry 2023)

Regardless, we have shut the gate after the horse has bolted: *students already do so* – and, if truth be told, *so do their teachers*. Yet formal education settings maintain the pretence, by continuing to prepare students in ways which align with the traditional format of the examinations rather than with their own and their students' preferred learning practices. Second Language Development (SLD) research tells us almost all we need to know about how humans develop proficiency in languages. But for classical languages examinations, the grammar-first model seems default, and gives young learners the strong impression that the subject discipline comprises little more than the memorization and recall of conjugations, declensions and esoteric terminology. It is wrong, of course. At the university level, the subject discipline is far more vibrant, often using highly sophisticated digital means of studying the ancient world. It is an exciting time to be a professional classicist: if only more could get there.

Outside the classroom and 'official Classics', the world of online tutoring may provide something of an answer. Online private tutors can provide a teaching experience highly tailored to the customer's needs. Unencumbered by the daily routines of life in the classroom, the students are committed, motivated and ready to learn, often at a time and pace that suits them. Meanwhile, the tutor picks the students and, undisturbed by external examinations and institutional oversight, choose teaching methodologies and resources which suit their own preferences. In many cases the traditional examination prescription is followed: learn vocabulary, memorize morphology, translate – an endless routine of question and feedback. But even a brief perusal will show that things are changing.

It is from the USA that I detect the most innovative approaches (especially active approaches) to teaching classical languages. Perhaps this is because, for most students in the USA, their only assessments will be internal: such freedom allows if not encourages improvisation, innovation, daring (Hunt 2018). One area of interest, which I think lends itself as an introduction for teachers to think more expansively about the potential of online teaching and learning, is that of movement towards so-called 'un-textbooking' the classroom. In a 2019 article, Rachel Ash, a Latin teacher in a public school in America, noting the critical factors identified by SLD research for successful language acquisition, explained:

> After ten years struggling to come to terms with my dissatisfaction, I finally admitted that the textbook could not provide me with the things I had grown to require for a successful class and curriculum. Namely, I wanted a textbook that would allow me to create a curriculum that was comprehensible, compelling, and caring, and no textbook currently exists for Latin that provides these things.
>
> (Ash 2019: 66)

Un-textbooking is not just about getting rid of the textbook and replacing it with another kind of book: it is a way of thinking *beyond* what the textbook can do. Oftentimes, the textbook has come to define the way in which Latin should be learnt, and the examinations align with them. The textbook is convenient: it is portable, easy to publish and use. There is nothing wrong with the textbook *per se* for subjects (like Geography or Mathematics) which have definitional consensus for substantive knowledge, the duration of courses, teaching methods and suchlike. But languages (and music, for example) are different. They have both substantive knowledge, according to intent and purpose difficult to define, and also personal and interpersonal skills. Reading, singing, speaking and listening are, one could argue, more difficult for a person to develop than learning how to distil a salt solution. SLD research has shown for a long time now that knowledge of grammar rules common to modern language textbooks does little to help learners gain proficiency in the language (Lichtman & VanPatten 2021). This is commonly noted in the teaching of ancient languages too, even though they are not 'used' (i.e. spoken) in the same way as modern foreign languages are. The result is that the focus of the teaching tends to turn to the rules of the language rather than to the language itself. Such books continue to hold sway in the classroom and the many other ways in which one can become proficient in languages are routinely ignored in the classroom, mainly, I suspect, because they are not able to be written in a textbook. It is as if they do not exist. Linguistics expert Professor Stephen Krashen considers this a conspiracy by textbook publishers:

> There is no financial profit in encouraging acquisition even though it works – students will rarely notice that it is happening or has happened [. . .] but there is a lot of profit in study and conscious learning. It results in a kind of competence that is difficult to access and use, but students blame themselves when they find it hard to understand, learn, and use.
>
> (Krashen, Facebook, 9 January 2024)

Whether Krashen's vision of a too-cosy publishing cartel is accident or design, the close alignment of textbook and examinations can be a problem. But there *are* teachers who are moving away. It is possible to reject the textbook / examination industry. Teachers can teach Latin not Latin-exams. Rachel Ash, for example, describes multiple routes, choosing from the ever-increasing range of easily-accessible stories, such as contemporary-authored 'novellas' set in Roman and non-Roman periods (Piazza 2017; M. Patrick 2019; Cooper 2023; Hunt 2022b), movie-talks (Ash 2017), and all sorts of active language approaches, including different forms of dictation, reading aloud, speaking, listening (including music, gesture, actions), variations on story-telling, story-asking and story-making activities and different types of composition, including personalized writing, collaborative story-writing and the writing of fan fiction (see Lloyd & Hunt 2021; Hunt 2022a; Letchford 2024; Trusted 2024; and Aguilar Garcia 2024 for an introduction to many of these).

Many chapters in this volume attest to the speed with which teachers are adapting their practice as a result of what they read about on the Internet and what they themselves do there. Can teachers set translation to be completed at home, when nearly every translation is easily downloadable for free, or quickly, ChatGPT or Google-translatable? Some have been setting students different sorts of task that make use of the tools available: the flipped classroom (where students prepare by watching, for example, video explanations, before the lesson proper), and vocabulary learning online and out of class to name but two. Some Classics teachers have been experimenting with Virtual Reality (VR) in the classroom (Johnson forthcoming; Barry forthcoming). VR has huge potential for embodied and experiential learning which may affect, engage and motivate students as drawings and photographs rarely can. Research by Sobocinski et al. (2023) suggests that carefully-constructed VR environments offer great potential for self-regulated learning activities. Can VR in the future provide prompts in Latin or Ancient Greek to students in VR temples and the fora of ancient Rome or Athens?

The role that Artificial Intelligence (AI) might play in teaching and learning is currently being debated. Whether it will ever pass the Turing Test or be nothing more than 'plagiarism software' (Chomsky 2023), AI is likely to be most valued as a one-to-one tutor and supplement to the usual classroom teacher. Chi and Wylie (2014) proposed the ICAP framework for thinking about how activities promote different types of student engagement, and therefore motivation and learning:

- **Interactive**: where the learner engages in dialogue with their tutor where both sides produce constructive responses, such as debating the justification for an answer.
- **Constructive**: where the learner generates or produces something new, such as self-explaining or problem-solving a question.
- **Active**: where the learner takes overt action, such as highlighting, paraphrasing or underlining.
- **Passive**: where the learner receives information, such as watching a video or reading an article.

The more interactive activities tend to lead to better learning outcomes than the more passive activities. Globally scaling these sorts of interactions is impossible using real-life teachers. But DiCerbo suggests that AI has a special place in the mix:

New AI technologies, particularly large language models, may help more students engage in interactive learning. [...] The AI-powered tutor can also engage either side of a debate on any topic and then offer a summary of each sides' points with feedback on the argumentation skills of the debater. It can take on the persona of a literary character and discuss their motivations with a learner.

(DiCerbo 2023)

The use of AI in education is only just beginning to be explored and understood. The ethical concerns about students' usage, its detectability and its accessibility to all students, not to mention its plundering of authors' materials, are all undergoing consideration (Booth 2024). On the other hand, teachers can use AI to reduce workload by helping them to create resources faster and more efficiently than before; and students can get support with homework, with planning, writing and creating images. There is huge potential for personalized learning, for assessment and for feedback and for developing analytics for learning gaps (Barran 2024). It seems to come down to whether we see AI as a threat to testing or an aid to learning.

AI's 'knowledge' of Latin lexis and syntax is currently restricted by the corpus of literature on which it has been trained (Burns 2023). Its accuracy as a tool for translation of Latin and Greek is variable (Ross 2023), but it is improving. If it is to provide a means of generating Latin text for specific classroom exercises, the authors and periods on which it is trained would need to be restricted (Cavaleri 2022). Díaz-Sánchez and Chapinal-Heras (2024) have proposed a model lesson whereby students' target language input to the Midjourney AI program generates representational images to test the accuracy of their composition. AI can generate images of historical figures or imitate them by providing answers to questions posed by students, including in Latin. We are at a new and somewhat wild frontier. Ross and Baines (2024) have consulted UK university students and recommended protocols for students to follow in their university; but, at the time of writing, there is no nationwide protocol for school students and guidelines are only just being considered (Patel 2024).

It is not yet clear how much AI may of itself affect and subvert current teaching and learning practices, especially with its ability to follow questions and provide answers in the target language. AI might prove the death of traditional approaches to teaching and learning Latin: the grammar-first method is easy prey to gaming or cheating the system, because lexical and syntactical analysis and translations both into and out of the target language are achievable with a click of the mouse. On the other hand, AI may be the catalyst teachers need to make them rethink their practices in ways which go beyond those which digital resources and online learning have already activated. AI is already able to read, write and even listen and speak in the target language. These capabilities might provide the means to develop the range of resources which deliver the sort of learning experiences which SLD tells us are effective for students to become proficient in languages.

The rise in interest in active approaches to the teaching of Latin and Ancient Greek has been well-documented (Carlon 2013; R. Patrick 2015, 2019; Bailey 2016a, 2016b, 2019; Hunt 2018; Ramsby 2020; Lloyd & Hunt 2021). While the debate about the efficacy of spoken active Latin in the modern age continues (see Moran 2022 for reservations and Lanzillotta forthcoming in response) the main challenge has been to find enough teachers sufficiently competent. Training can be found at the Paideia Institute's conferences at Fordham University, New York, and its Living Latin courses in Paris and Rome (Mistretta & Pedicone 2021); the Accademia Vivarium Novum in Frascati, Italy (Manolidou et al. 2023b); the Polis Institute in Jerusalem (Rico & Kopf 2021); the *conventicula* in the University of Kentucky (Minkova & Tunberg 2021) and courses run by *SALVI* and *Oxford Latinitas* (Letts 2021), among many others (see *passim* in this volume). YouTube videos and online tutoring spoken Latin or Ancient Greek courses have sprung up for those who cannot afford to travel: Andrew Morehouse's *Latinitas Animi Causa* (and *Lac: Grex Omnium*, a kind of social media community in Latin), Seumas Mcdonald's *SeumasU*, Luke Amadeus Ranieri's *polýMATHY* channel, Jenny Teichmann's τρίοδος *trivium / Argos Didaskei*, among many others.

Put them together, and what have we got? Dare I envisage Classics students of the future in VR headsets, chatting to AI Roman avatars and being set to find solutions to authentic problems such as the defence of the Dacian *limes*. . . .?

One thing that this vision lacks: learning is best not a solitary activity. It is not just about doing it; it is about doing it with other people. Practising on your own is not as fun as practising with others – education is more than just about cognition, it is the social aspect. It is about feelings and emotions, more so when one is learning a language and about other people. A research project found that middle school students processed extended texts better on paper than they did on screen (Froud et al. 2023). Meanwhile, US researchers discovered that Gen Z rather liked using the library as a place to study, relax and meet friends to learn together (Demopoulos 2024). I take heart from these two reports about how young people today are learning. Much of this interest in traditional reading is driven by #booktok, a social media hashtag on which teens and authors share book recommendations. No doubt Cicero would have much approved.

References

Adams, E., S. Capewell, C. Downes, S. Hunt and C. Ryan (2014), 'Apps for Classics Teaching and Learning', *Journal of Classics Teaching*, 29: 37–8.

Aguilar Garcia, L. (2024), 'Vocabulary Acquisition in the Language Classroom: what it is, how it works, which strategies and approaches are suitable for Latin instruction', *Journal of Classics Teaching*, 25 (50): 1–7.

Ash, R. (2017), 'The MovieTalk: A Practical Application of Comprehensible Input Theory', *Teaching Classical Languages*, 8 (2): 70–84.

Ash, R. (2019), 'Untextbooking for the CI Latin class: why and how to begin', *Journal of Classics Teaching*, 20 (39): 65–70.

Baddeley, S. (2021), 'Online teaching: a reflection', *Journal of Classics Teaching*, 22 (44): 109–16.

Bailey, J. S. (2016a), 'Teaching Latin to Humans; How to Honor both the Language and the Learner', *Eidolon*. Available online: https://eidolon.pub/teaching-latin-to-humans-4e6b489b4e17 (accessed 1 February 2024).

Bailey, J. S. (2016b), 'The "ars" of Latin Questioning: Circling, Personalization, and Beyond', *The Classical Outlook*, 91 (1): 1–5.

Bailey, J. S. (2019), 'Toward a Collegial, Post-Method Latin Pedagogy', *The Classical Outlook*, 94 (2): 94–101.

Barran, Baroness (2024), 'Our plan to ensure schools benefit from the AI revolution', *Schools Week*, 24 January. Available online: https://schoolsweek.co.uk/our-plan-to-ensure-schools-benefit-from-ai-revolution/ (accessed 1 February 2024).

Barry, G. (forthcoming), 'VR in Practice: Temples, teaching, and Year 11s', *Journal of Classics Teaching*.

Baty, C. (1962), 'Classics in the Schools. A survey of the position and prospects', in The Classical Association, *Re-Appraisal: some new thoughts on the teaching of Classics*, Supplement to Greece & Rome, 12 (1): 10–14.

Berthele, R. and I. Udry (2023), 'Digitale Übersetzungsprogramme und Online Wörterbücher im Fremdsprachenunterricht', *Linguistik Online*, 120 (2): 145–67.

Bond, S. (2018), [Blog] 'Teaching Roman Daily Life Through Animation: Spotlight on Ray Laurence', *Society for Classical Studies*. Available online: https://classicalstudies.org/scs-blog/ionic007/blog-teaching-roman-daily-life-through-animation-spotlight-ray-laurence (accessed 31 January 2024).

Booth, S. (2024), 'Five changes experts suggest on AI in schools', *Schools Week*, 24 January. Available online: https://schoolsweek.co.uk/five-changes-experts-suggest-on-ai-in-schools/ (accessed 1 February 2024).

Bozia, E., A. Pantazopoulou and A. Smith (2023), '"Translating" Classics for Generations Z and Alpha', *Journal of Classics Teaching*, 25 (49): 43–7.

Bracke, E. (2018), 'Taking Classics into Communities', in A. Holmes-Henderson, S. Hunt and M. Musié (eds), *Forward with Classics. Classical Languages in Schools and Communities*, London: Bloomsbury Academic, 187–204.

Burns, P. (2023), [Blog] 'How Much Latin Does ChatGPT "Know"?', *Society for Classical Studies*, 31 July. Available online: https://classicalstudies.org/scs-blog/patrickjburns/blog-how-much-latin-does-chatgpt-"know" (accessed 9 January 2024).

Cameron, H. (2022), 'Imagining Classics: Towards A Pedagogy of Gaming Reception', *Classical Journal*, 118 (1): 90–112.

Cannatella, P. (2021), 'Student and teacher perceptions of the value of Total War: Saga in motivating KS3 students in an all-boys state school', *Journal of Classics Teaching*, 23 (45): 22–32.

Carlon, J. (2013), 'The Implications of SLA Research for Latin Pedagogy: Modernizing Latin Instruction and Securing its Place in Curricula', *Teaching Classical Languages*, 4 (2): 103–22.

Cavaleri, D. (2022), 'L'enseignement du latin à l'aube de l'intelligence artificielle', *Association Suisse des Philologues Classiques Bulletin* 100, X.

Champion, E. and J. Hiriart (2023), '*Assassin's Creed' in the Classroom. Histpory's Playground or a Stab in the Dark?*, Berlin and Boston: de Gruyter.

Chi, M. and R. Wylie (2014), 'The ICAP Framework: Linking Cognitive Engagement to Active Learning Outcomes', *Educational Psychologist*, 49 (4): 219–43.

Chomsky, N. (2023), 'The false promise of ChatGPT', *The New York Times*, 8 March. Available online: https://www.nytimes.com/2023/03/08/opinion/noam-chomsky-chatgpt-ai.html (accessed 1 February 2024).

Classics for All (2023), *Classics Matters*. Available online: https://classicsforall.org.uk/sites/default/files/uploads/CM%20newsletters/Classics-for-All_ClassicsMatters-Spring23_Digital.pdf (accessed 16 December 2023).

Claughton, J. (2021), 'In Praise of Parsing', *Antigone Journal*. Available online: https://antigonejournal.com/2021/11/in-praise-of-parsing/ (accessed 11 January 2024).

Cooper, M. (2022), 'To Read or Not to Read: Trialling an Extensive Reading Program in a Year 10 Latin Classroom', *Journal of Classics Teaching*, 24 (47): 44–51.

Deary, T., P. Hepplewhite and N. Tonge (2009–14), [TV series] *Horrible Histories*.

Delaney, C., H. Smith, L. Tims, T. Smith and W. Griffiths W. (2021), 'Keeping the ancient world relevant for modern students with Suburani', *Journal of Classics Teaching*, 22 (43): 64–7.

Demopoulos, A. (2024), 'Books and looks: gen Z is "rediscovering" the public library', *The Guardian*, 26 January. Available online: https://www.theguardian.com/books/2024/jan/26/books-and-looks-gen-z-is-rediscovering-the-public-library (accessed 1 February 2024).

Díaz-Sánchez, C. and D. Chapinal-Heras (2024), 'Use of Open Access AI in teaching classical antiquity. A methodological proposal', *Journal of Classics Teaching*, 25 (49): 17–21.

DiCerbo, K. (2023), 'AI, Education, and Humanity', in E. Horvitz (ed.), *AI Anthology*, Microsoft. Available online: https://unlocked.microsoft.com/ai-anthology/kristen-dicerbo (accessed 2 February 2024).

Duchemin, L., A. Durand and B. Franceschetti (2023), 'The Nausicaa experience: Teaching Ancient Greek in French preschools and primary schools', *Journal of Classics Teaching*, 25 (49): 39–42.

Froud, K., L. Levinson, C. Maddox and P. Smith (2023), 'Middle-schoolers' reading and processing depth in response to digital and print media: An N400 study', *bioRxiv*. Available online: https://www.biorxiv.org/content/10.1101/2023.08.30.553693v1 (accessed 1 February 2024).

Giuffrida, A. (2021), 'Pompeii's new director: "Excavation is always a kind of destruction"', *The Guardian*, 26 February. Available online: https://www.theguardian.com/world/2021/feb/26/pompeii-vexes-board-with-appointment-of-german-director (accessed 20 February 2024).

Hall, E. and H. Stead (2020), *A People's History of Classics*, London: Routledge.

Hands Up Education (2020), *Suburani*, Haverhill: Hands Up Education.

Harvey, C. (2020), 'A peripatetic model for teaching Latin', *Journal of Classics Teaching*, 21 (41): 86–7.

Hunt, S. (2018), 'Latin is Not Dead: The Rise of Communicative approaches to the Teaching of Latin in the United States', in A. Holmes-Henderson, S. Hunt and M. Musié (eds), *Forward with Classics. Classical Languages in Schools and Communities*, London: Bloomsbury Academic, 89–108.

Hunt, S. (2020), 'Sight Unseen: Visible and Invisible teachers in online teaching', *Teaching Classical Languages*, 11 (2): 33–66.

Hunt, S. (2022a), *Teaching Latin: Theories, Contexts, Practices*, London: Bloomsbury Academic.

Hunt, S. (2022b), 'Novellas and Free Voluntary Reading: an overview and some starting points for further research into practice', *Journal of Classics Teaching*, 23 (46): 176–83.

Jenkins, S. (2024), 'England's secondary schools are Dickensian. No wonder children are staying away', *The Guardian*, 8 January. Available online: https://www.theguardian.com/commentisfree/2024/jan/08/englands-secondary-schools-are-dickensian-no-wonder-children-are-staying-away (accessed 9 January 2024).

Johnson, T. (forthcoming), 'Ten Minute Trips: A Case Study examining Student Perceptions of the Value of Virtual Reality in A-Level Classical Civilisation', *Journal of Classics Teaching*.

Jones, T. (1979), [Film] *Monty Python's Life of Brian*.

Kitchell, K. (2015), '"Solitary Perfection?" The Past, Present and Future of Elitism in Latin Education', in E. Archibald, W. Brockliss and J. Gnoza (eds), *Learning Latin and Greek from Antiquity to the Present*, Cambridge: Cambridge University Press, 166–83.

Lamb, M. G. (2020), 'Access and Opportunity: Technology Tools for Transitioning Online', *Teaching Classical Languages*, 50 (2): 109–14.

Lanzillotta, L. (forthcoming), 'Pro Latinitate Activa: A Student's Perspective on Active Latin', *Journal of Classics Teaching*.

Laurence, R. (2019), 'From Research on Roman History to cartoons and Outreach in UK Schools', in B. Natoli and S. Hunt (eds), *Teaching Classics with Technology*, London: Bloomsbury Academic, 107–20.

LeHur, C. (2022), 'A New Classical Greek Qualification', *Journal of Classics Teaching*, 23 (45): 79–80.

Letchford, C. (2024), 'Teaching Greek: from school to university via fifteenth century Florence', *Journal of Classics Teaching*, 25 (50): 1–5.

Letts, M. (2021), 'ars longa, vita brevis: Active Latin in the Classroom', *Antigone Journal*. Available online: https://antigonejournal.com/2021/10/ars-longa-vita-brevis-active-latin-in-the-classroom/ (accessed 16 December 2023).

Lichtman, K. and B. VanPatten (2021), 'Was Krashen right? Forty years later', *Foreign Language Annals*, 52 (2): 283–305.

Lister, B. (2007), *Changing Classics in Schools,* Cambridge: Cambridge University Press.

Lloyd, M. and S. Hunt, eds (2021), *Communicative Approaches for Ancient Languages,* London: Bloomsbury Academic.

Manolidou, E., S. Goula and V. Sakka (2023a), 'Ancient Greek for Kids: From Theory to Praxis', *Journal of Classics Teaching*, 24 (47): 3–11.

Manolidou, E., C. Rico, J. Teichmann, J. Coderch, M. R. Mistretta and S. Hunt (2023b), 'Insights on Classics in Praxis at the Delphi Economic Forum', *Journal of Classics Teaching*, 25 (49): 77–82.

McMenamin, C. (2022), 'Greek Club: Resurrecting Dead Languages in Secondary Schools', *Journal of Classics Teaching*, 23 (46): 121–3.

Mead, G. (2004), 'Video Conferencing Latin', *Journal of Classics Teaching*, 2: 14.

Minkova, M. and T. Tunberg (2021), 'Global Latin, Active Kentucky and Beyond', in M. Lloyd and S. Hunt (eds), *Communicative Approaches for Ancient Languages*, London: Bloomsbury Academic, 125–32.

Mistretta, M. R. and J. Pedicone (2021), 'New Approaches to Ancient Languages: the Paideia Institute's Pedagogy', in M. Lloyd and S. Hunt (eds), *Communicative Approaches for Ancient Languages*, London: Bloomsbury Academic, 180–9.

Mitchell, J. (2023), [Blog] 'How often do you think about the Roman Empire?', *Society for Classical Studies*, 3 October. Available online: https://classicalstudies.org/scs-blog/torilee/blog-how-often-do-you-think-about-roman-empire (accessed 15 December 2023).

Moore, D. (2020), 'Lessons from Online Modern Foreign Language Classes for the Classical Language Instructor', *Teaching Classical Languages*, 11 (2): 67–80.

Moran, J. (2022), 'Comprehending Comprehensible Input (CI): Some Observations', *Journal of Classics Teaching*, 23 (46): 124–5.

Moser, C. and C. Thomas (2024), 'Rome: The Game. Creating an Online Course as an Interactive Adventure Game', *Journal of Classics Teaching,* 25 (50).

Mullany, G. (2007), 'e-Latin', *Journal of Classics Teaching*, 11: 7.

Nesbit, J. (2021), 'ubi est piscina? Teaching Ancient and Modern Languages', *Antigone Journal*. Available online: https://antigonejournal.com/2021/09/teaching-ancient-modern-languages/ (accessed 11 January 2024).

Nightingale, A. (2004), 'Cambridge Online Latin Project: Distance Learning to GCSE', *Journal of Classics Teaching,* 3: 16.

Oulitskaia, V. (2024), 'Using Assassin's Creed: Odyssey to teach Olympia as part of the Classical Civilisation A Level', *Journal of Classics Teaching,* 25 (50): 1–7.

Parga Ormelas, I. and J. Parker (2021), 'Student-led initiatives at Oxford and Cambridge', in M. Lloyd and S. Hunt (eds), *Communicative Approaches for Ancient Languages*, London: Bloomsbury Academic, 179–88.

Patel, H. (2024), 'Five policies to make AI-enabled learning safe and equitable', *Schools Week*, 23 February. Available online: https://schoolsweek.co.uk/five-policies-to-make-ai-enabled-learning-safe-and-equitable/ (accessed 23 February 2024).

Patrick, M. (2019), 'Free Voluntary Reading and Comprehensible Input', *Journal of Classics Teaching*, 20 (39): 78–82.

Patrick, R. (2015), 'Making Sense of Comprehensible Input in the Latin Classroom', *Teaching Classical Languages*, 6 (1): 108–35.

Patrick, R. (2019), 'Comprehensible Input and Krashen's theory', *Journal of Classics Teaching*, 20 (39): 37–44.

Piantaggini, L. (2020), 'Grammar-Translation: What Is It—Really—For Students?', *Journal of Classics Teaching*, 21 (42): 92–4.

Piazza, J. (2017), 'Beginner Latin Novels: A General Overview', *Teaching Classical Languages*, 8 (2): 154–66.

Ramsby, T. (2020), 'Changing Methods in Latin Teaching', *The Classical Outlook*, 95 (1): 20–7.

Richardi, J. (2023), '"Neither Orthodox Nor Enlightened": Dorothy Sayers and Classical Education in America', *New England Classical Journal*, 50 (2): 9–28. Available online: https://crossworks.holycross.edu/necj/vol50/iss2/4/ (accessed 17 December 2023).

Rico, C. and M. Kopf (2021), 'Teaching Ancient Greek by the Polis Method', in M. Lloyd and S. Hunt (eds), *Communicative Approaches for Ancient Languages*, London: Bloomsbury Academic, 141–50.

Roberts, A. and D. Petrelli (2024), 'Experiencing Roman religion on Hadrian's Wall: embodied interaction in an antiquarian Museum', *Theoretical Roman Archaeology Journal*, 6 (1): 1–21.

Rollinger, C. (2020), *Classical Antiquity in Video Games*, London: Bloomsbury.

Ross, E. (2023), 'A New Frontier: AI and Ancient Language Pedagogy', *Journal of Classics Teaching*, 24 (48): 143–61.

Ross, E. and J. Baines (2024), 'Treading Water: New Data on the Impact of AI Ethics Information Sessions in Classics and Ancient Language Pedagogy', *Journal of Classics Teaching*, 25 (50).

Salapata, G., J. Tracy and K. Loke (2023), 'Teaching Greek mythology through a scenario-based game', *Journal of Classics Teaching*, 49: 1–11.

Scott, R. (2000), [Film] *Gladiator*, DreamWorks Pictures.

Searle, E. (2018), 'Widening Access to Classics in the UK: How the Impact, Public Engagement, Outreach and Knowledge Exchange Agenda Have Helped', in A. Holmes-Henderson, S. Hunt and M. Musié (eds), *Forward with Classics. Classical Languages in Schools and Communities*, London: Bloomsbury Academic, 27–46.

Seranis, P. (2004), 'E-tutoring for Independent Learners of Latin: Views & Reflections', *Journal of Classics Teaching*, 2: 11–13.

Slota, S. and K. Ballestrini (2019), '*Una Vita*: Exploring the Relationship between Play, learning Science and Cultural Competency', in B. Natoli and S. Hunt (eds), *Teaching Classics with Technology*, London: Bloomsbury Academic, 81–91.

SNL (2023), [YouTube video] *Rome Song SNL*. Available online: https://www.youtube.com/watch?v=P2nWlXlcO5I (accessed 15 December 2023).

Sobocinski, M., D. Dever, M. Wiedbusch, F. Mubarak, R. Azevedo and S. Järvelä (2023), 'Capturing self-regulated learning processes in virtual reality: Causal sequencing of multimodal data', *British Journal of Educational Technology*. Available online: https://bera-journals.onlinelibrary.wiley.com/doi/10.1111/bjet.13393 (accessed 28 January 2024).

Stead, H. (2023), 'Spennymoor Classics: Tales from the Pit University', *Working Classicists*. Available online: https://www.workingclassicists.com/post/spennymoor-classics-tales-from-the-pit-university (accessed 29 December 2023).

Stephenson, D. (2023), '43rd JACT Latin Summer School – 2023 Director's Report', *Journal of Classics Teaching*, 25 (49): 72–6.

Trafford, S. (2023), 'Reflections on the new International Baccalaureate Diploma Classical Languages Syllabus', *Journal of Classics Teaching*, 24 (47): 81–5.

Treasure, J. (2016), 'Retirement? What Retirement?', *Journal of Classics Teaching*, 17 (33): 45–7.

Trusted, A. (2024), 'Rewriting the Textbook: An investigation into students' practices with creative composition in a Year 7 Latin class', *Journal of Classics Teaching*, 25 (50): 1–6.

Vandewalle, A. and R. Cole (2023) [Conference presentation] '"As You Write Your Odyssey. . .": An Empirical Study of Classics Students' Play Interests and Ergodic Characterization in Historical Video Games', Conference: The Interactive Pasts 3, Leiden. Available online: https://www.youtube.com/watch?v=JbqEUesBQ_g&list=PLKbRwyeu6RQuLHDDDbZVf4ApCDOHBBxQ8&index=20 (accessed 11 January 2024).

Walden, V. (2019), 'Distance Learning and Technology: Teaching Latin, Greek and Classical Civilisation at a Distance from the UK', in B. Natoli and S. Hunt (eds), *Teaching Classics with Technology*, London: Bloomsbury Academic, 29–38.

Walker, L. (2015), 'The Impact of using *Memrise* on Student perceptions of learning Latin Vocabulary and on Long-Term memory of Words', *Journal of Classics Teaching*, 16 (32): 14–20.

Wright, A. (2016), 'Running a Greek Club – The Hereford Cathedral School Experience', *Journal of Classics Teaching*, 16 (32): 21–4.

Wright, J. (2022), 'Classical Christian Education and Classics: What's in a Name?', *Antigone Journal*. Available online: https://antigonejournal.com/2022/10/classical-christian-education/ (accessed 17 December 2023).

INDEX

Index

Index